Albuquerque

Albuquerque

A Narrative History by

Marc Simmons

University of New Mexico Press / ALBUQUERQUE

Library of Congress Cataloging in Publication Data

Simmons, Marc.
    Albuquerque: a narrative history.

    Bibliography: p.
    Includes index.
    1. Albuquerque (N.M)—History.   I. Title.
F804.A3S55 1982   978.9′61   82–11124
ISBN 0–8263–0627–6

Design by Emmy Ezzell

Manufactured in the United States of America.
Library of Congress Catalog Card Number 82-11124.
International Standard Book Number 0-8263-0627-6.
International Standard Book Number (paperback) 0-8263-0649-7
First paperback printing, 1983.

The research for this book was made possible by a grant from the
National Endowment for the Humanities.

To The Memory of
COACH JOHN BAKER
of
Albuquerque
(he made his own kind of history)

Contents

Illustrations

Preface

THE PURPOSE OF THIS BOOK is to tell the story of a city—Albuquerque—as it has unfolded through two hundred and seventy-odd years of history. Within the narrative, several underlying themes can be discerned. One, common to most municipal histories, deals with the ongoing process of population growth, boundary expansion, and economic development. Another theme focuses on cultural diversity and conflict. Still a third points to the random and unlooked-for incidents that at various times deflected the stream of events in such a way as to ensure that Albuquerque, rather than Santa Fe, Las Vegas, or some other town, would rise to a position of economic dominance in New Mexico.

To get an eagle's-eye view of the setting that will form the backdrop of this story, imagine yourself in a hot air balloon floating in the crystalline atmosphere high over New Mexico's Middle Rio Grande Valley. From your basket you can see the warped and wrinkled land sprawling below, like a vast mottled map whose edges fade fuzzily into smoky distance.

Off to the north, the horizon is rimmed by two great mountain chains—the Sangre de Cristos on the right overlooking Santa Fe, and the Jemez on the left, darkly mantled with a heavy growth of timber. Below the southwest corner of the Jemez, the open skyline is broken at intervals by isolated peaks, like the black knob of Cabezon, round-shouldered Mount Taylor, and soaring Ladron Mountain. It is marked, too, by mesas capped with volcanic basalt, whose steep sides appear from a distance to be walls of a man-made fortress. Closer to your drifting basket, on the east, loom tips of the Sandia and Manzano mountains, their somber crests dressed in blue-green pine.

At the very center of this landscape, seen from on high, the Rio Grande, its body bent in graceful and easy curves, moves south to disappear in the dim haze along the Mexican border. Between the Sangre de Cristos and the Jemez, the river slices through a lofty plateau to form White Rock Canyon. Not far outside the exit of that precipitous gorge, an eleven-mile-long, earth-filled dam has been thrown up to catch the silt-laden waters of the Rio Grande and form Cochiti Lake. Just below the dam begins a series of floodplains, each defined by its own valley and each strung along the silvery chain of the river like beads on a rosary.

The first of these long, narrow depressions, the Santo Domingo Valley, holds the Hispanic village of Peña Blanca and the Indian pueblos of Cochiti, Santo Domingo, and San Felipe. Near its southern extremity, close by San Felipe, the valley pinches out at a place the Spaniards called Angostura, The Narrows.

Shortly, a new floodplain appears, marking the beginning of the Albuquerque Valley. Wide and fertile bottom lands extend several miles on each side of the Rio Grande to ragged edges of sandhills. And a belt of cottonwoods, the *bosque,* spreads a canopy of shade along the river banks. Here in descending line are situated Bernalillo, Sandia Pueblo, Corrales, Alameda, Albuquerque, Atrisco, Armijo, Pajarito, and Los Padillas.

Near Isleta Pueblo, the Rio Grande is again constricted between encroaching bluffs. There commences the third concavity, the Belen Valley, which runs to a point below the village of Tomé. Downstream, other valleys decorate the chain. But these three, really subvalleys, closely linked and thinly separated, form their own larger physiographic unit called the Middle Valley of the Rio Grande.

The pivot, the heart and the soul of the Middle Valley, is the city of Albuquerque. From balloon height, its distended boundaries give the appearance of an enormous metropolis, reclining serenely on the axis of the river. Urban Albuquerque, whether viewed from the air or from the ground, seems at first glance to be a carbon copy of its sister cities in the Southwest—Denver, El Paso, Phoenix, and Tucson. It is afflicted with the same tumorous sprawl, chronic noxious vapors emanating from freeways, creeping asphalt, and endemic hubbub. It has a similar backdrop of mountains, a similar foundation of arid, buff-colored soil, and an almost identical measure of abundant sunlight.

But superficial comparisons, as we know, can be deceiving. Albuquerque at bottom has a character and a personality that go beyond the modern neon glitter of its look-alike shopping malls and the crowded acres of tract homes that have become the trademarks of all America's cities. It possesses, indisputably and immutably, what poetic writers have come to call "a strong sense of place."

The meaning of that phrase is clear to any native of Albuquerque who has been gone for a while and returns. Descending from an airliner or passenger train, his breath quickens at the first sight of Sandia Mountain on the east or the sentinel row of small volcanoes on the west. Driving through the streets, he feels the pulse and tempo of the city, beating with a rhythm that is peculiar to Albuquerque. The distinct "sense of place" emerges from a mix of landscape, climate, history, architecture, and cultural tradition. In Albuquerque's case, that combination, unquestionably modern in tone, is also uniquely New Mexican.

As much as anything, this book is intended to show that Albuquerque is tied to the past by a myriad of gossamer threads. Those lines, braiding together through many human generations, have produced the city today. Yet, the plain fact is that most of the time we are so boxed into the present, so preoccupied with the niggling details of daily life, we fail to remember where we came from. All that went before—the great silent gulf of history—is forgotten.

In no way should the present work be regarded as the final or definitive word on any aspect of Albuquerque's story. Serious scholarly investigation is still needed for every historical period. That is especially the case for the Spanish and Mexican years, of which our view remains cloudy and our information, as yet, imprecise.

In the writing of this narrative, I have tried to present, in broad outline, what is known at present about the history of Albuquerque, and to do it in such a manner as to appeal to the general reader. I have also attempted to include, here and there, new interpretations and evidence of my own original research with the hope that specialists in the field of Southwest studies may find the volume useful as well. It should go without saying that the selection of material and the conclusions reached reflect my perspective and tastes. Those who may find their views at variance with mine are free to write their own book.

One small but confusing matter should be clarified at the outset. The city took its name from the Duke of Alburquerque, Viceroy of New Spain, who spelled that name with an extra *r*. Spanish and Mexican documents continued to use the traditional spelling as late as the 1840s. But then, with the coming of the Anglo-Americans, whose tongues tripped over the long and unfamiliar word, the first *r* fell away and *Alburquerque* became *Albuquerque*. For the sake of consistency, I have employed the latter form throughout, except in those cases when reference is made directly to the Duke.

During the research and writing of this volume, I have incurred many debts. The project had its genesis in a conversation with Gerald George, now director of the American Association for State and Local History. The work was made possible through the assistance of a research grant from the National Endowment for the Humanities. The findings and conclusions presented here do not necessarily represent the views of the Endowment. Thanks are owed especially to Myra Ellen Jenkins, Richard Salazar, and John Baxter of the New Mexico State Records Center and Archive, Santa Fe; to Susan Dewitt and the staff of the Historic Landmarks Survey of Albuquerque; and to Jack Rittenhouse, John L. Kessell, Katherine Stamm, Sidney Brinckerhoff, Elizabeth Dear, David J. Weber, William Buchanan, and Jack and Polly Baker.

Librarian Stephany Eger of the Museum of New Mexico, Santa Fe, and the staff of the Coronado Room, University of New Mexico Library, Albuquerque, offered unstinting help. Byron Johnson, Curator of History, Museum of Albuquerque, assisted in assembling the illustrations and provided useful data on the early railroad era. The Museum of Albuquerque courteously supplied many photographs. Urban historian John Ellis made available to me two unpublished manuscripts of his, one on development of the trolley system and the other on the history of Blacks in Albuquerque. In several interviews, he also called my attention to significant points that I would otherwise have missed.

Anyone who writes about Albuquerque, and that includes myself, must acknowledge the splendid contribution of journalist Howard Bryan, who for many years has covered much authoritative material on the city's history in his column, "Off the Beaten Path," appearing regularly in the *Albuquerque Tribune*. He also provided me directions to the ruined hacienda of Spruce M. Baird in the South Valley.

Editor David Holtby and the production staff at the University of New Mexico Press deserve credit for seeing the manuscript through the difficult stages of publication. And, finally, a word of thanks to my research associate and typist, Susie Henderson.

MARC SIMMONS

Los Cerrillos, New Mexico
Summer 1982

Albuquerque

One of the earliest and most valuable lessons history teaches to such as can be taught anything is that you and I and our times are not the earth and the fullness thereof, but mere drops in an inevitable tide. Incredible as it may seem, there was some world before we got here. And when we can face and begin to grasp that inconsiderate truth, we are in a fair way to be able to get some good out of history.

— CHARLES F. LUMMIS

The Geography Behind History

THE SHAPE OF THE LAND, its composition, flora and fauna, variances in elevation and climate have all combined in an interlocking web to produce Albuquerque's physical setting. It is that geography which provides one of the master keys for understanding the way human activity has developed here. The land, in offering opportunities and imposing limitations, has determined, to a significant degree, the course of history in the Albuquerque Valley. But the influence has not been all one-sided. Man, for his part, has redesigned and remolded the landscape, so that he himself has become a forceful, and sometimes destructive, agent of geographical change.

Far back in the gray dawn of geologic history, perhaps two billion or more years ago, the unstable crust of the earth was twisted, wrenched, and pierced by violent forces of various kinds issuing from the depths of the globe. Intense concentrations of heat melted underlying rock and at many points burst through the surface as volcanoes, spewing ash and molten lava. In parts of New Mexico, massive mountains, of a height to rival Mount Everest, rose in smoking majesty above vast lenses of mud and beds of sandstone. Within time—time measured in millennia—the eroding action of wind, rain, and snow wore down those mighty peaks and cast the debris from them onto empty plains.

In that long-ago age, which geologists call the Precambrian Era, much of the underground heated rock failed to break through to the surface. Instead, trapped beneath the crust, it slowly cooled and solidified to form a heavy foundation of granite. But the rock tended to be brittle, so that when subsequent stress in the earth led to shifting and uplifting, the granite fractured into sharp blocks of various sizes. It was this basement granite that would one day form the core of the Sandias, Sangre de Cristos, and many of the other mountain ranges of New Mexico.

During later periods of landscape formation, great inland seas advanced and retreated in successive stages. Since their waters were teeming with marine life, and contained suspended sediments, they left behind thick beds of limestone, sandstone, and shale, capping the older Precambrian rock. At intervals, the land rose from the water to be subjected to the eroding forces of weather and wind. Then it would sink again to lower elevations, allowing the sea to return and renew the deposits that had been worn away. The process continued for hundreds of millions of years.[1]

Some 250 to 300 million years ago, in the period termed Pennsylvanian, another layer of limestone accumulated in what would one day be central New Mexico. At the same time, streams and rivers flowing into lagoons deposited sediments that eventually became sandstones. In the Pennsylvanian rocks, where they have been exposed today, one can discover marine fossils of diverse and strange forms—corals, crinoids, brachiopods, and trilobites, for example.

Plant and animal life of that time bore practically no resemblance to what we know now. There were no grasses or flowering plants and none of our common trees. Ferns of infinite variety choked the swampy lowlands. Trees, of a kind long extinct, soared 100 feet in the air. Mammals had not yet appeared, but an abundance of primitive amphibians and reptiles fed and reproduced in the primeval muck. The dank and heavy air was filled with flying insects, like the giant dragonfly with a wingspread of 20 to 30 inches. Armies of outsized cockroaches lumbered about amid the ferns, so numerous that some geologists speak of the period as "The Age of Cockroaches."[2]

Roughly 70 million years ago, late in the Cretaceous Period, land features that we would recognize began to emerge in New Mexico. An extensive upheaval of the earth's crust, referred to as the Laramide revolution, definitively raised the interior of the continent above the seas. Volcanic activity of considerable magnitude, thrusting from below, pushed up the Rocky Mountains, including its southern extension, the Sangre de Cristos. In the broad marshes filled with water lilies, rushes, and eucalyptus that stretched from the base of the highlands, gargantuan dinosaurs and needle-toothed reptiles found a congenial home. Interspersed among the ancient forms of plant life grew oak, poplar, ash, willow, and other examples of modern flora that were beginning to come into their own.

The main topographic landmarks in the vicinity of Albuquerque, however, were still to be erected. That did not happen until late Miocene and Pliocene times, between 25 and 5 million years ago. In other words, the area's mountains, volcanoes, and mesas, born toward the near end of the earth's historical scale, must be thought of as relatively young. Certainly in geologic time, they are not ancient.

The processes at work, which raised the land to new elevations, were the same ones that had operated intermittently since the beginnings of the planet. To the east of what would later be the Middle Rio Grande Valley, underground heat and compression forced a massive break in the earth's shell. On one side of the fault, or crack, that appeared, the land rose vertically, creating a sheer bluff facing west. The overall effect was of a great block jacked up on one end and with its tilted surface sloping eastward. At the outset, many discolored bands of rock representing deposition in previous ages must have been clearly visible on the fractured face of this promontory. They rested, layer upon layer, over a now exposed foundation of Precambrian granite. But almost at once, nature summoned its timeless agents of erosion and began stripping away the stratified levels of overburden. The cutting down and sculpting that continued for millennia ultimately left a pair of much diminished mountain ranges, which men would one day call the Sandias and Manzanos.

At the time of the original uplift east of the fault, the land immediately to the west began to drop, ultimately leaving an elongated sediment-filled cavity thousands of feet in depth. The simultaneous movement—up on one side, down on the other—may be compared to a terrestrial seesaw whose pivot point lay astride the fault line. The 90-mile-long depression, created on the down side, has been named the Rio Grande trough.

This earthshaking event did not occur overnight. The seesaw movement progressed slowly, if we rate it in terms of human lifetimes. Indeed, there is evidence that it continues to this day: imperceptibly the trough is still sinking, the mountains are still rising.

Similar examples of the same process took place both on the north and south. Beginning in central Colorado, a series of faults resulted in the formation of a string of troughs, sided by mountains or high plateaus, which extend southward to the vicinity of El Paso. The entire chain of troughs geologists have labeled the Rio Grande structural depression.

Almost as soon as the troughs appeared, they began to fill with sand, gravel, silt, clay, even rocks and boulders—whatever wind, gravity, and running water cared to dump in them from the surrounding highlands. Below the Sandia uplift, such material eventually accumulated to a thickness of 10,000 feet in the Rio Grande trough; at least, this is the best estimate of scientists. As massive a deposit as that leads us to believe that Albuquerque now rests upon the surface of one of the world's greatest troughs.

That fact is of more than academic interest. A trench in the ground, even when it is filled with sediment, acts as a huge natural reservoir. Here the loosely compacted sand, silt, and gravel are highly permeable. Through the ages water percolating downward has completely saturated many of the strata within the trough, so that such water now makes up an estimated 10 to 20 percent of the total fill. Albuquerque, as a result of this geological arrangement, is perhaps the best watered city in the Southwest. A single well has been known to pump up to 3,000 gallons per minute.[3]

While faulting was creating the Sandia uplift and the Rio Grande trough, volcanic action began to modify the landscape along the western skyline. In the Miocene, violent eruptions started to build up the San Mateo Mountains. The highest cone in this range, Mount Taylor, now

5

rises to an altitude of 11,389 feet, and is clearly visible from most sections of east Albuquerque. How much higher the old volcano may have been before erosion trimmed it down is open to speculation.

Although the most spectacular in terms of size, Mount Taylor was but one in a field of some 200 lesser volcanoes. Among a number of these, lava congealed in the throat of the cones and when, later, the outer surface weathered away, a volcanic plug, or neck, was left behind. The Puerco Basin, between Mount Taylor and the Rio Grande Valley, is littered with these geological curiosities. The best known example is Cabezon Peak.

The volcanoes of this region continued to rumble and pour forth flows of basalt and andesite for a long period. As a consequence, lava plateaus grew up on the flanks of the cones, forming broad, dark tables like the Mesa Chivato and Mesa Prieta. The most recent of such outflows, the lava beds near Grants, is perhaps no more than 1,000 years old.[4]

Fifty or so miles northeast of Mount Taylor, more volcanic activity built up the Jemez plateau. At its center arose a colossal smoking cone belching fire, lava, and ash. Estimates of its height range from 14,000 to 27,000 feet. In a series of cataclysmic eruptions, the mountain cast up great clouds of cinders and gases that darkened the sky. Held aloft in the atmosphere, much of the material drifted eastward, where it eventually settled to earth over Oklahoma and Kansas. In the country immediately surrounding the volcano, the ashfall accumulated to a depth of hundreds of feet, compacting and forming a thick layer of tuff.

Throughout its long tenure of violence, the mountain, fuming by day and glowing by night, literally coughed out its insides. Underneath, a spacious chamber was opened without pillars or support of any kind. Finally, the roof could no longer hold the volcano's weight and it gave way. The collapsing earth swallowed up the princely peak and the larger debris that had fallen at its foot. In the process, an expansive caldera, or craterlike depression, the Valle Grande, was left in the center of the Jemez plateau.

Straining to relieve internal heat and pressure that lingered, the forces of volcanism gave one last shuddering heave beneath the caldera and pushed up three rounded domes of rhyolite. These intruding domes, really mountains, divided the floor of the caldera into separate valleys. Later, melt water from winter snows collected in the lows, creating a deep crater lake in which tops of the domes became islands.

The lake began to drain, some 25,000 years ago, as breaches on the western rim of the caldera allowed impounded water to escape into the Jemez River and its tributary San Antonio Creek. Some of the moisture seeping into the ground was warmed by residual heat from the original volcano and under pressure reemerged at selected points as hot springs. Indeed, scientists now regard the vicinity of the caldera as a geothermal energy "hot spot." Test wells sunk in the grassy floor of the basin have led to the conviction that enough heat is available to supply Albuquerque's energy needs for the foreseeable future—if it can be harnessed to generate electricity.[5]

The latter phases of land formation in the Jemez, which we have been describing, took place during the Ice Age or Pleistocene, that is, within the last million years. From the direction of the north polar cap, sheets of ice invaded the interior of North America. Although the continental glaciers did not actually reach New Mexico or even Colorado, small mountain glaciers did form in the higher valleys. During periods of moderating climate, these ice masses tended to migrate slowly to lower levels, widening the valleys and gouging the earth as they moved. In their descent, the mountain glaciers began to melt. Their copious waters, carrying much broken rock, cascaded from the highlands to the country below. The force of the flood as well as the work of the cutting rock recarved the land surface into new shapes. It also opened new channels for rivers. One of the rivers, born in this way during the middle Pleistocene, was the Rio Grande.

High on the eastern slope of the Continental Divide in Colorado's central Rockies, glacial melt water collecting in a turbulent stream found an outlet southward through the structural depression left from a previous age. In a blind rush toward sea level, the headwaters moved quantities of rock and earth over vast distances, dropping them at those spots where the valley widened and the current slowed. At Albuquerque, the new river's first task seems to have been one of filling in, with its rich burden of sediment, the lows still remaining in the great trough. Afterward, owing to climatic change and additional uplift of adjacent regions, the Rio Grande started to erode its newly formed floodplain and carry the debris downstream. Indeed, a cycle of erosion and deposition was established that continues to the present.

During one of the deposition phases, the river laid down a band of mud and sand, more than 200 feet in depth, over what is now Albuquerque's downtown area. The valley surface then was well above the tops of today's tall buildings. In a subsequent stage of scouring and cutting, the Rio Grande again removed the assorted sediments, after which it initiated a new period of filling. This last phase, one of deposition, began roughly 20,000 years ago and is still in progress. Thus far the river current has returned approximately 75 feet of alluvium to the inner valley flanking its main channel. This constant raising of the land by accretion accounts for many of the flooding and drainage problems that have plagued human settlement here.

One other major feature of the land around Albuquerque is yet to be mentioned. Some time late in the Pleistocene, after the Rio Grande had set its course through the center of New Mexico, two nearly aligned fractures in the earth, about 4.5 miles long, opened west of the river and roughly parallel to it. Fiery lava, rising from deep in the earth, shot forth in at least eighteen separate eruption points along the line of the break. In five places the liquid rock and compacted cinders built up volcanic cones. From these, a series of lava sheets emerged and spread successively over the river lowlands to the east and north. Hardening into a basaltic cap, the old flows may have once covered upward of 50 square miles. But that is merely a guess, since the Rio Grande, using the cutting edge of erosion, has bulldozed away all but 23 square miles of the original sheath.

So recent was this eruptive activity (about 190,000 years ago) that the five volcanoes have not ceased their cooling. After a heavy snowfall has mantled the ground with white, these guardians of Albuquerque's western skyline, standing smartly in a row, show faces as black as ever. The remnant of heat locked within is still sufficient to melt off quickly any accumulation of snow.

Even now hot drafts can be detected issuing from vents and caves. Periodically over the past century the volcanoes have sent up clouds of gaseous vapors. In 1881, just a year after the founding of New Albuquerque, the local press reported that one of the volcanoes west of the city was emitting smoke. The sight may have caused mild alarm among recent arrivals, who perhaps wondered if the ground was not preparing for a major explosion.

That unhappy possibility seemed on the point of coming to pass some years later when Albuquerque residents were startled by a loud boom reverberating from the west mesa. One of the volcanic cones had begun to belch villainous clouds of black smoke and in preparation for a major disaster, the fire and police departments turned out in force. Panic, however, was as short-lived as the eruption. Investigation swiftly revealed a hoax: college boys had filled the crater with old tires and set them afire.

The Albuquerque volcanoes appear related to other recent volcanic fields north near Bernalillo and south in the vicinity of Isleta and Belen. All fall within an unstable belt that extends toward Socorro on the west side of the Rio Grande. Within this narrow zone, 76 percent of New Mexico's recorded earthquakes have occurred. Army surgeon John F. Hammond first called attention, back in 1850, to a concentration of seismic disturbances in this area. While stationed at Socorro, he noted a total of twenty-eight earthquakes during a fifteen-month period. A similar "swarm" (a series of quakes in rapid succession) shook the ground surrounding Belen during 1935–36. Since 1893 at least thirteen tremors have originated directly beneath Albuquerque. Seismologists predict that at least one major earthquake, of magnitude 6, can be expected each one hundred years.[6]

After a couple of billion years of preparation, the land around Albuquerque was ready to receive man. The period beginning, say, 20,000 years ago, when the earliest Paleo-Indian hunters may have wandered in, and continuing down to the present, must be regarded as but a brief moment in the total span of geologic history. Changes in the landscape during that recent time, whether produced by erosion, climatic variations, or by man himself appear insignificant matched against the cataclysmic alterations in the earth's surface that had gone before.

But now that the stage is set—that the river, the plains, the mesas, and the mountains have been shown to possess their own history—let us look at them, individually and, then, collectively, to see how they appear today and how they have influenced, in combination with weather, the growth and character of human societies.

First, to take a panoramic view at ground level, we can select no better vantage point than the banks of the Rio Grande. For Europeans, who began keeping a written historical record of the valley more than 400 years ago, the river furnished an attractive environment for settlement, and its long-trending valley running roughly north to south offered a natural avenue of travel. Without the Rio Grande, there would have been no Albuquerque—at least on its present site.

When Spaniards under Coronado first came to this valley in September of 1540, they heard the river called P'osoge by the resident Pueblo Indians, which in their language meant "Big River." The main stream channel then was much wider and deeper than it is today, and as there existed no other river anywhere close by that could rival it, in either size or volume, the name was quite apt. For Coronado's men, however, P'osoge proved too strange and heathen-sounding for their tastes, so they christened it El Río de Nuestra Señora, or the River of Our Lady.

But that name did not last. A Franciscan padre in 1581 proposed calling it Guadalquivir, after the foremost river in southern Spain. But it too, after a brief period of popularity, fell by the wayside. Later through common usage, Río Grande del Norte (or often simply, Río del Norte) emerged as the favored and accepted name—the Big River of the North. So, Big River it was to be after all.

Stacked against the Mississippi, the Missouri, the Columbia, or any one of a dozen other major American rivers that flow broad and deep, the Rio Grande makes a poor showing. But rated in terms of history and romance, it must be ranked near the top. Exuberant and starry-eyed young soldiers marching off to fight the Mexican War in 1846 caught its gilded color in the words of one of their popular songs:

> Oh, say were you ever on the Rio Grande?
> Way, you Rio!
> It's there that the river runs down golden sand.
> For we're bound for the Rio Grande.
> And a-way, you Ri-o! Way, you Rio![7]

Upon close inspection, golden sand is hard to come by along the river, at least near Albuquerque. Equally scarce is clear and shining water, which one expects, by rights, to find in any western waterway fed with winter's snowpack from the Rockies. The Rio Grande, of course, is crystal pure when it tumbles cold and sweet out of Colorado. But almost from the moment it enters New Mexico, silt and grit are swept up by the rushing current so that by the time it reaches the Middle Valley, its color, depending on the season of the year, lies somewhere in the range between lion-yellow and chocolate.

Through the valley above and below Albuquerque, the Rio Grande meanders over its inner floodplain, whose perimeter on either side is defined at many places by steep, sandy bluffs. At Bernalillo the river runs close to the western edge of the plain; but a few miles downstream at Corrales it makes a curve to the east, before swinging abruptly westward again as it approaches Albuquerque's upper limits. Northwest of downtown (at the Interstate 40 bridge) the Rio Grande flows against the base of confining cliffs. By lateral cutting, the current is eroding these cliffs, whose height varies from 25 to 150 feet, and in the process is enlarging the breadth of the valley. Immediately below, the channel assumes a southeasterly direction as it loops through the Barelas section of Albuquerque.

We know from geologic studies that the river has not always followed its present course. Until harnessed in the twentieth century by dams along its upper and lower reaches, the Rio Grande with each springtime flood leaped its banks and spread in a dark sheet across its inner valley. At some point, perhaps a thousand or two thousand years ago, the main channel ran in a fairly direct line south from Alameda through what is at present the downtown section of Albuquerque. An overflow then caused it to shift to a new and lower course, forming the westward bow that exists now.

Periodic flooding by the Rio Grande, together with the singular structure of the great trough through which it sweeps, have combined to produce severe drainage problems. At the time of the city's founding in the early eighteenth century, the valley's water table lay very close to the surface. The porous soil readily soaked up moisture seeping from the river, which, at low spots on the floodplain collected in mud flats, marshes, and ponds. With a careful eye, the first Spanish colonists selected scattered patches of high ground within the valley for use as farmland. On these the water table was down far enough so that it did not interfere with the raising of crops. Large areas of bog between the fields were simply neglected or used for occasional grazing. This was the case, too, with the wide Swamp of Mejía, which once covered much of the district from present Central Avenue south to the Barelas bridge.

One of the central paradoxes of the Albuquerque Valley is that in spite of the abundance of ground water a few feet below the surface, cropland must still be irrigated. Rainfall alone, currently averaging 8.06 inches per year, cannot sustain agriculture. Not only is the quantity insufficient, but it is unevenly distributed through the summer growing season. Colonial farmers met the challenge by constructing a web of *acequias,* or "irrigation ditches," so that thirsty fields could be watered when needed. This solution, however, spawned an added problem. Seepage from the ditches, like that from the river itself, contributed to the creation of new bogs and the increase of alkali in the soil.

The Rio Grande, throughout historic times, has possessed the character of an aggrading stream, which means that it is constantly in the process of depositing its heavy load of suspended sediments, thereby building up its bed. It also raises flanking banks, forming natural levees, so that the river in effect provides for its own confinement. At Albuquerque this resulted in a curious situation. The channel bottom actually reached an elevation several feet higher than that of the land paralleling it along the east side of the valley. The phenomenon was accentuated by the introduction of man-made levees, designed to hold back flood waters, and by the building of Elephant Butte Dam in 1916 (145 miles down-river), which slowed the current as far north as Albuquerque and caused more silt to be dropped. The progressive rising of the channel resulted in a corresponding rise of the water table, and, as a consequence, increasing numbers of fields in the surrounding valley became waterlogged and useless for agriculture. By the 1920s, the problem had rendered almost half the farmland lying 50 miles north and south of the city unfit for cultivation.[8]

The long belt of lowlands east of the river, which is astride the old abandoned channel that extends down from Alameda, constitutes what is usually termed a *Yazoo*. This is simply a depression that cannot drain properly because the adjacent river lies above it. Albuquerque's Yazoo, until recent diversion work was completed, received the runoff from at least eight major arroyos that headed in the Sandia Mountains. Since the ground was already saturated by the shallow water table and could absorb little of the inflow, the new water collected in thin ponds, which the Spaniards called *esteros*. The ponds sat, stagnating and breeding insects, until evaporation dried them up.

New Albuquerque, laid out in 1880, resided in the midst of the Yazoo. At the time a small *estero* was situated just north of Railroad Avenue (later Central) and town planners hastily cut a ditch toward the south to provide for drainage. Afterward, the dry bed of the *estero* served as a site for the city hall. Incoming residents who took up house lots discovered that digging a well within the Yazoo was the simplest of tasks. One merely had to scoop out a hole a few feet deep, insert a wooden barrel with the bottom knocked out to serve as casing, and a plentiful supply of water trickled into the cavity.[9]

The Yazoo, however, was more a bane than a boon. Albuquerqueans lived constantly under the threat of a major disaster from flood. The prime danger point was at Alameda where the Rio Grande began its westward curve. If the river at highwater ever broke through to its old channel, citizens knew that a torrent would pour into the Yazoo and inundate the city. As we will see later, they spent a great deal of time, effort, and money over many decades to prevent that very thing from happening.

Albuquerque's flood and drainage problems, associated with the river, were not attacked in any systematic way until creation of the Rio Grande Conservancy District in 1925. That entity, organized as a political agency of the state under the Conservancy Act, developed an elaborate system of riverside drains and diversion dams. These works, along with a drought in the 1930s and 1940s and heavy use of domestic and industrial wells, brought about a lowering of the water table and the reclaiming of much swampland.[10]

Like most rivers, the Rio Grande is a fickle lady. Some years, her tempestuous waters fed by deep snowpacks in the mountains or torrential summer thunderstorms, threaten the levees and ditches with which men have clothed her flanks. At other times when moisture is short, she shrinks away to nothing and children at play walk dry-shod from one shore to the other. It is this proneness to go to extremes that has made her the butt of jokes.

The river is usually so muddy, some Albuquerqueans are fond of saying, that a nearsighted farmer once tried to plow it. Humorist Will Rogers went one better when he visited the city in late summer and found that water in the Rio Grande had disappeared. "Why friend," he told Governor Clyde Tingley, "you ought to be out there right now, irrigatin' that river to keep it from blowin' away."[11]

Wit aside, the Rio Grande for all its devilish ambivalence remains Albuquerque's most estimable natural resource. The struggle by man— early Indian and Spanish farmers and modern engineers—to control her waters and turn them to productive use stands as one of the most significant and persistent themes woven through the city's long story.

Looking west from the Rio Grande anywhere within Albuquerque's city limits, one sees an ascending river terrace representing the remnant of an old floodplain. This feature is now spoken of as the West Mesa, but Hispanic folk long referred to it as *La Loma,* "the Hill." At its western rim, a second mesa rises like a giant step whose surface sweeps gently upward to the skyline. It is known as La Ceja del Rio Puerco because for a distance of 20 miles north and 50 miles south of Albuquerque this mesa forms the divide between the Rio Grande and the Rio Puerco. *La ceja* literally means a "brow" or "ridge," but the Spaniards of New Mexico were in the habit of applying the word to any flat country that lay above such a formation.

Along the east boundary of the Ceja stand the five volcanoes, which rest on a platform of black rock constructed during successive eruptions. From a distance, this basal rock appears to be a dark outspreading apron with scalloped edges and with a studded belt, formed by the volcanoes, at its waist. On the talus slopes below the apron, a multitude of boulders lie scattered, as if cast at random by the hand of some Goliath or of an Indian deity. The smooth faces of these stones attracted ancient Pueblo artists, who covered them with thousands of engraved and incised figures. This primitive picture gallery displays people, animals, birds, religious masks and symbols, as well as a profusion of abstract designs. Probably no other American city can boast of so much native art preserved at its doorstep.

On the opposite side of the Rio Grande, an eastward-stretching terrace grades upward toward the foot of the Sandia Mountains. At Albuquerque the terrace is some 8 to 9 miles wide, while farther north near Bernalillo it scarcely exists at all, the foothills of the mountains encroaching upon the river having squeezed it out. This table land is officially named the Sandia Mesa, but now it is commonly spoken of as the East Mesa, or The Heights.

As with the West Mesa, the East Mesa structurally represents a remnant of the Rio Grande's old floodplain. But because it is backed by the Sandias, the eastern terrace also contains strata of out-wash material from the mountains. Through time, heavy downpours have carried mud, gravel, and pumpkin-sized boulders out of the Sandias' canyons, depos- iting them in fan-shaped formations at the base of the mountains. From the canyon mouths, the intermittent streams raised by the rain have flowed toward the Rio Grande and in their progress have left the terrace seamed by arroyos. Tijeras Creek, draining a large catchment area at the southern end of the Sandias, has opened the deepest arroyo. At one point in its nine-mile course to the river it reaches 250 feet in depth.[12]

If the Rio Grande, its inner valley, and its lateral terraces or mesas are taken as half the equation making up Albuquerque's landscape, then that leaves the Sandia and Manzano mountains, walling the eastern skyline, to provide the other half. The lowlands are one environment, the uplands another. Of the two it is the mountains—their crests catching evening's last burst of sunlight or snagging zigzag bursts of bluish lightning from a summer shower—that fire man's imagination and evoke his wonder and awe.

Sandia, in the language of the Spaniard, means "watermelon." In Spain itself a portion of the majestic Sierra Nevada in the province of Granada goes by the name El Corazón de la Sandía because its appearance reminds one of the heart of a melon. The same imagery must have caught the eye of the seventeenth-century explorers in the Middle Rio Grande Valley. The overall shape of the main range certainly bears a striking resemblance to a neatly sliced wedge of watermelon and the effect is heightened by the pervasive coloration of red at sunset which lights up the coarse-grained Precambrian granite exposed on the western face. Near the ridge line at the summit, thin layers of pale Pennsylvanian limestone and a cover of dark timber even suggest banded green rind.[13]

If the Spaniards perceived a watermelon, the Pueblo Indians who peopled the country below saw something altogether different. For them, the outline of the sierra brought to mind the humped shell of a turtle and so they used the name Oku Piñ, signifying Turtle Mountain. In spite of its unglamorous title, Turtle Mountain was a holy place. Deities, including Wind Woman and Spider Woman, dwelled there. And sacred shrines were hidden in nooks within the foothills and up among the highest crags.

To the Pueblo way of thinking there was nothing incongruous in the fact that hallowed Turtle Mountain was also consecrated to war. The father of the Twin War Gods had his home there, and from a rocky lair near cloud level his pair of sons sallied forth to do battle with the monsters and demons that, according to Indian mythology, plagued the ancient world. While the Twins were expert warriors, they also received credit as consummate peacemakers, so in that capacity at least they contributed to Turtle Mountain's reputation as a birthplace of holy beings.[14]

From a distance the Sandia Mountains give the appearance of a single compacted mass rather than of an attenuated range, so that people are often inclined to speak of it in the singular, as the Sandia Mountain. Closer inspection, however, reveals separate and distinct peaks. The highest, North Sandia Peak, rises to an elevation of 10,678 feet. From its wooded shoulder a broad saddle, known as Sandia Crest, extends in a direct line to South Sandia Peak, at an altitude of 9,782 feet.

Below these heights on the west, knobs, columns, and pinnacles of granite have weathered out to form appendages on the main body of the range. Along the talus mound at their base, massive boulders, some round, some angular, lie in random profusion, having long before broken loose from the overhanging mountain. Ages of erosion, which molded the spires and cast off the boulders, were also responsible for the vigorous carving of short steep-walled canyons indenting the face of the western escarpment. It is runoff from these canyons that feeds the arroyos draining the East Mesa.

The opposite side of the Sandias offers a completely different picture. In place of the sheer cliffs that plummet abruptly to the floor of the Rio Grande Valley, the mountain east of the crest slopes at a comparatively gentle gradient toward the plains beyond. Light-gray limestone alternating with beds of dark shale cap the underlying foundation of granite. The general smoothness of the surface and a thick growth of evergreens convey the impression of a tilted table top covered with green baize.

One other important feature of the Sandia Mountains bears mentioning. At the northwest end of the chain, a series of low outliers joined by a continuous ridge forms a subrange, which can be likened to an arm fastened to the shoulder of North Sandia Peak. From the point of connection, the arm extends in a westerly direction toward Bernalillo on the river, but then at the elbow it bends south in a crook, creating an open-ended valley, of the kind the Spaniards referred to as a *rincón*. From that, the heights have taken their name: Rincon Ridge. The little valley is now designated the Juan Tabó Recreation Area.[15]

The Sandias, with an overall length of approximately 20 miles, end suddenly on their southern extremity at Tijeras Canyon. This narrow defile separates the Sandia Mountains from the Manzanos, which lead on southward, parallel to the Rio Grande, for another 40 miles.

Tijeras means "scissors." The name apparently derives from the forking of the canyon near the present village of Tijeras, which to some Spaniard must have suggested an open pair of scissors. An older and alternate name for the canyon is Carnué (also Carnuel). Origin of that term is obscure, but one guess is that it represents the corruption of some Tiwa Indian word.[16]

The canyon is drained by Tijeras Creek, an intermittent stream fed by small springs and seeps. The flow was probably once greater than it is today, for we know that Spanish farmers in colonial times tapped the creek for irrigation purposes. In late summer, cloudbursts occasionally fill the stream bed with a cascading torrent of runoff, resulting in erosion and down-cutting of the canyon floor.

As is the case on the west face of the Sandias, erosion here has exposed large areas of Precambrian granite as well as the overlay of Pennsylvanian rocks. The latter strata are quarried by the Ideal Cement Company, which has a large plant (built in 1957), consisting of mills and kilns, in the center of the canyon. Pennsylvanian limestone, dolomite, shale, and gypsum constitute the principal raw materials used in the operation.

For centuries, Tijeras Canyon has served as a natural passageway between the river on the west and the Estancia Valley on the east. Apaches and Spaniards long used a slender foot and horse trail threading the gap. In 1858, the United States Army opened a respectable wagon road, which was not significantly improved until the 1920s when it was expanded to a two-lane thoroughfare for automobiles. During the following decade, the road got its first coating of asphalt. In 1927, the entire length of U.S. 66, of which it formed a segment, was designated as the Will Rogers Highway. Today, the route through the canyon is marked by a modern six-lane interstate, a far cry from the primitive trail earlier travelers knew.

The Manzano Mountains below Tijeras are geologically similar to the Sandias. That is, they consist of a fault-block whose vertical face overlooks the Rio Grande Valley and whose tilted surface of Pennsylvania marine strata grades eastward into the Estancia Valley. The range is actually divided into several units. The northernmost, called the Manzanita Mountains, appears from a distance to be a fairly even ridge running south from Tijeras Canyon and connecting with the higher Manzano Mountains proper. At the western foot of the Manzanitas rise a sprinkling of lower detached hills, which have been incorporated in the Sandia Military Reservation. Their hollowed out interiors now serve as storage for atomic weapons.

At Guadalupe Peak (9,450 feet), the main Manzanos begin. Within the range's serrated profile, several peaks achieve elevations above 10,000 feet. Some 20 miles to the south, the sierra interlocks at Abó Pass with the less rugged Los Pinos Mountains. Abó Pass, southeast of Belen, was a main east-west artery of travel in colonial days, just like Tijeras Canyon.[18]

The Spaniards, in the beginning at least, did not recognize that the Manzanos were structurally independent from the Sandias, and so they spoke of both as the Sierra de Sandia, as if they were but a single range. Some time after 1800, a stray band of colonists planted a small settlement on the lower margin of the wooded eastern slope. Along with grain fields, they put in a couple of orchards of *manzanos,* small sweet Mexican apples. From those fruit trees, the new community as well as the entire chain of mountains south of Tijeras Canyon took their names.[19]

As the topography of the Albuquerque area has influenced the course of human history, so too has climate. Its effects—temperature, variations in rainfall, and storms—as we have seen, are a prime factor in shaping the physical landscape; but they also have a significant bearing on the activities of man. People are highly sensitive to weather. Their health and mental activity, it has been often demonstrated, are closely tuned to changing atmospheric conditions. Moreover, climate, as one of the chief determinants of soils, sets limits to the range of natural vegetation and to the kinds of agriculture that man can practice. An understanding of Albuquerque, both past and present, requires, therefore, some knowledge of her distinctive climatic situation.

Among those ingredients that go into the city's serving of weather, sunshine is the one that Albuquerqueans appreciate and comment upon the most. There is no question that sunlight is abundant: on an average there are only five days a year in which the sky is completely overcast and the sun does not break through. During one record stretch, between December 1961 and February 1964, the sun shone, at least briefly, for 779 consecutive days. Moreover, some one hundred days a year, on the average, are virtually cloudless.[20]

The beneficial effects of sunlight upon mankind have been recognized for centuries. New Mexico's Pueblo Indians have long sent village elders to the rooftops to welcome the sunrise with prayer and song. Spanish and Anglo-American newcomers to the Rio Grande Valley often spoke eloquently in their chronicles of the abundance of sunshine, even in winter. It was this invigorating and curative resource that lured thousands of sufferers of tuberculosis and other pulmonary ailments to Albuquerque in the nineteenth and early twentieth centuries.

The amplitude of sunshine, for all its benefits, is associated with scant and unevenly distributed rainfall, rapid evaporation, and low humidity. The valley and bracketing mesas receive only 8 to 10 inches of rain yearly, the higher elevations in Tijeras Canyon 14 to 16 inches, and the crests of the Sandias and Manzanos up to about 30 inches. Much of the city's annual quota of rain comes in short, violent thunderstorms crowded together during the wet season, from July to September. This pattern gives rise to flash floods and causes damage to soil, vegetation, buildings, and irrigation works. It also contributes to arroyo cutting on the East and West Mesas.[21]

The Rio Grande trough, with Albuquerque near its center, is an area of low precipitation, mainly for two reasons. One is that the mountain barriers on the east block much, though by no means all, of the moisture-laden winds that blow from the Gulf of Mexico. A second reason is that eastward-moving storms from the Pacific have already dumped their heaviest burden of rain before they reach central New Mexico. The same moderating factors also apply to the winter's snowfall. As frigid polar air swirls down the eastern plains, entering the state in the vicinity of Raton, it meets warm Gulf air and is pushed west. Cold and snow accompanying such storms hit the Sandia-Manzano barrier and are deflected back toward the Estancia Basin and the plains beyond. Occasionally some of the disturbance will break around the north end of the Sandias or through Tijeras Canyon, leaving a dusting of snow in the heights and funneling an icy wind into the Rio Grande bottoms. But without the sheltering mountains, the amount of snow and rain Albuquerque receives would be doubled, and temperature extremes would be far more severe. As it is, most of the city's yearly ration of snow, averaging 10 inches, comes from the tag end of Pacific storms.[22]

The mountains, proclaim meteorologists, also keep the Albuquerque Valley free from tornadoes. Their heights, by checking the full flow of warm, moist air needed to feed a gathering cyclone, shield the city from the kinds of violent storms that periodically ravage the flatlands of the central United States. But this is not to say that Albuquerque has been wholly spared from the disagreeable effects of high winds. Indeed, the intensity of its spring "windy season" has, through the years, evoked as much adverse comment as the exhilarating sunshine has promoted favorable applause.

During March and April, the stiff westerlies blow across New Mexico with velocities up to 70 miles per hour. Commonly this wind activity is confined to the daylight hours, commencing soon after sunup and picking up speed as the day advances. As the fierce gusts boil over mesas and prairie, they sift out powdery dust and coarser particles from the dry topsoil and lift it in dirty, billowy clouds that obscure the sky and sun. In a tone of disgust, a Confederate soldier with the rebel army that occupied Albuquerque in March of 1862, recorded his feelings toward the windy weather. "The sand and gravel . . . [flew] in a manner that I never saw before. I would compare it to a description that I have seen of the sand storms of the great desert of Sahara."[23] His displeasure was shared in larger measure by the housewives, immigrants from the East, who came later and faced the task of keeping airborne grit from their parlors and bedchambers. Lina Fergusson Browne, daughter of a pioneer family, remarks in her memoirs that fine furniture had to be draped with protective covers and that following a particularly blustery storm it was not uncommon to collect a dustpan full of sand from a single window sill.

The problem was one the Indians had coped with for ages, and learned to tolerate. Sandia Pueblo, just north of the city, was called Na-fi-at in the Tiwa language, a word whose aptness of meaning could scarcely be improved upon: "Dusty Place."

Brief winter winds can also be troublesome, especially when they build up tremendous pressure behind the mountains and then rush suddenly into the valley. It was that situation precisely which spawned the strongest gale ever recorded in the city. On December 9, 1943, the wind reached 90 miles an hour.[24] With that record in mind, one can better understand why old-timers claim, with a chuckle, that the most practical wind gauge for central New Mexico is an ox chain fastened to a post.

Albuquerque, at an elevation of 5,000 feet, experiences temperatures characteristic of high altitude, dry, continental climates. But here again, the presence of the Sandias and Manzanos exerts as much influence over temperature ranges as it does over storm and wind patterns. West of the mountains, the thermometer drops to zero degrees only once every two or three years, while at the village of Estancia 35 miles to the east, the mercury reaches zero on average seven times a year.

It is apparent that the Middle Rio Grande Valley has not always enjoyed the relatively mild winters and temperate summers in evidence today. During portions of the colonial period, a swing in the climatic cycle seems to have produced marked extremes in temperature and to have been accompanied by a lengthening of the winter season and an increase in snowfall. Men of the Coronado expedition, encamped near Bernalillo, suffered through shuddering cold late into March of 1541. Some ninety years later, the Franciscan friar, Father Alonso de Benavides, informs us that in winter the Rio Grande congealed to a marblelike solidity, permitting heavily loaded wagons and large herds of cattle to move across it in perfect safety. It was so cold, he complains, that sacramental wine froze in the chalice while he was saying Mass, even though two braziers burned upon the altar for warmth. And every year, the padre adds, many Indians froze to death and some Spaniards had their ears, feet, and hands frostbitten. "On the contrary," he notes, "in summer the heat is more intolerable than the cold in winter."[25]

A shifting of climatic zones resulting in wider variations of temperature, of the kind Father Benavides and his contemporaries knew, could happen again one day in the Albuquerque Valley. But for the present, the area, enjoying a daytime average temperature of 50 degrees in winter, and summer highs of less than 90 degrees (except in July), lays claim to one of the most perfect all-round climates in the United States.

Temperature and availability of moisture influence the biotic communities—the associations of plants and animals, which characterize the Albuquerque Valley and adjacent highlands. As one would expect from our previous references to abundant underground water in the Rio Grande trough, lands along the river are capable of supporting a rich flora. Urban sprawl accompanied by assorted pollutants has, of course, significantly altered the natural environment. But a remarkable amount of native vegetation and wildlife can still be found, particularly inside the levees that confine the river channel.

The most attractive feature of the lowlands are the *bosques*, the groves of Rio Grande cottonwood—sparse now within the limits of Albuquerque, but still thick both above and below the city. In summer their dense green foliage spreads a welcome lattice of shade upon the river's banks, and in autumn they become a blaze of gold. The trees are large: some reach 100 feet tall and grow trunks 4 feet in diameter. The bark of young trees is smooth and pale green, but as they mature it becomes rough and deeply furrowed. The cottonwood is rapid-growing; if the roots are plentifully watered, it can develop into a venerable giant within a quarter century.[26]

The Spaniards found the cottonwood to be one of the Albuquerque Valley's finest natural resources. The wood, lightweight, long-fibered, and soft but tough, provided fence posts, corral poles, timbers for architectural purposes, and material for a variety of agricultural and domestic implements, including carts, plow beams, and kitchen utensils. Cottonwood also makes a good fuel. Even now Pueblo Indians on the river like to burn it because it produces a hot fire and leaves little ash.

As a result of the heavy demand for wood in colonial times, the *bosques* became sadly depleted. By the time Anglo-Americans entered the valley, cottonwood was in short supply. Henry Smith Turner, who camped south of Albuquerque in the fall of 1846, informs us: "There is great

18

difficulty in obtaining sufficient fuel for cooking purposes—the men have to go to the distance of several miles to obtain a handful of wood." And then he adds, "We occasionally see a grove of cottonwood which is preserved with great care, as it furnishes the only material with which carts for the whole country are made. These groves are always private property."[27]

Another visitor, John Udell, found no firewood on the river at all when he reached Albuquerque in 1859. To cook his meals he was obliged to purchase wood packed from the mountains on burros.[28]

Such information as this conveys a picture of the Rio Grande Valley, almost stripped of its timber by the mid-nineteenth century. After 1880, when the railroad began to bring in milled lumber and brick for building and coal for home heating, the demand for cottonwood declined, allowing the *bosques* to start a slow recovery. But the twentieth century must have been well-advanced before the splendid groves that we know today had reestablished themselves.

While cottonwoods are predominant in the Middle Rio Grande Valley, other varieties of trees can be found. Willows, particularly shrub types, grow thickly in boggy places along the shores. Now they are interspersed with two ornamental trees that escaped from cultivation within the last century and spread throughout New Mexico's waterways: the Russian olive, with narrow, silver-backed leaves; and the tamarisk, also called salt cedar, which has thin wiry branches adorned with feathery leafage and clusters of tiny pink flowers in season.[29]

All of these trees provide nesting for doves and songbirds and cover for terrestrial wildlife. They also help stabilize the river banks during flooding and shield the levees from erosion and scouring. The same benefits are offered by stands of cattails, rushes, and sedges and by salt grass and horseweed, which form the vegetation under the shading trees.[30]

Just as the encroachment of man over the past several centuries has restricted and changed the flora, so too has it affected the habitat of small mammals and birds. Draining of ponds and swamps, conversion of unused land to agriculture or housing subdivisions, and expanded use of herbicides and pesticides take their toll. Rodent control measures, for example, have all but eliminated colonies of prairie dogs that once pocked the alluvial plain and lateral mesas.

Though in retreat, wild creatures nevertheless survive in surprising numbers, mainly in the sheltered areas inside the levees. Beavers and muskrats can be found on the river and along irrigation ditches where they make burrows in the banks. Raccoons, weasels, skunks, porcupines, squirrels, cottontails, and pocket gophers have all managed to establish an uneasy equilibrium between themselves and man. But they fall constant prey to guns, traps, poison, and, when crossing city streets, to automobiles.[31]

Many of the 400 species of resident and migratory birds recorded in the Southwest can be observed seasonally amid the *bosques* along the river. When George W. Kendall passed through Albuquerque in 1841, he took note of "immense flocks of blue and white herons and wild geese

. . . exceedingly tame." The Spanish folk only occasionally hunted the river bottom for ducks and geese, and then not to a degree that it ever made a dent in their numbers.[32]

During the last quarter of the nineteenth century, when the killing of birds became a national pastime and a national disgrace, the Rio Grande Valley's winged creatures seem to have escaped decimation only because the Anglo population remained relatively small. Author Harvey Fergusson, who as a boy at the turn of the century whiled away many an hour, alone or with chums, stalking birds in the fields and marshes that impinged on downtown Albuquerque, recalled years afterward that wild fowl abounded. In cloudlike swarms, they darkened the sky during spring and fall migrations. "I will never forget," Fergusson relates, "the first wild mallard drake I killed when I was about ten, with his plush-green head, the rich chestnut of his breast, and the iridescent purple of his wing-bars. He was beautiful as a jewel or a flower and I was proud of him as though I had created rather than killed him."[33]

From all reports, Albuquerque's youth failed to respond to emotional pleas put forward by leading conservationists, who, through the press and monthly journals, enjoined the vandal element among the nation's juveniles to spare "the feathered songsters of the grove." Nor do the city's young seem to have been attracted to the signing of pledges, then circulating, neither to kill birds nor to wear their feathers.[34]

Leaving the river and the valley and entering upon either of the inclining mesas to the east and west of the Rio Grande, one finds a distinctly different ecological zone. To travelers from the well-watered East, these mesas appear to be drab, barren, sun-baked patches of wasteland capable of sustaining little vegetation and even less wildlife. By contrast, the narrow belt of river bottoms seems like a flourishing garden, and the jutting peaks of the Sandias, robed with trees and shrubs, give the impression of a lofty oasis. But the mesas, for all their straw-colored bleakness and look of unrelieved aridity, are not an unwholesome environment. They support grass, woody shrubs, and a variety of small animal life. And they form an important ecological bridge between the valley and the mountains.

Soils of the mesas are generally of mixed sand, clay, and loam and are low in organic matter. They bear the short, semidesert grasses like grama, dropseed, muhly, and wheatgrass. After the brief growing season, coinciding with the rains of later summer, these grasses cure to a pale brown under the hot sun. Though withered and crackling underfoot, they retain their value as nutritional pasturage throughout the winter. Growing among the grasses can be found saltbush, rabbitbrush, the clumpy snakeweed, yucca, and the thorny cholla, prickly pear, and hedgehog cactus. As the mesas have been overgrazed by livestock, most noticeably within the last century, the hardy shrubs and cactus have expanded at the expense of the grasses. Another invader gaining ground is the Russian thistle, which dries and snaps at its root in the wind to become the common tumbleweed. Like the tamarisk and Russian olive, it was introduced from afar. It is known to the Indians as the "white man's plant."[35]

On the higher edge of the East Mesa, where the land rises to fuse with the squatty foothills of the Sandias, the vegetation receives conspicuously more moisture. Grasses are thicker and one finds a studding of piñon and juniper trees. Within this narrow girdle, at the mouth of Tijeras Canyon, the Spaniards were once able to practice marginal dry-farming.

The steady expansion of Albuquerque's suburbs has greatly reduced the animal habitat on the mesas. But before that fairly recent development was under way, many larger mammals, such as the pronghorn or antelope, deer, and wolf (lobo), had been hunted out. Even with the diminished range, however, creatures like the coyote, fox, badger, and striped skunk manage to survive. Yet, the most common mammals in the grasslands, today as in times past, are the rodents. This is not an unusual condition since rodents enjoy numerical superiority over other animals throughout the world. A dozen or more different varieties of mice and rats can be encountered in this zone, along with ground squirrels, rabbits, and an occasional prairie dog. To all these animals, which find a place on the mesas, we can add terrapins, toads, and several kinds of snakes.[36]

While the lowlands, comprising the valley and mesas, feel the constant pressure of man—a pressure that threatens one day to crowd out most of the native vegetation and wildlife—the Sandia Mountains, by comparison, appear to be an island refuge for flora and fauna. The reason can be found in the area's rugged terrain and in the fact that much of the range is public land cared for by the government. This is not to say that lumbering, mining, stock grazing, hunting, and roadbuilding have not, in years past, disturbed and even caused severe damage to the mountain environment—only that such tampering by man has been on a far smaller scale than in the surrounding region.

The Sandias bear a wealth of vegetation: more than 890 different plant species. Thirteen kinds of coniferous trees are represented, among them ponderosa pine, firs, and spruces. In association with the conifers occur broadleaf trees—at higher elevations the showy aspen along with locust, gambel oak, and elderberry, and lower down in the canyons, boxelder and cottonwood. A profusion of shrubs, grasses, and mountain flowers clothe the forest floor and occasional open meadows. Rarest of all plants in the upper Sandias are the native orchids. Numbering three separate species, they grow furtively in out-of-the-way nooks and are seldom seen by man.[37]

Along the sharp rib of Sandia Crest, living things take a severe beating from the pitiless wind, from snowblast, and from fierce solar radiation. Trees, twisted and leaf-spare, bend away from the prevailing gales, and small bushes seem to cling to life by a slender thread in the thin soil. But below on the sheltered east slope, the elements moderate, allowing timber and lesser plants to thrive in comparative calm.

The diversity of flora finds an echo in the great variety of animal life. Some 286 species have been recorded in the Sandias. Biologists declare with authority that good diversification of both plants and wildlife renders an area ecologically more stable than those less richly endowed.

If that be the case, then the mountains above Albuquerque can still claim possession of a healthy and hospitable environment.[38]

Except for a wedge of land encompassed within the old Elena Gallegos Spanish land grant, which intrudes on the west, the upper reaches of the Sandias all fall within the Cibola National Forest, established in 1931. That status has helped protect the local animal population. So, too, did the later creation of the Sandia Game Refuge. For several beasts, nevertheless, such protection came too late. By the opening of the twentieth century, the grizzly, black bear, wolf, antelope, elk, mountain lion, and Rocky Mountain bighorn sheep had all disappeared.

Two of these animals, the black bear and mountain lion, later returned by migration and reclaimed their old territory. Another, the bighorn sheep, was brought back by man, who can sometimes be moved to undo the mischief caused by his ancestors. During the years 1941–42, the New Mexico Department of Game and Fish transported nine sheep from Canada and released them in the Sandias. The transplant was so successful that the herd soon grew to 100 animals and furnished seed stock for reintroductions in additional New Mexico mountain ranges.

Other mammals that frequent the high precincts of the Sandias include the mule deer, bobcat, badger, ringtail, chipmunk, six varieties of squirrel, and eleven kinds of bats. Raccoons, rare creatures in all New Mexico before the mid-1940s, are now plentiful in these mountains. Seldom encountered by visitors, they betray their presence by footprints left near streams and springs. Another relative newcomer is the tasseleared, or Abert, squirrel, easily identified by prominent hair tufts on the tips of his ears. Although native to the nearby Jemez Mountains, this squirrel does not seem to have reached the Sandias until recent decades.[39]

The well-watered and liberally timbered heights also offer a congenial home to songbirds. Led by chirps and the flutter of wings, the wildlife enthusiast can catch sight of robins, nuthatchers, Stellar's jays, warblers, wrens, swallows, and such larger birds as hawks, golden eagles, and ravens. The most interesting winged inhabitant of the area, however, is not a bird, but a unique green butterfly, the Sandia hairstreak, discovered and named in 1955. The only other place it has ever been found is among the Davis Mountains of west Texas.[40]

The hovering Sandias, with their water, mineral, timber, and wildlife resources, and their recreational opportunities, have exerted an influence over the history and destiny of Albuquerque, second only to that of the Rio Grande. Without these mountains, there can be no doubt that the city below would have suffered both an aesthetic and economic impoverishment.

The Latecomers:
Indians and Spaniards

SOME TIME IN THE LAST STAGES of the Ice Age, man found his way into the Albuquerque Valley. Precisely when that happened, we cannot say. Archaeologists, after years of investigation, are by no means certain at what point the first Paleo-Indians crossed from Siberia to Alaska and began peopling the New World. Recent guesses by reputable scholars now range from 20,000 to 50,000 years ago. Be that as it may, no hard proof exists at the moment which places man on the Rio Grande much before 12,000 years ago.[1]

Still, that is within the last glacial phase of the Pleistocene—a time when a number of now extinct species of Ice Age animals roamed the well-watered and hospitable savannas of central New Mexico. These beasts, which would appear strange to our eyes, nevertheless, bore a strong resemblance to modern forms of life.

Among them, for example, was the camelops, whose fossil bones are found in abundance in the vicinity of Albuquerque. He had a short, compact body like the llama of South America, but long and thin legs and a heavy head similar to today's African camel. Competing for pasturage with the large herds of camelope were bands of New Mexico's early horse, a creature, then, probably not unlike the zebra. He was one of the region's most common Ice Age animals. This native horse disappeared by the end of the Pleistocene and thousands of years elapsed before Old World horses were introduced by the Spaniards.

There were bears, too—huge, shaggy things that stood 10 feet tall on their hind legs. Woolly musk oxen, sporting massive down-curving horns, and a strange species of longhorn bison (*Bison antiquus*) grazed alongside the camelops and horse. And the giant ground sloth, who would have tipped the scales at 8 or 9 tons, lumbered about browsing on leaves and possibly insects.

But of all the extraordinary beasts of that far-off age, none was more outlandish in appearance or more monstrous in size than the Imperial mammoth, an ancient elephant and largest animal inhabitant of the Rio Grande Valley. His statistics must be regarded as truly impressive: overall weight, 12 tons; height, 16 feet and above; weight of individual teeth, about 20 pounds. Added to those uncommon attributes were huge tusks that swept forward from the head in a flowing bend to overlap at their tips, forming a circle of ivory. In all, the mammoth was a true marvel of the Ice Age.[2]

He also must have been a source of awe and fear to the earliest groups of humans dwelling in the neighborhood of Albuquerque. The first Paleo-Indians, about whom we have definite knowledge, hunted the mammoth with spears. Indeed, all our meager information suggests that this animal may have been their principal food source. The "big-game hunters"—that is the phrase that fits these people best—probably concealed themselves in the marshes along the Rio Grande, waited until a mammoth waded in to drink or wallow in the mud, and then brought it down with a hail of their primitive missiles. At best, it was chancy business. Facing a wounded and enraged Imperial mammoth was no sport for the faint-hearted.

The ancient mammoth hunters, who were spread thinly over western North America, used a distinctive stone point to tip their thrusting spears and their long darts, which they propelled with a wooden launcher. These artifacts are known to archaeologists as Clovis points, because it was at Blackwater Draw near Clovis, New Mexico, that their antiquity was firmly established in 1934. Glacial lakes, which once existed in that corner of the southern plains, proved an attractive environment for the mammoth. And it is evident that Paleo-Indians were drawn to the area for that reason. Kill sites, places where the giant creatures were felled and butchered, are still being excavated. They yield Clovis points (typified by a channel or groove running from the base about halfway to the point) and quantities of stone blades used in cutting up the carcasses.

Clovis points, representing the oldest known hunting culture, are rare throughout the continent. In the country surrounding Albuquerque, only one site occupied by the Clovis people has been reported. What little we know about the habits and mode of living of these Paleo-Indians has been inferred from the few remaining examples of their Stone Age technology—the points and simple butchering tools. Of their perishable homes and clothing, and their religion and language, we know absolutely nothing.

One curious thing about the Clovis hunters: their culture seems to have been confined to a narrow span of time, between 9500 and 9000 B.C. At least by the latter date, the Clovis point was on the road to disappearance. And so too were the Imperial mammoth, the horse, the camelops, and most other Pleistocene animals. The reasons are still veiled in mystery, but a major part of the explanation may well be found in long-term climatic changes that led to progressively warmer temperatures and alterations in vegetation.[3]

In any event, the mammoth hunters who had made and used the Clovis point vanished and were succeeded by people who used the Folsom point. For some 1,000 years, from roughly 8500 to 7500 B.C., the Folsom hunters were the principal occupants of the Middle Rio Grande Valley. Their livelihood was also based on hunting—hunting of the single Pleistocene animal that survived into that time: the longhorn bison.

In the early 1960s, extensive suburban development on Albuquerque's West Mesa led to the discovery of many Folsom campsites. Bulldozers and road scrapers, churning up long-buried artifacts, brought archaeologists from the University of New Mexico to the scene. Their careful surveys, carried out over the next three years, disclosed the highest concentration of Folsom sites thus far found in America. The ancient hunters, it was clear from the scientists' findings, had placed their camps on low ridges overlooking shallow ponds. The advantages of such locations were twofold: they provided a good vantage point from which to observe herds of bison coming in to water, and they were situated downwind from the ponds.

In the one area of Rio Rancho Estates, northwest of Albuquerque, 40 or more Folsom camping places were identified. Clusters of lodges, probably built of pole frame and covered with bison skin, faced south toward the hunting grounds. Evidence of fire pits remained in front of the lodges, and scattered about each site were thousands of flint chips, discarded by Folsom tool makers. There were specimens, too, of the famous Folsom points. These projectiles are delicately, exquisitely made— the finest examples of art ever produced by stone workers in North America. So distinctive are they in design and form that their identity can never be mistaken. Each face of the point is deeply fluted; that is, pronounced grooves extend from the base almost to the tip. We mentioned channels indenting the Clovis points of an earlier day, but the workmanship in those artifacts is far inferior to that seen in the Folsom pieces. The fluting, as well as the parallel flaking along the sharp edges of the Folsom point, are superbly and precisely executed. The Folsom men, it is clear, had an eye for beauty as well as utility.[4]

Over a period of years, the big-game hunters of New Mexico appear to have undertaken a gradual withdrawal eastward until, at last, they were seen no more in the area. Their departure, however, did not leave the country empty of humans, for people with another cultural tradition and a different type of economy had already begun to establish themselves throughout the Southwest. But before referring to them, we should add a postscript to the story of the Paleo-Indians.

Thus far no notice has been taken of the so-called Sandia Man, alleged to have been a resident of the Albuquerque region some 25,000 years ago. The subject constitutes one of the most controversial matters in American archaeology. Beginning in 1936, a series of archaeological excavations were carried out at Sandia Cave, situated in Las Huertas Canyon on the north end of the Sandia Mountains. The stripping away of successive layers of deposits revealed a long record of human occupation. One lower level of material contained the classic Folsom points, demonstrating conclusively that man had used the cave as a shelter at least 10,000 years ago. Below the Folsom artifacts, a deeper layer yielded what appeared to be an older type of point—a leaf-shaped projectile with a shoulder on one side. These "Sandia points," it was postulated, had been left behind by the earliest Ice Age hunters discovered to date. The points were estimated to be roughly 25,000 years old.

The sensational news received wide coverage in both the popular and scientific media. Within a few years, Sandia Man had won a niche in archaeological textbooks and gained an honored place in New Mexico's tourist guidebooks. Almost at once, however, there were those who raised questions concerning the antiquity of the Sandia points and the propriety of assigning them to a separate culture.

A review of the original excavation methods pointed up numerous discrepancies in record-keeping and the analysis of material. Initial claims that the cave deposits had been undisturbed when work began were later shown to be untrue. Rodents burrowing through the debris had actually moved artifacts both upward and downward to different levels. And then, too, the dating, which had been based on the structure of geological deposits, was shown to possess a huge margin of error.

Some scholars reassessing the Sandia question now suggest that the shouldered points may be a local variant of the Clovis type. If that is the case, they form part of a culture already well-defined, not another, older culture as previously thought. The question of Sandia Man—Was he or wasn't he?—still remains a lively subject for debate.[5]

The Paleo-Indian hunters in western and central New Mexico were replaced, in time, by the Desert culture, which occupied the period known as the Archaic. One of their chief economic activities was the collecting of wild seeds and other plant products. Characteristic stone implements found in Archaic sites are the shallow stone basin, or metate, and the one-handed milling cobble, the mano, used to grind seeds into coarse flour. It should not be overlooked, however, that these people also pursued small animals, so that in reality theirs was a mixed gathering-and-hunting economy.

A great deal of information on the Desert culture has been uncovered within a 50-mile radius of Albuquerque. Immediately west of the city, on the Atrisco Land Grant, archaeologists began finding, in the early 1950s, a multitude of campsites containing fire hearths and the telltale metates and manos. Meticulous survey showed that these people had once inhabited most of the country between the Rio Grande and the Rio Puerco. Another center of their activity has been found farther north, on the Jemez River near Santa Ana Pueblo, where drifting sand dunes and eroding arroyos have laid bare ancient camping places. In 1954 evidence of the Desert culture came to light east of the Rio Grande when a child burial was discovered exposed in a wash on the eastern slope of the Manzano Mountains near the ruined Spanish mission of Quarai. Associated with the skeleton were the usual grinding implements together with several stone points used in hunting.[6]

While the study of all these sites has helped us learn much about how the ancient gatherers lived, it has not yet satisfactorily answered the question: when did they first settle in central New Mexico? It is now believed that people with a Desert culture were living in the deserts of California and Nevada as early as 9,000 years ago, and that they slowly spread eastward, filling in the vacuum left by the departure of Paleo-Indian hunters. Perhaps by 5,000 to 6,000 years ago—and this is only a guess based on the most recent evidence—the vanguard of the gatherers reached the country surrounding Albuquerque, found it inviting, and settled in to stay.[7]

Archaeologists of the future will continue to piece together the faint traces of that early migration so that one day a clearer story can be told. But while the history of the Desert culture at the far end of the scale remains cloudy, the picture at the near end is in fairly sharp focus. We know, for example, that in the centuries before Christ, the widespread gathering tradition of the Southwest commenced to undergo a major transformation. In the process, the Indians of the Archaic climbed a long step on the ladder of progress and became, in effect, a new people—the Basket Makers.

The key element behind the transition from Desert to Basket Maker culture was the adoption and expansion of agriculture. In the later stages of the Archaic, people began to raise small fields of corn, or Indian maize, to supplement their seed gathering and hunting activities. Incipient farming in the Southwest may go back as far as 1500 or 2000 B.C., but then and for many centuries thereafter it played only a minor part in the primitive economy. About the opening of the Christian era, however, agriculture came of age. The people shifted to a greater reliance on their crops and, correspondingly, gave less attention to the age-old foraging practices. The more reliable food supply and the accumulation of a surplus, which farming allowed, led to a noticeable expansion in population and to a marked improvement in the material well-being of the Indians. Because they produced a profusion of finely woven baskets, these new farmers have been named Basket Makers by archaeologists.

By A.D. 400 the Basket Maker people had added beans imported from Mexico to the maize and squash they were already raising. Not only did beans provide welcome variety to the menu, they contributed important nutritional elements to the basic diet.

One other significant acquisition of the Basket Makers was pottery, which also appeared about A.D. 400. They probably got the technical skills necessary to form and fire ceramics from advanced peoples living to the south. From the plain brown, orange, and red wares initially made, pottery styles would later evolve to become the highest art form of New Mexico's prehistoric Indians.

At the beginning, the Basket Makers dwelled in simple dome-shaped structures built of logs, brush, and mud mortar. In time they commenced to construct true pit-houses, semisubterranean lodges of either circular or square shape. Around today's Four Corners, the center of Basket Maker country, their villages sometimes numbered several dozen pit-houses. But along the fringes of their range, as in the Middle Rio Grande Valley, the communities were often much smaller.

On the West Mesa, opposite Albuquerque and stretching north to the vicinity of Santa Ana Pueblo, remains of Basket Maker sites are found superimposed upon the traces left by their predecessors, the Folsom and the Desert culture peoples. The earliest Basket Maker villages and farms here were placed on terraces above the river, but subsequently the Indians shifted down into the fertile alluvial bottoms. This short move must have occurred as techniques of water control and flood farming became known.[8]

In a transition period, A.D. 700 to 900, the Basket Makers abandoned their old pit-houses and occupied above-ground buildings made of puddled adobe or stone. This revolution in housing, attended by other cultural developments, was so profound that scholars see the emergence of a new style of life: the Basket Makers evolved to become the Pueblos.

When the Spaniards first visited the Southwest in the mid-sixteenth century, they were at once struck by the blocky, multistoried Indian apartments so unlike anything else they had encountered in the New World. They correctly named the buildings *pueblos,* meaning "towns," for that is just what they were. The entire population of a village was housed in a single structure. By extension, the tribesmen who resided in them were designated Pueblo Indians, and so they are known to this day.

The most spectacular pueblos, raised in the years after A.D. 900, were concentrated at Chaco Canyon in northwestern New Mexico, and in portions of adjacent states. Several of the well-designed towns situated along the Chaco River attained heights of four to five stories and sheltered hundreds of people. But many more pueblos—and this was true of the first ones built along the Rio Grande—were composed of small house blocks that grew slowly in a helter-skelter fashion as the need arose.

Surprisingly, the old Basket Maker pit-house survived alongside the new-style architecture, though it took on a different function. With some modification, the semiunderground pit-house, entered by a ladder through the roof, was transformed from a dwelling to a religious chamber—the feature that Spaniards would one day call an *estufa* (a "stove," perhaps because it resembled one), and Anglos would refer to as a *kiva.*

The rise of the great pueblos signalled a march by southwestern Indians toward a new cultural summit. The movement may well have been fueled by influences emanating from the high civilizations of Central Mexico. We know that the ancient Mexicans came to trade at selected villages in the Southwest. It was through such contact, no doubt, that architectural features, religious practices, and items like parrots and copper bells from the south were introduced to the Pueblos.[9]

A few miles southwest of Albuquerque, on the floodplain of the Rio Puerco, an extraordinary ceremonial and trading center flourished for some 175 years, from 1300 to 1475. It is known today as Pottery Mound because of the immense heaps of broken pot shards that literally buried the pueblo ruin before it was excavated. The site has produced evidence of Mexican influences, including an earthen flat-topped pyramid in two levels and a possible ball court. Even more remarkable are seventeen kivas whose walls, when exposed by archaeologists, contained more than 800 mural frescos, many of them in layers, one on top of the other. These colored paintings constitute the most extensive body of Pueblo religious art ever discovered, and they tell us much about the depth and richness of the Indians' spiritual life.[10]

Pottery Mound got its start just at the time when central New Mexico was receiving a great influx of people from the West. The late thirteenth century was a time of serious drought, especially in the plateau country of the Four Corners. Refugees, abandoning their splendid towns in Chaco Canyon and Mesa Verde, Colorado, drifted to other areas, less severely affected by the prolonged dry spell. Many reached the Rio Grande Valley, which must have appeared like Eden in the desert. As a consequence of this migration, new pueblos took root above and below Albuquerque in the years after 1300.

One such was Kuaua, located on the west bank of the Rio Grande, near modern-day Bernalillo. The ruins of the pueblo are encompassed within Coronado State Monument, so named because it is thought likely that here the sixteenth-century explorer spent the winter of 1540–41. From its perch on a sandy shelf above the river, Kuaua commands a panoramic view of the Sandia Mountains. Upon excavation, the pueblo was found to contain over twelve hundred rooms, two main plazas, and six kivas. All this was built in the three centuries before 1600. After the latter date, the inhabitants abandoned the village and moved in with their kinsmen at Sandia Pueblo, 5 miles south, at a time when Spanish colonists were first settling the valley.

Aside from its possible association with the Coronado Expedition, Kuaua wins special acclaim for the seventeen panels of murals in one of its kivas, brought to view by archaeologists in the 1930s. Though less numerous than those discovered at Pottery Mound, the Kuaua paintings depict a broad range of figures integral to Indian religious belief. There are flowing springs, clouds, streams, corn, the animals valued by hunters, and masked dancers, representing *katcinas,* or deities, believed to have been introduced originally from Mexico. The Pueblo Indians have always lived in a world of mysticism and symbolism, a world in which the supernatural joins man to his natural environment. As agriculturalists, their abiding concern was with cycles of weather and crop fertility. Not unexpectedly, thus, the kiva murals with all their multicolored details demonstrate the native belief in the interrelatedness of sacred and worldly matters.

Kuaua was one among a cluster of Tiwa-speaking pueblos lying athwart the Rio Grande from the vicinity of Bernalillo downriver to Los Lunas. Albuquerque is situated roughly in the center of this old native kingdom, which the Spaniards from the time of Coronado, knew as the Province of Tiguex. Several outlying Tiwa villages, on the east slope of the Manzano Mountains, formed a subdistrict. Other pueblos, populated by Keresan and Tano speakers, bordered Tiguex on the north, while on the southern limits of the province dwelled Indians whose language was Piro.

By the opening of historic times, the Pueblo people were concentrated in north central New Mexico and in several western enclaves, notably Ácoma, Zuñi (Province of Cibola), and Hopi (the Moqui Province). This represented a significant shrinking of the vast domain they had occupied in earlier centuries. Evidently a variety of factors had led to the shifting of population, the growth of larger communities in the East, and a trend toward congregating in fewer and fewer pueblos. Drought, as already mentioned, played its part in creating these new conditions, as did a cycle of intensely cold winters, which affected the length of the growing season. Development of improved and more complex irrigation methods in late prehistoric times expanded the food supply, allowing greater population densities. And finally, new defense needs impelled the Pueblos to unite in larger units. The Athabascans (Apaches and Navajos) became a threat in the period immediately preceding arrival of the Europeans, as did the nomadic Teyas (probably Caddoan speakers) who launched attacks from the plains.

The Spaniards found only twelve to sixteen Tiwa villages (accounts vary) making up the Tiguex Province. The archaeological record, however, has disclosed the location of at least 40 pueblo sites that once occupied the district. What is clear is that during the ensuing colonial era, the old trends leading to a shrinkage of territorial boundaries and concentration of the Indian people continued and, indeed, were accelerated.[12]

In late summer of 1540, Captain Hernando de Alvarado reached Tiguex at the head of a reconnaissance party sent by Coronado from his main camp, then at Zuñi. What the Tiwa Indians felt, at this, their first contact with the strange invaders, mounted on even stranger animals, we can only imagine. On the surface they appeared intensely curious and prone to be hospitable. Underneath, no doubt, lurked apprehension and a measure of bewilderment.

Alvarado informs us that the population of twelve pueblos turned out to greet him. The Tiwas came marching in good order, those from each village lining up behind their chieftains. In ranks they paraded around his tent to the music of a flute and then came inside where they presented gifts of food, blankets, and skins. In return, the captain says, "I gave them some small articles, whereupon they went away."[13]

From the quill pen of Hernando de Alvarado, we have our first description of the land and people along the Middle Rio Grande. "This river flows through a broad valley planted with fields of maize," he says in a letter to Coronado. "There are some cottonwood groves. The houses are of mud, two stories high. The people seem good, more given to farming than war. They have provisions of maize, beans, melons, and turkeys in great abundance. They dress in cotton, buffalo skins, and coats made with feathers from the turkeys. They wear their hair short. The old men are the ones who have the most authority among them. We thought they were witches because they said that they could rise to heaven, and other things of the sort."[14]

Through hindsight, it is possible to find in these few, simple, and seemingly innocent words the foreshadowing of great troubles that would soon afflict the native people. The docile Indians are more devoted to farming than war, Alvarado had noted. But future events were to force war upon them and destroy their apparent docility. The "provisions in abundance" that so impressed the Spanish captain would become a focal point of controversy as the hungry newcomers invaded Indian storerooms and carted away what they wanted. And the mistaken notion that the old men (that is, the religious leaders) were witches would lead to unspeakable tragedy, when, later, zealous missionaries backed by soldiers attempted to destroy Pueblo religion, which they saw as an amalgam of witchcraft, idolatry, and Devil worship.

The coming of Coronado and his brash cavaliers to Puebloland marked a watershed in the long history of New Mexico's Indian people. After centuries of comparative isolation, they were now to be drawn into close and irritating contact with Europeans, whose alien ways and beliefs would upset the old familiar pattern of native life, the roots of which traced back to the Desert culture of the pre-Christian era. Thus, the year 1540 was a turning point for the Indians. And it was also a benchmark in the story of Albuquerque, for the claiming and initial exploration of New Mexico set in motion the sequence of events that provide the background for the city's founding.

What kind of men were these who followed Francisco Vásquez de Coronado a thousand miles northward from Mexico into unknown lands seeking adventure and mythical kingdoms filled with treasure? In answering that question, we come a long way toward understanding the mentality and motives of those Spaniards who later became the founders and builders of the Province of New Mexico.

The Spanish conquistador of the sixteenth century was a restless, undisciplined, prideful, courageous bundle of energy with strict loyalties to his king and his religion, and with a consuming ambition for wealth and social status. His appetite for life and enthusiasm for adventure led him across the greater portion of two continents, making possible seemingly impossible conquests. The hereditary poverty and austere customs of his native Spain ably fitted him to endure without complaint the severe hardships met in the New World. Whether through an inborn sense of fatalism or a simple lack of foresight, the fact is, he was prone to improvidence, to impatience with long-range planning. As a man of action, he wanted immediate results. For him, the monotony of daily toil held no interest.

In spite of a poor showing in his treatment of the Indians, especially in the early years, the Spaniard at heart believed the native people possessed certain natural rights guaranteeing protection of their lives and property. But herein lay seeds of trouble: the conquistadores, along with the civil governors and missionaries who succeeded them, were also convinced that as chosen servants of God and the Spanish king, it fell to them to define and administer such rights and at the same time to reshape the Indian, for his own good, in the image prescribed by Hispanic Catholicism. These conceited and inflexible notions often bore bitter fruit, and nowhere was that harvest more unsweet than in New Mexico.

Coronado's knights, who, with Alvarado, made first contact with the Tiwa pueblos were by all accounts a bantam-sized lot, averaging probably under 5.5 feet in height, as did most Europeans of the day. Life's grinding hardships coupled with a meager and poorly balanced diet kept man physically small, but that did not prevent him from becoming tough and sinewy. To the Indians, themselves small in stature, the bearded Spaniards dressed in partial body armor, wearing helmets, and carrying harquebuses, crossbows, and swords must have appeared larger than life. As they would soon learn, these strangers were extraordinary men with extraordinary dreams. But at the same time, they were people accustomed to having their way, and woe to anyone who obstructed their path.

Coronado's expedition to discover and explore the mysterious realms of the far north had been organized with much fanfare in central Mexico. To his colors had come scores of young, footloose, rough-and-tumble Spaniards eager for the riches they felt certain abounded among the unknown tribes at the interior of the continent. Fernando Cortes, a mere twenty years before, had found and conquered the glittering Aztec empire, so it seemed entirely plausible that another El Dorado waited in the wilderness for those plucky enough to search it out.

Viceroy Don Antonio de Mendoza, chief representative of the king and the highest civil official in Spanish North America, journeyed amid much pomp and pageantry to the village of Compostela in western Mexico, the launching point for Coronado's grand project. Mendoza desired to bestow his personal blessing upon the undertaking, which he hoped would both expand and enrich the enormous Viceroyalty of New Spain over which he governed. But he, along with Coronado and the reckless army of adventurers, were all destined for supreme disappointment. New Mexico and the wide lands beyond were to prove barren of treasure.

The Spaniards' frustration and disenchantment help explain, but fail to justify, the treatment accorded the Indians dwelling along the Rio Grande. After the vanguard of the expedition reached the river and received its cordial welcome, Alvarado had hurried a messenger back to his commander, who remained at Zuñi, suggesting the Province of Tiguex as a suitable place to spend the winter.

Coronado accepted the recommendation and put his force in motion toward the Rio Grande. The bloom was off his enthusiasm, for after a punishing march across the deserts and mountains of southern Arizona, the rock and mud pueblos of the Zuñis had yielded no gold. Nor had a brief excursion by one of his lieutenants to the nearby Hopi villages produced anything of value. It had begun to appear that the fabled wealth of the north was pure myth. Yet, it was still too early in the game to give up altogether. With pennants flying and helmet plumes dancing in the breeze, he took up Alvarado's trail for Tiguex on the fond hope that there some faint success might be salvaged.

On the Rio Grande, the first units of the army of 300 Spaniards made camp close by the walls of the Tiwa town, Alcanfor, believed to be the place we now know as Kuaua. Their tent quarters provided adequate protection while the bracing autumn weather held, but late in the season stiff, chill winds began to creep around the upper end of the Sandias promising a rigorous winter ahead. As the cold deepened and set teeth to rattling, the distress of the soldiers grew. Their light clothes that served them well in the tropics offered meager defense against New Mexico's icy blasts.

The Indians of Alcanfor were asked to vacate their pueblo so that the Spaniards could move in. They did so without resistance, but with much muttering and open resentment. Their kin in neighboring towns took them in. This high-handed eviction left Coronado and his crew snug winter accommodations as well as storerooms bulging with native foodstuffs. But it also alienated the Tiwas and pointed them on the road that eventually led to armed struggle.

As gales howled among bare limbs of the cottonwoods and the surface of the river gradually froze to a brittle hardness, unrest in Tiguex grew. The sons of Spain had large appetites and soon they were making levies on other pueblos for additional supplies. Some trifled with Indian women, and all caused general offense by their arrogant swagger and boorish manner.

The Tiwas struck back. A war party attacked the Spaniards' horse herd, wounded a guard, and made away with a number of animals. A pursuit squad under one of Coronado's junior officers trailed the stolen stock downriver to the pueblo of Alameda, located on the northern outskirts of modern Albuquerque. The village was deserted, but several dead horses bristling with arrows were found. Riding back to report to their commander, the men passed another pueblo called Arenal. Inside the walls they could hear a great commotion where more of the stolen horses were being slaughtered.

The report delivered to Coronado was grim: the people of Tiguex were in open rebellion. At a council of war attended by the officers and chaplains of the expedition an agreement was reached to punish the Indians by force of arms.

Coronado ordered out his troops, and like avenging crusaders they marched to the conquest of Arenal. In a bloody and furious battle lasting many hours, they sacked and burned the pueblo. Some of the defenders were lanced to death or trampled under pounding hooves as they attempted to flee. Others taken captive were promptly tied to stakes and roasted alive. The few who escaped spread a message of terror across the land: the Spanish intruders were pitiless in battle, merciless in victory. That somber word was given further credence a short time later when Coronado's army laid siege to the pueblo of Moho, four leagues from Alcanfor, capturing it only after many of its inhabitants had perished from thirst.

As a result of these hostilities, the Province of Tiguex suffered almost total devastation. The remaining pueblos were abandoned as their people sought refuge in the mountains far from the bullets and blades of their enemies. It was a disaster from which the Indians of the Middle Rio

Grande Valley would never fully recover, and one they would never entirely forget.

Spring came late in 1541. On April 23 of that year the Spanish army walked its horses across the still solid ice covering the Rio Grande and headed east to continue the quest for the Golden Fleece. The residents of Tiguex were thereby granted an interval of peace in which they could begin putting their shattered pueblos back together. The respite proved all too brief.

A little over a month after taking up the trail anew, Coronado reached the center of the awesome Staked Plains in the Texas Panhandle. There, concluding that prospects for some major discovery looked dim, he sent the main expedition under Captain Alvarado back to New Mexico. With thirty select stalwarts to serve him as an escort, he pressed ahead. His reconnaissance eventually led to Quivira, the home of the Wichita Indians in central Kansas. But to the eyes of the treasure-hungry Spaniards, it had even less to offer than the lands already visited. The poverty of Quivira dashed their last hopes for glory and wealth.

Meanwhile, retracing his steps to the Rio Grande, Alvarado found that the Tiwas, hearing of his approach, had taken to the hills again, leaving their province deserted. Without opposition, he reoccupied the pueblo of Alcanfor. But unlike the previous winter, the storerooms were now empty. If starvation was not to overtake the expedition during the hard months ahead, new supplies would have to be found. To this end, Captain Alvarado began ranging up and down the Rio Grande demanding contributions of food in other Pueblo districts. The Spaniards' reputation for harshness had preceded them, so the provisions sought were furnished quickly, though grudgingly. Therefore, when Coronado, finishing his bootless errand to Quivira, arrived back at Alcanfor in September, he found enough supplies on hand to see them through until spring.

After weathering another frigid and uncomfortable winter, the disillusioned Coronado ordered the trumpets sounded and pointed his face toward home. So it was farewell to New Mexico for the Spaniards, at least for the time being, and it was good-bye to uninvited and thoroughly quarrelsome guests for the embittered natives of Tiguex. The entire enterprise, costing so much in money, lost lives, and human suffering, served no other purpose than to acquaint European map makers, who studied the expedition's chronicles, with the geography of interior North America. It also had the effect, unrecognized at the time, of indelibly engraving Coronado's name upon the pages of southwestern history. It is one of the small ironies of that history that the man who led this fiasco and whose expensive expedition returned not one centavo of profit should have his name, four centuries later, attached to New Mexico's largest shopping mall. Albuquerque's multimillion dollar Coronado Center commemorates the region's first entrepreneur, a man who went broke.[15]

Over the next forty years, the Pueblos of the Middle Rio Grande Valley slipped back into that unhurried, familiar rhythm of life they had known before the fire-eating Spaniards turned their small world upside-down. They remained free from outside meddling during that time largely because no one in the Viceroyalty of New Spain felt any inclination to retrace Coronado's trail. More than a generation would pass, dimming the unpleasant memories of his expedition, before Europeans again looked to New Mexico as a Promised Land.

Beginning in 1581, a series of new ventures launched from the south opened the next chapter in the history of the Tiwa Pueblos and the Albuquerque area. First, a small party of three priests escorted by nine soldiers, under the leadership of Fray Agustín Rodríguez, marched up the Rio Grande to examine the possibilities of initiating missionary work among the Indians. One of the fathers was killed by the Pueblos when he improvidently set out alone to carry reports back to Mexico. The remaining two, Fray Agustín and his companion Fray Francisco López, elected to stay in New Mexico at the conclusion of the tour, seeing, through rose-colored glasses, a horde of waiting converts. Either because of ignorance or carelessness, they picked the unlikeliest Pueblo group upon which to bestow their attentions, the Tiwas. Settling in at the village of Puaray, a short distance southeast of Alcanfor, Rodríguez and López met death very soon after the departure of their soldier guards. In the shedding of the friars' blood, the Indians exacted a small measure of retribution for the monumental miseries heaped upon them four decades before by Coronado.

The following year, 1582, another body of Spaniards, this one led by an adventurer, Antonio de Espejo, journeyed to New Mexico, ostensibly to learn the fate of the pair of missionaries left in Tiguex. Upon finding that the padres had perished, Espejo showed his true motive in coming. Prospecting was his game and for several months he scoured the sun-bleached hills and mesas for sign of gold or silver.

In his official report of the expedition, Antonio de Espejo tells us that Tiguex contained sixteen pueblos and that its people, through sign language, gave him a vivid account of their earlier troubles with Coronado. Many of the Indians, relates Espejo, thought that he had come to punish them for killing the friars, and in panic they skipped to the Sandias to hide. "We tried by all means possible," his report continues, "to persuade them to come back peacefully, but they refused. . . . We were unable to find out how many inhabitants there were, because they had fled."[16]

In 1591, still a third expedition entered New Mexico. The commander was Gaspar Castaño de Sosa. With him came families and wagons of supplies, for it was his intention to found a settlement among the Pueblos. The Tiwas, living in the shadow of the Sandias, he observed, were skittish as deer and fled at his approach. All their past experience seemed to confirm that the presence of the Spaniards spelled nothing but trouble.

Castaño de Sosa's plan of establishing a foothold on the Rio Grande came to nothing. He had embarked on the undertaking without the necessary government authorization, and soon after his arrival in New

Mexico, a military force dispatched by the viceroy suddenly appeared with an order for his arrest. He and his would-be settlers were escorted home. The Pueblos breathed a fresh sigh of relief. [17]

The brief visits of Rodríguez, Espejo, and Castaño de Sosa had little impact on the Middle Rio Grande Valley. From them, the Indians might have divined that Spanish penetration into their homeland was destined to grow. But the ephemeral nature of these early contacts scarcely prepared the native people for the cultural shock and psychological stresses they would experience when European colonization and evangelization got under way.

Don Juan de Oñate, governor and captain-general of the newly proclaimed Kingdom of New Mexico, was the individual who fastened Spain's hold on the land of the Pueblos. Journeying northward from his native Zacatecas at the head of a slow-moving caravan of colonists and missionaries, he entered the Province of Tiguex in late June of 1598, as the first ears of Indian corn were beginning to form on the stalk. Hard rains greeted his arrival and at one point he and his people got mired in the mud as they were crossing one of the many grain fields that lined both banks of the river. Oñate paused briefly at Puaray Pueblo, noting solemnly in his journal, that there the venerable Fathers Rodríguez and López had given up their lives. [18]

The governor was searching for a suitable site upon which his subjects could create a town and he could establish his military head-quarters and political capital. At first glance, the valley containing the Tiwa pueblos appeared ideal. The country was open and gave easy access to the trail south. And the wide bottomlands abutting the river were obviously fertile and simple to irrigate.

But other, negative considerations outweighed those positive points. For one, the Indian farms flanking the dozen or more pueblos already had most of the available ground under cultivation, and, as Oñate well knew, Spanish law carried strict provisions for protection of native lands. In any case, it was apparent that the Tiwas would have made churlish neighbors. Their previous meetings with Spaniards had left them distrustful and fearful, and certainly in no mood to welcome a community of these outlanders in their midst.

Juan de Oñate was in fact aware of the Tiwas' deep-seated hostility and he also knew, from reading the reports of earlier expeditions, that the Indians farther north, who had had less contact with Spaniards, possessed a more friendly disposition. Moreover, the same reports spoke of good mining prospects in the northern mountains, and the governor thought it best to have his new town close by any gold or silver mines that might be discovered. For these compelling reasons, he did not stop and settle in the Middle Valley of the Rio Grande. Instead, from Puaray, he continued upriver to the Española Valley, and there raised his capital of San Gabriel not far from the Tewa pueblo of San Juan.

During New Mexico's infant years as a new realm of the Spanish Empire, no settlers took up residence on or near the future site of Albuquerque. But there was much coming and going of travelers and supply caravans, since the Middle Valley lay athwart the main north-south road, or Camino Real, as it came to be called. Actually, the first people to show an authentic interest in the area were missionaries, not colonists.

Soon after setting up housekeeping in the Española Valley, Oñate divided up the band of Franciscan friars, which had accompanied him, assigning individuals to minister to the various groups of pueblos. Father Juan Carlos drew the southern Tiwas. He moved into one of the larger villages, probably Puaray, and began trying to win the Indians to Christianity. As far as the records show, he built no mission and, in fact, within a few years gave up his efforts.[19]

Don Pedro de Peralta, Oñate's successor as governor, arrived in New Mexico in 1609. Almost at once, he abandoned San Gabriel and commenced laying the foundations for a new capital at Santa Fe, whose location, near the foot of the Sangre de Cristo Mountains, was deemed better suited to the needs of the growing colony. At the same time, the Spanish crown began showing a more active interest in promoting the missionary program as a means to "civilize" and assimilate the Pueblo Indians. With considerable financial support from the government, the Church launched a massive drive to convert the native people and to erect more than a score of majestic missions throughout the region.

Two of the new churches were placed among the Tiwa, one at Sandia Pueblo and another at Isleta. Both had extensive auxiliary buildings, which included priests' quarters, workshops, and classrooms. Of the two missions, Father Alonso de Benavides wrote in 1630:"There are schools of reading and writing, singing, and playing all instruments. The pupils are well taught in Church doctrine and ways of civilized living. These two monasteries and churches are very costly and beautiful."[20] From other documents, we learn that each place had its own organ, the melodious strains of which must have sounded strange indeed to the Indians, whose only instruments were drums, rattles, and flutes.

A pair of lesser missions, referred to as *visitas,* were constructed at the pueblos of Puaray and Alameda. Initially, at least, they had no resident missionary of their own, but were served periodically by the padres stationed at Sandia. Alameda, in the 1660s, got its own minister, but continued to remain a mission of secondary importance.

Statistical information for the seventeenth century is extremely sketchy and unreliable, but from the data available, it would appear that the Tiwa population steadily declined. The same phenomenon was noticeable everywhere among the Pueblos of New Mexico and can be linked to the introduction of measles, smallpox, and other Old World diseases by the Europeans. Lacking any natural immunity to such maladies, the Indians succumbed in droves with each recurring epidemic. As their numbers dwindled in the many small and scattered pueblos, the survivors tended to congregate in fewer, but larger, communities. By the second half of the seventeenth century, the southern Tiwas had deserted practically all their outlying villages and joined their kinsmen clustered in the four pueblos of Sandia, Isleta, Alameda, and Puaray.

As this decline and concentration of the native population occurred, vacant Indian farmlands throughout the Middle Valley became available to Hispanic settlers. After the early 1650s, increasing numbers of colonists from the upper portion of the province, as well as new immigrants, obtained rural properties, or estancias, in this area. By the mid-1660s, such estancias seem to have numbered several dozen.[21] Their residents attended church at the nearest Indian·mission and journeyed to Santa Fe on periodic business trips or for social occasions. The capital, in fact, remained the realm's only formally organized municipality in the years before the Pueblo Revolt of 1680.

Although no real community existed in the Middle Valley, the region had its own alcalde mayor, or district magistrate, who handled minor judicial cases and measured the boundaries of land grants assigned by the governor. The office was customarily filled by one of the local estancieros. About 1660 it became the practice to divide New Mexico into two major subdivisions or administrative units—the Rio Arriba and the Rio Abajo, that is, the upper and lower portions of the Rio Grande Valley, together with neighboring districts. The dividing line between the two was the high east-west escarpment known as La Bajada, situated about 20 miles below Santa Fe. The lieutenant-governor of New Mexico was given direct command of the Rio Abajo, mainly to handle a growing problem there with hostile Apaches. The governor focused his attention on affairs in the northern district.[22]

In those early years, most of the Spanish estancias of the Rio Abajo were concentrated in two principal areas. The first was located toward the head of the valley, near The Narrows of the Rio Grande, and on the border between the Tiwa and Keres pueblos, which was between the mouth of the Jemez River and San Felipe. The Spanish folk spoke of this locality as La Angostura de Bernalillo, meaning The Narrows of Little Bernal. The Bernal family lived thereabouts, and doubtless the diminutive, Bernalillo, derived from their name.[23]

Somewhere in this quarter, the governor of New Mexico in 1643 established a temporary military post, the presidio of San Antonio, to guard a ford on the Rio Grande frequented by Apache raiders. The garrison consisted of one captain and fifteen soldiers. This defensive experiment must have been short-lived, for the San Antonio fort received only a single passing mention in documents of the period.[24]

Among those who carved out estates around The Narrows of Bernalillo were, in addition to the Bernals, such prominent families as the Bacas, Carvajals, Cuéllars, Sáenzs, Pereas, and Anayas. The mere listing of names tells us nothing about the people themselves, their tight-knit society, or the kind of life they led on their largely self-sufficient estancias. Information of this kind, which might have been recorded on paper, was almost entirely lost when the Pueblo Indians unleashed their holy war against New Mexico in 1680.

About one of the Bernalillo settlers, however, some fragmentary details have survived, mainly because his haughty and unconventional ways led to his trial and imprisonment by the Inquisition in Mexico

City. His name was Cristóbal de Anaya, and he was born in New Mexico in the late 1620s. Descended from grandparents who were natives of the Spanish city of Salamanca, Cristóbal had no claim to nobility, but that did not prevent him from building a career and putting on airs that were typical of many blue-bloods of the day. At the tender age of eleven, so the records inform us, he took up soldiering, a fact less astounding when we recall that frontier youth matured early, and often assumed the responsibilities of manhood before the onset of adolescence.

By his mid-thirties, fiery Cristóbal de Anaya was deeply embroiled in the intense factional squabbles that characterized colonial New Mexican politics. Evidently, he took the side of civil officials who attempted to curb the immense power of the missionary fathers, and this partisanship may well have contributed to his ensuing troubles with the Church. In 1661, he was arrested by agents of the Inquisition, for supposedly heretical remarks, and sent to Mexico City, in chains, we assume, since that was the practice then.

For four miserable years, Cristóbal remained confined in the Inquisition's dungeons, undergoing a series of trials. At last he was forced to march in a procession of penitents through the streets of the viceregal capital, as a token of his humiliation. Subsequently he was released. All things considered, he got off gently.

Back in New Mexico, among wife and children on his estancia at Angostura, Cristóbal de Anaya made light of the hardships suffered at the hands of the Inquisition. The experience seems to have taught him little, for shortly he resumed his old habit of speaking disrespectfully of the Church. One priest even brought charges against him, but this time the matter was not followed up. Before many more years passed, he and his family were to fall victim to the rage of the Pueblos, as our narrative will soon show.[25]

The other focal point of Spanish activity in the Middle Valley lay south of Sandia and Alameda pueblos, extending downriver past the future site of Albuquerque to the boundary marking the lands of the Isleta Indians. By the middle 1660s, twenty or more estancias existed in this area, which together with those to the north made a total of about forty-five estates for the entire valley. The main houses on many of these properties were referred to as haciendas, suggesting a rather spacious and commodious dwelling. But in truth, we know from archaeological and documentary evidence that most of the residences were of fairly modest size, and we can guess that comforts and anything approaching luxurious furnishing must have been few.[26]

Names of the owners of several of these haciendas, within or close by modern Albuquerque, are of considerable importance to the early history of the district. One was Alonso García de Noriega who in his early twenties had come to New Mexico from Zacatecas and begun developing lands, called the Estancia de San Antonio, on the west bank of the Rio Grande. He is mentioned in 1670 as being the local alcalde mayor, and ten years later he had become lieutenant-governor, ruling over the entire Rio Abajo and holding the military rank of *maese de campo* (equivalent to lieutenant-general).[27] His hacienda, no doubt among the foremost of such establishments, sheltered a wife and numerous children.

Approximately opposite Alonso García's property was the house of Francisco de Trujillo, on the east side of the river. Unlike his prosperous neighbor, the lieutenant-governor, Señor Trujillo, so far as is known, had no titles and little wealth. Evidently he died sometime in the 1670s, leaving the home to his wife. Thereafter, the place was known as the Hacienda de Doña Luisa de Trujillo, and formed the site upon which Albuquerque would be founded in 1706.[28]

Doña Luisa's name was attached not only to her hacienda but to the great stand of cottonwoods that thrived in the surrounding lowlands. Far into the following century, long after the woman herself had been forgotten and the hacienda had crumbled to dust, the trees continued to be known as the Bosque Grande de Doña Luisa. An alternate name for the grove, at least in the beginning, seems to have been the Bosque Grande de San Francisco Xavier, in honor of the patron saint of the locality.

The house of Francisco de Trujillo and Doña Luisa lay near the southern end of the cottonwood forest, for the next place below, the Hacienda de Mejía, was said in 1692 to be situated in open pastureland without trees.[29] Much of this area, now within south Albuquerque, comprised swamps and shallow ponds and was known as the Esteros de Mejía. The founder and developer of the hacienda was presumably named Mejía, but since no such family appears in the records of the day, it is possible that the owner, whoever he may have been, borrowed the name of the nearby swamp for his house. In any case, the Hacienda de Mejía was located square beside the Camino Real and was a designated *paraje,* which meant that it was a spot where travelers customarily stopped for the night. That fact alone lent it added significance.[30]

The Spanish colonists, dispersed on their estancias throughout the valley, must have felt keenly the lack of churches and communities of their own. The padres at the neighboring Indian missions could provide them the sacraments, but their interests and energies were directed mainly toward the Pueblos, not the settlers. Spaniards have an almost hereditary affinity for town life, with its round of religious observances, public markets, and social activity centered upon a plaza, all supported by a municipal political structure based on accumulated tradition. Formal creation of new communities was one of the first steps taken by the sixteenth-century conquistadores as they expanded the limits of New Spain.

Just why the Spaniards failed to establish a legal settlement in the Middle Valley prior to 1680 cannot be satisfactorily explained. The interest was there and one or more feeble attempts were made to do so, but they came to nothing. For example, in 1662, Governor Diego de Peñalosa traveled down from Santa Fe and at a meeting held on the estancia of Pedro Varela (or Barela) de Losada he drew up an order calling for the creation of a formal town, or *villa.* Twelve to fifteen persons, who agreed to participate in the venture, affixed their names to the document

along with the governor.[31] The Varela estate is believed to have been
somewhere inside present-day Albuquerque, perhaps within the area of the south valley now known as Las Barelas.

It is apparent that Governor Peñalosa as well as other prominent men of the day regarded the country along the Rio Grande between Sandia and Isleta as the best possible site in all New Mexico for establishment of a new town. But neither he nor his immediate successors in the governorship were able to bring about such a project. We can only suppose that their attention was diverted by the multitude of problems that plagued the province during the third quarter of the seventeenth century.

The most serious of these was the growing discontent and belligerence of the Pueblo Indians. In 1650, several villages formed a league with the Apaches for the purpose of rebellion. They planned to attack on the night of Holy Thursday when the Spaniards were assembled in the churches and would be defenseless. The plot, however, was discovered and nine ringleaders were hanged, including several Tiwas from the pueblos of Alameda and Sandia.[32] Although this first attempt at a general uprising fizzled, the seeds of resistance had been sown. Over the next three decades, hostile incidents multiplied at an alarming rate and should have sounded a clear and frightening warning to the colonists that they were in for rough sledding. But like most people, they preferred to live with their comfortable illusions rather than face facts, and so the signs of coming disaster went largely ignored.

The great Pueblo Revolt, when it broke forth with noise and fury in the summer of 1680, was sparked by multiple causes that had flowed together over the years to form a single well of bitterness among the Indians. Their largest complaint against the rulers of the land was directed at the padres, who, since the arrival of Oñate, had worked with fierce dedication to stamp out native religion. That religion, supported by an elaborate ceremonialism, permeated every aspect of the Indian's daily life, and to give it up, as the missionaries demanded, threatened to destroy not only the social and political structure of each village, but also the sense of world order and personal identity of the individual.

The Spanish fathers, operating within the framework of medieval Christianity, were inflexible and obdurate. The old pagan religion, a product of the Devil, they believed, had to go—in its entirety. No room existed for compromise. With Spanish soldiers backing them, they raided Indian kivas, burned the sacred masks and fetishes, and relentlessly persecuted the caciques, or native priests, whom they stigmatized as sorcerers. Predictably, such heavy-handed abuse did not achieve the goal intended. The ancient rites went undercover, the new religion of the friars was discredited, and wrathful indignation was kindled in the breast of the oppressed Pueblos.

From about 1660 onward, drought followed by famine added to the Indians' woes. In this calamity, they saw a direct connection with the work of the meddling padres: the traditional ceremonies, many of them devoted to rainmaking, were increasingly disrupted by outside interference, and the visible result was a withering away of summer showers and winter snows. The Pueblos concluded that if the missionary program continued unchecked, they would eventually perish.

But the Indians' displeasure was not directed solely at the friars. They had a strong case, too, against Spanish settlers and officials who, in violation of royal laws, habitually exploited the native people. Several Pueblo witnesses gave testimony, after the Revolt, as to their motives and the nature of their grievances. They spoke of beatings, theft of property, violation of their women. At those seasons of the year when they were most needed in their own fields, Spanish landowners had forced them to work on the estancias. Often they had not even been paid for this labor, as the law required. Among those accused of gross misconduct was the lieutenant-governor himself, Alonso García.[33]

Given the gravity of the complaints, it is hardly surprising that New Mexico's Pueblo Indians were driven to desperate measures. Under a shining bowl of blue sky, they raised the banner of rebellion throughout the land on August 10, 1680. Within a few days, most of the bloody work was done. Of the 32 missionaries in the province, 21 died. Among the colonists, 380 men, women, and children lost their lives, some in isolated estancias, others on the road where they were overtaken in flight. The retribution meted out was as merciless as it was widespread.

In the north, those settlers in the countryside who managed to escape hurried to Santa Fe, where the governor, Antonio de Otermín, rallied the survivors behind the fortified walls of his adobe palace. Besieged, the residents of the capital held out for ten days while Otermín tried in vain to get a messenger through to Lieutenant-governor García in the south, asking for aid. At last, when no help was forthcoming, the Spaniards gathered up what they could, abandoned their city, and fled down the course of the Rio Grande.

Reaching the head of the Middle Valley at La Angostura, the benumbed refugees were greeted by a picture of desolation and horror. Estancia after estancia lay sacked and destroyed, the gutted haciendas containing the mangled corpses of owners and workers. At the once proud house of Captain Cristóbal de Anaya, he who had defied the Church and suffered a trial before the Inquisition, Governor Otermín paused long enough to record in his journal the grim findings: buildings looted, all the livestock run off, and the naked bodies of the Captain, his wife, six children, and servants scattered before the main door.[34]

Continuing downriver, the Spaniards reached Sandia Pueblo. They found it empty, its people gone. The church and cells of the friars had been ransacked. The retreating Indians left a carved full-length figure of Saint Francis on the altar, its arms hacked off by an ax. Vestments and sacred vessels had been profaned with human excrement. And wheat straw was piled on the floor of the church and in the choir loft where it had been left ablaze. Otermín seemingly made no attempt to extinguish the fire, preferring to renew his march at once.

A short distance below the pueblo, a body of armed Tiwas appeared in the foothills skirting the road and commenced firing at the forlorn cavalcade. The governor brought his people to a halt and ordered 50 men out to engage the enemy. The Indians quickly faded into the furrowed slopes of the Sandia Mountains, driving with them a great herd of cattle and horses plundered from the mission and estancias. Otermín, casting a glance over his shoulder, observed a huge column of smoke issuing from the Sandia church. That sight, as much as the Tiwa attack, prompted him to send a party back with instructions to fire the entire pueblo. Given the magnitude of the disaster that had already befallen him, it was a comparatively small retaliatory gesture. But it carried a sting nevertheless, especially for the population of Sandia, which was left homeless.[35]

At the next pueblo, Alameda, the Spaniards obtained a bit of welcome news. From an old Indian found hiding in a cornfield, it was learned that Lieutenant-governor García and other colonists had survived, and believing everyone at Santa Fe to have perished, they were then on the road below Socorro, headed out of New Mexico. Otermín at once dispatched a squad of four men to overtake García with orders for him to stop until the governor's convoy could catch up.[36]

Leaving Alameda, Otermín marched to the estancia of Doña Luisa de Trujillo, three leagues away. En route his army passed in sight of the ruined hacienda of Alonso García on the west bank of the Rio Grande. Four leagues below Doña Luisa's house, they came to the shell of the Gómez hacienda. There the governor entered a brief note in his journal: "All along this road from the pueblo of Sandia to this estancia everything was found deserted and pillaged, alike of cattle and of household possessions, there being many haciendas on both sides of the river, all of which were sacked and destroyed by the enemy."[37] Much of the country of which he was speaking is now encompassed within the sprawling boundaries of Albuquerque.

Farther south, Otermín was at last able to unite his force with that of García and together they proceeded to El Paso. There a government in exile was established to await the time when upper New Mexico could be reconquered. The governor attempted that very thing himself late the following year, 1681.

Raising a small army, he set out with a blare of trumpets and rode north to Isleta, the first pueblo he found inhabited. Governor Otermín had expected to see the Indians remorseful and if not eager, at least willing, to be received back into the fold of Spanish Church and state. The bellicose and unrepentant attitude of the Isletas, however, swiftly dispelled that unrealistic hope. As Father Francisco de Ayeta, who accompanied the expedition, wrote, "They have been found to be so pleased with liberty of conscience and so attached to the belief in the worship of Satan that up to the present not a sign has been visible of their ever having been Christians."[38]

Venturing on, the Spaniards visited the Tiwa villages of Alameda, Puaray, and Sandia, the last having been rebuilt since its burning the previous year. Because the residents of all three had fled at his approach, Otermín took it upon himself to fire the villages, the only act of punishment of which he was capable. But with that deed, really a symbol of the governor's frustration, it was apparent that New Mexico was not to be reconquered, at least for the present. On giving up the project and withdrawing to El Paso, he paused at Isleta long enough to put the pueblo to the torch and carry away 385 of its inhabitants as prisoners.

For the next decade, the Pueblo Indians held on to their independence, enjoying that liberty of conscience which Father Ayeta had found so repugnant. But all the while, the Spaniards at El Paso were assembling men and supplies against the day when they could return and reclaim New Mexico. To carry out that much-desired mission, the Spanish crown appointed a new governor in 1691, Don Diego de Vargas Zapata y Luján. In August of the following year, he embarked for Santa Fe with a strong force at his back, intending to make a thorough reconnaissance of the land and, if possible, to win back the Pueblos through peaceful persuasion.

Traveling with an escort in advance of his main army, Vargas passed the bleak and burned out walls of Isleta and arrived at the ruined hacienda of Mejía. A brief survey showed the site to be plentifully furnished with water and good pasture, so he decided, as soon as his wagons arrived, to create a supply base there. In writing of this decision, he declared, "I leave at this place and hacienda called Mejía, Rafael Téllez Jirón, whom I appoint as campaign captain and leader of the camp. He is to be in charge of guarding and defending the stores which I leave in reserve at this hacienda, and also the cattle, oxen, and horses."[39] In thus ridding himself of excess baggage, Vargas gained greater mobility for his troops, an important advantage should he be obliged to fight at the portals of Santa Fe.

Happily for the Spaniards, that prospect was avoided. At the capital they discovered a large population of Pueblos occupying Otermín's old palace and neighboring buildings in the center of town. After lengthy discussions, a truce was arranged allowing Vargas and his soldiers to enter the courtyard of the palace. There the governor raised the royal banner, shouted "Long live our king, Carlos the Second!", and proclaimed New Mexico once again under the rule of Spain. His men joyfully tossed their hats in the air and the chaplains fell on their knees to give thanks for their good fortune.[40]

A significant first step had been taken, but much remained to be done. The far reaches of Puebloland had to be pacified. To that end, Vargas led his troops from one side of New Mexico to the other, addressing each pueblo in turn, as well as stray bands of Navajos and Apaches met on the road, urging submission. Responses varied from polite compliance to sullen silence. But the governor felt that in the main his errand was a huge success. With that, he guided his army back to El Paso.

Once there, Vargas began preparations to return upriver with a full contingent of settlers and missionaries, so that the province might be effectively repopulated. Some of the people who had survived the 1680 disaster were still in El Paso, ready to go and rebuild their homes. Their number was insufficient, however, for the large work the governor had in mind, and hence he set off on a quick trip to his native city of Zacatecas in central Mexico to launch a recruiting program.

By the fall of 1693, when Vargas departed El Paso for Santa Fe, his expedition boasted more than 800 persons, including seventeen missionaries. As the cavalcade passed through the Middle Valley, on its way northward, the governor gave some of the colonists permission to drop out in the vicinity of Alameda and Sandia and begin establishing homes. Presumably, most of these were old settlers who had lived there before the revolt.[41]

At Santa Fe, the Spaniards got a rude shock. Many of the Indians who had submitted the year before, now repudiated their allegiance and showed they were prepared to open a new war. The Pueblos still holding the capital resisted Vargas's entry and had to be expelled in a wild and bloody battle. Then, over the succeeding months, rebellious Indians in outlying areas were brought to bay in a series of campaigns that sapped Vargas's physical strength as well as his material resources. That he prevailed in the end was owing principally to help obtained from certain pueblos that remained friendly and provided him with auxiliary warriors who marched and fought alongside his own troops.

By early 1695, the governor had matters well enough in hand that he could write the viceroy of New Spain and exclaim exuberantly, "With sails full we forge ahead."[42] His confidence was buoyed by arrival of his second-in-command, Lieutenant-governor Juan Páez Hurtado, with more settlers, soldiers, and supplies from the south. Now he had the wherewithal to begin founding new towns. That was an aim uppermost in his mind, because Vargas knew that until New Mexico possessed more municipalities to serve as strongholds and symbols of Spanish power, it would remain vulnerable to the kind of rebellion that had swept over the province in 1680.

The first town he formed was the *villa* of Santa Cruz de la Cañada, just east of modern Española. Taking sixty-six of the recently arrived families, he rode north from Santa Fe on April 21, 1695, and placed them in possession of the new site. Since this was a frontier town, it was provided with a military government composed of an alcalde mayor, a captain of militia, and assorted junior officers. Settlers were given seeds, farm implements, and firearms. With this kind of support, Governor Vargas hoped that Santa Cruz would become the main bastion of Spanish defense north of Santa Fe.

Later the same year, he moved to create a similar protective bulwark in the south with the founding of Bernalillo. Details surrounding the town's birth are murky, but this much can be said: a group of colonists laid out a plaza and built a church and friary dedicated to San Francisco, at a site several miles north of present-day Bernalillo, and probably on the west side of the Rio Grande. The place became the residence of an alcalde mayor (the first being Fernando Durán y Chávez) who, initially at least, had jurisdiction over the entire Middle Valley. Roundabout, land grants were made to individuals who carved out ranchos, or small farmsteads. These took the place of the grand estancias that had characterized rural life in the valley before the revolt. The shift to landholdings of more modest size was due in part to the fact that lands were now to be cultivated primarily by farmers and their families, rather than by enforced Pueblo labor, as had been the practice before 1680. The government believed that the old system, with its assorted abuses, had helped stir up rebellion among the Indians.[43]

While Bernalillo was the first regular community developed in the Middle Valley, and the focal point of Spanish activity there during the final five years of the seventeenth century, settlers lost no time in applying for land grants and filling in the country south as far as the swamps of Mejía. One of their number was a man named Pedro López, who received a grant from the hand of Governor Vargas, dated March 4, 1695. The location of this farm, which Lopez called San Nicolás, was described as being "opposite the agricultural lands of Atrisco and on the edge of the Esteros de Mejía."[44] Thus, the property was very close to the lands upon which Albuquerque would be founded eleven years later.

Some confusion exists about the municipal status of Bernalillo during its first years. It is mentioned briefly in 1696 as the Real de Bernalillo, the term *real* being the legal title for a mining town.[45] Several small mines were operated fitfully in colonial times at the north end of the Sandia Mountains, and perhaps it was in anticipation that that area would become a major mineral producer which led to Bernalillo's original designation as a *real*. Be that as it may, the title quickly fell by the wayside and was heard no more. Father Juan Alvarez, in preparing a summary report of New Mexico communities and missions in 1706, referred to the town as the Villa de Bernalillo.[46] Now, a villa, under Spanish law, was a fully chartered town with specific rights and privileges extended to it by the crown. Santa Fe was a villa, as was Santa Cruz de la Cañada founded by Vargas in 1695. But in no other document known can we find confirmation of Alvarez's statement that such a rank was bestowed upon Bernalillo. One can only conclude that the good friar made a slip of the pen while preparing his report. In documents of the early eighteenth century, Bernalillo is most often cited as a *puesto*—in Spanish, literally, a "place," but in New Mexico it had the special meaning of a "small town."

If Bernalillo owned any signal claim to fame during its first decade of life, it came from a melancholy event that transpired there on April 8, 1704. The previous month Governor Vargas, then sixty years of age and worn thin by hard service, had set out with fifty Spanish soldiers and a contingent of Pueblo warriors to pursue hostile Apaches who had been raiding in the Middle Rio Grande Valley. Riding out from Santa Fe, he had chosen Bernalillo as his military headquarters and base of operations for the campaign.

From there he headed the main force downriver while his scouts ranged through the heights of the Sandias and Manzanos looking for signs of the enemy. Suddenly, some miles south of the site of Albuquerque, the governor fell deathly ill. Alarmed, his officers called a halt to the expedition and retreated hastily to Bernalillo with their ailing commander. The *alcalde mayor*, Don Fernando Durán y Chávez, took Vargas into his home. Realizing that death was at hand, the governor called for a quill and paper and beginning with the words, "In the name of God Almighty," wrote his last will and testament. Therein, he ordered that a mass be said for his soul in the Bernalillo church, with the body present, and that afterward the corpse be conveyed to Santa Fe for burial. Don Fernando and his eldest son, Bernardo, were among those who signed the will as witnesses. Scarcely had the document been composed when Don Diego de Vargas died. The passing of New Mexico's reconqueror marked the end of an era.

Looking toward the Rio Grande Valley and Sandia Mountains, 1941, before Albuquerque suburbs had spread over the East and West Mesas. Old U.S. Highway 66 in the center. (State Records Center & Archives, Santa Fe, DOD Collection)

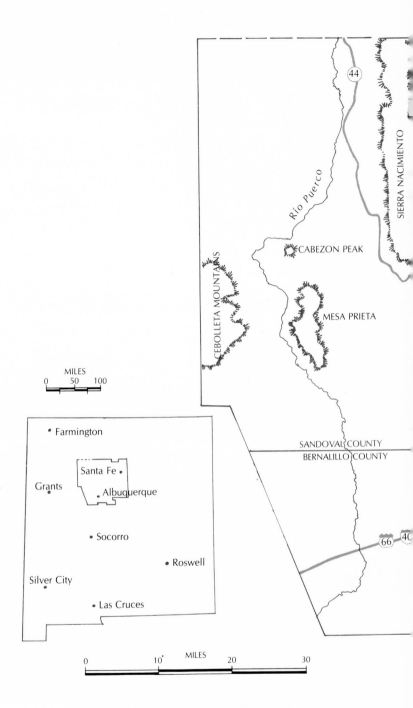

MILES

0   50   100

SANDOVAL COUNTY
BERNALILLO COUNTY

SIERRA NACIMIENTO

CEBOLLETA MOUNTAINS

Río Puerco

CABEZON PEAK

MESA PRIETA

44

66   40

• Farmington

Santa Fe •

Grants
•

• Albuquerque

• Socorro

• Roswell

Silver City
•

• Las Cruces

MILES

0   10   20   30

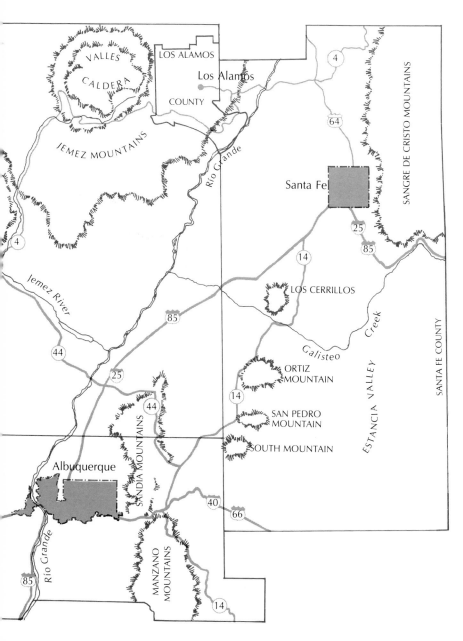

Geography of the Albuquerque Area

51

The Rio Grande. (Museum of New Mexico, photograph by T. Harmon Park-
hurst)

Juan Tabó Recreation Area, 1937, at the base of the west face of the Sandias. The giant boulders long ago fell from the overhanging mountain. (Museum of Albuquerque, photograph by U.S. Forest Service)

Escarpment on the West Mesa, whose fractured boulders contain a profusion of Indian rock art. (Photograph courtesy of Tracy Green)

Indian rock art (at left, a costumed figure) on Albuquerque's West Mesa. (Photograph courtesy of James G. Bain)

Laguna Pueblo, west of Albuquerque. (Museum of New Mexico)

Girls of Isleta Pueblo.
(Museum of New Mexico)

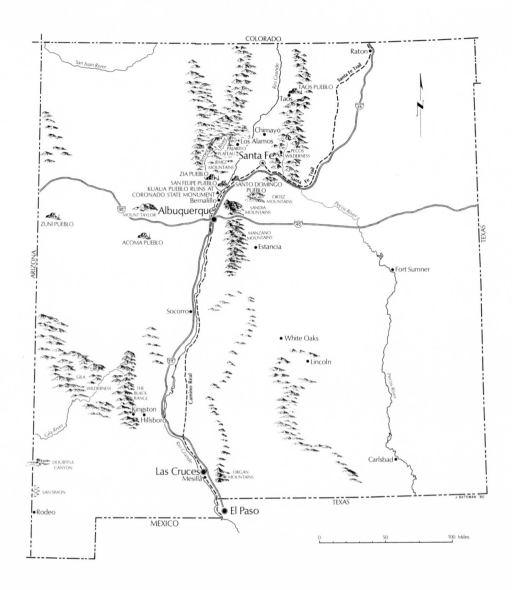

North Central New Mexico and Indian Pueblos

56

Zia Pueblo Mission, typical of the churches built near Albuquerque in the colonial period. (From a painting by Carlos Vierra)

Kuaua Ruins, Coronado State
Monument, on the Rio
Grande near Bernalillo.
(Museum of New Mexico)

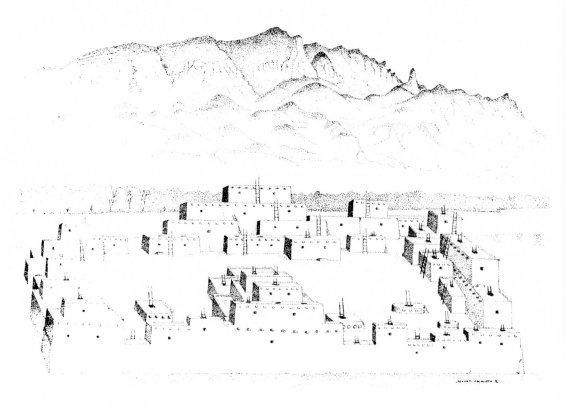

Artist's conception of Kuaua in 1540. (Courtesy of *El Palacio*)

Kuaua Kiva Murals, a fine example of Pueblo Art (Museum of New Mexico)

Kuaua Ruins. (State Records Center & Archives, Santa Fe, McNitt Collection)

Don Francisco Fernández de la Cueva Enríquez, Duke of Alburquerque, Viceroy of New Spain, 1702–11. (Courtesy of *El Palacio*)

Governor Diego de Vargas, reconquerer of New Mexico in 1692–93. (Museum of New Mexico)

Signatures of the Duke of Alburquerque and Francisco Cuervo y Valdés

60

Castle of the Duke of Alburquerque in western Spain surmounting a hilltop.
(Photograph courtesy of John L. Kessell)

Roadsign to Alburquerque, Spain.
(Photograph courtesy of John L. Kessell)

Spanish settlements in the Middle Rio Grande Valley, 1779 (from a map by
Bernardo de Miera y Pacheco)

Artist Jose Cisneros's conception of a Spanish caravan on the Camino Real between Albuquerque and El Paso. (Original art owned by the Museum of New Mexico)

Ranchos de Albuquerque Church, about 1900, thought to resemble Albuquerque's original San Felipe Neri Church on the west side of Old Town Plaza. (Museum of Albuquerque)

Navajo warriors and their wives. From the early colonial period to the mid-1860s, this tribe raided the area around Albuquerque. (Museum of New Mexico, photography by Ben Wittick)

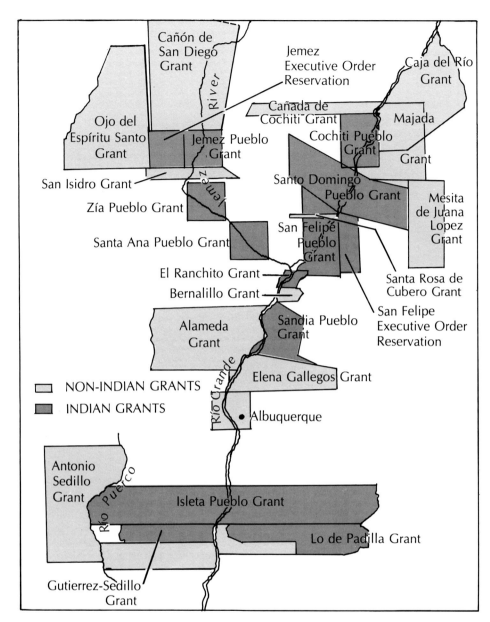

Spanish and Mexican Land Grants of the Albuquerque Area

In open courtyards, Albuquerque's colonial settlers baked bread in *hornos*, domed adobe ovens. (Photograph courtesy of Ward Alan Minge)

Facing page: Goods from New Spain were often brought to Albuquerque over the Camino Real in hide chests with iron fittings. Once there, they became pieces of furniture, used for storage in place of closets. (Photograph courtesy of the Colorado Springs Museum of Art)

Lt. Zebulon M. Pike stopped briefly at Albuquerque in 1807. He was one of the few Americans to visit the town in the Spanish colonial period. (Museum of New Mexico)

Gen. Manuel Armijo, Albuquerque's most prominent citizen during the 1830s and 1840s. (Museum of New Mexico)

Manuel Armijo's residence near the Old Town plaza. (Museum of Albuquerque)

Bishop Antonio de Zubiria of Durango inspected the churches in the Albuquerque area, and elsewhere in New Mexico, during the Mexican period. (Museum of New Mexico)

Gen. Stephen W. Kearny. With a portion of his Army of the West, he occupied Albuquerque in late summer of 1846. (Museum of New Mexico)

Albuquerque in 1853, the earliest pictorial view of the town. (After Whipple)

Judge Spruce M. Baird, leading Albuquerque figure in the 1850s and early 1860s. (Museum of New Mexico)

Gen. James Carleton, commander of the Albuquerque military post in the mid-1850s. (State Records Center & Archives, Santa Fe, McNitt Collection)

An Albuquerque street (Old Town) as early American merchants might have
seen it. (Museum of Albuquerque)

Franz Huning in his Santa Fe Trail trading days. (Photograph courtesy of Mrs. Alexander Caemmerer, Jr.)

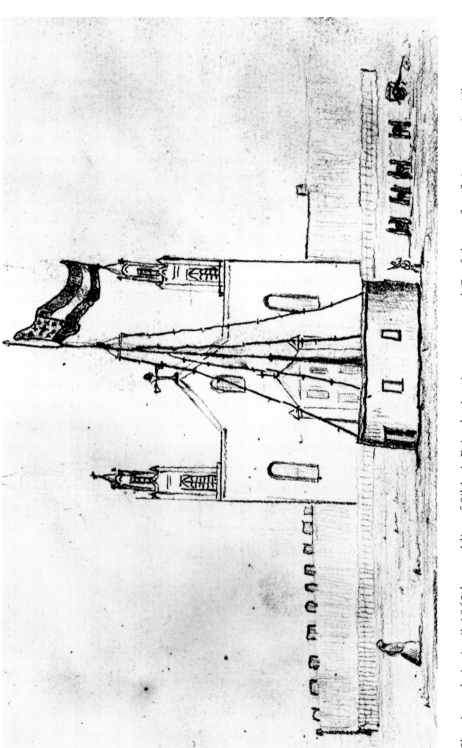

Sketch made in April 1862 by a soldier of Sibley's Brigade showing cannon and Confederate flag flying over the Albuquerque plaza. Walled cemetery at left later became the site of a convent. (Photograph courtesy of the Arizona Historical Society)

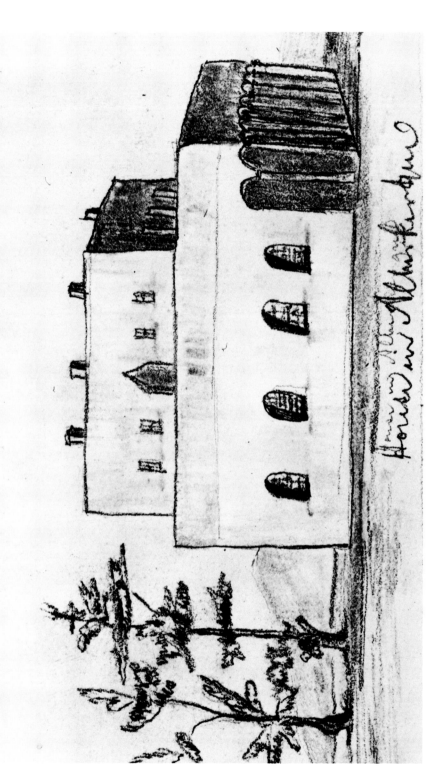

Confederate soldier's sketch done in April 1862 of an unusual Albuquerque house, of two stories and with portal columns supporting adobe arches. (Photograph courtesy of the Arizona Historical Society)

Famed frontiersman Kit Carson helped recruit
a volunteer regiment at Albuquerque to defend New Mexico from a Confederate invasion. (Museum of New Mexico)

James (Santiago) Hubbell, prominent South
Valley rancher, in a uniform of the Territorial
Militia. He fought against the Confederates
at the Battle of Valverde. (State Records Center & Archives, Santa Fe, Hubbell Family Papers)

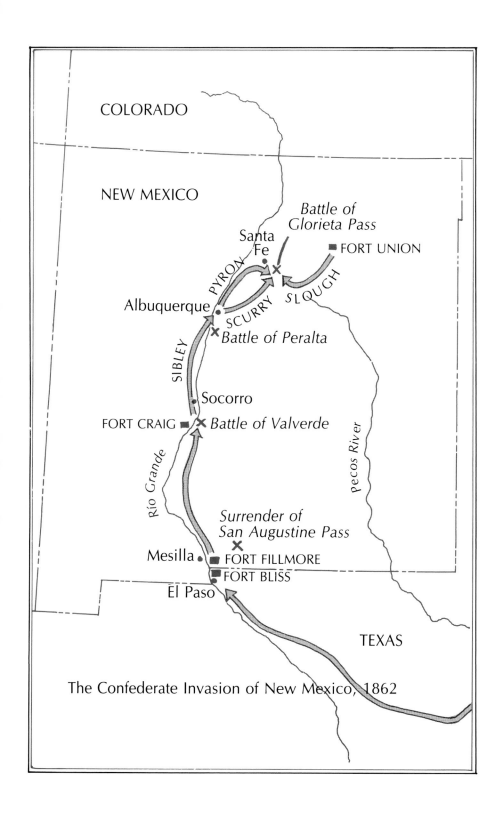

COLORADO

NEW MEXICO

*Battle of
Glorieta Pass*

Santa
Fe

■ FORT UNION

PYRON

SLOUGH

Albuquerque

SCURRY

✕ *Battle of Peralta*

SIBLEY

Socorro

FORT CRAIG ■ ✕ *Battle of Valverde*

Río Grande

Pecos River

*Surrender of
San Augustine Pass*
✕

Mesilla ● ■ FORT FILLMORE
■ FORT BLISS

El Paso

TEXAS

The Confederate Invasion of New Mexico, 1862

The Bosque Becomes a Villa

ON APRIL 23, 1706, seventy years before the American Revolution, Governor Francisco Cuervo y Valdés of New Mexico sat at a writing table in the dimly lit halls of his mud palace on the Santa Fe plaza. He was composing a formal document to his sovereign in Spain and to the viceroy in Mexico City, attesting to the creation of a new town. Deftly he wrote, "I certify to the king, our lord, and to the most excellent señor viceroy: That I founded a villa on the banks and in the valley of the Rio del Norte in a good place as regards land, water, pasture, and firewood. I gave it as patron saint the glorious apostle of the Indies, San Francisco Xavier, and called and named it the villa of Alburquerque."[1]

With a hint of pride in his words, Governor Cuervo went on to relate the progress that had been made to date. Thirty-five families, he asserted, had already taken up residence in the town, comprising 252 adults and children. A spacious church had been completed and a house for the priest was well under way. A start had been made on the *casas reales,* that is, the government buildings for local officials. The settlers had finished their houses, which were provided with corrals for livestock. Irrigation ditches were open and running. Crops were sown. The town was in good order, well-arranged, and all had been achieved without any expense to the Royal Treasury. This last implied that the people themselves had borne the entire costs for the town's founding.

The governor wished to emphasize the legality of his actions. Therefore, he declared that he had followed the procedures prescribed for the establishment of new municipalities as set forth in the royal laws contained in the *Recopilación,* the book of statutes that governed the conduct of colonial officials. Having said that, and having added a note attesting to the refounding of the Pueblo of Galisteo, which had been abandoned during the turbulence of the revolt and reconquest, Francisco Cuervo y Valdés affixed his signature to the paper, had it witnessed by his secretary, and sealed it with an impression of his coat of arms.[2]

The governor's words contained in this formal document of certification seem straightforward and clear: he founded the villa of Albuquerque in 1706, he provided his superiors certain details about the number of settlers and the buildings then under construction or already completed, and he stated that the project had been carried out in strict conformity with the law. The legal code, which he referred to as the *Recopilación,* was the celebrated *Recopilación de Leyes de los Reynos de las Indias,* Spain's monumental compilation of laws covering practically all aspects of colonial government and public life. One section dealt specifically with the procedures and requirements for creation of new towns.

According to that code, a minimum of thirty family heads was necessary to charter a villa. The site chosen should have good water, arable land, and some timber, if possible. The town received as much land as needed, measured with a cord. At its center, space was to be marked off for a plaza, a church, and government buildings. As soon as streets were laid out, each family should be given a lot for a house and assigned farm plots in severalty. After living upon the lots and improving the farmland for a specified number of years, residents obtained final title. Portions of the town grant, not distributed to citizens, were reserved as commons (ejidos) available to all for pasturing, wood gathering, or rock quarrying. Further, a villa was to have an elected council *(cabildo)* with jurisdiction over executive and judicial affairs of the municipality.[3] These major provisions, and other minor ones, were all designed to provide Spanish colonial towns with an orderly form of government.

Three days after certifying to the founding of Albuquerque, Governor Cuervo wrote a letter to Viceroy Francisco Fernández de la Cueva, Duke of Alburquerque.[4] In it he provided background information about the new villa that had not been included in the earlier notice of certification. Motivated by a desire to see New Mexico expand and prosper, Governor Cuervo said that he had issued orders for the placing of a villa on the river below Bernalillo and Alameda. In advance of actual settlement, he had sent one of his subordinates, General Juan de Ulibarrí, to scout the area and find a suitable site. The spot Ulibarrí selected possessed the necessary tillable land, water, pasture, and firewood, as the law required. It had other natural advantages, too, which though left unmentioned by Cuervo in his letter to the viceroy, could scarcely have escaped notice. For one, the center of the proposed villa was situated on ground slightly elevated above the surrounding bottom lands, affording some protection from periodic flooding by the Rio Grande, or Rio del Norte, as the governor called it. For another, the geographical position of the town appeared ideal as far as the practical needs of the future settlers were concerned. It lay astride the Camino Real, a good ford on the river existed near to the west, and a dozen miles due eastward yawned the mouth of the Cañon de Carnué (Tijeras Canyon), a pass giving access to the plains beyond the Sandia Mountains.

Once the site had been chosen, Cuervo explained that he made a public announcement throughout the province inviting citizens to join in creating the new community. Many families responded, he told the viceroy, bringing with them herds of cattle and flocks of sheep. For security, he detached a squad of ten soldiers from the Santa Fe presidio and sent it to escort the settlers while on the road and then take up permanent guard duty at the villa. The troops, accompanied by their families, were led by Captain Martín Hurtado. Their presence played an important part in attracting participants to the endeavor, because as the governor himself noted gravely, the country south of Bernalillo was alive with hostile Apaches. Even as few as ten soldiers stationed in the villa could offer considerable comfort to the Spanish colonists.

Thus far Governor Cuervo had provided the viceroy with simple information, but now he could not resist the temptation to make an optimistic forecast about his municipal creation. "I do not doubt, very excellent lord, that in a short time this will be the most prosperous Villa for its growth of cattle and abundance of grain, because of its great fertility and for my having given it the spiritual and temporal patrons that I have chosen: namely, the ever glorious Apostle of the Indies, San Francisco Xavier, and Your Excellency, with whose names the town has been entitled Villa de Alburquerque de San Francisco Xavier del Bosque."[5] Clearly the governor was bucking for favor when he gave the viceroy's name to the new town.

In conclusion, Cuervo declared, "The Villa was sworn, taking into account the things ordered by his Majesty in his royal laws."[6] By the word "sworn" he meant that the heads of households had taken an oath as charter citizens to live upon and improve lands allotted to them as a requirement for gaining final title of possession.

From the foregoing statements, it is clear that Governor Cuervo intended to show that, through his own efforts, he had assembled a respectable number of colonists and chartered the new villa of Albuquerque; that he had ordered delineation of the outer boundaries of the community as well as the marking of a site for a plaza; and that he had caused a church and government offices to be built. Unfortunately, other evidence indicates that the ambitious governor, in his claims, strayed several degrees from the truth. Indeed, as a subsequent review of other documents will show, he uttered numerous half-truths and several outright falsehoods. Some doubt is, therefore, cast upon the traditional belief that Albuquerque was founded as a lawful Spanish municipality.

The subject is of more than academic interest. As child and heir of the Spanish colonial villa, the modern city of Albuquerque has on occasion asserted claim to land and water rights in the courts by reference to Hispanic law governing the community at its founding. Such a stand has always been predicated upon the position that Governor Cuervo, true to his word to the king and viceroy, conducted the formal proceedings and followed the steps as stipulated by the *Recopilación* that were needed to establish Albuquerque as a legal entity.

In 1881 at the beginning of the boom occasioned by arrival of the railroad, the city of Albuquerque placed a petition before the state surveyor general asking that he survey a tract of four square leagues (roughly 17.2 square miles), centering upon the Old Town plaza, and then recommend to Congress that it place Albuquerque in possession. The claim was based upon a mistaken belief that old Spanish practice automatically granted four square leagues to each new villa. Although Governor Cuervo had never referred in existing documents to such a grant, attorneys for the city hoped to show that one had, indeed, been made.

The surveyor general of New Mexico evidently assumed as much, for he acted favorably upon Albuquerque's petition, surveyed the "imagined" four square leagues, and recommended it for confirmation by Congress. He was careful to explain to Washington, however, that, "No original documents constituting or creating the grant hereby are known to exist, and therefore no such document can be filed herewith."[7] What he supposed, as have most lawyers and historians since, was that the original grant papers, which Cuervo must have drawn up, had become lost over the years, but that unfortunate circumstance notwithstanding, Albuquerque was still entitled to its original allotment of land. The tough-minded congressmen, though, were not swayed by such an argument, and eventually the city's claim was disallowed.

The issue came up again in 1959, but this time in relation to water rights. The city became involved in a dispute with the state over use of waters in the surrounding Rio Grande Basin. It claimed that under Spanish law the villa of Albuquerque was conceded all the water necessary for its growth and development and that since the modern city was the legal heir of the villa, its right in this regard remained unimpaired. The New Mexico Supreme Court finally decided against the city on the basis of other legal points. Yet what is significant here is that much of Albuquerque's stand rested upon the popular assumption that in the year 1706 Governor Francisco Cuervo y Valdés officially established a valid community according to the laws of Spain.[8]

It is now possible to clarify, in some measure, the incidents attendant upon Albuquerque's beginnings, particularly the actions of Governor Cuervo. But since serious gaps still exist in the documentary record, our picture, though revised and brought into sharper focus, remains disappointingly fuzzy around the edges. Keeping that fact in mind, we can begin by taking a close look at what was going on in New Mexico, and especially in the Middle Rio Grande Valley, during the years immediately before 1706.

When Governor Diego de Vargas died at Bernalillo in April 1704, his second-in-command, Juan Páez Hurtado, a native of Andalucia and a staunch soldier, took charge of the province. At once he notified the viceroy, the Duke of Alburquerque, of Vargas's passing and then he set about holding things together until a replacement could be named.

Páez Hurtado had no easy task, for New Mexico was in a state of extraordinary disarray. Predatory bands of Apaches and Navajos stalked the small Spanish settlements and ranches, and nothing a few soldiers were able to do seemed to stem their constant attacks. Those same soldiers, in whose hands defense of the frontier lay, suffered from lack of provisions, a shortage of horses, inadequate pay, and low morale. Compounding the Indian problem, some of the western Pueblos still refused to submit to Spanish rule. The Zuñis, after first pledging loyalty, had changed their minds and, abandoning their pueblo, fled to a neighboring mesa top where they remained until a Spanish priest talked them down in 1705. The Hopis, still farther west, continued defiant and, indeed, would persist as a thorn in the side of Spanish governors throughout the remainder of the colonial period.

The settler folk who had come with Vargas in 1693 and others who arrived in a thin but steady trickle in succeeding years had not fared well. Government support in the form of provisions and tools sustained them initially, while they commenced to rebuild the province, but such aid was drastically curtailed in 1698 when officials of the royal treasury in Mexico City arbitrarily decided that New Mexicans should have made enough headway by then to go it alone. The loss of material backing unluckily coincided with the beginning of a severe drought, which stretched without relief from 1698 to 1704. Streams evaporated, scorched pastureland was grazed over and became ankle-deep in dust. Crops withered and produced at harvest scarcely enough seed for the next planting. Livestock wasted away. And hunger became a grim specter stalking the colonists. The stars, it seemed, were aligned against them.[9]

The miserable economic conditions led inevitably to social discord. Petty controversies split the populace into squabbling factions and produced so much poisoned air that many embittered persons threatened to pull stakes and return to El Paso.

It was this atmosphere of despair and gloom that Francisco Cuervo y Valdés found when he arrived at Santa Fe on March 10, 1705, to take over the reins of government. He had received his appointment to office directly from the viceroy, on condition that the king approve. But since such approval might be months in coming, owing to the slowness of transatlantic mail service, Cuervo had hastened on to New Mexico to begin at once putting affairs there in order. Until confirmed in office, he would be acting merely as the provisional governor. That temporary status perhaps explains his strenuous efforts to make a good showing during the first months after his arrival.[10]

Cuervo was well fitted by background and experience to follow in the footsteps of the lamented Governor Vargas. Born in Santa María de Grado in the province of Asturias, northern Spain, his family was evidently of the nobility, for noble lineage was one of the requirements for membership in the military order of Santiago, to which Cuervo was elected some time after 1698.[11]

He arrived in the New World in the year 1678 and proceeded to Sonora (which included much of present-day southern Arizona) where he took up duties as an infantry captain. Three years later, he became lieutenant-governor of the province. Thereafter, he served in succession as the military governor of the provinces of Nuevo León and Coahuila, which lay immediately south of Texas. It was his skillful performance in the handling of those offices and his wide knowledge of frontier affairs that led the Duke of Alburquerque to name him to the governorship of New Mexico late in 1704.

Once in Santa Fe, Cuervo made a hasty survey of local conditions and discovered excellent grounds for apprehension. The depth of his dismay is evident in words he addressed to the king. "I have never seen so much want, misery, and backwardness in my life," he wrote to His Majesty. "I suspect this land was better off before the Spaniards came."[12] Such a candid admission indicates that the new governor was something of a realist.

Since military defense was one of his prime concerns, Cuervo undertook a quick inspection of the one hundred regular troops attached to the Santa Fe presidio. Then he called for a general muster of the citizens' militia. Because of the constant danger from hostile Indians, all able-bodied men were enrolled in militia companies. Under orders of the governor, those from the towns of Santa Cruz de la Cañada and Bernalillo marched to the capital for a review and inspection. The Bernalillo contingent, the military records note, was led by three captains: Fernando de Chávez, Diego de Montoya, and Manuel Baca. All were destined to play a prominent role in the early history of Albuquerque.[13]

With a coldly professional eye, Governor Cuervo tallied up his forces, both regular and volunteer, and determined that their number was far too small to defend his broad domain. He fired off a letter to Mexico City asking for reinforcements, but, as he may well have anticipated, the economy-minded viceroy simply pigeonholed the request. No more soldiers were to be forthcoming.

The governor's next move was to take the troops already quartered in Santa Fe and spread them out on the frontier. He hoped that by patrolling the danger zones with small squads, he could stop the Apaches and other tribes from running roughshod over the New Mexican settlements. To that end, temporary detachments were stationed at the pueblos of Santa Clara, Cochiti, Jemez, Laguna, Acoma, and Zuñi.

As part of a broad policy to gain cooperation of the Pueblo Indians, Cuervo toured their villages, spoke to the leaders in conciliatory terms, and obtained promises of aid in the continuing war against the Apaches. From those meetings, he drew a high opinion of the Pueblo people, referring to them as handsome in appearance and industrious by nature.[14] The Indians, for their part, responded favorably to the governor's overtures. Indeed, they came to regard him as something of a savior, or so he tried to convince the king. By letter, Cuervo declared immodestly that Pueblo spokesmen who gathered at Santa Fe in January 1706 voluntarily composed a document urging that "don Francisco Cuervo y Valdés be continued and maintained in this administration for such time as is His Majesty's will. . . ."[15]

The implication is plain. Worried over his pending confirmation, the governor had contrived an endorsement from the Indians in a bid to polish his image and win approval from the crown. Something of the same motive, in part, was behind Cuervo's move to create a new villa in the Bosque de Doña Luisa. Certainly, he exaggerated on paper the dimensions of the project and his own role in its initiation, as we shall see shortly.

Actually, interest in founding a villa somewhere in the Middle Valley
of the Rio Grande had existed long before Cuervo y Valdés assumed the
governorship. The idea first surfaced in 1662 when Governor Diego de
Peñalosa made an unsuccessful attempt to promote a town in that area.
The matter came up again after the revolt and reconquest. The municipal
council of Santa Fe in 1698 called upon the governor to establish a villa
in the Rio Abajo, but once more, nothing was done.[16]

While officialdom may have been guilty of heel-dragging with
regard to organizing a formal villa, the same could not be said for
individual Spanish colonists who were eager to develop the potentially
rich agricultural lands of the Middle Valley. Some of them, as mentioned
earlier, had peeled off from Vargas's returning column in 1693 and
reoccupied portions of the valley, especially the Bernalillo district. During
the next several years, Governor Vargas had made a number of land grants
to persons who desired farms in the country between Alameda and the
swamps of Mejía. One of those grants, issued in the summer of 1704,
went to Luís García, who reclaimed the estate of his grandfather, former
Lieutenant-governor Alonso García.[17]

The pueblo of Alameda itself, which had been burned by the Spaniards in the aftermath of the Pueblo Revolt, remained untenanted until
1702 when missionaires gathered about fifty stray Tiwas and rebuilt the
village. This population, however, was evidently too small to maintain
a viable community and, six years later, the Indians moved downstream
and joined Isleta Pueblo.[18] That left the abundant and fertile farmland,
stretching south from Bernalillo, available to Spanish citizens who might
wish to apply for grants.

One nucleus of settlement, predating the founding of Albuquerque,
was the village of Atrisco, located on the west bank of the river and
facing the site of the future villa. At least by 1703, the place was
recognized as a community even though in form it was no more than a
collection of farms. Lacking any municipal organization, Atrisco was
attached for administrative purposes first to Bernalillo and, after 1706,
to Albuquerque. Throughout the remainder of the colonial period, the
village was a satellite of its larger neighbor, and, in fact, was often spoken
of as "Atrisco de Albuquerque."[19]

One thing is clear then: a number of Spanish property holdings
existed on both sides of the Rio Grande well before Governor Cuervo
certified to the king and viceroy in the spring of 1706 that he had
founded the villa of Albuquerque. But in spite of that start, there had
been no great rush of settlers from elsewhere in New Mexico to claim a
share of the plentiful cropland and pasture available in the region. The
vulnerability of the valley to Indian attack offered the major stumbling
block to expansion of settlement. That problem, Cuervo hoped to alleviate
by stationing the detachment of ten soldiers at the new villa. Their
presence plainly proved to be a key factor in luring colonists to Albuquerque.

Information surrounding the actual formation of the villa, including
the ceremonial taking of possession and distribution of lands to residents,

is very thin. Most writers have tried to reconstruct a picture of the event by reference to procedures set forth in Spanish law and to ceremonies, described at a later date, for the founding of other New Mexico towns.[20] There would seem to be justification for such guessing because Governor Cuervo, as noted, did give the king flat assurance that in establishing Albuquerque he had followed the laws as set down in the *Recopilación*.

In a remote area, such as New Mexico, however, some flexibility in application of the laws seems to have been permitted. General Vargas, for example, upon creating the villa of Santa Cruz in 1695, placed it under an appointed alcalde mayor, who also had the title of militia captain, rather than under the usual elective municipal council, or cabildo. As he pointed out, he gave the town "this style and form of government because of its being on the frontier."[21] In addition, he specifically decreed that Santa Fe, the first villa of the province, should alone have the privilege of operating under a municipal council. The precedent established by that order, as well as Albuquerque's status as a frontier community, perhaps explain why Governor Cuervo in chartering his new villa in 1706 provided it with an alcalde mayor rather than a cabildo.

A native born New Mexican, forty-six year old Captain Martín Hurtado, was the man Governor Cuervo selected to serve as the first alcalde mayor of the villa of Albuquerque, as well as the commander of the ten-man military squad to be garrisoned there. To Hurtado must go credit for partitioning lands among charter members of the villa, which he did during January 1706, and for conducting the founding ceremony on the following February 7. We would like to believe that the assembled populace gathered at the spot selected for a plaza, participated in the marking off of streets and town lots, and helped designate the sites for a church and soldiers' quarters. They would also have followed behind Captain Hurtado while the town's lawful boundaries were measured and marked. In conformity with ancient Spanish custom, they would have pulled up grass, thrown rocks in the air, and shouted, "Long live the king!", symbolic acts associated with the taking possession of new lands. Later, some of the colonists recorded that they had sworn an oath, which confirms that some kind of formal proceeding took place. But whether the boundaries were actually surveyed and whether plaza, streets, lots, and commons were marked is open to question.[22]

Further uncertainty surrounds the actual number of charter citizens. The governor's own declaration that there were thirty-five families with 252 people had generally been accepted by scholars. But Juan Candelaria, recollecting seventy years after the fact, stated that the villa got its start when twelve families from Bernalillo moved to the site, accompanied by the soldier escort that Governor Cuervo had assigned to them.[23]

A wholly different picture emerges from the records of an investigation into the governor's activities, conducted in 1712, long after he had left office and returned to Mexico. At that time the king's ministers, while reviewing documents in their archive, discovered discrepancies in some of the claims put forth by former governor Cuervo y Valdés of New Mexico. As a result, they prevailed upon the crown to issue a royal *cédula,* or decree, directing the current governor of the province, Juan Ignacio Flores Mogollón, to open an official inquiry. Specifically, they wanted to know whether Albuquerque had been legally founded and whether the charter families had numbered thirty-five, as Cuervo maintained. They also asked that his claims to having created another villa north of Santa Fe, called Santa María de Grado, and having refounded the abandoned pueblos of Galisteo and Pojoaque with displaced Indians be examined.

At Santa Fe, Governor Flores Mogollón, upon receiving the king's *cédula,* appointed Vargas's old friend and subordinate, General Juan Páez Hurtado, to carry out the investigation. The general spent several months traveling about the province taking depositions from citizens, and his findings, particularly as they relate to the beginnings of Albuquerque, are most illuminating.

Opening the judicial inquiry at the villa of Albuquerque on October 21, 1712, Páez Hurtado summoned witnesses and received their testimony "under the sign of the cross," that is, under oath. Here is the statement of Pedro Acenzio López:

Question: Was he one of the founding citizens of the villa which was settled by order of Don Francisco Cuervo?

López: That was true. He had joined with his father, Pedro López, when the governor founded it.

Question: How many persons were in his family?

López: Five.

Question: Did he know the total number of founding families?

López: There were nineteen original families, plus the ten soldiers, with their women and children, who served as guard for the vicinity. The nineteen families at the time comprised 103 people, not counting dependents of the soldiers. Now they totaled 129 people.

Question: Had the said Don Francisco Cuervo provided them any government aid *(ayuda de costa)* at the founding?

López: He knew of none.

Question: Had the villa been established in proper form with streets and a plaza?

López: He and the other settlers had moved into the houses abandoned by the Spaniards in 1680, occupying the same estancias and farms. What was called the villa stretched for more than two and a half miles (one league) from the first house to the last.

Question: Were there now any families here beyond those settled by Don Francisco Cuervo?

López: Yes. Seven additional families with twenty-two people.

Pedro López then declared that he knew no more about the matter and was dismissed. A succession of other witnesses gave similar testimony, in each case verifying López's population figures. From their statements, a few supplementary details can be gleaned. For example, Captain Fernando Dúran y Chávez, long one of the leading men of the valley, was asked if Albuquerque had been lawfully formed with streets and a plaza, as His Majesty required. He responded that from the day of its founding, the villa had the same layout as it did then, with the residents living in homes built before 1680. They were scattered for a league from the first house of Baltasar Romero on the north (at modern Ranchos de Albuquerque) to the last house on the south, that of Pedro López (below Central Avenue). All of this area, he noted, was heavily wooded (*en mucha alameda*). And, he reports that it was by the authority of Governor Cuervo that the prerevolt estancias and farms were allotted to the new citizenry.

From these declarations, it can be seen that the governor's original account to the king and viceroy in 1706 varied rather widely from that of the witnesses interviewed by General Páez Hurtado. Not only that, the General learned in his continuing investigation that Cuervo had fraudulently claimed to have created a new villa above Santa Fe, naming it after his birthplace in Spain, Santa María de Grado. No such town, in fact, had been founded. Further, while the governor had actually resettled the pueblos of Galisteo and Pojoaque in the north, he grossly inflated the number of Indians involved. All this, Páez Hurtado entered into the formal record of his inquiry.[24]

As already indicated, Governor Cuervo y Valdés seemed to have been intent upon currying favor among his superiors. No doubt, it was that simple motive which led him to color the truth. To the Spanish mind, the founding of a villa carried immense prestige, and the governor beyond question wished to add that accolade to his name. An eighteenth-century friar-scholar, Silvestre Vélez de Escalante, who composed a history of early New Mexico, wrote with biting sarcasm that Governor Cuervo, "eager to accumulate merits, falsified his reports."[25] It is difficult to disagree with that judgment.

But where does that leave us with regard to the status and early history of Albuquerque? Must all of Cuervo's utterances on its founding be dismissed, or did he mix truth with fiction? Is it possible to draw any satisfactory conclusions on the matter at this late date?

Assimilating all currently available information, this much seems evident. Governor Cuervo, in writing to his superiors, portrayed himself as the architect of the new and glorious villa of Albuquerque. He erroneously claimed a founding population of thirty-five families, when in fact there were little more than half that number. Perhaps the governor pumped up the figure so that it would surpass, by a comfortable margin, the minimum requirement of thirty families as specified in the *Recopilación*. Very few of the other stipulations pertaining to new villas seem to have been met. Whatever was done, must have been performed in the most casual, haphazard manner. At the time of the judicial inquiry of 1712, none of the witnesses indicated that even the elementary task of designating a plaza and streets had been carried out. Nor did they make reference to the building of a church, although other contemporary documents affirm that one was in progress during the villa's first years. Certainly, Governor Cuervo's solemn assertion to the king in 1706 that a church was already completed must be viewed with skepticism.

What appears to have occurred is this: Upon learning that ten soldiers were to be stationed in the area, nineteen families migrated to the Albuquerque Valley, probably coming in piecemeal fashion, and, upon arrival they were assigned individual land grants. Many of those, especially the twelve families Juan Candelaria mentions as coming from Bernalillo, were actually reclaiming properties that had belonged to their ancestors before the revolt of 1680. All households, so far as we can tell, received private grants of farm and ranch land. There is no evidence that any family was enrolled as a member of the community grant alleged to have been made to the villa of Albuquerque. As the settlers in 1712 made plain, Albuquerque was not the usual compact urban town one thought of in connection with the rank and title of a villa. Rather, it was a mere collection of farms spread along the Rio Grande. From all reports, this pattern of dispersal continued throughout much of the century.

General Pedro de Rivera, for instance, while on a military inspection tour of New Mexico in 1726, passed through Albuquerque and observed that the majority of its population, made up of Spaniards, mestizos, and mulattoes, lived on scattered farms. In 1754, Father Manuel Trigo, traveling upriver from Isleta spoke of reaching the villa, "or I might say the site of the villa of Albuquerque, for the settlers, who inhabit it on Sunday, do not live there. They must stay on their farms to keep watch over their cornfields, which are planted at a very pretty place three leagues distant, called La Alameda." And finally, as late as 1776, another priest, Fray Francisco Domínguez, spoke of the villa itself as consisting of only twenty-four houses located near the mission. "The rest of what is called Albuquerque," he wrote, "extends upstream to the north, and all of it is a settlement of farms on the meadows of the river for the distance of a league."[26] It bears mentioning that throughout the colonial years, New Mexico's other villas, Santa Fe and El Paso del Norte, and especially Santa Cruz de la Cañada, all showed similar characteristics of population dispersal and lack of genuine urbanism.

After a church was up and functioning, the Albuquerque citizenry evidently erected second homes, or "Sunday residences," on or near today's Old Town Plaza. Thereafter, for at least the first three-quarters of the eighteenth century, the community retained this loose and informal aspect. Only gradually in later years did a body of permanent residents take root around an emerging plaza. But notwithstanding its uncharacteristic and extralegal design, the town was known from 1706 onward as the Villa de Albuquerque, and no one appears to have challenged its right to use the prestigious title of "villa."

The reasons early Albuquerqueans fanned out to settle private grants rather than congregating around a plaza within the limits of a formal town grant are not hard to find. Irrigable land, restricted to a narrow strip along the river, stretched for several miles north of the villa. The farming folk, from a purely practical point of view, desired to live close to their fields both to save time, which would have been lost had they traveled daily from town, and to be on hand to guard their crops from thieves and predators. Also, with the houses widely scattered, each family could take advantage of the open rangeland nearby on the mesas flanking the valley. Simply put, the people saw more advantage in developing their own independent rural properties than in grouping together to form a standard Hispanic villa.

Self-serving Governor Cuervo covered the truth of the matter under flowery language and with sweeping claims about his strict adherence to the law, in his formal certification and in reports to Mexico City and Madrid. If nothing else, he had a flair for invention. But he also possessed a dash of cleverness, which lay behind his bid to gain the good will of the viceroy by naming the new villa in his honor. The governor's motive aside, the town was fortunate in acquiring a distinctive and illustrious name.

In Spain the town of Alburquerque (spelled with the extra "r") lies in the province of Badajoz, close to the Portuguese border. It contains an impressive walled castle, the traditional home of the Dukes of Alburquerque. Dating from Roman times, its original name was Albaquercus, which derives from the Latin *albus quercus,* meaning "white oak." The municipal coat of arms, even today, bears a single white oak on a crimson field.[27]

In 1464, Henry IV, king of Castile and León, created the Dukedom of Alburquerque. The first duke was Beltrán de la Cueva, and from him the title has descended in an unbroken line to its current holder, Beltrán Alfonso Osorio y Díez. Of interest to our story is the tenth man in the chain, don Francisco Fernández de la Cueva Enríquez, who served as viceroy of New Spain from 1701 to 1708. It was he, Governor Cuervo y Valdés of New Mexico sought to flatter by gracing the new villa on the Rio Grande with the noble name.[28]

By all accounts, Viceroy don Francisco Fernández proved an able and efficient administrator, a man known to be courtly and affable in manner. Soon after taking office in Mexico City, he shored up the coastal defenses of the viceroyalty as protection against pirates and the navies of rival colonial powers. When not busy with affairs of state, he and his wife entertained at their palace with lavish theatrical productions and splendid banquets. No doubt, upon receipt of Governor Cuervo's document of certification, attesting to the founding of the villa of Alburquerque, the viceroy experienced genuine pleasure at seeing his family name thus complimented.[29] But the news of the governor's action presented at least two legal problems. Therefore, he referred the matter for resolution to an appointed junta, or advisory council, which met in July 1706.

One point considered by the junta was the name selected by Governor Cuervo for his new villa. It so happened that a royal decree had just been received in Mexico City ordering that the next villa established in the viceroyalty be named San Felipe in honor of Felipe V, to commemorate his recent coronation. The members of the council found a way to comply with the decree by recommending that the name of Governor Cuervo's town be changed to San Felipe de Alburquerque, thereby honoring both the king and the viceroy.[30]

It will be recalled that originally Governor Cuervo had declared Albuquerque's patron saint to be San Francisco Xavier. Perhaps that was another ploy of his to please the viceory, whose given name was also Francisco. But it is possible, too, that the governor was thinking of himself: his own name was Francisco, and his personal saint, San Francisco Xavier, as suggested by the fact that he christened one of his sons, Francisco Antonio Xavier y Cuervo.[31] Then, there is still a third reason why this saint was a logical choice as the patron of Albuquerque. He had earlier been the patron of the household of don Francisco Trujillo (husband of Doña Luisa), whose home, before being sacked by the rebellious Pueblos in 1680, lay on or near the future site of the villa. As mentioned, one of the several popular names for the adjacent cottonwood grove was the Bosque Grande de San Xavier. Therefore, among the settler folk, the locality in 1706 was already strongly identified with that particular saint.

Be that as it may, the viceroy's advisors decided in favor of San Felipe. But they neglected to state whether the name now to be linked to the villa of Albuquerque referred to San Felipe Apostol, one of the Twelve Apostles, or to San Felipe Neri, a sixteenth-century Italian saint. Confusion over this omission lasted for many years. Since the matter was cloudy anyway, the people of Albuquerque and their priests did as they pleased and called their church, San Francisco Xavier. At least that is what Fray Francisco Domínguez discovered when he arrived in 1776 to conduct an official ecclesiastical inspection. He found that a painting of San Francisco Xavier, as principal patron, occupied a prominent place over the main altar. Rummaging about in the storerooms of the church or friary, he turned up a tattered oil canvas of San Felipe Neri and ordered that it be installed over the altar, to replace the image of San Francisco Xavier. From that time forward, Albuquerqueans recognized San Felipe Neri as the town's official patron.[32]

The viceregal junta in the summer of 1706 also took up a request submitted by Governor Cuervo that a bell, vestments, chalice, and other altar furnishings be sent to equip Albuquerque's first church. Since the law provided that such things should be given by the government, the advisors approved and authorized appropriate expenditures.[33]

They were not so generous, however, when it came to the procedures Cuervo had followed in founding Albuquerque. In their report to the viceroy, they pronounced the governor wrong for establishing the villa without consulting Mexico City. But inasmuch as the town was already up and growing, the members judged that, for the general welfare of the realm, it could be permitted to continue. To avoid a similar misstep in the future, they ruled that the governor of New Mexico should refrain from establishing any more settlements unless he informed the viceroy in advance. That order was to be recorded in the archives of the villa of Santa Fe.[34]

The Duke of Alburquerque, in accord with the conclusions of his junta, dispatched a lengthy mandate to Governor Cuervo, dated July 30, 1706, advising him of the foregoing rulings. He also included an unhappy piece of news. Shortly before the mail reached Spain bringing word that the viceroy had appointed Cuervo provisional governor of New Mexico and recommending that his position be made permanent, the king had given the job to someone else. Rather, he had sold the office to a wealthy admiral, Don Joseph Chacón, who was the Marqués de la Peñuela.[35] This was not an uncommon practice. Whenever the crown was short of cash, it simply sold an overseas post to the highest bidder. Governor Cuervo, who had come up the hard way through long service on the frontier, was left out in the cold.

After waiting some months for his successor to arrive, Cuervo packed up his trunks and departed for Mexico City, late in 1707. As he passed downriver, through his scattered villa of Albuquerque, he must have been low in spirit. Sadly, there was no way he could peer into the future and perceive the legacy he was leaving behind: the small, badly formed town whose founding he had authorized and upon which he had bestowed the name Albuquerque was destined to flower one day into a great city.

Years of Struggle

ALBUQUERQUE, DURING THE FIRST CENTURY after its founding, witnessed sporadic episodes of high drama: Indian attacks and reprisals, violent quarrels among the colonists, famines, and plagues. But behind such troubles flowed the quiet, unsensational stream of ongoing daily life that characterized all New Mexican communities in the days of Spain's colonial rule.

A traveler from Mexico coming up the Camino Real for the first time, say in the decade of the 1790s, and pausing for a day to stroll through Albuquerque's plaza and along the wobbly, ill-defined streets would have been struck by the mellow atmosphere of somnolence and by a prevailing sense of timelessness. It was a place where every phase of work and leisure was governed by age-old custom, and where major events in man's life cycle—birth, marriage, and death—were attended by ceremonies encrusted with tradition.

The citizens of Albuquerque, as our traveler might have seen, walked to their tasks in full sunlight, thinking their own thoughts, swayed by their own emotions, and wholly unconscious of being a part of the great tide of history. They were not cardboard men and women, flat and bloodless, existing in a dim twilight, as we often in our imagination tend to see people out of history. They were alive with purposes and desires of which we have only a small inkling.

The dusty, sunburned Albuquerque seen by our Mexican visitor was composed of a jumble of squat mud houses, neither stylish nor comfortable; an earth-walled church, whose cavernous interior held a funereal silence and a musty odor of antiquity that all adobe structures seem to acquire the day after they are built; and, to the west of the church, a cluster of barracks for the soldiers, which local citizens had graced with the title of El Presidio, though it was not really a fort.

These dun-colored buildings in the bright glare of midday seemed poor and humble. But when evening's last burst of sunlight shot a fan of long red streamers from the dark edge of the West Mesa, their walls grew rosy and from a distance the glow gave Albuquerque the aspect of a rich and wonderful town.

Ambling about the plaza, upon which faced the church and several of the most important residences, the traveler absorbed the sights and sounds and smells of colonial life, all merging to form a pleasing medley of impressions. Pure, untainted air, laced with the faint fragrance of juniper smoke from cooking fires, assailed the nostrils. From the distance came the sound of bleating goats, the wheezing, protesting bray of a burro, and the rhythmic thunk, thunk of an ax biting into sticks of firewood. On all sides could be heard the bubbling noises of children at play and the occasional yowling of an infant. From neighboring houses issued the rasping sound of women grinding corn on stone metates and the bump and clack of weavers at work on heavy Spanish looms. Each of these sounds, together with the hollow ring of the church bell at noontide, was clear and distinct. They punctuated the heavy silence that enveloped all the land—the silence that has become one of our lost and now unremembered luxuries.

The people one saw, passing through Albuquerque's early-day plaza, formed a cross-section of the Rio Abajo population. There were big-hatted ranchers, with silver buttons on their clothing and a bright sash at the waist, who were mounted on small and wiry horses. Men of more humble station walked, carrying crude farm implements on their shoulders. They dressed in loose-fitting shirts and trousers made of *sabanilla,* a rough white cloth produced locally. Or sometimes they wore *gamuza,* the tanned skin of deer and elk as soft to the touch as velvet. Younger women, lithe and shapely, decked themselves out in blouse and skirt, and like the men shod their feet with *teguas,* the hard-soled moccasin used everywhere in New Mexico. Matronly ladies of advanced years, their faces lined and gullied by time and the weather, were usually attired in conservative black with a fringed *tápalo,* or shawl, wrapped around the head hood-fashion. Small children ran naked·and were quickly tinctured nut-brown by the sun.

Leaving the plaza and moving up the valley on the Camino Real, our visitor from Mexico would have encountered the patchwork of farms that helped feed the villa of Albuquerque. Upon the fields, the Rio Grande's seasonal floods deposited a layer of fine alluvial soil. One New Mexican in 1773 remarked graphically that, "The water brings with it a thick mud which serves as manure for the land, leaving on top of the irrigated earth a glutinous scum resembling lard."[1] The plots, thus fertilized, yielded bountiful crops of corn and wheat, vegetables like chile, squash, beans, and onions, and, of course, *punche,* the brown and acrid native tobacco smoked by everyone in little flat cornhusk cigarettes. In addition, one could find wondrously green vineyards that grew grape-heavy in late summer, and orchards of peach, apricot, plum, and apple.

A veritable net of *acequias,* or irrigation ditches, allowed the fields to drink between rains. Where they crossed the Camino Real and smaller feeder roads, the acequias were spanned by clumsy log bridges. The main

ditch, the *acequia madre,* siphoned off water from the Rio Grande several
miles above the villa, then ran along the eastern edge of the valley, near the foot of the tumbled sandhills. From it, tributary ditches dropped down to the individual fields where farmers, using wide-bladed hoes, caused the water to spread evenly over the thirsty soil. The ditch system had been started by the pre-Revolt settlers, and it had been restored and expanded by the tillers who reclaimed the valley in 1706. At the gurgling acequias, Albuquerque's populace drew water for drinking, and in them they bathed, washed their clothes, and watered livestock. Beyond such purely practical functions, the ditches, sparkling under the sun and shining like yellow ribbons by moonlight, lent much to the pastoral beauty of the countryside north of the villa.

Journeying up the Camino Real, following the deep ruts cut by cart caravans, the wayfarer passed a succession of ranchos, the small farmsteads with a two- or three-room adobe house, an outdoor beehive oven, and out back a few sheep and burros quartered in tight little pens of juniper pickets (coyote fences, they are still called). Occasionally larger establishments could be seen: the multiroomed houses with a portal and tiny chapel belonging to aristocratic families who set their tables with a few treasured pieces of silver and were waited upon by Indian servants captured from the Apaches or Navajos.

This was the small, close-knit, almost self-sufficient Albuquerque of two centuries ago. The villa, its neighboring farms, and the way of life seen by our Mexican visitor have been swallowed up by the past, all but a few traces and faint echos of that earlier time buried under the bustling hubbub of today's sprawling city. Yet, among the faded and fragile colonial documents, carefully preserved in public archives, can be found a record, spotty and incomplete though it is, of history's high points during those years when the Spanish flag floated over the Albuquerque plaza.

Most abundant in the old papers are references to Indian raids that kept the Middle Valley in constant turmoil far into the nineteenth century. Governor Vargas's last illness in 1704 had overtaken him while pursuing Apaches through the Sandia Mountains, and although none of his successors fared so badly as to die on a campaign, they all had to devote a considerable portion of their time to keeping the hostile tribes in check.

During his brief administration, Governor Cuervo y Váldes prosecuted the war "with all vigor," as he put it.[2] He mounted two campaigns against the Navajos on the west, and three against the Apaches of the south and east. His military efforts met with some success, for as he wrote to the Duke of Alburquerque in mid-1706, "By these operations, the kingdom has attained the quiet, peace, and tranquility which it now enjoys."[3]

In the interval of calm, which is all it proved to be, an Apache arrived in Albuquerque and spoke to the alcalde mayor, Captain Martín Hurtado. He said that members of his band camping in the Sandias had a vision in which they were encouraged to accept Spanish authority and to trade with the people of the new villa. It was an obvious and disarming ploy on the part of the Apaches to gain a breathing spell from the constant harassment they had lately suffered at the hands of the governor's forces. But it was also an expression of their desire to engage in honest trade—that being an acceptable alternative when the preferable business of raiding proved too risky.

Captain Hurtado doubtless put little stock in the "vision" claimed by the Indians, but he was warm to their proposal for opening commerce. Shortly, he notified Governor Cuervo of "the peaceful visits made by the pagans of the Apache nation," and described their repeated trips "to barter with the Spanish inhabitants of the villa of Albuquerque and with the Christian Pueblos . . . of this district and jurisdiction."[4] The colonists, whose markets were extremely limited, eagerly sought traffic with the nomadic Indians, knowing full well that the tribesmen had stolen from them in the past and would for a certainty steal from them again in the future. The arrangement—alternating war with trade—became an established practice on the New Mexican frontier.

On numerous occasions, the Hispanic settlers, not content to wait for the Indians to come to them, carried mule loads of merchandise into the wilds looking for customers. The royal governors ineffectually attempted to regulate such commerce by requiring traders to get licenses. Governor Juan Ignacio Flores Mogollón, for example, issued an order in 1712 providing that persons caught at illegal trading would be jailed for four months, and that alcaldes mayores who winked at such activities in their districts would be removed from office and given a two-month jail term. The stern order was proclaimed by town criers in Albuquerque, Bernalillo, and other communities in the province. But no one paid it much attention.[5]

The peace Governor Cuervo had won in 1706 lasted barely a year. About the time he was transferring the reins of government to his successor, the Marqués de Peñuela, late in 1707, Apaches and Navajos resumed attacks upon Albuquerque's Middle Valley with all their old ferocity. At the end of the year, a war party of Apaches seized one hundred head of cattle belonging to residents of the villa and disappeared toward the southwest. Martín Hurtado got a hurried message off to Santa Fe asking for help, and Captain Félix Martínez, commander of the Santa Fe presidio, responded promptly. With thirty crack troops and sixty Pueblo militiamen, he arrived in Albuquerque where he enlisted a number of local settlers to give his punitive force still more muscle. Then he went pelting off on the trail of the thieves. He surprised them in their lair, situated in the Ladron Mountains 35 miles below Albuquerque, and delivered a knock-out punch. His men killed some of the warriors and scattered the rest of the band.[6] Such chases were repeated innumerable times in the years following, but only rarely did the Spaniards earn a clear victory as they had on this occasion.

The Albuquerque folk experienced added raids in 1708, and their losses they blamed on the Marqués de Peñuela. Soon after taking office, the new governor had called in the small squads of soldiers that had been

98

stationed around the province, believing that it was better to have the Santa Fe garrison at full strength. Incensed at losing the ten-man guard given them by Governor Cuervo, residents of Albuquerque authorized two of their leading spokesmen, Fernando Durán y Chávez and Baltazar Romero, to petition for redress.

In a formal document sent to Peñuela, the petitioners declared, in part, "The governor has been pleased to take away our squad, for which reasons the enemy, seeing our weakness, has dared commit barbarous robberies, daily running off stock from our corrals. And now, knowing they will not be punished, they may be planning to surprise and destroy us and our wives and children. Before, they did not venture such an attack because of the presence of the soldiers. So for these reasons, we pray that the governor will be pleased to grant the return of our squad."[7] After some indecision and delay on the part of Peñuela, the Albuquerqueans, much to their relief, got back their contingent of troops.[8]

The people's fear of the Apaches and Navajos, when the tribes were in a warring mood, was fully justified. On June 8, 1709, an enormous army of Navajos fell upon Jemez Pueblo northwest of Albuquerque, sacked the small government building and church, and made away with the priests' vestments and sacred vessels from the altar. Two squads of soldiers went in pursuit. In a running fight, they killed a few warriors and wounded others, but, owing to the large numbers of the enemy, failed to inflict a decisive defeat. The very next month, Navajos struck again at Santa Clara Pueblo north of Santa Fe. In retaliation, Governor Peñuela summoned the provincial militia (including, presumably, citizens of Albuquerque), and sent it with a strong body of regular troops on a major sweep through western New Mexico. The campaign chalked up several major victories, and as a result the Navajos sued for peace, which as expected, proved only temporary.[9]

The Apaches, bellicose as ever, continued to plague the New Mexicans. Members of the Faraon band haunted the Sandias, seizing every opportunity to cause mischief among settlers in the Middle Valley. In 1714, Juan Ignacio Flores Mogollón, who had succeeded Peñuela as governor, mounted a major expedition against them, composed of 36 soldiers, 11 residents of Albuquerque, and 321 Pueblo auxiliaries drawn from villages as far north as Taos. This force, bristling with weapons, followed the trail of the Faraon Apaches who had stolen some cattle in the vicinity of Bernalillo. The Spaniards with their Pueblo allies marched through the Cañada de Carnué, scouted the mountains and came up empty-handed.[10] Time after time, the story was repeated. The Indians, knowing the country and the best escape routes, would make a lightning raid, and then skip away, staying two jumps ahead of their pursuers.

As the leading community in the Rio Abajo, Albuquerque became a main assembly point for campaigns launched against hostile Indians in the lower half of the province. Its open square facing the church was designated a *plaza de armas,* a parade ground where troops could be mustered and stand in review. Military operations occurred with such frequency that people of the villa came to regard the clank of arms and the rattle of drums as a familiar, if unwished for, part of life. Like families everywhere in time of war, women and children must have gathered solemn-faced at the edge of the plaza each time their menfolk mounted up and rode off to do battle. They would have made an impressive sight, those citizen volunteers of Albuquerque. Each reported for duty bearing his own weapons, wearing a padded leather vest meant to fend off arrows, and leading extra horses and mules, which would be needed on forced marches. Those of substantial means brought along a personal servant to wait on them along the trail and to do double-duty as a soldier in case of a fight.

Although the Albuquerqueans willingly responded when called by the governor to take the field, they seem to have been downright negligent when it came to defending their immediate locale. At least that was the opinion of Governor Tomás Vélez Cachupín who took office in 1749 for a five-year term. "The settlers of Albuquerque," he remarked acidly, "wish to have a soldier for every cow and horse they pasture so that they would have nothing to worry about and could live in slovenly indifference. I have tried to accustom them to the idea that each one should take care of the defense of his own hacienda. The number of settlers in that area is sufficient to do so. Besides, they are well trained and experienced in war."[11]

The fact was, the residents of the villa were so spread out and their livestock was allowed to graze so far on the mesas that they were vulnerable to any stray war party looking for easy pickings. They received an upbraiding from Vélez Cachupín's successor, Governor Francisco Marín del Valle, who issued a formal order calling attention to the carelessness shown by the people of Albuquerque in the guarding of their animals. Often, he said, they just turned the horse herds loose to forage, leaving them prey for the Indians. The governor threatened to fine and jail anybody guilty of such irresponsibility.[12]

But the Indian troubles endured by the valley colonists in the first half of the eighteenth century paled when stacked against what followed. A new and more deadly foe, the Comanche, appeared out of the north, unleashing frightful assaults all along the Spanish frontier. For three decades after 1750 the New Mexicans suffered a series of maulings, and not through any failure of nerve on their part. The settlers were peppery enough. As Governor Vélez Cachupín had suggested of the Albuquerqueans, they were trained and knew how to hold up their end in a scrap.

The problem lay with the Comanches themselves. Unlike the Apache and Navajo, who usually came by stealth in small bands and were content to grab a flock of sheep and maybe a captive or two, then break for the hills, the Comanches rode in massive parties of several hundred and ravaged the entire countryside. Woe to anyone who tried to follow them when their bloody work was done, for they were masters at manuevering in the open and at laying deadly ambushes. That became gruesomely apparent when a befeathered Comanche host devastated the Middle Valley between Sandia and Alameda in June of 1775. Walled Sandia Pueblo easily repelled the invaders, but as they departed, the Comanches drove off virtually every horse, cow, and sheep belonging to the village. Unstrung by the crippling loss, thirty-three Pueblo men improvidently set off on foot after the attackers. The Comanches at first feigned retreat. But as the Pueblos became exhausted by their running, the Comanche warriors turned and slew them to a man. Afterward, they wantonly butchered the slow-moving cattle and sheep and then disappeared with the captured horses. The episode left little Sandia Pueblo benumbed, and increased the fear already stalking neighboring Albuquerque, Bernalillo, and the other Spanish communities. [13]

The Pueblo Indians, as long as they stayed in their fortresslike villages, were safe enough, but the colonists, dispersed on their farms, were as exposed as always. A keen-eyed priest, Father Damián Martínez charged that, "Every compact pueblo, even those with a small population, is capable of mounting a vigorous defense. This can be seen at the pueblo of Sandia, which has the smallest number of fighting men. The strongest of our enemies, the Comanches, dare not attack it, but instead raid Albuquerque with impunity because the population there, although more numerous, is badly scattered." [14]

In the teeth of the Comanche threat, New Mexico's governors regularly issued proclamations encouraging the beleaguered people to abandon their dispersed farmsteads and unite in defensible towns. From the government's viewpoint, such a course was eminently practical because it meant the citizens themselves could shoulder most of the responsibility for repelling the war-hungry Comanches. Farmers and ranchers, loath to leave their property unattended, would have preferred to see an increase in soldiers and an expansion of military patrols, with the added expense footed by the royal treasury. That attitude explains penny-pinching Governor Vélez Cachupín's earlier complaint that "the settlers of Albuquerque wish to have a soldier for every cow and horse they pasture." [15] When it became manifestly clear that such was not to be, many of the rural folk, under the spur of Comanche pressure, began to move into compact settlements. Spanish colonists in the Taos Valley, which was extraordinarily accessible to invasion, left their far-flung homes and took up quarters behind the walls and towers surrounding Taos Pueblo. On the frontier east and west of the Rio Grande, some hamlets regrouped and built fortified quadrangles with homes around the perimeter facing inward on an enclosed plaza.

At Albuquerque, there is no evidence of the building of any walls, bastions, or other military defenses during this troublous period. But there does seem to have been some shift of population from outlying areas to the inner precincts of the villa. Father Domínguez, as already quoted, could observe no more than twenty-four houses in the center of Albuquerque as late as 1776, but even that represented significant urban clustering when compared to the straggled condition of the villa in earlier decades.

There was not the slightest doubt in the mid-1770s that the Rio Grande Valley was caught in a deadly bear hug, with the Comanches of the north applying pressure on one side and the Apaches and Navajos doing the same from the opposite direction. On June 18, 1774, two hundred Comanches hit Albuquerque, killing two Spaniards and three friendly Indians, abducting four sheepherders, and stealing the villa's horse herd. The offenders made an easy escape because the militia was absent at the time campaigning against the Navajos. The following summer Apaches pillaged the country below the villa, leaving fifteen dead. At the village of Valencia, also downstream, twenty-three lost their lives in a Comanche incursion of May 1777.[16] On August 27, ten Albuquerque men and a woman were massacred in still another blood bath. The galling casualties produced by such onslaughts made many people wonder if the colony could survive.

Happily for New Mexico, a savior arrived in the person of don Juan Bautista de Anza, who assumed the governorship in 1778. A seasoned Indian fighter with previous experience in Sonora and California, Anza knew what he was about. A serious face, highlighted by a prominent nose, broad forehead, and pointy chinbeard gave him the appearance of a philosopher. But the peaceful exterior belied the stern, unyielding qualities of the inner man. When he observed the New Mexicans, worn to a frazzle, and perceived the disastrous state of the local economy, reduced to near ruin by continuous Indian warfare, he acted with decision and dispatch.

First, he inspired and reorganized available provincial forces—the regular troops, citizen volunteers, and Pueblo auxiliaries. Then, by careful deployment and adroit manuevering, he managed to blunt the worst inroads of the Indian foe. Concentrating on the Comanche threat, the governor within a year brought about a drastic curtailment of their raids, allowing the settlers and Pueblo Indians a much overdue respite from terror.

For the tenacious Anza, however, that was only the beginning. In hopes of achieving a permanent solution, he decided to carry the fight into the home country of the Comanches. In late 1779, he mustered an army of 600 men, led it over the Rockies to the main Indian camps in eastern Colorado, and administered the enemy a resounding defeat. His action broke the back of Comanche resistance and paved the way, a few years later, for a general peace with the entire tribe.

During the 1780s, Albuquerque commenced a slow recovery. Apaches still committed petty raids on occasion, but with the Comanche threat lifted, the men of the villa cooperating with the king's soldiers were able to establish a measure of security that had heretofore been entirely lacking. The welcome calm, relative though it may have been, encouraged the birth of new settlements in the Middle Valley and allowed others, which had been started earlier but withered owing to Indian hostilities, to gain a new lease on life. A brief look at these small satellite communities of Albuquerque will be useful for achieving a better understanding of the history of the villa in later colonial times.

First, though, mention must be made of the troubled story of the Tiwa Pueblos. Their once thriving and populous province of Tiguex had, by the end of the seventeenth century, been thoroughly demolished by the shattering upheavals of the Pueblo Revolt and reconquest. In 1700, not a single Tiwa village remained in the Middle Valley. Many of the original inhabitants survived, however, and lived as refugees among other pueblos around the province. The largest body of Tiwas had fled west to the Hopis during Vargas's reconquest, and there built a pueblo called Payupki on Second Mesa.

The Spaniards felt some remorse over the fate of these dispossessed people, and, in 1702, they made the first of several attempts to reestablish the Tiwas along the Middle Rio Grande. In that year, as we have previously noted, Alameda was refounded near its original site with about fifty Indians. Father Juan de Zabaleta, minister at Bernalillo, directed the project and saw to the building of a tiny church dedicated to San Joseph. Later the population was swelled by arrival of a handful of Tiwas from Hopi, but even so the pueblo was too small to ward off Apache attacks. Hence, in 1708 or 1709, the whole endeavor was given up and the people joined Isleta Pueblo downriver, which was in the process of reforming.[17]

Lands abandoned by the Alameda Tiwas soon attracted the attention of Spanish settlers. In 1710, Governor Peñuela made a large grant, which became known as the Alameda tract, to Captain Francisco Montes Vigil as a reward for military service. Two years later the captain sold the grant to Juan González, who built a small chapel, containing a belfry, in honor of Our Lady of the Conception. Smaller parcels of land were given to other families, mainly from Albuquerque, for the development of ranchos. From these beginnings, the hamlet of Alameda soon emerged. Its nucleus was the house and chapel of the González family. In 1744, the community contained only eight families, but by the 1770s, it had grown to sixty-six families with 388 persons.[18]

At the ruins of Isleta Pueblo south of Albuquerque, the Spaniards made their second attempt to congregate the displaced Tiwas. It will be recalled that back in 1681, Governor Antonio de Otermín, upon failing to retake New Mexico from the rebellious Pueblos, had burned Isleta and marched 385 of its people south to El Paso. There the captives had been installed in a new community, Isleta del Sur. Father Juan de la Peña was serving as their priest when, in May 1708, the Franciscan Order selected him to be chief prelate, or head, of all the New Mexico missions. Traveling upriver to assume his new duties, Father Peña conceived the idea of repopulating old Isleta. By late 1708 or early 1709, he was able to collect a fair number of Tiwas, including the residents of Alameda, refugees scattered among other Rio Grande Pueblos and among the Apaches, and some of the people who had been living with the Hopis. It is quite possible, too, that a few of the members of his former parish at Isleta del Sur may also have moved up and joined in the new venture.[19]

To launch the reborn pueblo of Isleta, Father Peña provided its founding residents with cattle and supplies and directed rebuilding of the old church, which he named San Agustín. The village was settled and fully functioning at least by the winter of 1709, for the first reference to an Apache raid on the place appears at that time. Peña seems to have initiated and carried out the refounding solely upon his authority as head of the provincial church. Governor Peñuela did not give his formal consent and offers of aid until January of 1710.[20]

Isleta, unlike the pueblo of Alameda, survived and prospered. Its population, increasing slowly but steadily, reached 304 by 1760, and finally climbed to 1,000 in 1880. In the latter half of the colonial period, the pueblo served as a partial buffer between Albuquerque and the Apaches who roamed southern New Mexico. And the ample produce of its grain fields and vineyards contributed materially to the developing economy of the Middle Valley.[21]

At Sandia, the Spaniards made one more try at resettling the Tiwas in their old homeland. The pueblo and its adjacent farms, lying between Albuquerque and Bernalillo, had remained vacant since the time of the great revolt. In 1733 a group of *genízaros* asked the governor for permission to occupy the deserted village. Genízaros comprised a class of Indians peculiar to New Mexico: they were people who as children had been purchased or captured from far-roaming nomadic tribes—Apache, Ute, Kiowa, Pawnee, and Wichita. Growing up in the New Mexican settlements, they became thoroughly Hispanicized, losing all traces of their former tribal identities and languages.

Properly speaking, they were bound servants, not slaves. Upon deaths of their masters, many genízaros were freed. At first they tended to take up residence with the Pueblos, but having abandoned most of their Indian ways, they were not happy there. Feeling a common kinship among themselves, they began petitioning the governor for lands to form their own communities. One of the first such requests was for the tract containing the ruins of Sandia Pueblo. In this instance, the governor, Don Gervasio Cruzat y Góngora, denied their petition, but a few years later, in 1740, the genízaros were given land at Valencia, near Tomé Hill, a few miles south of Albuquerque.[22]

The governor's reluctance to regrant the Sandia tract no doubt reflected his hope that some of its original Tiwa occupants could one day be collected and induced to rebuild the old village. That hope, in fact, was fulfilled in the following decade through the efforts of a pair of Franciscan missionaries.

In September of 1742, Father Pedro Ignacio Pino, resident priest at Albuquerque, and Father Carlos Delgado, missionary to the Isletas, journeyed westward to the land of the Hopi villages. The Indians there, independent since 1680, had repeatedly rebuffed attempts by the Spaniards to bring them back into the fold of the church. What was more, they offered refuge to Rio Grande people like the Tiwas who had fled rather than accept Spanish rule. The two padres intended to try again to convert the Hopis and to lure back the dislocated Tiwas. Unexpectedly, they met with some success.

At Payupki, the new Tiwa village built, like its Hopi neighbors, high on a mesa top, Pino and Delgado discovered that a majority of the Indians were longing for their old homes and were willing to return with the friars. Moreover, a group of Hopis, who had recently been ousted from their village of Oraibi in a factional dispute, also asked to go. Although some of the very old and very young could not be taken, because of the lack of riding animals, a total of 441 people accompanied the missionaries back to the New Mexican settlements.[23]

It was the intention of Fathers Pino and Delgado to install the new arrivals at a site near Albuquerque, preferably Sandia. But the then governor, Gaspar Domingo de Mendoza, refused to allow it, saying that permission would have to be obtained from the viceroy. In the meanwhile, the footsore refugees were given temporary shelter at Jemez and other pueblos.

Six years passed before the required license was obtained from Mexico City, but at last in 1748 it came, and the governor issued a decree providing for the reestablishment of the pueblo of Sandia. In May the lieutenant-governor, Don Bernardo de Bustamante Tagle, went to the site and placed the Indians in possession, distributing lands, waters, and pastures, and marking the corners of the grant with stone monuments surmounted by a wooden cross. He also announced that the pueblo would be under the administrative jurisdiction of the alcalde of Albuquerque. Several Spaniards, who were landowners on the west side of the Rio Grande opposite Sandia, appeared before him, worried that the new pueblo might encroach on their property. Bustamante explained to these men that the law allowed the Indians to have a league (2.6 miles) in each direction from their village. But he said that on the west he would measure only as far as the river, and since that distance was not a full league, he would compensate the Indians by a larger measurement to the east. In consideration of this, however, the Spaniards would have to agree to allow the Sandia people to graze stock on their side of the river where it was safer from seizure by Apaches. To that proposal, they willingly assented.[24]

Thus, Sandia got its new beginning and became Albuquerque's nearest Pueblo neighbor on the north. Of the seventy families making up its original population, the majority were Tiwa and the remainder Hopi. For many years, the two groups lived in separate and distinct precincts of the pueblo. By keeping slightly apart, each was able to maintain its own language and customs. But in the mid-1770s, with the Comanche war at its height, the governor at Santa Fe ordered the Hopis to move in with the Tiwas so as better to resist attack. With that, the Hopis were rapidly absorbed, although in the process they left a strong mark on Sandia's culture. Even today, each May 15 the pueblo performs kachina ceremonies in its plaza (to which white men are not admitted) that are strictly Hopi in origin.[25]

Once the matter of the Tiwas was settled—Sandia being the last project of the Spaniards to reestablish them in the Middle Valley—colonists quickly filled in the few remaining areas of cropland available above and below Albuquerque. Between Sandia's southern boundary and the northern limits of the villa, a cluster of farms soon became recognized as the community of Ranchos de Albuquerque. Its lands had been granted initially to Captain Diego Montoya by Governor Peñuela back in 1712.

Shortly afterward they were conveyed to Elena Gallegos, the widow of Santiago Gurulé. (As was often done in colonial New Mexico, she retook her maiden name upon her husband's death.) The property, which became known as the Elena Gallegos grant, amounted to an estimated 70,000 acres, much of it on the East Mesa and in the Sandia Mountains.[26] When she died in 1731, Elena asked in her will to be interred inside Albuquerque's parish church, "near the font of Holy Water," and requested that her burial be solemnized with a High Mass and wake. More to the point, she willed her estate to her only child, Antonio Gurulé. He lived on the grant, in a six-room house, until his own passing in 1761.[27]

As the eighteenth century wore on, the descendents and heirs of Elena Gallegos and her son, Antonio, subdivided the irrigable bottomlands along the Rio Grande into long, narrow strips that ran from the river to the foot of the sandhills. Some of the strips were passed onto children of the next generation, while others were sold to outsiders. The greater portion of the grant, that part lying on the mesa and in the mountains, continued to be held and used in common. Anyone owning even the smallest particle of land within the grant was permitted to pasture his stock there.[28]

The farms known as Ranchos de Albuquerque constituted only one of several little settlements that took root on the Elena Gallegos grant in later years. Most were populated, at the outset at least, by a single extended family that gave its name to the hamlet—such places as Los Griegos (just inside the southern boundary of the grant and hence closest to the villa of Albuquerque), Los Montoyas, Los Poblanos, and Los Gallegos. The Spanish custom of naming communities after the leading resident family was widely followed in the Middle Valley, so that in addition to those just mentioned, one could encounter, moving south from Albuquerque, place-names like Los Barelas, Los Armijos, Los Padillas, Los Lunas, and Los Chávez.[29]

One exception was Los Corrales, which, according to local tradition, took its name from the extensive corrals built on the west side of the Rio Grande by rancher Juan González, founder of Alameda. It was actually two communities: Santa Rosalía de Corrales, or Upper Corrales, opposite Sandia Pueblo; and San Ysidro de Corrales, or Lower Corrales, immediately to the south. Of the two, Lower Corrales was more prosperous, possessing wider fields and better grazing. Father Domínguez counted twenty-six families there in 1776, as compared to only ten families for Upper Corrales, which, he observed, had "not very good lands."[30]

By 1750, Albuquerque and its satellite communities were beginning to feel the pressure of overpopulation. Many of the valley farms, divided and redivided through inheritance, were reduced to long strips stretching from the river to the acequia madre at the foot of the sandhills, a pattern necessary so that each piece of land bequeathed to a child would touch the main irrigtion ditch. Moreover, growth of the livestock industry, which had proceeded apace in spite of the dents made by Indian marauders, was placing a heavy strain on nearby graze. Increasingly, sons of large families, finding their economic prospects dim in the Middle Valley, began to cast hopeful glances west, toward the Rio Puerco.

Among the earliest to pull stakes and migrate westward were twelve men, most of whom were related to the villa's first families. They included five Montaño brothers, a Chávez, a Gallegos, a Baca, and a Candelaria. In petitioning the governor for a grant of land on the Rio Puerco, Bernabé Montaño acted as spokesman for the rest and filed the necessary papers because, as he explained it, "the others don't know how to sign their names."[31]

In doleful terms, he informed the governor on October 21, 1753, how he and the remaining petitioners were being nudged out of their native Albuquerque because of diminished opportunities for making a living. The few lands they owned were not sufficient to sustain their families, and pasturage on the mesas was so thin, they feared the coming winter would see their weakened livestock perish. To make ends meet, some of their number had gone to work at pueblos close by, weeding the fields and hauling firewood from the mountains in return for a few ears of corn, which is all the Indians paid them.

Plainly, it rankled Bernabé Montaño and his companions to find themselves in such a demeaning and impoverished condition, though they may well have exaggerated their woes a bit to gain the sympathy of the governor. They reinforced the appeal with a reminder of their own merits and those of their forebears. "We are worthy of this concession," wrote Bernabé, "since our grandfathers and fathers served His Majesty in the conquest and reconquest of New Mexico, while we, all our adult lives, have aided the king by taking part in every campaign against enemy Indians to which we were called. All this service notwithstanding, up to this moment we have never asked the government for a single bit of land [*ni un pedazo de tierra*]."[32]

These impassioned arguments could not have failed to stir the governor, Tomás Vélez Cachupín. We know anyway that later in the year he issued a large grant on the Rio Puerco to Montaño and the others and instructed them at the same time to erect a fortified settlement with a square plaza and a single gate as entrance, so that "the families might defend themselves from invasions by barbarous Apaches."[33]

In December, normally the coldest month in New Mexico, the twelve Albuquerqueans rode to their grant, about 20 miles west of the villa, and there met the alcalde mayor of Jemez who was to conduct the appropriate legal ceremony. He dutifully inscribed in the official record: "And they all entered into possession thereof by plucking up weeds, scratching up the ground, casting stones, and shouting in loud voices, 'Long live the King and Sovereign Don Fernando VI,' and we all shouted simultaneously, 'Huza! Huza!.' "[34]

Upon their new town, located a short distance east of the Puerco, the settlers bestowed the name Nuestra Señora de la Luz, San Fernando y San Blas, though in common parlance it came to be simply San Fernando. By that title, the people obviously wished to honor the king for whom they had so warmly uttered their "Huzas."

Before many years elapsed, the San Fernando folk had a batch of unwelcome neighbors on the south. These later arrivals also originated in the Middle Valley, but they came from Atrisco rather than Albuquerque. Since the Rio Grande and the lands of the villa hemmed them in on the east, the Atrisqueños had been forced by necessity to expand their stock-raising activities toward the Puerco. As they spread farther and farther westward with their flocks and herds, across the desert grassland where Folsom men had once hunted the longhorn bison, they approached San Fernando and the boundary of what had come to be called the Bernabé Montaño grant. There they got a hostile reception, for the old settlers were not eager to share their large domain with the newcomers. In fact, they rudely chased them back to Atrisco.

In 1768 the Atrisqueños complained to the governor about the ill treatment they had received, and they asked for their own grazing grant south of the Bernabé Montaño grant. There was plenty of room along the Puerco for everybody, they contended—with considerable justification. And, beside, their presence would serve as a bulwark for the defense of both San Fernando and the Albuquerque area, since along the Puerco "barbarous Apaches," as well as Navajos, were as thick as thorns on a cactus. The governor saw the logic in this, and they got their grant.[35]

The reference to the Indian danger was well founded. Indeed, the Puerco Valley settlers suffered such a volley of ferocious attacks, principally from the Navajo, that by 1774 practically all of them had been driven back to the Rio Grande. In subsequent years, the Spaniards reclaimed the area for short terms, but its continuing status as an exposed and perilous frontier zone discouraged any extensive settlement during the late colonial period.

The story was repeated, on a smaller scale, immediately east of Albuquerque. In 1762, some nineteen poor and landless inhabitants of the Middle Valley obtained a grant at the Cañon de Carnué. They planned to build homes there, grow crops, taking advantage of springs and a small stream in the bottom of the defile, and turn their stock on the heavy grass that grew along the base of the Sandias and Manzanos. All of the prospective settlers had families, except bachelor Joseph Antonio Baca. Before he could be confirmed as a grantee, the governor ordered him "to marry for the increase and concord of the settlement." Since Baca wanted his land, he quickly hunted up a bride and got married.[36].

On February 12, 1763, the assistant alcalde of Albuquerque accompanied the people to their grant, where they went through the familiar ceremony of possession. Boundaries of the tract were delineated and house lots assigned to individuals. The new village, established near the mouth of the canyon, was formally named San Miguel de Laredo, but because of its location, most people called it San Miguel de Carnué, or simply Carnué.

Ethnically, the settlers were a mixed lot. In addition to the Spaniards, there were several *coyotes,* that is, mixed bloods, and a handful of genízaros, the Hispanicized Indians who formed a kind of floating population in many New Mexican towns. Carnué had no church, or any public official, so it was dependent for its religious and political needs upon the villa of Albuquerque, 12 miles away. The lack of any supervising agency left the residents to stray, when they chose, from the straight paths of lawful behavior. In 1763, for example, they were accused of illegally trading with Apaches who had come to the doorstep of the village to swap salt, corn, and deerskins for horses and cattle. Albuquerque's assistant alcalde, Baltasar Griego, who had known about the trade but kept quiet, was arrested and sent to Santa Fe, where he spent three days in the guardhouse. He was jailed mainly because he neglected to require the Carnué men to get the proper business license.[37]

A more serious incident occurred in the spring of 1768. Two of Carnué's *genízaros* were taken into custody by provincial authorities on charges of cattle rustling. At their trial in April, they confessed to taking animals from the pueblo of Zia on the Jemez River, but declared they had been put up to it by their Spanish neighbors who were trafficking in stolen stock. The pair was sentenced to labor on public works at low pay until they had earned enough to make restitution for the cattle. Their Spanish accomplices got off scot-free. The little episode suggests that the Carnué citizenry ran more toward the off-scourings of the frontier rather than toward the upright and moral folk one usually associates with pioneering ventures.[38]

The people of the Middle Valley were eager to see Carnué succeed. Situated as it was near the opening of the only pass through the eastern mountains, the struggling little village offered a first line of defense for the villa of Albuquerque. Some of the less belligerent Apache bands, as we have indicated, were willing to trade peacefully at Carnué, but others saw the village as a golden opportunity for indulging their appetite for robbery and murder. In 1770 a flurry of raids occurred, culminating during October in a major assault on the community. Several of the settlers fell and the disheartened survivors bundled up their families and fled back to Albuquerque.

Upon receiving the dismal news that Carnué had been abandoned, Governor Pedro Fermín de Mendinueta ordered the people to return or face loss of their grant. Thirteen of the braver souls, though poorly armed and insufficiently provisioned, gave it a try, but they lasted only two days before scurrying anew for the relative safety of Albuquerque. In a letter addressed to the governor, sent in early April of 1771, they attempted to explain their loss of heart. The place was swarming with Apaches, the letter said. Four of the settlers did not even have weapons, and few as they were, it was impossible "to oppose the great boldness which the barbarous enemy now displays." Hungry and broken in spirit they had given up.[39]

Hard-fisted Governor Mendinueta viewed the matter in a different light. Perhaps recalling that the inhabitants of Carnué already possessed a blackened reputation owing to their shady dealings in the past, he now cited them for cowardice. In a stern decree (issued April 12, 1771), he charged that the settlers had grossly exaggerated the risk as a way to hide their own want of courage. To Don Francisco Treból Navarro, alcalde mayor of Albuquerque, he gave orders that unless Carnué was resettled at once, he was to nullify the grant and force its displaced citizens to hire out in the valley as laborers to prevent them from becoming vagrants.[40]

Twelve days later, the Carnué grantees held a stormy meeting with Treból Navarro. It took place in the casas reales, or municipal buildings, on the Albuquerque plaza. Also in attendance was a new group of landless genízaros whom the alcalde, with a specific purpose in mind, had managed to round up. Knowing that they were good fighters, he attempted to persuade them to join the old settlers and reclaim Carnué where they would be given house lots and farms. If they all worked together, he assured the assembled throng, then the place could be retaken and held.

Hot debate produced near tumult there in the council chamber. The genízaros were unanimous in refusing to volunteer for so dangerous an enterprise. Nor did the alcalde receive even a particle of encouragement from the settlers. Nothing had changed, they wailed. Carnué was a death trap. They were not about to lose their lives at the hands of the Apaches as had already happened to some of their number the past October. As for the grant, they were prepared then and there to give up all rights to it. For them it had been an accursed gift. In the face of such determined opposition, Treból Navarro disbanded the meeting and acknowledged failure.

A few weeks later, he notified the former residents of Carnué to bring their wrecking tools and assemble at the casas reales in Albuquerque. On the appointed day, he led them out across the East Mesa to the silent walls of the town and set each man to demolishing his deserted house. By nightfall, the place was a pile of rubble. The New Mexican authorities wanted nothing left that might serve as a base of operations for roaming Apache war parties.[41]

Governor Mendinueta was much put out by the whole affair and evidently hoped that he would hear no more of Carnué. The Albuquerqueans, on the other hand, still wished for some kind of outpost at the site to afford them a bit of security when they grazed their extensive flocks on El Llano, as they called the East Mesa. Therefore, they gave their full support to a new resettlement plan offered in 1774. The proposal to reestablish Carnué came from thirty-five families who had just been chased out of San Fernando and the Rio Puerco Basin. Adrift and out of work now in the Middle Valley, they selected Antonio Montaño, brother of Bernabé, to make their appeal to the governor. They also solicited the aid of Treból Navarro, who was enthusiastic about the idea but unhappy over the paltry material resources the petitioners could contribute to the project. As he apprised the governor, only five of the men owned muskets, the remainder having nothing more than spears, bows and arrows, clubs, and shields. That was precious little in the way of weaponry to stand off well-armed Apaches. To make matters worse, the thirty-five poverty-stricken families together possessed a mere twelve riding animals and eight ox teams. The numbers, as any experienced frontiersman could see, were far from enough to defend and sustain a new town.[42]

That was Governor Mendinueta's conclusion, too. He had worries aplenty trying to protect his vast jurisdiction and the last thing he desired was the addition of another liability, which from past experience, he knew Carnué would turn out to be. Not unexpectedly, he denied the application for a new grant with the explanation that the settlers failed to demonstrate that they had sufficient arms and provisions to carry through. And that was that—for the moment, at any rate.[43]

Carnué, in fact, was not resurrected until well into the nineteenth century. A group of Albuquerque citizens in 1818 applied for a grant in the canyon, and since the Apache threat had subsided, it was approved. They built a new San Miguel de Carnué just inside the mouth of the pass and went to farming the tiny patches of flatland strung along the creek. Eastward above the Tijeras, where the canyon forked, other settlers entered the following year and founded the village of San Antonio. Thus, by the end of the colonial period in 1821, three miles of the canyon floor were under cultivation.[44]

All of this shifting about of people and expansion of settlement in and around Albuquerque was typical of the entire colonial period. Every bit of good land within the villa was preempted during the first decade or so following 1706 and, thereafter, as population grew, colonists either had to make do with smaller farms or move farther out. In a small inbred community like Albuquerque, petty quarrels proliferated, and much of the bickering involved disputes over property boundaries. Knowing full well his fellow countrymen's penchant for fussing about land rights, Albuquerque's first alcalde, Martín Hurtado, when issuing grants, gave specific instructions that owners should avoid raising controversies. Those who did not, he promised to fine 20 pesos, the sum to be applied to the building of the church and the town jail.[45] But for all the effect his order had, the alcalde might as well have commanded the spring winds to cease blowing. Boundary squabbles, leading to bitter family feuds and endless litigation, irritated Albuquerque's early social life like recurring canker sores.

The chronic shortage of farmland was exacerbated by the hostile Indian problem—people afraid to appear in the fields and plow oxen lost to raiders—and by periodic droughts, which left insufficient irrigation water to go around. Crops failed completely due to drought at least three times between 1714 and 1734. Under those stressful conditions, it is scarcely surprising that, periodically, tempers flared and men picked fights with their neighbors. The colonial court records list cases that range from creating a public disturbance to homicide.

One incident, indicative of the times, took place during the summer of 1719. It involved respected members of the community—original founders of the villa—a fact which, when combined with the violent nature of the affair, promoted much raising of eyebrows and tongue-wagging. Don Nicolás de Chávez, scion of one of the oldest families in the Middle Valley, was at the center of the rumpus. Son of Fernando Durán y Chávez, former alcalde mayor of Bernalillo and developer of large properties at Atrisco, don Nicolás had expanded his patrimony to include lands on the southern limits of Albuquerque and in the Isleta area. Prosperity and an aristocratic lineage—the Chávez were descended from a noble family of Spain—produced in him an attitude of haughtiness and a corresponding disdain for others' sensibilities. But in the summer of which we speak, he was still in his late twenties, so that some of what followed may actually be attributed to the hotheadedness characteristic of youth.[46]

The man who raised don Nicolás's ire, thereby becoming the second protagonist in the story, was seventy-year-old Pedro López. His farm, the southernmost within the nebulous boundaries of Albuquerque, lay near the Camino Real and adjacent to the brushy quagmires of Mejía. The citizens of the villa, as previously noted, were accustomed to turn their livestock loose to graze the lush grasses of the swamp, and evidently some of the animals were wont to stray from time to time into the unfenced fields of Pedro López. On the occasion in question, Don Nicolás had ridden down to check on his roaming cattle and, while about it, he had run into López.

Harsh words were exchanged. The older man ordered Chávez to remove his cows from the vicinity, claiming they had trespassed on his farm. Don Nicolás refused. He could see no damage that had been done, and suggested that if there were some, then Pedro López should take the matter to court. The argument grew in intensity. It finally became violent.

Each man claimed later that the other had seized a stick and struck the first blow. Chávez belabored López and vice versa. In the midst of the altercation, the elder's son, Pedro Acenzio López, dashed up. An Indian servant had come running to his house crying that somebody was beating his father to death with a stick. Grabbing his sword he had leaped on a horse and rushed to the rescue.

On arrival, Pedro Acenzio recalled afterward, he politely greeted Don Nicolás with a *Buenas tardes* and removed his sombrero. Dismounting, he asked him why he was attacking his father, an old man ill and weighted down with years. Chávez responded insolently and brandished his stick, whereupon the son met him with a sword thrust. At that point, Don Nicolás dropped his makeshift weapon and took to his heels.

True enough that Pedro Acenzio had doffed his hat, Chávez reported, but then he launched an unprovoked attack inflicting a stab wound. He had fled into the dense underbrush of the bosque and there armed himself with a larger stick. Returning again to the open fields, he met Pedro Acenzio and they renewed their combat. Old Pedro López, his grandson, and several neighbors now came up and joined the meleé. Don Nicolás sustained another cut from his opponent's sword, and his clothes were soon drenched with blood. López, the father, looked scarcely better for blood gushed from his mouth and nose as a result of his earlier drubbing. Someone might have been killed but for the timely interven-

tion of Captain Alonso García, who chanced to be passing by along the
Camino Real on his way from Isleta to Albuquerque. Seeing the tumult, he galloped up and put a stop to the whole affray. The captain took Chávez up behind him on his horse, together they went in search of the Don's mount, and then they rode into Albuquerque to get medical attention.

The matter was serious enough to warrant the governor sending a judicial investigator, Alonso Rael de Aguilar, down from Santa Fe to conduct a formal inquiry. He collected testimony from Pedro López at his farm, from Nicolás de Chávez, convalescing in his home, and from the other witnesses. But getting to Pedro Acenzio, he who had carved up Don Nicolás with a sword, took a little doing, for after the assault, the son had taken refuge in the Albuquerque church, claiming the Spanish right of sanctuary. This meant that as long as he stayed inside the church, no law officer could arrest him.

Rael de Aguilar knew, however, that if he obtained the consent of the local minister, he was allowed to enter and take a statement from the fugitive. But the right of sanctuary also allowed the fugitive to refuse to answer, if he chose, by repeating the phrase "church is my name" to all questions. "Going to the friary of Nuestro Padre San Francisco," Rael de Aguilar says, "I requested with all kindness and due courtesy of the Reverend Father Andrés de Zevallos that as a good servant of His Majesty he should grant me permission to go into the church, and he graciously assented."[48]

As it turned out, Pedro Acenzio was willing to waive his right to answer "church is my name" (equivalent to the modern practice of taking the Fifth Amendment), and consequently the investigator was able to get a declaration from the last witness. When his work was completed, Rael de Aguilar submitted the entire record of the proceedings to the governor who, in addition to his political and military duties, served in effect as the chief justice of the province. The judgment he handed down seems relatively mild, given the amount of blood that had been spilled: both Pedro Acenzio López and Nicolás de Chávez were fined, the money going into the building fund for the Albuquerque church. To boot, Don Nicolás was instructed to keep a closer watch over his livestock hereafter. And so the case was closed.

Though but one small incident of mayhem in the history of the villa, it tells us something about the nature of those all too human Albuquerqueans of the eighteenth century—about their fierce Spanish pride, which showed when a personal insult was involved, and their quickness to anger and take up arms against a neighbor. Naturally, not everyone went for a stick or a sword at the first sign of a disagreement; most, in accepted fashion, carried their problems to court. Even there, however, the records are sufficiently complete to suggest that during the long years of the Spanish regime the waters beneath the seemingly placid surface of Albuquerque's social life were fraught with discord.

The Chávez-López squabble pitted the stockman, who turned out his animals to graze at will, against the farmer, forced to be on guard constantly lest wandering cattle and horses devour his unfenced crops. It was a familiar problem, like the persistent haggles over land boundaries. With stockraising and agriculture as the twin mainstays of the villa's economy, some competition between the two occupations was no doubt inevitable. The rancher, as in any society of Spaniards, enjoyed greater standing in the community than did the farmer. His flashy dress and prancing horse set him apart. And the size of his herds and flocks proved an easily visible measure of his wealth, as is still the case among the Navajo, who accumulate livestock to enhance their reputations in the tribe.

Much of Albuquerque's colonial population consisted of subsistence farmers who raised enough for their family's needs, with maybe a tiny surplus in good years that could be traded at nearby pueblos or in Santa Fe, two days' journey to the north. The Albuquerque census for 1790, the most detailed one we have for the colonial era, lists fifty-seven farmers, and only four ranchers. Across the river, however, little Atrisco had twelve ranchers and but seven farmers.[48] The emphasis on stockraising there can be attributed to the dearth of farmlands on the west side of the river and, conversely, to the abundance of pasture stretching league upon league toward the Puerco Basin. Given the high proportion of ranchers at Atrisco, it would not be amiss to suppose that the place was regarded as a "prestige suburb" of Albuquerque.

Although both cattle and sheep were raised in the Middle Valley and its environs, most people engaged in ranching strongly favored sheep. One reason was that cows were easily stampeded by hostile Indians and, if captured, they could be driven away swiftly. Sheep, being slower of foot, were somewhat less attractive to raiders. Also, the shepherds had the habit when attacked of scattering their flocks, a practice that seemed to cut down on losses.

Many sheep raisers turned their flocks over to herders on shares, the so-called *partido* system. The shepherd (called a *partidario*) entered into a contract with the owner, agreeing to pasture and care for the sheep year-round in exchange for a specified share of the increase. From the flock he got meat and milk to feed his family and plenty of wool to be spun into yarn for blankets and clothing. The drawback was that out of his share he had to make up for animals lost to Indians, wolves, or rattlesnakes. Many of the men who went with Bernabé Montaño to settle the Puerco country were *partidarios* who drove sheep belonging to ranchers in the Middle Valley. But the Navajos cut into the flocks so deeply that most of the *partidarios* went broke, one of the reasons they later abandoned their homes and came back to Albuquerque.

In the beginning, even the most prosperous owners had no more than a few hundred head of *ganado menor* (small stock), by which was meant flocks of sheep with a few goats mixed in. For instance, Josepha Baca, a well-to-do widow and mistress of an hacienda at Pajarito just below Albuquerque, in 1746 claimed ownership of 600 *ganado menor,* all let out on shares to residents of the Rio Abajo. At the same time, another rancher of the district, Luís García, brother of Captain Alonso García, listed 747 sheep and goats in his possession. As the years advanced the size of the flocks grew larger in spite of the toll taken by Indians. Aristocratic Manuel Durán de Armijo of Albuquerque in 1764 made provision in his will for over 1,200 head of sheep and goats; and that was in addition to 24 plow oxen and more than 100 cows and bulls. By the opening of the nineteenth century, sheep were plentiful and the standard size of each flock let to *partidarios* came to be 1,000 ewes and 10 breeding rams.[49]

Very little hard money circulated among the colonial New Mexicans and, as a consequence, sheep, valued at one to two pesos depending upon the period, customarily served as a unit of exchange. There existed a great temptation on the part of ranchers to ship as much wool clip and as many sheep as possible for sale to the presidios and mining communities of northern New Spain. But in the early years after Albuquerque's founding, the royal governors clamped tight controls on export of both products, as well as on grain and cattle, fearing that New Mexicans would be left short. While well-intentioned, the prohibition placed a severe strain on the provincial economy. In 1737 Albuquerqueans got up a petition asking for relief: they desperately needed to sell more than woven blankets and stockings and piñon nuts in the Chihuahua markets.[50] The ban continued, nevertheless, and it brought them in 1744 to a small crisis.

During that year, Albuquerque suffered an infestation of moths, and the hungry insects were attacking large stores of raw wool that the citizens had accumulated. Unable to sell the fiber locally, because of a temporary glut on the market, they were on the point of losing their entire investment. Then a heaven-sent opportunity appeared. Francisco de Vargas, manager of a large mule train from Mexico City, arrived in Albuquerque by way of the Camino Real. He represented himself as an agent for a wealthy merchant of the capital and he announced that he was prepared to purchase all the wool he could get hold of. The rub, of course, was that the Albuquerqueans could not sell without violating the law.

In an urgent letter to the governor at Santa Fe, they related the details of their moth problem and begged permission to turn their surplus wool while they had the chance. Fortunately, the governor was a man of flexible nature, not completely bound by the iron chains of bureaucracy, so he suspended for the moment the usual restriction on exports. But he stated clearly that his action applied to the present emergency only. Not until later in the century did the controls finally come off, leaving the people of New Mexico free to dispose of their goods unhindered.[51]

The Camino Real, the principal artery of travel and trade, connecting New Mexico with the southern provinces, proved one of Albuquerque's leading economic assets, even in those first years when the volume of exports was severely limited. Caravans and pack trains, like the one from Mexico City headed by Francisco de Vargas, as a matter of course, passed through the villa on their way to Santa Fe and points beyond. The road was of equal significance to intraprovincial traffic, tying together, as it did, the Rio Abajo and the Rio Arriba. Sooner or later, everyone in New Mexico who had business that took him away from home passed through Albuquerque.

By an order dated October 12, 1732, the New Mexican governor directed alcaldes throughout the land to inform their citizens that the annual trade convoy would leave for Mexico on the following November 1. Those with goods to sell (legal goods, that is) should rendezvous at Albuquerque, where they would be provided a military escort for the dangerous trip down the Camino Real. He also reminded the alcaldes that everyone who planned to go was obliged to obtain a travel permit, another one of the many petty restrictions imposed upon Spanish subjects.[52]

Departure of the merchant convoys, loaded with local products, was an annual event. In those years when the assembly point was Albuquerque, the villa's plaza for a few brief days in the fall became a scene of bustling activity. Most of what went on in the way of preparation must, unhappily, be left to our imagination, for no traveler of that colorful era, so far as we know, recorded his impressions in a diary or letters. As the area downriver from Albuquerque sprouted new settlements, the rendezvous shifted southward. For a time in the latter eighteenth century, the favored site was La Joya, a village on the east bank of the Rio Grande below Belen. Albuquerque, besides sending many of its people with the caravans as traders, also contributed, when requested by the governor, some of its militia to reinforce the regular soldiers who served as a mobile guard.[53]

From all reports, finished textiles constituted the chief commodity produced in Albuquerque and sold in the *tierra afuera,* the "outside country"—at least until export of sheep and wool were freed from mercantile restraints late in the colonial period. Father Miguel de Menchero, writing in 1744, mentions that the principal occupations of the one hundred families, who then comprised the combined populations of Albuquerque and Atrisco, were farming and "weaving hose and blankets."[54] That he failed to include stockraising is evidently an oversight on his part, for it was a relative abundance of sheep that made possible the thriving weaving industry. By 1790, as the census records show, Albuquerque supported forty-seven weavers, twenty-five carders, and fifteen spinners.[55] Other villages and towns in the Middle Valley listed additional persons dedicated to these trades, so it is apparent that textile production was the chief cottage industry of the region. Second in importance, though far down the line, was shoemaking, with thirteen cobblers counted in Albuquerque. Their products, the New Mexican moccasins or *teguas,* were sold mainly within the province, but some were also exported to Chihuahua and Sonora.

From the beginnings of Albuquerque down to the end of Spanish rule in 1821, the villa experienced slow but steady population growth. Over the years a number of censuses were compiled by military officers, alcaldes, and missionaries, but many of them are unreliable either because of the haphazard manner in which they were made, or because the taker failed to state whether his figures applied to the villa alone, or included adjacent villages under its jurisdiction.[56]

Each new governor at the start of his administration was required by law to conduct a *visita,* or general inspection, of every town and village in New Mexico. In the course of his tour, he heard complaints from citizens, reviewed the militia, and took a census. The population data obtained during these formal *visitas* was generally far more accurate than that from other sources. But unfortunately, only a few of the governors' censuses survive.

One that we do have, taken by Governor Fernando de la Concha in 1789, is worth quoting in full as it provides interesting disclosures about the composition and character of Albuquerque's colonial population. On October 3 the governor summoned the villa's people to assemble and be counted, and at the same time he had the local militia march in review. The military parade must have been something less than inspiring since Concha wrote tersely in his log: "Out of the entire population, I considered only 220 fit for war, and of these only a very small number were properly mounted and armed. All the rest appeared in a most deplorable condition."[57]

The census figures collected by the governor represent the number of inhabitants in Albuquerque and fourteen dependent plazas in the valley above and below the villa. They are as follows:

Men over the age of 60	15
Married men	226
Widowers	16
Bachelors	126
Boys 14 years and under	293
Women over the age of 60	17
Married women	233
Widows	60
Unmarried women	147
Girls 12 years and under	214
Total	1347

The discrepancy between the number of married men and women, which should have been the same, is not explained by the records.

From these data, several interesting facts emerge. One is that more than one-third of the population are children. Boys of 15 and older are counted as bachelors until they marry, usually in their early 20s, while girls 13 and older are listed as unmarried women, which explains the large figures in those categories. People over the age of 60, a total of 32, compose less than 5 percent of the population. Thus, the average life span of these early Albuquerqueans fell somewhere between 30 and 40 years, as was true in much of the western world at the time. How that somber fact affected the thought and outlook of the villa's residents we can scarcely calculate.

One other point bears noting. As Governor Conchas's census demonstrates, widows outnumbered widowers nearly four to one. The higher mortality rate among men was probably owing, at least partially, to deaths at the hands of the Indians while tending stock, doing militia duty on campaigns, and serving as escorts for the trade caravans. The possibility also exists that males suffered more fatalities from epidemic disease, which periodically ravaged the Rio Grande Valley.[58]

Now that epidemics of infectious disease have largely been brought under control, it is difficult to recall the catastrophic effects they once had on colonial society. Church burial records, which show sudden spurts in the number of deaths during a major epidemic, bear the grim testimony. Measles depleted the ranks of children on several occasions. The common cold and acute respiratory diseases—pleurisy and pneumonia—were widespread. Impure water drawn from irrigation ditches was the source of dysentery and typhoid. Body lice, prevalent among the New Mexican population until well into the nineteenth century, carried typhus fever. But of the leading ailments, none was more feared or more deadly than smallpox, *el peste* as the Spanish folk knew it.

From the days of earliest settlement, smallpox seems to have been endemic among settlers on the Upper Rio Grande. The annual spring outbreak was usually a mild one, but about every ten years or so the disease would gather strength and burst forth in a particularly virulent form, causing great loss of life. In 1780, when a terrible pandemic of smallpox reached across the Southwest, thousands of people, many of them Indians, succumbed to the pestilence. In Albuquerque, thirty-one persons died, and during another flare-up the following year fifteen more, including four children, perished.[59]

Because the scourge was so common and highly contagious, New Mexicans expected inevitably to come down with the disease. Statistics compiled in 1805 by Albuquerque's alcalde mayor, Manuel de Arteaga, convey an accurate picture of the magnitude of the problem. The larger Albuquerque district then had a total population, Arteaga reported to the governor, of 6,930. Of these, 2,202 were children under 12 years of age, of whom only 929 had not had smallpox. Among the remaining 4,728 people, only one had not been afflicted.[60]

These gruesome figures represent the survivors. Since the fatality rate in a smallpox epidemic could range anywhere from 10 to 50 percent of those infected, we have to assume that in the several decades before 1805, hundreds of Albuquerqueans had fallen victim to the disease. If we were able to travel in a time machine back to that year, surely one of the first things catching our attention would be the faces of the people, all bearing the disfiguring scars of smallpox. Some folk, especially comely young women, tried to hide the pitted skin on their cheeks by liberal application of a red mineral paint or white flour as a cosmetic. But to our modern taste, that artifice would probably have appeared more grotesque than the honest scars of disease.

Even as Alcalde Arteaga was gathering his statistics, however, relief was on the way. Back in 1798 Englishman Edward Jenner had discovered an effective vaccine, made from cowpox virus, which rendered humans immune from smallpox. Recognizing the importance of this break-through, the Spanish king in late 1803 equipped an "expedition against smallpox" to sail around the world and distribute the precious vaccine to his colonial subjects and to all others who desired it. The vaccine was carried in the arms of six orphans and each eight days it was passed in relay to six others, so that the fluid remained fresh and available. In this way, the vaccine was disseminated via groups of children until it was carried thoughout the Spanish empire.

By the summer of 1804, it had reached Chihuahua City, where Dr. Cristóbal Larrañaga, military surgeon from Santa Fe, was waiting to claim his share of vaccine for the people on the Upper Rio Grande. By the following winter, he was moving slowly northward from El Paso vaccinating as he went. All those he treated were children, for they were about the only ones who had not already had the disease. Those living through a bout of smallpox gained lifelong immunity, and hence did not need the vaccine.

At Albuquerque, Dr. Larrañaga vaccinated 37 children. He would have done more, but dysentery, measles, and whooping cough were all raging at the time and he dared not administer the vaccine to sick youngsters since it created a mild infection of its own.[61] At intervals over the next ten years, however, he returned to the villa to continue the immunization program. Records dating from 1810, for example, indicate that in that year he vaccinated in the villa proper and six neighboring hamlets 124 children, ages 1 to 6 years.[62]

In Spain and the rest of Europe, introduction of Jenner's vaccine brought a rapid fall in the death rate and led to an accelerated growth in population.[63] A similar phenomenon can be noted for New Mexico generally and for the Albuquerque area in particular. During the first half of the nineteenth century, the population of the province more than doubled. While some of the increment can be attributed to immigration, the greater part may well be credited to an ongoing program of vacci-nation against the dreaded killer smallpox.[64]

In the face of sickness and the constant threat of Indian raid, Al-buquerque's people found solace in religion, which has always been the touchstone of Hispanic life. For the first few years after the villa was founded, and while the first church was slowly going up, they were ministered to by the priest at Bernalillo. As remarked, the church was constructed largely of adobes donated by local citizens or given by them as fines for various infractions of the law. By 1718 or so, the building seems to have been far enough along that services could be held, and the residence of the priest, the *convento,* was probably complete, or nearly so. In the early 1750s, Father Manuel José Rojo added a walled cemetery in front, with a large wooden cross standing on an adobe platform at the center. This same sort of arrangement, in which worshippers must walk through the cemetery to enter the main door of the church, can be seen today at some of the Pueblo Indian missions.[65]

Fray Francisco Atanasio Domínguez inspected the Albuquerque church in 1776 and left us a full account of its appearance, furnishings, and operation. The structure faced east toward the Sandia Mountains and fronted upon a large rectangular plaza. There were no bell towers but at the top of the facade a small adobe arch had been erected to hold two bells, both of them cracked. Hewn beams and carved corbels supported the roof. Upon entering, one passed under the choir loft, a kind of balcony at the east end of the nave, facing the sanctuary. The space above the high altar was decorated with a painted screen containing pictures of the saints. Four side altars, two on the left and two on the right, a crudely put together confessional, a pulpit, and a baptismal font near the door completed the furnishings. Pews were absent: the congregation stood or knelt on the hard packed-dirt floor, women on the right side of the invisible aisle, men on the left.[66]

The quick eye of Father Domínguez took note, during his brief visit, of the "lethargy and laziness" displayed by some Albuquerque parishioners toward their religious duties.[67] His observation is reminiscent of Governor Marín del Valle's earlier complaint that Albuquerqueans were extremely careless in the guarding of their livestock. These two statements suggest that apathy and a negligent attitude may have characterized life in the villa. That would help explain the astonishing fact that in the winter of 1792–93 the people of Albuquerque allowed their church to collapse!

In a proclamation issued on February 18, 1793, Governor Fernando de la Concha referred to the occurrence as a public disgrace. He also spoke of the urgent necessity of getting the church back up and lamented the paltry resources of the parish. To accomplish the task at hand, he ordered everyone in the Middle Valley to pitch in, either with labor or contributions. So the message would get around, he directed that copies of his proclamation be posted in the *convento* of Albuquerque, at Isleta Pueblo, Belen, and Tomé.[68]

Exactly what brought about the fall of the church is not revealed. Apparently earlier in 1792, it had shown signs of distress, for the villa's alcalde mayor had solicited help from local residents in making repairs. Adobe structures need constant maintenance—replastering of walls, mending of the packed-earth roof, attending to drainage around the foundations. The villa's citizenry probably let these things slide so far that their minor repairs failed to forestall the disaster and provoked the governor's charge of "a public disgrace."

The wreck must have been complete because plans were formulated at once to begin construction of an entirely new building, *"un nuevo edificio"* in Concha's words. Inexplicably, the builders failed to clear the rubble and restore the church to its original site. Instead they moved around to the north side of the plaza and commenced work on a structure that faced south. The project, likely extending over a period of years, produced a church quite unlike the original one viewed by Father Domínguez in 1776. The new building lacked the walled cemetery in front, but it was conspicuously graced with twin bell towers at each corner. It also had an interior in the form of a cross, with a shallow apse behind the sanctuary and transepts on either side. The former church, by contrast, had possessed a simple rectangular plan.[69]

The San Felipe Neri Church, begun in 1793, is the one that stands today on Albuquerque's Old Town Plaza. After almost two centuries of remodelings and additions, it bears scant resemblance to the original, yet under a false ceiling and beneath layers of paint and cement plaster, there remains much of the early fabric put in place by the villa's colonial residents.

Until almost the very close of the Spanish period, Albuquerque's religious ministry was in the hands of members of the Franciscan Order. The Franciscans, of course, were missionaries, having come initially with Juan de Oñate to convert the Pueblo Indians. Since they were the only priests in the province, they also took care of the spiritual needs of the colonists. Practically all their expenses were paid by the royal treasury, including an annual stipend for each missionary of 330 pesos. Understandably, this proved a serious financial strain on the government, which was nevertheless willing to shoulder the burden as it offered the best means for "civilizing" the Indians and incorporating them into the Spanish social and political system.

The intent always was that as soon as the Indian people had been fully converted, the missionaries were to be withdrawn and their place taken by ordinary, or secular, priests under authority of a bishop. With that change, the Indian parishioners were then expected to pay the salary and living expenses of their minister, as was the custom in any community of Spanish Catholics.

In New Mexico, as well as in other provinces on the northern frontier, the missionaries proved to be a stumbling block in carrying through this plan. Having become well-entrenched, they were loath to give up their churches and congregations to the Johnny-come-lately secular priests. Therefore, they simply reported year after year that the Indians were not completely converted and that missionary work must go on. That meant also, as they were well aware, that their nice government stipends would continue.

The Franciscans found it much more difficult to justify their prolonged ministry in the Spanish towns. In its first years when New Mexico was a poor and struggling province, the royal treasury was willing to underwrite expenses for new churches and their priests as one means to help the colonists. But the government's charity had limits. It wanted the subsidized missionaries out as soon as possible, and secular priests in, who would be supported by the local parish.

To that end, an order was promulgated in the year 1767 calling for the replacement of the Franciscan friars in New Mexico's four villas of Santa Fe, Santa Cruz de la Cañada, Albuquerque, and El Paso with secular priests to be sent by the Bishop of Durango.[70] The Diocese of Durango, of which New Mexico was a part, covered a vast area of the northern frontier. Its bishop, residing in the city of Durango, about 800 miles south of Santa Fe, generally showed little interest in his subjects in the remote Upper Rio Grande Valley, although at least two holders of that office did make a tour of New Mexico during their terms. The first was Bishop Benito Crespo y Monroy, who passed through Albuquerque on his way to Santa Fe in 1730. The second, Bishop Pedro Tamarón y Romeral, stopped at the villa on May 21, 1760, long enough to hold ecclesiastical ceremonies and to record in his journal one of the problems faced by the resident priest.

"Because some of his parishioners are on the other side of the river," wrote the bishop, "this parish priest of Albuquerque, called Fray Manuel Rojo, is obliged to cross it when summoned. This kept him under apprehension, and above all he emphasized to me that when the river froze, it was necessary to cross on the ice. He elaborated this point by saying that when the ice thundered, he thought he was on the way to the bottom, because when one crosses it, it creaks as if it were about to break."[71]

The order of 1767 obliging the Bishop of Durango to send priests to New Mexico's villas was only partially implemented because of the shortage of clergy. Secular priests did take over in Santa Fe and El Paso, but Franciscans were left, at least for a time, to administer the churches of Albuquerque and Santa Cruz de la Cañada. At both places, however, the government suspended the fathers' stipend, forcing them to depend for their livelihoods upon money exacted from the congregations. The main revenues came from fees (generally referred to as "offerings"), which the priests collected for baptisms, marriages, funerals, and other spiritual activities. They also charged extra for the privilege of burial inside the church. The going rates, given by Father Domínguez for Albuquerque were: 4 pesos for burial at the back of the church, 8 pesos in the center; and 16 pesos up front near the sanctuary steps.[72] Such marketing of services, an old practice in the Spanish Church, was later to shock the newly arrived Anglo-Americans.

Finally, in 1802, Bishop Francisco Olivares appointed one of his priests, Juan José de Sida, to go to Albuquerque and replace the Franciscan there, Fray Ambrosio Guerra. For fifteen years, Guerra had ministered to Albuquerqueans, and it must have been with pangs of regret that he departed the villa for a new post. If so, his grief was of short duration, for less than two years later Father Sida was recalled to Durango and Guerra was reassigned to Albuquerque.[73]

He was there in 1806 when the villa passed its first century mark (no evidence exists that Albuquerque took note of the occasion), and he was still there the following year when a young army lieutenant from the United States, Zebulon Montgomery Pike, passing down the Camino Real stopped by the San Felipe *convento* to pay him a social call. For a hundred years, Albuquerque had been a small backwater villa in the Spanish empire, but the day of Hispanic rule was fast approaching an end. Neither Father Ambrosio Guerra nor Lieutenant Pike, as they sat amiably conversing in the priest's quarters, had any inkling of that fact,

for as yet no hint was in the air of the profound transformations that
would soon shake Albuquerque and all New Mexico. For the moment it was enough that a hospitable Spanish priest and an eager American officer should enjoy each other's company and sip wine there in the largest town of the Rio Grande's Middle Valley.

The Winds of Change

FROM THE DAYS OF FERDINAND and Isabella, Spain and its overseas colonies lay under the tight control of the crown. The succession of kings in the seventeenth and eighteenth centuries reigned as absolute monarchs, exercising the last word in political, judicial, economic, military, and even church matters. Through a vast network of officials, the sovereign kept tabs on his subjects everywhere in the huge empire. And an enormous body of royal laws regulated the smallest details of human activity.

One portion of those laws, imposing a strict prohibition on foreign trade, had a serious impact upon New Mexico in the late colonial period. As the province grew in population and its economy expanded, it desperately needed new markets for its raw products and new and cheaper sources for imported manufactured goods. But under the existing system, the New Mexicans were permitted to do business only within New Spain, which meant all their trade had to be funneled down the Camino Real to the city of Chihuahua, 500 miles south of Albuquerque. As early as 1778, Father Juan Agustín de Morfí called attention to the inequities that resulted.

"The people of New Mexico," he pointed out, "are truly puppets of the Chihuahua merchants, from whom they get credit to run their own businesses and to whom they must repay with raw products of the country. The Chihuahuans, knowing perfectly well the ins and outs of this commerce, overcharge for the goods they sell and knock down prices on what they buy. As a consequence, there is scarcely any margin with which the New Mexicans can pay freight and still support themselves, even at a poverty level. Since they have no alternative, they are forced to accept the rules laid down in Chihuahua."[1]

The best way for New Mexico to break this onerous monopoly would have been to open trade with French, British, and, later, American merchants in the Mississippi Valley. But that practical course was effectively blocked by stern royal laws, which kept the gates at the borders of the empire firmly locked. Several small parties of Frenchmen did sneak into New Mexico to barter their wares in the years after 1740, but their few illegal intrusions did little to satisfy the local hunger for foreign goods.[2]

Then in 1803 France sold the vast Louisiana Territory to the United States. That brought the new American nation to the very edge of northern New Mexico and raised the prospect of a foreign market being developed close at hand. Spain, however, gave no sign of dropping her long-standing trade barriers. Indeed, nervous over America's headlong expansion, she tightened her restrictive policies and redoubled her watchfulness.

Lieutenant Zebulon Pike was the first American to fall afoul of the Spanish law against trespassers. Handsome and dashing, the twenty-six year old officer in 1806 was placed in command of a small party to explore the headwaters of the Arkansas and Red rivers. Those streams, it was thought then, formed the boundary between the Louisiana Purchase and New Spain. Late in the year, Pike crossed the plains to the foot of the Colorado Rockies where he and his men made camp and shivered through a miserable winter. With the spring thaw, they crossed the mountains and Pike ordered construction of a small stockade on the Conejos River, an affluent of the Rio Grande. He professed to believe that he was on the upper reaches of the Red River and, hence, inside territory of the United States. But that notion was quickly dispelled by a force of one hundred Spaniards, who marched up from Santa Fe and took the American intruders into custody.

There is some reason to think that Lieutenant Pike actually invited capture as the best means for gaining admittance to New Mexico and seeing what lay behind the Spanish veil. If that was the case, then the ploy worked, for during his enforced tour of the Upper Rio Grande Valley, he got an eyeful.

The Spaniards were a model of courtesy. At Santa Fe, Governor Joaquin Real Alencaster questioned Pike at length concerning his motives and intentions and dined him in the old mud palace facing the plaza. It was not like a captivity at all, for the Americans were allowed to keep their personal possessions, including sidearms, and to explore the streets of the capital. Later the governor informed Pike that he was sending them with an escort to Chihuahua City for further interrogation by the commandant general. Alencaster made clear, however, that the Americans were going as guests of the Spanish government, not as prisoners of war. To show his friendly intent, he hitched up his state coach with six mules, invited Lieutenant Pike inside, and accompanied him several miles on the road leading south from Santa Fe.

At the end of the first week of March 1807, Pike, his men, and the military escort reached Albuquerque. Throughout the Middle Valley people were at work opening and cleaning the irrigation ditches in preparation for spring planting. "We saw," Pike recalled afterward, "men, women and children of all ages at the joyful labor which was to crown with rich abundance their future harvests and ensure them plenty for the ensuing year. Those scenes brought to my recollection the bright descriptions . . . of the opening of the canals of Egypt. The cultivation of the fields was now commencing and everything appeared to give life and gaiety to the surrounding scenery."[3] His words provide us the first reference to colonial Albuquerque by an American visitor.

Upon reaching the center of the villa, the officer and his companions were hospitably entertained by Father Ambrosio Guerra. Leading his guests into his own quarters, the priest introduced the members of the household, who, to the astonishment of the Americans, turned out to be beautiful young damsels. "Our host," wrote Pike, "ordered his adopted children of the female sex to appear, when they came in by turns, Indians, of various nations, Spanish, French, and finally, two young girls who from their complexion I conceived to be English."[4] Noting that the two fair maidens had caught the officer's eye, Father Guerra directed them to give him a hug, as a mark of friendship, which they did most willingly. Then they sat with him on the sofa. To the flustered lieutenant, the priest explained that the girls had been seized somewhere in the east and traded from tribe to tribe. He had purchased them as infants and now they could recollect neither their names nor original language.

The party shortly sat down to dinner at a table bountifully supplied with a variety of dishes and an assortment of wines. Pike, somewhat breathless, declared eloquently: "We were waited on by a half dozen of those beautiful girls, who like Hebe at the feast of the gods, converted our wine to nectar, and with their ambrosial breath shed incense on our cups."[5] For a young man fresh from the wilderness, the Roman-style banquet in the humble precincts of Albuquerque was as stimulating as it was unexpected.

With many expressions of thanks, Zebulon Pike took his leave of Father Guerra and continued his enforced march to Chihuahua, arriving there on April 2. Again he was subjected to prolonged interviews by the military authorities. But a few weeks later, he learned that his company was to be taken north and deposited in American territory at Natchitoches, Louisiana. Much to Pike's displeasure, Spanish officials decided to keep the bulk of his personal papers, including the maps and journals compiled during the preceding months of exploration.

Once again in the United States, Lieutenant Pike discovered that his fellow countrymen were keenly interested in what he had seen along the southern border of the Louisiana Purchase. From memory he assembled a report of his experiences and had it published in 1810. His work gave Americans their first inside view of Hispanic life and customs on the Rio Grande and demonstrated the bright trade prospects offered by New Mexico. The cost of manufactured goods throughout the province was exorbitant, Pike reported. Fine-quality textiles sold for twenty-five dollars per yard, and other imported articles were commensurately high. The message, for canny Yankee traders, was plain. The New Mexico market offered an untapped bonanza, but only if Spain's wall of restrictions on commerce and travel could be pierced. Pike's expedition had raised a tantalizing possibility, but more than a decade was to elapse before anyone in either the United States or New Mexico was to benefit from it.

When Lieutenant Zebulon Montgomery Pike visited Albuquerque and partook of Father Guerra's generous hospitality, he had no way of knowing that he represented the vanguard of an American wave that in the course of the century would storm the fortress of Hispanic culture on the Rio Grande. His appearance in the villa was a portent of change, but not all of the change the town was to experience, especially in those early years of the nineteenth century, derived from contact with the United States. The Spanish empire itself was in turmoil, the rigid system of an absolute monarchy under attack from within. Political upheaval in the mother country and in colonial New Spain sent ripples all the way to the northern frontier, touching the lives of Albuquerqueans and the residents of other communities in New Mexico.

The new era in Spain was ushered in by the Napoleonic Wars, which witnessed an invasion by French forces in the spring of 1808 and the capture of King Ferdinand VII. At the southern port city of Cádiz, which escaped occupation by the French, a regency was installed to rule until such time as Ferdinand could be returned to power. In 1810 that body issued a call for the meeting of a *cortes,* or congress, to be attended by representatives from each province in the empire. The liberal nature of the regency was underscored by one of its decrees, which declared that, henceforward, all citizens at home and abroad should consider themselves elevated to the status of free men. That revolutionary notion, growing out of liberal ideas emanating from France and the United States, was indeed a novel one for Spanish subjects, who for three centuries had been enchained by the absolute power of the monarchy.

In New Mexico, don Pedro Bautista Pino, a distinguished resident of Santa Fe, was selected to travel to Spain and represent his province in the cortes. He arrived at Cádiz in time to assist in the promulgation, on March 18, 1812, of a new constitution for the empire. The document imposed strict curbs on the power of the king, whenever he should return to the throne, creating in effect a limited or constitutional monarchy. The cortes also issued a law directing all towns within the Spanish realm to elect municipal councils, called *ayuntamientos,* which could provide true representative government at the local level. It was this particular measure that had the most noticeable impact on Albuquerque.

By 1814, the villa had conducted an election, the first free balloting in its history, and installed an ayuntamiento. The council was composed of the required officials: magistrates, councilors, and a secretary. The neighboring communities of Bernalillo and Belen were also entitled to ayuntamientos, and their elections were carried out at about the same time as the one in Albuquerque.[6]

Unhappily, this experiment in municipal democracy was short-lived. Napoleon suffered defeat and Ferdinand VII regained the Spanish throne. Looking askance at the liberal policies that had flowered in his absence, he promptly did away with the cortes and abolished the laws limiting his authority. Specifically, he ordered that the ayuntamientos be extinguished and that the former officials who had preceded them be returned to office. For Albuquerque, when it received the king's decree in 1815, this meant dissolving the elective council and reinstating the alcalde mayor, the appointive officer who had directed all the villa's affairs since its founding in 1706.

Ferdinand was badly out of touch, both with the times and his New World subjects. Spanish Americans, having tasted the sweet fruit of liberty, were in no mood to return to the autocratic rule of a pompous king. Abolition of the cortes and repeal of its enlightened laws helped spark independence movements throughout North and South America. After an interval of revolutionary wars in which his royal troops generally got the worst of it, Ferdinand made a belated attempt to save his empire by restoring, in 1820, the cortes and the constitution. His action was a classic case of too little, too late. Mainland America was lost to Spain, leaving her only Cuba and Puerto Rico in the Caribbean.

The Viceroyalty of New Spain broke with the empire in September of 1821, taking the name Mexico. Until a new form of government could be worked out, it was proclaimed that the Spanish constitution formulated by the cortes in 1812 should remain the law of the land. Ahead of Mexico lay years of political turbulence and instability, conditions that would affect the destiny of New Mexico far out on the northern rim of the new nation.

For Albuquerqueans, this drawn out series of revolutionary events touched their lives only marginally. Workaday tasks associated with the changing of the seasons, which put bread and meat on the table, were of far greater concern than the marches and countermarches of distant armies and the heated speeches of remote politicians. No document has come to light confirming that the residents of the villa celebrated the consumation of independence with the ringing of church bells, firing of cannons, and the delivery of patriotic speeches as was done by their countrymen up in Santa Fe. But such may have been the case. They did, however, make one gesture of record: Albuquerque's plaza was formally named the Plaza de la Constitución.[7] The town also got back its elective ayuntamiento, as did Bernalillo and Belen. Two other communities of the Middle Valley, Pajarito and Alameda, picked up municipal councils as well.

In September 1822, the Albuquerque ayuntamiento formulated a detailed census, probably the first taken following independence. From it, we are given one of our best glimpses of the early-day character of the villa's population. The ayuntamiento's secretary, Antonio Ruíz, who is author of the census, defined the area covered by the tabulations: "This jurisdiction [of Albuquerque] extends three leagues from north to south and thirteen leagues from east to west. It should be understood that [the area] in the latter direction is unpopulated, serving only for firewood collecting and pasturage." And he added, "The inhabitants are engaged in agriculture and the tending of their livestock. There is no industry whatsoever."[8]

The population given for the Albuquerque jurisdiction is 2,302, of which 1,415 are unmarried males and females (this includes children), 796 are married persons, and 91 are widows and widowers. Of the total, more than half (1,361) are under the age of 25. A separate listing of occupations shows: 297 farmers, 15 merchants, 13 craftsmen, 121 day laborers, 3 teachers, and 1 priest. An appended property valuation discloses 416 houses worth 5,006 pesos, and farm land (acreage not mentioned) valued at 7,181 pesos. If nothing else, such data illustrate that the area remained essentially rural in character, farmers and farm laborers far outnumbering the few members of the business, artisan, and professional class.

The quarter century (1821–46) that New Mexico remained under the Republic of Mexico proved to be a period of innovation and revolutionary change. A faltering national government in Mexico City alternated between ill-advised intervention in New Mexico's internal affairs and gross neglect of her economic and defense problems. Beyond question, the province was more on its own during these years than it had ever been under the old Spanish regime.

One thing Albuquerqueans quickly noticed was that they were going to have to pay more heed to their own military security. A bankrupt national treasury and a Mexican army in disarray were able to provide even less aid in dealing with hostile Indians than that once supplied by Spain. Soon after independence, for example, moneys in the *fondo de aliados* dried up. This "alliance fund," long furnished by the royal government, had been used to purchase gifts for annual distribution to friendly tribes, such as the Comanches, Jicarilla Apaches, and the Utes. It served as the chief instrument in maintaining peace with those Indians, leaving the New Mexicans free to deal with the still unpacified southern Apaches and Navajos.

When the funds and gifts were cut off in 1821, the old alliances, especially the important one with the Comanches, were placed in jeopardy. Albuquerque and its sister communities on the Rio Grande wanted no return to those bitter days of warfare that had existed before Governor Anza struck a peace with the Comanche in 1786. But for a time, it appeared things might go just that way. In August of 1821, a band of Comanches showed up in Santa Fe seeking their accustomed allotment of gifts, but now they were turned away empty handed. Heading back for the plains, they vented their anger upon the village of San Miguel, where they killed livestock, sacked several homes, and raped two women. Governor Facundo Melgares, aware that this outrage might be a harbinger of things to come, circulated an appeal throughout New Mexico, soliciting donations from private citizens to replenish the alliance fund. His actions, which brought in some revenues, evidently forestalled any major breakdown of the Comanche peace, although stray members of the tribe made small raids on the Upper Rio Grande Valley during the decade of the 1820s.[9]

The real threat to Albuquerque's security, however, came not from the Comanche, but from the Navajo, who were flexing new muscle beyond the Rio Puerco. After raiding Spanish flocks on the Rio Grande for two or more generations, the tribesmen had developed a pastoral economy based on the grazing of thousands of head of sheep. This placed them in direct competition for pasturage with stockmen from the Middle Valley, who kept edging westward looking for new ranges. As early as 1804 Spaniards out of the Albuquerque-Atrisco area had built the fortified settlement of Cebolleta on the eastern flank of Mount Taylor, in the very heart of Navajo country. Although more than once nearly overwhelmed by hostile Indians, the little town managed to hold its ground and survive. [10]

By 1818 warfare between the New Mexicans and the Navajo was unremitting, and brutal in its intensity. Each side launched attacks on the other, slaying, stealing livestock, and taking captives. The battle-hardened men of Cebolleta soon came to specialize in the seizing of Navajo prisoners who could be sold as servants for 500 pesos apiece to wealthy landowners in Albuquerque. The Navajos, for their part, grabbed youngsters from the settlements, adopted them, and put them to herding sheep. This two-way traffic in human lives kept the flames of resentment burning at white heat.

In the early years of the nineteenth century, Albuquerque had begun to beef up her local militia. The ten-man contingent of Spanish soldiers that protected the town in its infancy and youth were long since gone, so that the ranks of volunteer troops, recruited in the immediate district, shouldered the full burden of defense. In 1815, fifty-year-old Captain Bartolomé Baca, a seasoned campaigner and soon-to-be governor of New Mexico, was listed as commander of Albuquerque's Cavalry Company of Volunteer Militia. [11]

Four years later, a complete muster list was compiled of the villa's citizen forces, and it showed more than 360 officers and men under arms. Within the provincial-wide militia organization, Albuquerque's home guard was designated as the Second Squadron. It comprised three companies of cavalry totaling 150 men, plus a large infantry company with 212 members. Persons of wealth and influence, of course, gravitated to the cavalry, whose officer corps was dominated by the prominent Armijo family. The ranks of the infantry, under the command of Captain José Mariano de la Peña, were filled, in the main, by poor folk from the farming class. [12]

As the tempo of strife with the Navajo increased in the years following independence, the role of the large Albuquerque militia assumed ever greater importance. It responded, for instance, to a general call-up issued in the summer of 1823 by then Governor José Antonio Vizcarra. Assembling an army of 1,500 men, the governor conducted a wide sweep through western New Mexico, killing thirty-two Navajos and taking thirty prisoners. [13] Similar campaigns, undertaken periodically throughout the Mexican period, did little or nothing to check that tribe's harassment of the New Mexico frontier. Indeed, the Navajo remained a perennial menace to settlers in the Middle Valley until their final defeat by American soldiers in the mid-1860s.

The year 1821 proved a watershed, not only because it marked the formal break with Spain, but also because it signalled the opening of the overland trade with the United States. When William Becknell of Missouri reached Santa Fe in late summer at the head of a mule train loaded with merchandise, he found that Mexico, reversing the old restrictive policies of the colonial government, had flung open the doors to foreign commerce. Disposing of his wares at a fat profit, he hastened home to restock and to spread the word that New Mexico was now welcoming Yankee merchants.

A minor rush followed as Americans pointed their caravans of white-topped freight wagons up the 900-mile-long trail to Santa Fe. Within two years, however, New Mexico was fairly glutted with American goods and the Missouri traders began looking southward toward Chihuahua and Durango in hopes of finding new markets. For many of them Santa Fe soon became not the end of the trail, but a waystation at the junction with the old Camino Real, which led on to Mexico's rich mining frontier.[14] Albuquerque, handily situated astride the road south, found itself in a good position to benefit from the increased flow of traffic up and down the Rio Grande Valley.

Among pillars of the community who moved quickly to share in the booming commerce were Mariano Chávez and his brother, Antonio José. They were sons of Francisco Javier Chávez, a native of Belen and an influential voice in provincial politics.[15] By this period, the 1820s, the Chávez surname was one of the most common in the Middle Valley, the many members of the clan all being descendants of pioneer settler don Fernando Durán y Chávez. Mariano and José, already among the social elite owing to their prestigious name, each enhanced their standing further by marrying into powerful and wealthy families. Mariano wed a sister of José Leandro Perea of Bernalillo, who was on his way to becoming one of the leading sheep barons of New Mexico. Antonio José married Barbara Armijo of Los Ranchos de Albuquerque, the Armijos, as our narrative will show, being among the most energetic and opportunistic citizens of nineteenth-century Albuquerque.[16]

The two Chávez brothers owned large properties at Los Padillas just below the villa and were already prosperous in ranching before they entered the Santa Fe trade. As their mercantile interests expanded in the 1830s and early 1840s, Antonio José assumed charge of the Missouri end of the business, traveling yearly to Westport and St. Louis to purchase manufactured articles.[17] Mariano, for his part, superintended the export of these goods, plus flocks of sheep, from New Mexico south to Chihuahua and other cities. In 1844, for which we have specific information, Mariano conducted $26,474 worth of merchandise and six thousand sheep valued at $3,000 down to the Chihuahuan markets.[18] These figures, and similar ones for other local merchants, indicate that New Mexico at last was beginning to enjoy a long overdue prosperity.

The new wealth meant that at least upper-class families in the Middle Valley could acquire some of the frills and luxuries that had been in such short supply while Spain ruled. When people like the Chávezes, Armijos, Pereas, Oteros, and Bacas hitched up their wagons and journeyed east to buy trade wares, they usually tacked onto their shopping

lists knick-knacks for their own homes and fine gifts for the wife and
children. A visitor in 1846 to the Hacienda de Padillas, owned by Mariano
Chávez, described its elegant furnishings, most of which had been
freighted in over the Santa Fe Trail. "The house is very large . . . with
handsome Brussels carpet, crimson worsted curtains, with gilded rings
and cornice, white marble slab pier tables—hair and crimson worsted
chairs, and candelabra. Since all the Mexicans have the greatest passion
for framed pictures and looking glasses, in one room of Chávez's house
are eight or ten gilt-framed mirrors all around the wall. All is exceedingly
neat and clean."[19] The aristocracy of Albuquerque, materially speaking,
had finally come into its own.

The upper crust of the Rio Abajo formed a powerful clique that
easily dominated political, economic, and social life between Bernalillo
and Belen. Within this tight circle of families—linked in innumerable
lines through constant intermarriage—none was more ambitious or shrewd
than the Armijo clan. For the better part of the nineteenth century, the
personal fortunes of the Armijos were closely interwoven with the history
of Albuquerque.

Founder of the family in New Mexico was José de Armijo, one of
the citizens of Zacatecas recruited by Vargas in 1695 to help resettle the
Rio Grande Valley. His grandson, Vicente Ferrer Armijo, according to
the 1790 census, was a respected rancher living at the Plaza de San
Antonio, on the northern outskirts of Albuquerque.[20] Vicente and his
wife, Bárbara Chávez, had eight children.[21] Four of their sons, Francisco, Ambrosio, Juan, and Manuel served brief terms as alcalde, or
magistrate, of Albuquerque during the 1820s and 1830s. They also held
officers' rank in the militia. In 1819 Francisco, for example, commanded
the town's Second Squadron. In addition, Ambrosio, Juan, and Manuel
were heavily involved in the Santa Fe trade.[22]

By means of family connections, influence in the militia, and his
own political acumen, youngest of the brothers, Manuel Armijo, thrice
jockeyed his way into the governor's chair, and, by the sheer weight of
personality and cleverness, became the dominant figure in New Mexico
during the Mexican period. His true character is difficult to assess because
most of those who wrote about him were Americans who, for a variety
of reasons, held him in low esteem. One of the most unflattering indictments of his conduct was penned by George Wilkins Kendall, a
reporter for the *New Orleans Picayune*. Kendall in 1844 described the
governor as a pompous despot, guilty of "assassinations, robberies, violent
debauchery, extortions, and innumerable acts of broken faith." He also
pictured him as an errant coward whose personal motto accurately reflected the governor's want of courage: *Vale más estar tomado por valiente
que serlo*. "It is better to be thought brave than to really be so."[23]

On the credit side, Manuel Armijo unquestionably possessed a strong
instinct for survival. Setbacks dogged his career, but repeatedly he managed to recover and turn ill-fortune to his own advantage. Amid the
storms and quicksands of New Mexican politics, that was no mean feat.
At best, then, it can be said that he was a man of energy, but of few

scruples. Some would have added that he was a clever politician, but one with all the personal charm of a snapping turtle.

Armijo's first term as governor, 1827 to 1829, ended under a cloud. He resigned in the latter year apparently to avoid a federal investigation of irregularities into the conduct of his office. At that point, he retired to his home in Albuquerque to become alcalde, but having tasted the power that went with the governorship, he kept casting wistful glances toward Santa Fe.[24]

An opportunity to reenter the political arena finally came in 1837. A new governor, brash and young Albino Pérez, from Mexico City had been ordered by the national government to impose direct taxes and at the same time reform the New Mexican's lackadaisical ways of administering provincial affairs. These measures, regarded as outside interference, sparked deep resentment on the Upper Rio Grande and fueled a plot among certain sectors of the populace to overthrow Pérez. Since conspiracies are conceived in secrecy, names of the participants, their plans, and motives are often lost to history. Nevertheless, circumstantial evidence strongly points to Manuel Armijo as one of the ringleaders. He was hoping, it seems, to step in and claim Albino Pérez's place, should the governor be ousted. But in the sequence of bloody events that followed, matters took an altogether unexpected turn.

Open insurrection broke forth in August 1837 among farming folk and Pueblo Indians north of Santa Fe. Governor Pérez mustered a small force of reluctant followers and confidently marched out to disperse the rebels. In a skirmish near San Ildefonso, his men were defeated and he was obliged to race for the capital with a frenzied mob at his heels. Shortly thereafter, the governor was captured and decapitated while members of his staff were tortured and killed.

News of these barbarous doings upriver threw the rich dons of the Rio Abajo into a panic. As much as they may have disliked Albino Pérez, they were in no mood to support a rabble movement that defied established authority. Catching the drift of sentiment among his neighbors, Manuel Armijo perceived at once where his own interests lay. He now announced his opposition to the uprising and invited others to join him in putting it down. At a meeting held September 8 at Tomé, just below Albuquerque, the elite of the Middle Valley convened and issued a manifesto calling for vigorous suppression of the forces of anarchy that had seized control of Santa Fe. Armijo was the first to affix his signature and rubric to the document.

Mariano Chávez, also in attendance, addressed the gathering and made a dramatic nomination. "I know of no one better qualified to lead our army than Manuel Armijo, " he declared in stentorian tones. "Therefore, I ask this assemblage to declare him to be our leader."[25] And without a dissenting vote, that was done.

With the entire militia of the Rio Abajo at his back, Armijo grandly marched away and within a few days occupied the capital, which the rebels had vacated upon his approach. Promptly he dispatched couriers to Mexico City with an exaggerated account of his exploits. He portrayed

himself as the savior of New Mexico, a claim that soon won him confirmation as governor and supreme commander of military forces. With
his hand thus strengthened, Armijo the following January led his soldiers
north to the Santa Cruz Valley where the insurgents had again collected,
scattered them in a fierce battle, and summarily executed the captured
leaders.

Over the next several years, Manuel Armijo, who now sported the
title of general as well as governor, consolidated his political power,
stepped up his commercial activities in the Santa Fe trade, and acquired
significant new land holdings. When in 1841 an expedition of 320 men
from the newly independent Republic of Texas invaded eastern New
Mexico, he took the field with his troops and soon had the entire party
under wraps. Newsman George Wilkins Kendall was one of the prisoners,
and it was largely because of the abuse he and his companions suffered
at the governor's hands that he later wrote about Armijo in such uncom-
plimentary terms.

Marched south under heavy guard toward Mexico where a jail awaited
them, the Texan captives passed through Albuquerque. There, as Kendall
later informed his readers, Governor Armijo maintained a hacienda, a
fine estate he had purchased with the proceeds of his cheating, stealing,
and gambling transactions.[26] The governor resided at home only part of
the time—for the rest, being occupied with his duties in Santa Fe—but
his family remained at Albuquerque year around. Armijo's wife, Trinidad
Gabaldón, he described as a "gross, brazen-faced woman . . . contaminated with every depraved habit to human nature."[27] Evidently, the
newsman's hatred for the governor spilled over to include the governor's
wife. Other Americans subsequently spoke of Señora Armijo in gentle
and charitable terms.

To other ladies he met, Kendall responded more favorably. Albuquerque, he averred, was famed for the beauty of its women. "It was
there that I saw a perfect specimen of female loveliness. The girl was
poor, yet there was an air of grace, a charm about her, that neither birth
nor fortune can bestow. She was standing upon a mud wall, the taper
fingers of her right hand supporting a large pumpkin upon her head,
while her left was gracefully resting upon her hip. Her figure was faultless
and even the chisel of Praxiteles himself never modeled ankles of such
pure and classic elegance. . . . Among the crowds of beauty her image
will stand out in bold relief, and not one of those who saw her on the
day we passed through Albuquerque will ever forget her."[28]

While the Armijos, Chávez's and other patrician families of the
valley devoted themselves to politics, military affairs, and commercial
enterprises, Albuquerque's peasant folk—which included Kendall's pretty
pumpkin girl—carried on the even tempo of their simple lives, much
as they always had. Times were changing, but as yet at such a slow pace
that the average man was scarcely aware of it.

Free, public schools, for example, had been introduced by the
government of the Mexican Republic, something that had been lacking
under Spain. But in Albuquerque, as elsewhere in New Mexico, these

135

were never more than feeble and ineffectual institutions, completely incapable of banishing the illiteracy that almost universally prevailed. The town's alcalde and municipal council exercised administrative responsibility over the school, teacher, and pupils, but they were dependent for operating funds upon appropriations by the legislative assembly in Santa Fe. Such funds, for the teacher's salary and school supplies, came irregularly, when at all, and in paltry sums.

Ambrosio Armijo, alcalde of Albuquerque in 1828, in desperation wrote the governor, his brother Manuel, asking him to pull strings on behalf of the local school because it possessed no paper or books. If the governor could not procure both of these necessary items, then Ambrosio declared he would settle for "one or the other."[29] Three years later, it is recorded that the provincial assembly allocated the magnificent sum of 40 pesos so that Albuquerque's teacher, Antonio Ruíz, might purchase a year's worth of supplies for his pupils.[30] The niggardly support of education seems to have caused no great outcry among the public, mainly because of a general apathy toward the entire issue. Alcaldes, who doubled as truant officers, found that parents were uncooperative—children were needed at home and time spent in school was time lost from work. The gentry, unlike the common folk, placed a high value on education, but aware of the deficiencies of the local system, they sent their sons east to St. Louis or south to Durango to be enrolled in tuition-supported church and private schools.[31]

Conditions of the churches in the Middle Valley very nearly matched those of the schools. Among the Franciscans, the missionary zeal that had animated the Order during the colonial years practically vanished during the Mexican period. As the older friars died, none were sent to replace them. Those few who remained were forced to ride an ever wider circuit, spreading their labors thin. When in 1833 Bishop José Antonio Laureano de Zubiría journeyed up from Durango to make an episcopal visit, he found spiritual life among the New Mexicans in a sad and neglected state. At each community he inspected the furnishings and property of the church and conducted the sacrament of Confirmation (at Albuquerque this occurred on August 9), but nothing he saw gave much room for hope. Religious services were imperfectly and irregularly performed, attendance was down, and attention to the needs of the Indians was in serious decline.

The bishop took special exception to the Brotherhood of Penitentes, an order of laymen that engaged in bloody acts of penitence and held mock crucifixions on Good Friday. Most of the Penitentes resided in remote villages of the north, but some were scattered through the Middle Valley, with a heavy concentration around the village of Tomé. In a stern pastoral letter, Zubiría denounced the Brotherhood, terming it illegal and calling for its suppression. In the same document, he exhorted the people to pay closer heed to their religious duties.[32]

By 1846, New Mexicans were in dire need of whatever comfort their religion could afford. Even greater was a need for wise and inspired leadership to help them confront a crisis developing in the East, one that carried the potential punch of a cyclone. United States–Mexican relations had deteriorated steadily after American settlers in Mexico's province of Texas declared for independence in 1836. Refusing to acknowledge loss of the territory, Mexico made several unsuccessful attempts to recover it, prior to the United States annexation of Texas late in 1845. When the Mexican government sent troops across the lower Rio Grande to defend its claim in the spring of 1846, a fight with American troops ensued. A few weeks later, on May 11, President James K. Polk went before Congress and read a formal declaration of war. From that moment forward, the fate of New Mexico and other territories on Mexico's northern frontier was sealed, though some months elapsed before citizens there were made aware of that fact.

Albuquerque's Manuel Armijo, in the midst of his third term as governor, appeared to be New Mexico's man of the hour when war broke forth. With his customary bluster, he issued high-sounding patriotic appeals to the populace, warning them to be ready, at the first sign of an American invasion, to answer a call to arms. In consultation with his lieutenants, the governor laid plans to fortify the mountain pass at the mouth of Apache Canyon, 15 miles east of the capital. That strategic site, commanding access to the final leg of the Santa Fe Trail, seemed the best place to try and hold back an invading army.

And an army, indeed, was on its way—from Fort Leavenworth, Kansas. Under the command of General Stephen Watts Kearny, the force was composed of regular infantry, dragoon, and artillery companies, plus a large contingent of hard-fighting Missouri volunteers. These men knew of Manuel Armijo by reputation—of his mistreatment of Texas prisoners in 1841, and of his high-handed dealings with some of the Santa Fe traders. So as they marched west to the conquest of New Mexico, there was a spring in their gait, put there by the expectation that they would soon have the chance to call Manuel Armijo to account.

Perhaps fearful of just such an eventuality, the governor took elaborate pains to ensure that nothing like that would happen. Upon learning that Kearny's troops had occupied Las Vegas on New Mexico's easternmost fringe of settlement and were en route to the capital, Manuel Armijo ordered the trumpets sounded. At the front of a rag-tag army composed of regulars, militiamen, and a scattering of Pueblo Indians, he rode out to Apache Canyon, where he had a few breastworks built. Before the construction proceeded very far, the governor called a halt and announced that he was withdrawing and giving up the game. Several of his officers, made of sterner stuff, threatened to shoot him if he did not stand and fight. Armijo paid no attention, and instead calmly climbed into his American-built carriage and drove south to the village of Galisteo, headed for Mexico. In his haste to be gone, it seems the governor neglected making a side-trip to Albuquerque, to bid his wife Trinidad good-bye. Rather, he directed his flight down the east slope of the Sandia and Manzano mountains, crossing into the Rio Grande Valley at Abó Pass. He must have gotten some message home, however, for he was soon joined on the road by a wagon train bearing personal possessions and a goodly stock of merchandise brought earlier over the Santa Fe Trail. If he must retreat into exile, Manuel Armijo had no intention of going as a pauper. Señora Armijo was not with the wagons. She had been left in Albuquerque.

Far down in the desert wastes of Chihuahua, a young British adventurer, George Ruxton, heading toward New Mexico, encountered the fleeing official. "The runaway governor of New Mexico, General Armijo," he informs us, "was traveling in company with his caravan on his way to Mexico City, to give an account of shameful cowardice in surrendering Santa Fe to the Americans without a show of resistance. I stopped and had a long chat with Armijo, who . . . rolled out of his American dearborn, and inquired the price of cotton goods in Durango, he having seven wagonloads with him."[33] The former governor, it would appear was more interested for the moment in business than in politics.

The failure to show resistance, of which Ruxton spoke, had allowed the army of General Kearny to march unopposed into the streets of Santa Fe and hoist the American flag over the plaza. But Armijo's flight had also deprived the Missouri boys of their opportunity to settle accounts. A few days after fall of the capital, however, a rumor circulated that suggested there might yet be a chance to meet the governor in battle.

General Kearny received word that Manuel Armijo had returned with troops from Chihuahua and was in the vicinity of Albuquerque, rallying the Abajeños (as people of the Rio Abajo were called) with a view to recovering Santa Fe from the Americans. Although the report was entirely without foundation, Kearny thought it wise to lead part of his troops downriver for a personal look at the situation. As he emerged with his cavalcade of 700 men from The Narrows at the upper end of the Middle Valley, the general was greeted by a throng of people, representing not an opposing army, but a horde of venders eager to sell their baskets of grapes, melons, and eggs. The soldiers, who had been on short rations for days, grabbed the opportunity to swap a straight pin for a bunch of grapes, or a button off their blouse for a melon.

As the Americans marched toward Albuquerque, the crowd of sellers and curiosity-seekers swelled into the hundreds. The whole affair had the air of a Fourth of July frolic. Nowhere was there the slightest sign of hostility. "The people received us kindly," remarked one young soldier. "They seem to be well pleased with the change of government & the idea of being considered as citizens of the American Republic. They say that Armijo has gone to the Devil."[34]

At Bernalillo, Kearny and his officers were entertained in the largest house of the district, the residence of the lordly Perea family. Most of the adult members had been over the Santa Fe Trail to Missouri on more than one occasion, and several younger sons, fluent in English, had attended Catholic schools in St. Louis and New York City. While servant girls pattered about, the American officers accepted plates and spoons of solid New Mexican silver, "clumsily worked in the country," and helped themselves to a table loaded with grapes, sponge-cake, and local wine.

Lieutenant W. H. Emory, mingling with the others took reproving note
of the *sala,* or large reception hall. "The walls are hung with miserable
pictures of the saints, crosses innumerable, and Yankee mirrors without
number. These last are suspended entirely out of reach; and if one wishes
to shave or adjust his toilet, he must do so without the aid of a mirror,
be there ever so many in the chamber."[35]

It was early September as the men approached Albuquerque. The
corn was being taken in, the yield of the vineyards borne to the wine
presses, and droves of mules driven to the open threshing floors where
their flinty hooves would separate the newly harvested wheat from its
chaff. The valley swarmed with waterfowl—ducks, wild geese, sand
cranes, blue heron, and even a few pelicans—but for the most part they
remained undisturbed except, as Emory comments, "when some American levels his rifle."[36] The curious adobe fences bordering the road, their
tops planted with cactus to keep trespassers out of the fields, drew the
attention of the marchers, as did the elaborate network of irrigation
ditches that appeared strange to men raised in a land of abundant rainfall.

Among the half dozen or so of Kearny's followers who were keeping
a daily journal, most mentioned the high density of farms in the Middle
Valley. As one diarist phrased it: "On both banks of the river, the towns,
villages, and ranchos or farm houses cluster so thickly together that it
presents the appearance of one continued village from Algodones to San
Tomé, a distance of nearly sixty miles."[37] Albuquerque itself, the writer
related, stretched some 7 or 8 miles up and down the river. To get to
the plaza, another soldier complained, "I rode for miles as through a
straggling village."[38] Evidently the helter-skelter layout of the old villa,
referred to by eighteenth-century writers, still prevailed.

When the general and his command paraded into the center of
Albuquerque, they received an unexpectedly cordial welcome—one, in
fact, that bordered on the tumultuous. The long lines of men followed
by the artillery and baggage train formed ranks in front of the church.
Brown faces pressing close on all sides seemed duly impressed by the
American banner and the company colors, which streamed and snapped
in the fall breeze. There was much cheering and noise and at one point,
in the best tradition of a Hollywood musical script, "a song of welcome
by the inhabitants."[39] At least that is how a youthful trooper remembered
it years afterward. Adding to the uproar, members of the Albuquerque
militia, positioned on the flat roof of the church, fired a twenty-gun-
salute, using old Spanish *escopetas,* or muskets. With these demonstrations
of friendship, Kearny rose before the assembled populace and administered the oath of allegiance to the United States government. Henceforth,
for good or ill, Albuquerqueans were American citizens.

We can but wonder what the town's first lady, Donã Trinidad
Armijo, thought of these ceremonies, which witnessed the transfer of
the province, formerly ruled by her husband, into the hands of foreigners.
Upon meeting the lady a few months before Kearny's arrival in Albuquerque, Alfred Waugh, a traveling Irish artist, described her as an
intelligent woman who deported herself with much propriety.[40] Later,

the Britisher Ruxton caught a glimpse of her seated in the window of her home: "I had a good view of the lady who was once celebrated as the belle of New Mexico. She is now a fat, comely dame of forty, with the remains of considerable beauty, but quite *passée*."[41] Bereft of her husband and of her social position because of his hasty flight, Señora Armijo appears, nevertheless, to have preserved her equanimity and pride. And she possessed also the large town house, referred to in some accounts as an adobe mansion, similar in style to the Governors Palace in Santa Fe, with a *portal* entirely across the front and ornamental tinned doors.[42]

Others of Manuel Armijo's Albuquerque relatives evidently suffered not the slightest disturbance in their households or business affairs as the town passed into American hands. In truth, like most of New Mexico's privileged dons, they were well situated to take advantage of the new order. For them, the political change meant more profits. A conspicuous example was offered by one of Manuel's nephews, whose store on the plaza Susan Magoffin, wife of a merchant, visited late in 1846.

"At Albuquerque," she jotted in her diary, "we stopped for a few moments at the store of Don Rafael Armijo, which notwithstanding the Sabbath was opened. While they were counting some money my husband was receiving, I stepped in to take a look at the premises. The building is very spacious, with wide portals in front. Inside is the patio, the store occupying a long room on the street. This is filled with all kinds of little fixings, dry goods, groceries, hardware &c."[43]

Leaving the town on Saturday, September 5, Kearny and his column proceeded south to the village of Tomé to complete their survey of the Middle Valley. By chance, a religious fiesta was in progress so that the men from Missouri received an introduction to merrymaking, New Mexican style. All roads leading into Tomé were crowded with people, some walking, others riding in ox carts, in carriages, or on horseback or burro. At nightfall the entire place burst into flame as a myriad of skyrockets, trailing zig-zag streams of sparks, soared hundreds of feet into the air, and small bonfires of pine knots were lighted on every housetop and on the roof of the church. A discharge of musketry and a clattering of the mission bell, creating a thunderous din for four continuous hours, were meant to contribute to the festive atmosphere, although to the awe-struck Americans the decibel of noise seemed more likely to render the throng of fun-seekers totally deaf. Fifteen hundred persons, according to one estimate, squeezed into the public square, took seats on the bare, hard-packed sod, and watched entranced as a Spanish folk comedy was performed by a group of actors on an improvised stage. At the same time, the side streets were filled with people dancing, gambling, horse-racing, or selling baskets of baked goods and fruit. The pandemonium persisted without let-up far into the evening.

At sunup, the fiesta was renewed with appropriate religious observances. The church, packed to overflowing, was lighted by twenty-four candles. General Kearny and his staff officers, who thought it politic to attend, were handed tapers. As one of the enlisted men observed with a snicker, "They looked and no doubt felt supremely ridiculous, each one holding a long, greasy tallow candle in his hand, which was to be blown out and relighted at certain intervals during the ceremony."[44] Throughout the service, loud singing, instrumental music, and the firing of musketry shook the rafters, so that the voice of the priest on the altar was scarcely heard. "Was this serving God in spirit and in truth," asked one of the soldiers rhetorically.[45]

The local congregation must have thought so, for when the ritual inside was done, they moved outdoors where there was nothing to confine their pious enthusiasm. The padre led the way, accompanied by four men who held a gilded canopy over his head and used their elbows to nudge a path through the crowd. In the train went also lads with muskets, who kept up a steady firing into the air, and altar boys, throwing skyrockets aloft. "With their continual racket," said Private John T. Hughes, "they made the heavens dizzy with streams of fire."[46]

Next day, General Kearny, much relieved to be done with the business of fiestas, and having ascertained that no sentiment for resistance existed in the Rio Abajo, faced his men about and pointed them toward Santa Fe. The first night on the backtrail they spent at Albuquerque, where many of the troops were lodged in the extensive barracks adjacent to Manuel Armijo's home. Young Ruxton advises us that the former governor had constructed these quarters to accommodate the large military escort that always attended him on frequent trips down from Santa Fe.[47] The barracks must have been frugally built and with little thought for comfort, as was the prevailing custom in New Mexico. Said one of the Americans who found shelter there: "In order to show the limited size of our quarters, the room that I and eight others were in was only fourteen feet by eight. Here we cooked, ate, and slept; and had, as it may well be presumed, close stowage at night. It was lighted by a window hole about fifteen inches square."[48]

Rough as these lodgings were, they were destined to see more service, for within a few weeks a detachment of the First Dragoons was posted at Albuquerque under the command of Captain J. H. Burgwin, for the purpose of protecting the surrounding countryside from the Navajos. One of the things Kearny had promised, upon taking custody of New Mexico, was to put a stop to hostile Indian raids. But that was a gift far beyond his capacity to deliver, as he was soon made aware. Through the early weeks of September 1846, reports of Navajo forays in the Middle Valley reached his ears almost daily. In the environs of Albuquerque, 12,000 sheep were stolen on a single day, and while that was considered something of a record by local ranchers, the news was greeted with no great astonishment, so common had large-scale thefts become.[49] In frustration the general endorsed guerrilla warfare against the Indian miscreants. His proclamation on the subject read, in part:

> In consequence of the frequent and almost daily outrages committed by the Navajo upon the Persons & Property of the Inhabitants of the Rio Abajo, . . . now be it known that I, Brigadier General S. W. Kearny, hereby authorize all the Mexicans and Pueblos living

in the said . . . Rio Abajo, to form War Parties, to march into the Country of their enemies, the Navajos, to recover their property, to make reprisals and obtain redress for the many insults received from them.[50]

Kearny departed for the conquest of California on September 25 after erecting the scaffolding of a civil government in New Mexico. He left the territory under the care of Colonel Alexander Doniphan, who had instructions to take some of the American garrison and invade Navajoland. His goal was to arrange a peace treaty if possible, and if not, then to wage war. On a snowy November 21, Doniphan met with some 500 members of the tribe at Ojo del Oso (Bear Spring), a noted landmark 150 miles west of Albuquerque, and concluded a treaty. Unfortunately, it held up for less than a year, because while the Navajos were perfectly willing to regard the Americans as friends, they could not bring themselves to make peace with their hereditary enemies, the New Mexicans. So the raids on Albuquerque and other valley towns continued, and their peoples soon grew accustomed to patrols of blue-jacketed soldiers dashing back and forth over the dusty roads girding the Rio Grande.

In the short space of a quarter century, Albuquerqueans had seen their land shuffled from the rule of Spain to that of Mexico, and finally to the United States. These political changes, fundamental though they may have been, were quickly overshadowed by far greater social, economic, and cultural changes. The growth of the Santa Fe trade and Kearny's conquest of 1846 marked the beginnings of the Americanization of Albuquerque. That process, developing slowly at first, would not come full circle to completion until 1949 when the Old Town, centering on the plaza of colonial days, would finally be annexed and absorbed by the New Town, the twentieth-century metropolis that sprang from the railroad boom of the 1880s.

New Masters, New Ways

IN THE FOUR YEARS following New Mexico's conquest, from 1846 to 1850, the province remained in an uneasy political limbo. General Kearny appointed a civil governor, trader Charles Bent, before he departed for California, but Bent had fallen victim to assassins early in 1847 during a brief and bloody uprising at Taos. The region was then ruled by a succession of American military commanders who held power by presidential appointment. Serving in effect as acting-governors, they were more concerned with the hostile Indian problem than with politics, though inevitably they were drawn into the fireworks that lit up the developing political arena.

Influential New Mexicans, that is, members of the old Hispano ruling class together with wealthy Anglos who had long been prominent in the Santa Fe trade, at once fell to bickering over the province's future status. One citizens' faction issued a call for immediate statehood, noting that New Mexico already contained the necessary population of 60,000. Another faction argued that the area should be made a territory because the large number of Spanish-speaking people needed a period of apprenticeship before they would be ready to participate fully in the American democratic system. However they might disagree on this issue, New Mexicans were unanimous in condemning the continuation of military rule. One and all they wanted Congress, which held final authority in the matter, to come to some decision and provide New Mexico with an orderly government.

Congress, though, was doing a good bit of foot dragging. Other weighty issues were hammering for attention, and several of these, directly or indirectly, bore upon the New Mexico question. Foremost was the slavery controversy—one aspect of which involved the vexing problem of whether slave-owning should be allowed in the Southwest territories newly won from Mexico. The bitter North-South fight in the halls of the Senate was already opening a rift that would ultimately lead to civil war. Another bone of contention, requiring a congressional remedy, was an old claim by Texas to jurisdiction over all land east of the Rio Grande. If recognized, that claim would have delivered the eastern half of New Mexico into the hands of the Lone Star state, something New Mexicans opposed as did abolitionists in the East, who were against any expansion of slave territory.

Washington lawmakers addressed these problems, at least so far as they concerned New Mexico, in several clauses of the Compromise of 1850. The Texas claim to lands on the Upper Rio Grande was denied and the present boundary between the two states defined. As compensation for the territorial loss, Congress provided Texas 10 million dollars. On the status of slavery in New Mexico, the Compromise side-stepped the thorny issue by leaving it up to the people of the area to decide in a future election. Finally, and most significantly, New Mexico was organized as a territory, thus ending the prolonged period of military rule.

All the political debate in Washington and Santa Fe was of little immediate interest to the populace of Albuquerque, even though what was decided would soon bear directly upon their lives. Albuquerque, from the best evidence available, entered the second half of the nineteenth century with an air of nonchalance that one would have expected from a town that had, in point of years, reached staid maturity. Among her citizenry, however, a careful observer could probably have detected an underlying sense of unease brought on by the slow-dawning realization that the Hispanos, descendants all of Albuquerque's colonial families, were no longer quite the masters in their own house. The Anglos had taken the country and the effects of their coming were beginning to be felt in the Middle Valley.

One of the most noticeable and disturbing consequences was a new turbulence in political and social affairs. Young John Greiner of Ohio, appointed Indian agent for New Mexico, came to the Rio Grande in 1851 and was promptly taken aback by the highly combustible atmosphere that he found. "In New Mexico," according to his earliest recorded impression, "everybody and everything appears to be at cross purposes."[1] It was a statement that seemed to presage an even more perceptive comment uttered a few years later by territorial Governor Lew Wallace, who with solemn resignation declared: "Every calculation based on experience elsewhere, fails in New Mexico."[2] A violent episode in Albuquerque during the fall of 1851 graphically illustrates the truth behind the remarks of Mr. Greiner and Governor Wallace.

The affair of bloodshed grew out of the first territorial election, held to select New Mexico's delegate to Congress. The delegate from a territory had no voting powers, his function being merely to represent the views of his constituents in Washington. But which views were promoted was of considerable interest to New Mexicans, so the election generated a surfeit of heat and acrimonious debate.

The leading candidate was Major Richard H. Weightman, a strong spokesman for the statehood faction and a partisan of the large Hispano population. Weightman had come to New Mexico as a volunteer artilleryman with Kearny's conquering army in 1846. Liking the country and its people, he settled in Santa Fe, practiced law, and was soon embroiled in local politics. He possessed delicate features framed by short, curly hair and a neatly barbered beard, which lent him the distinguished air of a Roman senator. Impulsive by nature, he was known for his hair-trigger temper, a trait that had drawn him into several duels.

Weightman's opponent was Captain A. W. Reynolds, a retired army quartermaster, and the candidate of the territorial faction, composed mainly of Anglos. In the balloting, Major Weightman won an easy victory, but Reynolds claimed fraud and in a memorial to Congress leveled charges of voter intimidation, violence, and irregular procedures. Evidence, however, pointed to Reynolds's own supporters as being guilty of disrupting the election.

Judge Spruce M. Baird, a resident of Albuquerque and an ally of Weightman, gave a full account of what happened there on voting day. A rowdy gang of twelve Americans, drunk and waving whiskey bottles, appeared at the polling place and demanded to be allowed to vote. Most of them had ridden down from Santa Fe to support their candidate Reynolds, and the election judges told them that they could not legally vote in the Albuquerque precinct. Another one of the men, a local soldier named Burtinett, was denied a ballot because members of the military did not have the franchise in territorial elections. The Americans then began to threaten the judges, who were thoroughly intimidated. At that point, Spruce Baird intervened and saved the day. Accept their votes, he urged the judges, but beside each name in the poll book enter a protest. That was done and the situation was defused.

The conduct of native Albuquerqueans at the voting place, Baird found exemplary. "I must say," he wrote later to Weightman,

> that the Mexican population, when left to themselves, are the most orderly people I have ever seen at an election. Their custom is to open the polls by reading the proclamation of election aloud. They all take their seats, draw their *ojas* (cornhusk papers), tobacco, flint and steel, and, like philosophers, fall to smoking, and conversing in the most courteous and affable manner, about everything but the election. One party gets through voting before the other intrudes. Then the judges announce that they are ready to receive the votes of the other party. It must be understood that this is the case only in precincts where Americans are absent."[3]

His fellow countrymen, Judge Baird discovered, constituted a highly disruptive influence, their much-vaunted devotion to the democratic process notwithstanding. "Breaking up an election in this country," he stated, "is regarded as a masterly political movement," and he added that part of the strategy of Weightman's foes was to create chaos at all those precincts expected to give large majorities against them.[4]

Foiled in their attempts to stir up a tempest in Albuquerque itself, the disorderly American gang moved upriver a few miles to Ranchos de Albuquerque, also known to be a Weightman stronghold. Though they had already voted the same morning, they demanded new ballots, which they were promptly denied by the judges. Harsh words followed, then a scuffle, then a full-scale riot. Burtinett, the soldier, was shot dead, and several Americans and New Mexicans fell wounded. The unprecedented incident created a news sensation. It also led some Anglos, unacquainted with the circumstances, to call for harsh punitive measures against the people of the Ranchos. Spruce Baird was one who took up the cudgel in their defense. "If anyone doubts the hospitality and kindness of the people of the Ranchos, he has but to go there as a gentleman, to change his opinions. I live neighbors to them, and have never had better neighbors in any country."[5]

One more tragic incident remained to be added to the story. From Santa Fe, William C. Skinner, a prominent member of the Reynolds party, went down to Ranchos de Albuquerque to investigate the election riot. It was a task that called for caution and restraint, but in Skinner there was about as much restraint as in a charge of gunpowder. Fortified with liquor, he entered a local store belonging to Juan Cristóbal Armijo, a nephew of the former governor. He commenced to use abusive language and wave a pistol in the air, actions that quickly cleared the store of customers. Armijo attempted to grab the pistol. The two men grappled, the weapon discharged, and Skinner dropped, mortally wounded.

The Santa Fe *Gazette,* a staunchly anti-Weightman paper, spread an inflammatory headline across its front page: "Another Horrible Assassination in Bernalillo County." It described Skinner's death as "murder most foul" and urged territorial Governor James S. Calhoun (New Mexico's first governor by presidential appointment after the Compromise of 1850) to call out the militia. Its reporting of the affair strongly intimated that the Rio Abajo was on the brink of rebellion.[6]

Governor Calhoun, a level-headed sort, took the chief justice of the territory and quietly rode to Albuquerque to have a first-hand look at the situation. His findings confirmed the earlier observation by Spruce Baird that the "people were most orderly." Since calm reigned, the *Gazette's* wild charges proving baseless, Calhoun headed back to the capital and left the winding up of the matter to the normal judicial process. Subsequently, a grand jury examined the circumstances of William Skinner's death and refused to bring a charges against Juan Cristóbal Armijo. It was clearly a case of self-defense.

Major Weightman, whose election in 1851 engendered so much ill-feeling, served a single two-year term in Washington and then returned to New Mexico. This time he settled in Albuquerque and launched a newspaper, *El Amigo del País,* the town's first.[7] Its Spanish name emphasized Weightman's continuing alliance with the native Hispano population. Indeed, the main reason, it seems, that he started his paper was to support the candidacy of Padre José Manuel Gallegos as his replacement in Congress.

Padre Gallegos at that moment was one of the most controversial figures in the territory. When in 1851 French-born John Baptiste Lamy arrived to be New Mexico's first resident bishop, Gallegos had been serving as pastor of the Albuquerque parish. His personal conduct, according to whisperings within the American colony, was licentious in the extreme. Among his closest cronies were the rich stockmen at Ranchos de Albuquerque and Bernalillo, at whose ebullient house parties he danced, drank, and gambled. He knew all the politicians and leading merchants and had business dealings with many of them. On the side, he ran a string of freight wagons to Chihuahua and operated a general store in Albuquerque. A store owned by a man of the cloth was bad enough, but Gallegos added insult to injury by keeping it open Sundays and by having his mistress help out at the counter.

No one was more appalled at the Albuquerque pastor's light-hearted way of living than the new bishop. Promptly he delivered a series of stern warnings to Gallegos, ordering him to mend his ways. Father Joseph Machebeuf, Lamy's right-hand man who had accompanied him from France, spoke of the clergyman and his lady in the sourest terms. "It was," said Machebeuf, "a great scandal for the people to see a woman such as that in the rectory, traveling along with the priest in his coach, and active in his business. . . . The parish administered by a priest so scandalous and so given to business and politics finds itself plunged in the most profound ignominy and corruption."[8] His harsh criticism and that of the stiff-necked Americans, though, was not shared by native Albuquerqueans. Padres had long indulged their worldly appetites—one has only to recall the fair nymphs surrounding Father Ambrosio Guerra during Pike's visit in 1806—so that the faithful scarcely paid any attention to it.

Padre Gallegos paid even less attention to the rebukes of Bishop Lamy. In late summer, 1852, he filled seven wagons with merchandise and set off for a trading excursion to Chihuahua. As far as Lamy was concerned, that was the final straw. He issued a decree suspending Gallegos and forthwith dispatched Father Machebeuf to assume charge of the Albuquerque parish. Members of the San Felipe Neri Church were outraged. Nine hundred and fifty of them, with Probate Judge Ambrosio Armijo as their spokesman, filed a protest with the bishop and included a vigorous defense of their beloved Gallegos. Moreover, they wanted nothing to do with Machebeuf, for they had heard him in the pulpit, and as they wrote Lamy, they disliked his "boring and annoying preachings."[9]

The wishes of the people did not prevail. Father Machebeuf moved into the Albuquerque rectory, taking advantage of Gallegos's absence, and on the following Sunday formally announced the bishop's sentence against him. In the spring (1853), Machebeuf set out on an extended visit to Indian pueblos within a 75-mile radius of Albuquerque. Soon after his departure, Gallegos returned home, his wallet bulging with the profits of a successful winter's trade. Upon learning of the recent turn of events, he appeared anything but daunted. Installing himself in the rectory, he let it be known that he planned to challenge the right of Bishop Lamy to remove him.

On the road, Father Machebeuf got wind of Gallegos's plans. His own strategy, as he explained later, was as follows: "I heard that the Padre had returned and was going to dispute the possession of the church with me the next Sunday. This did not alarm me, but I thought best to be prepared, so I sent a messenger in haste to the Bishop to get a confirmation in writing of the sentence pronounced upon the Padre, and my authorization in clear terms to administer the affairs of the parish."[10]

Armed with the proper documents, Machebeuf got back to Albuquerque late on Saturday night. Intending to get a jump on his rival, he went to San Felipe Neri Church the following morning an hour before the scheduled service. But much to his chagrin, he saw that the wily Gallegos had outflanked him. "What was my astonishment," Father Machebeuf informs us, "upon arriving there to find the Padre in the pulpit and the church filled with people whom I knew to be his particular friends. These he had quietly gathered together, and now he was exciting them to revolt, or at least to resistance."[11]

Attempting to enter the side of the church through the sacristy door, Machebeuf found it locked. Then he went to the main entrance, and, as he says, "Assuming an air of boldness, I commanded the crowd to stand aside and make room for me to pass."[12] Jostling his way toward the altar, he mounted the sanctuary platform just as Father Gallegos was concluding a diatribe against him and the bishop. Then, Father Machebeuf delivered his own sermon, refuting Gallegos's accusations, reviewing the moral scandals that had brought his suspension, and, as a concluding flourish, pulling from his pocket and reading the letter of the bishop confirming the padre's removal. Gallegos spoke not a word in reply, but acknowledging that the game was up, as Machebeuf tells us triumphantly, "he went out as crestfallen as a trapped fox and left me in peaceful possession of the church."[13] The French priest, in time, completely won the hearts of the once hostile Albuquerque parishioners, and when in 1854 Bishop Lamy transferred him back to Santa Fe, many of his flock came weeping and begging him not to desert them.

Of Father Gallegos, after the confrontation at San Felipe Neri, Machebeuf wrote acidly, "Abandoning the Church, he went into politics."[14] It was Gallegos's entry into the political arena, as a candidate for congressional delegate, that led Major Weightman in 1853 to begin publishing *El Amigo del País,* as a vehicle to aid the padre's cause. Except for Weightman and a few other Anglos of the old statehood party, Gallegos was opposed in his bid by most of the American community, as well as by Bishop Lamy. Their opposition, formidable as it was, proved insufficient to overcome the padre's popularity among the Hispano electorate, which allowed him to squeak by with a narrow victory over his opponent William Carr Lane.[15] Gallegos, who journeyed to Washington by stage over the Santa Fe Trail, then by boat up the Mississippi and Ohio rivers, and finally by stage again, eventually took his seat in the House of Representatives, not speaking a word of English. When the priest from Albuquerque asked permission to bring an interpreter with him to the floor of the chamber, his request was denied. Owing to his linguistic deficiency, Gallegos for all practical purposes was unable to represent the interests of New Mexico during his two-year tenure.[16]

Territorial elections and the problems that grew out of them proved unsettling to Albuquerqueans, but it was another change wrought by the new Anglo-American presence that more profoundly affected the routine of life in the Middle Valley. In the years following annexation of New Mexico by the United States, Albuquerque became an important hub of military activity. Its location very near the center of the territory meant that troops there could move quickly to all points of the compass whenever Indian hostilities required. Furthermore, the town's position, in the midst of a fertile and productive agricultural region, allowed the army to acquire food and forage close at hand, cutting down on the amount of supplies that had to be freighted in, at great expense, from the East. Finally, it can be said that the various companies of soldiers stationed in Albuquerque during the 1850s and 1860s did much to break down the community's insularity and to introduce its population to a new language, customs, and tempo of social and economic life. Among the units posted at Albuquerque until 1867, when the regular garrison was discontinued, were companies of the First and Second Dragoons, Third Artillery, Third Cavalry, and Third, Fifth, and Seventh Infantry.[17] Some of the men became so enchanted with Albuquerque that after being mustered out of service, they took up residence in the town, becoming prominent businessmen and civic boosters.

The formal beginnings of the military establishment began in 1848 with the creation of the Albuquerque Post, garrisoned by a single company of the First Dragoons. Neither at that time nor in succeeding years did the army attempt to build a true fort. Rather it rented housing for officers and men, buildings for offices, a hospital, and quartermaster's depot, and space for stable and corrals from local citizens. Hence, the military was scattered rather liberally throughout the community, although there existed some concentration of facilities, notably the stables and depot with its warehouses, on the west in the area between the plaza and the river.

When Colonel George A. McCall, inspector general of the army, visited the Albuquerque installation in 1850, its strategic importance was not readily evident to him. Having reviewed New Mexico's defense needs, he concluded that the soldiers, to render any real service, would have to be stationed in the midst of the Indian country, not on its fringe. Mounted troops, even with their horses in first-class condition, seldom overtook raiding parties, simply because the distances were too great. The Albuquerque Post, Colonel McCall noted in his official report, ought to be abandoned and its garrison sent to the hinterlands.[18]

Albuquerque citizens, smarting as they always had from Indian attacks in their own backyards, were well-qualified to challenge the colonel's recommendation. According to one estimate, in the four years from 1846 to 1850, the Navajos had plundered the Rio Grande Valley of more than 450,000 sheep, 31,000 cattle, 12,000 mules, and 7,000 horses.[19] If that did not place Albuquerque square in the center of a battle zone, the townsfolk would like to have known what more was required to qualify.

Several particularly damaging raids in the Albuquerque vicinity, both immediately preceding and shortly after Colonel McCall's inspection, underscored the clear need for a strong military presence. Early in 1849, Navajo marauders swept through the Puerco Valley grabbing between 6,000 and 8,000 sheep. Ranchers south of Albuquerque raised a civilian pursuit party, and with the support of nineteen soldiers from the garrison, went chasing after them. As usual, the thieves made a clean getaway. Later in the same year, another Navajo band struck at ranches near Sandia Pueblo, killed five New Mexicans, and seized valuable booty.[20]

Then in January 1851, a few scant weeks after McCall first urged abandonment of the Albuquerque Post, the Navajos were back, leaving death, destruction, and empty corrals at Isleta Pueblo and at Corrales, 7 miles north of the Albuquerque plaza. Taking official note of the forays, Governor James Calhoun remarked, "The daring of these Indians produced quite a sensation in that neighborhood."[21] The Albuquerque dragoons were sent after the offenders—Calhoun expressed the hope that "the cunning of the Indians will not avail them on this occasion"—but once again they made good their escape. McCall had at least been correct when he pointed out that chases, after a raid had been committed, were, by and large, useless.

One of the few things that allowed the soldiers to earn their keep was providing escort service for travelers and freight wagons moving in and out of the Middle Valley. A Baptist minister, Reverend Hiram Read, for example, asked for a detachment of troopers when he passed through Albuquerque in March 1851, on his way to pay a missionary visit to the village of Cebolleta beyond the Puerco. Not trusting to the soldiers alone to protect his hair, the reverend confided in his diary: "I was mounted on my horse, gun in hand, a brace of pistols in the holsters on my saddle."[22] Though no doubt he put plenty of faith in divine protection, the good clergyman, like everyone else venturing beyond the precincts of Albuquerque, went amply supplied with powder and lead.

Finding a way to deal with hostile Indians was uppermost in the mind of Colonel Edwin Vose Sumner when he marched over the Santa Fe Trail from Fort Leavenworth in the summer of 1851 to assume command of the military department of New Mexico. In his satchel he carried instructions from Secretary of War Charles Conrad to revise the system of defense, relocate military posts, and—this sounds quite modern—to cut costs wherever he could. Upon arrival, Sumner went vigorously to work. First he began construction of Fort Union on the trail east of Las Vegas, and as quickly as possible transferred to it most of the troops stationed in Santa Fe. The capital, with its gambling dens, grog parlors, and loose women, he considered "a sink of vice and extravagance," and he wanted his men removed from its evil influences. The same motive animated him in his decision, in line with Colonel McCall's earlier recommendation, to close down the garrison at Albuquerque. Sumner explained his zealous move in these terms: "I consider the withdrawal of the troops from the towns, a matter of vital importance, both as it regards discipline and economy. It is unquestionably true that most of the troops in this territory have become in a high degree demoralized, and it can only be accounted for, by the vicious associations in those towns. These evils are so great, that I do not expect to eradicate them entirely until I can bring the troops together, in considerable bodies, for discipline and instruction."[23]

In part it was this preoccupation with the morals of his soldiers that led Colonel Sumner to shift his own departmental headquarters to Fort Union. But it did not take him long to discover that the move had been a mistake. His new position was just too far east of the principal theater of hostilities, the Navajo country, to permit him to keep tabs on the situation. Therefore, he reluctantly admitted, "I find it indispensably necessary to remove my headquarters from this post to Albuquerque, on the Rio Grande."[24] And thither he went in February of 1852. Albuquerque thereby became the nerve center for all military operations in the territory and the primary supply depot for new forts erected along the southern and western frontier.

The magnitude of New Mexico's security problem had been spelled out by Governor Calhoun in a plaintive letter he addressed to Secretary of State, Daniel Webster (February 29, 1852): "It is a lamentable fact that [Indian raids] are increasing rapidly, to such an extent, that if such outrages continue much longer, our Territory, instead of becoming settled with an industrious and thriving population, will be left a howling wilderness, with no other inhabitants than the wolf, and the birds of prey hovering over the mangled remains of our murdered countrymen."[25]

Colonel Sumner, from his new vantage point at Albuquerque, began developing a strategy that he hoped would prevent the land from reverting to the "howling wilderness" Calhoun had prophesied. A show of military force, he decided, might intimidate the Indians, at least enough to slow their terrorizing of the Rio Grande Valley. To that end he dispatched troops downriver to Socorro where Apaches had been raising havoc, and he personally took command of a large expeditionary force, pointing it westward from Albuquerque into the lair of the Navajo. Sumner's campaign, in spite of much marching to and fro, proved disappointing. Unable to make contact with any large bodies of the enemy or even to locate their cornfields, which he wanted to burn, the colonel finally returned to headquarters, virtually empty-handed. Though he probably remained unaware of the fact, it was the same story of fruitless manuevering that had attended Spanish expeditions a century before.

Sumner received some solace from the fact that Navajo leaders the following November met him and Governor Calhoun at Jemez Pueblo, where they signed a new peace treaty. On the face of it, their willingness to submit seemed to derive from the recent spectacle of uniformed soldiers marching at will through their homeland. At least, that is how Colonel Sumner chose to interpret the sudden interest in peacemaking. But the truth of the matter was that the Navajos were after the liberal gifts bestowed upon them at the signing, and almost before the ink had dried on the treaty document, they returned to their customary raiding habits.

The territorial press went at the colonel with a hatchet. The Santa Fe *Weekly Gazette* dubbed him "The Big Bug of Albuquerque," and accused him of buying a peace rather than obtaining one by conquest. "It was not Colonel Sumner," the paper continued, but the gifts, "the red cloths and calico shirts that cowed the Indians." And the editor characterized the commander's policies as "one series of blunders and absurdities."[26] Such criticism, which was widespread in the territory, led to Sumner's removal and his replacement, in July 1853, by General John Garland. Though Garland showed no greater aptitude in stemming the tide of Indian incursions, he did at least manage to retain command of the department for an unprecedented term of five years.

While Albuquerqueans may have had ready complaints themselves about the ineffectual leadership provided by the military, they had no quarrel whatsoever with the decision to place departmental headquarters in their town. The garrison purchased local farm products, provided civilian jobs, rented quarters, and, of course, patronized merchants and saloon keepers. As to the flourishing liquor business, a seemingly necessary appendage to every post in the territory, one American commented, "The average soldier *will* take his tod—as often as he can get the chance."[27]

In 1853, the year of Sumner's leaving, the Albuquerque Post employed thirteen civilians, including a clerk, a forage master, a ferryman, one herder, four teamsters, and five day laborers. Their yearly salaries amounted to $42,000. Further, the quartermaster paid out $2,000 annually for rented buildings. Other funds went to valley farmers for corn, flour, beans, and mutton. And even the poorest peon could cut hay (which sold to the army for $30 the ton) or bring in burro loads of firewood from the Sandias. The infusion of hard money, in a town where simple barter had long been the rule, understandably had a stimulating effect upon the economy, and it would continue to do so until removal of the army post in 1867.[28]

One area that greatly benefited was the milling industry. The simple water-powered tub mills of the New Mexicans, whose output was scarcely more than a few quarts of flour per day, could not meet the large demands of the quartermasters. Nineteen-year-old Private Josiah Rice saw one of the local machines and described its primitive construction. "In Albuquerque, whilst rambling around the town, off one side of the main street where the *acequia* happened to cross, I heard a low grumbling noise which on going to it, proved to be a mill. This was a curiosity. What will our mechanics say to a flourishing mill built entirely without iron? All of the wheels and other parts are of wood, of course excepting the mere stones, which are made from the ironstone boulders found in all parts of the country. The flour ground by this mill was very coarse, the bran not separated."[29]

The inefficiency of the native mills was not to the army's liking, so it put in an order for gears and other metal parts to be shipped to Albuquerque over the Santa Fe Trail. With these, and locally cut mill-

stones, a modern grist mill was in operation by June 1850. But milling
was not in the usual line of military activity. Competent millers were difficult to find in Albuquerque, there were no facilities for storing great quantities of flour, and soon large private mills, hastily constructed by energetic businessmen, were producing enough flour to meet army needs. Hence, toward the close of 1851 the military mill was closed down, dismantled, and the pieces were shipped to Fort Union, where they were converted into a sawmill.[30] One of those who helped take up the slack was Antonio José Otero, whose Peralta Mills, a few miles south of Albuquerque, supplied the quartermaster with 145,000 pounds of flour in 1852. Otero held a series of contracts for additional deliveries extending into the 1860s.[31] The Peralta Mills and others that soon sprouted in the Middle Valley must have all been furnished with equipment imported from the East. One newspaper correspondent viewing the loading of freight wagons in 1858 at Westport, Missouri, reported seeing "all the machinery necessary for a new flouring mill at Albuquerque."[32]

In the 1850s, Anglo merchants and developers were drawn to Albuquerque by the minor business boom that sprang from the increased military activity in the Middle Valley. They had competitors, of course, in the old Hispano families who were already well entrenched. Relatives of former governor Manuel Armijo owned several stores in Albuquerque and Los Ranchos; the one run by Rafael Armijo was reputedly stocked with $200,000 worth of goods. But with the town growing, plenty of room existed for newcomers to get a toe hold and claim a share of the ever widening market.

In 1852 Simon Rosenstein was operating a small store on the south side of the plaza, in an adobe building rented from Manuel Romero. Rosenstein was among the vanguard of Jewish merchants who within a few years would spread across the territory and play a major role in bringing economic progress to New Mexico. A pioneer tradesman, he was, nevertheless, a minor figure in Albuquerque's history. But by chance, he proved instrumental in luring another man, Franz Huning, to settle there, and Huning in time became one of the pivotal figures in reshaping the face and fortunes of Albuquerque.

Born in 1827 in the province of Hanover, Germany, Franz Huning was one of thirteen children sired by prosperous farmer and landowner Johann Huning. Studious by nature, young Franz had a passion for books. The father, recognizing that his son was not cut out to be a farmer, sent him to a private school, where he mastered English and French, among other subjects. Upon completing his formal education, the youth apprenticed to a mercantile business. Though he would claim later that during the three years of his apprenticeship he "did not learn much besides weighing groceries, sorting tobacco, and packing linen goods," the experience gained was destined to prove useful down the road.[33]

At the age of twenty-one, a craving to immigrate to America overtook Franz Huning, and in the company of his brother Charles he set sail for New Orleans. From that city, the pair went up the Mississippi by steamer to St. Louis. Charles was content to take up clerking in a local store, but Franz still had the wanderlust. California was then on everyone's lips. The year being 1849, gold fever had spread its contagion along the entire western frontier, and Franz Huning was one of those who caught the bug. Short of funds, Franz decided to work his way west and he landed a job as bullwhacker with an ox train hauling government stores to Santa Fe. His notions of geography were so foggy, he recorded afterward in his memoirs, that at the time he was uncertain whether New Mexico was in Santa Fe, or Santa Fe was in New Mexico. No matter. He was pointed in the right direction.

Franz Huning landed in Santa Fe in mid-winter, where snow covered the ground and nothing was moving toward California until spring. The enforced wait proved fatal to his original plans: odd-jobbing to support himself, struggling to learn the local Spanish dialect, and all the while enjoying the "novelty of his situation and surroundings," the German youth fell under New Mexico's spell. By the time snowmelt had begun in March, thoughts of California had been banished. After some ramblings about the territory, Franz made the acquaintance of a Santa Fe merchant Gaspar Ortiz who was preparing to depart for Mexico with several wagons filled to their side boards with trade goods. If the young man felt adventuresome, Ortiz told him, he was welcome to tag along for the ride.

"I accepted his offer," Huning relates. "When we reached a point opposite Albuquerque on the foothills road, we went into camp as he [Ortiz] had business in town. I went along with him to see the place. Here I happened to meet one Simon Rosenstein, who kept a small store. He persuaded me not to go to Old Mexico, but to stay in Albuquerque, and offered me a situation in his store. I accepted."[34] That chance decision sealed Franz Huning's destiny—Albuquerque was to be his home, thereafter—and it weighed large in the town's future development.

His first years as a clerk in Rosenstein's store were memorable ones for Franz. The colorful parade of customers were a constant source of entertainment, and in off-hours Albuquerque offered enough lively amusement to occupy even a bookish emigrant lad who had seen something of the world. Best of all, there were fellow Germans with whom he could talk. Most served in the regimental band that came to Albuquerque with Colonel Sumner in 1852. Notable among them was Major Melchior Werner. He had joined in the German Revolution of 1848, and for his participation was condemned to be shot by the military authorities. At the last minute, his sentence had been revoked, but after that narrow escape he abandoned his homeland and sailed for America. Here he resumed his military career because the life of a soldier was the only one he knew. Army duty had brought him to Albuquerque. Like his fellow countryman Franz Huning, Major Werner took to life in Albuquerque with zeal, and a few years later, upon being mustered out of service, he launched a successful mercantile firm and served a stint as postmaster.[35]

Melchior Werner was but one of many former soldiers from distant states and countries, who, when their tour was done, would decide that budding Albuquerque promised a better future and would settle in to stay. It was a phenomenon destined to recur on a far vaster scale almost a century later as servicemen stationed in Albuquerque during World War II returned in droves after 1945 to build new lives in the sun-drenched Middle Valley.

Another man to whom Franz Huning was drawn in his early years, one quite different from the Germans in the band, was Justice Kirby Benedict, who at Albuquerque presided over New Mexico's Third Judicial District. That district, thirty times larger than Benedict's native Connecticut, covered nearly two-thirds of present-day southern New Mexico and Arizona. Physically, Kirby Benedict looked the part of a judge, with his habitual taciturn expression, his backbone ramrod stiff, and a wavy beard that spilled onto his chest. But he possessed one serious defect that belied his upright calling: he cheated at cards.

When the judge was in town, not riding circuit, Simon Rosenstein usually took the lead in getting up a friendly game in the back rooms of his store. Franz Huning, not much given to gambling, took no part in these affairs, but always retired early to his small quarters next door. One night he was awakened by loud voices and a rumpus in the store. Presently one of the party, a man named Peter Saxel, rushed into his room and asked him for a pistol. "I'll shoot the damned son of a bitch," he hissed.

"I at once understood the situation," recalled Huning. "I, of course, knew that the judge had been cheating. Saxel knew that I had a pistol, but I pretended not to remember where it was. He commenced to look for it himself and I slipped out of the room into the store, took the judge by the arm and shoved him out the door. Mr. Rosenstein was too drunk to interfere."[36]

Though Kirby Benedict may have been sly at cards, he was not an ingrate and he never forgot the rare presence of mind young Franz had shown in getting him out of harm's way. In fact, the following year, 1857, he invited Huning to accompany him as deputy clerk and interpreter when he set out on circuit. That entailed a difficult and dangerous ride along the Rio Grande to Tomé, Socorro, and Mesilla, with a stop in each place to hold court. In addition to Franz Huning, the judge's party included the United States attorney, the United States marshal, several lawyers, among them Spruce Baird, as well as a cook and mule packers. Huning had to quit his job with Rosenstein, but loss of employment was a small price to pay for a jaunt down the Rio Grande in the company of some of the most eminent men in the Territory.

Back in Albuquerque, after his interlude of travel, Franz bought a small stock of goods with his earnings and opened a store, his first, on the main plaza. The initial year, with business slim, he economized by dining on such simple fare as beans, boiled eggs, coffee, and bread. But he had a talent for merchandising, one not evident during his early apprenticeship in Germany, and his establishment grew. Brother Charles was enticed to New Mexico with promises of a partnership in the business, and the now thriving firm took the name F. & C. Huning. Franz cut costs and enlarged his profits by purchasing oxen and wagons with which he traveled regularly to Kansas City. There he bought directly from the commission houses at wholesale and freighted his goods back to Albuquerque. By hard work and careful management he had, by the end of the 1850s, laid the foundations for a personal fortune and established himself as one of Albuquerque's new merchant princes.

During the period that Franz Huning was launching his career, he occasionally had business dealings with three men who, like himself, had found New Mexico to be a land of opportunity. They were Spruce M. Baird, Henry Connelly, and James Lawrence Hubbell. Each acquired a large estate in the valley south of Albuquerque, engaged in extensive ranching and commercial activities, and each shared in the gathering of forces that would soon propel the town and surrounding countryside into a new and progressive age.

Of the three, Spruce McCoy Baird seemed the least likely, at the beginning anyway, to make a go of it in New Mexico, for he was a Texan. And since the days of the abortive Texas–Santa Fe Expedition of 1841, persons from that quarter were not well thought of in the Territory. Indeed, it was said that local mothers threatened their children by proclaiming: "If you are not good, I'll give you to the *Tejanos* when they come back."[37] The cavalier treatment many Texans customarily accorded persons of Mexican ancestry did nothing to ameliorate their sinister reputation among folk on the Upper Rio Grande.

Spruce Baird, however, was not cut from the standard Lone Star mold. One could have guessed that by his spirited defense of the character and conduct of valley Hispanos at the time of the election riot in 1851. By then he was already firmly ensconced with his family in a spacious hacienda 7 miles below the Albuquerque plaza, and he had political and social connections with many of the region's most influential people. As in the case of his acquaintance Franz Huning, an eventful chain of circumstances had led him in a roundabout way to a new home in the Middle Valley.[38]

Kentucky born, of Scotch ancestry, Spruce Baird left his native state in the early 1840s to seek a fresh start in the then independent Republic of Texas. He was a bluff man with curly red hair, a trait that would prompt his Albuquerque neighbors at a later date to nickname him *El Chino Tejano*. In New Mexican Spanish, *chino* was slang for "curly-haired." On his migration to Texas, Baird carried a fiddle under one arm and a load of law books under the other. There is no record that he possessed any formal training in jurisprudence, but he had read considerable law on his own and that was quite enough in the backwoods town of Nacogdoches in eastern Texas to qualify him as a lawyer. His practice over the next several years was mildly profitable, if unsensational, and it earned him enough to send for his Kentucky sweetheart and to marry her. Following the admission of Texas to the Union in 1845 and the subsequent outbreak of war with Mexico, he enlisted with a local company under Captain George T. Wood and saw service south of the border.

Baird was back in Nacogdoches in 1848, apparently destined to remain an obscure small-town lawyer, when fate intervened. His old company commander George Wood had become governor of the state. Texas at that moment was trying to assert its sovereignty over that portion of New Mexico east of the Rio Grande, and so on paper it had created Santa Fe County and a new judicial district to give substance to its claim of ownership. Governor Wood appointed Spruce Baird as judge of the district, with instructions to go to Santa Fe, organize the county under the laws of Texas, and represent the interests of the State in the hullabaloo that was sure to follow.

Thus, at age thirty-four Spruce McCoy Baird climbed aboard a stagecoach and headed west, on a mission that in advance gave every sign of being futile. The prediction was borne out during the first few weeks after his arrival in the New Mexican capital. Political and military leaders rebuffed him, the people ignored him, and the press, intimating that the judge from Texas was a public nuisance, suggested a tar and feathering. For two years, Baird rambled about the Territory, serving as a spokesman for the Texas claim and achieving no tangible results. Then with the Compromise of 1850, which resolved the matter largely in New Mexico's favor, Spruce Baird was out of a job.

Instead of returning to Nacogdoches and an unexciting law practice, he decided to stay in New Mexico. Actually, that decision may have been made soon after his initial arrival, because we know that as early as 1848 he was investing in local properties and making plans to develop the salt lakes in the Estancia Valley.

William H. Chamberlin, a Forty-Niner bound for California, wrote in his diary, upon passing through Albuquerque: "Two American gentlemen, Messrs. West and Baird, from Kentucky, settled here two [sic] years ago. They purchased the governor's palace and expect to make a fortune in a few years."[39] The "palace," of course, was Manuel Armijo's old residence. He had returned from exile in Mexico in 1848, sold his Albuquerque property, and retired to Lemitar, near Socorro. If Spruce Baird did acquire an interest in the historic "palace," as Chamberlin says, then he must have sold it within a few years, because later records show that several relatives of Manuel Armijo were in possession.[40]

The man West, mentioned by Chamberlin, was Elias P. West, a Kentucky lawyer who came to New Mexico in his late twenties. In stray accounts of the day, he is referred to as a business partner of Spruce Baird, a not unlikely association since both were Kentuckians by birth and shared a common enthusiasm for law and politics. In the early 1850s, West operated a small gristmill in Albuquerque and Baird owned a sawmill, so that even their interests in milling coincided.[41]

It was in 1852 that Spruce Baird purchased a 33,696-acre tract of land east of the Rio Grande and opposite the tiny community of Pajarito, which lay on the west bank. The seller was Antonio Sandoval, claimant of a 500,000-acre land grant, whose residence was in Las Barelas on the southern outskirts of Albuquerque. Baird's property, known locally as El Rancho del Chino Tejano, extended from the river east to the foothills of the Manzanos, and thus contained both an abundance of irrigable farmland and pastures. At once he began construction of a two-story house, fabricated not of adobes, but of *terrones,* which were sod blocks cut from the river bottoms. His wife had come from Texas to join him, and subsequently four children were born to the Bairds in their sod mansion.

The house, according to Major James Carleton, who stopped by in 1853, was located precisely 7 miles, 694 yards below Albuquerque.[42] As the main river road ran approximately 100 feet west of the front door, travelers often found it convenient to camp at the ranch overnight, and Spruce Baird was usually able to furnish them with wood and hay. William W. H. Davis, an attorney riding the judicial circuit in 1854, was one of many who, in his words, was "treated with genuine Southern hospitality" at the Bairds' home, and "passed a pleasant evening with the host and hostess."[43]

Like other ranchers in the Middle Valley, Spruce Baird must have worked his lands under the age-old system of debt peonage. Poor laborers, peones, were given advances of money and were required, by law, to remain with their employer until the debt was paid. Since they continually borrowed against the future, many of them remained bound to their jobs for years, held in a state of menial servitude. In 1853, one of Baird's female peons (they were generally employed in housework), ran off to Socorro and was jailed there on a charge of larceny. He went down to retrieve her and the court docket for May 7 shows: "Personally appeared . . . in open court S. M. Baird who after being duly sworn declared upon oath that Doloris M. Miral . . . is a Peon of his and indebted as such to him in the sum of between sixty and seventy dollars. [It was ordered by the Court that] upon full satisfaction by the prisoner of the fines and costs imposed by the Court that she be delivered to said Baird as his Peon."[44] The peonage system, along with the widespread practice of raising captive Navajo children as servants, answered most of the New Mexicans' labor needs and explains in part why Negro slavery never became a real issue in the Territory.

In addition to his business enterprises and the management of his ranch, Judge Baird—long after he had left the employ of Texas he continued to be known by that title—was admitted to the New Mexico bar and resumed the practice of law. He represented a number of parties in cases involving the settlement of Spanish land grants, and he was the attorney for Acoma Pueblo in a dispute over water rights with neighboring Laguna Pueblo. But Baird's most celebrated case was his defense in 1854 of his old friend and former territorial delegate, Richard Weightman, for the killing of François X. Aubry.

A small feisty French Canadian, Aubry for many years was engaged in the Santa Fe trade. An appetite for adventure earned him national fame when in 1848, as a stunt, he rode horseback nonstop from Santa Fe to Independence, Missouri, in the unheard-of time of five days and sixteen hours. Later, in 1852 and again in 1854, he explored a route from Albuquerque to California then being proposed for a transcontinental railroad. Weightman, in the pages of his *Amigo del País,* wrote about both trips and included some disparaging remarks, since he happened to favor a more southerly route for the railroad (through El Paso and Tucson).

On the afternoon of August 18, 1854, François Aubry rode into the Santa Fe plaza and entered a store to have a drink. Weightman had been sitting on the corner, saw him arrive, and remarked to some friends that he must go and welcome Mr. Aubry back from California. Inside they exchanged cordial greetings and chatted awhile. After a bit Aubry asked what had happened to the *Amigo del País* and Weightman answered that it had died a natural death for lack of subscribers.[45]

Aubry retorted that such a lying paper deserved to die. It had abused him and misrepresented his survey of the railroad route. When Weightman denied this, the little French-Canadian pounded his fist on the counter and shouted angrily, "I say it is so!" Richard Weightman, who had fought duels with men for less, took a tumbler of liquor from the counter and pitched it in Aubry's face. Aubry then pulled a pistol, but it discharged prematurely sending a bullet through the ceiling. In another moment, Weightman stabbed him in the belly with a Bowie knife, and Aubry collapsed on the floor and died within ten minutes.[46]

A month later, Richard Weightman went to trial with Justice Kirby Benedict—he who cheated at the card table—presiding. Spruce Baird rode up from Albuquerque to defend him. The jury deliberated an hour and returned a verdict of not guilty, judging his actions to have been in self-defense. That decision was just, most New Mexicans believed, but still they grieved over the loss of the highly popular Aubry. Even the distant *New York Times* devoted an entire column to the tragic affair: "All who are or have been on the Plains will hear of Aubry's untimely death with a feeling of deep sadness."[47] None was more heartstricken than Weightman himself. As far as New Mexico was concerned, he felt himself a ruined man. Shortly after his acquittal, he left for Missouri never to return. He was later killed in the Civil War at the Battle of Wilson's Creek.

For Spruce Baird, the Aubry episode was almost as painful, since Weightman's departure cost him a good friend. But he had his family, ranch, and Albuquerque business dealings to preoccupy him, and soon politics were once again engaging his attention. From 1852 to 1853, he had served by appointment of the governor as special agent to the Navajos, but that minor post had scarcely satisfied his desire to play some larger role in New Mexico's administrative affairs. In 1857 he ran for delegate to Congress, but lost, partly because of his former Texas connection. Then in 1860, he won appointment as New Mexico's attorney general. As it happened, the Navajos were particularly troublesome that year and after six months in Santa Fe, Spruce Baird resigned his office so that he could return home and see to the protection of his property. It was to be the last official position he would hold in New Mexico, for the Civil War's gathering storm clouds were soon to sweep away with their unbridled fury all that he had built on his Rancho del Chino Tejano.

The second of the south valley ranchers to capitalize on Albuquerque's economic boomlet of the 1850s was Dr. Henry Connelly. Like Baird, raised in Kentucky, he had received a medical degree before entering the Santa Fe trade in 1828. Two years later, he settled in Chihuahua, opened a store, and married a Mexican woman. A few years after that he formed a partnership with Edward J. Glasgow at St. Louis to operate freight wagons over the Santa Fe Trail.

In the mid 1840s, during the turbulence of the Mexican War, Connelly transferred his business interests from Chihuahua to New Mexico. His first wife having died, he married Dolores Perea, the widow of a well-to-do rancher, José Chávez, of Peralta.[48] Through his wife he became an in-law of Manuel Armijo, whom he had known for years as a result of his mercantile activities on the Santa Fe Trail. Indeed, upon Armijo's death in December 1853, it was Connelly, then serving in the Territorial Council (equivalent to the Senate), who offered a resolution in tribute. It read in part: "Resolved that this Council has heard with profound regret of the death of our distinguished citizen, Gen. Armijo. . . . The Council offers the most sincere condolence to the family and friends of Gen. Armijo and to the territory for the loss of one of its greatest benefactors."[49] Evidently the passage of years had served to blunt much of the unsavory criticism of Armijo's career, because Connelly's flowery resolution passed the Council unanimously.

Although records on the matter are sketchy, it would appear that Dolores Perea brought to her second marriage the imposing hacienda called Los Pinos, which had belonged to her late husband. It was located on the east side of the Rio Grande, a few miles below Spruce Baird's ranch. After the wedding, Henry Connelly made Los Pinos both his home and the headquarters for a chain of commercial houses he founded in the Territory. William Davis, the lawyer, had this to say about the hacienda in 1854: "A few miles from Peralta we came to the residence of Doctor Henry Connelly, an American, . . . His house is a large establishment in the old Spanish style, and the buildings for his peones and other purposes which surround it make up quite a little village. He has acquired wealth and influence, and is at this time a member of the Legislative Council."[50]

Much of the wealth Davis refers to at this time came from stores that Henry Connelly had opened in Peralta, Albuquerque, Santa Fe, and Las Vegas. He sold a good deal of corn and other local products to the army, but since he was still running wagon caravans from the East, he also had a respectable assortment of imported goods on his shelves. An invoice which survives from his Albuquerque branch shows that to one customer he sold: "8 pr White blankets, 1 Doz Spades, ½ lbs Clark beads red, 4 Axes, and 42 lbs Copper kettles."[51] A business slump in 1857 and dishonest managers in charge of the Albuquerque and Santa Fe stores caused a serious decline in Connelly's fortunes late in the decade. But his sterling reputation was not tarnished by the financial reversals, and in fact continued to shine with such luster that President Lincoln was led in 1861 to appoint him Territorial governor. It thus fell to Henry

Connelly, as we will see, to shepherd New Mexico through the toilsome days of the Civil War, a chore he performed so ably that later writers would credit him with saving the Territory for the Union. Fittingly perhaps, the last battle of the war fought in New Mexico was on his Los Pinos Ranch.[52]

James Lawrence Hubbell, known to his Hispano neighbors as Santiago, was the third American entrepreneur residing immediately downstream from Albuquerque. Of Danish ancestry on his father's side, James had been born in Connecticut, where the family had long engaged in fur trading and mercantile pursuits. When he enlisted in 1846, at age twenty, for a year's army service, he was described as 5 feet 9 inches tall and of fair complexion. Sent to New Mexico on garrison duty, James Hubbell was mustered out at Santa Fe in the summer of 1847. For a New Englander, the land and people were as foreign as anything that could be imagined. But since youth often responds to the adventuresome and exotic, Hubbell concluded to stay and make a new life for himself. Within a year, he wed Julianita Gutiérrez, daughter of Juan Gutiérrez, and heiress to the 45,000-acre Pajarito land grant.[53]

James, or Don Santiago, settled in with his bride at the tiny community of Pajarito, located on the eastern edge of the grant, directly across the river from Baird's Rancho del Chino Tejano. Soon he obtained government contracts to supply beef to the army and began making trips down the Chihuahua Trail to buy large herds of cattle in Mexico. As his resources grew, he branched into the freighting business and in time became owner of forty-eight ox-drawn wagons.

Like everyone of means in the Middle Valley, Hubbell was highly vulnerable to Indian attack. In early February 1851, a small raiding party of Navajos crept onto his lands and ran off sixty-five cattle and ten mules. With some of his hastily assembled neighbors, he went in pursuit. Near the Rio Puerco, they caught sight of the culprits and a wild chase ensued. When the Navajos saw they were losing ground, the captured stock holding them back, they lanced most of the animals to death and scattered into the hills. Don Santiago called a halt and he and his companions headed back toward the Rio Grande. On the way, they met a troop of dragoons from Albuquerque, who having gotten word of the foray, had started out to lend a hand. As usual, the soldiers were too late, something the beleaguered valley ranches had come to expect.

James Hubbell was neither as politically ambitious nor as economically prosperous as his neighbors, Spruce Baird and Henry Connelly. But through several of his progeny, the Hubbell name was destined to make a large mark upon the subsequent history of Albuquerque and the Greater Southwest. Sons Lorenzo and Charles would become successful traders to the Navajo, and another son, Frank, would rise to political power in turn-of-the-century Albuquerque.

As important as private individuals proved to be in enlarging the base of Albuquerque's economy, it was actually the activities of the United States government that sparked and then fueled the sudden spurt in commercial development at mid-century. Traditionally, western historians have overlooked the large role of the federal government on the frontier, but neglecting that aspect of the story, especially in Albuquerque's case, leaves us with a picture that is incomplete.

The growth of the military establishment, as already explained, funneled government money and manpower into pre–Civil War Albuquerque. So, too, did new road building programs and a series of official railroad surveys undertaken at Washington's expense. Albuquerque, located at a natural crossroads in the center of New Mexico, was in a far better position to benefit from the opening of new transportation routes than was Santa Fe, whose position in the north at the foot of the Sangre de Cristos was less accessible.

Following the Mexican War, work began at once to chart wagon roads across the newly-acquired Southwest territories. Well-defined and passable thoroughfares had to be established, both to expedite military supply of newly founded forts, and to serve emigrants on their way to the Pacific Coast. As a result, Congress passed a series of appropriations to provide funds for the survey and construction of western roads. The army, since it could furnish protection for construction crews, as well as technical support through its Corps of Topographic Engineers, was handed the main responsibility for carrying out the programs.

Early in the spring of 1849, Captain (later General) Randolph B. Marcy received orders to open a wagon road from Fort Smith, Arkansas, to New Mexico. The new route, leading across the Oklahoma and Texas plains, was considerably south of the old Santa Fe Trail and was intended to offer the Forty-Niners a more direct way to California. Marcy was accompanied by Lieutenant James S. Simpson of the Topographical Engineers, who served as chief reconnaissance officer.

Their expedition in late June reached Anton Chico on the Pecos River, the first New Mexican settlement. Just beyond, at a place called Laguna Colorado, Marcy discovered that the trail used by local residents forked, one branch heading northwest to Santa Fe and the other southwest to Albuquerque by way of the village of San Antonio and Carnué Canyon. His records show that the total distance from Fort Smith to Albuquerque was 814.75 miles.[54] This route, which became known as Marcy's Road, proved highly popular with the California gold seekers. Its volume of traffic, however, never approached that of the Santa Fe Trail, which remained the favored artery of travel from the East. Two branch roads on that historic trail were built by the army in the 1850s to by-pass the capital and take travelers directly to Albuquerque. One left the main Santa Fe Trail a few miles west of Las Vegas and angled down to join Marcy's Road. The other split off at the Rock Corral, a stage station 12 miles east of Santa Fe, and ran through Galisteo and the mining camps north of the Ortiz Mountains before continuing on to San Antonio and the pass at Carnué.[55]

Beyond Albuquerque, across the far western ranches of New Mexico and Arizona, a direct route to California was slow in developing. Most westbound travelers in the late 1840s and early 1850s, upon reaching

the Rio Grande, continued downriver until they could pick up the Gila
Trail running from El Paso to Tucson and San Diego. A great saving in
miles would be made, by those entering the Southwest on the Santa Fe
Trail or Marcy's Road, if the long swing south could be avoided and a
straight bead taken on California from Albuquerque. That route west,
lying along the 35th parallel, had the enthusiastic backing of Albuquerque's business community, who were eager to see it surveyed and
marked as a wagon road, and who even entertained hopes that it would
one day find favor as the path for a transcontinental railway.

The army, on its early expeditions against hostile Navajos, collected
considerable information about terrain, waterholes, and pasturage in
western New Mexico. Lieutenant Simpson, who upon completing his
service with Marcy had been assigned to duty in the Territory, went on
one such campaign late in 1849. The trail from the Rio Grande to Zuñi
Pueblo, he observed, was well defined since it had long been used by
New Mexicans. But what was needed was a survey of the country west
of Zuñi, for the seemingly limitless desert reaching toward California
remained an uncharted wilderness.[56]

In September 1851, Captain Lorenzo Sitgreaves, also of the Topographical Engineers, was ordered to follow up on Simpson's recom-
mendations and conduct a reconnaissance of the unknown lands beyond
Zuñi. He and his party of fifty men struck out across northern Arizona,
but wanderings in search of water and Indian troubles, particularly with
the Mojaves, deflected them from a direct westward course. They reached
Fort Yuma on the lower Colorado River and thence marched on to San
Diego, but the trail pioneered by the expedition had far too many
meanderings in it to appeal to travelers setting out from Albuquerque.[57]

The next attempt at a western survey, conducted by Lieutenant
Amiel W. Whipple in 1853–54, was a great deal more ambitious and,
as far as Albuquerqueans were concerned, offered larger promise for the
future of their town. Whipple's work was an outgrowth of the Pacific
Railroad Survey bill passed by Congress on March 2, 1853. That measure
directed the secretary of war to report on all practicable railroad routes
from the Mississippi Valley to the Pacific Ocean. The study was to be
based on field surveys made by parties under the supervision of the army's
Topographical Corps, and was to ascertain the relative merits of the
proposed routes. Two of the routes under consideration crossed New
Mexico: one on the 32nd parallel hugged the Mexican border; the other
followed the 35th parallel west of Albuquerque. Survey of the latter was
assigned to Lieutenant Whipple, an able astronomer and trailblazer.

The young officer's expedition was staffed with several scientists,
among them Dr. Jules Marcou, a Swiss geologist, and Heinrich Baldwin
Möllhausen, a German artist-naturalist and a protegé of the famed
scholar Alexander von Humboldt. Besides Whipple's official report of
the journey and survey, Möllhausen wrote his own personal and highly
entertaining account. In later years, he produced forty-five books in
German on the American frontier, all immensely popular in Europe,
which earned him the title of "the German Fenimore Cooper."

In the first stage of his undertaking, Whipple led his men from Fort Smith, Arkansas, to Albuquerque virtually retracing the steps of Marcy's 1849 expedition. But now he was taking careful measurements with scientific instruments, so that future railroad builders would have accurate data on grades and passes. Reaching Albuquerque on October 5, 1853, the party settled in for a month's stay to prepare for the second and more difficult stage of their task. Richard Weightman's weekly paper, *Amigo del País,* then in the midst of its brief life, welcomed the pathfinders in glowing phrases and pronounced the first half of the survey an unqualified success.

Up to this point, Lieutenant Whipple had seen nothing that would prove a major obstacle to the laying of track. The Carnué Pass through Tijeras Canyon he described as deep and narrow, but added that "it would not be impracticable to cut through it a passage for a railway, and thence proceed to the Rio Grande near this place [Albuquerque] with a grade of eighty feet to the mile."[58] In addition to the pass through the Sandias, he also examined the banks of the river as far south as Isleta, looking for places that might be suitable for a railroad bridge. The number of inhabitants around Albuquerque he estimated at 2,500, exclusive of Atrisco on the west side of the Rio Grande. Möllhausen, however, advises us that the town proper had no more than 700 or 800 people.

After three months on the trail, members of Whipple's command made the most of recreational opportunities available to them in Albuquerque. Soldiers of the regular garrison and local citizens went out of their way to accord the explorers a warm reception and to laud their mission, as the *Amigo del País* had already done. They were introduced to the finest wines, the most becoming señoritas, and the liveliest fandangos. Some of them also fell prey to the gamblers hanging about the military post, the card sharps that Baldwin Möllhausen described reprovingly as being "always on the watch to relieve the soldiers of their pay."[59]

"Albuquerque," Möllhausen related, "lies about five hundred yards from the Rio Grande, and has a rather ruinous aspect; the only building at all conspicuous is the church, which, with its two towers, might lead to the expectation of a more important settlement. Church, houses, barracks, and the stables of the garrison are all built of the same material, namely adobes, or bricks dried in the air in the usual Mexican fashion."[60] Perhaps because he was accustomed to the sophisticated stone and frame buildings of his native country, the German adventurer cast a critical eye upon the mud houses whose floors were no more than "hard stamped clay, which only the wealthy cover with straw mats and carpets."[61] His distaste for New Mexican architecture, however, was quickly put aside when the post surgeon offered him use of a room in his home. Möllhausen had found the expedition's tent encampment, pitched several hundred yards west of the plaza, a most uncomfortable place, because, as he said, "The ground was only two or three feet above the level of the Rio Grande and was constantly wet and cold."[62]

At this date the youthful Franz Huning was still a clerk in Simon

Rosenstein's store, and although neither he nor Möllhausen mention a meeting in their memoirs, it seems scarcely plausible that the two bright and articulate Germans would have failed to find one another in such a small community. If there was an encounter, it likely occurred when Möllhausen went shopping, which he seems to have done on frequent occasions. He writes: "As Albuquerque is a western frontier town, the stores of the traders exhibited a curious variety of all imaginable articles in ordinary use, &c. Clothes and medicines, dried fruits and iron goods, linen and pastry, brandy and prayer books, were to be had in abundance for hard cash, literally hard cash, for paper money is not taken. We found, therefore, every facility for fitting up the gaps in our wardrobes or other possessions."[63]

As the month's stopover drew to a close, the gentlemen of Whipple's expedition threw a lavish party to pay off their social obligations. Invitations were extended to all the "educated and presentable folk of Albuquerque," which included a flock of charming señoritas who appeared in "their white dresses and simple but tasteful ornaments."[64] General Garland, commander of the military department, was there. "He mingled in the dance with as much frolicksome activity as the youngest lieutenant," and along with the other guests he enjoyed the champagne and oysters that overflowed the refreshment table. The memory of this superfandango would linger and buoy the tired spirits of the surveying party when later the trials of the wilderness wore them down. In a sentimental passage, Heinrich Baldwin Möllhausen wrote in his journal, "Often afterwards, as we lay round the flickering campfire, . . . we thought of that pleasant night of revelry in Albuquerque: and every weary wayfarer brightened up a little as he called it to mind, and told of some remarkable anecdote connected with it."[65]

West of the Rio Grande, Whipple and his companions laid out a route along the 35th parallel, plotting negotiable passes through the main mountain ranges of Arizona and encountering, as on the first half of their journey, no major barriers to future railway construction. Their course between Albuquerque and present-day Needles, California, was almost exactly the same as that followed a few decades later by the Santa Fe Railroad.

Whipple's final report of his exploration clearly showed his enthusiasm for the path he had marked on the 35th parallel. "There is no doubt remaining," he asserted, "that for a railway, the route we have passed over is not only practicable but in many respects eminently advantageous."[66] The geographical advantages that he claimed for the route were its directness from the Mississippi Valley to California, its low passes unobstructed by snow in winter, and its reliable watering places at strategic locations. These things added up to the shortest and cheapest route across the continent. Unfortunately, before progress could be made on plans for any transcontinental railroad, approach of the Civil War put an end, for the time being, to all talk of tying the East and the West together by track.

Albuquerqueans, whose hopes had been raised by the Whipple

project and then dashed by the period of inactivity which followed, received some comfort from the fact that the government continued to underwrite development of wagon roads and new transportation systems. In 1854, Congress came up with a yearly subsidy of $80,000 for a monthly mailstage from Missouri, via Albuquerque, to Stockton, California. The precise route through New Mexico is unclear, but it appears to have reached Albuquerque by way of Marcy's Road and from there headed south to strike the Gila Trail. The private company operating the stages took in only $1,255 during its first nine months, and as a result it discontinued the operation. Another firm, the Kansas City and Stockton Overland Mail, attempted to revive the mail service in 1859 by transferring the postal pouches at Albuquerque from its coaches to the backs of pack mules and sending them over the rugged miles along the 35th parallel to California. After five runs or so, the company folded.[67]

Although there was no immediate prospect of a railroad along Whipple's trail west of Albuquerque, the United States government in the late 1850s was eager to develop that route for wagon caravans. In 1857, Lieutenant Edward Fitzgerald Beale, a man thoroughly familiar with the Southwest, was ordered to mark and build a road on the 35th parallel. His project was to be combined with a novel experiment conceived by the War Department, that of using camels as beasts of burden on the western deserts. Several dozen animals imported from the Near East were landed with their Greek and Turkish handlers on the Texas coast. From there they were marched to San Antonio, where Lieutenant Beale was waiting, and the so-called Camel Brigade was born.

Beale led his company of road builders, a soldier escort, and the camel train across Texas to El Paso and ascended the Rio Grande to Albuquerque. To the simple farmers of the Middle Valley, the line of humpbacked beasts with their colorfully garbed attendants presented the strangest spectacle ever seen in New Mexico. At every small community, the inhabitants rushed out to see the free show pass by and wave. One of the men noted in his diary that below Albuquerque the expedition reached "a splendid grove of cottonwood, in the center of which was a small town known as 'Connelley'."[68] This, of course, was Dr. Henry Connelly's hacienda and store near Peralta. He appeared at the door and invited some of the party inside for a glass of cognac. "When we came to pay for it," one of the men wrote later, "the old fellow said the sight of the camels was ample compensation, and would not take a cent."[69]

After a three-day stay in Albuquerque, during which the camels were quartered in the army corrals near the plaza, Beale pressed on westward to Fort Defiance, northwest of Zuñi, where he began marking and improving the new road. In time it became known as Beale's Wagon Road, the first officially designated thoroughfare leading from Albuquerque to California. The improvements Lieutenant Beale and his workers made on the route must have been very minor indeed, but that did not prevent the citizens of Albuquerque from touting it as a marvel of engineering and as a most acceptable way to reach the Pacific Coast. John Udell, sixty-four year-old leader of several California-bound fami-

lies, listened to the glowing accounts of the new road when he arrived
in Albuquerque during June of 1858. "Through the influence of the
citizens of this place," he records, "our company, all except myself, agreed
to take Mr. Beale's newly explored route, and leave the old traveled road
here, and undertake to travel nine hundred miles through an altogether
savage and mountainous country. All the way was without any road
except the trail of a few explorers, which could not be found much of
the way by a stranger. I thought it was preposterous to start on so long
a journey with so many women and helpless children, and so many
dangers attending the attempt."[70]

In spite of his misgivings, Udell went along with the majority when
they set out on Beale's Road. His prophesy of trouble proved all too real,
as the party suffered hunger and thirst, repeatedly lost the way, and
finally saw some of its members cut off and massacred by the Mojave
Indians. News of their misfortunes, however, did not deter later emigrants from taking the same route.

The new east-west road along the courses pioneered by Marcy and
Beale meant that Albuquerque grew in importance as a waystation for
transcontinental travelers. But it failed to overshadow the fact that the
Valley Road, what had been the old Camino Real bisecting the Territory
from Taos and Santa Fe south through Albuquerque to El Paso, remained
the chief highway serving the Middle Valley. Below Albuquerque, this
road split into several parallel branches, offering travelers a choice of
routes southward. In dry weather, most people took the one descending
the east bank of the Rio Grande that led from the Albuquerque plaza
and passed close to Spruce Baird's house. But sometimes, this way proved
so sandy that wagons sunk to their axles. When that was the case, many
caravans forded the river near Barelas and followed firmer ground on the
west shore as far as Socorro, where they recrossed the river and got back
on the main road. During what was known as the annual "June rise" of
the Rio Grande, both of the valley branches were apt to be under water.
Then the only sure passage was by a rough and difficult road through
the sandhills forming the eastern edge of the river bottoms.

Crossing the Rio Grande, in the absence of bridges, had presented
a major problem since colonial times, at least at certain seasons of the
year. Dr. Frederick Wislizenus, a Swiss physician who drifted through
Albuquerque in July 1846, reported that, "The Rio del Norte is here
about 100 yards wide, and, as usual, sandy, shallow, everywhere fordable
and nowhere navigable, not even for canoes."[71] He was seeing the river
after the June rise and evidently in a dry year because many who later
followed in his footsteps spoke of the difficulties and dangers involved
in crossing from one bank to the other.

The Forty-Niner William Chamberlin encamped near Albuquerque
on June 20, not long after the Rio Grande had crested. "This noble
river," he jotted in his diary, "is nearly a mile wide at this point. Its
waters have been higher this season than ever known before, and although
considerably abated, is still very much swollen, and more than bank full
in many places. A pack mule company of 80 men is crossing at this

place; they ferry their baggage and swim their mules. The current is very swift, the water cold, and of a muddy or turbid nature."[72]

Samuel Cozzens, who forded the river in 1858, is even more graphic in his recital of perils to be faced. "The Rio Grande is one of the most uncertain streams in the known world, owing to the peculiar nature of the soil through which it runs. Its bottom is nothing less than a mass of quicksand; and as we had been informed that the ford here was hazardous and very uncertain, it was with no enviable feeling that we looked at the muddy turbid water."[73]

When the river was low, the rural folk on their way to market or church in Albuquerque simply rolled up their trousers or skirts and waded across. But at other times, they had recourse to log canoes or skiffs, which they propelled with long poles. Then about 1856, Albuquerque got its first ferry boat, a boon provided by Major James Carleton, acting-commander of the military post. Carleton had come to New Mexico with Colonel Sumner in 1851 and served at Fort Union before being transferred to Albuquerque in 1853. General John Garland, who succeeded Sumner the same year as department head, arrived at his headquarters, took one look, and promptly declared Albuquerque to be "the dirtiest hole in New Mexico."[74] Thereafter, during his five-year tenure, he managed to spend most of his time in the field campaigning, or in Santa Fe, which he found more agreeable. In his absence, he left Major Carleton to command the Albuquerque garrison. The selection of Carleton may have had something to do with the fact that he was married to the general's niece, Sophia.

Major Carleton, it is clear, had a greater liking for Albuquerque and its people than did his priggish uncle-in-law. The evidence can be found in his sponsorship of civic improvements, one of which was the much-needed ferry boat. Actual building of the craft was assigned to a young private named Church who was being held in the guardhouse on a charge of desertion. A former ship's carpenter, the soldier was released, given tools and furnished timbers, and in a short time produced a sturdy, water-going vessel. The job was completed with such success that Carleton granted Private Church a full pardon.[75]

The new ferry was launched at a convenient crossing about 3 miles downstream, near the present Barelas Bridge. It remained under government ownership, but operation was delegated to local workers who were paid by the month. Around the docking site on the east bank, a small community called Placers grew up. It later was washed away by one of the Rio Grande's spring floods.

For more than two decades, until the first bridge was built, Private Church's ferry continued to haul people, livestock, stagecoaches, and freight wagons over the river's muddy waters. A news correspondent riding a coach from Santa Fe to Fort Craig in 1870 spoke disparagingly of the boat as "an extremely primitive craft, being a low, narrow barge, evidently of considerable age, and somewhat shaky as to its deck timbers. The motive power . . . consisted of two brunettish individuals, who after depositing their garments upon the prow, took to the water, rope in hand, and drew us across by main force."[76] A nun stationed at Albuquerque, Sister Blandina Segale, tells a bit more about the method of navigation: "Manpower is used to propel the raft from the river bank as far as it is safe for the men to wade. They then go on the raft and with long poles worked the 'ferry boat' until we were near the opposite bank of the river, when they jumped into the water again and used their physical engines to land us."[77]

The most vivid picture of the boat in service comes from an early-day tourist, J. H. Beadle, who saw it loaded to capacity on a Sunday morning. "The women, in gay robes and black *rebosos,* were laughing, shouting, and singing, while the men screamed, swore and shouted directions all at once to the four boatmen, as the flat drifted in circles down the swift current. Fortunately, the actual channel is not more than two hundred yards wide, and the flat only descended half a mile in making the passage. A boat load of New Mexicans on the way to church can make more noise than two circus shows."[78]

The ferry was only one of Major Carleton's contributions to Albuquerque. He also had young Church apply his talent to the construction of a large flagpole made of timbers carried from the mountains and spliced together to a height of almost 150 feet. The difficult task of raising such a heavy pole was assigned to another carpenter, John A. Hill, a former soldier who had settled in Albuquerque. The tricky work was accomplished, and Carleton's flagpole, erected on the plaza opposite the entrance of San Felipe church, became a town landmark.[79]

Two other of the major's civic projects fared less well. One was a sundial that he purchased and installed on the plaza for public use. It was vandalized not long after Carleton left on a new assignment late in 1856. He had also begun the digging of a well near San Felipe Neri so that women of the town would be spared the daily chore of hiking to the river and bearing home jars of silty water on their heads. The well was unfinished at the time of his departure, and no one bothered to complete the excavation. Carleton's example of enterprise had not been sufficient to overcome citizen inertia.[80]

During her stay in Albuquerque, Sophia Carleton, the major's wife, perhaps believing that the town was destined for prosperity, did a bit of dabbling in real estate. From Henry H. Wheeler, in 1854, she purchased a tract of land southeast of the plaza for the sum of $550. On it were twelve buildings and corrals, which she rented to the army for use as a hospital, shops, storehouses, and stables. Soldiers dying in the hospital were buried in a small graveyard out back. Given Mrs. Carleton's position—wife of the post commandant and niece of the departmental commander—it is safe to say that a clear conflict of interest existed in this business arrangement. In those days, however, such things were widely tolerated and no suggestion of impropriety was ever raised. When the Carletons were transferred, they had to leave the care of this valuable property to others. Of its sad fate during the subsequent Confederate invasion of Albuquerque, we shall learn shortly.[81]

Apart from the military garrison, outlanders from the East who settled in and around Albuquerque during the 1850s numbered no more than several dozen. The time when the town would fling wide its doors to welcome the host of entrepreneurs and developers destined to transform the old Spanish community into a new and very different place was still a quarter of a century off. General Garland had thought it "the dirtiest hole in New Mexico," but others in those early years agreed with the opposite view of traveler William Chamberlin, who judged Albuquerque to be one of the cleanest and most respectable municipalities in the Territory.[82] Samuel Cozzens, there in 1858, thought it neat and tidy and observed with admiration that "nearly every house in the city had a piece of land or garden filled with peach, apple, and plum trees of nearly every variety, or with vines growing the most luscious grapes."[83] The Garden of Eden aspect, however, was marred, according to a visiting lawyer, by "flies and mosquitos swarming in and out of doors in untold millions which neither day nor night allowed man or beast to live in peace."[84]

The plaza, as in former days, continued to be the center of town life. Several acres larger in area than today, it extended farther to the east and to the south almost to present Central Avenue. Once the *plaza de armas* where Spanish militiamen marched in review, it served during Carleton's tenure as a parade ground for the United States garrison's infantry and cavalry units. On regular market days and on religious holidays, especially the feast of San Felipe Neri, May 26, the plaza filled with a boisterous throng of townspeople, farmers, and Pueblo Indians. The constant traffic ground the soil to a fine powder, which was picked up, layer by layer, with each spring wind and borne to some other place. The plaza thereby had become a shallow depression, which rains or overflows from the nearby river periodically converted into a temporary pond. At such times, plaza merchants opening their doors in the morning were able to shoot wild ducks from the porches.

By 1860, according to the United States census, Albuquerque's population had reached 1,760, a figure which shows that residents scattered along the town's irregular streets and out in the neighboring countryside still had plenty of elbow room. The palmy days of the 1850s, it is evident from the census, had been good to the valley's better class. Men like José Leandro Perea, the sheep king of Bernalillo, and Mariano Yrisarri, a Ranchos de Albuquerque merchant, owned estates worth more than $200,000. The property of Cristóbal Armijo of Albuquerque was valued at $82,000, while that of the Huning brothers was far down the list at $30,000.[85] The Hispanos may have lost political control to the newcomers, but some of them at least were managing to profit quite nicely under the new political and economic regime introduced by the Anglos. Placid days, however, were drawing to a close; Albuquerque's calm would soon be shattered by the noise and din of war. The pending storm, touched off by the issues of slavery and secession, was blowing west, and it promised considerable disruption in the lives of people along the Rio Grande, before its fierce gales were exhausted.

Tug of War

IN THE SPRING OF 1862, Albuquerque found itself under the muzzles of opposing guns, those of the Union and Confederate armies. It was a conflict—begun with the firing upon Fort Sumter a year before—in which the majority of native New Mexicans had little stake and less interest. Black slavery, for them, was scarcely an issue since New Mexico held fewer than two dozen slaves, and most of those were personal servants of army officers from the South. Nor were they stirred by the question of states' rights, a favorite rallying slogan of Southerners, for as residents of a territory with no immediate prospect for statehood, they saw nothing in the phrase with which to identify.

When hostilities appeared inevitable, the territorial delegate to Congress, Miguel Antonio Otero, went as far as to suggest publicly that New Mexico should take the lead in forming a separate confederation of western states, which could stand aloof from the coming fight in the East. That represented something of a switch on his part. Married to a belle from South Carolina and sponsor of a slave code passed by the territorial assembly in 1859, which provided for the return of fugitive slaves, he appeared to have had distinct prosouthern leanings. But when it actually came to choosing sides, Miguel Otero elected to back away from the problem, and like his fellow countrymen in the Rio Grande Valley, avoid involvement as long as possible. That seemed the best course to follow in preserving both his political standing and the thriving Otero family hacienda, La Constancia, located downriver from Albuquerque, past Spruce Baird's ranch. Miguel Otero's proposal of a nonaligned confederation in the West never got off the ground, but coming from a Hispano, it was indicative of the isolationist sentiment prevailing in New Mexico.[1]

That sentiment did not extend to the Anglos, either the small civilian population or the men in military service. When the quick plunge toward war commenced, they could not escape making a choice, based on past loyalties, between the North and the South. And, once the lines were drawn, leaders on both sides began to manuever for the support of the hesitant New Mexicans.

Governor Abraham Rencher, a North Carolinian, perhaps wishing to hold onto his chair in Santa Fe, professed to be neutral, but other officials, like Territorial Secretary Alexander Jackson and Surveyor General William Pelham worked openly to push New Mexico into southern ranks. They were supported by a corps of ranchers and merchants of similar persuasion, many of them former Texans, who were concentrated in the Mesilla Valley above El Paso.

Even more damaging to the Union cause was the strength of secession sentiment among the military officers stationed in New Mexico. With organization of the Confederacy, many of them resigned their commissions and, as the saying had it, "went South." Among the most prominent were the commander of the department, Colonel William W. Loring, and the quartermaster at Albuquerque, Major James Longstreet. The latter went on to become one of the foremost Confederate generals in the eastern theater. Another of the defectors was Colonel Henry Hopkins Sibley who had served at Albuquerque and at the time of his resignation was in command at Fort Union. Upon him the Confederacy was soon to pin its hopes for the conquest and annexation of New Mexico.

Since Governor Rencher's loyalty was in doubt, President Abraham Lincoln, on September 4, 1861, removed him from office and appointed a man who could be trusted to defend Union interests in the Territory: Henry Connelly of Peralta. Not only was he a solid Federalist, but because of his long residency on the Rio Grande, he knew and had the sympathy of the native New Mexicans. Five days after his inauguration at Santa Fe, Connelly issued an urgent call for the organization of militia forces in each county. The old militia squadrons that had existed under the Mexican Republic had been allowed to lapse after 1846, mainly because the United States government was fearful that they might become a training ground for some future native rebellion. But in the current emergency, Governor Connelly decided that a strong milita, or home guard as he chose to call it, was absolutely necessary for the defense of the territory.

In a message to the legislative assembly at the capital, he left no doubt as to the identity of the enemy. "The enemy is Texas and the Texans," he thundered. "They threaten under the pretense that they are under the authority of a new arrangement they call a Confederacy, but in truth is a rebel organization." After adroitly raising the specter of an invasion by the hated Texans, the governor appealed to the racial vanity of the Hispanos: "Be true, be faithful, and be courageous; then . . . New Mexico will blaze with fame, and her sons and daughters glow with pride. . . . Now is the day to feel the tingling of the ancient and unconquerable Castilian blood that our ancestors brought to this land,"[2] Plainly, if President Lincoln had wanted a man who could rally the lethargic New Mexicans and convert them to staunch Unionists, then he had found the best possible governor in Henry Connelly.

172

With the departure of the departmental commander, Colonel Loring, the ranking officer in the Territory was Major Edward R. S. Canby, who was soon promoted to colonel and entrusted with the task of defending New Mexico from the expansion-minded Confederacy. An experienced frontier soldier, Canby, one of his men would recall, stood tall and straight and, in spite of a tendency to portliness, presented a dignified appearance that inspired confidence and respect among the ranks. In an age when much facial hair was the fashion, he went clean shaven. In the manner of General Ulysses Grant, Colonel Canby habitually chewed on a cigar that he never lit. When he wished to smoke, he brought out a pipe. By temperament, he was a methodical and cautious planner, qualities which when brought to bear on the rough-and-tumble military operations that were soon to follow would raise questions concerning his tactical abilities and capacity for aggressiveness.[3]

The Texan enemies that Governor Connelly had warned about in such ringing tones had plenty of trouble in store for Colonel Canby and the Territory of New Mexico. That had become apparent in the summer of 1861 when Lieutenant Colonel John R. Baylor of the Confederate Army swept north from El Paso with 350 Texas Mounted Volunteers and occupied the Mesilla Valley. Fort Fillmore, under the command of Major Isaac Lynde of Vermont, fell after a half-hearted struggle, even though the federal garrison there outnumbered the invaders better than two to one. The easy victory convinced the Confederacy that the more populous regions of upper New Mexico were also ripe for plucking.

To Henry Hopkins Sibley, now promoted to brigadier general, went the task of seizing Albuquerque, Santa Fe, and the strategic Fort Union for the South. In many ways, Sibley was the exact opposite, in both appearance and disposition, of his counterpart, Colonel Canby. Sporting mutton-chop sideburns, a thick mustache, and curly chin beard, he cut something of a romantic figure, in spite of an overall grizzled mien. On horseback in his stiff gray uniform and with polished spurs and buttons that glinted sunlight, the general looked as dauntless as Hannibal. But the comparison is deceiving, for behind the glitter of appearances and starchy military manner that he affected, Sibley was plagued by serious defects of character. Unlike Canby, who was a model of caution, Sibley had a tendency to be impulsive and rash. When things went awry, he showed indecisiveness and too quickly sought the advice of junior officers. And most significantly, as far as the outcome of the New Mexico campaign was concerned, he was denied a clear head, which all generals must have in plotting strategy, by a near-fatal addiction to the bottle. That weakness would lead one of his officers to blame him for the ultimate failure of the invasion and to suggest that a court martial was appropriate for a commander who "when the bullets began to whistle stayed in comfortable quarters soaking himself with rum and whiskey while others did the work."[4]

From the moment he got the nod from the Confederate government at Richmond, Sibley brimmed with confidence. New Mexico, he felt, was his for the taking. From previous service in the Territory, he knew that the quartermasters' depots at Albuquerque and Fort Union bulged with war supplies and that the number of regular troops on duty was too few to halt a determined attack. He would make a swift drive up the Rio Grande Valley, rally southern sympathizers to his banner, and pocket New Mexico before Washington was even aware of the danger. Then when this formula for victory had provided him a secure base, he would launch assaults upon Colorado and California, whose productive goldfields could help finance the South's struggle. It was a starry vision and one that General Sibley earnestly hoped would come to pass.

In August 1861, he arrived in San Antonio, Texas, and began recruiting volunteers for an invasion force to be known formally as the Army of New Mexico. With three regiments of cavalry and a battery of artillery, the Texan general marched to El Paso, established a temporary headquarters, and issued a proclamation to the people of New Mexico. In it, he announced his intention to take possession of the Territory "in the name and for the benefit of the Confederate States." To the native people, he pledged freedom from taxes and protection of their religion and civil and political liberties. He promised to pay for forage and supplies that his army might require, but warned that anyone providing goods to the federal government would be treated as an enemy. And having heard that some New Mexicans had enlisted as volunteers in the Union Army, Sibley urged them to throw down their arms and go home. "But persist in the service," he warned, "and you are lost."[5]

The general was counting heavily on the territorial populace remaining neutral in the coming fray and perhaps even showing support once the Confederate steamroller gathered momentum. In a sardonic tone, he would afterward write that the ricos, or wealthy citizens of New Mexico, cared only for their pocketbooks and had no concern for the burning issues of the war.[6] Be that as it may, Sibley was to find that in the main the ricos as well as members of the peon class, under the motive of self-interest if not of patriotism, gravitated to the Union cause. That was to be one of several miscalculations destined to derail his carefully laid plans.

In late January 1862, Henry Hopkins Sibley put his regiments in motion and began slowly ascending the Rio Grande Valley. His immediate destination was the federal stronghold at Fort Craig, perched on the west bank of the river midway between Albuquerque and Mesilla. There he expected to meet Colonel Canby in battle, and, if things went well, to settle the question of New Mexico's political allegiance.

The loyalist civil and military leaders of the Territory, however, had not been idle. Throughout the previous summer, when it was apparent that a strike would be made from Texas, Canby sought to bolster his defensive capabilities by calling for formation of volunteer infantry and cavalry regiments to be paid and equipped by the United States government. Four companies were to be raised at Albuquerque, and other towns and districts were to contribute men according to their means. Recruitment proceeded slowly during the following winter, but picked up in the spring when word of Sibley's approach aroused the New Mexicans to the peril at hand. Famed mountain man and pathfinder Kit Carson, a resident of Taos, was placed in command of the First Regiment of New Mexico Volunteers, and Colonel Miguel Pino and Lieutenant Colonel Manuel Chaves, the Second. In filling the officers' positions, Canby gave preference to Hispanos, believing that their presence would aid in attracting volunteers to the ranks. Carson was an exception because he enjoyed immense popularity with the local people.

For a number of years, Kit Carson had been a frequent visitor to Albuquerque and was well known to the town's leading citizens. Samuel Cozzens saw the scout there in 1858 and described him as "a little weazen-faced, light-haired, wiry, active frontiersman, who wore his hair long and swore in a horrible jargon of Spanish and English, and who didn't 'fear no Injun a livin.' "[7] In the spring of 1861, Carson was stationed in Albuquerque, filling out the quota for his volunteer regiment. Franz Huning approached him one day and showed him a copy of a sensational dime novel, then in wide circulation, entitled, *The Life and Exploits of Kit Carson*. Thumbing through the pages and seeing a fictionalized picture of himself clad in buckskins, wearing a long beard, and in the act of killing two Indians at once, Kit exclaimed in his soft, distinctive voice, "Why, is that me?"[8]

Scarcely less active than Carson in urging the New Mexicans to answer a call to the colors was Governor Henry Connelly. Not content with mustering the militia and delivering patriotic messages to the legislative assembly, he traveled widely around northern New Mexico exhorting men to enlist in the Volunteers. As word of Sibley's advance circulated toward the end of January 1862, Albuquerque became a rendezvous for recruits, who were placed in companies and sent hastily down river to beef up Canby's forces at Fort Craig. Connelly himself soon passed through town on his way south, accompanied by an escort of militia. Not one to cool his heels in the background when a battle was in the offing, he had decided that his presence among the troops was essential to keep their dander up. "The spirit of our people is good," he soon wrote the secretary of state in Washington. "They have displayed a commendable spirit in the present emergency, and I have great confidence that they will do good service."[9] His assurance seemed to stem from the enthusiasm shown by the elite of the country, "our best citizens," he called them, who had come flocking with their weapons and with servants to wait upon them during the campaign. The governor may have been less easy in mind about the mettle of the rank and file, composed mainly of poorer folk who had little military training and less experience with stand-up fighting. But if he entertained worries in that direction, he did not express them. That was left to one of the officers of the regular army who ventured the opinion that "These Mexican Volunteers are more afraid of the Texans than they are of death."[10] He added that in case of attack, it was doubtful they could be relied upon to hold their lines.

Once at Fort Craig, below Socorro, Connelly conferred with Colonel Canby and learned to his satisfaction that the post contained some 4,000 men under arms, of which 1,200 were regular army troops. That number, the governor felt certain, was sufficient to parry any thrust the Texans might make. On February 21 came the opportunity to see if that belief would hold true.

General Sibley, after marching across the desert of central New Mexico, reconnoitered the stout adobe walls of Fort Craig and decided that he could not take them by storm. A better move, he concluded, was to draw Canby's blue-coated army into the open, where, in a pitched battle, the Texan odds would be greatly enhanced. With that object, he led his men up the east river bank five miles or so north of Craig to a ford on the Rio Grande called Valverde. Canby, observing the movement of the enemy and fearing that he would be outflanked, grabbed the bait and ordered out his troops. So off they went, the volunteers led by Colonels Carson and Pino, the artillery under the charge of Captain Alexander McRae, and Colonel Canby heading up the regular cavalry and infantry and directing the movements of the entire force. From the mud redoubts, Governor Henry Connelly watched their departure. His mood was one of hopeful expectancy mixed with apprehension. Canby and Carson, he knew, would be in the forefront of the fighting, as would many of his friends and neighbors: men like James Hubbell (serving as a captain of one of the volunteer companies) and his own stepson, José Francisco Chávez (who had been given a lieutenant-colonelcy). In their hands that day, as the governor was only too aware, rested the security of New Mexico.

At the river crossing, the two armies collided head on in what became known as the Battle of Valverde. All morning under the rattle of musketry and the booming of artillery, the Union men outmaneuvered and outfought the Rebels. The bewhiskered Sibley, stalking behind the lines, took a new nip from the bottle with each setback suffered by his men. By afternoon, he was so drunk he had to retire to his tent, leaving one of his subordinates, Colonel Tom Green, in command. Those men close enough to notice the general's state of intemperance referred to him derisively as "the Walking Whiskey Keg."[11]

Green, although he had fought in the Texas Revolution and the Mexican War, had little acquaintance with tactics. The only thing he knew to do was order an all-out charge, which, perhaps because it was bold and unexpected, proved the correct stratagem. The Texas fighters gave their rebel yell and rushed forward, firing shotguns and brandishing lethal-looking Bowie knives. At the sudden onslaught, the Union regulars broke and when the native volunteers saw them give way, they fled the field in panic. Captain McRae, courageous to the last degree, refused to abandon his artillery and fell, riddled with bullets. Canby, after futilely trying to stem the rout with the aid of Carson, Pino, and Chávez, retired to the fort accompanied by the demoralized remnant of his force.

General Sibley, who sobered quickly when he heard of the triumph, emerged from his tent to resume command. A quick assessment led him to the conclusion that storming Fort Craig would still prove too costly. Therefore, he determined to leave the battered Canby holed up behind its walls and continue upriver to complete the conquest of northern New

Mexico. If things went as planned, he could return and deal with the colonel at a more propitious time. Urging him onward was the Confederates' desperate need for supplies. They had counted on living off the country, but thus far the pickings had been exceedingly slim.

The Union defeat at Valverde opened the Rio Grande's Middle Valley to the invaders and placed Albuquerque squarely in the war zone. As soon as Colonel Canby realized he was being by-passed, his concern shifted to the security of the military stores housed in Albuquerque and Santa Fe. Should they fall into the hands of the hungry enemy, it would mean a major setback. By starlight, he sent his quartermaster, Major James Donaldson, to slip past the rebel army, warn the token forces holding Albuquerque and Santa Fe to remove or destroy supplies on hand, and do what they could to slow Sibley's progress. The militia and volunteers inside Fort Craig Colonel Canby disbanded, believing they could be of no further service.

Another man who left the fort by stealth was Governor Henry Connelly. With a few militia officers as an escort, he skirted the Texans and pressed up the valley, warning folk along the way to send their livestock to the mountains and hide any goods that might be of use to the enemy. Pausing briefly at his home in Peralta, he disposed of what he could in the way of possessions, but because of his hurry was obliged to leave much behind.[12] The governor rode on to Albuquerque, where all was pandemonium, and from there made his way to Santa Fe. Immediately he began preparations to abandon the capital and go to Fort Union and even out of the territory if that became necessary. "I feel no disposition to be taken prisoner," he exclaimed in a letter hastily dashed off to Washington. And in the same message, he reported ominously, "Albuquerque is defenseless . . . it is very likely the enemy will succeed in taking that place."[13]

In the town of which he spoke, the situation was indeed bleak. News of Sibley's approach filled most Albuquerqueans with dismay and fear. Following the advice of Governor Connelly, ranchers and small farmers gathered their sheep and cattle and drove them across the East Mesa to places of concealment in the Manzano Mountains. Each household collected its valuables and either spirited them out of town or found a safe burial place. A few families thought it best to desert their homes altogether and escape to Santa Fe. The savage Texans, according to rumors on the plaza, were "blue-eyed monsters with long hair and fierce mustaches, long caped coats, great guns, and everything frightful but horns and tails." These demons, it was said, were *mucho mas grande que los Americanos,* "a lot bigger than the Americans."[14]

In 1923, author Erna Fergusson, granddaughter of Franz Huning, interviewed old-timers who remembered, as youngsters, the terror inspired by the advent of the rebel troops. One of them, Mrs. Ambrosio Sánchez of Barelas, said that her family was living in Atrisco when the Tejanos came and all the women and children were hustled into the chapel, where they remained for hours in the dark and cold awaiting the horrors they knew would soon assail them. Another lady, Encarnación

Romero, was just a tiny girl when her wealthy parents loaded their offspring into carriages and joined other refugees streaming north. A short distance on the road, little Encarnación remembered that she had left her doll behind. At her insistence, the family went back to retrieve it, lest it fall captive to the Texans.[15]

The sense of impending doom which disconcerted the majority of Albuquerque's populace was not shared by a tiny group of prosouthern sympathizers who viewed with considerable pleasure the prospect of a Confederate takeover. Chief among them was Spruce McCoy Baird, who was much in evidence in those days, passing information to spies sent forward by Sibley and drumming up support where he could among a handful of local Hispanos whose loyalty to the Union appeared to be wavering. His seditious activities were so notorious, in fact, that Major Donaldson at Santa Fe issued an order for his arrest. But there was no person of authority in Albuquerque willing or able to carry it out.[16]

Another grave problem was posed by a sudden rise in banditry along roads in the Middle Valley. After Valverde, some of the native volunteers had deserted and the remainder, as mentioned, had been released by Colonel Canby. Carrying arms originally issued by the army and finding the country in turmoil, a number of the less scrupulous turned to raiding. "A general system of robbery and plunder seems to be the order of the day," lamented one United States military officer.[17] This criminal activity coming on top of the Confederate push dealt added misery to citizens in flight and to Union authorities attempting to engineer an orderly retreat of their scattered forces.

To Captain Herbert M. Enos, assistant quartermaster and ranking officer in Albuquerque, fell the task of evacuating as many supplies as possible from the military depot and destroying those he was unable to move. For this work, he had only twelve regular soldiers and some local militiamen and volunteers under Colonel Francisco Perea. On the morning of March 1, Enos still had no definite news on the location of the enemy, and assuming they were as yet several days to the south, he sent six wagons off to the Sandias with their crews to bring in firewood. But at 6:00 that evening an express rider galloped into the Albuquerque plaza with word that an advance column of Texans had reached Los Lunas, a scant 20 miles away. The gray-clad foe were breathing down Captain Enos's neck.

Immediately, he sped a messenger to the wood-cutting party in the mountains, advising it not to return to Albuquerque, but to escape through Carnué Pass and proceed by way of Galisteo to Santa Fe. Then, he ordered some of the army wagons, already filled with arms and ammunition, and guarded by the skeleton force of regulars, to pull out for Santa Fe. Keeping the volunteers, the captain had them work into the night loading several remaining vehicles with baggage.

In the icy predawn darkness of Sunday, March 2, as Albuquerqueans were beginning to stir up their breakfast fires and prepare themselves for early Mass, Captain Enos saw to the harnessing of his baggage wagons. The warehouses were still crammed to the rafters with military equipment, but with Sibley's pickets already making noise at Albuquerque's south gate, in the vicinity of Barelas, there was no time to remove them outside for burning. Hence, at 6:30 A.M., he directed his men to put the torch to the buildings as well as to the neighboring stables and corrals. Many of the structures were those belonging to the absent Major Carleton and his wife.

Some of the town's poor, anticipating the firing of the warehouses, had hung in the shadows throughout the night. As Captain Enos mounted up and signaled his wagons to roll, a mob of scavengers raced past him and commenced to plunder the flaming buildings. Heedless of scorched faces and singed hair, they carted away quantities of molasses, vinegar, soap, and candles, along with a few saddles, carpenter's tools, and even office furniture.[18] The wild scrambling, the noise, and blazing light left no doubt that the Civil War had at last come to Albuquerque.

The federal retreat northward was carried out without interference from Sibley's vanguard, but it experienced severe reverses from another quarter. As the baggage train labored up the sandy valley road near Sandia Pueblo, a party of deserters from the militia and volunteers who had turned to outlawry, swooped down and captured three wagons and a portion of the spare mules. To that loss, Captain Enos had to add the wood-cutting train, which, as he learned later, had been seized by other bandits as it attempted a getaway along the east slope of the Sandia Mountains. Union fortunes, indeed, were at a low ebb.

Those of General Sibley's army, as it approached the southern outskirts of Albuquerque, however, were scarcely in better shape. The men were hungry and cold and their horses had been drawn razor thin by fast marching and a shortage of pasturage. New Mexico was just coming out of a two-year drought, and grass, always short in the Middle Valley, was now practically nonexistent. The gray-coated officers had pushed their soldiers hard after Valverde, spurring them on with promises of abundant supplies that would be theirs for the taking in Albuquerque. Then, a mile below the plaza, they received a shock. "As we came in sight," one of the enlisted men wrote plaintively, "we beheld three large columns of smoke ascending, as it were, to the very heavens. This told the tale for us."[19]

Surveying the smoldering wreckage of the federal warehouses, the first Confederate officers to occupy Albuquerque might well have concluded that the tale of their bold venture was, in truth, finished. But as was to happen so many times east of the Mississippi, when the South found itself in desperate straits and on the point of expiring, the wheel of chance made an unexpected and favorable turn, giving the gray host a new lease on life.

Sibley's forward column had been in town less than an hour when a courier galloped in from the west with a heaven sent piece of news. The rider reported to Major Charles Pyron, then in command, that Southerners living at the small village of Cubero, 60 miles west of Albuquerque, had formed an impromptu regiment and captured a large quantity of military supplies stored there. The equipment had been collected earlier for a projected Navajo campaign and evidently was forgotten by the Union Army in the tumult following Valverde.

Dr. F. E. Kavenaugh, a Cubero storekeeper and a dyed-in-the-wool rebel, engineered the coup. With three companions—the sum total of his so-called regiment—he audaciously strode up to Volunteer Captain Francisco Aragón, head of a forty-man guard, and demanded an immediate surrender of the supplies. Aragón, lacking instructions for such a contingency and wholly uninterested in the conflict at hand, replied, 'Sí, señor. They're all yours," or words to that effect. The bluff netted Kavenaugh and the Confederate Army 60 small arms, 3,000 rounds of ammunition, medical stores, and enough other desirable goods to fill twenty-five wagons. When two dozen soldiers sent by Major Pyron arrived to escort the booty back to Albuquerque, Dr. Kavenaugh gave further evidence of his southern patriotism. Opening his store, he distributed food, clothes, and whiskey to the starving and threadbare men.

The plums won at Cubero restored Texan spirits, yet they hardly compensated for the government stores whose fire-blackened remains covered several acres west of the Albuquerque plaza. But other events soon helped to replenish the Confederate larder.

General Sibley, at the head of the main army and several days behind Major Pyron, reached Peralta about March 6. There he received such a cordial reception from former territorial delegate Miguel Otero and his South Carolina–born wife that he invited the couple to accompany him on the last leg of his march to Albuquerque. Otero, who had been vacillating in his loyalties, seems to have shifted southward, now that the Confederate star was in the ascendant. The next day the Texas force encamped at Spruce Baird's ranch, and on the morrow it paraded in triumph into the hollow square facing San Felipe Neri Church. Thirteen cannon roared a salute, opening a formal ceremony that was highlighted by an unfurling of the Confederate banner atop the flagpole erected six years before by Major Carleton.[20] Having taken a large and important New Mexican town, Sibley felt a soaring of that confidence which had been so badly damaged during the hot moments on the Valverde battlefield.

His optimism had been bolstered by first reports of the Cubero feat, and his elation must have expanded when, soon after arrival in Albuquerque, another unlooked-for blessing was dropped in his lap. Five or six of his Texan scouts, probing the depths of Carnué Pass, encountered a twenty-three–wagon caravan from Fort Union on its way to Colonel Canby at Fort Craig, and it was loaded with provisions. The civilian wagonmaster, William B. Tipton, had been on the road so long that he was completely unaware of the Union defeat at Valverde and the Confederate occupation of Albuquerque. But the half dozen Texans quickly brought him up to date and at the same time relieved him of the wagons.

Of the incident, the loyalist *Santa Fe Gazette* remonstrated indignantly: "Small as was the force that demanded the train's surrender, it was given up without the least show of resistance, from which the enemy received much aid and comfort."[21] The inference was plain. Mr. Tipton's sympathies must lie with the South, else he would have put up a fight. Whatever the truth of the matter, Sibley had more Yankee loot to add to that acquired at Cubero.

Now that he was in Albuquerque, new opportunities arose for obtaining material support from the civilian population. First in importance was the voluntary aid furnished by collaborators. The powerful merchant Rafael Armijo and his younger brother, Manuel, welcomed the Texans with open arms and, according to later testimony of Franz Huning, were "deep in the plot of the invasion."[22] At the Armijos' insistence, General Sibley used their sprawling adobe house near the plaza as his headquarters. Nor was that all, as he pointedly noted in a report to Richmond. Those two gentlemen "on our arrival in Albuquerque came forward boldly and protested their sympathy with our cause, placing their stores, containing goods amounting to $200,000 at the disposal of my troops."[23] Sibley made payment to Rafael Armijo in drafts redeemable in gold, but when the paper was later presented to the Confederate government, it was not honored.[24]

Natives who welcomed the invaders, in addition to the Armijo pair, were an assorted lot. They included Father José María Chávez of Peralta and Julián Tenorio, a property owner in Ranchos de Albuquerque and poet of local repute, who composed some doggerel verse in praise of *Los Confederados del Sur*. But the strangest figure surely was Manuel Barela. The previous winter, long before Sibley's army had entered New Mexico, Barela had been accused of "violently seditious and incendiary conversation, and blatant denunciation of the Federal government."[25] His treasonous utterances had led Colonel Kit Carson to arrest him and confine him in the guardhouse. But after only a few days in the lock-up, Barela was released, at the urging of friends who guaranteed his loyalty and excused his behavior on grounds that he was crazy.

Demented or not, Manuel Barela proved a willing and useful tool for the Texan general. As soon as Sibley was settled in the Armijo house, he presented himself and volunteered information on supplies he knew to be hidden in Albuquerque households. Most of the goods were those salvaged from the flaming Union warehouses. The general promptly issued an order requiring all persons to deliver their plunder to Confederate headquarters.

Apart from Barela, who may have been unsettled in mind, it is difficult to explain why some Albuquerqueans chose to cast their lot with their traditional enemies, the Texans. Spruce Baird, working hand-in-glove with Sibley and applying his powers of persuasion, perhaps had something to do with it, for, as we have observed, he was held in high regard by the Hispano community. In the case of the Armijo brothers, who had a great deal to lose, it would appear that they simply wanted to be on the winning side and with the easy fall of Albuquerque injudiciously concluded that the Confederates were invincible.

Be that as it may, the overwhelming majority of the town's residents remained strict partisans of the Union cause, and some of them suffered accordingly. In the days before the federal retreat, a significant number of Albuquerqueans had brought forward draft animals, harness, and wagons which they voluntarily donated to United States government use. In response to Governor Connelly's suggestion, they moved much, though by no means all, of their livestock to mountain hideaways. And they took measures to cache their money and goods.

As Sibley extended his control over the town and surrounding country, he put his soldiers to work confiscating any property that might prove useful to the campaign. Businessman Salvador Armijo (cousin of Rafael and Manuel) is listed among the big losers, along with fellow merchant Tomás Gonzales. Between them they saw the rebels haul away large stocks of staples, including corn, wheat,flour, sugar, coffee, and beans, plus fourteen barrels of whiskey and brandy. Evidently they had not had time to dismantle their stores or, for that matter, send all their draft stock into hiding. Sibley's foragers got 75 horses and mules and 67 oxen.[26]

Many persons, as remarked, had closed up their houses and left before the capture of the town, but some of those who stayed, when they observed the predatory nature of the Texans, resolved to slip away. Their plight was noted on March 23 by Governor Connelly, who had betaken himself to Las Vegas. "On yesterday there arrived at this place," he recorded, "some 20 of our most prosperous and respectable citizens from the neighborhood of Albuquerque and Bernalillo, fleeing from the exactions of Sibley; among the number a gentleman of eighty years of age, Don Pedro José Perea, and his three sons, upon whom a demand had been made for a large sum of money, which they had not in their houses, having advanced all their available means to the disbursing officers of the Government but a short time before. The threat of personal violence in case of refusal so alarmed them, that they left their homes and entire contents at the mercy of the enemy."[27] The burdensome war was taking its toll.

It seems to have weighed less heavily, however, on the small American colony in Albuquerque. Franz Huning happened to be absent at the time of the invasion, having gone east to purchase mules and freight wagons. He was walking down a street in St. Louis when he heard a newsboy shouting, "Read all about the battle in New Mexico!" Grabbing a paper, he learned for the first time of Valverde. "The report of this fight caused me much uneasiness," he said later. "I knew it could not take the Texans long to reach Albuquerque, and I was afraid they might commit depredations." To be more specific, what he feared was that his store, left in the charge of brother Charles, would be pillaged. That it was not, Huning afterward credited to some of Sibley's junior officers, "former Albuquerqueans, who intervened to protect our citizens."[28]

But Franz Huning did not escape completely unscathed. His home, La Glorieta, an old adobe with walls 3 feet thick located southeast of the plaza, was occupied by the Texans. In an open courtyard, Franz had planted a cottonwood. Under its spreading branches, the intruders slaughtered large numbers of cattle. The ground became soaked with blood to a considerable depth, fertilizing the tree and, in following years, producing rampageous growth. Huning's grandson would declare after the turn of the century, "I have observed cottonwoods closely for years and I never found another more than five or six feet through the trunk, but this one reached a diameter of about fourteen feet and developed a crown of great height and luxuriance, completely covering the courtyard and stretching long limbs across the roof."[29]

Franz Huning erred a bit when he stated that American merchants at Albuquerque were not molested by the Confederate despoilers. As reported by the pronorthern *Santa Fe Weekly Gazette,* "The contents of the stores of Mssrs. Clark and Spiegelberg Bros., sutlers for the regulars and volunteers, were appropriated by the Texans."[30] The first gentleman referred to, Mr. Clark, as soon as the Civil War passed by, seems to have sold out what remained of his establishment to Franz and Charles Huning.[31] The Spiegelberg brothers, leading Jewish merchants of Santa Fe, operated a branch store in Albuquerque and served as sutlers to the garrison. Their losses to the Texans placed no serious strain on their well-capitalized firm.[32]

Tallying up the supplies, those bagged from the United States government and wrested from Albuquerque's hapless populace, General Henry H. Sibley calculated that he now had enough provisions to last his army for three months, plenty of time in his estimation for completing the proposed sweep through northern New Mexico. But the strong-arm methods that he had used on people like Salvador Armijo and the Pereas ensured that there would be no mass rallying to his standard, a hope he expressed in a new public proclamation released in Albuquerque on March 13. In spite of widespread mistreatment of civilians and confiscation of private property, he blandly declared in that document, "The conduct of this army since its entrance into the Territory of New Mexico attests the honesty and integrity of our purpose, and the protection it has and can afford to the citizens of the country.[33]

One problem Sibley still faced was finding a pasture for his cavalry mounts. A week after establishing headquarters in Albuquerque, he sent most of the men and horses to a temporary camp at a spring in Carnué Pass. Wood and grass were plentiful there and it was a good place to rest up for the coming drive against the last Union strongholds in the north. As it turned out, the encampment proved less than an ideal site for relaxation, because the rising westerly winds, owing to the lateness of the winter season, carried a chill bite along with their usual ration of flying grit. But the movement to Carnué did serve, for the moment at least, to cork the eastern gateway through the Sandias, thereby preventing Canby at Craig from getting supplies from Fort Union, via the mountain road.[34]

Until Albuquerque, the Confederate sweep up the Rio Grande had been a touch-and-go affair. But General Sibley, lolling comfortably in the house of Rafael Armijo while the bulk of his men shivered from the wind sluicing through Carnué Pass, pored over his maps and contemplated the sweet taste of what now seemed an inevitable victory. Everything hinged on seizing Fort Union, as he knew full well, so at the end of two weeks he called in the troops from the mountains and prepared to launch the next phase of his offensive. Major Pyron and his men, the spearpoint of Sibley's seizure of Albuquerque, had already been sent northward where they occupied the capital unopposed. Before following, the general divided his army, sending one wing under Lieutenant-Colonel William Scurry circling to the east through Carnué with instructions to rendezvous on the Santa Fe Trail. The main column he sent marching directly up the Rio Grande at a leisurely pace, while he himself remained for the time being in Albuquerque, with a stripped-down garrison of two companies. As yet, Sibley had no inkling of the size of the federal force then mustering to oppose him.

Earlier in the winter, as the threatened incursion from Texas began to materialize, Colonel Canby had dispatched desperate appeals to the governors of Colorado and California asking for aid. In response, Colorado Governor William Gilpin at Denver called up a volunteer force and started it on the road for New Mexico. En route, the citizen soldiers received news of the Union debacle at Valverde, causing them to double their speed, so that they reached Fort Union on the evening of March 11. Now it was the turn of the blue army to take the offensive. Twelve days later a mixed column of regulars and Colorado volunteers filed out of the fort and headed west, prepared to brace the gray veterans of Valverde.

Traversing Glorieta Pass, the federals, near the mouth of Apache Canyon, ran straight into Major Pyron, who was once again far in the front of his tardy commander. As mentioned earlier, Sibley, according to a rebel lad, was usually to be found in comfortable quarters soaking up rum and whiskey when the bullets started to fly. And that was the case once more, for during the hard fought engagement at Apache Canyon the general could be found 70 miles to the rear, safely in Albuquerque.

In the day-long fight, March 26, the out-gunned Confederate troops got the worst of it. But at dusk, both sides pulled back to lick their wounds. Pyron promptly sped a rider toward the southwest to search for Colonel Scurry, coming up from Carnué Pass. The messenger found him at the village of Galisteo, explained Pyron's predicament, and led the entire force at quick-time back to Apache Canyon. With those reinforcements, the Texans were ready to surge forward once more.

At the summit of Glorieta Pass, on March 28, was fought the decisive battle of the Civil War in New Mexico. The rebel soldiers emerged as the apparent victors, for as sun set they held the field. But a raiding party of Colorado volunteers actually decided the issue in favor of the Union, when they slipped behind the Confederate lines and burned the huge train of supply wagons that had been so arduously assembled at Albuquerque. The pillar of black smoke, visible for 25 miles, signaled, with the emphasis of a giant exclamation point, the end of Sibley's dream.

The Texan army, which fell back to Santa Fe after the battle of Glorieta, found itself in a bind, to put it rather mildly. The men, if asked, would have made a last-ditch fight to hold the capital, but General Sibley, making a belated arrival, lamely ordered a withdrawal to Albuquerque. His supply train having gone up in smoke, he could think of

no way to feed his men. Besides, Santa Fe might easily become a trap.
The Union force that had engaged his troops at Glorieta still hovered
menacingly in the east. And there seemed a distinct possibility that
Colonel Canby, upon receiving news of the Confederate setback, would
finally leave the protection of Fort Craig and come charging up the valley
to launch an attack from the rear.

Canby, indeed, had that very thing in mind. On April 1, he started
slowly upriver, following the tracks Sibley had left five weeks before.
Kit Carson remained behind with a token garrison to hold Craig. After
ten days' march, Colonel Canby drew his troops up along the southern
perimeter of Albuquerque. His scouts informed him that the main rebel
force had not yet arrived from Santa Fe, and the town seemed to be
guarded by a small but stubborn Confederate contingent armed with
cannon. The colonel had four pieces of artillery of his own and with
these he decided to make a noisy "demonstration," as he called it.

The Texan guns were situated at Franz Huning's mill, south of his
home (near present Central Avenue and Laguna). When the Union cannon
began booming, they returned the fire and thus commenced the so-called
Battle of Albuquerque. It proved to be little more than a skirmish, an
artillery duel of several hours' duration. The only casualty was Union
Major Thomas Duncan, struck in the head by a shell fragment. Canby's
indiscriminate bombardment of the town, however, threatened to produce victims among the civilian population. A citizen delegation came
out finally and explained that the Texans would not allow the women
and children to seek refuge. So the colonel gave an order to cease firing.
That was the end of the battle.[35]

As darkness fell, nervous Albuquerqueans and the Confederate defenders could see the yellow glow of Canby's campfires in the vicinity of
Las Barelas. The strains of tattoo floating on the night air reached their
ears as the Union buglers, drummers, and fifers signaled the end of day.
Whether an assault would be made on the following morning, no one
inside the town dared venture to predict.

As it happened, there was no cause for concern. Colonel Canby was
not yet willing to confront Sibley's entire army, which might reach
Albuquerque at any time. Hence, under the mantle of dusk, he and his
thousand or so men silently stole away, leaving the musicians temporarily
behind and the fires blazing to cover their exit. Dawn had come before
anyone in Albuquerque knew of their departure.

The federals, far from retreating, were moving through Carnué
Pass. They were looking to join the body of regulars and Colorado
volunteers from Glorieta whom Canby earlier had summoned south by
messenger. Once the two forces were united, the colonel felt certain he
could deal with Sibley. Reaching the village of San Antonio, 20 miles
northeast of Albuquerque, he went into camp. Within hours, the reinforcements appeared and soon afterward scouts came in from Bernalillo
to report that the main Texan army had passed through going south and
was by then in Albuquerque. Colonel Edward R. S. Canby could not
have been more pleased. For the first time, he had the lion's share of

territorial troops under his direct command, Sibley was off balance, and the way seemed clear for a final resolution of the conflict—in his favor. He, therefore, issued orders that set his army marching back over the road through Carnué.[36]

While Colonel Canby was exerting efforts to come to grips with his foe, Sibley, newly arrived in Albuquerque from Santa Fe, was doing his best to avoid another fight. Morale in the ranks remained good, and in fact the men assumed that after a respite, a new offensive would be mounted directly against Fort Union. By firelight, one of them scribbled in his journal, "Now comes the tug of war."[37] But when Sibley called a meeting of his staff officers to plan the next move, he had something other than tugging in mind. For the benefit of his subordinates, he spelled out the extremity of their situation: food for fifteen days at the most; only thirty-five or forty rounds of ammunition per man; and, to top it, intelligence reports claimed that Canby's force had made a hookup with the Colorado volunteers and would soon be angling for a striking position.

To save the army, the only reasonable course was to evacuate Albuquerque and retreat down the valley, out of the Territory. None of the officers gave General Sibley any argument. Some of the wounded would have to be left behind, as well as eight brass howitzers for which ammunition had been exhausted. The Valverde battery, those guns captured in battle the previous February, were taken, partly owing to the refusal of the men to give them up. In the middle of the night before the retreat, Sibley sent his chief artillery officer, Captain Trevanion T. Teel, to bury the howitzers in secret at a corral behind San Felipe Neri Church. If he had to abandon the cannon, he wanted to be sure they would not be turned against the Confederacy at some future date.

On the morning of April 12, the first units of the rebel army marched to the river ford southwest of town, crossed to the opposite bank of the Rio Grande, and commenced the withdrawal toward El Paso.[38] With them rode the crestfallen brothers, Rafael and Manuel Armijo, leaving behind them their homes, fortunes, and reputations. In a subsequent report to his superiors, Sibley lauded their sacrifice and the decision that led them "to join their fate to the Southern Confederacy." He concluded with the words, "I trust they will not be forgotten in the final settlement."[39]

The evacuation of Albuquerque proceeded in stages. The general and the main body of troops followed the advance column across the river, leaving Colonel Tom Green, the hero of Valverde, to bring up the rear with an escort for the baggage train and artillery. Green did not start until the next morning, April 13, and when he did, he soon discovered that the Albuquerque ford was too quicksandy to get his overloaded wagons through. Hearing that a better ford existed about 30 miles downstream near Peralta, he decided to stay on the east bank and try it. By dark, he had gotten no farther than Spruce Baird's ranch. A layover there gave Judge Baird and his family time to pack up their belongings, including his library, and join the exodus. With the sudden reversal of Confederate fortunes, New Mexico was no longer a safe place for them.

In the morning Green moved out again with the Bairds added to his train. Loose sand on the road greatly impeded progress and caused the once tight column, in the course of the day, to lapse into widely separated and disorganized units. Reaching Governor Connelly's now deserted hacienda near the Peralta ford, the colonel called a halt. He wanted to allow the entire night for his stragglers to catch up. On the morrow, he intended to cross the Rio Grande and join Sibley, who was awaiting him at the community of Los Lunas. Colonel Green, however, had not reckoned upon the abrupt appearance of the Union Army.

From San Antonio, the emboldened Canby had threaded his way through the pinched defile of the Cañon de Carnué emerging at its mouth about noon on the 14th, where he called a lunch stop. Before him stretched the sun-browned slope of the East Mesa descending uninterrupted to the attenuated line of the Rio Grande. The weather, until now wintry and mean, had suddenly turned mild and the transparent air beneath an indigo sky allowed the colonel, as one of his soldiers put it, to view with a spy-glass "the river like a silver thread glistening under the slanting beams of the sun."[40] From his scouts Canby knew that Albuquerque, resting in the valley immediately below, was now free of Texans. So swinging his glass toward the south, he must have been able to pick up the tell-tale plumes of dust trailing behind the fractured segments of Green's column as they labored down the sandy trace below Baird's.

By forced marching, Colonel Canby brought his battle-ready troopers to a row of squatty sandhills overlooking Governor Connelly's sprawling estate. They arrived at midnight, the last few hours of travel having been accomplished under the floodlight of a radiant full moon. The noise of songs and the strains of violins greeted their ears. Colonel Green's boys, in full possession of the governor's house, were in the midst of an uproarious fandango. Their pickets failed to discern the federals whom Canby was busily deploying on the heights above.

As a gray dawn lighted the sky behind the eastern mountains and gradually seeped into the valley, illuminating the rebel camp, the Union colonel saw that his opponents held a strong position. The Connelly house lay in a thick grove of trees, and was surrounded by open fields crisscrossed with irrigation ditches and adobe fences. All were obstacles to effective maneuvering of infantry and cavalry and to advancement of the artillery. Under the circumstances, Canby thought it imprudent to launch an assault, although some of the Colorado men urged exactly that; instead he instructed his cannoneers to commence firing. Their first thunderous volleys awakened the Confederates who rubbed the sleep from their eyes and raced for their own Valverde battery. The brisk cannonade, continuing throughout the forepart of the day, did little damage to either side. At one point, the rebel gunners, running low on shot, began firing glass bottles. An outraged officer of the Colorado volunteers sent them a curt note saying if they fired another bottle, he would "kill and scalp every S of a B of them."[41]

The Union soldiers, angered because their colonel held back from a full attack, did get one piece of action that helped cool their war fever. A file of seven Confederate wagons was observed approaching the battle site, the last of the stragglers left over from Green's march of yesterday. With a whoop and a cheer, part of the federal line peeled off and went pelting forward across the dry valley floor. The unfortunate Baird family, which chanced to be with the train, took to its heels and escaped. But the thirty-five–man rebel escort fanned out and prepared to repel the bluecoats. A brief skirmish ensued. It quickly ended when the outnumbered Texans ran up a dirty white handkerchief on a ramrod to signal surrender. Canby's men seized the wagons, one piece of artillery, and the household possessions and books of Spruce Baird.[42]

About two in the afternoon, one of New Mexico's murderous spring winds came up. A Colorado volunteer described the air as "one solid cloud of moving sand and dust in which we could scarcely breath."[43] All military operations became impossible and Canby drew back to wait out the storm. Under the shielding canopy of airborne dirt, Colonel Green and his lads slipped down to the edge of the Rio Grande, waded its icy waters with the Valverde guns on their shoulders, and succeeded in reaching Sibley at Los Lunas. The Texans, now reunited, resumed their flight southward. Colonel Canby, following at a discreet distance down the east side of the valley, was content to let them go. In their present desperate straits, he knew they could do no more harm to New Mexico.

The ill-fated attempt by General Henry Hopkins Sibley to snatch control of the Territory left the Middle Valley devastated. Inside and outside Albuquerque, families had been uprooted, the livestock population had drastically declined, and much personal property had been lost. Spruce Baird's showplace of a ranch lay deserted and stripped. Henry Connelly traveled down from Santa Fe to survey the damage to his home, and the capital press reported what he found. "We understand that the Texans during the night they stopped at his house demolished everything in the shape of furniture they could lay their hands on. Other articles of family use and convenience shared the same fate. The Governor's loss in consequence of these outrages is heavy."[44] Later sources give it as about $30,000.[45]

In the aftermath of the dismal affair, territorial officials took stern measures to punish those citizens who had been so ill-advised as to collaborate with the enemy. One person eager for retribution was Colonel James H. Carleton, commander of the famed California Column. Carleton had been stationed on the West Coast when word came of the Confederate hostilities in New Mexico. Largely because of his prior service on the Rio Grande, he was handed charge of 2,350 California volunteers, and told to march east by way of Tucson and assist Colonel Canby in liberating New Mexico from the clutches of rebeldom.

By the time Carleton reached the Mesilla Valley, on August 10,

1862, General Sibley and his haggard Texans had long since abandoned the Territory. After a brief swing south to El Paso and Fort Quitman, Texas, Carleton and his staff rode northward at a fast clip to Fort Craig. A rest stop there and they were on their way again climbing the Middle Valley to Albuquerque. En route the party passed by Spruce Baird's silent ranch house where Carleton in years past had been a guest. It stood now, a silent reminder of friendships sundered by civil strife.

Entering the old villa surrounding San Felipe Neri Church, James Carleton made an unsettling discovery. On the site of his wife's property, instead of shops, warehouses, stables, and corrals, he found heaps of ashes and charred timbers, the legacy of Captain Herbert Enos's retreat of the previous April. The rental of those structures to the United States Army, $105 monthly, had formed an important supplement to his regular salary. The extra sum had helped support Mrs. Carleton and three children, who had remained behind in California, and the general (he had been promoted to brigadier general while on the trail to New Mexico) knew that his family would feel the loss keenly.

In later years, he tried vainly to dispose of the empty acreage, but a quarter of a century elapsed before it was finally sold to Santiago Baca for $1,000. A board of survey meeting at Albuquerque on September 12, 1862, assessed the value of the Carleton's property loss, due to the war, at $7,600. With the interminable delays to which Congress seems always prey, however, the just claim against the government was not recognized and paid until 1890, seventeen years after the general's death.[46] Ironically, the land, which brought the Carletons so little in profit, later became a valuable piece of real estate, first as the site of the county jail (on the southwest corner of Central Avenue and Rio Grande Boulevard), and afterward as the location of the Territorial Fair Grounds and the municipal streetcar barns. In 1938, when all memory of the Carletons' earlier ownership had faded, the land was subdivided into residential lots to form a suburb known as Traction Park.[47]

Carleton received a warm and enthusiastic reception from Albuquerqueans, who gratefully recalled his sponsorship of town improvements at the time he commanded the local garrison a half dozen years before. But the general's stay was short, for Canby had summoned him to Santa Fe. In the capital, he learned that he had been designated as the new commander of the military Department of New Mexico, replacing Edward Canby, who was being transferred to another post. Thus, General James Carleton commenced his second stint of service in the Territory, but this time he bore the full burden of a formidable responsibility.

One part of his new duties, and something that must not have been wholly unpleasant given the financial loss he had sustained, involved the identification and prosecution of New Mexicans who had traitorously lent assistance to the gray-clad invaders from the South. Almost immediately upon his arrival in New Mexico, Carleton had begun confiscating the property of disloyal citizens, his first seizure being the contents of a branch store in Mesilla owned by Rafael Armijo. Later, the general issued a formal decree ordering such property sold at public auction and the money it brought credited to the army quartermaster. The highly irregular procedure violated due process of law, but soon even the territorial judiciary became involved in retaliatory measures of dubious legality.

When it became known in Albuquerque that a grand jury would be impaneled to bring indictments, a black cloud settled upon the town. The civil authorities invited accusations, neighbor against neighbor, and anticipating that many would be charged, they prepared in advance large numbers of indictment forms. These had the crimes already entered and left blank only the space awaiting the name of an accused party. Albuquerque took on the kind of air, pervaded with suspicion and fear, that usually accompanies a witch hunt. Persons with old grudges to settle made the charges fly thick and fast, so that many who were innocent were summoned to defend themselves against allegations of high treason. The standard indictment read, in part, "Said accused did conspire to stir up and excite insurrection, rebellion and Civil War, against the United States and to overthrow and subvert the Government . . . together with General Sibley and diverse other false traitors."[48]

At the February 1863, term of the United States District Court, Bernalillo County, the trials began on twenty treason indictments already returned. But bringing charges proved to be one thing and obtaining convictions quite another. The United States Constitution expressly prohibited a conviction for treason except upon the testimony of two witnesses, and in practically none of these cases could two be found. Furthermore, as the territorial press complained, families in Albuquerque and the Middle Valley were all interrelated, either closely or distantly, so that it was impossible to convene a wholly impartial jury. Consequently, in trial after trial, the verdict returned read, *El acusado no tiene culpa!* Not guilty! Such leniency was not restricted to native New Mexicans. One Thomas J. Hill, an Anglo resident of Albuquerque, was tried and acquitted by a jury of twelve Hispanos.

The most sensational trial, and one in which conviction seemed sure, was that of Manuel Barela, the man bereft of reason who had caused such mischief by acting as an informer for Sibley. Barela had been indicted the previous October, but soon afterward disappeared. United States Marshal Abraham Cutler later arrested him in Mesilla and brought him back to Albuquerque for trial. In Barela's case, his disloyal acts had been committed so openly that plenty of witnesses could be found. Among them were such prominent Albuquerqueans as Salvador Armijo, Charles Huning, and Louis Zeckendorf, a German merchant. But the overwhelming evidence notwithstanding, the all-Hispano jury acquitted even Manuel Barela. The newly established *Rio Abajo Weekly Press* declared bitterly that the culprit had friends on the jury who "shielded him from merited punishment."[49]

Repeated failures to convict dampened the enthusiasm of government prosecutors, although indicted persons continued to be brought to trial as late as 1867. Notable examples were the hapless brothers Rafael and Manuel Armijo. They and their families had accompanied Sibley out of New Mexico, eventually reaching San Antonio, Texas. From there

Manuel had traveled on to the Confederate capital at Richmond in an unsuccessful effort to win recognition of their claims against the rebel government, which, according to Rafael's own statement, totaled $400,000.[50] Impoverished, they returned to New Mexico and settled first in Las Cruces. Then in 1866, Manuel voluntarily appeared in District Court at Albuquerque to plead not guilty at his belated arraignment. On May 4, 1867, Rafael also presented himself in court and posted bond to the sum of $10,000, a very high amount in those days. By this late date, however, the political climate had changed, their crimes were regarded as ancient history, and neither of the pair was ever brought to trial. Others against whom longstanding charges were dismissed included Spruce M. Baird and Dr. F. E. Kavenaugh, the individual responsible for capturing commissary supplies at Cubero and turning them over to Sibley's forces.[51]

The prolonged judicial proceedings taken up with the ugly treason charges touched many Albuquerqueans and, no doubt, left some lasting scars. Even the highly esteemed Hunings did not escape unscathed. Franz, as remarked, had been in the East on a buying trip during the rebel occupation. While returning over the Santa Fe Trail, he encountered a friend who had hurried out from Albuquerque to bring distressing tidings. "I learned," recounts Franz, "that some mischievous person with a grudge against my brother had gone before the grand jury and accused him of conspiracy against the Government with the Texan invaders. In spite of the ridiculous nature of this charge, a true-bill was found, the store was attached and Charles was thrown in prison."[52]

Hastening home, Franz Huning discovered the report was all too true. "I found my brother in jail together with several others. Sidney Hubbell was the judge then, and I prevailed on him to call an extra session of the court and try those cases of conspiracy. The Judge acquitted them all without calling a jury. This trouble caused us a considerable amount of damage. The store had been in possession of the U.S. Marshal and a deputy had charge of it. It was no secret that he had helped himself."[53]

The marshal was Abraham Cutler, a native of New York who received his post by presidential appointment and took office August 16, 1862. It was his job, originally begun by Carleton, to attach and dispose of the property belonging to the collaborators. Unfortunately, Cutler had few scruples and he used his position to victimize the innocent and guilty alike. The confiscations were made quite apart from the treason trials, with the result that persons cleared in the latter, still suffered a seizure of their land and goods by the marshal. Among abuses credited to Cutler were purchasing condemned property for his own use under fictitious names, paying himself exorbitant fees out of public monies for processing spoils seized, and forging documents, all for the purpose of personal profit. When he left office in 1866, an Albuquerque grand jury indicted him for embezzlement. But Marshal Cutler had plenty of friends and good counsel; the native jury let him off.[54]

Federal court records in Bernalillo County for 1862 and years immediately following show that more than 160 residents of the Middle Valley were subjected to some confiscation.[55] After condemnation, most of the property was ordered sold at auction by the Albuquerque court, and the *Rio Abajo Weekly Press* published the appropriate legal notices preliminary to public sale. From the tenor of its editorials, it is clear that the stridently pro-Union paper derived immense glee from the prospect of seeing traitors' property going to the auction block. In printing notices relating to real estate of Spruce Baird, Julián Tenorio, and Father José María Chávez, the editor chortled: "The property referred to will be desirable to purchasers not only as being the late residences of an oratory, a poet, and a devine, but also on account of the intrinsic value." The possessions of S. M. Baird, the orator, were listed as a private acequia for irrigation, good range for stock, and a commodious and conveniently arranged dwelling house and other buildings. "Just the place," said the editor, "for a purchaser who delights in rural life."

The residence of poet Julián Tenorio at Ranchos de Albuquerque, he noted ecstatically, was favored with a large garden, vineyard, and orchard. That property he recommended to a buyer who wished "to recline under his own vine and peach tree." And of the property at Peralta of Father Chávez, "the devine who acted more like a devil than a minister of the Gospel," the paper praised it as "suitable for a farmer or retired business man."[56] Such touting by the press must have helped bring out a respectable crowd, the curious as well as buyers, when at 10:00 on the morning of March 31, 1863, Baird's and Tenorio's estates were auctioned off from the courthouse doorway in Albuquerque. Chávez's home was sold from the steps of the Valencia County courthouse in Tomé.[57]

When General Carleton arrived in New Mexico with his California Column and assumed command of the department, his first concern had been for the protection of the Territory from a new Confederate invasion rumored to be in the mill. According to ominous reports, Spruce M. Baird had been commissioned to raise a regiment in Houston and San Antonio for the purpose of making another try at New Mexico. Such a plan was actually afoot for a time, but as the fortunes of war began to go against the South, Baird's men were diverted in the opposite direction to assist in defense of the Texas coast and Louisiana.[58] The Upper Rio Grande Valley, therefore, was spared further direct involvement in the civil conflict. But it was left with that older, abiding problem of Indian hostilities, which had plagued the land since the advent of the Spaniards in the late sixteenth century. To that, General Carleton now turned his attention.

The warring tribes had been quick to take advantage of the white man's disarray during the Confederate incursion, and they stepped up their attacks as never before. In April 1862, in a letter to Washington, Governor Henry Connelly spoke of the Indians as having "during the last three months entirely desolated the Territory of all the stock within their reach."[59] Navajo forays against Albuquerque and Mescalero Apache raids from Peralta southward persisted through that year and into the next. But all the while Carleton was preparing for a major offensive by which he intended to bring such rapacious activities to an end.

The first to feel the cudgel were the Mescaleros, concentrated in the mountains of southeastern New Mexico. Against them General Carleton sent Kit Carson and five companies of the First New Mexico Volunteers. In the late fall of 1862, Carson harried the tribe into submission and forced its people to move to a new reservation at Bosque Redondo on the Pecos River. Then, with that success under his belt, he headed into the Navajo homeland west of Albuquerque.

During the summer and autumn of 1863, Kit Carson led his troops from one end of the Indians' country to the other. He engaged in little fighting, but managed to shatter the Navajo economy by relentlessly destroying waterholes, fields, orchards, and livestock. Off and on for a year, small bands and large, starved out, came in to surrender. Piecemeal they were sent eastward under army escort on the Long Walk, as it is remembered in tribal history, to the flat, arid, and utterly cheerless Bosque Redondo Reservation. Passing through Albuquerque, the captive Navajos, suffering from disease and malnutrition, must have given pause to residents of the town, who saw their once proud foe reduced to such saddened straits.

When the Navajo round-up was completed in 1865, Colonel Kit Carson rode into the Albuquerque plaza and mustered out most of the companies in his volunteer regiment. The several companies retained in service were sent north to garrison Fort Garland in the San Luis Valley.[60] With the conclusion of the Navajo campaign, inhabitants of the Middle Valley breathed a sigh of relief, believing that their Indian fighting days were a thing of the past. But their elation proved a bit premature.

Young Navajo warriors, chafing under the close confinement at Bosque Redondo, began slipping away to seek sport and profit in raids along the Rio Grande. In one instance, a renegade band stole all the livestock from Casa Colorado, a small settlement 33 miles downriver from Albuquerque. Another party drove off 2,000 sheep belonging to the Otero family at Peralta. Indeed, stockmen all along the eastern fringe of New Mexico began to feel the bite of Navajo depredations. In response, a Santa Fe newspaper published a petition signed by 1,974 citizens urging the closing of the Bosque Redondo Reservation and removal of the Navajo, either to Arizona or to the Indian Territory. That call echoed the criticism leveled earlier by Albuquerque's *Rio Abajo Weekly Press* against General Carleton and the military, who, in the editor's view, had been short-sighted in placing the Indians on the Pecos amidst prime ranch land that was ripe for development.[61]

The Navajos, perpetually hungry on short government rations and longing for the red mesas and smoke-colored mountains of their traditional homeland, were the first to admit that Bosque Redondo was not the place for them. Finally, in 1868, the government agreed, and upon delivering solemn promises that they would raid no more, the Navajo tribesmen began the second Long Walk, but under happier circumstances than their first, since it represented a return from exile.

At dawn on June 15, 7,000 Indians marched out of Bosque Redondo trailed by 100 military supply wagons and a herd of 6,000 head of livestock. Their route lay up the Pecos River to the village of San José, thence westward to Tijeras Canyon and the pass at Carnué. Although the pace was grueling, the Navajos kept urging the government teamsters to whip their mules up a little faster, so eager were they to get home. Twenty-one days after leaving the reservation, the column reached the mouth of Tijeras Canyon. The Indians in the lead gazed out across the East Mesa, now greened by unusually abundant spring rains, and they saw the spires of San Felipe Neri Church lifting above the distant line of Albuquerque's rooftops. But what stirred them to their mocassin soles was the sharp, sparkling outline on the far horizon of their sacred mountain, Tso Dzil, the whiteman's Mount Taylor, home of the Navajo deities Turquoise Boy and Yellow Corn Girl. At the sight of that holy place, still 70 miles away, people wept openly and one man became temporarily deranged and had to be tied to a wagongate by the soldiers until he regained his senses. Recalling that moment, long after, an aged Navajo said: "When we saw the top of the mountain from Albuquerque, . . . we felt like talking to the ground, we loved it so."[62]

For their entry into Albuquerque, the town where they had so often raided in the past, the Navajos did their best to make a dignified showing, donning beforehand what little finery remained after their years of captivity. The women put on their velvet blouses and dresses, hoping the fading and patches would not be too noticeable, while the men bedecked themselves with the hand-hammered silver ornaments for which the tribe was already famous. The Navajo cavalcade stretched in a procession 10 miles long and presented never-to-be-forgotten pageantry. The leaders strode into the outskirts of Albuquerque, Sunday, July 5, 1868, at the same time that those in the rear were just emerging from Carnué Pass. At last on the edge of their own country, the Navajos' arrival in the old Spanish town by the Rio Grande marked something of a homecoming.

Because of high water and the great multitude of people, crossing of the river west of the plaza required seven days. Eight small rafts were hastily constructed and Indians, livestock, and wagons were ferried across a few at a time. In the interval, the Indians camped among the scattered cottonwoods along the shore, each band waiting its turn. By day they wandered freely about the plaza and at night they sat up late around their fires drumming and singing the throaty chants inherited from their ancestors. At week's end, the last of the native visitors braved the muddy waters of the Rio and disappeared on the rutted road over the West Mesa. Their departure marked the end of an era. From then on, Albuquerque and the Middle Valley enjoyed a lasting peace with their Indian neighbors.

In the summer of 1968, some of the grandchildren of the people who had made the Long Walk home, retraced their steps as a centennial commemoration of that historic event in Navajo history. The modern-day caravan of Indians, garbed in native raiment, paraded down Central Avenue, treading on concrete streets, shaded by tall buildings, cheered on by a smiling throng of spectators. The profound changes that had come to Albuquerque and to the Navajo themselves in the lapse of a mere century were almost more than any individual could grasp. But the reenactment of the Long Walk, perhaps as nothing else could have, helped bring history full circle, and for a brief moment recalled to mind one of the more poignant pages in the city's life story.[64]

Although the Civil War and the resolution of the Navajo problem highlighted Albuquerque's history in the 1860s, other events of some import also left their mark. One, long remembered, was the series of natural disasters that fell upon the Territory in 1865. In late spring, heavy frosts nipped the blossoms and buds on fruit trees throughout the Upper Rio Grande Valley. Then came torrential rains and pelting hailstorms, which battered the new crops in the fields. Spring floods, the worst in living memory, swept away most of the remaining wheat and corn in Bernalillo county, inundated Atrisco, Pajarito, and Padillas, and so threatened Albuquerque that virtually the entire population fled briefly to high ground in the sandhills. Perhaps because of the wetness of the season, a plague of grasshoppers and corn worms descended upon the land and devoured every blade of grass and leaf from Albuquerque westward to Fort Wingate. Appeals for help were made to the government, and the Pueblo Indians, whose custom it was to store up grain against famine, were asked for donations of foodstuffs. The Middle Valley, usually a producer of surplus crops, harvested practically nothing. The Santa Fe *Gazette* characterized the calamity by saying: "Properly to describe the misery created by frost, flood and other combinations of earth and sky this year, a man ought to write with tears instead of ink."[65]

But in a day when catastrophes were almost as common as needles on a piñon tree, inhabitants along the Rio Grande had learned to bounce back. Albuquerque, though more than a century and half old, was still a frontier town in spirit, and its people, being of the pioneer breed, knew how to shrug off losses and build and plant again.

Even while war and the weather were disrupting their lives, Albuquerqueans went quietly about fulfilling their civic responsibilities. On March 2, 1863, they ambled to the polls and elected seven aldermen, four Hispanos and three Anglos. The results provided an ethnic balance of sorts, since natives were in the majority, but in another sense, the ranks of the town fathers appeared topheavy with newcomers. There was clearly a disproportionate representation of Anglos, who as yet constituted only a tiny fraction of the population. Two of the new office holders were Salvador and Cristóbal Armijo, still recovering from the wartime ruin of their mercantile businesses, but working hard to maintain the influence of their family name in community affairs. William T. Strachan, proprietor of the local Sutler store in partnership with William Pool, was another alderman, a man who soon was to make a reputation for himself as a developer and entrepreneur.[66]

In the same election that brought the aldermen to office, Albuquerque voters approved a set of police ordinances. These covered animal and traffic control, sanitation, public works, zoning, and established a magistrate court and the office of town marshal to handle misdemeanors. All of these matters were to be under supervision of the aldermen, who also collected legal fines on behalf of the municipal treasury. Some of the prohibitions inserted in the ordinances graphically pointed up the primitive conditions that even yet prevailed in the old villa.

> All houseowners, or heads of families within the city limits of the town of Albuquerque, shall have especial care that their servants do not cast dirty water, sweepings, ashes or kitchen residue in front of the plaza, roads, streets, or alley-ways.
>
> All persons whose animal, or animals, shall die within the limits of Albuquerque, are required to remove them, within twenty-four hours after death, to a distance from said town, so their sight and stench may not cause any inconvenience.
>
> Any person making water, or depositing any excrement, under any porch, or upon any sidewalk or wall in front of the plaza, or within the cemetery, or in any street, road, or alley-way, upon conviction of the same before the Police Magistrate, shall be fined not less than five dollars. . . .
>
> Every person who shall keep a disorderly house within the limits of the town, or allow riots or other disorderly conduct on their premises, when convicted thereof, shall be fined not less than five dollars. . . .[67]

These and other provisions obviously addressed problems that had long gone unattended. But prompt enforcement of the ordinances demonstrated to Albuquerqueans that their former careless habits would no longer be tolerated. On April 14, the *Rio Abajo Weekly Press* informed readers that, "Last week, Alderman Salvador Armijo did a 'land office business' in the way of fining sundry individuals for offences against town laws. The consequences will be that, when hot weather comes, a person will be able to walk through any of our streets without his nostrils being saluted by odors incompatible with the relish of a good dinner."[68] Clean environment, the catch phrase of a later day, had become a public issue in nineteenth-century Albuquerque.

The man who helped make it so was the founder and editor of the *Rio Abajo Weekly Press,* Pennsylvania-born Hezekiah S. Johnson, who came to New Mexico in 1849. In 1853 he became an apprentice printer on the *Santa Fe Weekly Gazette* and six years later the editor. Upon moving south and launching the *Rio Abajo Weekly Press* in January 1863, Johnson modestly wrote in the inaugural editorial: "We do not think the brilliance of our style of writing will throw any considerable number of readers into ecstatic raptures, or set the Rio del Norte on fire. However, . . . we can master enough simple English words to manifest our meaning to the generality of the readers of the language."[69] While it is true that H. S. Johnson's paper did not set the river afire, it was nevertheless a landmark enterprise, representing the beginnings of professional journalism in

Albuquerque. Richard Weightman's short-lived *Amigo del País,* as noted, qualified as the first paper, but it scarcely made an impact on the community and left no successor.

Distinguished Albuquerque historian William A. Keleher once described the *Rio Abajo Weekly Press* as "a fairly well edited paper, although a bit shabby looking at times, while suffering from what its editor noted as a 'lack of political pap.' "[70] At the start, Johnson was the entire staff. He printed the paper during daylight hours on a small army press, and spent much of the night preparing copy. One Sunday in June 1863, a youth named Albert Franklin Banta wandered into Albuquerque looking for a job, and when Johnson learned that he had some experience in printing, he told him to report to work the following morning. The paper now had a staff of two.

Johnson soon sent to Philadelphia for a small Washington model hand press, capable of making 250 impressions of a two-page form per hour. It was a decided technological improvement. Banta installed the equipment when it arrived and went joyously to his task. "After I had put up the little Washington press," he recorded, "I think almost every woman and child in town came to the office to see the curly haired boy work that wonderful machine."[71] The *Weekly* lasted a year and a half, being succeeded in the summer of 1864 by *The New Mexico Press.* Thereafter, Albuquerque was never to be without some kind of a newspaper. H. S. Johnson, after a term in the territorial legislature, went on to become judge of New Mexico's Second Judicial District, a position he held until his death in 1876.

Franz Huning and his brother, Charles, had made a quick recovery following the disruption of their business during the Civil War. In 1863 Franz was back on the Santa Fe Trail headed for Missouri. Prairie travel had laid hold of his affections and he was never happier than when riding the endless miles along the old trail. In St. Louis, he made his annual purchase of trade goods, and to them added machinery for a new gristmill and a sawmill. The expenditure for heavy equipment was an investment in Albuquerque's future, for he felt certain a boom was just around the corner. The purchases were turned over to his wagonmaster for freighting back to New Mexico, but Franz himself was not returning, at least for the moment. He had another trip to make, one that his newfound prosperity now allowed. After an absence of more than fifteen years, he wanted to see again the land of his birth.

From St. Louis, Franz Huning made his way to New York and there took a steamer for England. Crossing the English Channel, he landed in France. Speaking of the journey later to his children, he related: "From Paris I went by the way of Cologne to my old home near Osnabrück in the province of Hanover. My father had died some years before, also my oldest brother. Most of my old acquaintances, schoolmates and others had scattered or died. It made me sad to see the changes that had been wrought. . . . I stayed with my mother about 20 days and visited brothers and sisters, old familiar places, etc."[73] It was all a pleasant and nostalgic interlude, but Franz was eager to be on his way. His destiny was now firmly wedded to the mud town half a globe away on the banks of the Rio Grande, whose name his German relatives could scarcely pronounce.

During the return to New Mexico, an event of considerable significance occurred in Franz Huning's life. At St. Louis, he paused to wed a German immigrant girl, Ernestine Franke, and together the newlyweds embarked upon a two-month journey over the trail to Las Vegas and Santa Fe. Home in Albuquerque by the summer of 1864, Franz had much to do. First he installed Ernestine in La Glorieta, along with ten canaries brought from St. Louis. As a wedding gift, the records show, he deeded her the rambling old adobe house, with its cottonwood under which the Confederates had butchered their cattle. Here in La Glorieta would be born the Hunings' son and three daughters.

Ernestine Huning must have been a bit startled by the rustic life into which she had entered, but she met daily challenges with good humor and strong determination. Water for household use was brought from the river in a large barrel fitted with wheels. Often it was so muddy that she found it necessary to drop in a broken egg to settle the contents. Some of the precious liquid went to water the lilacs and other flowers she planted to bring color to the bare interior placita. Later, devoted Franz would provide her with elegant furniture, a grand piano, and paintings.

In the mid 1860s, Albuquerque had a resident Anglo population of about fifty, and, of these, only a dozen or so were women. Ernestine quickly became the acknowledged social leader of the English-speaking ladies. Gatherings at her home each Thursday afternoon to sew and partake of coffee and cake became a sacred ritual. Sometimes Franz, handsome now in middle age with a sandy mustache and goatee, would drop in on those weekly fetes to entertain with his dry wit. Addicted to coffee, he always drank from a large bowl, which the guests referred to humorously as his "double-cup."[74]

Soon after his return from St. Louis, Franz saw to the uncrating of the mill machinery, and he began plans for construction of a new store. The Huning Brothers mercantile business had continued to expand and more spacious quarters were imperative. In the summer of 1864, Franz and Charles, on what must have been a ceremonious occasion, laid a cornerstone for the store on the west side of the plaza. Sensing perhaps that it was an historical moment, they deposited a document with the stone. When the building was demolished in 1903, the paper came to light. It read:

> August 31, 1864
> Fourth year of the American Civil War
> General Grant trying to take Petersburg and Richmond
> Gold at 260 %
> Indians on the Santa Fe road to the States very hostile
> We built this house and the steam mill in Rancho Seco
>   at the same time
> [signed]   F C   Huning[75]

The Hunings' new establishment was not without serious competitors, for in the late 1860s, at least nine other mercantile houses vied for the Albuquerque trade. Several of the most prosperous belonged to nephews of the late Governor Manuel Armijo. One, Juan Cristóbal Armijo, ran a store, built in 1857, on the southeast corner of the plaza. He resided nearby (at present 110 San Felipe) in the house that had once belonged to his illustrious uncle. Another, Salvador Armijo, had a store and warehouses in Albuquerque, with branches scattered in towns around the Territory. And a third shopkeeper, Ambrosio Armijo, gained renown as a leading importer and owner of freight wagons plying the Santa Fe Trail.

To stay even with their business rivals, Franz and Charles also opened branches outside Albuquerque, the first at Zuñi Pueblo, and a second at Pinos Altos near Silver City. The steam-powered flour mill at Rancho Seco, immediately south of La Glorieta, brought added profits and helped diversify the interests of the firm. As early as 1867, Franz Huning also began speculating in land, an activity that had become all the rage in the Territory. One of his first investments, in an old Spanish land grant 8 miles below Albuquerque, went awry and he lost $8,000.[76] But the fiasco failed to dampen his ardor for the acquisition of real estate. He had an abiding faith in the future of Albuquerque, and when the boom came, as it surely must, he hoped to have a share of the profits that would inevitably be reaped by those with vision who had gotten in on the ground floor. On the road to prosperity, Albuquerque and Franz Huning would march hand in hand.

"Clarion Notes of Progress"

"ALBUQUERQUE IS THE COMING TOWN of New Mexico, if it has a coming town, which I am much inclined to doubt."[1] Those were the words of J. H. Beadle, a visitor to the Middle Valley in the early 1870s. Like many contemporary Americans, Beadle looked upon the Territory as an arid and remote wasteland inhabited largely by backward people who cared more for the past than the future. While he conceded that Albuquerque's "wealthy families have whitewashed houses, stone windowsills, pine floors, sometimes carpets, and live perhaps as well as farmers in Ohio," he also admitted condescendingly that he had to smile at "the solemn humbug" of their aristocratic pretensions based on "what somebody did two or three centuries ago."[2]

Ever since New Mexico had fallen into the hands of the United States, it had its detractors who seemed intent upon giving the place an unsavory name. As early as 1853, Secretary of War Charles Conrad, whose knowledge of the Territory came wholly from official reports filed in Washington, wondered aloud if the government should not persuade its benighted people to abandon "a country which seems hardly [fit] for the inhabitants of civilized man."[3] Although no one but the secretary seriously considered abandonment as the proper fate for New Mexico, the *Chicago Evening Journal* in its pages of May 3, 1870, was constrained to inform readers that "no man of sense and sanity would go there to settle."[4] Scarcely less disparaging were comments of the *New York Times,* which, in speaking of Santa Fe, noted, "Here, upon the plains, in the heart of our worst civilization is an American city 300 years old . . . seventy miles south is Albuquerque, younger, but with all the signs of ignorance and sloth."[5] If everyone believed what they read in the papers, then New Mexico would have been shunned like a leper. But as always there were a certain number of independent spirits who saw beckoning opportunity where others perceived none. From the ranks of the adventuresome, there came to New Mexico during the decade of the 1870s, men ready to win a share of whatever destiny had in store for this, the oldest of southwestern territories.

For those who chose Albuquerque and the surrounding valley as home, the immediate problem was how to make a living. Agriculture, at least in the beginning, held little appeal, for as Beadle sagely observed, "An American cannot live here as a farmer; he cannot compete with the natives. They can live too cheap."[6] That would change in time; the end of the century would find several large truck-gardening enterprises north of the plaza in the hands of industrious farmers from the East. But for the moment, new residents to Albuquerque looked elsewhere for a source of livelihood.

Sheep raising, the other pillar of the local economy, also did not appear attractive. Hispanic methods of handling the stock, well-suited to New Mexico, were thoroughly unfamiliar to Anglos, as was the custom of contracting flocks on shares, the *partido* system. Moreover, the old sheep barons of the Middle Valley held a virtual monopoly over the industry. What profits existed in wool, hides, and mutton, they meant to keep for themselves.

Easterners who drifted to Albuquerque in the post–Civil War years, therefore, entered into the life of the community as merchants, tradesmen, artisans, and innkeepers. There was even a sprinkling of doctors and lawyers. As providers of goods and services in what was predominantly a Hispano town, they found it both expedient and desirable to adapt wholeheartedly to prevailing custom. Many of these men married native Albuquerqueans and gained thereby important social connections. At no extra trouble, they also acquired what was then termed a "sleeping dictionary," that is, a wife who could teach them Spanish. Practically all business and social discourse was in that language, as were political speeches and sermons in San Felipe Neri Church. No Anglo could function in Albuquerque of the 1870s without at least a working knowledge of Spanish.

The town, in spite of a quarter century of American rule, retained its Hispanic-Mexican aspect almost intact. Lydia English, an immigrant woman on her way to Arizona in 1875, thought that Albuquerque differed little from other Mexican adobe towns, "It is very old and has a tumbledown look," she said.[7] An overriding sense of antiquity was heightened, according to others, by activity in the streets that reminded one more of medieval Spain or colonial Mexico than it did a town owned by the modern American nation. As they always had, men still wore sombreros with tall crowns and draped their bodies with serapes. Of the latter, one passerby remarked caustically: "Men [wear] a serape of all the glaring colors, looking as if it might be the American flag kicked over the shoulders by a government mule."[8] For the ladies, full dresses and enveloping shawls, or rebozos, remained the model of good attire, although garments of imported print cloth and even a few slat-brimmed sunbonnets were beginning to find favor among the younger set.

The streets of the old villa overflowed with a constant moving stream of wagons, carriages, horses, burros, and pedestrians. Peddlers were everywhere, hawking wares in the center of the plaza and occupying porches in front of the business houses where they spread piles of fruit, vegetables, cheese, piñon nuts, and leaf tobacco. On most any day, vendors took over the hitching racks, using them to hang meat carcasses, both wild game and mutton, so that finding a place to tie a horse or saddle mule required a diligent search. Gamblers roamed about with decks of cards in hand, hoping to entice some visiting farmer or sheep-herder into a fast game of three card monte. And almost every store, whether it specialized in dry goods or bakery goods, also sold liquor by the bottle over the counter.

The English-speaking newcomers slipped smoothly into Albuquer-que's Old World tempo of daily life, but being inclined toward progress and dedicated to profit, they soon began to introduce changes that bit by bit altered the character of the town. William Brown, a former soldier, took up business quarters in a low adobe building near the center of the plaza, known popularly as The Fort. From its roof projected the towering flagpole donated by Carleton. To the public, Brown advertised his services as barber, dentist, and chiropodist. As a tonsorial artist, he offered "first class service in the smartest and latest styles."[9] When he hung out a sign reading Flag Staff Barber Shop, his customers ignored it. His building was The Fort and that was what they would call it.

Major Melchior Werner, who had come to Albuquerque with the army back in the 1850s, in 1876 opened a hotel west of the plaza, which he named, appropriately, The Centennial. In addition to lodgers, it housed the post office—since 1867 Werner had been the Albuquerque postmaster—and the telegraph office, after the wire reached town in February 1876.[10] Melchior Werner was a staunch Catholic and a liberal contributor to San Felipe Neri Church. On the feast of Corpus Christi in June 1873, he was one of several prominent citizens erecting altars in front of his place of business so that the religious procession, passing through the streets, could pause for a brief service.[11]

Hotels were a fairly new luxury for Albuquerque, although The Centennial was not the first such establishment. That honor belonged to the Atlantic and Pacific Hotel, which opened its doors soon after the Civil War. One of its earliest guests was a Denver newspaper reporter who proclaimed it the "worst-kept hotel in the Territory."[12] Perhaps a reputation for slovenliness, with a corresponding shortage of customers, prompted owner John Murphy in 1874 to sell his hostelry to John B. Brophy. Mr. Brophy made a gallant bid to turn the business around by adding modern furnishings, better housekeeping, and by putting his wife in charge of the kitchen. But his best efforts proved unavailing, and the following year he sold out to Thomas D. Post.

Like so many Americans who went west in this era, Tom Post was something of a jack-of-all-trades. When he landed in Albuquerque after the war, he first opened a butcher shop on the plaza. By 1874, he took over the ferry business immediately west of town, and in the following year, he purchased the failing Atlantic and Pacific Hotel. His first act was to change the name to Post's Exchange Hotel, which proved all that was needed to turn its fortunes around. Overnight it became the favored stop in the Middle Valley, and stagecoaches running from Las Cruces to Santa Fe regularly called at its door. In 1879, Post sold the building to Nicolás Armijo, but kept the name which he transferred to a structure, purchased from Paula Montoya, situated just south of the plaza. Much of Post's trade must have followed him, for the second Exchange Hotel, with rates of $1.50 a night, proved to be as popular as the first. It continued to do a banner business until the owner's death in 1893.[13]

From the moment he entered the ferry business in 1874, Tom Post was alert to the commercial possibilities of erecting a toll bridge on the Rio Grande that could benefit from the growing flow of traffic between Albuquerque and Atrisco. In 1876, the year after opening his Exchange Hotel, he constructed a pontoon bridge on the site of the present Central Avenue Bridge. It was the first such structure to span the river anywhere in the Middle Valley. At the east end he built a two-story house, store, and toll station. A local paper commented that Post, not content to give guests the best accommodations at his hotel, was eager to furnish them with every means to get there.[14] Though a financial success, the pontoon bridge apparently did not long survive the ravages of Albuquerque's annual spring floods. When railroad surveyor Henry Allen Tice crossed at the site in 1880, there was no sign of the bridge and he was obliged to pay $.25 to be ferried across on one of several clumsy, flat-bottomed barges.[15]

Another man leaving his mark on Albuquerque in those years was William McGuinness, who had come out with the army in the early 1860s. In 1870 he launched the *Republican Review,* a bilingual newspaper and the only one to serve the town during the ensuing decade. From a small adobe office (which still stands at 202 San Felipe SW), he struggled with single-minded devotion to meet his Saturday afternoon deadline and to keep the enterprise afloat. Delinquent subscribers and advertisers, habitually in arrears with payment, were one source of worry. His health impaired by overwork was another. Mrs. McGuinness, the former Encarnación Romero, occasionally had to get the paper out on her own. As a child, it will be recalled, she had been the one who had obliged her family to return and rescue her lost doll when the Confederates invaded Albuquerque.

While most frontier journalists were notoriously contentious and abrasive, William McGuinness harnessed his pen with uncharacteristic restraint. In an inaugural issue, he proclaimed that the *Review* had "no axes to grind." Generally, throughout his editorship he avoided acrimony, although once he departed from his usual moderate stance long enough to denounce the correspondent for another newspaper as a "mendacious lickspittle."[16] In one matter close to his heart, McGuinness must be classed as an extremist: promotion of economic progress for Albuquerque. For ten years or more, he was at the forefront of those praising the natural advantages of the Middle Valley and urging capital investment and improvement. It was the timeless cry of men who dreamed of building and innovating and prospering. His sentiments, while new to New Mexico, were quite familiar to the rest of the United States. They had been voiced at every stage of the nation's development and had motivated generations of aspirants to wealth and influence. Expansion, progress, and growth, ballyhooed to the heavens, were the catchwords of the day, and they produced the authentic vision of the American pioneer. [17]

One category of new arrivals well positioned to reap rewards were the lawyers. In frock coats, boiled shirts, and bat-wing collars, they were drifting into Albuquerque, as well as other territorial towns, in hopes of gaining a firm foothold before an anticipated economic boom overtook New Mexico. Since little money could be made in legal work at this early date, many of them branched out to speculate in mining, land development, or merchandising. A case in point was William C. Hazeldine, who left Arkansas in his late twenties, after serving as a state legislator and district judge, and made his way to Santa Fe. There in 1875, he formed a partnership with another lawyer, William Breeden, and two years later he moved to Albuquerque, where McGuinness's *Review* announced that he was opening a branch office of the firm.

Over the next few years, Hazeldine's name was to be associated with a variety of speculative ventures. In a number of these he was linked to another rising star on Albuquerque's economic scene, Elias S. Stover. On a bright day in 1876, Stover had climbed off the stagecoach in front of Tom Post's Exchange Hotel, beat the dust from his clothes, and looking about told himself that this sun-blistered, dirt-coated Albuquerque had the pulse of a town with a future. A Union veteran, former lieutenant-governor of Kansas (1872–74), and a merchant by trade, Elias Stover, at age forty, believed in keeping ahead of the crowd. Kansas, before he left, had been in a frenzy of railroad building, and at least one of the lines, the Atchison, Topeka, and Santa Fe, was pointing toward the Southwest. Stover's nose for business must have told him that once the rails reached New Mexico, the land's vast reservoir of resources would be ripe for tapping, and that could only be done by the men who were out front. Whether by chance or by unerring instinct, he had singled out the one town ordained by circumstance to become the chief metropolis of the Territory. Quickly he set himself up in a store on the plaza and by the spring of 1878, Stover and Co. was being referred to in print as "the most liberal, enterprising, and public spirited of any house in town," second only to the venerable Huning Mercantile. [18] In an unbelievably short time, Elias S. Stover had won a slot among the ranks of the community's business elite. And from that position, he was on his way to becoming a central figure in the lively events that were soon to follow.

One fact worth noting about the "Anglos" who settled in Albuquerque before the railroad era is that so many of them were foreign born. Immigrants flooded the eastern United States on the heels of the Civil War, and it is scarcely surprising that many of the more daring and visionary followed the wagon tracks of older Americans leading toward the blooming West. Among the earliest of such arrivals at Albuquerque, as we have seen, were the Germans Franz and Charles Huning (later joined by another brother, Louis) and Melchior Werner. Other prominent German merchants of the 1870s included Henry Springer and Joseph Pohmer, both from Bavaria, and William Eront, a Prussian. John Murphy, who opened a drugstone on the plaza after the failure of his Atlantic and Pacific Hotel, was an Irishman, as was William McGuinness. Thomas Keleher, wool merchant, was the son of Irish immigrants. Fritz Greening, a blacksmith, came from Poland, and lawyer William H. Henrie, who first gained public notice upon his election as an Albuquerque alderman in 1863, was a native of France.

But the most conspicuous group of foreigners were the Italian Jesuits who took charge of San Felipe Neri Church in 1868, replacing one of Bishop Lamy's French priests, Father Augustine Truchard. The previous year, while on an official visit to Rome, the bishop had requested that the Jesuit Order open a new missionary field in New Mexico and thus help ease a continuing shortage of priests. In response, several Italian fathers and brothers who had been serving in Spain were assigned to Lamy's charge, and together they sailed for the United States. After a harrowing trip over the Santa Fe Trail, in which the party narrowly escaped an Indian massacre, the Italians reached New Mexico and were placed in the church at Bernalillo. Then in April 1868, the bishop ordered them to move to Albuquerque, since he considered that place more suitable for the educational programs the Jesuits were proposing. Father Donato Maria Gasparri assumed the reins as superior and the Albuquerque rectory became the Mother House for other Jesuit missions that were soon established in the Territory. [19]

Father Gasparri, fluent in Spanish and zealously progressive, set the tone for all the Jesuits who were to come after him. On acreage belonging to the church north of the plaza, he developed truck gardens, orchards, and vineyards, the last eventually containing twelve hundred vines grown from imported Italian cuttings. The bountiful "Fathers' Gardens," as they were known to residents, became the pride of Albuquerque. [20] Education was always one of the prime interests of the Jesuits, and Gasparri in 1873 launched a school for boys, headquartered in the house of Ambrosio Armijo. Another of his projects, a school designed to train local youths for the priesthood, failed for lack of applicants and financial support. Albuquerqueans, marveling at the priest's breadth of learning, nicknamed him, "The Walking Encyclopedia."

The Jesuit Order, founded in the sixteenth century following the Protestant Reformation, had as its principal aim the protection and expansion of the Catholic faith. That goal made it one of the most aggressive and dedicated missionary orders in the Church. As soon as he had the Albuquerque parish functioning smoothly, Father Gasparri began casting wistful glances toward the "pagan" Navajos, who, since their return from Bosque Redondo, had scattered over the far reaches of western New Mexico and Arizona. Hearing that the Presbyterians were making efforts to introduce missions among the tribe (Protestants were the special foe of the Jesuits), Gasparri in 1870 left Albuquerque to conduct a quick tour of the Navajo homeland. His journey proved disappointing since it revealed that the Indians were dispersed too widely to make establishment of a mission practical. He then considered a new program for the Pueblos close to Albuquerque. Through work of the Spanish Franciscans in colonial days, they had supposedly been converted, but their current commitment to religious duties and doctrine left much to be desired. One Sunday Father Gasparri rode upriver to Sandia Pueblo to say Mass and assess the spiritual state of the people. The Sandias let their hostile sentiments be known with a most unequivocal gesture: they placed a rattlesnake under the altar. Gasparri got the hint, beat a hasty retreat, and promptly abandoned all thoughts of working with the Pueblos.

Father Gasparri lent his voice to those Albuquerqueans who, throughout the 1870s, worked in hopes of seeing a railroad extended to their town. He was too strong an advocate of community development to do otherwise. But at the same time, he knew that rail transportation from the East would inevitably bring in a horde of Protestants and their ministers and that would produce, in his estimation, a serious threat to those members of the Albuquerque parish not already firm in the faith. Such fears, in part, lay behind his concerted drive to build parochial schools wherever the Jesuits founded missions in the Territory. And they also prompted him to raise money and purchase a small press from the United States to be used for printing religious tracts and schoolbooks. The Imprenta del Río Grande, as the new press was called, commenced operation during the fall of 1872 in a shop set up in the San Felipe Neri rectory. Father Enrico Ferrari, one of a new contingent of Italian priests that reached Albuquerque in that year, served as printer. After a severe flood in 1874 threatened the plaza and church, Father Gasparri had the press dismantled and moved to a Jesuit mission in Las Vegas where it would be safer.

The most noticeable effect of the Italian presence was in the remodeling of the interior of San Felipe Neri Church. James F. Meline, attending Mass back in 1866, had been struck by a new board floor in the nave, apparently the only one then in a New Mexican church. Aside from that innovation and a half dozen kneeling benches near the altar, the interior architecture and furnishings looked about the same as in colonial days.[22] The Jesuits decided to change all that by doing away with the old Franciscan Pueblo Mission style and introducing, as best their limited means would allow, an imitation of the Italian Baroque style. The undulating lines, characteristic of adobe walls, were straightened and masked with plaster and wood wainscoting. Pulpit and altar received coats of paint, applied to resemble Italian marble. The rough altar screen installed by the Franciscans disappeared and large plaster statutes of San Felipe Neri, San Francisco Xavier, and San Ignacio de Loyola (founder of the Jesuits) were substituted. It was almost as if the transformation of San Felipe Neri Church was preparing the Hispanic people of Albuquerque for more sweeping changes that would soon touch every other aspect of their lives.[23]

During the 1870s the town emerged as one of the leading commercial centers of the far Southwest. With the demand for manufactured goods growing, Albuquerque merchants expanded their retail business by accepting payment in hides, wool, and farm products, a practice necessitated by the local shortage of cash. They also developed a lucrative wholesale trade by supplying smaller firms in southern New Mexico and the Arizona Territory. Their volume of business in one of the palmiest years, 1872, was estimated at $300,000.

But commercial development did not proceed at an even pace. In the middle years of the decade, Albuquerque experienced a severe economic slump, which spread hardship throughout the community. It was precipitated by the disastrous flood in the summer of 1874, the one that frightened Father Gasparri into moving his cherished printing press to Las Vegas. At Alameda, the swollen Rio Grande broke into its old channel and swept down the east side of the valley, leaving Albuquerque marooned on an island. Although the flood waters retreated within a few days, the adobe town and its surrounding farmlands sustained a staggering amount of damage. Some exaggerated newspaper reports published elsewhere in the Territory and in the East suggested that Albuquerque had been nearly washed away and that its recovery was in doubt. Indeed, two years after the disaster, roofless and windowless houses could still be seen in outlying suburbs.

Local businessmen and lawyers in a spirit of cooperation formed the Albuquerque Association to plan the town's resurrection. But the task was so monumental and funds needed were so scarce that little came of their effort. Each shopkeeper and farming family simply had to rebuild slowly as he was able. In the interval, a fall-off in business brought some Albuquerqueans to the verge of bankruptcy. Henry Springer, after struggling for a time, closed out his store and accounts and went to work for the Huning firm. The Huning brothers themselves had been hard hit, and probably as a result of economic strains of the period, they dissolved their partnership in 1875. Charles returned to Germany, and Franz, regrouping what was left of the business, began working to regain the ground that had been lost. At that time he owed a $300 debt to Editor William McGuinness and being strapped for funds, he offered a sizeable chunk of real estate on the East Mesa in lieu of payment. McGuinness, who was in even worse financial shape, rejected the offer claiming that he needed the cash to see his newspaper through the economic crises. The land that he turned down became, a few years hence, the Huning Highland Addition, one of the most valuable properties in Albuquerque.[24]

In time the town began to recover the buoyant optimism that had prevailed in the early 1870s. The overspreading waters of the Rio Grande, which had done such harm to man-made structures, also performed their usual beneficial service by leaving behind a thick deposit of rich alluvial soil. As soon as the fields had been cleared of debris, farmers and the Jesuit fathers commenced to restore crops, fruit trees, and vines with the certainty that future harvests would far surpass those of previous years. A leader in the restoration of agriculture was Salvador Armijo, who, with his partner and son-in-law, Santiago Baca, was the largest employer of farm workers in the valley. He had some 300 acres under cultivation, and because he imported steel plows and improved seed corn from the States, his yields far exceeded those of his neighbors. Armijo also brought in a mechanical reaper, the first ever seen in Albuquerque. In spite of the small commercial revolution sparked by the rising merchant class, the Middle Valley's economy continued to rest firmly on a farming and pastoral base.[25]

Albuquerque suffered a second major blow during this period which, while not as physically damaging as the flood of 1874, was, nevertheless, almost as dispiriting. The setback was the loss of the county seat to an upstart rival, the town of Bernalillo, second largest community in the Middle Valley. Bernalillo County had been one of the original nine counties created by the territorial legislature in 1852. Initially Ranchos de Albuquerque was designated the seat of local government, probably because of its convenient location near the center of the county. But it soon became apparent that Albuquerque, as the business and military center of the Rio Abajo, was the logical place for county offices, and thither they were moved in 1854.[26] The courthouse, a rambling adobe building, was built north of the plaza on Main Street (today's Rio Grande Boulevard) at the corner of Santiago.[27] "Our courthouse is nothing to boast of, in the architectural point of view," acknowledged McGuinness in the columns of his *Republican Review*.[28]

The threat to Albuquerque's position as the political hub of the Valley first surfaced in the spring of 1875. It came from a coterie of powerful ranching families, led by the Pereas, who were headquartered at Bernalillo. Seeing no reason why their town should be left behind while Albuquerque surged to prominence, they began casting about for some means to make Bernalillo a serious competitor. A good first move, they concluded, would be to gain possession of the county seat. Most Albuquerqueans did not take the challenge seriously, although when word got about, Franz Huning went so far as to place a petition on his store counter asking support in opposing any transfer of the county offices.

As the first step in their battle strategy, the Bernalillo faction managed to persuade the territorial legislature to pass a bill annexing Santa Ana County, adjoining on the north, to Bernalillo County. The maneuver was touted as an economy measure, but what it did was place the town of Bernalillo close to the geographical center of the newly enlarged county. That paved the way, during the next session of the legislature in 1876, for the Pereas and their friends to ask for a change in the county seat. Albuquerqueans, now thoroughly alarmed, mustered their forces at the capitol and managed to block a bill providing for outright removal. They had to accept a substitute bill, however, which required that the issue be submitted to county voters for a final decision. That gave Albuquerque a breathing spell, but not much more.

After a series of delays, the county commissioners called an election for March 23, 1878. The votes of citizens in Albuquerque and Bernalillo were a foregone conclusion, so it was clear that the question would be decided in the small villages and rural areas of the county. At a public meeting on February 27, Albuquerque's town fathers gathered to form their own plan of battle. Salvador Armijo's energetic young son-in-law, Santiago Baca, was selected presiding officer, and when he delivered a ringing speech denouncing the "Bernalillo conspirators," his words were greeted with enough cheers and shouts to shake the roof.

A balanced committee of Hispanos and Anglos, twenty-three persons in all, was appointed to draft resolutions expressing the sentiments of the meeting. Franz Huning won the chairmanship hands down, and the membership included such community stalwarts as Thomas Post, James L. Hubbell, William Hazeldine, and Elias Stover. One of the resolutions they presented for adoption clearly shows that they entertained grave fears for their pocketbooks. It read: RESOLVED that, as by removal of the county seat from Albuquerque serious loss will incur to its citizens . . . and that the value of real estate in and within a circuit of fifteen miles of Albuquerque will necessarily become depreciated and of very little value, that existing business enterprises will be comparatively ruined, that it will be the means of stopping all improvements and the investiture of capital, and that it will deprive the poor of employment and a market for their labor and its products."[29]

Another worry expressed was that, should the county seat be lost, the United States District Court might be the next to leave, thereby depriving Albuquerque of one more source of employment, money, and trade. The town, just as it was beginning to recover fully from the flood, now confronted a new peril that once again could plunge the economy into a tailspin.

In the weeks before the election, Albuquerqueans fanned out over the county, from the mountain villages on the east to the Rio Puerco settlements on the west, trying to line up votes. Passions ran high and two Albuquerque supporters were severely beaten when they attempted to speak at a rally in a small community on the Puerco. The fact was, the Pereas had most of the county residents firmly in their corner. Many owed them debts or favors; few were willing to incur their displeasure. When people from Bernalillo rode down river to shop at Albuquerque, they traveled in groups and went heavily armed. On election day, Editor McGuinness wrote somberly, "Happily there were no lives lost as was anticipated by many."[30]

But the election was lost—by Albuquerque. Los Ranchos, Los Griegos, and Barelas voted with it, as did the villages beyond the Sandias and Manzanos. Every other place in the county, however, went overwhelmingly for Bernalillo, even Albuquerque's neighbor across the river, Atrisco. It was a bitter, stinging defeat. After an effort fizzled to stop the removal through court action, the county records and offices were quietly transferred to Bernalillo.[31]

If Albuquerque failed to wither on the vine and blow away with its annual spring winds, as preelection rhetoric suggested it might, the reason was not that the prediction had been overstated or unwarranted. It was rather that events from another direction suddenly turned favorable for Albuquerque; so favorable, in fact, that they not only prevented the town from sliding into the business depression previously forecast, but actually launched it on a new road of plenty. The occasion was the approach of the long-dreamed-of railroad. And one of the key decisions, determining upon which community that railroad would bestow its major blessing, happened to fall to the indomitable José Leandro Perea of Bernalillo. By a serious miscalculation, he was destined to parley away the future of his own home town, deliver an irretrievable advantage to rival Albuquerque, and in so doing alter the course of history in the Middle Valley.

Since the 1850s, when Whipple had surveyed the 35th parallel route across central New Mexico, Albuquerqueans had looked forward to the day when rails would reach their town and link them to the great market centers of the nation. That hope had to be put aside temporarily during the Civil War, but with end of the conflict, interest in railroad development was reborn. It also became an imperative need, not only for Albuquerque, but for the entire Territory.

The war had created a demand for New Mexico wool, a demand that increased rather than lessened after peace was declared in 1865. Active freighters, like Manuel Yrissari and Juan Estevan Barela of Los Ranchos de Albuquerque, Felipe Chávez of Belen, and José Leandro Perea and Mariano Otero of Bernalillo saw their fortunes grow as the volume of wool transport expanded. During the spring of 1867, Perea, in partnership with Nesario González, shipped thousands of pounds of raw wool in ten freight wagons to the Kansas City market.[32] Although records are sparse, we can easily suppose that he made similar shipments in succeeding years. Wool, which had brought $.04 a pound in 1862, had skyrocketed to $.18 a pound by 1871.[33] The message was clear: the voracious cloth mills of America could take all the wool that New Mexico might send them.

For the Middle Valley, the boom in prices came at a most fortunate time, coinciding as it did with the cessation of Navajo hostilities. Indian troubles had long retarded growth of the sheep industry, but now stockmen were free to expand their ranges both east and west of Albuquerque. New seed flocks were driven through Tijeras Canyon into the Estancia Valley and the Pecos Basin beyond. And westward, sheep raisers, largely from Atrisco, poured into the, until now, thinly settled grasslands along the Rio Puerco.

A new Anglo resident of Albuquerque, taking his family one day for a picnic in the Sandias, describes a sight that was then becoming common on the East Mesa. "Toward evening, as we were driving out of Tijeras Canyon on the way back to Albuquerque, we came upon a flock of sheep, about 10,000 they told us. We watched the sheepherders bed them down for the night. The sheep were divided into four or five flocks, and, around each flock the sheepherders stationed dogs, each dog on a sheepskin."[34] New Mexico had vacant pasturage in abundance to accommodate many more flocks such as this, but its freighting capacity was becoming strained to the limit. To handle the ever larger volume of wool, railroad cars were needed, not more ox-drawn wagons. And until they were available, the Territory's full potential as a sheep producer was not going to be realized.

In a like manner, the mining industry was also in limbo, awaiting the day when improved transportation would make possible the importation of heavy machinery and the shipment of ore. Many of the men in Carleton's California Column, which had come to the aid of New Mexico in 1862, settled in the Territory, and because they had previous experience in the Pacific goldfields, they took to prospecting. But their finds had been small and their operations, generally superficial. Without a railroad in the Territory, little incentive existed for the large-scale capital expenditures that mining required.

Forty miles or so northeast of Albuquerque existed a gold mining district called the Placers, which had been opened in the Ortiz Mountains early in the Mexican period. Closer at hand, some promising mineral prospects were reported in the Sandias and Manzanos, and valuable coal deposits had been discovered nearby in the Puerco Basin. Yet, investors were doing little or nothing about them. During the entire decade of the 1870s, scarcely a half dozen mining claims were filed in Bernalillo County. That the lack of interest was attributable directly to the transportation problem is shown by the fact that in 1880, the year the railroad reached Albuquerque, a total of 137 claims were suddenly filed in the county.[35]

New Mexico also possessed vast forest resources, but no lumbering enterprise was possible without railroads. Agriculture and mercantile business, although well-established, likewise felt the pinch. If the Middle Valley was ever to rise to greatness as a commercial center, it must have the iron horse, or so opined William McGuinness in the pages of the Albuquerque *Review*.[36] Few of his readers were willing to challenge him on that point.

Rails in the direction of Albuquerque had actually been laid as early as 1866. In that year, a group of speculators led by General John C. Frémont formed the Atlantic and Pacific Railroad Company and obtained a charter from Congress that allowed them to build a transcontinental line from Springfield, Missouri, to San Francisco via the 35th parallel through central New Mexico. The announcement brought unbounded joy to Albuquerqueans, but the elation proved premature. After laying only 361 miles of track into the northeast corner of the Indian Territory, the A&P in 1872 went into receivership. Four years later, however, another company, the St. Louis and San Francisco Railroad (the Frisco), took over the A&P track, obtained possession of its original charter, and revived the plan to continue on to the Pacific. But in so doing, it had to reckon with a powerful new competitor, the Atchison, Topeka and Santa Fe Railway.[37]

Begun in 1868 as a small project to connect the two Kansas towns embodied in its name, the AT&SF very shortly expanded its sights and commenced aiming toward New Mexico and the Pacific Coast. By 1872 it had reached roaring Dodge City, and by the summer of 1878 its rails stretched to Trinidad, Colorado, near the northern approach to Raton Pass. The struggling Frisco had been left far behind, but it had not been forgotten by the Santa Fe company officials. In 1879, they arranged an agreement to bring together the interests of their railroad with those of the Frisco and the A&P so that jointly they could build a transcontinental railway using the old A&P charter. Under the plan, the Santa Fe was to install track as far as the Middle Valley of the Rio Grande and from that point, work would continue westward under the Atlantic and Pacific name. The agreement, complex in its manifold details, was not untypical in an era when railroad magnates resorted to the most intricate man-ueverings in a bid to win rights of way and spheres of influence over giant slices of the country.

One problem still confronted the AT&SF: it needed a charter from the territorial legislature to build into New Mexico. To that end W. B. Strong, general manager of the company, and Miguel A. Otero, who had extensive business interests in the East and had long been involved in railroad promotion, went to the capital and shepherded the charter through. It was granted to the New Mexico and Southern Pacific Railroad Company, the name of the subsidiary the AT&SF had formed to handle its operations in the Territory.

Like many western railroads of the period, the Santa Fe, in its haste to be first into a new region and to reach the Pacific, was building track faster than it could raise capital in the East. The enormous sums expended in construction were done in anticipation of future profits, but while work was in progress, the company had to scrimp to meet payrolls and bills. That fact was not always appreciated by territorial citizens, who tended to view the railroad as a giant corporation with access to unlimited funds. A misunderstanding of the point was to cost several New Mexico towns dearly.

As the Santa Fe, for example, approached Las Vegas, the first major community in the Territory, it presented the town fathers with a request for enormous concessions. The railroad wanted an outright gift of $10,000, a free right of way, thirty free acres of ground for a depot, and one-half interest in 400 acres of land for a suburb addition to Las Vegas. Local property owners were stunned, for they had expected to reap small fortunes selling land to the company. Now they were asked to make substantial donations for the privilege of being served by the railroad. Unwilling or unable to meet the demands, they watched in dismay as the AT&SF built a mile east of the plaza, an act that soon resulted in the growth of New Town and the withering away of the old business district.[38]

Even the city of Santa Fe, despite its rank as the political and mercantile hub of the Territory, faced difficulties with the AT&SF, as well as with another line, the Denver and Rio Grande. The D&RG, which was proposing to run track from Colorado down the center of New Mexico, sent its representatives to the capital in the spring of 1878. They came with their hands out, wanting $200,000, half in cash and half in county bonds; land donated for a depot; and free right of way

213

through the county. To the people of Santa Fe this looked unpleasantly like a demand for tribute. They also knew that any attempt to see the D&RG's terms would require unprecedented public expenditures, which could only be met by hiking the local tax rate. The feeling of the town was perhaps best expressed by a sage journalist who observed, "Better a cool adobe house free from debt, than a palace plastered all over with mortgages."[39]

Santa Fe's men of affairs rejected the D&RG proposals. For one thing, they believed that the railroad could not afford to pass them by and hence would soon have to soften its demands. For another, the advancing AT&SF seemed to offer a more promising alternative. Its agents were also in the capital, and rumor had it that the company was surveying passes through the Sangre de Cristo Mountains due west of Las Vegas, which would bring their line into Santa Fe. One report circulated that if Santa Feans continued to spurn the overtures of the D&RG, the AT&SF would be willing to build to the capital without asking for subsidies, since they would have a monopoly on all rail traffic.

As it happened, by 1879 the D&RG, beset with internal problems, temporarily shelved plans for further expansion into northern New Mexico. At the same time, the AT&SF began to question the wisdom of trying to reach the capital with its main line. As General Manager Strong announced publicly, "Our company are anxious to use all their funds in pushing west as fast as possible."[40] What he meant, reading between the lines, was that the railroad's primary goal was to reach the Pacific Coast and desires and needs of New Mexicans were only of minor concern. Surveyors, in fact, had determined that the best rail route lay through the Galisteo Basin and thence down the Rio Grande to the Middle Valley. That left Santa Fe, situated on its high plateau at the foot of the mountains, in isolation eighteen miles north of the track.

Appalled by the unexpected turn of events, civic leaders in the capital hurried to salvage what they could. After getting a pledge from the railroad—which, after all, was not eager to alienate potential customers—to build a feeder line from the main track, they called an election to approve issuance of bonds. The money raised, earmarked for construction costs, represented a significant contribution on the part of Santa Fe toward obtaining rail service. It was clearly a measure taken in desperation: the same measure, indeed, that had been rejected a year earlier during negotiations with the D&RG. With enthusiastic passage of the bond issue, work on the branch line commenced at a point known as Galisteo Junction (later renamed Lamy, in honor of the archbishop). And in the second week of February 1880, the last spike was driven at Santa Fe amidst tumultuous cheers from townspeople.[41]

Albuquerqueans looked with both consternation and alarm upon the treatment accorded Las Vegas and Santa Fe by the AT&SF. In the case of the former town, Editor William McGuinness had exclaimed early in the game: "The managers of the AT&SF Company have told the people of Las Vegas that they are not quite so liberal and considerate as most folks were led to believe by newspaper reports. They have given Vegas to understand that if she wants a railroad, she must pay for it, and then she may not get it to her liking. . . . What then must Albuquerque be prepared to do if she wants to have a finger in the pie?"[42] After seeing Las Vegas bypassed by a mile and Santa Fe missed by a good deal more than that, with the main line at least, nervous Albuquerqueans knew one thing for a certainty: haggling with the AT&SF was risky business.

José Leandro Perea had found that out in February 1878. At that time, the railroad was still at Trinidad, Colorado, preparing for the push over Raton Pass and first entry into New Mexico. Its "advance men," however, were far out front, surveying the route and arranging for rights of way. Five of them rolled into Bernalillo one afternoon on the Concord mail coach and alighted at the stage station. Among their number was Lewis Kingman (for whom Kingman, Arizona, would later be named), chief surveyor of the AT&SF, and Albert Alonzo Robinson, the company's chief engineer. Merchant Nathan Bibo, who was also the Bernalillo postmaster, saw them arrive and recalled afterward that the railroad men were impeccably dressed, prepossessing in appearance, and gave every indication of being "true representatives of the American man-of-the-world type, full of pep and energy."[43]

Their brisk manner suggested they were on an important errand, the precise nature of which was soon spread throughout the town. The company, it seemed, had selected Bernalillo as the chief division point on its transcontinental line, so here a bridge would be built across the Rio Grande, and offices, a roundhouse, and extensive yards established. By a touch of the AT&SF's magic wand, Bernalillo would be transformed into a shining metropolis, the foremost in the Territory.

Francisco Perea, former territorial delegate to Congress and nephew of José Leandro, was quickly summoned to a brief private meeting with the railroad representatives. After a bit, the entire delegation left on foot for the nearby house of Bernalillo's premier citizen. At the door, José Leandro Perea gave them a wintry smile and stiffly conducted the party into the main *sala*. Kingman and Robinson unrolled maps and in their direct, efficient manner commenced to explain the land needs of the company. Besides a right of way through Don José's vast domain, considerable acreage would be required on the eastern outskirts of Bernalillo for the offices and yards. The going price for such land, they said, was known to be $2 to $3 per acre, and they were fully empowered to negotiate a purchase.

To this offer, Perea's response was as startling as it was unwelcome. If the railroad wanted his land, it should be prepared to pay $425 an acre. Now it was the turn of the AT&SF men to grow frosty. Unaccustomed to receiving ultimatums, they were of no mind to continue the discussion any further. Rolling up their maps, they strode hurriedly back to the stage station. The coach, which had waited while the important passengers conducted their business, was soon rumbling south on the road toward Albuquerque. The whole affair had taken no more than forty-five minutes, but the events that transpired in that brief time were to have far-reaching consequences.[44]

Was it simple avarice and greed that led José Leandro Perea to set his exorbitant price? His personal wealth at the time was reputed to be in the neighborhood of 2 million dollars, a fortune representing the accumulated profits of his wide ranching, mercantile, and freighting activities.[45] Perhaps he was one of those men whose burning passion in life is to acquire money for its own sake; yet, if that was the case, he committed a serious error of judgment. Placing the railroad yards in Bernalillo, and the flowering of the town that must have inevitably followed, would have profited him enormously.

In all likelihood, José Leandro Perea's action toward the railroad was inspired by other motives. Now in his late fifties, he had witnessed the coming of the Americans in 1846 under General Kearny, seen the disruption of Hispanic life-ways, and, with his father and brothers, experienced the embarrassment and hardship produced by their humiliating flight during Sibley's Confederate invasion. Under the circumstances, he may well have viewed the AT&SF's advance men as a new breed of invaders introducing changes as unpalatable as those that had gone before. According to one tradition, Don José proved uncooperative because he could not bear to face the noisy disturbance that shops and switch engines would bring to drowsy Bernalillo.[46] Another objection was that the advent of trains would put him out of the freighing business. Among wealthy Hispanos of the Middle Valley, he was not alone in that fear. For example, José Francisco Chaves (stepson of Civil War Governor Henry Connelly) made public speeches opposing railroads because they threatened to drive freighters into bankruptcy.[47] What men like Perea and Chaves failed to perceive, as some farsighted Anglos were swift to point out, was that railroads, while eliminating long-distance business for wagons, actually created new opportunities for short hauling, through stimulation of the local economy.

The Albuquerque *Review* did not mince words when it took to task those New Mexicans who had raised a cry against the train. "Certain it is, to speak impartially, that in our opposition to a RR, some of us exhibit our supreme selfishness, as strikingly as others of us do our profound ignorance and almost superhuman indolence. Alas! Some of us do not wish to advance at all, but prefer to remain either stationary or to make a retrograde movement. But we've got to go, like it or not. We've got to advance anyway, even if we have to be dragged along by the triumphal ear of Progress."[48] The paper's words doubtless sounded reasonable to English-speaking Americans raised on the homilies of Ben Franklin. But to native Hispanos, whose lives were grounded in age-old customs and who by cultural upbringing were resistant to change, the new philosophy of enforced progress would take some getting used to.

In the tangled skein of historical events, the element of chance often carries more weight than the carefully articulated plans of men. But for the intransigence of José Leandro Perea, we can plausibly assume that Albuquerque would have been relegated to the status of a whistle-stop on the mighty AT&SF and that in its place Bernalillo would have soared onward, through mushroom growth, to become New Mexico's stellar city.

For a while it was by no means clear that Albuquerque would be able to capitalize on the opportunity that Bernalillo had so recently lost. Surveys showed that the best site for a railroad bridge to span the Rio Grande lay a dozen miles to the south, near Isleta Pueblo. At that point, the tracks would fork, after crossing the river, with the transcontinental line (under the A&P name) heading toward California, while the other branch continued down the west bank toward El Paso. The key question was where the AT&SF would decide to place its offices and yards—in the vicinity of the fork, in which case a new town could be expected to grow up; or near Albuquerque, where commercial facilities were already available.[49]

A happenstance of geography had pretty well precluded the possibility of tracks reaching the old Albuquerque plaza. The town, nestled in a bend of the river, was approximately a mile and a half west of a straight line the surveyors drew down the eastern side of the valley. Construction engineers preferred building along the straightest and most direct course. So even before any route decision was announced, Albuquerqueans were reconciled to the fact that policy-makers of the AT&SF were unlikely to allow a curve in the tracks just to accommodate the scant 2,000 residents of a backwater town on the Rio Grande.

During late June 1879, agents for the railroad arrived and began sounding out landholders to see if they would be willing to guarantee a right of way up to 200 feet in width.[50] Community leaders saw that now was the time to whip up public support, create a hospitable atmosphere, and show the company that its needs would be met, all by way of avoiding the disappointments that had plagued towns farther up the line. To this end, an open forum was held in the courthouse on July 5, with merchant Ambrosio Armijo presiding. One after another, influential citizens took the floor, expounded upon the benefits that would flow Albuquerque's way once it obtained rail service, and urged compliance with whatever the AT&SF demanded. There was even strong sentiment for granting the company a free right of way through the town's eastern limits as a goodwill gesture.[51]

By the end of the year, tracks had advanced from Las Vegas to within 80 miles of Albuquerque and the air was electric with excitement. There was an unaccustomed stir in the narrow dirt streets. New faces were seen at every turn, many of them belonging to opportunists who, anticipating a boom, were on the prowl for bargains in real estate. Rents rose steadily in value, and storekeepers expanded their establishments and enlarged the supply of merchandise. Henry Springer, having recovered following his financial reversals in 1874, opened the Mint Saloon on the southwest corner of the plaza, which featured, among other elegant furnishings, a Monarch billiard table.

Among those rushing to gain a favorable position before the railroad worked its miracle upon the town, Franz Huning was in the vanguard.

Now fifty-three years old, he had literally grown up with Albuquerque and knew, as well as any non-Hispano could, the temper and inner workings of the community. Even before the railroad fever had taken hold, he was quietly buying land, a tract that came to total about 700 acres, south and east of the plaza. In a short time, the property, ripe for subdivision, was destined to increase in value manyfold, allowing Franz to include in his memoirs a masterful understatement: "My investment in town lots yielded good profits."[52]

Early in January 1880, Chief Engineer Albert Robinson made the formal announcement that the AT&SF would build its depot and yards on the east side of the valley, a little over a mile from the plaza and astride the road leading to Carnué Canyon. In expectation of that decision, Franz Huning in the weeks before had taken the lead in improving the road as far as the depot site, and by December it was already known, appropriately, as Railroad Avenue (the present Central Avenue). Wise heads all agreed that it would become the principal thoroughfare in the Albuquerque of the future. Franz Huning was quite in favor of that, since both his mill and his home, La Glorieta, faced upon it.[53]

Just east of the Huning property, the road south to Las Barelas crossed Railroad Avenue. Beyond that road and stretching to the foot of the sandhills, the open floodplain as far as the proposed depot site contained scattered marshes interspersed with farm plots owned by sundry Albuquerque residents. Beginning in March 1880, three local citizens, claiming to represent the newly organized New Mexico Town Company, began purchasing that land at a furious pace. The three were Franz Huning, William C. Hazeldine, and Elias S. Stover. The Town Company was a subsidiary of the New Mexico and Southern Pacific Railroad Company, which in turn was an auxiliary of the AT&SF.

Officers of the railroad had formed (March 3) a real estate firm, the New Mexico Town Company, to serve as a thinly disguised shield for the acquisition of lands required in the vicinity of Albuquerque. Huning, Hazeldine, and Stover (acting as agents) were able to purchase properties at modest prices and these they deeded to the Company for the sum of one dollar. More land went to the railroad in this manner than was actually needed for a right of way, depot, and shops. Officials planned to sell the surplus after commercial development along the tracks had greatly inflated its price. By previous arrangement, the trio of agents was to get one-half of the profit received in those later sales.

Huning, Hazeldine, and Stover apparently suffered no censure by fellow citizens for their speculative activity on behalf of the railroad. In the climate of the day, such actions were looked upon merely as good business practice. Indeed, their conduct bore the mark of civic enterprise since it helped guarantee a sound working relationship between Albuquerque and the AT&SF. From that, all residents would benefit, although plainly some would benefit considerably more than others.[54]

By February 9, 1880, the new tracks had reached Galisteo, 67 miles to the north, and were pushing toward Albuquerque at the rate of a mile a day. On Wednesday afternoon, March 31, community leaders assembled to chart plans for a welcoming celebration. In the reception committee which they formed, we find familiar names of the men who held Albuquerque firmly in their grasp. On a motion of Elias Stover, Franz Huning was elected committee chairman. Stover and don Santiago Baca won election as vice-presidents on the motion of Judge Hazeldine. And Major Melchior Werner was elected secretary on a motion of Stover. The reins of power were indisputably concentrated in a few hands.[55]

On April 3, Editor McGuinness with unrepressed glee wrote, "This Saturday afternoon word came to this office that the construction train with its locomotive was puffing and fizzing half a mile south of don Juan Cristobal Armijo's house, thus placing the end of the track about two miles north of town. This makes it probable the train will be able to run up to the depot grounds on Monday next, at noon."[56] Exuberantly, he continued: "Let the day of our railroad reception be one ever to be remembered, and let all vie with each other in adding to its gaity, its decorum, and its hospitality to invited guests. There should be no ungenerous rivalries, no disorder, no inebriety, no offensive reflections cast upon anyone."[57] In a free-wheeling, frontier town such as Albuquerque, his call for restraint was quite in order.

The last rail was laid to the depot grounds by 4:00 P.M., April 5, 1880. From Alameda, where the Rio Grande commenced its U-bend to the west, the tracks shot south in a direct line to the site. The route roughly followed the course of the ancient riverbed, which the Rio Grande had abandoned long before the Spaniards came. At once, freight trains began to arrive with supplies and heavy materials for the contractors. A boxcar, pushed on to a sidetrack, served as temporary depot. And with scarcely a pause, grading continued down the valley toward the spot, below Albuquerque, selected for a river crossing. The gala ceremony and reception was delayed until April 22 to allow ample time for the arrival of railroad officials and invited dignitaries from Bernalillo, Santa Fe, and Las Vegas.

Dawn of the appointed day found the Albuquerque plaza bedecked with fluttering flags. By late morning, practically the entire population was jamming the streets, while parade marshals bustled about trying to sort out the units for a procession. At noon, a battery of artillery let loose a thunderous volley signaling the commencement of festivities. With cheers resounding from the housetops and spirited music floating on the midday breeze from the Ninth Cavalry Band, which had traveled down from Santa Fe for the occasion, the parade began wending its way along Railroad Avenue toward the depot. At the head marched the Grand Marshal and Army band, followed in turn by President of the Day Franz Huning in his carriage; orators and distinguished guests in their carriages; schoolchildren; horsemen with flashing silver ornaments on their bridles and saddles; and, finally, plain citizens, garbed in holiday finery, on their burros or on foot. Albuquerque's intense and universal jubilation was unmatched by anything that had ever gone before.

Once at the tracks, people crowded around two flat cars, rolled in earlier to serve as a speakers' platform. Franz Huning, attired in starchy formal dress, called the crowd to attention and opened the proceedings with these words: "We with one voice welcome the arrival of the first train of cars to the Central City of New Mexico. And [we] tender greetings and gratitude to the wisdom, capital and labor . . . of the AT&SF Railroad for placing us on the highway of nations."[58] "Central City of New Mexico" was just one of several catch-phrases then bandied about by local boosters. Albuquerque was also being called the "Queen City of the Rio Grande," and the "Chicago of the West," no doubt with the hope that such rhapsodic sloganeering would help attract the attention of eastern investors as well as ordinary folk looking for a town with a future. That sentiment, Huning encompassed in his concluding remarks: "We invite to her salubrious climate, to the immense and rich domain of New Mexico, the capital and the skilled and unskilled labor of the world."[59]

Other speeches followed, half in English, half in Spanish. Don Miguel Otero, now a vice-president of the AT&SF, spoke on behalf of the railroad. And even J. Francisco Chaves, who had once opposed railroad development, took the stand to praise the sunrise of a new era. Highest plaudits of the day, however, went to Judge William Hazeldine for his flowery address presented with the flourish of an ancient Greek senator. With voice upraised, he cried, "Today the new civilization of the East is brought into direct contact with the ancient civilization of New Mexico. Today the bell of the locomotive tolls the death knell of old foggyism, superstition and ignorance, and proclaims in clarion notes that henceforth knowledge, education, advancement and progress shall be the right of our people. Are we of Albuquerque prepared to take advantage of this opportunity and make this the epoch in the history of our town? I answer unequivocally, we are . . . !"[60]

The "clarion notes of progress," by which the judge would banish "old foggyism and superstition," was nothing less than a veiled call to cast off the Old World mores that had governed Albuquerque in the past. It was his wish, and that of many men like him, to see the new town brought into the mainstream of America as speedily as posible. With the railroad as an instrument of change, that goal now seemed within reach. The death knell, then, was really for Hispanic culture, which, despite Anglo rule since 1846, had continued to predominate in the Middle Valley. But if Albuquerque's Hispanos recognized in Judge Hazeldine's sugar-coated phrases a forecast of doom for their own cultural heritage, they failed to show it. Instead, they joined in the wild applause that greeted his retirement from the platform.

When the speeches and an assortment of lively tunes from the band had been completed, as many people as possible climbed aboard the ten cars of an excursion train, draped with patriotic bunting, for a free trip to Bernalillo. For many of the poor rural folk who crowded on, the thirty-minute ride at unheard of speeds was an experience never to be forgotten. Bernalillo welcomed its visitors with banquet tables spilling over with food and drink. In the front rank of greeting dignitaries stood none other than José Leandro Perea. Under the mellow atmosphere of the occasion, spokesmen of both towns agreed to put aside past differences and henceforth live in peace and goodwill.

The excursionists, well fed and primed with alcohol, were soon on their way back to Albuquerque. From the depot grounds, they hastened to the plaza to continue the celebration. There, barrels of native wine (with tin cups chained to them) had been placed at convenient points and an open invitation issued to anyone who wanted to drink his fill. At sunset the artillery roared anew, the military band struck up more brassy airs, and fireworks filled the dark dome of sky with a brilliant display. As the festivities and the day drew to a close, Father Donato Gasparri gave one last speech. In a fitting metaphor, he pointed out that the railroad had first entered the capital of Santa Fe, which represented the head of the Territory. But then it had reached Albuquerque, a town no less important because it served as the heart and center from which the blood of life flowed to nourish the whole body.[61]

The good father's allusion to Albuquerque as the circulatory organ sustaining all the Territory did not quite apply at the moment, but as a prophesy of things to come, it was right on target. No single event of the nineteenth century touched the town more deeply than the advent of the railroad, nor ultimately played a greater role in catapulting it to a position of preeminence among New Mexican communities. In the decades ahead, Albuquerqueans would look back upon 1880 as a benchmark year. Among the exhausted and intoxicated revelers who struggled home in darkness following Father Gasparri's speech were many who would play a key role in the city's transformation.

Growing Pains

PETER ("SHORTY") PARKER KNEW a promising opportunity when he saw one. On the day Albuquerqueans gathered around the flatcars to hear jubilant speakers bid the railroad welcome, he had mingled in the crowd with the rest. But his mind had been on business, not on the roistering of the moment. The bare, sandy land on either side of the tracks contained not a single building then, only stacks of rails, ties, and other construction materials. Yet, he could foresee that in a brief time the empty ground around the depot and tracks would be bustling with activity.

Early the following morning, while much of the populace was still abed nursing hangovers, Shorty Parker went diligently to work. Near the point where Railroad Avenue crossed the tracks, he paced off a lot 6 feet square and claimed it by squatter's rights. Using a shovel, he scooped a hole in the sand and into this makeshift cooler deposited bottles of beer. Several broken boards scavenged from the environs of the boxcar depot served both as a lid for the cellar and a floor for the proprietor to stand on. A large wooden barrel turned up-side down became a bar. Upon its surface was placed an open valise filled with liquor. The "saloon" had no name, no roof, no canvas awning, nor any chairs, tables, or spittons. The last item would have been superfluous anyway, since customers were free to squirt tobacco juice on the bare ground wherever they chose. Henry Tice, a surveyor who debarked from the railroad the very next day, was quite astonished by Shorty's primitive establishment, and commented: "With his ten-rod stuff in a suitcase and his beer under his feet he was ready for business and ballyhooed his delectables at two bits a drink—take your choice."[1]

But for his novel and short-lived saloon venture, Shorty Parker's name would certainly have been lost to memory. With his eye riveted on the making of a fast buck, he probably cared not a whit, even if he could have perceived it through some second sense, that history would honor him as the first merchant in the up and coming city of New

Albuquerque. Rather quickly, another saloon, the Concannon House, muscled in on Shorty's early monopoly by opening for business in two spacious tents pitched several hundred yards to the south and adjacent to the tracks. Likely, Shorty Parker loaded stock and fixtures into his barrel and caught a train to one of the towns down the valley near the tracks' end. At least, he was heard of no more in Albuquerque.

For the first few months, the new townsite beyond the depot grounds consisted of little more than surveyors' stakes set out in neat rows among the wheat stubble and dry corn stalks of the previous year's crop. Scattered here and there were numerous small signs advertising lots at $10 each, "Make your own selection." "Talk about acres of diamonds!" exclaimed one early visitor. "They were right there in the sand, but we didn't see them."[2]

Land speculators and potential businessmen, arriving daily to look over prospects, either slept in boxcars along with railroad employees or paid $.50 for a buckboard ride to the plaza 2 miles away where proper lodging could be found. As the year progressed, a cluster of tents, shanties, and even a few substantial frame and adobe buildings sprouted along Railroad Avenue. And the price of land began to rise.

The prime real estate surrounding the tracks and known as the "original townsite" began to be developed by the New Mexico Town Company, which, as we have seen, was the railroad corporation that acquired the property through the aid of Huning, Hazeldine, and Stover. The Company soon assigned Colonel Walter G. Marmon, a civil engineer who had done occasional work for the railroad, to survey, mark, and name new streets for the townsite. Marmon, a native of Ohio and Union veteran, eventually settled and married at Laguna Pueblo, 40 miles from Albuquerque.[3] Streets running north to south between the railroad and the border of Old Town, he unimaginatively named First through Six-teenth. Since First faced the tracks, it was referred to by practically everyone as Front Street. To the cross streets paralleling the already established Railroad Avenue, Colonel Marmon gave the names of min-erals—Copper, Gold, Silver, Lead, and Coal—no doubt a reflection of the hope then current that Albuquerque was on its way to becoming a major shipping point for the mining industry. To no one's surprise, the three streets south of Coal were designated Huning, Hazeldine, and Stover.

Moving east of the depot grounds, Marmon marked off a wide thoroughfare in line with the tracks, which he called Broadway because, as one observer wrote, he thought every city worth its salt ought to have a street by that name.[4] The next streets, parallel to Broadway, were Arno (in honor of a son of Franz Huning), Edith, Walter, and, finally, High street, so dubbed because it ran through the gravelly hills edging the valley. Actually the colonel had gotten carried away with his surveying and laid more streets than were called for in the original instructions. When he got to High, the Town Company, believing Albuquerque would never reach that far, ordered him to stop.[5] The broad, straight streets thus formed crossed each other at right angles and stood in marked contrast to the narrow and meandering thoroughfares that extended in a maze from the old plaza, just to the west.

While the New Mexico Town Company had preempted the choicest property adjacent to the railroad yards, certain visionary individuals snapped up available tracts nearby and started to plat new subdivisions. Elias Stover was one. On lands southeast of the plaza, he began plans for a housing addition, but before he had gone very far, he saw a chance to reap a quick profit, and he sold out. The buyers were Mariano Armijo (son of Ambrosio Armijo) and a newcomer, William E. Talbott. They divided the tract into 800 residential lots, but sales, in what continued to be known as "Stover's Addition," were slow for many years, mainly because of the distance from the railroad.[6]

Several subdivisions directly south of the Town Company's property fared better. They included the Atlantic & Pacific Addition, which attracted railway employees; the Baca Addition, owned by Santiago Baca, whose investments in real estate and a thriving wholesale liquor business were causing his fortunes to snowball; and subdivisions owned by various members of the old Armijo clan. But the project that showed the most promise was the Huning Highland Addition, founded east of the tracks and facing the depot. It was convenient to the railroad and had the added advantage of being on elevated ground that sloped upward toward the sandhills. Well-drained and safe from flooding, the addition quickly became a prestige suburb. Franz Huning was the main backer, although his junior partner, Thomas F. Phelan, a young lawyer recently arrived from Michigan, proved to be the driving force that ensured the development's success. Elias Stover also had a small financial interest in the project. By 1888 some 63 percent of the 536 lots had been sold, bringing Huning more than $35,000.[7]

By 1881 a building boom was well under way in what would become the business district of New Town. The first substantial structure was raised by Lyman Beecher Putney. In 1876, Putney, a retailer in Lawrence, Kansas, decided to move west and sell supplies to contractors for the AT&SF. He first located at Trinidad, Colorado, where he built a store of pine panels, 100 feet long and 70 feet wide. The following year, wishing to keep ahead of the railroad, he dismantled his building, section by section, loaded it in ox-drawn wagons, and rolled down to Las Vegas, where he put the thing back together and was in business. Next door was a dance hall in which the favorite sport on Saturday night was shooting out the lights. The walls of Putney's store were soon amply ventilated with bullet holes.

In 1880 he moved again. Loading his now well-traveled store on flatcars, he betook himself to Albuquerque. On the corner of First and Railroad Avenue (later the site of the Y.M.C.A.), Putney raised the bullet-ridden walls once more. For several years, his place of business also doubled as a residence. Nights, Indians who had come in to trade were allowed to roll up in their blankets on the floor. The proprietor slept in

225

a hammock slung close to the rafters. Putney claimed later that he kept his bed high in the air to escape bed bugs and stray lead fired by rowdies who went on sprees in the streets.[8]

Like the Putney Store, others of Albuquerque's earliest structures arrived on railroad cars. They were called "perhaps houses," because they could be easily taken apart and removed, in case greener pastures beckoned the owners to another place.[9] Before long, however, the tents, shanties, and "perhaps houses" gave way to more durable and attractive buildings. Lumber, fired brick, cut and cast stone, and iron, brought in by train, were now available for construction, although adobe, owing to its cheapness and accessibility, also continued to be used. During 1882 alone, 5,000 tons of quarried stone reached Albuquerque builders by freight car.[10]

The first structure to reflect the new elegance in architecture was the Armijo House, an eye-catching hotel of frame, three stories high with a mansard roof. Owner Mariano Armijo thought that the up-to-date "city style" would attract guests more quickly than the traditional adobe architecture of the hostelries near the plaza. A. S. "Scott" Moore, the manager, set out to make the Armijo House the best in the Territory, and, according to testimonials of satisfied customers, he succeeded. One of his first rules was that patrons must wear coats in the dining room. Two work-clad cowboys immediately challenged the edict by forcing their way to a table. When Moore ordered them to leave, they came at him with their fists and a brawl erupted, of the wild free-swinging variety usually seen only in saloons. The manager bested both men and sent them flying through the front door. It was a small victory for gentility in rough-and-tumble Albuquerque.[11]

The genial and popular Moore was a loyal civic booster. Vermont tourist C. M. Chase, who spoke with him soon after the hotel opened, remarked, "Scott Moore is full in the faith that Albuquerque is the New Mexico pivot. He is fully confident that every dollar in real estate will improve 50 to 100 per cent every six months for two years at least. Having seen it improve 100 to 300 per cent during the past six months, his conclusion does not seem so very extravagant, after all."[12]

The Armijo House, perched on the southwest corner of Third and Railroad Avenue, shortly faced another symbol of town progress, the A. A. Grant Building. It comprised two stories: the lower floor provided space for four stores, and the upper floor housed the justly famous Grant Opera House. With a seating capacity of 1,000, it offered Albuquerqueans their first taste of dramatic and musical performances. Canadian Angus A. Grant came to New Mexico as a bridge contractor for the AT&SF in 1880. For a time, he worked on the railroad 60 miles west of Albuquerque at a site that became known as Grant's Camp, which was the beginning of the modern town of Grants. By 1882, he had moved to Albuquerque where he launched his own construction firm (called Grant Brothers Construction Company, after his brothers Lewis and John joined him in 1886). He also invested heavily in municipal utilities. For the next twenty years, until his departure for Los Angeles,

Angus Grant was to figure prominently in shaping the new Albuquerque.[13]

In 1882, a group of local business men organized the Albuquerque Hotel Company to underwrite a new hotel, the San Felipe. Located on the corner of Fifth and Gold (site of the present Dennis Chávez Federal Building), it was erected over a two-year period by pioneer Albuquerque builder Edward Medler, at the then staggering cost of $103,000. The three-story brick structure contained eighty rooms, including ornate "bridal parlors." A tower rising 40 feet above the ornamented roof lent substance to its claim of being the foremost hotel in the Territory, outstripping in luxury even the Armijo House.

One of the promoters of the San Felipe was Colonel Gurdon W. Meylert, a stern moralist. Probably at his behest, the architects provided the building a separate ladies' entrance with stairs giving access to the upper levels. The intention was to spare female guests the ordeal of passing through the main lobby and mingling with uncouth, cigar-smoking men. Colonel Meylert was also a temperance advocate, an unpopular position among hard-drinking Albuquerqueans. By force of argument, he was able to prevail upon his associates to ban liquor from the San Felipe's premises. In the space that would normally have been used for a club or saloon, he introduced a library. When the territorial legislature in 1889 established the University of New Mexico at Albuquerque, Colonel Meylert managed to have the first meeting of the Board of Regents convene in the San Felipe's library room. Perhaps he saw it as a vindication of his belief that education had the power to crowd out intemperance and immorality?[13]

While impressive edifices, such as the San Felipe and the Grant Building, were rising at scattered points within the new townsite, more modest business houses were going up in the intervening spaces. As early as 1882, Front (or First) Street facing the tracks boasted a solid line of stores and saloons for several blocks. There and on Railroad Avenue, merchants ran up false fronts, painting fake windows near the top, to give the appearance of a second story. It was a curiously pretentious gesture, common in frontier communities. Many places were built 4 to 5 feet above ground level, with high steps leading to their porches, as a hedge against flooding. That same year, a correspondent for *Harper's Magazine* noted that, "Buildings stood in sturdy ranks . . . outlining the anatomy of the town that was to be."[15]

At first, Railroad Avenue, since it was the main artery leading to the old plaza, gave fair promise of becoming Albuquerque's prestige business street. But before long, many new firms were gravitating to Gold, one block south, and putting up handsome office buildings, thereby challenging Railroad's early position of dominance. The shift was no doubt sparked by the AT&SF's decision to place its depot near the lower end of Gold.

Privately owned utilities were soon providing Albuquerqueans with a number of the amenities residents of more cosmopolitan areas had come to expect. The Albuquerque Gas Company, whose board listed Huning as president and Hazeldine as secretary, erected a plant that took coal, brought in by railway, and converted it to gas. Illumination of the streets by gas lights proved not only a decided convenience, but it helped, if only in small measure, to check crime in the dance-hall district that had sprouted near the tracks. By 1883 a rudimentary telephone system (started the previous year by Miguel Otero, Sr.) was in operation, although the total number of subscribers was just thirty-four. There was no long-distance service until 1905. Also, a water works had been organized. It catered mainly to large establishments, such as hotels, since most citizens found it simpler and cheaper to sink a shallow well in their back yards.

The pride of Albuquerque, however, was the Street Railway Company, incorporated late in 1880. By the end of the first year, it had eight mule-drawn cars and 3 miles of track connecting the plaza with "New Town" and the suburb of Barelas. Again, Huning and Hazeldine were among the founders, but the president and guiding spirit was Oliver E. Cromwell, a New Yorker who had arrived in 1879 and begun investing in real estate.[16] For $.10 passengers could ride in the open cars from the railroad depot to the end of the line at Elias Stover's house near the plaza. The vehicles were so light that high winds often blew them off the tracks. Riders grew accustomed to assisting the conductor in lifting them back on.

The mule cars operated in the most casual manner, reflecting more the slow pace of old Albuquerque than the hurried pace of the new. Hispano drivers, perched on stools and leisurely puffing cornhusk cigarettes, gladly held their mules while ladies finished their shopping. When the need for a drink came upon them, the drivers were in the habit of stopping for a half hour or so in front of a handy saloon. Anyone who climbed aboard and lacked the fare was allowed to charge it. Another custom, which caused much raising of eyebrows, received comment in the local press: "It is a common occurrence to see females of questionable reputations seated boldly on the front platform, ofttimes holding the reins."[17]

In the 1890s, a single draft horse replaced the pair of mules as motive power. The sturdy animal wore a large brass bell around its neck, the loud jingling alerting passengers a half mile ahead to the streetcar's approach. The line had a rush hour each morning and evening when it hauled workmen to and from the railroad yards. "But for the rest of the time," recalled one early-day patron, "it was mostly a sporting proposition for the young and agile who would leap aboard the rear platform while the conductor-driver was busy at the other end."[18] Speed was not part of the service. Quite likely, a popular refrain of the day, uttered wherever horse and mule systems operated, was often repeated in Albuquerque. "If you're in a hurry walk, but if you have time, take the streetcar."[19]

The light, narrow-gage tracks ran down the center of Railroad Avenue on an elevated grade that varied from a few inches to 2 feet. The street itself was a stretch of loose sand and dust during dry weather and a quagmire of mud when it rained. For the benefit of pedestrians, rough planks were nailed to the ties between the rails in the three blocks from

First Street to the Armijo House. That was the only sidewalk Albuquerque
had for several years.[20]

The Street Railway Company, despite all its inefficiency, assumed an importance that went far beyond the primary function of providing transportation. Its car tracks served as a visible umbilical cord, linking the aging parent drowsing around its plaza to the bumptious infant taking on new life in the shadow of the railroad depot. Old-timers had banked heavily on the old and new towns growing together to become a single thriving metropolis. They envisioned a solid line of stores and residences walling both sides of Railroad Avenue, lured there by easy access to the streetcars. True, the community would still have an east end and a west end, with concentrations of business at either extremity, but at least Albuquerque would be one.

That fond hope was to founder in the decade of the 1880s, for unseen economic and social forces set loose by the coming of the railroad were to promote division rather than unity and leave Albuquerque seemingly fractured beyond repair. Also, the great distance between the original town and the AT&SF tracks, almost 2 miles, precluded joining the separate parts to form a unified municipality. From upper stories of the Armijo House or the Grant Building, New Towners could look westward across the depressingly bare floodplain, to the low cluster of adobe buildings huddled around the towers of San Felipe Neri Church. Even the most optimistic among them could scarcely imagine that population growth would ever bridge the yawning gap.

The first serious breech between the people of east and west Albuquerque was precipitated, inadvertently, by the United States Post Office. On February 10, 1881, it issued a charter establishing a post office in the new town and naming F. H. Kent (a junior member of the Town Company) as postmaster. Immediately the office was installed in a small structure owned by Kent, located on Third Street, across from the Armijo House.[21] It contained a mere twelve boxes and the lobby was so tiny that patrons, often as many as a hundred at a time, had to line up outside and await their turn at the delivery window.[22] Even greater inconvenience was caused by the difficulty of directing letters to the proper post office, since incoming mail, addressed simply to "Albuquerque" could be meant either for the office on the plaza or the new one on Third Street. A visiting postal inspector in 1882 concluded that the best way to deal with the problem was to close down the old station and let the new handle all Albuquerque's business—and he did just that.

The fury of the folk who lived around the plaza broke like a storm. The railroad town, scarcely two years old, seemed on its way to relegating the original community to second-class status, so the old-timers fought back. By burying the postal department in petitions and by enlisting the sympathetic intervention of New Mexico's territorial delegate in Washington, they applied sufficient pressure to have the plaza post office reopened. But their victory was not complete. Still grappling with the knotty problem of two Albuquerques, the postal service, invoking its formal power to certify community names, ordered the old plaza area to be called, henceforth, Armijo, and granted the new town sole right to use Albuquerque. The grasping trackside community was not only taking away the plaza's commerce, but was being given license to steal its name, or so it appeared.[23]

The matter, nevertheless, was far from settled, and local controversy over who was entitled ownership of Albuquerque's historic name continued for several years. Then, in 1886, the post effected a compromise by designating the west station, Old Albuquerque, and the east station, New Albuquerque. It proved an easy way out, particularly since by this time people had developed the habit of referring to the former as Old Town and the latter as New Town. Later, of course, as New Albuquerque reached out to engulf the plaza, the day came when it could legitimately drop the qualifying adjective. The elastic expansion of boundaries, through urban sprawl, would finally create one Albuquerque, but not before the mid-twentieth century.[24]

Early discord arising from the post office squabble spilled over and fueled another debate in the widening rift between east and west enders. Involved was the return of the county offices, which, it will be remembered, had been transferred to Bernalillo in 1878. Albuquerque, never reconciled to the loss, plotted constantly to get them back. Facing both Old Town and the booming New Town, Bernalillo's partisans evidently decided they could not prevail, so they put up virtually no resistance when, in May 1883, the county commissioners held an election on removal. By a huge majority, 1,395 to 18, Albuquerque won back the county seat.[25] Bernalilloans may have acquiesced so easily because they figured that the courthouse would actually go to New Albuquerque, not their archrival of long standing, Old Albuquerque.

As might have been foreseen, both sides of town wanted the courthouse and were willing to put up a struggle for it. People on the west end moved with dispatch and obtained a petition signed by citizens willing to underwrite the cost of "a suitable Court House in the Old town of Albuquerque."[26] Quite unexpectedly, officers of the Street Railway Company, mostly New Towners, came out in their support. They had determined that a location near the plaza would mean added passengers (and profits) for the streetcars since residents on the east side would be continually running over to conduct county business. The unseemly quarrel dragged on for several years, during which New Town supporters attempted, unsuccessfully, to gain possession of the county offices through the courts. By the spring of 1886, backers in Old Town, following through on their earlier pledge, had raised a sizeable building fund. That was enough, apparently, to sway the county commissioners, who ruled that the courthouse should go to Old Albuquerque. The overjoyed victors draped the plaza with bunting and flags and ignited nighttime bonfires to show their approval.

In the years between the removal from Bernalillo and the construction of a permanent courthouse, the county offices occupied several temporary locations. For a time, they were domiciled in a building owned by Santiago Baca. Next they were moved to Ambrosio Armijo's spacious house on the east side of the plaza. Finally, the offices borrowed rooms in New Town on the first and second floors of the Medler Building on south Second Street.[28] By late 1886, the new courthouse, situated just southeast of the plaza, facing Railroad Avenue and the streetcar tracks, was well under way. The firm of Bernardinelli and Palladino erected the three-story brown sandstone structure at a cost of approximately $62,000.[29] A county jail, also of sandstone, was built a short distance away (on the southwest corner of Central and Rio Grande) at the same time.

New Albuquerque may have lost the courthouse fight because its attention was diverted by the prospect of bigger game: the bagging of the territorial capital, which it wished to see transferred from Santa Fe. In recent years, competition between Albuquerque and Santa Fe for leadership in political and economic affairs had nurtured the growth of petty jealousies and envy. The situation was aggravated by the press in each place, which took delight in malicious attacks upon the rival town. Depth of the bitterness that developed over the years is revealed by an editorial in the *Santa Fe New Mexican* following a fire that destroyed part of the paper's offices during July 1888. An Albuquerque newspaper had used the occasion to deliver some unkind jibes, and the *New Mexican,* in printer's ink fortified with acid, responded in kind. "One paper, and that a disgrace to journalism in New Mexico, has taken advantage of the situation . . . and made lying and dirty remarks about the misfortune which befell the *New Mexican* and the people of Santa Fe. The *Albuquerque Democrat,* that Judas Iscariot of New Mexico and professional blackmailer, was that paper. Of course nothing else could be expected from that source."[30]

The first concerted effort by Albuquerqueans to win the capital away from Santa Fe came at the meeting of the legislative assembly in February 1884. Santa Fe political boss, lawyer Thomas Benton Catron, helped push a bill to appropriate money for a new capitol building to replace the Spanish colonial Governors Palace, then still in use. Passage, he believed, would guarantee that the capital, for the foreseeable future anyway, would stay put. A representative from Socorro, who wanted it moved to his town, brought up his own bill to settle the question by a territorial election. Even the members from Albuquerque voted against that. They also worked to defeat Catron's bill, but at the final ballot found themselves outflanked. Diego Archuleta, an assembly member from Rio Arriba County, and a man closely allied with the Santa Fe faction, was suffering from an extreme case of pneumonia. Nevertheless, he had himself carried into the House of Representatives so he could deliver an important vote, one that helped pass the appropriations bill and keep the capital in Santa Fe. His exertions, however, led to his death a few days later.[31]

Even though their first efforts had been stymied, Albuquerque partisans refused to give up. Through the remainder of the 1880s and well into the 1890s, they poured money and energy into an intense lobbying effort designed to bring the capital south. Santa Feans wailed that the sums they had to expend at each new legislative session to block a capital removal bill amounted to thousands of dollars. Yet, in the long run their money was well spent. In the final years of the century, Albuquerqueans abandoned the campaign as hopeless.[32]

The protracted scrimmaging with Santa Fe over the capital question, and with Old Town over the issues of the courthouse and location of the post office, reflected New Albuquerque's acute yearning to add luster to the town name. Unabashedly, civic leaders sang hymns of praise to the community's future, while lending their influence and pocketbooks to any movement dedicated to bringing in new business, whether government or private. The boosterism, crass in tone and self-serving in purpose, was aimed largely at eastern investors and prospective eastern emigrants. If the pitch was often shrill and the slogans, extolling Albuquerque's charms, often exaggerated, the reason could be found in the competition the town fathers faced. It came not only from Santa Fe and Las Vegas, but from outside the Territory. El Paso, Tucson, and the nascent cities of southern California were all booming, thanks to new railroad service, and all were elbowing forward in a race to become a key center of business in the Southwest. The spirit of the age seemed to be expressed by Los Angeles ministers who left their Sunday pulpits after the sermon to mingle with the congregtion and sell real estate.[33]

During the first five years of its infancy, from 1880 to 1885, New Albuquerque's promoters labored under a severe handicap, owing to the fact that the town remained unincorporated. The Townsite Company, as an auxiliary arm of the AT&SF, was concerned wholly with land speculation, and it provided citizens with no legal governing body. The United States marshal and county officers, including the sheriff, had jurisdiction over the townsite, but they could scarcely give their undivided attention to New Albuquerque's needs. Citizens themselves partially filled the gap by forming a county precinct and electing on February 1, 1881, a constable and justice of the peace.[34] One year later, local business men moved to take up more of the slack by creating the Board of Trade. Ostensibly a "chamber of commerce" composed of practically all leading merchants and professional men, this body in effect became the town government. Among other things, it established a Merchants' Police Force to maintain order, and assessed members for funds to pay for municipal projects. Conspicuous on the Board were the names of Huning, Hazeldine, and Stover.[35]

This situation was tolerated until 1884, when, coinciding with the push to gain the county seat from Bernalillo, Santiago Baca and William Hazeldine, along with a young lawyer newly arrived in town, Harvey B. Fergusson, spearheaded a drive for incorporation. On July 28 of that year, Grant's Opera House hosted a public meeting, which led to the securing of a town charter and the issuance of a call for an election to incorporate. In the balloting, held June 4, 1885, New Towners approved the action almost four to one. At a follow-up election, July 4, merchant Henry N. Jaffa became Albuquerque's first mayor.[36]

Jaffa had served as president of the Board of Trade, so he was as qualified for the job as anyone. Moreover, he was hand in glove with the tight coterie of men who occupied the town's topmost rung on the economic and social ladder. Like many Jewish merchants, Henry Jaffa, a native of Germany, had come to the Southwest in prerailroad days and shared in the general prosperity that followed. Before moving to Albuquerque, he and his brother Samuel had developed a prestigious mercantile firm in Trinidad, Colorado.[37]

With Jaffa, four trustees were elected to constitute a municipal governing board. All were small business men; none had held positions of prominence before. Indications are that they had come to office with the approval of persons like Hazeldine and Stover, who preferred to stay in the political background and attend to their commercial empires. The Board of Trustees abandoned the old policy, employed by the former Board of Trade, of raising revenues by assessing merchants for "voluntary" contributions. Instead, it obtained municipal funds through the lucrative sale of business licenses. Saloon keepers paid the largest fee for a license and bond, $450, but that charged hotel managers, shop owners, and professional men, though smaller, was commensurately stiff.[38]

The Board of Trustees was empowered to pass municipal ordinances—the first ones were concerned with regulation of dance halls, gambling dens, and saloons—and to grant franchises to utility companies.[39] The Albuquerque Electric Light Company, founded in 1883 by Angus Grant, asked for and received a forty-eight year contract to furnish the town with arc light.[40] Grant also owned the Water Works Company, which received a franchise to develop a municipal water system, consisting of a reservoir (built in 1886 in the East Heights at a cost of $110,000), pumping station, underground mains, and hydrants. Other franchises went to the Street Railway Company and the Gas Company. The Board of Trustees by floating bond issues, assumed reponsibility for development of sewers, a fire department, and street maintenance. By 1890 most of the streets in the business district were graded, guttered, and lined with boardwalks.

In 1890 the territorial legislature passed a new law allowing larger towns to reincorporate as a city, governed by a mayor and aldermen. New Albuquerque, ever vigilant for advantage, seized the opportunity and scheduled an election on the first Tuesday in April 1891. By a thumping majority, the populace declared in favor of city status. As a result, New Town (now with a population of 3,785) was divided into four wards, each ward having the right to elect two aldermen to the city council.[41]

At about the same time, Albuquerque was drawn into legal proceedings involving the municipality's original Spanish grant. In 1891, the United States House of Representatives established a Court of Private Land Claims to settle the validity of land grants in New Mexico and Colorado. Members of the traveling court reached Albuquerque on December 8 of that year and began examining evidence that would support the city's claim to a legal grant, believed conceded to it under Spanish law. The plaza would have been at the center of the grant, but New Town fell well inside its supposed boundaries. Confirmation of the claim seemed to hinge upon finding the original grant papers of 1706, and so city officers offered a reward for their recovery. Even though the documents never came to light, the court, on the basis of secondary evidence, ruled in favor of confirming the grant.[42] The gratification that judgment brought to Albuquerque's city government, however, was of short duration. Congress, reserving the right of final confirmation, reversed the court's decision and disallowed the claim. Had it stood, the municipality would have received a valuable block of land, and the pattern of urban growth might have assumed a different direction. Little Atrisco, which had filed for approval of its own grant, had better luck and, after considerable litigation, received approval and a new patent in 1905.[43]

Inevitably, as New Albuquerque filled out and prospered during the 1880s and 1890s, the Old Town declined in importance and influence. Some of the original merchants at first tried opening branch stores in the new railroad town, but when commercial activity rapidly waned in the plaza area, they closed down their establishments there and moved all business to the branches. Many of them, however, continued to maintain their residences in Old Town, commuting to work each day on the streetcar. They often shared seats with native folk who had found steady employment in the railroad yards and crowded the streetcars each morning, lunches in hand. The sudden flurry of jobs provided by the railroad, both in the Albuquerque shops and on section gangs, as tracks were laid south and west, offered the first real opportunity for working-class New Mexicans to break free of the grinding and unprofitable labor that for centuries had bound them to their own small subsistence farms or to the estates of the powerful dons. The economic impact of the railroad thus created waves that touched the lives of practically all who lived in the Middle Valley.[44]

Scarcely less far-reaching were the effects, some good and some bad, upon the old social order. The horde of Anglos, freshly arrived from the East, brought with them attitudes and prejudices poorly tuned to New Mexico's traditional society. As Roy A. Stamm, who came as a boy in this uneasy period, wrote years afterward, the natives of Old Albuquerque looked upon "the discourteous newcomers in New Town as loud-mouthed, money-mad, and so restless they have neither leisure nor appreciation of the things life grants to those who value them."[45]

The new residents, for their part, tended to view Hispanic Albuquerqueans as strange and backward, and to disparage their unfamiliar language and customs. Unlike their predecessors, who before 1880 had congenially embraced life in Old Town, the latest breed of Anglos was impatiently progressive and smugly confident that it was their manifest destiny to build a new community trackside that would be a perfect model of the standard American midwestern or eastern town. Editor William McGuinness, a loyal member of the old guard, found the intolerant notions prevailing in New Albuquerque particularly disturbing. In print, he condemned rowdyism common in the saloons along Front Street and contrasted it, much as Spruce Baird had done on the occasion of the election riot back in 1851, with the law-abiding character of the local Hispano population.

In the late 1870s, McGuinness had been one of the leading boosters of the railroad, even when it announced its intention to place the tracks 2 miles east of the plaza. He had championed growth in both the old and new towns, believing that "the magical changes wrought by American enterprise" could be channeled toward the making of a single harmonious community.[46] His optimism, however, dissipated quickly. The majority of his fellow countrymen, it became apparent, lacked the editor's enthusiasm and respect for the Middle Valley's original inhabitants. McGuinness bravely took up the cudgel on behalf of his Hispano neighbors and used his paper in their defense. To cite a single case: he unmercifully flailed the "many Americans who . . . act towards Mexican women as if they, as a class, were a race of harlots."[47] And later in large type, he issued A WARNING, to wit, "Respectable native New Mexican families should be very guarded in allowing their marriageable daughters to associate with or form alliances with strangers coming into the Territory."[48] His liberal crusade, unfortunately, bore little fruit.

A few of the more adventurous Hispanos boldly entered the aggressive business and political world of the Anglos in New Albuquerque and won a respected place. Notable in this regard were several members of the resilient Armijo family and Santiago Baca. Personally ambitious, Baca became a power in Republican politics and led the fight to wrest the county seat from Bernalillo. His widespread popularity allowed him to win the office of county sheriff in 1884, beating out three-term incumbent Perfecto Armijo. His name also cropped up with some frequency on boards of directors of various civic associations, but usually he was a lone Hispano in a sea of Anglos. The fact was, New Town and Old Town, though closely joined by economic ties, gradually drifted apart socially. By the end of the century, the polarization had crystallized so that, culturally anyway, Albuquerque was more a divided community than ever.

William McGuinness had discerned the drift of things at an early date. His dream of a town that borrowed the best from its two ethnic elements and combined them to form a new and unique social fabric went a glimmering. Late in 1880, he put the *Review* up for sale, and in a farewell to readers, expressed his disappointment that Old Town, as he so accurately perceived, was destined to become a stepchild in its own house. "Goodby!" he wrote. "The time has come for us to yield up those expectations because we see no longer any hope for their fulfillment."[49]

On the southwestern frontier, after the railroad came, small presses and small newspapers seemed to sprout like weeds. In new boom towns they offered their owners a quick source of influence and a tool for gaining political power. So, even as William McGuinness was closing shop (he sold the *Review* and it was moved to Santa Fe), others rushed in to fill the vacuum. Among the earliest was E. W. Deer, a health-seeker from the East, who launched Albuquerque's first daily, the *Golden Gate,* on June 4, 1880. Unhappily, after putting out only two issues, he fell critically ill and thirty-three days later died.[50]

Deer's press was acquired by the Albuquerque Publishing Company, a firm organized by a group of local business men who wanted to start their own paper as a forum for the promotion of the Republican party and the fortunes of New Albuquerque. The first issue of the Company's *Albuquerque Daily Journal* hit the streets on October 14, 1880. Its masthead listed a former Missouri printer, James S. Spradling, as manager and editor, Franz Huning as president, and William C. Hazeldine as secretary. Spradling left for Las Cruces the following year and William S. Burke was brought in as the new editor. Burke had landed in Albuquerque in 1880 as superintendent of the Pacific Coal Company. Formerly a newspaper editor in Kansas, he seems to have known Elias Stover there, and doubtless it was Stover who recommended him to Huning and Hazeldine for the top job on the *Journal.*

William Burke had practically no formal education, but he could dash off stories with crispness and an elán that won readers. Nor was he hesitant about criticizing and rewriting his own work. According to the *Journal* staff, his favorite saying was, "The scissors are mightier than the pen." A fellow journalist, Horace B. Hening, once declared that "Burke could take the hide off in an editorial cleaner and deeper than any editor I have ever known."[51] Perhaps because of his own educational deficiencies, Burke led the drive to organize the first public school system in Bernalillo County. Upon being elected county school superintendent in 1884, he left his position with the *Journal.*

Long before that, Huning and Hazeldine had concluded that publishing a newspaper was not in their line and so they arranged for the sale of the *Journal,* March 2, 1881, to Tom Hughes, a journalist recently arrived in town from Maryville, Kansas. The Las Vegas *Optic* neatly summed up the matter in an editorial. "The *Journal* has had an uphill career, and has been floated, of late, by a stock company, composed of the solid men of the city. Things were not of the pleasant tenor, and a sale was the most advisable thing that presented itself. Tom Hughes is a self-made boy, and knows how to run a newspaper to the top notch. . . . He will make a good paper of the *Journal* and we are glad to learn of his assession."[52]

When Burke quit his editor's post in 1884, Hughes himself took over the job and swiftly won the reputation as an incisive reporter and commentator on local and territorial affairs. It was said that "he could write more in three lines than most men could say in a column."[53] The old Albuquerque Publishing Company, meantime, had reorganized, with Elias S. Stover as president, had put together a new lump of capital, and repurchased the paper from Hughes. Also the name had been changed to the *Albuquerque Morning Journal.* After remaining for a while as editor and manager, Tom Hughes departed, in 1887, to become co-owner and editor of another paper, the *Albuquerque Daily Citizen.* In that capacity, he remained a powerful voice in the city's affairs until his death in 1905.[54]

During Hughes's tenure with the *Citizen,* a sensational incident occurred that made his name a household word throughout the Territory and lifted him to hero's rank among Albuquerqueans. On October 9, 1895, he published a front page story entitled "Is It Honesty or Partisanship?" which was highly critical of the territorial Supreme Court. The article was unsigned and Hughes later claimed that he had found it amid the clutter on his desk one day and after only a casual reading had sent it off to be printed. Suspicion arose that the author of the inflammatory piece was lawyer Thomas B. Catron, the Republican boss of Santa Fe and a close friend of Hughes.[55]

Subsequently the *Citizen* ran an apology, contending that the story had appeared through gross carelessness and without malicious intent. Notwithstanding, Editor Hughes was brought to trial, charged with contempt of the Supreme Court. He might have gotten off free, but for his refusal to divulge the name of the man who wrote the article. On October 23, 1895, the Court convicted Thomas Hughes and handed down a sentence that many New Mexicans considered severe and unwarranted—sixty days' imprisonment.[56]

Locked up in the Bernalillo County jail, the editor received a train of well-wishers who kept him liberally supplied with fine cigars and whiskey, and through whom he smuggled out editorials for the paper lambasting the Court. Young Will Keleher, later a prominent Albuquerque lawyer and historian, recounts his own visit to the jail one Sunday. "My father took me to Old Town to call . . . on Thomas Hughes . . . who was serving a sixty-day sentence because he elected to stand fast and adhere to the code of the press." Keleher continues: "Father introduced me to him, and then handed him several cigars, explaining to me that Mr. Hughes was a 'great smoker.' They talked for what seemed to me to be a long time."[57]

His unwavering commitment to maintain the confidentiality of his journalistic sources made Tom Hughes a popular celebrity. On the night of his release, he was met at the door of the jail by a mob of friends. In a torch-light procession led by a military band engaged for the occasion, they conducted him down Railroad Avenue, which was thronged with cheering spectators. Hughes rode in state in a hack pulled by two white horses and puffed happily on a big cigar while waving to the crowd. He was deposited at Grant's Opera House, where eminent politicians, all Republicans, delivered speeches in his behalf. It was the kind of noisy demonstration common to the American political scene of that era.[58]

In the two decades before the turn of the century, Albuquerque saw a spate of other small newspapers come and go. They included the *Daily Democrat,* founded by the fiery editor J. G. Albright, who in 1882 brought his press down from Santa Fe on an ox cart; the *Albuquerque Republican;* the *Daily Herald;* the *New Mexico Nugget;* and several Spanish-language weeklies, like the *Hormiga de Oro* and *La Bandera Americana,* headed by an old resident, Nestor Montoya (brother-in-law to Salvador Armijo). One paper, the *Advance,* was published for a few short weeks in 1880 and would doubtless have left little mark on history but for the tragic fate of its proprietor and editor, A. M. Conklin. In early summer, Conklin decided to move his staff and press to Socorro by floating them down the Rio Grande on a raft. A rude craft was built and christened *The Advance.* On it the editor and crew sailed safely to Socorro on a voyage that might have appealed to Mark Twain. There he founded a new paper, the *Socorro Sun.*

On the following December 24, Conklin with his wife attended Christmas Eve services at the Methodist Church. There he fell into an argument with three young ruffians who were causing a disturbance. Afterward as he walked out the front door he was felled by a bullet through the heart, while Mrs. Conklin looked on in horror. Two of the culprits were captured and lodged in the Socorro jail. One of them was killed while trying to escape and the other was spirited away by vigilantes and hanged from a gate in the court house placita. The *Albuquerque Journal,* which had followed the incident closely, commented tersely, "Moral: 'Tis a bad thing to assassinate editors in New Mexico."[59]

The whirl of activity in the newspaper industry during the first two decades of New Albuquerque's existence was accompanied by a corresponding bustle in other phases of business endeavor. Investors established the Rio Grande Woolen Mills, the Albuquerque Foundry and Machine shop, the Southwestern Brewery and Ice Company (making Glorieta Beer), the Rio Grande Flour Mills, the American Lumber Company, and many smaller concerns such as carriage and blacksmith shops, cigar factories, and brick yards. Further, many of the large wholesale firms, referred to as commission houses, began moving to Albuquerque from Las Vegas. From the day in 1879 when the railroad had reached Las Vegas, that town had blossomed as the chief supply and distribution point for eastern New Mexico. In time, though, the wholesalers saw that Albuquerque, because of its central location, was fated to become the business center of the Territory and so they began shifting their interests to that city. Among the best-capitalized of such firms were the Ilfeld Brothers (Louis, Noa, and Bernard) and Gross, Blackwell and Company, which transferred its headquarters to Albuquerque in 1893 and built a warehouse alongside the tracks on the future site of the Alvarado Hotel.[60]

Also contributing to Albuquerque's rising prominence were surges in the mining and the wool trades. The sudden availability of rail transportation, followed by an influx of capital, encouraged prospecting ventures that had heretofore languished. Closest to the city were the Hell Canyon and Coyote Canyon mining districts, both located on the western slope of the Manzanos and accessible by a good wagon road. After traces of gold, silver, and copper were reported in the area, Elias Stover and William Hazeldine joined with a long-time resident of Old Town, Major Henry R. Whiting, to form the Manzanito Consolidated Mining Company. They laid plans to build a stamp mill in Hell Canyon. The miners they imported from Colorado declared, according to the Albuquerque press, that prospects at the site "looked as good as those in Leadville or any other crack mining camp."[61]

Gold fever apparently infected much of the local populace, for weekends would find a multitude of amateur prospectors scrambling among the rocks in both the Manzanos and Sandias, hoping to strike it rich. Excitement was fed by discovery of small placer deposits in the latter range at Bear Canyon and Tijeras Canyon. William T. Strachan, who had come to Albuquerque in the 1860s as an army sutler, saw an opportunity for a different kind of enterprise. On a low knoll by the entrance to Hell Canyon he erected the Hotel Strachan to serve the miners from Colorado and weekend visitors. The *Albuquerque Review* suggested that another good site for a hostelry was at the Soda Springs in nearby Coyote Canyon, "where a splendid hotel could be built for the accommodation of invalids or pleasure seekers, and which place could easily be connected with town by a line of stages."[62] No one followed up on that idea, but Adolph Harsch, who opened the first bakery in New Town, bored a well at Coyote Springs and using its mineral laden waters developed a prosperous business under the name, Harsch's Coyote Bottling Works. His mineral water was long the favorite chaser for whiskey in Albuquerque saloons.

Enthusiasm for the Manzano and Sandia mines was largely misplaced for they never fulfilled their initial promise. Indeed, speculators buying and selling claims probably made more money than purchasers who tried to develop them. Disappointment with the district close at hand was largely offset by successes in other areas, more distant from Albuquerque. Gold or silver booms spawned mushrooming camps at New Placers and Los Cerrillos, northeast of the Sandias; in the Cochiti mining district amid the Jemez Mountains; and in the south at Socorro, White Oaks, Hillsboro, Lake Valley, and Pinos Altos. Stagecoaches collected passengers at the Albuquerque railroad depot and carried them to many of these mining centers. And from all of them, developers came to Albuquerque with their freight wagons to stock up on supplies. In 1881, a Mining Bureau was established on Railroad Avenue, between First and Second Streets, to promote exploration and supply information to new arrivals interested in the mineral resources of the Territory.[63] The presence of the office was simply one more indicator that the town viewed itself as the coming commercial and industrial hub of the region.

The economic importance of mining, however, took second place to sheep raising and the wool trade. The year the railroad reached Albuquerque, official estimates placed the number of New Mexico sheep close to 4 million, with the largest concentrations in Bernalillo and neighboring Valencia counties. The Perea and Otero families alone were credited with a combined total of 500,000 head or one-eighth of all the sheep in the Territory.[64] Most of the stockmen continued to employ traditional Hispanic practices, but a few like Solomon Luna, who ran 150,000 sheep in western New Mexico, adopted progressive methods of cross-breeding and wool grading introduced by the Anglos.

Although the demand and price for wool fluctuated radically over the years, the sheep population continued to expand well into the twentieth century. Albuquerque's convenient location in the midst of the sheep country, and its excellent marketing, processing, and shipping facilities soon made it the focal point of the Southwestern wool trade. As early as October 1880, local merchants shipped forty freight cars of wool and hides, some of it brought from as far away as eastern Arizona.[65] As Albuquerque's involvement in the business grew, the sight of wagon trains heavily laden with wool wending their way toward town became commonplace. William McIntosh, a Scotchman who founded a sheep ranch in the Estancia Valley in the mid-1890s, each year brought in a caravan of forty wagons containing the fall clip. With part of the fortune he made, he financed a baseball team, the renowned Albuquerque Browns (later renamed the McIntosh Browns, in his honor).[66] As late as 1904, the *Albuquerque Morning Journal* reported: "Messrs. John Pflueger and Dick Heller's wool clip consisting of 40,000 pounds arrived yesterday from Cabezon, in the north Puerco district, and was sold on Railroad Avenue to the highest bidder. . . . The sight was an imposing one, the wool being loaded on seventeen wagons drawn by 67 horses."[67] Early residents later recalled with pride that the wool caravans were sometimes half a mile long.

Initially all wool from Albuquerque was shipped east "in the grease," that is, uncleaned or unscoured. Since the weight of raw wool might be increased by as much as 60 to 70 percent by dirt and grease adhering to the fleeces, considerable money was lost through payment of extra freight costs. Shipping of raw wool to market also played into the hands of dishonest dealers, who concealed rocks in the sacks to add to the weight, or rubbed sand into the fleeces for the same purpose. As early as the 1860s, when shipment was still being made over the Santa Fe Trail by wagon, the *Rio Abajo Weekly* had urged establishment of a scouring plant in Albuquerque, a cry taken up in the following decade by William McGuinness in the pages of the *Review*.[68] The first plant, however, was not established until 1883. A second and larger operation, the Albuquerque Wool Scouring Mill, was opened by Angus Grant and two partners in 1896, and still another mill, built by the Arnot Wool Company, followed soon after. In extensive warehouses owned by these companies adjacent to the railroad tracks, crews of native women sorted the wool and then moved it to the scouring machine, an electric-powered device that thoroughly cleansed the product in six minutes before sending it to the drying rooms. Until 1912, Grant's mill treated about 5 million pounds of wool annually. It closed in that year because new methods of wool-combing made it unprofitable to scour.[69]

A related industry, the Rio Grande Woolen Mills, also proved a boon to Albuquerque's commercial development. Its small plant, located close to the scouring mills, gave employment to carders, spinners, and weavers who manufactured fabrics, and to tailors and seamstresses who produced garments for men and women. Albuquerqueans benefited by being able to buy locally made blankets and clothing, free of the added costs that were common to imports from the East.[70]

Chapter 9 continues on page 273.

A busy day on the Old Albuquerque Plaza, from a painting in 1885 by Leon
Trousset. (Museum of Albuquerque)

TABLE OF ADDITIONS

ADDITION	SURVEYED BY	DATE OF FILING
*Atlantic & Pacific	Otto Dieckman	April 24 · 1888
do	Crowley & Mack C.E.	None
do Subdivision	J.K. Livingston	November 24 · 1882
do	Crowley & Mack C.E.	None
do Supplemental	do	November 22 · 1882
do do	Otto Dieckman	April 7 · 1882
Juan Armijo	Pitt Ross C.E.	April 28 · 1888
*P.M.&J. Armijo	Ch. J. Quetil C.E.	July 8 · 1887
do Supplementa'	do	April 26 · 1884
do		April 18 · 1882
Perfecto Armijo Bro's		September 26 · 1883
Severo Apodaca	M.J. Mack C.E.	February 28 · 1887
N.T. Armijo	do	August 15 · 1881
A.B.	do	September 16 · 1882
Severo Apodaca	do	January 21 · 1882
Baca & Armijo	Pitt Ross C.E.	April 28 · 1888
Belvedere	M.J. Mack C.E.	December 18 · 1883
Baca	C.W. Sanders C.E.	December 20 · 1880
*Baca	do	April 15 · 1881
Baca & Trimble	M.J. Mack C.E.	August 15 · 1883
County	C.L. Hubbs C.E.	June 21 · 1888
Duran & Alexander	Cha's A. Marriner C.E	September 18 · 1884
*Eastern Amend & Sup.	Martin Rapp C.E	October 24 · 1888
do	Pitt Ross C.E.	April 28 · 1888
Eastern	M.J. Mack C.E.	May 31 · 1883
Fritz Greening	do	June 18 · 1881
P.& H. Highland	R.L. Davies C.E.	December 11 · 1880
*H. Highland Amend. & Sup.	M.J. Mack C.E.	February 9 · 1883
H. Highland	M. Bro's & Pradt and R.L. Davies C.E., made by Otto Dieckman.	May 12 · 1887
Highland & Highland So.	Otto Dieckman	September 1 · 1882
do	M. Bro's & Pradt	
Highland South	by Otto Dieckman	February 15 · 1882
*	do	April 8 · 1887
do	do	January 10 · 1887
Homestead & Garden Spot	Wm. F. Hill C.E.	May 5 · 1885
*C.W. Lewis No 3	C.L. Hubbs C.E.	December 26 · 1888
do	M.J. Mack C.E.	January 21 · 1882
C.W. Lewis Highland No 1	do	January 7 · 1882
Lewis & Simonds	C.W. Sanders C.E.	March 24 · 1881
Mandell B. & R.	Wm. F. Hill C.E.	February 3 · 1886
New Mexico Town Co.	John A. Fulton C.E.	April 18 · 1882
* do	M.J. Mack C.E.	December 29 · 1882
do	John A. Fulton C.E.	May 5 · 1880
*Nichols & Bowden		March 4 · 1882
do		January 7 · 1882
Northern	M.J. Mack C.E.	May 15 · 1883
Franco Armijo y Otero	P.H. Bianchi C.E.	March 10 · 1881
Powell & Prager	T. Kuhn C.E.	June 18 · 1881
Perea	M.J. Mack C.E.	March 21 · 1881
Romero	Wm. F. Hill C.E.	December 5 · 1884
W.A. Rankin	J.R. Sutherland	April 6 · 1888
Springer	M.J. Mack C.E.	February 28 · 1881
*U.D.F.	M.B.& P. by O.D.	February 29 · 1888
do	O.D.	June 4 · 1884
do A.& S.	M.B.& P.	April 19 · 1883
do	do	February 9 · 1882

* In making Deeds use this survey.

Chart of New Albuquerque subdivisions platted in the 1880s. (Museum of Albuquerque)

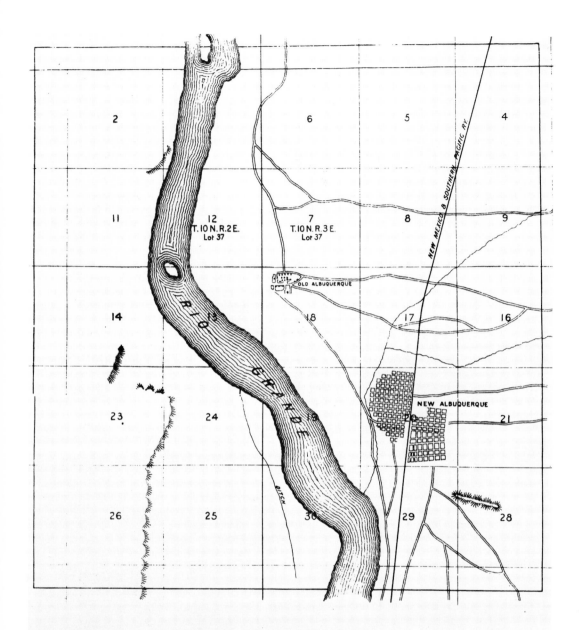

TOWN OF ALBUQUERQUE GRANT. NO. 130.

SCALE 50 CHAINS = 1 INCH.   AREA 17361.06 ACRES.

The field notes of the survey of Private Land Claim No. 130 the
Town of Albuquerque Grant, from which this plat has been made
have been examined and approved and are on file in this office.
   U.S. Surveyor General's Office
Santa Fé, New Mexico.
November 28·1883.

   Henry W. Atkinson

   U.S. Surveyor General

Town of Albuquerque, 1883 Survey Map

Father Donato Gasparri, rector of San Felipe Church from 1868–83. (Museum of Albuquerque)

Plan of San Felipe de Neri Church in the Nineteenth Century

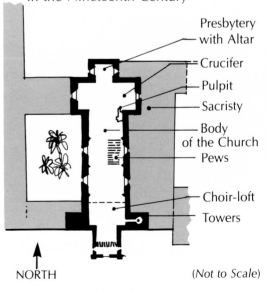

Presbytery with Altar

Crucifer

Pulpit

Sacristy

Body of the Church

Pews

Choir-loft

Towers

NORTH

(Not to Scale)

Adapted from a drawing by George Pearl.

244

An early bridge across the Rio Grande connecting Albuquerque and Atrisco.
(Museum of Albuquerque)

Above: Beginning in the 1870s, truck gardens in the North Valley supplied the city with a variety of farm products. This one, developed by Herman Blueher, was on the site of the present Museum of Albuquerque and Tiguex Park. (Museum of Albuquerque)

Below: Molina de Glorieta, Franz Huning's flour mill on West Central, 1875. (Museum of Albuquerque)

Above: Muledrawn streetcar on Railroad Avenue, July 1881. (Museum of Albuquerque)

Below: Earliest known photograph of New Albuquerque, April 1881. Looking south on First Street. (Museum of New Mexico, photograph by Ben Wittick)

Above: New Albuquerque was three years old when this photograph was taken in 1883. View from the sandhills, looking west toward the volcanos. (Museum of New Mexico)

Below: Railroad yards and warehouses looking west toward First Street about 1888. (Museum of New Mexico, photograph by J. R. Riddle)

The Armijo House, Albuquerque's first so-called luxury hotel. (Museum of Albuquerque)

A wool train entering Albuquerque. (Museum of New Mexico)

Bernalillo County Courthouse near Old Town, built in 1886. (Museum of Albuquerque)

Volunteer firemen of the Scott Moore and Angus A. Grant Hose Companies, 1890. (Museum of Albuquerque)

Flooding on North Fourth Street, September 1929. (Museum of Albuquerque)

A memorial statue in Robinson Park to the hero John Braden, who died in 1896. (Author's photograph)

Temple Albert, Jewish synagogue at Seventh and Gold, built in 1899. (Museum of Albuquerque)

Above: Turn-of-the-century students at work in the tailor shop, Albuquerque Indian School. (Museum of Albuquerque)

Below: The Albuquerque Indian School, completed in 1884. (Museum of Albuquerque)

254

The University of New Mexico's first building, Hodgin Hall, about 1900, before remodeling to a Pueblo Revival style. (Museum of Albuquerque)

Above: White frame exhibit hall, Territorial Fair Grounds, west of Old Town. (Museum of Albuquerque)

Below: An early balloon ascension in the 1880s from Second Street. (Museum of Albuquerque)

Above: Albuquerque's first baseball team, the Browns, about 1882. (State Records Center & Archives, Santa Fe)

Below: Pilot Roy Francis (left) and his tractor biplane at the Territorial Fair, 1913. (Museum of Albuquerque)

The Commercial Club at Fourth and Gold, built in 1892. Long a center for business and social life, it was demolished in the early 1950s and replaced by the Simms Building. (Museum of Albuquerque)

Above: Santa Fe locomotives, like No. 69, were once common in the Albuquerque yards. (Museum of New Mexico, photograph by Emil Bibo)

Below: Albuquerque's famed Alvarado Hotel, opened in 1902. (Museum of Albuquerque)

Above: Gold Avenue looking east toward the railroad depot, about 1890–1900. (Museum of Albuquerque)

Below: Electric streetcar, shown here at the Fair Grounds, began service in 1904. (Museum of Albuquerque)

By the 1890s, many Albuquerque men were riding to work on bicycles. (Museum of Albuquerque)

Bicycles and carriages in front of the First National Bank, Second and Gold, 1905. (Museum of New Mexico)

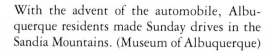

The Whitney Hardware Company's delivery truck. (Museum of Albuquerque)

With the advent of the automobile, Albuquerque residents made Sunday drives in the Sandia Mountains. (Museum of Albuquerque)

Birdseye view of Martinez Town, about 1898, looking northwest across fenced
fields toward the Rio Grande. (Museum of Albuquerque)

President William Howard Taft (seated, in light coat) on the speaker's platform, Alvarado Hotel, 1909. (State Records Center & Archives)

Erna Fergusson (d. 1964) was the granddaughter of Franz Huning and one of Albuquerque's most distinguished regional writers. (Museum of Albuquerque)

Kate Nichols Chaves, prominent Albuquerque socialite and architect. She is wearing a pale blue satin gown embellished with small pearls, made especially for a ball in the Alvarado Hotel about 1912. (Photograph courtesy of Consuelo Chaves Summers)

The Castle Huning on West Central remained the center of Franz Huning's life, until his death in 1905. (Museum of Albuquerque)

Franz Huning in his later life after having built Castle Huning. (Museum of Albuquerque)

Elfego Baca, before his death in 1945, was one of Albuquerque's most colorful citizens. (Museum of Albuquerque)

266

Above: The Albuquerque Airport had its beginnings in 1928 on the empty East Mesa. (Museum of Albuquerque)

Below: Mayor Clyde Tingley (right) greets flier Charles Lindbergh, March 17, 1929. (Museum of Albuquerque)

The Kimo on a January night in 1933. Albuquerque's leading landmark motion picture theater was built in 1927. (Museum of Albuquerque)

Downtown Albuquerque in the 1930s. (Museum of New Mexico)

Old Town about 1950. Original Bernalillo County Courthouse at lower right.
(State Records Center & Archives, Santa Fe, DOD Collection)

Modern Albuquerque with the Rio Grande in the foreground. (Albuquerque
Chamber of Commerce)

Henry Jaffa, elected Albuquerque's first mayor, July 4, 1885. (Museum of Albuquerque)

Mayor Harry Kinney assumed office in December 1981. Both Jaffa and Kinney spent formative periods of their lives in Trinidad, Colorado.

Although the sheep and wool business far outdistanced other forms of stock raising in importance, the cattle industry, nevertheless, made a significant contribution to economic growth in Albuquerque. Large ranches, many of them owned by eastern or foreign syndicates, had sprung up in New Mexico in the wake of the Civil War and, appropriating free grass on public lands, had prospered. Large cattle drives originating in the far corners of the Territory made their way to New Albuquerque's stockyards to take advantage of the excellent shipping facilities offered by the railroad. Alfalfa, grown in the Middle Valley, enabled steers and heifers to be fattened at home, enlarging the profit on cattle loaded aboard stock cars for markets in Kansas City, St. Louis, and Chicago.

Cattlemen, more than most other members of New Mexico's business community, suffered in the financial panic that gripped the nation in 1893. Unlike the more conservative sheep raisers, they had overstocked their ranges and borrowed heavily from banking institutions. During the panic, the market became depressed, with steers selling in Albuquerque for $4 a head. Many ranchers who were overextended simply went under. It is told that two cattlemen, deeply in debt to the Albuquerque National Bank, were unable to repay their loans; as a result, the bank was forced temporarily to close its doors on October 3, 1893.[71]

The hard times did affect to some degree every phase of business enterprise in town. Even the AT&SF, once considered the strongest industry in the Territory, suffered such a drastic decline in revenues that it passed into receivership. Fortunately, after the depression passed, the company was able to regroup and recover.[72] Although the panic produced deflation and low prices, numerous Albuquerqueans lacked even enough money to purchase basic food and clothing. Urged on by the press, Welfare and Ladies Aid Societies were organized to see the town's poor through the crises.

Something else that helped soften the pinch was the Middle Valley's agricultural production, which, like most other activities, had been given a vigorous boost by the arrival of the railroad. As already noted, the Jesuit fathers together with innovative individuals, such as Salvador Armijo, had lent encouragement to truck gardening and the expansion and diversification of orchards back in the 1870s. They had been followed by others who appreciated the advantages of a mild climate and rich soil that lands in suburban Albuquerque offered. Among the new wave of farmers was Herman Blueher, an Illinois gardener who got off the train in 1882, and within a few years developed an extensive truck farm and nursery on fields northeast of Old Town (at the site of present Tiguex Park).[73]

Albuquerque's vegetables, grain, and fruit were much in demand by miners in isolated gold and silver camps and by all classes of citizens in the northern part of the Territory where the shorter growing season limited the varieties of crops raised. Grocers in Santa Fe, 60 miles to the north and 2,000 feet higher in altitude, as late as the turn of the century sent their own wagons to Albuquerque to bring back produce for the capital trade. Because of the abundant sunshine in late fall, valley fruit could be left on the trees longer, thereby improving its flavor and appearance. As a result, it commanded a price 30 percent above California fruit when shipped by rail to eastern markets.[74] By comparison with the rest of the country, many Albuquerqueans would have acknowledged, even during the panic of 1893, that they dwelled in a suburb of Eden.

An important aspect of New Albuquerque's burgeoning business community was the birth and growth of several commercial banks. The Territory had no bank at all until the First National Bank of Santa Fe opened its doors in the capital on April 17, 1871.[75] The earliest banking on the Albuquerque plaza was handled informally by merchants, who accepted deposits from their customers, used the money in their business, and paid a fair rate of interest. Most shop owners had safes or lock-boxes in their establishments. Some citizens preferred to travel, as quietly as possible, by stage or private carriage with money packed in the bottom of a valise for deposit in a real bank at Santa Fe.

Such inconveniences continued until 1878 when the Central Bank was opened in a small adobe building on the southwest corner of the plaza. The president was Jefferson Raynolds who with his brothers, Frederick and Joshua, had two years earlier launched their first bank in Las Vegas. Initially, the Central Bank did only a meager business, but that changed quickly when railroad construction spurred the local economy. In 1881, the Raynolds began construction of a two-story brick building on the corner of Second and Gold, and as soon as it was completed, they abandoned Old Town, transferring their offices to the center of commercial activity in New Albuquerque.

The Central Bank soon had a competitor in the First National Bank of Albuquerque, chartered by a group of wealthy Bernalillo County residents on December 24, 1881. Mariano S. Otero of Bernalillo served as first president and Elias S. Stover, Nicolás T. Armijo, and Cristóbal Armijo were listed as directors. Other prominent names that appeared among the founders included Franz Huning's brother Louis; Felipe Chávez, a Belen merchant; José Leandro Perea; and Justo Armijo. The predominance of Hispano names shows that old leaders in the native community were actively seeking to retain some influence in the postrailroad era.

After several years of ups and downs, stockholders of the First National chose to sell out to the Raynolds brothers, which they did on December 19, 1884. With the merger, the new owners decided to use the name First National Bank, as being more prestigious than Central Bank. Although other, smaller banks came and went in the waning years of the nineteenth century, none gained the stature of the First National. It continued to occupy the office at Second and Gold until 1922, when a new eight-story building was erected at Third and Central at a cost of $580,000. That structure was described by Harvey Fergusson as "sticking up like a baby's first tooth, incongruous but promising."[76] It was Albuquerque's first skyscraper.

Albuquerque's bankers, merchants, journalists, and professional men not only guided the political and economic destiny of the town, but they also set the pace and defined its social life. Among fraternal orders, the

Masons led the way, founding a temple in New Town as early as 1881.[77] They were followed in later years by the Elks, Odd Fellows, and the Knights of Pythias. But the authentic social center of Albuquerque and the pride of the business community was the Commercial Club, organized in 1890. Its declared purpose was as broad as it was serious: "To encourage scientific and literary pursuits, to estabish a library, to maintain reading rooms, assembly halls, and club rooms . . . ; and to promote the commercial and industrial development of the city of Albuquerque and the surrounding country."[78] In its promotional aspect, the Club, like the earlier Board of Trade, resembled a Chamber of Commerce; but as a place of cultural activity and dignified entertainment, it had more in common with fashionable men's clubs so popular in the East. Certainly, nothing remotely like it had ever existed in Old Town.

The initial membership roster of thirty names listed practically everyone of power and means and was accepted as Albuquerque's unofficial social register. A few Hispanos, like Justo Armijo and Mariano Otero, movers in the launching of the First National Bank, were included, but they constituted a conspicuous minority.[79]

Colonel G. W. Meylert, who had earlier organized the library room in the San Felipe Hotel, served as the first president of the Commercial Club, and it was largely through his influence that a decorous tone was set. Rigid house rules restricted smoking, regulated the dispensing of alcohol, and prohibited gambling. Banquets and monthly dances attracted the elite among the younger set. Many a romance that had its beginning under the roof of the club eventually led to a wedding, which forged still another link in the widening chain of relationships joining the town's eminent families.[80]

In spite of its great variety of businesses and its modest social pretentions, New Albuquerque remained above all else a railroad town, with all that the phrase implied. The coming and going of the trains, their management and repair, formed an industry unto itself. Before long, proud Albuquerqueans were referring to their vast complex of railroad shops as the largest west of the Mississippi and no one found reason to challenge their claim. Directly or indirectly, every inhabitant of New Town owed his livelihood to the rail company. And it was the prosperity bestowed by the railroad that ultimately allowed Albuquerque to outstrip in importance other towns in the Territory.

The supreme symbol and ever-present reminder of Albuquerque's dependence upon the railroad industry was the shop whistle. Its sleep-murdering shriek, echoing through the valley and across the mesas, aroused workers from their beds at 6:00 A.M. At 6:45, another blast uttered a warning to get on the job. And a final summons came at 7:00 sharp, announcing that every man who expected to be paid must be at his post. At the close of the ten-hour work day, the whistle screamed again, releasing the shop crews promptly at 6:00. Day in and day out, men marched smartly to their labor with the precision of a machine. And the regimen was infectious. Recalled one local resident years afterward, "Railroad time was the most accurate time we could get, so everyone set his clock or pocket watch, and started his day's activities by the shop whistle."[81]

Viewed from the sandhills on the east, the cluster of railroad buildings with their tall stacks presented a formidable sight. The primary focus of interest was the station, initially a small red frame building containing a ticket office, baggage room, and freight office. Flanking it closely on the south was a Harvey Eating House, an adjunct of AT&SF stations throughout the West. The "little red depot," as it was affectionately known, soon proved inadequate, so it was loaded on a flatcar and rolled down track to a new home at San Marcial. In its place was built a new two-story station, which served community needs until 1901 when the present depot arose as part of the passenger complex that included the Alvarado Hotel.

From the station site, and stretching toward the south and west, were the switchyards, car shops, roundhouses for locomotive repair, warehouses, offices, and other accessories required by a main plant in the railway system. Counting the construction and maintenance crews that worked out of Albuquerque, as many as 1,500 employees might on occasion report for the morning whistle.[82] More than any other class, the railroad men, wearing grimy blue overalls, work shirt, a striped denim cap, and a red bandanna at the neck to keep out cinders, personified the new times.

In their role as civic boosters, the people of Albuquerque liked to declare that their town was served by two major railroads, the Santa Fe and the Atlantic & Pacific. Technically, that was true since the companies maintained separate organization and management, but as already explained, the A&P operated, in fact, as a subsidiary of the AT&SF.[83] That relationship was to continue until 1902 when the A&P was absorbed by the parent company.[84]

The peak years of railroad construction in New Mexico were between 1878 and 1885 when section gangs laid more than 1,200 miles of track.[85] In its furious drive to advance the rails, the Santa Fe had scarcely paused upon reaching Albuquerque in early April 1880. Pushing rapidly down the Rio Grande Valley, it reached Socorro by July and San Marcial, an important cattle shipping point 20 miles to the south, on the following September 10. From Atchison, Kansas, the beginning of the line, to San Marcial, the tracks stretched 1,000 miles, a fact that lent confidence and added vigor to the AT&SF's expansion program.

At Rincon, 75 miles below San Marcial, the rails branched, with one line continuing on to El Paso and the other proceeding west to a link-up at Deming with the Southern Pacific, which had built eastward from California. On March 8, 1881, officials of the Santa Fe drove a silver spike at the Deming junction, a ceremony signalling completion of the nation's second transcontinental rail system.[86]

Meantime, the A&P had been doing its best to reach California along the old 35th parallel route. Originally, its engineers had looked at the possibility of erecting a bridge in the vicinity of Old Town and building in a direct line to the Rio Puerco. But the steep grade over the West Mesa rendered that plan extremely costly. As an alternative, they elected to span the river at what became known as the A&P Junction, 12 miles below Albuquerque near Isleta. The gentle grade west of that point was ideal for laying track. On May 1, 1880, the bridge was completed, and the following October the *Albuquerque Daily Journal* reported that rails had advanced 50 miles beyond. "Speed the good work!" admonished the editor.[87]

Construction of the A&P brought money and employment to New Albuquerque, just as the town was getting off the ground. Huge quantities of construction materials were accumulated in the yards to be sent to tracks' end when needed. At least 800 carloads of rail were funneled through the Albuquerque freight office by contractors. The company paid track layers and graders $2.25 a day, and spikers and iron layers, $2.50. Also, many Navajos and Apaches were hired as shovelers and day laborers. The wages were considered exceptionally good for the time. Men who worked all week laying 52-pound steel rails at the rate of one mile per day were ready to let off steam and squander their pay when Saturday came.[88] From construction camps, they rolled into Albuquerque on flatcars and in boxcars, prepared to take possession of the saloons and bawdy houses running the length of Front Street. Their sprees enriched Albuquerque and gave the place the air of a fast and wicked town.

In the summer of 1883, the A&P bridged Arizona's Colorado River and entered Needles, California, where it connected with a branch of the Southern Pacific. By previous arrangement, it was allowed to use the SP tracks to San Francisco. With that, the "thirty-fifth Parallel Trans-Continental Line" was finished and ready for business.[89] On October 21, two hundred Albuquerqueans gathered at their depot to see the first Pullman train start over the Atlantic & Pacific route to San Francisco and the Golden Gate.[90] It was another landmark day in the history of the Middle Valley.

For Franz Huning, the man whose fortunes had been intertwined with those of Albuquerque since the early 1850s, the last two decades of the century were given over largely to family matters and the development of personal properties. At first, his name appeared as an officer or board member on the letterhead of numerous civic and commercial enterprises. But more and more, as he aged he withdrew from active participation in public affairs. One gets the impression that despite his stolid German manner, he was not a shrewd manipulator, nor a cutthroat business man, as were many of the Anglo tycoons of New Town. And apparently he entertained no aspirations for political office. If he had, there can be little doubt that any municipal or county post would have been his for the asking.

A series of bad investments made during the speculative hurly-burly of the railroad boom was one of the major factors causing Huning to pull in his sails. His failures, mainly in real estate deals, he attributed to a lack of experience.

One project that had showed great promise at the outset, but turned into a financial disaster in the end, was the Albuquerque Bridge Company. Since Tom Post's pontoon bridge had been swept away by floodwaters in the late 1870s, people had been obliged to ford the Rio Grande or use the clumsy and uncertain ferry boats. Once Albuquerque had won its laurels as a railroad terminal and was bidding to become the first city of the Territory, civic leaders found it unconscionable that travelers should suffer such inconvenience in crossing the river. Therefore, the Bridge Company was incorporated in 1879. Elias Stover served as president, Franz Huning as vice-president, and William Hazeldine as secretary.[91]

Through sale of stock, $22,000 was raised and construction got under way in 1881. Work continued late into the following year and on December 12, 1882, the bridge was opened to the public.[92] The river span was 600 feet, with approaches across the marshy bottomland adding another 500 feet. A tollhouse in the center collected $.05 per person. Horsemen were required to walk their mounts; no trotting was allowed. Violators suffered a stiff fine.[93]

The new bridge proved a major economic asset to the community since it provided easier access to the Albuquerque markets for ranchers and miners from the Puerco Basin and beyond. But as a commercial venture, it was a disappointment. In dry weather when the river was low, most of the rural folk preferred to roll up their trousers and wade across, thereby saving the $.05 toll. During the rainy season when the bridge was most needed, it was often damaged beyond use by high water. The costly repairs kept the company constantly in the red. A particularly destructive flood in May 1891, finally smashed the bridge to pieces and carried its timbers toward Socorro.[94] The company went out of business, and Franz Huning, as a principal investor, lost the entire sum he had put in, seemingly several thousand dollars. Not until 1910 did Albuquerque get a permanent steel bridge.[95]

Soon after the founding of New Town, Huning had sold out his store on the plaza and opened another, dealing principally in hardware, amid the bustle around the tracks. But the informal and friendly trade to which he had become accustomed in Old Albuquerque was not in evidence here. Growth and the changing times brought a fierce competitiveness to the mercantile business that was not to his liking. So, at the first opportunity, he disposed of the hardware store and resolved to devote himself to management of his mill, La Molina de la Glorieta.

Located on Franz's acreage south of Railroad Avenue, the mill was a tall and gabled frame building shaded by cottonwoods. The machinery, which had been freighted in pieces over the Santa Fe Trail in the mid-1850s, consisted of a fifteen horsepower steam engine. It burned forty-five cords of wood annually, suggesting that the operation produced a considerable quantity of flour.[96] The mill was the largest and best patronized in the Middle Valley and it was the pride of Franz Huning.

In spite of reverses, Huning's overall financial position remained strong. Perhaps that fact inspired him to begin thinking of a new and more elegant home for his wife, Ernestine, and their four children. The couple's eldest child, Clara Mary, had been born in 1865, the year after Franz brought his bride from St. Louis and installed her in the rambling adobe house, La Glorieta. Clara, reputedly the first Anglo child born in Albuquerque, was something of a curiosity among Hispanos, who crowded about to stare at her fair features whenever she appeared in public. Three other children soon blessed the Huning household: Arno, the only son, in 1869; Lina, in 1873; and little Elly, who died in 1881 at age five.[97]

When Franz Huning began plans for building a new house in the early 1880s, he was at the peak of his career. So, the structure he designed was intended not only as a worthy domicile for his family, but also, in the words of his grandson, as "a monument to his success and a memorial to his past."[98] Huning commenced work on his dream house, on the border between Old and New Towns, in 1881. According to his own claim, "I drew the plans, was my own builder and supervised all cabinet work."[99] Upon a concrete foundation, Hispano laborers began to lay up three foot thick walls of *terrones,* or sod blocks, dug from an adjacent meadow. Franz, figuring his expenses closely, recorded that the *terrones* cost him $11.00 per thousand to lay in the wall and that in the final tally the house required 250,000 of the blocks. Progress was slow, stretching over a period of three years, for the meticulous builder wanted the heavy walls to settle, so as to minimize cracking later.

The finished product was a wonder to behold. Newcomers, taking the horse cars at the depot and traveling for the first time down Railroad Avenue toward Old Town, never failed to gasp in astonishment as the white battlements of the house suddenly appeared to view. The rough outer walls had been veneered with wood paneling and the arched doorways and windows, shipped from Chicago on flatcars, lent a touch of eastern sophistication. The main body of the building rose two stories to a flat roof, trimmed around its perimeter with ornamental grille work. A tower embellished with balconies was located in the center of the façade and lifted to an extra story above the level of the roof. From a great iron gate at the entrance to the grounds, a cement walk (the cement imported from Portland, England) led past a marble fountain to the front porch and main doorway.[100]

Franz called his creation Castle Huning, emblazoning the name over the door and upon all the window shades. It was often said in later years that he patterned the place after German castles along the Rhine River familiar to him in his youth. But in truth the design seemed to have more in common with an Italian villa, while the flat roof and square tower bore some faint resemblance to New Mexico's colonial missions. But to Albuquerqueans, unused to such architectural novelties, the residence was truly a castle.

The European influence was also apparent in the landscaping. Around his four hundred acres, extending from Railroad Avenue south to an incurving bend of the Rio Grande, Franz put up a protective fence to keep out wandering livestock. Within this princely estate, he planted hundred of trees—decorative varieties such as catalpas, Persian walnuts, Japanese umbrella trees; long rows of Lombardy poplars and Osage orange as windbreaks; and fruit trees that flowered profusely, like cherries and crab apples. Every kind of shrub, flower, and tree that would thrive in Albuquerque found its way into Huning's man-made forest and garden.

There were other touches, too, that seemed more in keeping with the Old World than the New: a grape arbor, a city block in length; an aviary, bowered with vines and containing a notable collection of birds; a winery where barefoot natives tramped the juice from grapes; grassy lawns; winding, gravelled paths; rustic seats; and fountains. Along the edge of an open meadow, Franz dug a narrow, meandering pond. It contained a wooded island joined to the shore by an artful bridge, and upon its glassy surface floated serenely a flock of white geese. Said one of his descendants who recalled playing at the lake as a child, "The scene lacked only a blond maiden to sit in a boat, trailing her hand in the water, and it would have been an almost perfect imitation of old German chromos."[101]

Inside the grounds were structures of purely utilitarian nature. West of the castle, Franz constructed stables, carriage houses, and corrals. There were rows of storerooms and also cellars, built by necessity above ground because the shallow water table would not let them be placed below. And, of course, there was the flour mill, conveniently situated a few hundred yards from the castle.

If Franz Huning had created a monument to his career, he had also built a haven from the modern world that was fast destroying the pioneering life he had known and loved. His distaste for the new ways grew with the years, and toward the end he seldom left the sheltering arms of his estate. Along the eastern boundary facing New Albuquerque he posted a chilling sign that warned in large letters, "Trespassers will be shot." Though he regularly patrolled his domain, double-barreled shotgun in hand, there is no record that he ever fired at intruders, who persisted in raiding the orchard. His testiness derived mainly from an impatience with fools and with the new breed of men who were short on gentility and morals. One account, which well expresses Franz Huning's sentiments, declares, "For the sharp and tricky trade of the railroad world, he had a strong dislike and for the corrupt politics of the period, a rather violent contempt. When the local political boss sent to his mill for a sack of corn, he sent the sack back empty with the simple message, 'Go to Hell.' "[102]

There were some Albuquerqueans ready to argue that what Franz Huning had wrought inside his fences was not only foreign to the Middle Valley, but ostentatious and pretentious as well. Yet, Franz was not a pretentious man. He built not to impress, but as his inborn tastes and desires dictated. If the ample and easy mode of life on his estate had a patriarchal character about it, the result was unquestionably in tune with the age-old pattern found in the homes of the Valley's Hispano aristocrats. And there was dignity and beauty in the Castle Huning, qualities noticeably deficient in the majority of structures, residential and business, that were being feverishly hammered together with little forethought in New Albuquerque.

Late in life, Franz Huning expressed the hope that his castle would stand for many years to be enjoyed by his descendants. Perhaps he also wished it to serve new generations of Albuquerqueans as a reminder of his own, not inconsequential, role in the early development of their city. Some of his heirs continued to occupy the mansion until the 1930s. Then it was sold, to become first a private school, and in 1942 the regional office of the United States Corps of Engineers.[103] The surrounding acreage, where once orchards and gardens had bloomed and geese floated on a storybook pond, was subdivided, a part going to the Albuquerque Country Club and the remainder converted to a luxurious residential section. In 1955, the Castle Huning, callously condemned as unsightly and unsafe, though it was neither, fell to the blows of a wrecking ball. Its demise offered a grim commentary on the new society, so dedicated to the philosophy of getting and spending that it seemingly had no desire left to protect and make room for one of its few remaining legacies of the past. Today (1980), the site of the Castle Huning on the southwest corner of West Central and Laguna is a bare and ugly vacant lot, scoured by the winds and unnoticed by speeding motorists who have never heard of Franz Huning.

When the Hunings moved from La Glorieta across the road to the newly completed castle shortly before Christmas, 1883, there was no thought of the distant future. They were content to enjoy the holiday amid the lovely surroundings that Franz's three years of effort had produced.

In contrast to their old home with its mudded walls, the rooms were sided with wallpaper, and instead of Navajo rugs and Spanish *jerga* matting on the floor, there were imported carpets. The furnishings included gilt-framed mirrors and pictures, heavy brass-hooded coal hods, crimson drapes, a grand piano, and pipe organ. Ernestine resumed her time-honored Thursday afternoon socials. Franz, who had provided the house with a ballroom, arranged lavish entertainments for visiting dignitaries who shuttled through town on the railroad in increasing numbers.[104]

One problem that long beset the Hunings was that of securing a proper education for their children, since Albuquerque possessed no public schooling and private facilities were minimal. When the eldest daughter, Clara, reached the age of six, a local Hispano teacher was engaged to instruct her in the reading and writing of Spanish. Thus as a child, she spoke German, the language of the Huning household, and Spanish—but no English. When she was nine, Franz placed her in the Loretto Convent in Santa Fe, but shy Clara was so miserable under the strict discipline of the nuns that he brought her home after a year. Next he escorted her by stage to Trinidad, Colorado, where they caught the train for St. Louis. Clara spent two years there in the Kirkwood Seminary and then went on to Germany for another two years to be taught "excellent German, an erect carriage, proper manners, embroidery, all kinds of needlework, piano, organ—the graces."[105] While she was away, her father built the Castle Huning. Clara arrived back in Albuquerque from her foreign studies late in 1883, just in time to share Christmas with her family and christen their new home.

The boy, Arno, was also sent away to school, to Kemper Military Academy at Booneville, Missouri, near the head of the old Santa Fe Trail. Later he went to Washington University in St. Louis and received a degree in electrical engineering. Returning to Albuquerque, he inherited the Castle Huning upon his father's death and lived there with his own family for twenty-five years. [106]

A new dimension was added to the history of the Hunings in 1887 when Clara, now twenty-two, married one of Albuquerque's ascending political stars, Harvey B. Fergusson. The fact that he was also a lawyer and a southern gentleman, being Alabama born, probably helped make the match acceptable to Franz, whose aversion to politicians in general has already been noted.

Harvey Fergusson had been a boy of thirteen when the Civil War broke out, just a few years too young to fight for the Southern cause. But he had come under the influence of its romantic traditions, especially during the immediate postwar years when he worked for a law degree at Virginia's Washington College. General Robert E. Lee was president of the institution and most of the students were sons of Confederate officers. One summer when young Harvey was working in the fields near the college to make tuition, General Lee rode up on his famous white horse, Traveler, called the young man to him, and praised his courage and persistence. The general's words, Harvey told his grown children half a lifetime later, were like the benediction of a god. [107]

In 1881, while working for a law firm in Wheeling, West Virginia, he was sent to attend a mining case in the town of White Oaks, located in the New Mexico Territory's Lincoln County. The stark landscape and the bubbling excitement of the boomtown captured Harvey Fergusson's affections. He resigned his position with the eastern firm and stayed, hanging out a shingle and attracting clients easily. During his two years in White Oaks, he wore a six-shooter on his hip, prospected for gold on weekends, and shared bachelor quarters with three other bright young men of limited means. They were William MacDonald who was to be a future governor of New Mexico; Albert B. Fall, later the secretary of interior and a central figure in the Teapot Dome Scandal; and Emerson Hough, destined to be a popular western novelist.

White Oaks, like most mining camps, was a place without a future, so in 1883 Fergusson moved to Albuquerque whose future at that moment seemed assured. Being a personable man endowed with considerable Southern charm, he was able to make his new law practice flourish. And as a "thorough-going Democrat" and gifted orator he was lured to politics, winning election as district attorney in 1885. His gentle manner and comely appearance, highlighted by a walrus mustache, caught the eye of Clara Huning and they were married on April 14, 1887. [108]

A year later daughter Erna was born at the Castle, in rooms the doting Franz had offered the Fergussons as lodging. So pleased was he with his first grandchild, that in celebration he gave Clara and Harvey his old adobe home, La Glorieta, across the road. Though the building, in traditional New Mexican style, was a far cry from the plantation home Fergusson had known as a boy, nevertheless, its historical association with the Confederate occupation of Albuquerque furnished a tenuous link with his origins, by which he set such store. La Glorieta, once the focal point of Franz Huning's life, now became the center of his son-in-law's political career, and a fitting residence in which Clara could raise her children. Behind its heavy protective walls were born in succession, Harvey Jr., Lina, and Francis. Erna and Harvey would grow up to become two of Albuquerque's most significant regional authors.

In political philosophy, Harvey Fergusson, Sr., was a progressive liberal, and in temperament a dreamer and romantic. That orientation made him a champion of lost causes and a worshiper of the past. His personal code required that he befriend the weak and oppose the wicked. And it led him to defy the railroads and big mining companies bent on dominating New Mexico. Though his attachment to the South was well known, the few Blacks in Albuquerque invariably chose him to deliver a speech on Emancipation Day. He would return to La Glorieta following such occasions musing to himself that he had extolled freedom and Abraham Lincoln and caused his father to turn over in his grave.[109]

Strangely, Fergusson never learned to speak Spanish and never showed any genuine interest in the native culture of the Middle Valley. When running for political office, he always communicated through an interpreter. But the deficiency failed to lower his popularity among the Hispanic folk. His idealism, his dramatic gift of oratory, his gallantry and democratic spirit, and, above all, his aristocratic bearing won him friends and votes across the barrier of language. The same attributes allowed him to attain high political office, as a Democrat in a Territory that was predominantly Republican. At Grant's Opera House, whenever he rose to address a political rally, the crowd, reversing the usual order of things, burst forth with a wild ovation even before he spoke.[110] Remarked Erna Fergusson, long after her father's death, "He would sacrifice everything—money, his family, himself—to his idea of public duty, and his conception of the public included all the people."[111]

When Harvey in 1896 defeated the powerful Republican Thomas B. Catron for the office of territorial delegate to Congress, he was granted an opportunity to perform his self-chosen duty on a grander scale. Packing the family off to Washington, he delivered his maiden speech before the House of Representatives in which he urged quick passage of a statehood bill for New Mexico. It was an issue that engaged him tirelessly until 1912, when the Territory finally won the coveted status. His greatest triumph came in 1898 when he guided through Congress a land measure known as the Fergusson Act. It set aside 4 million acres of the public domain in New Mexico for the benefit of schools and earned him such plaudits at home that he became, unquestionably, Albuquerque's most illustrious son.[112]

Franz Huning and Harvey Fergusson sprang from widely divergent backgrounds and their attitudes toward life were poles apart. But they both shared an abiding love for their adopted city and both left their imprint upon it. Huning epitomized the pioneer settler-merchant of the old era; his son-in-law, as a professional man and crusading politician, represented the coming modern age. Together they helped shoulder the burden of inching Albuquerque forward along the bumpy road of a new era.

The magnitude of Albuquerque's growth in the postrailroad period is best expressed in her decennial population figures. The United States Census for 1870 listed the total number of inhabitants at 1,307.[113] By 1880, the railroad's magnetic pull had lifted the figure to 2,135, and that did not include satellite communities like Barelas (350), Los Griegos (300), and Ranchos de Atrisco (740), which now form suburbs of the city.[114] The population of New and Old Towns combined had climbed to 6,059 by 1890.[115] The trend toward rapid population expansion, established in this period, would continue throughout the twentieth century with the number of residents practically doubling every ten years.

The distinguished speakers who had mounted the flatcar platform on April 22, 1880, to hail the advent of the railroad repeatedly referred to the progress and expansion that was sure to come Albuquerque's way. But in their wildest imaginations none of them could have foreseen that one hundred years hence, their small community clinging to the banks of the Rio Grande would have spread in a continuous blanket across the East Mesa and into the foothills of the Sandias, and that the population would be edging toward 400,000. It is one of the disadvantages of man's brief life span that he is denied the opportunity to witness the long-range results of his own creativity and efforts at building.

Desperadoes and Disasters

IF ALBUQUERQUE CAN BE SAID to have enjoyed a true golden age, it must have been during those ebullient years falling between 1880 and 1900. Fine periods would follow, but none quite to match the up-beat, exurberant, dazzling decades that unfolded back to back in the wake of New Town's founding. Though the times were magnificent in the prosperity and opportunity they held out to men of industry and imagination, they were also hectic and sometimes dangerous.

Lawlessness, while it cannot be said to have reigned unchecked, was, nevertheless, an unpleasant fact of life and one that persisted longer in Albuquerque than in many other towns of the wild West. There was the matter, too, of disasters—the man-made variety like fires, and the natural sort such as floods. Albuquerque, basking under the territorial sun, bore its share of tragedies before the turn of the twentieth century.

The railroad workers with silver coin to throw away were the magnet that drew professional gamblers, ladies of ill repute, bunko men, saloonkeepers, and outlaws of several stripes. Their ilk, in fact, was common throughout the Territory. Miguel Antonio Otero notes the reason in his memoirs. "New Mexico," he declares, "was located so as to receive the backwash from two streams. From one side Texas, Kansas, Colorado, and the Indian Territory deposited their flotsam and jetsam of humanity, while from the other side Utah, Arizona, and California spewed their human refuse. New Mexico became a sort of catch basin for this type."[1]

Early visitors observed that the streets of New Albuquerque were lined with gin mills from whose dark, smoke-filled interiors issued the warbling strains of accordions and the tinny notes of honky-tonk pianos. Saloons, by all accounts, were more numerous than any other business. The novelty of their names would have done credit to the wildest Kansas cowtown: White Elephant, Bucket of Blood, Silver Dollar (with actual silver dollars embedded in the floor), Jay Eye See, St. Elmo, Four Roses, Blue Indigo, and Alamo, to mention a bare sampling. Owners of such parlors threw away their keys and operated at madcap pace night and day.

Men lined the polished bars in solid ranks, downing straight whiskey at fifteen cents a shot. They paid in silver or gold coin—banknotes or "greenbacks" were rarely seen—and received change in house tokens, good for more drinks. Decent women were forbidden to enter the swinging doors, and even ladies of the evening were required to come in by a side door, known as the "family entrance." Hispanos and a sprinkling of Chinese gained admittance upon terms of equality with Anglo patrons, but Albuquerque's few Blacks were usually barred. [2]

For sheer elegance and snob appeal, the White Elephant Saloon had no peers. Situated on the corner of Second and Railroad (site of the present Sunshine Theater), it boasted a solid mahogany bar long enough to accommodate fifty men at once. The sumptuous furnishings cost $12,000, the shiny brass cuspidors were worth $15 apiece, and the glassware was imported from Belgium. The gambling tables enjoyed fame as the finest and straightest in the Territory. For thirty years, New Mexico's political and business leaders, along with visiting national dignitaries, drank, gambled, and hatched deals in the White Elephant's comfortable atmosphere. [3]

In contrast, the Bucket of Blood on First Street facing the tracks catered to the rougher element, mainly the railroad section gangs. Proprietors John and Mary Boyle offered no frills, but they took a personal interest in their customers. When a man drank away his paycheck on the weekend, they faithfully saw to the task of sobering him up on Monday morning so that he would be ready for the 7 o'clock whistle. [4]

Like the White Elephant, most Albuquerque saloons offered a variety of opportunities for gambling. A significant number of their employees were always "sporting men," as professional gamblers were called. Roulette, keno, faro, chuck-a-luck, fantan, craps, stud poker, and Mexican monte were the favorite games. Commented one astonished Easterner, "The saloons, with three to ten gambling tables each, are in the lead, and the ring of bottles, the rattle of high ball, the click of billiards and the shake of dice accompanied by the roundest and loudest profanity fill the air." [5]

For long, gambling was both legal and wide open in Albuquerque. Town authorities relied heavily upon the sale of saloon licenses and upon the fines imposed for disturbances at the gaming tables to help maintain the municipal government. [6] Since no stigma was attached to games of chance, distinguished pillars of the community indulged openly. One prominent gambling addict was Judge William C. Heacock, who could be found most nights whiling away his time at three-card monte. Whenever he went broke, he called in a town deputy and said, "Get me a drunk with money in his pockets who is guilty of disorderly conduct." [7] Upon the deputy's return with a qualified miscreant, the judge held an impromptu trial, imposed a fine that matched the amount of money in the culprit's wallet, and, thus enriched, continued his game.

In 1907, gambling in Albuquerque was a 15 million dollar annual business. But in that year, New Mexico politicians, in preparation for a major campaign to attain statehood, decided that to put their best face forward, they must prohibit gambling. An act was so passed in the territorial legislature. On the last day of the year, before the measure went into effect, Albuquerque's saloons threw open their bat wing doors, and men and women who had never been inside a gambling place flocked to the roulette wheels and card tables. In the final hours before midnight, the revelry reached an intensity that would not be seen again until the day before National Prohibition was instituted in 1919.[8]

Brothels, which the local press archly termed "palaces of forbidden pleasure," were as common as saloons. Regulated by municipal ordinance, they were concentrated along First Street, Railroad, and Copper.[9] The ladies—"soiled doves" as polite churchgoers called them—hung about the barrooms and gambling dens in the evening hours. Faces dusted with rice powder, lips and cheeks heavily encarmined, and a black beauty patch near the corner of the mouth provided clear evidence of their trade. Little Lina Fergusson, who was accustomed to travel up Copper Avenue with her chums to play on the mesa, once remarked innocently to her mother, Clara, that "it was funny so many ladies sat around in their doorways wearing kimonos in the middle of the afternoon."[10] Thereafter, Mrs. Fergusson saw to it that her daughter used the more respectable Tijeras Avenue.

"All Western towns are vicious but none of them flaunt their vice so openly in the faces of strangers as Albuquerque."[11] So wrote one of New Town's pioneer newsmen. The good and timid element in the community not only had to contend with drinking, gambling, and prostitution, but with an alarming rise in opium smoking. By 1883, four opium houses operated unmolested in the center of town. The habit, no doubt, was introduced by Chinese laborers on the railroad and by Chinese immigrants who at an early date established several laundries in New Albuquerque. An indignant editor of the *Albuquerque Journal* condemned the smokers, who could be seen from the street lying on double-deck bunks in dimly lit rooms puffing the pipes, their necks supported firmly in head-rests.[12] W. F. Saunders, crusading publisher of the *Daily Review,* delivered a public rebuke in evangelical tones. "Many a father, many a mother, and many a wife," he cried, "will wish before long that such fire as that which fell upon Sodom and Gomorrah had come down upon the temples of iniquity which invest this town."[13] Confirmed smokers, however, paid little attention to his rantings. A soiled dove told a reporter that she consumed from 20 to 100 pipes each afternoon at an average cost of about $2. "If I live until opium kills me, I'm satisfied," she declared brazenly.[14]

In such a society, it is scarcely surprising that most men carried arms. In the jargon of the day, a six-shooter went with every pair of pants. Local custom dictated that guns must be worn in plain view on the streets, although in one's office or place of business, it was permissible to keep them concealed. Upon entering a saloon, a universal rule required firearms to be checked with the bartender. Also, known outlaws were usually relieved of their weapons upon entering the town limits, provided the presiding law enforcement officer was brave enough.

As noted in an earlier chapter, the United States marshal for the Territory maintained his headquarters in Albuquerque because of its central location. But since he and his several deputies had jurisdiction over such a vast area, their efforts were spread exceedingly thin.[15] County law enforcement was in the hands of the sheriff, whose office during the last part of the nineteenth century was usually held either by Perfecto Armijo or Santiago Baca. The two men were staunch political rivals and it is said that at election time they garnered votes in a most unorthodox manner.

Preceding the balloting, both candidates rode into the surrounding county to enlist the aid of their brawniest and toughest supporters. On an appointed day, partisans of each man gathered in a vacant lot west of the Armijo House, between Third and Fifth Streets. On signal, the two sides flew at one another with sticks, stones, gun butts, fists, and profane language. Judge William Heacock, who took time out from his game of three-card monte to referee, recalled later that "though nobody was ever killed, the fights were real."[16] A throng of Albuquerqueans regularly assembled on the steps of the Armijo House to watch the fray. To the winner, whether Armijo or Baca, they gave their votes.

Soon after the founding of New Albuquerque, business leaders organized and funded a Merchant's Police Force, staffed by a town marshal and deputies. The first man to hold the marshal's job was an unlikely rogue who went by the assumed name of Milt Yarberry. Before coming to Albuquerque in 1881, he had already won a shady reputation as a dishonest saloonkeeper in Cañon City, Colorado, and in Las Vegas and Bernalillo. But he was known to be quick with his guns, and that qualification, it seems, took precedence over moral rectitude.

The town fathers, however, soon had occasion to question their wisdom in hiring Mr. Yarberry. The first serious incident occurred on March 27, 1881, and involved a man named Harry Brown, son of a former Tennessee governor. Both the marshal and Brown shared the attentions of a pretty widow named Sadie Preston. On the evening of the 27th, Yarberry called his rival into an alley off Railroad Avenue, they argued over Sadie, and it ended with the marshal pulling a gun and pumping four shots into Brown. At once he turned himself in to Sheriff Perfecto Armijo.

At a preliminary hearing, Yarberry claimed self-defense. Although no gun had been found on the victim, he was acquitted.

On the following June 18, the marshal was patrolling the streets when a shot was heard. "Who's firing?" he demanded to know. Someone pointed to Charles Campbell, a railroad carpenter who had the misfortune to be strolling down the street at that moment. Yarberry whipped out his pistol and shot the man dead. According to witnesses, he gave a little dance and shouted gleefully, "I've downed the son-of-a-bitch."[17]

The town marshal again entered a plea of self-defense, but this time it failed to hold water. He was convicted of murder after a trial in May

1882 and sentenced to hang. Some one hundred Albuquerqueans, hoping to speed the course of justice, assembled one evening in a livery stable on First Street and laid plans for a lynching. Sheriff Armijo got wind of the meeting, fearlessly barged in, and forced the crowd to back down.

Yarberry's attorney made an appeal to the Territorial Supreme Court and, while it was being decided, the condemned man was lodged in the Santa Fe jail. The Court upheld the conviction and sentence. Early on the morning of February 9, 1883, Milt Yarberry was herded aboard a special railroad car and under heavy guard sent back to Albuquerque. At the depot he was met by a mob of curious spectators and an escort from the Albuquerque Company of the state militia. Loaded on a street railway car, he made his last ride to the yard of the county jail in Old Town. Scores of citizens had been sent engraved invitations to the hanging, and others, not so favored, paid as much as a dollar for standing room on nearby rooftops. Instead of the solemn mood one might have expected from the crowd, an almost carnival-like atmosphere prevailed.

Still protesting that he had killed only in self-defense, the marshal was led to a special hanging device modeled after plans published in a recent issue of the *Scientific American.* A black hood and noose were fitted over his head and as a 400-pound lead weight dropped, he was hauled into the air, or "Jerked to Jesus," as the press fittingly put it. The body was carried to Santa Barbara Cemetery at the foot of the East Mesa and buried with the rope still in place. Milt Yarberry's hanging was the first and last execution of a peace officer in the New Mexico Territory.[18]

Albuquerque's second town marshal, Robert McGuire, was a man of very different character. He, too, died in office, but in performance of his lawful duty. On November 20, 1886, McGuire got word that two swaggering young outlaws, Charlie Ross and John ("Kid") Johnson had been seen at a dance hall in Martinez Town, a suburb inhabited mainly by Hispanos, which had grown up near the north end of Broadway. The two were part of a gang of rustlers and hold-up artists who had been terrorizing the countryside, and the marshal held warrants for their arrest.

Taking a deputy, E. D. Henry, McGuire went to the dance hall and searched the premises without finding the men. Upon leaving, the officers chanced to see the outlaws through a window of a small adobe house nearby. Rushing the door, they were met by a hail of lead. Deputy Henry fell dead with two bullets in his chest. McGuire received a bullet in the liver and died a few days later from internal hemorrhaging. The two assailants escaped, but young Ross was later captured by Santa Fe Railway detective Carl F. Holton. He was placed in the Bernalillo County jail, although he afterward escaped when a girl friend slipped him a key to the cell. Grief-stricken, Albuquerque lowered its flags to half staff and hung out mourning crepe along the streets to honor the slain officers.[19]

The episode, which contributed to Albuquerque's notoriety as a popular haunt of desperate badmen, was only one of many such dreary happenings. Even the momentary visitor was apt to draw the conclusion that the town's main pastime was gunfighting in the streets. Lieutenant

John G. Bourke, going through on the train in April 1881, descended from his car during a short layover. "At the moment of stepping upon the platform," he records, "two high-toned gentlemen of the town were blazing away with pistols at each other a little farther up the street." "Unfortunately," he adds sardonically, "neither were [sic] killed."[20]

Billy the Kid once went on a spree in Old Town and shot up the Martínez Bar. That was in the days before he worked himself into the history books through his participation in the bloody Lincoln County War.[21] The next look Albuquerque had of the Kid was in March 1881, when he was at the height of his fame. Billy was then a prisoner on a southbound train that paused briefly at the depot. Recently captured, he was being sent from Santa Fe to Mesilla to stand trial for the killing in 1878 of William Brady, sheriff of Lincoln County. Sightseers at the station craned their necks for a glimpse of the Kid through the coach window. The slight young man sat handcuffed under the watchful eye of Deputy United States Marshal Bob Olinger. Olinger had a couple of forty-fives in his belt and rested a sawed-off double-barreled shotgun between his knees. Billy the Kid was to slay the deputy with that same shotgun a month later when he made a daring break from the Lincoln jail, where he had been sent after the Mesilla trial.[22]

Among citizens of modern Albuquerque, the name of "Judge Lynch" means nothing; but a century ago, the phrase was universally understood to signify justice dealt out by a vigilance committee. New Town never possessed the powerful and well-organized vigilante groups that stretched so many necks in Socorro and Las Vegas. But when the occasion demanded and passions flared, Albuquerqueans were not above donning masks, fashioning a hangman's knot, and marching forth in the dead of night to see quick justice done in the court of "Judge Lynch." One celebrated case that resulted in several after-dark hangings was that involving the murder of Colonel Charles Potter.

A United States Geological Surveyor, Potter arrived in New Town during October 1880. His mission was to study the mineral resources of the Territory and compile data for the forthcoming census. He was a prominent resident of Newport, Rhode Island, and the stepson of an ex-Governor of that state, F. S. Van Zandt. The colonel established headquarters in Albuquerque and formulated plans for the carrying out of his survey. But with an eye to lining his own pockets, he also began speculating in mining shares on the side. One of his investments was in stock of the San Pedro Mining Company.

That firm had brought in a mining engineer and was in the process of building a dam across the mouth of one of the canyons on the east slope of the Sandias. The plan was to impound a large quantity of water and pipe it across the valley to the placer gold deposits in the San Pedro Mountains for use in washing out the precious metal. Though the scheme seemed a bit far-fetched, Potter and others were willing to gamble money in the venture.

While in Albuquerque, the colonel ran up a sizeable bill at a Chinese laundry owned by an immigrant named Quong Lee. Being temporarily short of cash, he offered several of the San Pedro Mining certificates in lieu of money to settle his account. The Chinaman took one look at the fancy engraved documents with their bright gold seals and agreed. What might have been worthless stock was, a few months later, converted into a genuine bonanza. General Ulysses S. Grant arrived by train to inspect the San Pedro mining property and was so impressed with its prospects that he agreed to serve as president of the company. On the strength of his name, the stock certificates soared heavenward. Quong Lee immediately sold his shares, married a harlot off Front Street, and departed for San Francisco to begin a new life. Colonel Potter, no doubt, would have experienced considerable regret over the loss of a portion of his investment to the Chinaman, but by the time the stock moved up, he was dead.[23]

As best as Sheriff Perfecto Armijo could piece the matter together, this is how it began. Against the advice of all his friends, Potter had set out alone horseback to visit mines east of Albuquerque. Bandits had been preying on travelers of late, but the colonel professed confidence in his ability to defend himself. First, he made a brief swing to the Hell Canyon diggings. Then a rider reported seeing him headed east through Tijeras Canyon on the road to the San Pedro district. That was the last sighting of Colonel Charles Potter, alive. He simply vanished.

Weeks dragged into months and no clues surfaced. The *Albuquerque Journal* ran a daily advertisement offering a $1,000 reward for the colonel alive, or $200 for information leading to the recovery of his body. Part of the money was put up by Governor Van Zandt, who came out from Rhode Island to aid in the search. Washington was also applying pressure on local authorities, since Potter had been a government employee.

On January 27, 1881, Sheriff Armijo got his first break. He learned that a Bernalillo resident, Pantaleón Miera, had pawned a gold watch in Albuquerque the previous November that matched a description of one belonging to Potter. Going to the loan shop of J. K. Basye, he was told that the watch case and chain had already been melted down, but the interior works had been saved. With them was a small oval picture of Colonel Potter's wife. Inconveniently, Miera was not available for questioning. He had been lynched the month before in Bernalillo for horse stealing.

A little probing, however, disclosed that the deceased had been a member of a rapacious gang of highwaymen led by the notorious Marino Leyba. A six-footer, with handle-bar mustache and steely blue eyes, Leyba operated out of Golden, a ramshackle mining town at the western foot of the San Pedro Mountains. Author Charles F. Lummis, who chanced to see him there in the early 1880s, described the outlaw as "a herculean man of astonishing agility and almost matchless skill with the revolver—one of his favorite pastimes being to spur his fleet horse through a village, shooting off the heads of chickens as he galloped past!"[24] All signs pointed to Colonel Potter having met foul play at the hands of Leyba and his cutthroats, and warrants were issued for their arrest.

Shortly, one of the gang, Escolástico Perea, was seized at Isleta and conveyed to Albuquerque, where, in a full confession, he revealed the fate of the missing surveyor. On his trip up Tijeras Canyon, the colonel had stopped at a hut belonging to a seedy character named California Joe and asked road directions. As chance would have it, Marino Leyba and some of his companions were inside the dwelling enjoying a meal. They quickly hatched a plot of ambush and robbery. One of the men slipped out and whispered to California Joe, enlisting him in the plan. As a result, Colonel Potter, who had no knowledge of the country, was steered onto a side road where later that afternoon he was waylaid and murdered by the bandits. Afterward, they piled logs over his body and set them afire.

With this information, Sheriff Armijo went to Tijeras, found the colonel's remains, and returned them to Albuquerque. He also brought in two of the villains, California Joe and Miguel Barrera, who were locked in a cell with Perea. But their stay there was a short one. Albuquerqueans awoke on the morning of February 1, 1881 to read a startling headline in the *Journal*: "Dancing on Air." Under that grim announcement, the tale was eloquently told. "This morning dawned clear, bright and beautiful over the city of Albuquerque, and as the sun came up from behind the peaks of the Sandias and shed its bright rays over the roofs and flat-topped adobe buildings, they fell on three human forms, stark and stiff, dangling from a wooden beam in front of the county jail."[25]

As the story ran, the town had been swept by the greatest excitement the previous evening when it became known that California Joe and Barrera had added their confessions of guilt to the one already supplied by Perea. Predictions were heard in the saloons that the assassins would never see the light of day. A traveling minstrel show had scheduled a performance that night, however, and the light-hearted entertainment, attended by much of the citizenry, seemed to dispel the talk of violence. Appearances proved deceiving.

At a late hour, a mob of some two hundred men, mostly Hispanos, and with their faces concealed by handkerchiefs, marched resolutely to the jail. The prisoners, struggling desperately, were removed, born to the yard, and, as the press reported it, "lynched into eternity."

"Though lynching in general is to be condemned," editorialized the *Santa Fe New Mexican* a few days later, "yet to every case there is an exception which simply proves the rule, and in cases such as the cowardly and dastardly murder of Colonel Potter, it is very doubtful whether justice can be too swiftly meted out." And the paper further remonstrated, "The sooner the same fate overtakes the remaining culprits the better will it be for that section of the country and New Mexico at large."[26] As if in response to that call, another of the outlaw band, Faustino Gutierres was apprehended a few weeks later, and on the night of February 24 was dealt the same fate as his accomplices by the Albuquerque vigilantes.

That left only the leader, Marino Leyba. With four hangings already accomplished, he evidently concluded that the Territory was too hot for safety, and he fled to Mexico. Returning several years later to his old roost north of the Sandias, he formed a new gang and resumed his misbegotten ways. Lawmen finally killed him in a gunfight near Golden in 1886.[27]

The extralegal execution of the Potter murderers received wide press coverage, but another triple hanging by the vigilantes got scarcely a mention. That was because the men who carried it out were the nabobs of the community. Three ruffians with six-shooters belted to their waists came to town one day and while drinking whiskey at a saloon were heard to make threats against the life of Franz Huning. The nature of their quarrel with Albuquerque's premier citizen is not known. Quietly, Huning and his friends gathered behind closed doors in the living room of his home. When the meeting was over, Franz told his wife that he would remain out late that night, but not to worry. The entire party then mounted up and rode away. At sunrise the following day, bodies of the three gunmen were found dangling from the huge cottonwoods shading the Huning flour mill. The act seems to have had the complete approval of the citizenry, and the manner in which it was carried out enhanced Albuquerque's growing reputation as a graveyard for professional badmen.[28]

Vigilance committees flourished throughout the American West whenever people lost faith in the normal judicial process. That was unquestionably the case in Albuquerque, where it was long said that any jury could be bought for $20 and a gallon of whiskey. C. D. ("Doc") Favor, a former Albuquerque justice of the peace and part-time undertaker, in an interview given to the *Chicago Tribune* in 1890, confirmed the unseemly fact. He told of sitting on the bench a few years earlier when a known horsethief and killer was brought to trial. Although the evidence for conviction was overwhelming, the jury returned a verdict of not guilty. Favor, who knew that four of the jurors had been bribed, was on the point of dismissing the case when a violent electrical storm came up. Suddenly, a bolt of lightning crashed down the chimney, entered the room, and struck the accused dead. "I had been in New Mexico for five years," Favor acknowledged solemnly to the *Tribune*, "yet that was the first time I had ever seen justice meted out in an Albuquerque courtroom."[29]

Random murders and hangings attracted attention in the years after 1880, while a variety of lesser crimes were so common as to pass virtually unnoticed. One popular racket involved the sale of bogus mining claims at the foot of the sandhills just east of the railroad yards. Bunko men staked out patches of ground, salted them with a little gold dust, and conducted thither unsuspecting dudes who had recently debarked at the depot. The formula of deceit called for an accomplice to come up, while buyer and seller were discussing terms, and bid up the claim. After many an innocent Easterner had been fleeced by this game, the vigilantes took a hand and drove the crooks from Albuquerque's limits.

Among the most unsavory of lawbreakers were the so-called dealers in second-hand coffins. One such dealer was Sam Fike, who also doubled as the town dogcatcher. Following a funeral, he would sneak into the cemetery, dig up the grave, strip the body of valuables, rebury it, and then take the coffin to the undertaker and sell it back. Accounts say that for over a year after the founding of New Town, Albuquerque got by with a single coffin.[30]

One buyer appears to have been Doc Favor, who before being elected justice of the peace, ran an undertaking parlor in the back room of an Albuquerque saloon. In time, before the town's reputation was be-smirched beyond repair, legitimate undertakers opened for business and ended the illicit trade in stolen coffins. At the forefront of the reformers were the brothers C. H. and Oren Strong. In 1881, they were passing through Albuquerque with their families in three covered wagons when one of the oxen dropped dead on the corner of Second Street and Copper. That chance mishap caused the Strongs to decide to settle where they were. They first opened a furniture-making shop, then branched into the mortuary business when they were able to buy out Doc Favor upon his election as a petty judge. The Strongs and their descendants (who have continued the old firm to the present day) gained considerable wealth and influence after the turn of the century. Their rise to prominence, along with other undertakers, was linked to a unique phenomenon in Albuquerque. As the city became a Mecca for health-seekers from the nation's more inhospitable climes, persons in the funeral trade became numbered among the busiest and most prosperous members of the community.

In the years Albuquerque was struggling to become a cradle of respectability, it was also called upon to face periodic threats to public safety posed by fires and floods. As New Town took shape, with rows of frame buildings lining its main streets, the question of fire protection assumed increasing importance. An observant visitor in 1881 took note of the "tinder-box style of building" and prophesied that, "after a great fire has swept all the wooden structures, as it inevitably must, a return to the comfortable and rational adobes may be expected."[31] Santa Fe, because of its adobe construction, was then regarded as the only fireproof city in the United States, and at least a few practical Albuquerqueans thought a mistake had been made in not following the capital's example.

Most newcomers, however, were unfamiliar with the merits of adobe and expressed a preference for wood frame structures. Their unwillingness to give adobe a try may have been heightened by an incident that occurred just as downtown construction was beginning to accelerate. On April 6, 1881, the press reported this small catastrophy: "Last night the new Lail Building was blown over by a whiff of wind. The edifice was a large two-story adobe, plated with iron to make it fireproof. The wind came from the west, struck the block broadside, and it toppled. Martsoff, the builder, and six or seven workmen had just left the ground floor before the gale hit. Martsoff is said to have lost $3000 by the tumble, and it is very likely he will feel the loss deeply."[32] No doubt, there were those who concluded that adobe buildings, at least ones of the two-story variety, were unsound.

Devastating fires that gutted entire cities were an acknowledged fact of life in nineteenth-century America. And so, the people of Albuquerque lost little time in preparing their defenses. A volunteer fire company was organized, but in the beginning, having no equipment, it relied solely on the tried-and-true bucket brigade. The principal source of water was an old irrigation ditch that crossed Railroad Avenue between Second and Third. Its flow was not always reliable, and, to make matters worse, residents commonly befouled the waters with sewage. The latter practice prompted the *Albuquerque Journal* to lament, "A person feels like having a clothes pin on his nose to keep out the disagreeable odors."[33] But contaminated water proved just as effective in quenching a fire as fresh.

In 1882 enough contributions were raised to purchase the town's first fire cart. Sheriff Perfecto Armijo and several business men donated materials for a station, a small wooden building erected on First Street opposite the Central Bank. Pranksters often stole the cart, or the ladder and leather buckets. Locking the station failed to curb such mischief since practically everyone in town had a key.[34]

With creation of a formal town government in 1885, purchase of additional equipment was authorized and a new and larger station was rented on Railroad Avenue.[35] Also, a formal fire zone was designated in the center of downtown, comprising the area between the tracks and Fifth, and between Copper and Lead. Ordinances prohibited further construction of frame buildings and the storage of oil, gunpowder, and other flammable materials inside the zone.[36] Limits of the district were progressively extended until, by 1906, they covered 2.25 square miles, within which were some 1,800 buildings.[37]

The number of volunteer companies soon expanded to three. Each bore the name of a prominent resident who acted as sponsor. There were the H. B. Fergusson Hook and Ladder Company, the Scott Moore Hose Company Number 1, and the A. A. Grant Hose Company Number 2. Membership in these companies was highly coveted by the men in Albuquerque. Part of the attraction must have been the flashy uniforms, sure to attract any lady's eye. The costume included a billed cap, red shirt with blue collar, black belt (with the name of the company stitched on), black trousers, and an engraved silver badge to be worn on the chest. A full company was composed of twenty-five men, plus two young boys, one serving as mascot and the other as lantern boy, who ran ahead of the cart at night to light the way.

The principal fire alarm was a bell suspended from a steel tower where the tracks crossed Railroad Avenue. When it sounded, the Santa Fe shop whistle and the bell on the switch engine at the depot chimed in. Passersby fired pistols in the air and set up a frightful yelling to add to the din. As people crowded into the streets, excitement swept the entire town. At the first alarm, the volunteer firemen raced to their stations. Fierce rivalry existed between the companies to be first on the scene.

The earliest fire vehicles were pulled by the men themselves, not by horses. Hence, all volunteers had to be strong and hardy runners.

The first arrivals at the station dragged out the cart and started it rolling toward the fire. Each unit, whether hook and ladder or hose cart, was mounted with a bell of different tone. This allowed latecomers to locate their company as it dashed through the streets and to take up their places on the team. To facilitate men joining in on the run, the leather harness was provided with quick-release snapout fasteners. These devices were not only useful for getting into harness swiftly, but also for getting out. As the vehicles built up speed, slower men in the rear of the team were in danger of being run over. Standard practice called for them to release the fasteners and dodge out of the way, leaving the stronger leaders to carry on.[38]

The twenty years following 1880 were punctuated by a number of major fires in New Albuquerque's central business district. Fortunately, in every case a combination of luck and the skilled efforts of the volunteer companies prevented them from spreading and becoming monumental disasters. In the early morning hours of March 6, 1882, for example, a fierce blaze broke out in the W. L. Trimble Livery Stable. "At 2 A.M.," said the news accounts, "the blowing of whistles and unearthly yells broke upon the slumbers of the threatened city. At first appearance, the impression was that the burg was doomed. This was made more evident by the fact that the wind was blowing a perfect gale."[39] Although several neighboring buildings, among them the Munro Millinery Shop and the Star Clothing Store, succumbed to the flames, a change in the direction of the wind allowed firemen to contain the blaze and save Albuquerque from an even greater loss.

Before the turn of the century, three of New Town's best-known landmarks were destroyed by fire: the Armijo House in 1897, the Grant Building in 1898, and the San Felipe Hotel in 1899. At the time of the Grant Building's demise, the Ilfeld Brothers store, then the largest mercantile firm in the Territory, occupied the entire first floor, while the second floor held the opera theater. Volunteers directed eight streams of water on the burning building until the pressure failed, whereupon the structure was abandoned to its fate.[40]

Twelve-year-old Will Keleher, playing in the streets, was the first to spot black smoke billowing from the roof of the San Felipe Hotel late one August afternoon. Gamewell alarm boxes had recently been installed on convenient poles around town and the alert youngster ran to one of those. "I broke the glass on the box," he recalled many years later, "pulled the lever, and set in motion a chain of events visualized by every small boy, but seldom realized in actuality."[41] His prompt action brought the Volunteer Fire Department with lightning speed, but it failed to save the venerable San Felipe. By nightfall, only the smoking skeleton of its walls remained standing.

On the night of October 19, 1896, there occurred a spectacular incident which gave Albuquerque a publicly acclaimed hero. The Territorial Fair, held on grounds southwest of Old Town, was ending its run with a final parade that led from the plaza eastward along Railroad Avenue. In the center of the procession, a man named John Braden drove an "ammunition wagon" loaded with fireworks. Suddenly, there was a loud explosion and the wagon was enveloped in flames. Rockets went off, struck the horses, and sent the terrified animals careening down the center of the avenue. For a moment, it appeared as if a float carrying the fair queen and her attendants would be hit, but Braden gamely held to the reins and avoided a collision.

At Railroad and Third the way was blocked by the Scott Moore Hose Company cart and Braden's runaways were forced to halt. At the same moment, he fell to the ground, his body aflame, and crawled toward the sidewalk begging bystanders to tear off his clothes. But help came too late. A few hours after the terrible accident, he died.

Albuquerque was plunged into mourning. At the largest funeral seen to date, Town Marshal Fred Fornoff expressed the grateful sentiment of the whole community: "No doubt that John Braden saved the young ladies on the Queen's float from death or serious injury. I never saw or heard of such heroism. He could have jumped from the wagon when the explosion occurred and saved himself, but he stayed at his post and prevented the frightened horses from trampling upon and doubtless killing a number of people."[42]

Although occasional fires did grave damage to Albuquerque, it was the seasonal floods that inspired the greatest dread and proved costliest in terms of lives and property lost. Renowned archaeologist Adolph F. Bandelier, riding the train up the Middle Valley during the seething flood of 1884, reflected upon the effect such inundations probably had had on the early Pueblo Indian population. "It is exceedingly interesting," he entered in his journal, "for the past history of the country and explains many features connected with the occupation and abandonment of the valley. It shows that the Rio Grande bottom, perfectly habitable and safe during long periods of time, may suddenly be swept by a flood obliterating human habitation and burrowing new channels, thus permanently changing the distribution of arable plots and sites for pueblos. Such floods as the one now are not frequent, but they have occurred before."[43]

The colonial settlers of Albuquerque must have been flooded out with some regularity, but the Spanish records are so spotty that little information remains concerning their travail. After independence, in 1828 a major flood spilled down the valley from Bernalillo all the way to El Paso. Although no details are available, we can guess that the devastation to towns and farms was of considerable magnitude.

As Albuquerque began to grow in the post–Civil War years, the economic repercussions of flooding took on new meaning. Reference has already been made in an earlier chapter to the setback Old Town businesses suffered when the Rio Grande overflowed its banks in the summer of 1874. On that occasion, shopkeepers loaded what merchandise they could salvage into wagons and fled, while the majority of residents escaped to the hills on the east, where they lived for days in tents.

From the outset, the site of New Town showed itself to be even more vulnerable to floodwaters than the area around the plaza. Not only was it several feet lower, but it lay astride the abandoned river channel, which hugged the eastern edge of the valley from Alameda south to Barelas. The Santa Fe tracks roughly paralleled the channel, and, after heavy rains, the barrow ditches on either side of the rails became small raging rivers. Runoff from summer cloudbursts in the Sandias posed still another hazard. Normally dry arroyo indenting the East Mesa emptied into the valley immediately above and below New Albuquerque. When filled with flash floods, acccording to the description of one astonished observer, they produced a "deep and distant roar, momentarily growing louder until the noise is deafening, a foaming and hissing sheet of water tearing down from the mountains, filling from bank to bank the broad beds, empty a moment before. Great boulders are tossed about like eggs, and are crushed and ground with a booming and crashing like the thunder of artillery."[44] Railroad bridges spanning the lateral arroyos caught the full force of these sudden floods and were often hurtled into the torrent.

Although New Albuquerque experienced some inconvenience from high water during the first three summers after its founding, it was not until 1884 that the town got a real taste of flooding. Early in the spring, travelers coming out of the northern mountains reported an unusually heavy snowpack, and by mid-May the *Santa Fe New Mexican* was warning: "Unprecedented snows in southern Colorado the past winter are melting and floods on the Rio Grande are creating alarm along the valley."[45]

The previous year, Bernalillo County had formed a River Commission, with power to levy a small assessment on all property within 5 miles of the Rio Grande. The money thereby derived was earmarked for the construction of earthworks at points where the river was prone to break through its banks. By June 1883, only $250 had been spent on such projects, which scarcely made a dent in the problem. But at least an agency with funds was in place and was prepared to take larger action when it could.[46]

As word circulated the following spring that the annual thaw might lead to enormous flooding, members of the Commission, joined by Angus Grant, Santiago Baca, Civil Engineer W. F. Hill, and other civic leaders, undertook a tour of inspection upriver. They wanted to look over the terrain and see what precautionary measures could be taken to prevent an overflow into the lowlands bordering Albuquerque on the north. Their survey revealed, not unexpectedly, that the greatest danger lay 2 miles above Alameda, where the river started its loop to the west and the old channel had its beginning. They suggested building a dike at that point, one that would hold back the river's swell and prevent it from breaking through into the abandoned bed that pointed like a dagger at the vitals of New Albuquerque. The proposed structure would also shield Alameda, which had been practically erased by the big flood of 1874 and was only now beginning to look like a community again. The people there wanted no repeat of the earlier disaster, if such could be avoided.

Workers were enlisted and by mid-May a lengthy dike was in place. It commenced at the railroad track on the east side of the valley, extended

5,000 feet nearly due west, and then angled toward the south in a short leg that terminated at the river bank near the mouth of the main irrigation ditch (popularly called the Chamisal Ditch). The embankment averaged 4 feet in height, 6 feet in width across the top, and was faced with sod blocks, or *terrones*.[47] But was it strong enough and high enough to do the job? Albuquerqueans were worried, and not without reason, for as May advanced and the press reported the Rio Grande increasingly "on the boom," no one doubted that this would be the mightiest flood in memory.

By the last week of the month, much of the river bottom from the Española Valley south to Mesilla was inundated. A view from out in space would have shown a narrow lake, turbid and roiling, bisecting the heartland of New Mexico. For all the power of the flood, the Alameda dike held, except for an occasional break here and there, which was quickly repaired.

On May 27, Angus Grant and Scott Moore made one of the many inspection trips to the dike conducted by anxious business leaders. Grant afterward informed a reporter for the *Albuquerque Journal,* "The water is higher now than it has been at any time, heretofore, and if the dike had not been built it would just about have filled the low places north of Alameda. The dike is standing splendidly and is turning all the water right back into the current of the river."[48]

The success of the barrier delighted the *Journal,* not only because it afforded protection for the town, but also because it provided ammunition in an ongoing war of words with newspapers in Santa Fe. The bitter rivalry that would soon develop between Albuquerque and Santa Fe over location of the capital was foreshadowed by the petty and almost inexplicable trading of insults during the dark days of the 1884 flood.

The unsavory tone of the squabbling is plain from this commentary by the *Journal*:

> Our good friends in the *Santa Fe Review* office are undoubtedly very much dissatisfied with the manner in which nature is managing her snow business this season. From the expression of the paper over the last two months, there is no reasonable doubt of the fact that they have been looking forward in high glee to an opportunity for a general rejoicing over the flooding of Albuquerque, about this time, and to find now that the river at its highest stage has not been within a mile of the town, undoubtedly causes them sore disappointment. True, the water is running through some of the streets of Socorro and San Marcial, but all that doesn't count, for it wasn't Socorro or San Marcial that they wanted to drown out. They staked everything on the inundation of Albuquerque, and Albuquerque persists in standing at a safe distance and serenely contemplating the river at its highest stages, without so much as wetting her feet.

Now thoroughly aroused to the loftiest pitch of journalistic indignation, the paper continued: "Our Santa Fe neighbors have given unmistakable evidence of the fact that nothing would afford them more solid comfort than to be able to chronicle a calamity to Albuquerque, especially by flood, and it is undoubtedly very galling to them to find Albuquerque sitting high and dry, while other towns are in the water."[49]

The *Journal's* remonstrances to the contrary, the community and its environs did not escape unscathed. The bridge west of Old Town went out, as did most other bridges in the direction of El Paso. The A&P railroad bridge at Isleta survived, but in such shaky condition that trains dared cross it only during daylight hours and at a crawl. Rail service north and south of Albuquerque was continually disrupted by washouts during much of May and June. At the depot, stranded passengers waited long and impatiently for service to resume, and huge quantities of mail and freight accumulated.

Below Barelas, the villages of Peralta, Valencia, Tomé, and Belen were almost completely submerged. Their residents, forsaking crumbling adobe houses, sought refuge in the neighboring hills. An appeal for aid went to Governor Lionel Sheldon at Santa Fe, and he in turn wired Washington requesting assistance. Four men attempting to cross the treacherous waters opposite Barelas in a skiff were swamped by an ocean-size wave and drowned.[50]

On May 30, railway engineeer Lewis Kingman en route through Albuquerque was prevailed upon to visit the dike and give an opinion as to its trustworthiness. After a personal examination, he pronounced it sound, saying that the entire earthwork was correctly placed and should withstand any rise in the river, except one that went over the top. The one weak section was at the lower west end, which received the greatest buffeting from the eroding current. Special watch should be kept there, he advised.[51]

On June 5, the Rio Grande crested at Albuquerque. Three days before, when it appeared the peak was approaching, a rumor flew through town that the dike had given way. Instantly, the alarm bell sounded, whistles wailed, and men rushed to the train station with shovels and gunny sacks in hand. Elias Stover, Angus Grant, William Hazeldine, and others of influence burst into the AT&SF office with an urgent appeal for transportation. In less than an hour, an engine with two flatcars was puffing toward Alameda carrying 200 volunteers.

The dike was found to be intact, but the turbid water had climbed to within inches of the top. At the west end, where Kingman had earlier warned of trouble, the current, said one man, "was rushing and roaring like a miniature Niagara."[52] The work crew from Albuquerque joined Alameda residents and Indians from Sandia Pueblo who were already on the scene. The force, totaling some 500, toiled through the night, reinforcing the embankment with sandbags and brush.

A small section of the dike at its western extremity did give way, flooding Alameda. But the frantic efforts at sandbagging preserved the remainder and spared New Albuquerque from serious harm. A few days later, the welcome news was received from Taos that most of the snow had at last melted off the mountain peaks. Receding of the flood waters, however, proved disappointingly slow. Much of the Middle Valley remained inundated through June and the first half of July. Not until August 18 did the railway succeed in restoring normal train service in and out of Albuquerque.[53]

The Rio Grande again went on the rampage in 1885 and 1886, although the havoc was less widespread than in 1884. One memorable calamity, which occurred in the early morning hours of July 19, 1885, was produced, not by overflow of the river, but by runoff from a sudden downpour in the Sandias. A stream of water cascading from the heights burrowed a hole 15 feet deep under the Santa Fe tracks about 9 miles north of Bernalillo. Darkness hid the damage and a perfect trap was set for the first train to come by.

By 11:59 Saturday night, the eastbound train departed Albuquerque. Behind the engine rolled a Wells Fargo express car, a freight car loaded with valley fruit, a day coach, and three Pullman cars. Less than an hour later, all were either smashed or derailed at the washout in what headlines the following morning proclaimed, "A Railroad Horror." One of the first reporters on the scene re-created, for the benefit of readers, the moment of the wreck and its grisly aftermath. "The ponderous engine sank as if into the earth, the air was filled with an unearthly rattle and crash, and the fiend-god of terror, death, and destruction smiled in ghastly satisfaction over a scene which pen cannot describe, or human imagination depict. Amidst the groans of wounded men, the screams of women and children, and the hissing of escaping steam from the now powerless engine, confusion and terror reigned supreme."[54]

A wrecker train that hurried to the site from Albuquerque next morning found the cars up-turned and scrambled, the engineer and a fireman dead; another fireman badly scalded by the ruptured boiler; and the express messenger severely injured. Miraculously, the passengers in the coach and sleeping cars, who had been flung about like cornhusk dolls upon impact, had all escaped with bruises and minor cuts. A survey by daylight disclosed the cause of the misfortune, and a subsequent verdict by investigators absolved both the deceased engineer and the railway company of blame. It was just the sort of accident to be expected during flood season in the Middle Valley.[55]

For the next half century the threat of periodic flooding was to hang like a sword over the heads of the people of Albuquerque. But while taking the danger in stride, they did not sit idly by and await the consequences dealt them by fate and the weather. Even before the high water of 1884 had subsided, residents gathered at a public meeting to formulate a resolution asking Congress for an appropriation to fund flood control. Specifically, they wanted a series of levees built along the river bank to provide security for both Old Town and New.[56] Perhaps aware that any federal help was apt to be a long time coming, Albuquerqueans, in the best pioneer tradition, decided in the short term to look to their own defenses.

They initiated construction of levees, installed rip-rap where the river was prone to bank-cutting, dug drainage ditches, and reinforced bridges. In 1891, through the joint efforts of the city and county, a larger and more substantial dike was completed at Alameda, to replace the original 1884 structure. Rows of willows were planted in front of the new barrier to serve as a breakwater, and the earthworks were seeded in hope that a grasscover would forestall erosion.[57]

These dogged efforts to bridle the Rio Grande met with only partial success. In wet years, emergency crews remained on constant alert, ready to dash to any point on the Alameda dike or ancillary levees where the river tried to break through. Their effectiveness was proved in 1902 when heavy rains sent the Rio Grande over its embankment. The trouble was first discovered by a farmer, Juan Barela, who in the style of Paul Revere leaped on his horse and galloped into Albuquerque, shouting that the dike was out and water was rushing toward the city. Firemen, policemen, and citizen volunteers grabbed their equipment and raced northward. They worked the night away, fortified with bottles of Monogram whiskey and hot coffee, sent by Albuquerque saloons "to ward off pneumonia." By dawn, the flood waters, reaching almost to Mountain Road just above downtown, had been stopped and turned back to the river. Barela's ride, speedy work, and perhaps the Monogram whiskey had prevented a disaster.[58]

The flooding problem in the Middle Valley was not attacked in any comprehensive manner until organization of the Rio Grande Conservancy District in 1925. Even then, while a master plan for drainage and flood control was devised, more decades were to pass before the massive sums of money became available for the needed work. As late as 1941, a segment of the levees gave way, funneling a mighty stream of tawny water down First Street and causing a million dollars worth of damage.[59] Not until mid-century, after the Air Force and Atomic Energy Commission had settled upon Albuquerque as the site for vast installations, did the government assault the flood problem on a grand scale. In 1950 the Army Corps of Engineers initiated work on the Jemez Canyon Dam to check flash floods on the Jemez River. That was followed by construction of Abiquiu Dam on another tributary of the Rio Grande, the Rio Chama. And finally, in the late 1970s, the huge Cochiti Dam was completed on the Rio Grande itself. These structures not only permit the impounding and controlled release of flood waters, they hold back the silt that otherwise would be carried to the Middle Valley and deposited in the main channel, thereby increasing chances of the river leaving its banks during the spring and summer runoff.

The dam-building program, coordinated with other Corps projects, such as dredging the Rio Grande's main bed and upgrading the levees, are all aimed at controlling the entire river system so as to save communities within it from disaster. Yet, in spite of all accomplishments to date, there persists the potential for a major flood in Albuquerque.

The Finer Things

HAD A GROUP OF no-nonsense experts been commissioned in the early 1880s to study New Albuquerque and to submit a forecast as to its possibilities of one day attaining the respectability that goes with the development of religious, educational, and cultural institutions, the experts might well have concluded, on that score at least, that the town had little future. Like frontier communities throughout the West, Albuquerque at the start seemed to feed and grow on its saloons, gambling parlors, and brothels, and to derive a certain perverse vitality from gunfights, public hangings, and night rides of vigilantes. But here, as elsewhere, both the loose living and the violence were to prove a transitory stage in the ongoing process of forming a new municipality in the standard American mold.

Some years were to elapse, admittedly, before Albuquerque was vested with the full quota of churches, schools, theaters, and parks that supplied the usual requirements for a town claiming a legitimate degree of sophistication and urbanity. But the movement toward such amenities, while slow in gathering steam, was under way almost from the moment the first train came huffing and hissing into New Town. The civic leaders, who held in their minds' eyes a picture of Albuquerque as it ought to be, were determined that in the rush to promote material prosperity, the religious and educational aspects of community life should not go unattended.

One piece of evidence supporting that fact can be found in action taken by directors of the New Mexico Town Company. In platting the original townsite along the tracks, they made a conspicuous show of offering free lots for the construction of churches.[1] The first church in New Albuquerque, however, was founded in the east highlands, outside the townsite, and on a lot donated by Franz Huning. It was a Congregational church headed by the Reverend Jacob Mills Ashley. An English-born missionary who had earlier been chased out of Catholic Ireland,

Ashley showed up in Old Town in March 1879. His eldest son, Alfred, appeared to be suffering from terminal consumption, and the father had brought him to New Mexico in hopes the mild climate would ease his last days. Alfred, to everyone's surprise, made a moderate recovery, allowing the Reverend Ashley to turn his attention to the organizing of a Protestant congregation.[2]

It was an uphill task, not only because the Reverend found few members of his sect in Albuquerque, but also because his stident anti-Catholicism earned him the enmity of the local priests. In a letter to his cousin in London, Ashley remarked with bitterness, "The people are blind Catholics and the Jesuit Priests have complete control over them. There are about a dozen of them here and you may see one or another of them, with their long black robes in the street at any time." And he added that the fathers were mostly Italians who had been kicked out of their own country (which was patently untrue), and they would be kicked out of Albuquerque if they did not behave themselves.[3]

As it happened, it was the Reverend Ashley himself who suffered expulsion—from temporary quarters in which he had begun services in Old Town. As he tells it, "I commenced a mission . . . first preaching in the County Court room; but the Catholics soon got us out of there. Then we furnished a room partly built, leasing it for six months and they got us out of there as soon as our lease was up, and for a time we could find no place to preach in, except now and then a dark hall."[4]

The birth of New Town the following year, peopled mostly by Protestants, gave the beleagured Ashley a chance to find a place for himself. The small, white-framed church he raised there was a deliberate and glaring departure from the architectural style of New Mexico's Catholic edifices. Completed and dedicated in April 1881, the Congregational Church opened its doors with a total membership of three persons.

Although the Reverend Ashley remained at loggerheads with the Jesuit priests, he got along well with other Protestant ministers, especially the Reverend Nathaniel Hawthorne Gale who organized a mission of the Methodist Episcopal Church (later the First Methodist Church) on April 18, 1880. The previous year, Ashley and Gale had held services jointly in the court house before being turned out of those quarters. Once the Congregational Church was up in New Town, Ashley allowed the Methodists to share use of his building until they could get one of their own. Under the Reverend Gale's dedicated guidance, a structure was finished late in 1881, the funds coming in part from contributions made by employees of the A&P Railroad. Land for the church, located at Lead and Third, was donated by the Townsite Company.[5]

The Episcopalians were another Protestant denomination that showed an early interest in Albuquerque. Ordained clergymen made occasional visits to Old Town in the 1870s, but between those visits Judge Hezekiah S. Johnson, whom we first encountered as editor of the *Rio Abajo Weekly Press* in the Civil War years, conducted lay services each Sunday in the dining room of Tom Post's Exchange Hotel.[6] In February 1880, a separate room was furnished as a chapel, representing the beginnings of St. John's

Episcopal Church. Two years later, the congregation acquired its own building in New Town, and thereafter, under the ministry of the Reverend Henry Forrester, became one of the most solid religious denominations in the community.[7]

Other Protestant sects soon made their presence felt in Albuquerque. The Reverend Sheldon Jackson, a celebrated missionary, formed the first Presbyterian congregation in 1880 by assembling five members who met regularly in a private home in Old Town. Shortly, the Reverend James A. Menaul arrived and led a drive for construction of the first Presbyterian Church in New Albuquerque on lots given by the Town Company at Silver and Fifth. The Baptists chartered a church in 1887, and were followed by the Lutherans, who established St. Paul's Church in 1891. The Lutheran congregation was spearheaded by two residents of German ancestry, Herman Blueher, famed for his bountiful truck gardens near the plaza, and Jacob Korber, a blacksmith and carriage maker, who later developed one of Albuquerque's most prestigious mercantile firms.[8] Blacks, though few in number at the beginning, managed in 1882 to form an African Methodist Episcopal Church with the Reverend Spotwood Rice as pastor. The congregation floated about, using temporary quarters, until a permanent church could be built in 1892.[9]

Albuquerque's Jewish community went without a place of worship until 1897, when fifty families organized a congregation and laid plans for erecting a synagogue. Three years later (September 14, 1900), the new Temple Albert, at Seventh and Gold, was dedicated in solemn services presided over by Rabbi Pizer Jacobs. The ceremony included handing of the temple key to the president of the congregation, Henry N. Jaffa, first mayor of Albuquerque.[10]

The Catholic Church, given new life by Bishop Lamy in the 1860s, and enspirited by the tireless ministry of the foreign Jesuits during the 1870s, continued to dominate religious life in Old Town where the population remained predominantly Hispano. But in 1882, it followed the lead of the Protestants, and opened the Immaculate Conception Church in the fast-growing town beside the tracks. The new parish attracted members from all levels of the business community, from the families of railroad workers, and from the few Hispanos who took up residence in New Town.

The proliferation of churches was mirrored by a corresponding growth in schools sponsored by the various religious denominations. Free public education came late to the Territory of New Mexico, leaving private schools, most of them church-sponsored, to fill the vacuum. The Catholics had the edge, not only because they enjoyed a long head start and possessed numerical superiority, but because their prelate, Bishop Lamy, channeled much of his surplus energy into fostering a parochial educational system.

Beginning in 1851, Lamy enticed several religious orders—the Sisters of Loretto, the Christian Brothers, and the Sisters of Charity—to send him teachers to staff the English schools he was busily setting up. In 1866, he went to Europe to enlist Jesuit priests for the same purpose. While returning the following year over the Santa Fe Trail, accompanied by the Italian fathers and six Sisters of Charity recruited in Cincinnati, his wagon train was attacked by hostile Indians. The eastern press, on the basis of unsubstantiated rumor, reported to the world that the bishop and ten priests had been killed, scalped, and mutilated, and that the sisters had been ravished and carried into captivity. Happily, the story was without foundation, and the party reached its destination eager to get on with the task of educating the youth of New Mexico.[11]

As earlier noted, the Jesuits took charge of Albuquerque's San Felipe Neri Church in 1868. After several false starts, they managed to open a school for sixty boys in quarters rented from County Commissioner Ambrosio Armijo. The year was 1872. The school only got off the ground because it was funded by $600 of public money, which made it, in theory, a public school. The territorial legislature earlier in the year had appropriated that sum and offered it to Father Donato Gasparri as an inducement to open an educational facility for the youth of Albuquerque.[12]

The Jesuit school stumbled along fitfully through the 1870s, kept alive by periodic shots of government money. The subsidies involved Father Gasparri in a bitter controversy with territorial Secretary William G. Ritch, over the question of Church participation in public education. The matter also sparked resentment among Protestants, after the founding of New Albuquerque, for by then county tax revenues were also being allocated to the Jesuits to support their educational endeavors.[13]

In those first years, only one serious challenge was mounted against the Jesuit monopoly over education, and it proved short-lived. The Reverend Patrick D. McElroy in January 1872 opened a Protestant academy near the plaza. A Presbyterian minister, McElroy was referred to by the Catholic fathers, with some derision, as "a renegade Irishman." Having little monetary support and fewer pupils, he was forced to close his school in the spring of 1874.[14]

What slim educational opportunities existed in the Albuquerque of the 1870s were reserved exclusively for males. Franz Huning's daughter Clara, relfecting upon the situation years afterward, declared acidly, "Schools were kept by the priests for boys only. Girls did not need an education."[15]

In 1880, Father Gasparri invited the Sisters of Charity to come to Old Albuquerque and take over the Church's education program. His request, in part, represented a tacit acknowledgment that schooling under his Order had not fared well. But it was also prompted by the Jesuits' desire to concentrate their attention on regular ecclesiastical duties in the expanding San Felipe Neri parish. At any event, the arrival of six sisters the following year provided a healthy boost to the educational fortunes of both the Catholic Church and Albuquerque.

The nuns discovered, to their dismay, after taking the train down from Santa Fe and being shuttled to the plaza, that their living quarters were still under construction. Father Gasparri had hired workmen to build a two-story adobe convent along the west side of the church (on the site of the former parish cemetery), but rains had slowed the work and caused a corner of the walls to collapse. A perky young nun, Sister Blandina Segale, a native of Genoa, Italy, made some suggestions to improve progress, and when he saw that she knew what she was talking about, Father Gasparri eagerly exclaimed, "For God's sake, Sister, please take it in hand."[16]

And that is what Sister Blandina did. Returning to Santa Fe, she engaged an Italian stonecutter, who had been imported to work on Lamy's new cathedral, led him back to Albuquerque, and gave instructions to put the convent right. "I had him lay a stone foundation," she wrote, "and carry the stonework half way above the first story. Naturally, there was no more collapsing."[17] The convent building stands to this day, on the northwest corner of the plaza, a monument to her spirit and enterprise.

By September 1881, with construction complete, the Sisters were ready for the fall term.[18] In rooms of their convent they opened not one, but two, schools: the parochial Our Lady of the Angels Private School, and the separate Old Town Public School. Girls as well as boys were admitted to the public school, the nuns teaching the former and the Jesuit fathers the latter.[19]

Never ones to rest on laurels, the Sisters of Charity soon cast an appraising eye on the rising bustle near the tracks. Recorded Sister Blandina: "Here our New Albuquerque is a town of intense mushroom growth. . . . Citizens encouraged each other to 'Build Albuquerque.' We secured sixty-four lots to do likewise. We fully realized that Old Albuquerque would remain in *status quo* and New Albuquerque would progress."[20]

Upon a portion of the sixty-four lots, cornering on Sixth and New York Avenue (modern Lomas), the nuns in 1882 initiated work on a new academy, which was completed and opened as a public day school the following year. Sister Blandina, her qualifications now firmly established, served as chief architect and construction superintendent. Referring to herself as the "fit-in-to-any assignment sister," she also took charge of erecting an annex in 1885 to house a boarding school.[21] From these efforts evolved the highly esteemed St. Vincent's Academy for girls.[22] In those years, the Sisters of Charity also developed small day schools in nearby Barelas and Los Duranes.

On December 18, 1882, while the sisters' new education program was speeding forward, the Albuquerque church received a sudden jolt with the death from a stroke of Father Gasparri. Of the dedicated Italian priest, who for more than a decade had played an integral role in the town's history, Sister Blandina wrote piously in her diary, "God took the man of Faith to himself. I trust his life will be written for the encouragement of others."[23]

The year before the coming of the railroad, the Reverend Charles R. Bliss, representing Colorado College of Colorado Springs, appeared in Old Town with a proposal. His institution, as he explained, was lending support for establishment of private academies in the western territories, where public school systems had not yet come into being. Should some of Albuquerque's wealthy and influential citizens be willing to organize an academy, then he would promise to provide teachers and guarantee their salaries. The offer met with ready acceptance. The Albuquerque Academy was promptly incorporated under the laws of the Territory, and received its first pupils on October 14, 1879. Initially, it occupied a small adobe building northeast of the plaza. Professor Charles W. Howe of Colorado College served as the first principal, and he and two assistants taught twenty-six students the opening year. Among them was Franz Huning's son, Arno. The Board of Trustees included such beacons of civic enterprise as Elias S. Stover, William Hazeldine, Franz Huning, and Adolph Harsch, owner of the Coyote Bottling Works.[24]

As the only school in the area offering a complete curriculum for grades one through twelve, the Academy grew rapidly and flourished. With an eye to the future, the trustees transferred the main campus to New Albuquerque in 1881, although a branch continued to be maintained in Old Town. Another branch was operated on Arno Street in the Highlands. By 1890, with enrollment expanded to 385, the Academy consolidated and moved into a new three-story building, Perkins Hall, located at Railroad and Edith. At the dedication, it was heralded as one of the finest educational plants in the Southwest, a boast not without some justification. Unexpectedly, its tenure in the new facilities was cut short. The next year, 1891, the territorial legislature finally got around to extending its full jurisdiction over public education, which meant that the mission the Albuquerque Academy had set for itself had now been completed. The same year, the city rented Perkins Hall to house the new Albuquerque High School and hired the Academy's last principal, C. E. Hodgin, to be the first school superintendent.[25]

Another effort to educate Albuquerque's youth during the 1880s was mounted by the Methodists. Mrs. Thomas Harwood, wife of a pionerr missionary, launched a girls' school in 1887 with a faculty of six teachers and a student body of sixty-eight. Two years later, the Methodists established the Albuquerque College, in conjunction with Mrs. Harwood's school, and offered the degree of Bachelor of Arts. At least they had planned to offer it—for two years after the college began, it closed.[26]

For some years before 1880, the government had expressed an interest in opening an industrial school for Indians somewhere in central New Mexico. Several sites on public land had been considered and rejected as being unsuitable. Franz Huning volunteered to donate forty acres about 10 miles south of Albuquerque, but government officials declined the offer when, upon examination, the tract was found to be barren, windswept, and utterly devoid of improvements.

Meanwhile, Presbyterian missionaries had learned of the planned institution and expressed an interest in establishing and operating it. The government at that time was in the habit of contracting with various Protestant denominations to run Indian schools. The Reverend Sheldon Jackson, regional head of the Presbyterian Board of Home Missions, submitted a proposal to the secretary of interior to found such a school at Albuquerque and manage it until the federal authorities were prepared to assume full charge. His plan won quick approval.[27]

On January 1, 1881, the United States Indian Training School (known commonly as the Albuquerque Indian School) opened in rented quarters at Los Duranes, a mile north of the Old Town plaza. The first class of about forty pupils was composed mainly of Pueblos, Apaches, and Utes. The youngsters, who boarded at the school, were taught a variety of academic and vocational subjects, designed mainly to hasten their integration into the American economic and social systems. The curriculum was modeled after that of the celebrated Indian Industrial School at Carlisle, Pennsylvania.[28]

Albuquerque businessmen, eager to see the new institution find a permanent home, raised $4,500 and purchased a sixty-six acre farm a half mile east of Los Duranes, which they donated to the Department of the Interior. Contractor Edward Medler began construction of the necessary buildings, and in the fall of 1882, the school moved to the new campus. Since agriculture was one of the vocational subjects taught, male students worked a part of each weekday in the fields, producing most of the food needed for the school's tables. Boys also received instruction in such crafts as carpentry and stonecutting, while girls studied cooking, sewing, and care of the sick. Both the government and the Presbyterians were motivated by a keen desire to see the Indian youth transformed into upstanding American citizens. The time had not yet come when the valuable aspects of native culture and folkways would be recognized and respected. The prevailing view of the day was expressed by local Indian agent Pedro Sánchez, who told the commissioner of Indian affairs in Washington: "The boys and girls that return from the Carlisle school as well as those who attend the Albuquerque school, are the pride of every man that appreciates education and desires the welfare of these Indians; but when they return home they have to join hands with the agent, and thus deal with the gross ignorance so deeply rooted in their people."[29]

In October 1886, the Presbyterians voluntarily withdrew from management of the school, and the United States government took control, appointing its own superintendent, New Yorker P. F. Burke. Politics, dissension among employees, and the refusal of some pueblos, notably conservative Santo Domingo and Jemez, to enroll their children created ongoing problems for the Albuquerque Indian School. But withal, it grew and improved to become one of the finest educational facilities for Native Americans anywhere in the West.

Although the Presbyterians relinquished control over the Indian School, their interest in Indian education at Albuquerque remained strong. For more than a quarter century, they had been engaged in building denominational schools to serve both Native American and Hispano youth throughout the Territory. So in 1886, upon ending its association with the government program, the Church acquired a two-hundred-acre tract just below the sandhills north of downtown Albuquerque and launched the Presbyterian Industrial School, a mission trade school for Indians. Originally, the barren site, pocked with prairie dog holes and infested with rattlesnakes, appeared wholly unpromising. But within months, the raising of a four-story brick building and three frame structures provided evidence that a campus was in the making—lingering prairie dogs and snakes notwithstanding.

A disastrous fire practically destroyed the school in 1887, but rebuilding was swift. That challenge, in fact, proved easier to meet than the one posed by increased competition from the federal Indian School, which was expanding at an accelerating rate a short distance to the west. By 1891, that institution showed itself capable of caring for all the educational needs of Indian students, so the Presbyterian Home Mission Board elected to close its own mission school.

The old facility, however, was soon reopened with a new orientation and purpose. In 1896, a Presbyterian boarding school for boys and girls in Las Vegas, which had foundered because of opposition from a local Jesuit school, was transferred to Albuquerque. The abandoned Indian campus was refurbished and a new institution, dedicated to educating Hispano students, launched. It took the name Menaul Training School, to honor the memory of Reverend James A. Menaul, who had served sixteen years as a missionary in the Territory and established Albuquerque's First Presbyterian Church. From the year of its founding to the present day, the school (located at 301 Menaul Boulevard) has occupied a preeminent place among New Mexico's private educational institutions.[30]

On February 12, 1891, the territorial legislature belatedly passed a law extending its control over a public education system. The key provision allowed local districts to issue bonds to pay for construction of school buildings. For a decade or more, Albuquerque had been relying on private schools, funneling dabs of money to them, from sources such as the sale of saloon licenses. But now the town's power elite lost no time in creating a Board of Education (its first meeting convened April 14, 1891), and instituting a regular public school system.

While the Board took steps to find suitable sites and initiate the raising of buildings, elementary and secondary schools opened in temporary rented quarters at various locations around the community. For districting purposes, New Albuquerque was divided into four quadrants, or wards, with Railroad Avenue forming the division line from east to west, and the tracks from north to south. Practically identical elementary schools—two-story, red brick buildings—were soon erected in each ward, offering classes in grades one through six. Overnight, fierce athletic rivalries developed among the ward schools, producing fist-swinging brawls and adding an unforgettable new dimension to growing up in Albuquerque.[31]

As remarked, the first public high school took over the facilities of the old Albuquerque Academy on east Railroad Avenue. In 1893, it moved to a frame building on south Edith, and seven years later to the Central School Building at Third and Lead. Finally, in 1914, the Al-

310

buquerque High School acquired a permanent campus on the corner of
Broadway and Central. It was built to accommodate 500 students, and
popular sentiment held that that should be sufficient to take care of the
community's growing population for at least the next century. But in
spite of several additions, the school was bursting at the seams within
a decade. Albuquerque did not acquire another secondary school until
1948 when Highland High was constructed in the East Heights.[32]

The early years of the Albuquerque public school system, under the
direction of Superintendent Charles E. Hodgin, were difficult ones, mainly
owing to a perennial shortage of funds. There were not enough supplies
or textbooks, but the resourceful administration made do—by passing,
for example, a single small set of readers from one ward school to the
other. Even with a tight budget, Superintendent Hodgin managed to
introduce such "extras" as a kindergarten and instruction in music and
manual arts. He also saw that Albuquerque complied with a federal law
requiring the teaching of temperance and the effect of alcohol upon the
body. The solid foundation for public education laid in the 1890s paved
the way for a system that by 1980 numbered more than 110 primary,
middle, and secondary schools.[33]

By the late 1880s, a movement was afoot among Albuquerque
business leaders to get a university for New Mexico and to have it placed
in their town. Many citizens regarded them as impractical visionaries,
for, after all, the Territory was perilously poor, no public education system
then existed, and the legislature in Santa Fe, which must authorize a
university, was preoccupied, as always, with the continuing struggle to
achieve statehood. The idea, therefore, seemed not only premature, but
entirely unrealistic. Nevertheless, the dreamers and planners refused to
allow their scheme to be pushed onto a side track.[34]

The guiding force behind the effort to gain a university was a thirty-
two-year-old lawyer, Bernard Shandon Rodey, an Irishman who had first
come to Albuquerque as a stenographer for the A&P Railroad. Early in
1889, Rodey went to Santa Fe as Bernalillo County's senator in the
territorial legislature. The political climate was decidedly hostile to proposals for a university, but the young lawyer was not deterred. With the
rough draft of a bill given him by Albuquerque attorney Neill B. Field,
Rodey locked himself in his room in Santa Fe's elite Palace Hotel and
in the space of thirty-six hours hammered out legislation creating the
University of New Mexico. Three days before the end of the legislative
session, the bill was presented. Suddenly, other towns, sensing a commercial advantage that must certainly go with such an undertaking,
became contenders for the home of the new school. By adroit manuevering, Albuquerque's partisans managed to allot other public institutions
to their rivals, and thus preserve the university for themselves. Socorro
got a School of Mines; Las Cruces, a College of Agriculture; and Las
Vegas, the Insane Asylum. It has long been believed that Santa Fe, because
of its political power, could have had the University of New Mexico for
the asking, but chose instead the penitentiary, believing it would prove
more profitable. The story, however, is pure myth, since, as contemporary

newspaper accounts demonstrate, the penitentiary was opened in August 1885, several years before the location of the university became an issue.[35]

Rodey's bill, supported by a coalition of progressive forces, succeeded in overcoming the opposition and won passage on February 28, 1889, in the waning hours of the session. One provision provided that the new school was "intended to be the state university when New Mexico shall be admitted as a state into the Union."[36] That designation guaranteed it the donations of land and other assorted benefits that Congress had already granted state educational institutions.

In the weeks before the measure passed, when it appeared likely that the university plum would fall to Albuquerque, heated discussion had developed over finding an appropriate site for the campus. Some people wanted it placed near the river in the vicinity of Old Town, while others supported a location in Barelas. Mindful that debate over the issue might cause future problems, Bernard Rodey resolved the question by adding a clause to his bill specifying that the university should be situated on still a third site, which he and many community leaders favored. The location was described as being, "near the town of Albuquerque, in the County of Bernalillo, within two miles north of Railroad Avenue, upon a tract of good, high and dry land, of not less than twenty acres."[37] This was well outside the limits of Albuquerque, which meant there was room to grow, and was far up on the East Mesa, well removed from the floods that plagued the valley.

The farsighted Rodey knew precisely what he was doing. He even carefully spelled out the method of land acquisition. "The said land," according to his act, "shall be donated and conveyed, free of any cost and expense, to the Territory of New Mexico, by G. W. Meylert."[38] Undoubtedly, the generous offer of free land was inserted to help ensure that Albuquerque got the university and that the bill would pass. Colonel Meylert, it will be recalled, was one of the promoters who built the San Felipe Hotel and the man who convinced his fellow investors that it should be supplied with a library in place of a saloon. Now that the university was in the offing, he seems to have acted as a front man, persuading at least four different property owners on the East Mesa to deed him parcels of land so that he might donate them to the state, as provided in the educational bill. One of the principal donors, who has never been recognized, was C. W. Kennedy, upon whose gift of land the first buildings of the university were constructed.[39]

After the acceptance of Rodey's bill by the territorial legislature, it was signed into law by Governor Edmund G. Ross. That was singularly fitting because, before his appointment to office in 1885, Ross had resided in New Albuquerque, where he was closely associated with several of the most powerful men in the community. He had come to the Territory in 1882 as a political exile from Kansas. While a Republican United States Senator thirteen years before, Edmund Ross cast the deciding vote in Congress against the impeachment of President Andrew Johnson. Almost unbearable pressure had been brought to bear—to vote the other way—but following his conscience and believing that a presidential impeachment would irreparably rend the fabric of America's constitutional government, Ross chose principle over political expediency. At the moment of casting the ballot that would save a president, he declared, "I looked down into my open grave." Long afterward, writers would refer to his deed as "the most heroic act in American history," and John F. Kennedy would include Ross among the uncommonly brave citizens lionized in his book *Profiles in Courage.*[40]

At the time, however, Ross was reviled, not only in his native Kansas, but throughout the nation, and the Republicans drummed him out of the party. Returning home, the frail, delicately handsome ex-senator found himself censured by the Kansas legislature, snubbed by former constituents, and even threatened with violence. Unwilling to crawl in an hole and hide, he tried to rebuild his political fortunes. But upon suffering a resounding defeat when he ran for the senate again on the Democratic ticket, he gave up and headed for New Mexico.

That he picked Albuquerque as a place of exile was no accident. Ross had been a founder of the AT&SF Railroad, and his association with the company made him thoroughly familiar with conditions and business prospects in the Territory of New Mexico. Furthermore, two notable former Kansans, staunch friends of his who had taken up residence in Albuquerque, stood ready to receive and aid him. One was Elias Stover, the former lieutenant-governor, and the other was W. S. Burke, editor of the *Albuquerque Morning Journal,* who promptly gave Ross a position on the paper's editorial staff.[41]

Before long, Edmund Ross was again dabbling in politics, but as a Democrat, since the Republicans still considered him tainted and turned him a cold shoulder. Then, in 1885, Democratic President Grover Cleveland appointed Ross to the governorship of New Mexico. The next four years in Santa Fe were stormy ones. The governor, an idealist and reformer, became a champion of women's rights, an advocate of temperance (he refused to allow liquor in the Governors Palace), and a hounder of corrupt politicians. The local Republican machine, known as the Santa Fe Ring, spared no effort to make his life miserable.

Leaving office in 1889, soon after signing the bill creating the University of New Mexico, Ross returned to Albuquerque and spent the last years before his death (May 8, 1907) living quietly as a small farmer and job printer. In 1906, just in time, he learned that Kansas at long last had forgiven him. The word was carried by General Hugh Cameron, an old friend who arrived in Albuquerque bearing a sheaf of letters from aging Republicans, vindicating Ross's antiimpeachment vote and expressing regret for the mistreatment accorded him.

Cameron had gotten the letters in a most unusual way. When Ross had left Kansas in disgrace, the general announced that he was withdrawing from society and would live in a tree on a bluff above the town of Lawrence until Kansans repented and admitted that they had done their senator wrong. Except for occasional excursions for supplies, he stayed perched among the lofty boughs winter after winter, while his hair and beard grew waist-length. Such eccentricity caused General Cameron to become known as the "Kansas Hermit." The turning of the century and waning of old political grudges prompted Ross's surviving enemies to rethink their earlier harsh actions toward him. By late 1906, Cameron was satisfied that he had enough documents and, descending from his tree, he made a long-delayed pilgrimmage to Albuquerque. Edmund G. Ross, at age eighty, saw his name rubbed clean of stain. As if anticipating his own passing a few months afterward, he is reputed to have exclaimed, "I will be a bigger man dead than I have been alive."[42]

Considerable time was to elapse between Ross's endorsement of the university bill early in 1889 and the actual beginning of classes. An administration had to be organized, buildings erected, a faculty hired, and students enrolled. To oversee these elementary preparations, Ross's successor, Governor L. Bradford Prince, appointed the university's first Board of Regents on September 2, 1889. Members included Mariano S. Otero of Bernalillo, elected president of the Board by acclamation; Gurdon W. Meylert, named secretary-treasurer; and Elias S. Stover, who was subsequently selected to serve as the school's first president. Month after month, the Board met in a room of the San Felipe Hotel feverishly laying the groundwork for the Territory's first institution of higher learning.[43]

The campus site, utterly bare of improvements, rested in the midst of a sandy tableland, studded with knee-high yucca that stretched uninterrupted to the toes of the Sandias. The most optimistic viewer could scarcely have imagined that this bleak ground would soon be transformed into an oasis. One of the first acts of the regents provided for the fencing of land, to exclude wandering livestock, and the setting out of trees, "not to exceed one hundred and fifty."[44] Next, bids were advertised in Denver, Kansas City, Santa Fe, and Albuquerque newspapers for contractors to raise the first building. Completed in 1892 at a cost of $30,568, the three-story gabled structure of red brick was in the Richardsonian Romanesque style, a contemporary variant of Victorian architecture. It reflected the reigning passion in New Albuquerque for things up-to-date. Above the arched entrance, carved in stone, large letters read simply: "University N.M." Later, the building would bear the name Hodgin Hall, in honor of Charles Hodgin, who, after filling a seven-year term as superintendent of the Albuquerque school system, became a distinguished professor and administrator at the university.

A provision in Bernard Rodey's original legislative bill stated that the purpose of the university was to offer the inhabitants of New Mexico "the means of acquiring a thorough knowledge of the various branches of literature, science, and arts."[45] At the outset, however, that aim, common to general programs of higher education, had to take a backseat to two more immediate needs. Since the Territory lacked public high schools, a serious question existed as to whether qualified candidates could be found to enter the new university. The school itself addressed the problem by establishing a Preparatory Department, the first in the curriculum, to prepare students for regular university work. This department, offering courses at the secondary level, continued functioning until 1905.[46] A second branch, the Normal Department, was designed to train teachers to staff the public schools just then beginning to appear throughout New Mexico. Thus, when the first classes were inaugurated in the summer of 1892, the University of New Mexico was a university in name only.

That situation rapidly changed, however, as a small flood of students toward the end of the century permitted expansion of both faculty and course offerings. Most of those who enrolled were from New Mexico, but increasingly the University lured students from other parts of the country. For one thing, it became known as a good place to learn Spanish, and its program in that language soon gained national recognition. For another, the school's desert setting and its salubrious climate attracted Easterners suffering an assortment of respiratory ailments. Clarence Luther Herrick, a scientist from Minnesota, came as a health-seeker in 1894, and three years later became the second president of the university, succeeding Elias Stover. Under his leadership, a science building, Hadley Hall, the second permanent structure on the campus, was erected. It housed both a laboratory for bacteriological research, and the new Department of Climatology, devoted to study of the effect of climate on disease. From that modest beginning, the university—and Albuquerque—would advance steadily to become one day a major center for scientific investigation.

Young Dr. William George Tight of Ohio, a recent graduate of the University of Chicago, succeeded Herrick as president in 1901. A geologist and an accomplished scholar, he was also an innovative thinker, a rare quality for academics at that time. In the small and still largely empty campus, he perceived a gilded opportunity to create a university both visually attractive and unique. Enlisting students as helpers, he donned work clothes and set out hundreds of trees and native plants dug from nearby mountains. Tame squirrels imported from his old home in Ohio were released on the campus. (Their descendants continue to thrive among the same trees to this day.) The president's beautification program required large quantities of water. He bored a deep well, experimented with irrigation, where none had heretofore existed on the mesa, and put up a tall windmill, for years a university landmark.[47]

It was in the design of new buildings, however, that President Tight chalked up his greatest achievement, and at the same time unexpectedly touched off an avalanche of public criticism. Coming directly from the East, the impressionable scholar had at once been captivated by the remarkable Pueblo Indian culture surviving at Albuquerque's doorstep. On frequent visits to nearby villages, with camera and sketchbook in hand, he carefully studied the methods used in native adobe construction. From such excursions, he began to formulate a distinctive type of architecture, based on the Pueblo model, that could be adapted for the university. Local buildings, he firmly believed, should reflect the local culture, not mimic styles borrowed from elsewhere, which were ill-suited to New Mexico.

With the assistance of Albuquerque architect Edward Buxton Christy, who provided him with working drawings, Tight launched his campaign to transform the University of New Mexico into "the pueblo on the mesa." A start was made on the new power plant, a flat-roofed adobe building constructed by the president and students. The result, equally handsome and practical, gave inspiration for a larger undertaking—the erection of dormitories. Until now, most of the student body as well as the faculty had resided in downtown Albuquerque. Each morning they boarded a horse-drawn hack and for a $.05 fee were conveyed up steeply graded Railroad Avenue, 2 miles to the campus. Housing on the university grounds, eliminating this time-consuming trip, President Tight knew, would be a decided boon.

The twin dormitories, for men and women, that rose from the soil looked much like the Pueblo apartments seen by Coronado four hundred years before. Projecting roofbeams, or vigas, supported the terraced upper stories, which, from the outside, could be reached by a series of ladders. Inside, the exposed woodwork was decorated with Indian symbols, applied by President Tight and Miss Ethel Hickey, an English teacher. Traditional corner fireplaces furnished heat. In a burst of romantic zeal, Miss Hickey dipped into her book of "pretty Indian legends" and came up with the name Kwataka, signifying "man-eaglet," for the boys' dormitory, and Hokona, meaning "virgin butterfly," for the girls'.[48] One concession to modernity was a solar heating system, placed on the roofs, and designed to furnish both space heat and hot water.

In his next building, Dr. Tight carried the grand scheme a step farther. On the east side of the campus, he installed a circular *estufa*, a replica of the ceremonial kiva at Santo Domingo Pueblo. The semisubterranean chamber, entered by a ladder through the roof, initially served as a hall for social gatherings. But later, in 1915, it became a meeting place for the university's first national fraternity, Alpha Alpha Alpha.

Riding the wave of his own evangelistic enthusiasm, the president cast an appraising eye upon the three-story, red brick administration building (Hodgin Hall). Its stern Victorian lines stood out among the soft contours of the pueblo satellites like a contemporary painting in a gallery filled with folk art. To achieve a harmony of style, Tight concluded that the structure would have to be remodeled, or to be more specific, "pueblo-ized." The facelift, commissioned at a cost of $16,000, was dramatic. Off came the gables, cornices, and chimneys. On went log vigas, pillars, and balconies. Earth-colored stucco hid the brick exterior. These improvisations, while not wholly satisfactory, did at least integrate the university's main building into President Tight's master plan. But it also ignited a furious controversy that brought his downfall.

Citizens of New Albuquerque had watched with undisguised alarm while the university head indulged his fancy for maverick architecture— "a reversion to the primitive," many called it. Sneered one critic: "If you are going to be consistent, the president and faculty should wear Indian blankets around their shoulders and feathered coverings on their heads."[49] The professors and students generally approved of the novel experiment, and in its defense, Dr. Charles Hodgin declared reasonably that "people did not seem to think it odd to go back several thousand years to copy

Greek architecture, but they could not tolerate what belonged to their own land."[50]

Public tolerance, in fact, dissolved completely when President Tight set out to redo the administration building. The furor that broke, as he plunged ahead, reverberated to the craggy crest of the Sandias and its echo reached Santa Fe. Businessmen muttered angry disapproval over their late afternoon mugs of beer. Journalists published ringing editorials expressing indignation. And finally, in 1909, the Board of Regents, consumed with indignation, demanded the president's resignation. The excuse was that he had fired two faculty members without consulting the Board, but the real cause was his architectural indiscretion.[51]

A few months after his dismissal, William George Tight died, and his dream of a pueblo on the mesa seemed destined to perish with him. His successor, Dr. E. Dundas McQueen Gray, mindful of the recent tempest, commenced adding buildings that resembled concrete boxes of "good foundation and good walls but no architectural style."[52] These tasteless monstrosities were simply made so that at some future date they could be easily remodeled to conform to whatever new and uniform plan of architecture might be adopted.

Actually, the university was left to drift in limbo for the next decade or so. But gradually Tight's discredited notions were revived and won new adherents. The Santa Fe Railroad in the intervening years had seized upon the Pueblo style, and incorporated it in the construction of many of its own buildings. People in the capital also found the Pueblo design compatible with a new popular movement to preserve the historic charm of old Santa Fe. Regional architecture was becoming respectable.

Its official rebirth at the university occurred in 1927 when the Board of Regents formally adopted the Pueblo architectural style for the campus. A final stamp of approval was given the following year as the new president, Dr. John F. Zimmerman, chose to be sworn in while standing on the steps of the estufa, surrounded by Indian leaders from five pueblos dressed in full native regalia. In 1933, John Gaw Meem of Santa Fe, one of the foremost proponents of the Pueblo style, was engaged as the university architect. Over the next quarter century, under his enlightened guidance, the distinctive campus, rooted in New Mexico's own cultural tradition, and which President Tight had conceived and fought for, at last became a reality. Ironically, Albuquerqueans whose fathers had shouted down the very concept a generation before, now pointed to the university with pride and called attention to its unique architectural character in promotional brochures designed to lure tourists and their dollars to the city. After many a season, William George Tight's heroic efforts bore a bountiful harvest.

Another public institution, which lent credibility to Albuquerque's desire to attain some degree of cultural standing, was the library. Colonel Gurdon Meylert, as noted, got things started in the early 1880s when he saw to it that the swank San Felipe Hotel made space for a library room. It was not until the spring of 1891 that a small group of socially prominent women, led by Clara Fergusson and Mrs. William Hazeldine, met in a parlor of the San Felipe and formulated plans for creating a free public library. Encouraged by editorials in the local press, they formed an association and commenced to solicit funds. In time, quarters were found in the Commercial Club and donations of books were received from the East.

The immediate problem proved to be one of finding money for yearly operating expenses, amounting to approximately $1,000. The dauntless ladies met the challenge by organizing a series of elaborate charitable functions. Their first venture was a grand ball held on May 13, 1891, in the Armory, then a frame building near the center of downtown Albuquerque. Working with the precision of an ant colony, they festooned the bare hall with evergreens, flags, ribbons, flowers, and Chinese umbrellas and lanterns; engaged an orchestra; and heaped the tables with small mountains of food. The crowd that swarmed in to dance and dine under the brilliant glare of electric lights promptly became loyal library supporters. Reported a newspaper the following day: "It was estimated last evening that the ball would clear nearly $500, a very snug sum and a splendid starter for the free library."[53]

Other fund-raising events—dances, plays, operas, concerts, and garden parties—were given every two or three months over the next decade. In addition, substantial contributions came from generous individuals, like banker Joshua Raynolds and D. B. Robinson, acting president of the AT&SF Railway. In this manner, New Albuquerque during its formative years developed one of the best libraries to be found anywhere in the southwestern territories.

Nevertheless, as the city grew, it became apparent that a private library association dependent upon charity would soon become inadequate for the task. Plainly, the municipality must assume the expanding weight of responsibility and take the library under its wing. The impetus for that move came from Joshua and Sarah Raynolds, owners of Perkins Hall at Railroad and Edith. The building, it will be remembered, had briefly housed the Albuquerque Academy in 1890–92, and for a while afterward, the Albuquerque High School. In 1900, the Raynolds agreed to deed Perkins Hall and four adjacent lots to the city for use as a new public library. The gift, coinciding with the merger of the private library association and a newly established municipal library board, marked the authentic beginning of the Albuquerque Public Library. Its home remained Perkins Hall until 1923 when a small fire damaged the structure. Believing repairs would prove too costly, the city commission demolished the building the following year and put up a new library (which still stands) in the by then fashionable Pueblo-Spanish architectural style.[54]

In their early efforts to raise money, ladies of the library association had promoted social events that combined entertainment with a worthy cultural project. That successful formula was much used by other groups of citizens in turn-of-the-century Albuquerque. For example, young persons devoted to music formed the Mandolin Club, both to play an assortment of instruments and to socialize. And persons of German an-

cestry founded the Club Germainia to keep alive the customs and language of the old country and attract German immigrants to the Territory.
Amateur societies for opera, drama, and literature (such as the Clio Club)
flourished, and many were the balls, oyster suppers, and strawberry socials
given to lure support. Showing of the first motion picture in Albuquerque
was one event staged purely for amusement. The film, presenting the
championship fight between Bob Fitzsimmons and James Corbett, was
shown for two consecutive nights in 1897 at the Armory on First and
Gold. Although the picture was unbearably fuzzy and often jumped
wildly on the screen, the novelty of the occasion produced a minor
sensation about town.[55]

By the mid 1880s, Grants Opera House and the Albuquerque Opera
House offered excellent facilities for a variety of theatrical productions.
Grants was launched in November 1883, with a grand opening that
featured a performance of the operetta *H. M. S. Pinafore.* Profits from
the evening went into funds for the hospital, library, and Indian school.[56]
The competing Albuquerque Opera House, in spite of its high-toned
name, leaned toward popular entertainment such as melodramas, mus-
icals, current plays, and minstrel shows. One troupe of traveling actors
in 1883 provided a most memorable performance when, in the course
of the show, they became angry with one another and staged a barroom
brawl. Both men and women swung fists and threw props. Some members
of the audience became so excited, they rushed on stage to join in the
battle. Patrons who remained in their seats to watch the bloody spectacle
agreed afterward that it was the liveliest production seen on an Albuquerque stage to date.[57]

Other popular diversions of the day included the glittering Montezuma Ball, held annually by the town's best-dressed socialites; riotous
and boozy Fourth of July celebrations; and, of course, the tradition-filled
San Felipe Neri festival on the Old Town plaza, which each May, as in
times past, mixed religious solemnity with secular merry-making. But
the high point of the year for rich and poor, for businessmen and servant,
Anglo and Hispano, was the Territorial Fair.

As early as 1854 the legislative assembly of New Mexico designated
the town of Albuquerque, no doubt on account of its central location,
as the site for an annual fair to commence May 28 and continue for eight
days.[58] Either because of prevailing poverty in both Albuquerque and
the Territory, or because of lack of interest, no fair was held until 1881,
and then in October rather than May. Stimulus to the local economy
fueled by the newly arrived railway, must have provided the major incentive for organizing the first fair in that year.

The inaugural fair, October 3–8, 1881, bore the grand name, New
Mexico Agricultural, Mineral and Industrial Exposition. Elias Stover took
the lead in promoting the event and served as first president of the fair
commission. He easily enlisted the financial backing and active support
of such respected men as editor Thomas Hughes, William Hazeldine,
A&P manager F. W. Smith, livery operator W. L. Trimble, Perfecto and
Cristóbal Armijo, Franz Huning, Angus Grant, and merchants Noa

and Louis Ilfeld. These and others saw in the fair a chance to advance their own business interests along with the civic fortunes of Albuquerque.

Land was acquired along Railroad Avenue, immediately west of Old Town, for a permanent fairground. Some of the area lay within the old Carleton property, which had contained the military buildings burned at the time of the Civil War. The first improvement, and the only one that was ready for the initial fair in 1881, was a large grandstand facing the half mile oval of a racetrack. Exhibits had to be placed in a series of tents, which proved unequal to the occasion. Unseasonal October rains fell with sufficient force to bring down the canvas and ruin most of the displays.[59]

The fair's maiden run, however, proved so rosy, in attendance and financial returns, that little trouble was had in raising permanent buildings for the accommodation of future exhibitors. The structures were mainly clapboard frame painted white with pitched roofs and occasional turrets—of a nondescript style popular in the East, but appearing singularly out of place adjacent to the earth houses of Old Town. A high board fence, reaching almost to the Rio Grande on the west, surrounded the fairgrounds. A ticket window and large gate faced Railroad Avenue, just to the left of the county jail, which, according to one early fairgoer, served as "a grim reminder to behave."[60] When the car barns of the street railway were later placed inside the fence, the fairgrounds became known as Traction Park.

The racetrack, known in those days as the "speed ring," was the focal point of fair activity. Horses were brought from as far away as Colorado and Arizona to run and participate in the sulky races, featuring both trotters and pacers. For several years, Santiago Baca's horse, Revenge, took most of the first prizes.

Underneath the length of the grandstand stretched what proud Albuquerqueans claimed to be the longest bar in the Territory. A few feet in front of the bar hummed roulette wheels, interspersed with faro, dice, and monte tables. And in one corner of the sheltering stand, almost unnoticed, stood the brave little booth of the WCTU, the Woman's Christian Temperance Union. The temperance movement in Albuquerque was led by Miss Frances E. Willard, a slim, firm-jawed woman who dressed plainly and spoke with the force and conviction of an old-time abolitionist. Hard-drinking men addressed her and her two or three supporters with respect, but they steered a wide path around the WCTU fair booth where only ice water was served. If Miss Willard was ignored when she tried to dispense ice water and hand out white ribbons, symbols of temperance, she received somewhat more attention with her annual floats in the fair parade. One of her moral efforts that brought in a grand prize was a float built around a water wagon. A tall-hatted Uncle Sam in tails drove the rig. Above the tank swung an empty demijohn of whiskey, upended, and bearing a sign with the stern warning, "The ways of the wicked He turneth upside down."[61]

The large oval space inside the racetrack and facing the grandstand became the staging field for a variety of outdoor fair events. The largest

draw was the baseball games, held every day of the fair. The home team,
the Albuquerque Browns, had been founded in the same year as New
Town, 1880, by W. T. McCreight. A former player for the St. Louis
Browns, McCreight still owned his old shirt with "Browns" emblazoned
across it when he organized the Albuquerque team. So, for thrift and
convenience, he decided the new club should also be the Browns. He
put together a training club as well, made up of aspiring youth who
played under the name McCreight's Colts.[62]

The national baseball season was over in the East at the time of the
New Mexico fair, and, therefore, big league stars could be recruited at
$100 each and expenses. Sometimes they were formed into a separate
team to play an exhibition game against the Browns, and on other
occasions, they joined the home club in contests with rival New Mexico
towns. Heavy betting accompanied every game. The umpire was usually
the Bernalillo County sheriff, resplendent in blue-serge suit and sparkling
gold badge.[63]

Albuquerque's fiercest foe, and the one that could be counted upon
to generate a frenzy of wagering, was the team from San Marcial. During
the 1894 fair, the Browns beat the highly favored San Marcial nine by
a score of six to five, which prompted a wild celebration among Albuquerque fans and forced the defeated team, impoverished by a loss of
bets, to walk the hundred-odd miles home.[64]

Another specialty of the fair was the contests between volunteer fire
companies, some of whom came from Arizona to participate. Events
included coupling team trials, wet and dry hose tests, and hose cart and
foot races. Individual races frequently brought bets totaling $15,000 or
more. Civic pride and the gambling instinct made companionable bed-
fellows.[65]

For many years a troop of cavalry rode over from Fort Wingate near
Gallup, pitched camp on the fairgrounds, and gave daily exhibitions of
mounted drills and simulated war manuevers. A local militia unit, the
Albuquerque Guards, performed additional military drills and escorted
the territorial governor each year during the parade that opened the fair.
The Guards had been enlisted in 1881 upon a flare-up of Apache trouble
in southern New Mexico. After that ended, they were used to chase
outlaws and perform a variety of ceremonial functions. The unit was the
apple of Albuquerque's collective eye, and businessmen unstintingly sub-
scribed large sums of money to pay for showy blue and buff uniforms.
At the second fair in 1882, the Guards in competitive drills beat out
the Laguna Militia to win a gold medal.[66]

The fair always attracted large numbers of Indians, who performed
dances and foot races in front of the grandstand. Pueblos living in the
Rio Grande Valley usually arrived by train, taking advantage of free
passage charitably offered them by the AT&SF. The Navajos, scattered
through the mesa lands to the west, came by horseback. During the
1903 fair, some 200 rough-looking members of the tribe rode in from
the remote Chaco Canyon area of northwestern New Mexico. Colonel D.
K. B. Sellers, president of the fair that year, saw them and conceived

the idea of staging a sham battle, modeled after the Buffalo Bill Wild West Show, then immensely popular throughout the country.[67]

He had little trouble gaining compliance of the Indians, the Fort Wingate cavalry troop, and a crew of stray cowboys. According to a hastily devised program, the colonel would ride across the baseball diamond in the center of the racetrack mounted on his stout gray horse. On signal, the Indians were to ambush him with much shouting and shooting. Then enter the cowboys firing six-shooter volleys. When it appeared they were getting the worst of it, the cavalry would rush to the rescue amid another crescendo of gunfire. The United States Army commander willingly supplied a plentitude of blank cartridges for all this staged mayhem.

It was early afternoon and the stand was packed with spectators contentedly downing sack lunches. Just as the performance was about to begin, Colonel Sellers received a shocking bit of news: some of the warriors were planning a genuine massacre. The Indian wars had long been over, but a number of these particular Navajos, it seems, still nursed a grudge against white men in uniform. They had thrown away their blanks and substituted live cartridges.

The colonel moved quickly. Slipping up behind the band leader he snatched his pistol from the holster, broke open the cylinder and, sure enough, real bullets. Summoning members of the Albuquerque police, Sellers conducted a hasty search and found thirty other loaded revolvers. The culprits were marched off to jail. The crowd, unaware of the near tragedy, waited impatiently for the start of the show. Colonel Sellers, as scheduled, rode his big gray onto the field and the battle went on according to plan—with one minor adjustment. The remaining Indians confined their demonstration to loud whooping; they had been relieved of all their firearms.

The curious incident at the Albuquerque fair was reported to Washington. As a result, the army issued explicit orders that no troops should ever again be allowed to join in a sham battle with Indians.[68]

Among the assortment of entertainments the Territorial Fair offered through the years, none won greater public applause than the periodic balloon ascensions. The first flight took place in 1882, nearly a century before Albuquerque would proclaim itself "Balloon Capital of the World." The town's pioneer balloonist was a tall, blond saloonkeeper whose title and name, Professor Park A. Van Tassel, sounded more fitting for the proprietor of a traveling medicine show. His maiden flight occurred at the Fourth of July celebration, 1882, from a vacant lot on Gold, between Second and Third Streets. The 30,000 cubic foot balloon bore the name "City of Albuquerque." The thing took two days to inflate with coal gas from the Albuquerque Gas Works. Excitement had reached such a pitch that local residents willingly went without illumination in their homes so that the gas might be diverted to the Professor's bag. On the evening of the Fourth, he cut the anchor rope and the balloon, like a giant air bubble released suddenly on the ocean floor, shot upward with tremen-

322

dous velocity. Hundreds of onlookers cheered in unison while Van Tassel
leaned from the basket excitedly waving the stars and stripes. At 10,000
feet, one of his flags dropped overboard and came down like an arrow,
fortunately missing viewers on the ground.[69]

This flight evidently was a preview for another ascension scheduled
the following fall during the fair. That one, however, did not go as
expected. The professor again inflated his balloon downtown and, with
one hundred men and boys hanging on to the ropes, had it walked to
the fairgrounds. Press reports tell what happened next: "As the balloon
was being moved a knot slipped and it got away. It ascended almost
perpendicularly and, after being up almost a quarter of an hour, burst
and slowly descended. Professor Van Tassel had just placed some clothing
and provisions in the car and was going to get in when it escaped."[70]
The balloon crashed north of the fairgrounds and Van Tassel sadly picked
up the pieces and walked away.

Later, the professor obtained a new balloon and went on a world
tour. On his last flight, he fell into the Pacific Ocean off Hawaii and,
according to word that filtered back to Albuquerque, sharks ate him.

Professor Thomas Scott Baldwin was the next balloonist featured
at the Territorial Fair, in 1889, and he, too, had his problems. First the
bag would not inflate properly because, as Baldwin explained, he had
not taken into account the rarified air of New Mexico. That difficulty
was eventually solved and he prepared to lift off. Lacking a basket or
car, he tied himself to the bottom of the balloon with a rope. No sooner
had he shouted, "Let her go!" than the rope broke and he dropped a
couple of feet to the ground, landing on his backside. In that embarrassing
position, red-faced, he watched as the balloon soared into the blue en-
ameled sky and disappeared.[71]

Merchant Roy A. Stamm was fascinated with aeronautics and upon
becoming secretary of the 27th annual fair in 1907, he arranged for
Joseph Blondin to bring a hydrogen balloon from New York for an
exhibition. In Albuquerque, Blondin tried converting a street sprinkling
wagon to a hydrogen generator. But the experiment proved unsuccessful
and his balloon had to be filled with coal gas at the city gas works.
Flying solo, he drifted 18 miles up the valley past Alameda where he
was shot at eight times by superstitious farmers, who, luckily, were poor
marksmen.

Stamm subsequently bought the balloon, but retained Blondin as
pilot. At the 1909 fair, they offered rides at $1 apiece. These were captive
flights in which the balloon was tethered to the ground by a 500-foot
cable. Even with this restraint, Roy Stamm remarked, "Most of our
passengers came down slightly white around the gills." Later in the fair,
he and Blondin made a free flight that carried them 11,000 feet over
the crest of the Manzanos to a landing in the Estancia Valley.[72] From
these early flights began Albuquerque's long infatuation with ballooning.

The following year, 1910, Roy Stamm went a step farther and
brought in an airplane, billing it as the finest attraction ever shown at

the fair. Visitors got a close look at the strange craft as it sat on the ground, but they never saw it fly. At Albuquerque's high altitude, the plane's engine power was insufficient for a take-off.

Compensating for that minor fiasco, the fair commission next year contracted with famous stunt pilot Charles F. Walsh to make three flights of fifteen minutes each in his single propeller Curtis biplane. The craft was shipped in by railway express, assembled at the fairgrounds, and made a series of flights over the city during fair week. On the final run, Walsh agreed to take Roy Stamm's younger brother, Raymond, aloft. A short board was wired to the lower wing to serve as a seat and an anvil was tied to the end of the biplane as a weight equalizer. They were unscientific perhaps, but the additions proved quite functional. With Raymond Stamm seated on the board, his feet hanging free and his arms clutching a wing strut, Walsh soared on a 3-mile circuit from the fairgrounds. The brief trip set a world's record—the first time a passenger had been lifted and carried from 5,000 feet above sea level.[73]

On one of his earlier fair flights, Walsh had circled over the baseball diamond while a game was in progress, dropping small sacks of flour on the players. Intended as a playful gesture, the Albuquerque press took note of the more ominous implications: "It demonstrated clearly the practicability of the use of the biplane as a implement of war, since it would be possible to drop bombs on an army or battleship with deadly effect."[74]

The aerial show was rated a resounding success and an attempt was made in 1912 to get Walsh back for a repeat performance. He had already accepted an engagement at the New Jersey State Fair, however, and so he sent as a replacement his former teacher and the man who had led him to stunt flying, the renowned barnstormer, Lincoln Beachey. The day after Beachey arrived in Albuquerque, word was received of Walsh's death. Before a crowd of 65,000 at Trenton, he had been making a spiral maneuver when the plane went out of control and crashed from an altitude of 2,000 feet. Said the grisly news reports, "Practically every bone in the aviator's body was broken."[75]

Shortly afterward, Walsh's remains, accompanied by his young widow, passed through Albuquerque en route to burial at his home in San Diego. Lincoln Beachey and Raymond Stamm were at the depot, flowers in hand, when the Limited made a brief stop. Mrs. Walsh cried on the elder man's shoulder when they met.

"Lincoln, if it wasn't for you, Charlie would be alive today," she said.[76] She had never approved of air acrobatics.

The moment was solemn for Raymond Stamm as well. By coincidence, the encounter with Mrs. Walsh occurred one year to the day after his world record flight with her husband. Filled with remorse, Lincoln Beachey swore he would never fly again. But the pull of the skies was too strong. Two years later while stunt flying at the San Francisco Exposition, a wing fell off his plane and he dropped into the bay and was lost.

One other landmark in Albuquerque's aeronautical history must be noted. In 1913, Roy N. Francis of California brought a twin propeller tractor biplane to the fair. It possessed far more power than the Curtis plane used by Walsh and was capable of carrying three or four passengers. Roy Stamm went on one of the flights with a high-speed camera and took the first aerial photographs of Albuquerque, probably the first ever made anywhere in the Southwest.[77]

On balance, the Territorial Fair emerged as one of Albuquerque's chief economic and social assets. Its success did not pass unnoticed in Santa Fe where civic boosters, encouraged by loyal newspaper editors, could not resist taking ungracious swings at their upstart rivals 60 miles down the Rio Grande.

The tenor of Santa Fe's jealous spite was reflected in an abusive diatribe printed by the capital's prestigious *New Mexican Daily* on September 23, 1887. "In the past few years," declared the paper, "the shoddy work of the fair association has disgusted everybody, and Albuquerque came so near losing the respect of every progressive citizen of the Territory outside of Bernalillo County that it was thought its people would have the good sense to improve on their conduct."

Warming to his self-righteous task, the editorial writer continued: "Santa Fe County recently sent 250 visitors to the fair this year, and these contributed to the capacious maw of that notorious institution, not less than $2,500. . . . The experience of the visitors was anything but pleasant; the money they spent was filched from them by fraud and misrepresentation, and altogether their treatment . . . has been such as to send all home in disgust."[78]

No evidence exists that the carping criticism from Santa Fe discomfited Albuquerque's fair promoters in the slightest. On the contrary, enthusiasm for their project grew with each passing year, as the popularity of the fair also increased. In 1910, with a Constitutional Convention at work in preparation for statehood, the *Albuquerque Morning Journal* jumped the gun and proclaimed the Territorial Fair of that year to be the "First State Fair."[79]

The dislocations and economic strains imposed by World War I put an end to the fair. Its revival, delayed by onset of the Great Depression, did not come until 1938, under a mandate from the state legislature. By that time, the original grounds near Old Town had long since been abandoned and the structures dismantled. Hence, a new site for the fair was selected on the barren East Mesa, 2 miles above the university. With aid supplied by the Works Progress Administration (WPA), a grandstand and racetrack along with pavilions and exhibit halls, in accepted Spanish-Pueblo style, rose amid the tumbleweeds and yucca. As in times gone by, Albuquerque again played host to New Mexico at its cherished State Fair.

Trumpeting the City

As the United States entered the twentieth century, the most striking characteristic of national life was the unparalleled rise of the cities. Vigorous growth had been made possible by the explosive expansion of industry and new improvements in transportation, both of which enabled business to wax fat and rich in the urban environment. Among leaders in the dozen or more communities on the east and west coasts with populations above 200,000, it became an article of faith that growing cities translated into burgeoning personal fortunes—that a thriving municipality, by definition, was endowed with a heady, aggressive business climate.

The message was not overlooked by the men of Albuquerque who had staked their futures and invested their bankrolls on the fond hope that the small trackside town in New Mexico's Middle Valley would one day soon become the financial and industrial hub of the region. By 1900, Albuquerque had already displaced Santa Fe as the commercial center of the Territory, and its civic promoters were pushing hard to ensure that the community continued on its steady upward course. The census in that year placed New Albuquerque's population at 6,326, with an additional 1,191 in Old Town, and 12,042 for Bernalillo County as a whole. Inside of five years, the county population shot up another 5,000, with most of that gravitating to New Albuquerque.[1]

The Commercial Club, as previously noted, assumed the functions of a Chamber of Commerce and in the 1890s began the campaign to lure investors and new residents. But soon after the turn of the century, a formal Booster's Association was organized for the purpose of fostering a more energetic and dynamic development program. It published a small journal, appropriately titled the *Albuquerque Booster,* and assorted other promotional literature, all of which extolled Albuquerque's virtues in extravagant and sometimes misleading terms. The Boosters also went to great lengths to encourage emigration. Swept away by their enthusiasm, they advertised the community as a natural paradise for health-seekers, and thereby drew thousands of ailing Easterners to the city. As later discussion will show, not all Albuquerqueans agreed that the quest for profit justified filling out municipal ranks with infirm, and, in many cases, terminally ill people.

The intensely loyal, optimistic, and versatile Booster's Association was prepared to take any step that would prime the business pump and heighten Albuquerque's reputation as a progressive city. Thus, when the Santa Fe Railway found it necessary to expand the freight yards outside the city limits and add a large tie-treating plant, with a capacity of 150,000 ties per month, it was the Boosters who provided a tract of land below the old yards, south of the Hispano suburb of San Jose.[2] Moved by a spirit that animated all of America's urban developers, they sang in chorus of the opportunities awaiting manufacturing, merchandising, wholesaling, banking, and other business interests that had the foresight to locate in Albuquerque. As a postscript, the promoters were willing to add that agricultural prospects in the surrounding valley glimmered brightly, promising sure rewards for those wishing to invest capital in a farming venture.

A much-used slogan of the day held that, "Ten acres of irrigated land near Albuquerque will beat 100 acres of prairie land in Missouri or Illinois."[3] Real estate boomers were obliged to include such a comparison in their sales pitches because eastern buyers were completely ignorant of the high productivity of valley acreage under irrigation. Figures for the first decade of the century reveal that prime truck garden land on the outskirts of Albuquerque was selling for $500 an acre and yielding an annual return of $500 to $2,000, "depending on the crop and the hustle of the farmer."[4]

The traditional cereal, vegetable, and fruit crops, whose production had been expanded by Salvador Armijo and the Jesuit fathers back in the 1870s, continued as the mainstay of the valley economy. But the get-rich-quick atmosphere of the time also encouraged experimentation with new commercial crops. About 1897, Old Town gardener Herman Blueher began putting out test plots of tobacco, including Sumatra, Turkish, Havana, Virginia, and Kentucky burley varieties. The plants fared well and according to one outside estimate produced 3,000 pounds of tobacco per acre. With tobacco then worth $.25 a pound, it appeared that Albuquerque was on the verge of reaping a bonanza. A group of local businessmen backed by the Commercial Club in 1903 formed the Rio Grande Tobacco Company, acquired lands about 5 miles north of the city, and commenced construction of curing sheds and the seeding of fields. Wrote one participant in the enterprise, "The prospects are now most flattering."[5]

At about the same time that Herman Blueher started his trial planting of tobacco, other growers were taking a look at sugar beets. Colorado had already made great profits in raising beets and had erected six processing plants. But to this point, little had been done with the crop in New Mexico. Albuquerqueans claimed that the soil and climate of the Middle Valley were ideal for producing beets with a high sugar content, and that the area offered a plentiful source of cheap labor. Encouragement came from the industrial development department of the Santa Fe Railway, which was ready in the wings, as usual, to encourage any new industry that would become a freight shipper. The Santa Fe announced that it would extend special reduced rates to beet farmers in the Middle Valley wishing to ship their product to sugar refineries in Colorado.

For a variety of reasons, neither tobacco nor sugar beets gained a permanent toehold in the environs of Albuquerque. Disappointed boosters blamed a shortage of outside capital, slow to enter the region because of New Mexico's continued status as a territory. But a greater impediment, and one referred to in an earlier chapter, was the steady decrease in arable land in the Middle Valley during the first quarter of the twentieth century. That was owing largely to the rise of the stream bed of the Rio Grande by increasing sedimentation, a process that led to the elevation of the adjacent water table so that many fields became waterlogged and no longer suitable for cultivation. With fewer farms remaining in operation, little opportunity existed for introduction of large-scale commercial crops like tobacco and sugar beets.

If agriculture failed to live up to expectations, then ample compensation was provided by unprecedented growth in the railroading industry and in manufacturing firms. In 1908, an average of 52,000 freight cars annually were passing through Albuquerque, and eight passenger trains traveled in and out of the city every day. The Santa Fe Railway's Albuquerque property, containing offices, repair shops, the tie-treating plant, and stockyards, covered several square miles and was valued at 3.5 million dollars.[6]

The shining jewel in the Santa Fe's crown was the Alvarado Hotel, begun in 1901 and named for Coronado's lieutenant, Hernando de Alvarado. Built at a cost of $200,000 alongside the tracks facing First Street, it was touted as the finest railroad hotel on earth. The design adhered to the California Mission style, which made use of towers, balconies, and arcades supported by arches. Inside, carved beams, massive fireplaces, and black oak paneling in the dining room lent an elegant tone to the southwestern theme. On May 11, 1902, the press announced that the newly completed Alvarado opened in "a burst of rhetoric, a flow of red carpet, and the glow of myriad brilliant electric lights."[7] Instantly, it became the social center of Albuquerque and, among other things, the host of the glamorous Montezuma Ball held yearly during the fair.

The hotel formed the anchor of a rambling railroad complex stretching for two blocks and incorporating the depot and offices, a restaurant, and the famed Indian Building (which doubled as a gift shop and museum). The legendary Fred Harvey managed both the guest accommodations and food services under contract with the AT&SF, as he did for all hotels along the line. At a time when most western trains handed out cold and stale box lunches, passengers on the Santa Fe were treated to a leisurely layover at Albuquerque, where a white-coated man summoned them to a royal dinner by sounding a gong, and Harvey girls in fresh, starched uniforms dished up all you could eat for a dollar.

John Frederick Huckel, a son-in-law of Fred Harvey and a senior member of the firm, was the one who furnished much of the inspiration for the regional design of the Alvarado and other Harvey railroad hotels built later. And it was he who made the Indian Building at Albuquerque a showplace for Native American craftsmen. Pueblos and Navajos were hired to demonstrate weaving and jewelry-making to the thousands of travelers who made a meal stop in Albuquerque, and for many it was their first introduction to the beauties of Indian art. The program helped spark a revival in native crafts and created a market where practically none had existed before.

The stimulation of a nationwide interest in the well-preserved cultures of Southwestern Indians was precisely in line with the desire of both the Santa Fe Railway and the city of Albuquerque to promote the tourist industry. Easterners were just beginning to discover the wonders of the Far West, and New Mexico possessed marvels aplenty to lure the traveling public. The volume of tourist traffic increased steadily through the first decades of the twentieth century and Albuquerque, opportunely located in the heartland of the Southwest, profited accordingly. By 1922, the Alvarado had to be enlarged to take care of the swelling tide of visitors. New rooms were added, as were shaded patios, water lily pools, and trickling fountains all carefully calculated to create the romantic atmosphere of old Spain. Upon petition of two hundred Albuquerque businessmen, the Santa Fe in 1925 initiated a program of bus tours through New Mexico's scenic Pueblo country. Called "Indian Detours," they allowed rail passengers to make a stopover of several days for a side excursion into the back country. Albuquerque became the center of operations for what proved to be a highly successful venture.[8]

By that time, the railway and the city had already compiled a respectable record in joint cooperation, having found over the years that their respective commercial interests often dovetailed. An instance of that can be seen in the elaborate promotion given to the meeting of the Sixteenth National Irrigation Congress held at Albuquerque in the fall of 1908.

Each year the congress was conducted in a different western city for the purpose of expanding knowledge and disseminating information on all aspects of irrigation, land reclamation, and water rights. The United States government supported the effort and in 1908 appropriated $30,000 to underwrite an exposition, coinciding with the Congress, which would exhibit the products of irrigated agriculture.[9]

Albuquerque was elated at being designated the host city, and it formulated elaborate plans to put its best face forward. Not only would people from around the nation be in attendance, but also "men of international reputation from across the globe."[10] Territorial Governor George Curry moved down from Santa Fe and set up a temporary office and residence so as not to miss any part of the momentous event. In it, he saw political and economic advantage for New Mexico. "People will be coming to the Congress from all parts of the United States," he was quoted as saying. "They will be persons looking for investment, for homes. . . . I believe the influence of the Irrigation Congress upon our chances for admission to the union will be tremendous."[11]

At this time, New Mexico was vigorously pushing for statehood and any favorable publicity, picturing the Territory as progressive and energetic, could not fail to assist the cause. C. L. Seagraves, an official of the Santa Fe Railway, aptly summed up the matter: "The National Irrigation Congress in Albuquerque is going to prove just the influence that has been needed to remove the last false impression about New Mexico from the minds of the people east of the Mississippi. . . . The impression of sagebrush and cactus, lizards and badmen has clung with discouraging tenacity. Recently, however, as people have come to know something of the real conditions, this new impression has been rapidly fading."[12] Plainly, the Congress had the potential for delivering a death blow to the outdated notion that New Mexico was the nation's backward stepchild.

Acting from a policy of enlightened self-interest, the AT&SF did its part in adding luster to the affair. Special trains at favorable rates were run, to transport the throng of in-coming delegates. A total of 4,000 eventually arrived, including representatives from Germany, South Africa, Mexico, Chile, and Brazil. The company sent and installed a special art exhibit composed of paintings from its vast collection. And the railway's president, E. P. Ripley, flanked by an entourage of officials, journeyed out from Chicago to lend support by his presence. When he stepped off the train at the depot, he was greeted by a Mexican band, dispatched by the governor of Chihuahua, which blared forth loudly with strains of "Dixie."[13]

The Santa Fe's contribution to the gala occasion was far overshadowed, however, by Albuquerque's own lavish preparations. The twelve-day congress, September 29 to October 10, had been scheduled to co-incide with the Territorial Fair as a way of providing a bonus of entertainment for the guests. Beforehand, all streets in the downtown area were paved and 3,000 red, white, and blue incandescent lights strung above the main thoroughfares. A new convention hall was hastily constructed and classes at the university dismissed so that the buildings there could be commandeered for exhibit purposes. A sparkling industrial parade opened the congress and was highlighted by marching cavalrymen from Fort Wingate. Days of tedious speeches and conference meetings that followed were interspersed with more parades, baseball games, firework displays, and sumptuous parties. Famed Indian trader and frontiersman Richard Wetherill rode in on horseback with more than a hundred Navajo men, women, and children from Chaco Canyon. Led by the aged Chief Peschlikline, they performed the Navajo Sacred Fire Dance one evening at the fairgrounds. Afterward, the Albuquerque press enthusiastically pronounced it "the most weird dance indulged in by any living Indians and was never before given in the presence of white people. Over ten cords of wood were used in one fire."[14]

The auspicious congress ended with the rousing Montezuma Ball at the Alvarado, staged with pomp and glitter unequaled in the history of the Territory. The toniclike effect of the entire affair buoyed spirits of Albuquerque Boosters and reinforced the conviction that their city, in the century stretching ahead, was marked for bright and wondrous things.

While the Santa Fe Railway served as the backbone of New Albuquerque's economy, a healthy manufacturing and merchandising industry furnished its lifeblood. By 1900, many of the industrial firms that had been established in the early railroad era were solidly entrenched and flourishing. They included everything from brickyards, tanneries, flouring mills, packing houses, and foundries to wagon factories, steam laundries, woolen mills, bottling works, and a cement plant. All offered jobs and helped attract new residents to Albuquerque. The Southwestern Brewery and Ice Company brewed 30,000 barrels of Glorieta Beer a year and turned out 45 tons of ice daily, requiring a work force of thirty men. The Albuquerque Foundry and Machine Works employed sixty men in the production of $100,000 worth of iron goods annually. But the pride of the city and the behemoth among all industrial concerns was the American Lumber Company.

Founded in the early 1880s, the Company was listed by 1908 as the largest manufacturing firm in the Southwest and one of the largest lumbering enterprises in the entire country. Many Easterners would have been surprised to hear that arid New Mexico possessed any lumber at all. But in fact the Company owned a vast tract of virgin white pine in the Zuñi Mountains 100 miles west of Albuquerque. The land contained an estimated 1.5 billion board feet of timber, which was cut at the rate of 50 million feet a year. In the woods, the Company maintained 55 miles of track and operated 6 of its own locomotives and 160 logging cars. Thirty to forty carloads of logs were shipped to Albuquerque daily. At the headquarters camp of Kettner could be found a roundhouse and machine shop, a hotel, and a commissary. More than 500 men were employed there and in other logging camps.

The main plant, situated on one hundred acres northwest of downtown Albuquerque, boasted sawmills, a box factory, and sash and door factories. Inside the yards were 5 miles of railroad track, huge ponds capable of holding 4 million feet of logs, and a self-contained electric plant. During the first years of the century, the Company, according to its own claim, had more than one thousand men and youths on its payroll at Albuquerque alone, so that it surpassed even the Santa Fe Railway in number of employees. And not only was it a key economic institution in the life of the city, but because of ancillary activities related to the welfare of workers, it also emerged as a major social force. The Company funded its own fire-fighting corps and a medical department. It ran a comfortable hotel and provided lodging for men who did not wish to live in town. And it sponsored social and musical organizations and athletic clubs. Such paternalism helped foster loyalty among employees.

Also, the sheer size of the Company's operations tended to create a small but distinct community within the larger community.[15]

To city Boosters, success stories like those of the American Lumber Company and the Alvarado Hotel furnished welcome grist for promotional brochures. But there were other examples of change and growth, after century's turn, which presented further evidence of civic headway. One that attracted a good deal of attention was the replacement of the antiquated horse trolleys with electric streetcars.

Development of electric traction in the late 1880s represented a significant advance in urban transport and within a few years streetcars, drawing power from overhead cables, became the rage throughout the country. Albuquerque, always lagging somewhat behind the times, was late in getting its own system, but even so, when it was installed in 1904, excited local citizens saw in the innovation another sign that they were square in the mainstream of American progress. They may also have gloried in the fact that Albuquerque had gotten a jump on Tucson, one of its rival cities in the Southwest, which would not obtain electric streetcars for another two years.

In 1903, promoter William H. Greer of Bakersfield, California, obtained a franchise from the city council and formed the Albuquerque Traction Company. O. E. Cromwell's old mulecar system was acquired, the entire line electrified, and the original lightweight tracks replaced with heavier rails. The system introduced ten green double-ended cars, each served by a motorman and a conductor.[16] A swift expansion in patronage led to addition of new routes, including one that ran north on Twelfth Street to the gate of the Albuquerque Lumber Company. A jubilant press voiced the hope that appearance of the high-speed electric cars would banish from the city's precincts "the last vestige of villagery."[17]

In 1908 a competing traction company inaugurated the Highland Line, which served the East Mesa. Its yellow cars traveled as far as the University, providing students and faculty rapid access for the first time to the downtown area. Later, the two streetcar firms merged to form the City Electric Company under the presidency of George Roslington.[18] The move reflected a gradual decline in the financial fortunes of the electric transportation system. Advent of the automobile had brought a cut in patronage, while the low fares—$.05 for adults and children free— scarcely provided enough revenue to meet expenses. A boost in fares to $.06 in 1918 offered only temporary relief and was not enough to raise motormen's salaries above the old rate of $.27 an hour.[19] The heaviest blow fell in 1922 when the city council assessed the Company $50,000 for new cement paving between the tracks. Unable to meet this obligation, Roslington warned that without aid his firm would have to discontinue service.[20] The council refused to lift the assessment, and after muddling along in the red for another few years, the City Electric Company went out of business in 1928. Its twelve electric cars were sold and suffered the indignity of being converted to motel rooms at Napoleone's Deluxe Service Station and Auto Camp.[21]

Upon demise of the streetcars, businessman John Morrow teamed with several associates to bring a bus company franchise to Albuquerque from Casper, Wyoming. One of the first vehicles was a "four-banger," that is, a four-cylinder, twenty-passenger bus purchased from the White Truck Company of Cleveland. It incorported such unique features as a large wooden steering wheel and a canvas top. Embarrassingly, the new bus lacked the power to climb the steep grade up the East Mesa to the University, so the four-cylinder engine had to be replaced with a six-cylinder model. The Albuquerque Bus Company remained in private hands until 1965, when it passed to city ownership and became the Albuquerque Transit System.[22]

Evolution of public transport, beginning in the early 1880s with the mule trolleys, had been paralleled through the years by innovations in private transportation. Many pioneer families of New Albuquerque owned saddle horses or a buggy and team, while the more substantial business houses kept delivery and freight wagons. Several livery stables provided boarding and rental service both for residents lacking their own means of getting about and for tourists or traveling businessmen.

In 1881, W. L. Trimble, a Kentuckian who had come West by mule train, built the first livery stable in Old Town.[23] He prospered as a livery man and soon opened a spacious new stable on Second Street (later the site of the Hilton Hotel, now the Plaza Hotel). His establishment (rebuilt after a fire in 1882) at once became a public institution where, in Erna Fergusson's words, "the town's socially unambitious fore-gathered."[24] Idlers loafed about the dark cavern of the livery barn shooting craps or swapping stories and gossip. An occasional cockfight in the large corral out back provided more lively amusement and drew the betting crowd. Teamsters, coal and ice men, and fly-by-night real estate brokers found the congenial atmosphere of the stables a handy place to conduct business deals.

A portly, affable man, Trimble was in the habit of standing in front of his livery barn to greet passers-by. Decked out in a tailored suit, derby hat, and with a gleaming gold watch chain looped across his ample paunch, he was a picture of success. Besides his lucrative stables, he owned cattle, speculated in land, and operated a feeder stageline to the Cochiti Mining District in the Jemez Mountains 50 miles northwest of Albuquerque. But of all his assorted enterprises, none won him more favor with the public than his rental of two giant tallyhoes—touring wagons capable of hauling twenty to thirty passengers at a time. Named Jumbo and Minne-haha, the vehicles conveyed school classes to picnics at Bear Canyon in the Sandias and loads of wide-eyed tourists to Pueblo Indian dances upriver. Little wonder that the news media of the day spoke of Mr. Trimble pridefully as "a self-made man and one of Albuquerque's most substantial citizens."[25]

The livery trade, however, was destined to wither away in the face of technology's relentless march. The first challenge to the horse's supremacy came from the bicycle, which, by the 1890s, was becoming a national fad. Some social observers thought it appropriate to refer to the times as the Bicycle Age and to suggest, metaphorically speaking, that the twentieth century rolled to its opening on two wheels.

In Albuquerque, men in starched collars and bowler hats rode bicycles to their offices. Other men, wearing overalls, pedaled to the Santa Fe shops or to the yards of the American Lumber Company. Ladies draped in full skirts and petticoats manfully climbed aboard bicycles to go shopping, and youngsters, at least those of means, rode them to the ward schools. Henry Brockmier sold Phoenix bikes on West Gold Avenue. Nearby, Tom Insley's Bicycle Shop offered repairs and presently came to rival Trimble's livery barn as a popular hangout. Insley's services were much in demand before the numerous bicycle races, which filled the year and were regarded as major sporting events. Excitement reached its peak with the annual spring race to the mountains, a grueling 20-mile round-trip over a rutted road loaded with treacherous sand. Albuquerqueans, always keen for a good competition, made every race a gala occasion.[26]

But in the long run it was to be the horseless carriage rather than the bicycle that transformed the city and eventually put men like W. L. Trimble out of business. The new contraptions were first spoken of derisively as "buzz wagons," or as "Devil wagons," and not without good reason. Unlike bicycles, automobiles, at least the earliest models, possessed several disagreeable drawbacks. Their uproarious noise frightened horse teams, scattered cattle and sheep, and disturbed what had been, until now, a relatively tranquil urban environment. Motor cars also had an infuriating tendency to break down, get stuck in the sand, and suffer flat tires. A simple afternoon's excursion onto the mesa often resulted in two or three flats, and one of the first lessons learned by novice motorists was to carry a repair kit. The combustion engines also gave off a high odor, doubtless made more offensive because it was so unfamiliar. "Cussed more than admired," was the way one early-day resident described Albuquerque's initial sprinkling of automobiles.[27]

J. L. Dodson, a local bicycle dealer, gets credit for introducing the motor car to the city, a small Locomobile with wire-spoke wheels. In November 1897, he went to Denver to collect his purchase and to begin a drive home that would take five days. His was the first automobile to enter New Mexico and the first to surmount Raton Pass where a few scant years before Santa Fe traders had guided their wagons. The trip produced a litany of hardships. Horses met along the way panicked and ran off with their drivers. The unmarked road caused Dodson to take wrong turns, and when he attempted to ask directions at isolated ranches, the rural folk, not liking the looks of his strange conveyance, slammed doors in his face. Gasoline had to be sent in by railroad and picked up at towns along the way. Layovers were necessary when the gasoline failed to arrive on schedule. Yet, in spite of all, Mr. Dodson and his Locomobile prevailed and reached Albuquerque safely.[28]

For the next two years, as the city's lone owner of an automobile, he campaigned tirelessly to convince his fellow citizens that the age of motorized transportation was at hand. His efforts met stiff opposition and, indeed, city councilors even debated passing a law prohibiting "buzz wagons" on municipal streets. Gradually the tide shifted: in 1899, T. C. Kern brought in a Yale car, and the following year prominent banker M. W. Flournoy had a second-hand Winton shipped out from New York. The Winton, a shiny maroon, broke down on one of its first runs to the East Mesa and the owner, in total humiliation, was obliged to engage a team of oxen to tow him home. Banker Flournoy promptly purchased a new red Thomas Flyer. In 1906, whosesaler Louis Ilfeld received a shipment of three Maxwells and took one for his own use. While teaching himself to drive, Ilfeld lost control on a main street and attempted to stop by yelling "Whoa! Whoa!" and pulling on the steering wheel as if it were a pair of reins. The only casualty was a pedestrian knocked into a mud puddle.[29]

The motor cars had caught on and buyers were confronted by a bewildering number of varieties, according to some estimates as many as 150 different makes. They included the Pierce Arrow, Columbia, Sterns, Rambler, Northern, Baker Electric, Pope Toledo, Stoddard-Dayton, Peerless, Stevens-Duryea, and Ford, to mention a bare few. By 1910, Albuquerque had thirty-two automobiles. At least, that number showed up for the fair parade, and they probably represented every car in town. By 1920, the city directory listed over sixty automobile-related businesses downtown.[30]

With the proliferation of vehicles inevitably came regulation. The municipal council in September 1908 thought it time to pass an ordinance regulating the equipment, operation, and speed of automobiles. As yet, the Territory had no licensing system, so the city, under authority of the new ordinance, issued its own licenses for a fee of $3.[31] It also set speed limits: eight miles an hour for automobiles; ten miles an hour for horse-drawn vehicles. Another discriminatory regulation prohibited motor cars from using the viaduct, which overpassed the dangerous braid of switching tracks at the railroad crossing on Coal Avenue.[32] There was no restriction on buggies and wagons. The viaduct had been constructed in 1901 by the Missouri Valley Bridge and Iron Works and financed through passage of municipal bonds. The structure was wood frame and hence susceptible to fire. As a safety precaution, city authorities kept six wooden barrels filled with water on the viaduct, and all citizens were authorized to use them in case of fire.[33]

The introduction of the automobile had a direct influence on law enforcement. The Albuquerque chief of police gloomily told a news reporter in 1908 that since "the police department has no Devil wagon, I fear the old family horse will not have the speed to catch a racing automobile."[34] It was not long, however, before minions of the law were provided with motor cars. Creighton Foraker, the United States Marshal stationed in Albuquerque, got the first one in 1910; a Studebaker. The *Albuquerque Morning Journal* expressed the hope, editorially, that "the buzz wagon, the benzine buggy, the gasoline vehicle . . . would speed the delivery of court process."[35] Scarcely a month later, word came that the sheriff of Phoenix, in the neighboring Arizona Territory, had used a

motor car to pursue and capture two train robbers. The news helped
confirm that the day of horse chases was nearly at an end.

The automobile's impact was also felt in other ways. High-speed, motorized transportation telescoped New Mexico's vast distances, making it feasible for persons in remote areas to conduct commercial business in the major urban centers instead of in isolated trading posts and small towns. An arduous trip that had once taken several days now became a pleasant journey of a few hours. Albuquerque, favorably placed in the middle of the Territory, was the chief beneficiary. That geographical advantage, combined with its status as a railroad center, first led the city to attract wholesalers and retailers, and the trend toward a concentration of business accelerated as the ownership of automobiles became commonplace. The result, as a resident of the period sagely took note, was that, "Albuquerque developed and grew prosperous, while many of the formerly prosperous towns shrank in population and came upon hard times. Some resentment and bitterness towards Albuquerque developed, persisting even until today."[36]

Automobiles made imperative the long-delayed surfacing of streets and roads. Albuquerque began a half-hearted paving program for downtown streets in the early 1890s, but no attention at all was given to the residential suburbs until the pending Irrigation Congress in 1908 spurred a frantic effort to upgrade the outlaying thoroughfares and thereby prevent visitors from getting an adverse impression of the city. Improvement of highways, although vigorously pushed by the New Mexico Automobile Association, was even slower in coming. As late as the 1930s, portions of U.S. 85, north and south through the valley, and U.S. 66, a primary transcontinental route, remained unpaved. Slow, too, were some New Mexicans in jumping the hurdle from horse-drawn to horseless carriages. Well into the 1950s, Pueblo Indians living near the city continued to drive wagons and teams on weekly shopping excursions to downtown Albuquerque.

The transportation revolution, set in motion by the railroad and progressing through street cars, bicycles, and automobiles, had a direct bearing on Albuquerque's pattern of municipal growth. As we have seen, city devlopers in 1880 had expected the Old and the New Towns to undergo parallel expansion until the space between them was filled, and they merged to form a single metropolis. But in fact, New Albuquerque spurted ahead, leaving its aging sister lolling in the doldrums over by the river. Old Town became like a barnacle clinging to the hull of the fast-moving central city, going nowhere on its own and glad for a free ride on the swelling tide of progress. The street railway, and later bicycles and motor cars, gave its citizens easy access to jobs and shopping facilities in New Albuquerque. But that plus was offset by the disadvantage of being excluded from the growing array of municipal services enjoyed by residents of New Town.

A similar situation prevailed in other communities, which, like Old

Albuquerque, were relegated to second-class status on the periphery of New Town. Barelas, a Hispano settlement of long standing, lay immediately to the south and close to the river. Very early, it was linked by street railway to New Albuquerque, where its people found employment in shops, factories, and the Santa Fe yards. To the east of Barelas and below the railroad yards, stood the little community of San José, which probably did not exist as a distinct entity until after 1880 when Hispano and a few Black workers at the Santa Fe shops and tie-treating plant took up residence there. Martinez Town, first called Dog Town because of its large canine population, was crowded into a marginal patch of land northeast of downtown, between Broadway and the sandhills. Its helter-skelter collection of adobe houses and irregular streets gave it the appearance of a traditional New Mexican village. But its people, contrary to tradition, were largely Protestant rather than Catholic, a fact owed mainly to the influence of the neighboring Menaul Presbyterian School. They had their own Presbyterian Church by 1889. After the turn of the century, an influx of Catholics created the Santa Barbara parish on the northern edge of Martinez Town. Westward, amid residual swamps, the surviving colonial hamlets of Los Griegos, Los Candelarias, and Los Duranes completed the chain of satellite communities on the fringes of New Albuquerque. Most would remain unincorporated and neglected until annexed by the sprawling city in the late 1940s.[37]

Albuquerque's civic boosters and real-estate promoters, if they paid any attention to the outlying villages at all, must have regarded them as an embarrassment, for neither their poverty nor their rustic architectural style helped in creating the image of a modern and typical American city. The developers were all newcomers who wanted a platted and regimented municipality indistinguishable in every respect from the places they had left. And that was largely what they built. As Harvey Fergusson phrased it, "By 1910 Albuquerque was almost a model of what a small American town should be. In all essentials it was just like a town in Iowa or Kansas and not strikingly different from one in Pennsylvania or Michigan."[38] In time that attitude would abate and some effort would be mounted to recover a measure of regional charm, but at the beginning, Yankee efficiency and sense of appropriateness dictated that the face of Albuquerque should be a careful imitation, not an original creation.

Around the original townsite staked out in 1880, which contained both the core of the business district and the earliest homes, land speculators developed a series of additions. As the new tracts were subdivided and built up, the city boundaries reached out to encompass them. The Huning Highland Addition east of the tracks, platted in mid-1880, was the first suburb added to the townsite. The architecture was principally Victorian in style, and the people, initially at least, almost exclusively middle-class professionals, who were thoroughly American and modern in their outlook and values. Only later did Hispanos and a few Blacks reside there. South and southwest of downtown could be found working-class neighborhoods with small dwellings of Santa Fe employees, machinists, boilermakers, and tradesmen—an ethnic mix of both Anglos and Hispanos. The Armijo and Perea additions, filling in a portion of the space between Old Town and New, drew people of varying economic backgrounds, but were especially attractive to younger people just beginning to make their marks in the community. A section of Railroad Avenue in that area, just east of the Huning Castle, was popularly known as Honeymoon Road.[39]

In Albuquerque, the process of suburbanization took its cue from a rising national dissatisfaction with life in densely populated central cities. The builders of New Town wanted none of the crowding, excessive noise, and tenement blight that in the East had driven out affluent urban dwellers. The new ideal emphasized the benefits of a semirural environment that could be had in the suburbs without giving up employment and cultural opportunities of the city. A cottage on a wide lot in a thinly settled neighborhood with all the pleasures of natural surroundings offered the best of both possible worlds. Albuquerque real-estate vendors made their pitches accordingly:

> Have a nice garden, raise your own chickens, keep a horse and a
> cow. Bring up a big family.
> 　　Be independent . . .
> 　　Enjoy life while you live
> For you will be a long time dead.[40]

What made the out-migration to the suburbs possible, not only in Albuquerque, but across the country, was the introduction of rapid transport. Contrary to an oft-stated belief, the streetcar and not the automobile precipitated the shift of population from the inner city to the more spacious fringes. Traction companies were often owned by large real estate concerns, who viewed them not as public utilities, but as promotional devices essential to luring customers for lots to the suburbs. Obtaining a traction franchise, developers would lay streetcar tracks in areas of anticipated growth. In any new addition, the first residential lots sold were those closest to the tracks.

Hoping to capitalize on that prescription for success, William H. Greer organized the Albuquerque Traction Company in 1903 and the following year put the city's first electric streetcars in operation. Greer and an associate, Henry A. Jastro, were from Bakersfield, California, where they had been key figures in the formation of a huge development corporation, the Kern County Land Company. The firm's holdings included extensive land and cattle interests in New Mexico. Both Greer and Jastro saw in Albuquerque an opportunity to profit by promoting subdivisions through expansion of streetcar service, a procedure they had become familiar with in California.

Once the Albuquerque streetcar franchise was securely under wraps, the two men put together a realty firm, the Traction Land and Improvement Company, to serve as the principal agency for their promotional schemes. To ease their entry into the community, they persuaded several prominent citizens to become officers in the new company. Among them were financier Matthew W. Flournoy; Solomon Luna, president of the Albuquerque Bank of Commerce and the largest individual sheep raiser in New Mexico; and Colonel D. K. B. Sellers, secretary of the Territorial Fair Association, who was already heavily invested in real estate and would later win a term as mayor (1914–16).[41]

Plans called for an extension of the main streetcar line on Railroad Avenue northward to New York Avenue (Lomas), thereby forming a loop around a major section of the business district and around proposed subdivisions where the Traction Land and Improvement Company intended to sell lots. The Company had control of land remaining in the old Perea Addition and had staked out a new addition, Luna Place (named for Solomon Luna) immediately to the east. A portion of the streetcar extension was built up Twelfth Street to the vicinity of the American Lumber Company, but the loop itself was never completed. The reason was, the developers were beset with problems that cut into land sales and discouraged the carrying through of their original design. One of those was the slowness of getting city services, particularly water mains, extended to their suburbs. Another was the company's requirement that buyers in Luna Place, which was advertised as a prestige addition, must make a minimum of $3,000 in improvements. Most of Albuquerque's new arrivals, who were in the market for residential lots, were either small tradesmen, workers, or health-seekers. The elite property being offered in Luna Place was far beyond their financial means.[42]

The selling of real estate, as a handmaiden of boosterism, proved attractive to others besides William Greer and Henry Jastro. Soon after the turn of the century, regional author Mary Austin wrote, "In southern California boosting has become a religious duty; and the divine right of that section to all it can get, by any method whatever, is unquestioned."[43] Her statement could have applied just as well to the sentiment prevailing among many Albuquerqueans with their eyes fixed on a fast dollar. Colonel Sellers, for example, launched his own hard-sell realty business after his participation in the Traction Land and Improvement Company failed to reap the expected rewards. One of his typical advertisements placed in the *Albuquerque Morning Journal,* September 26, 1908, proclaimed in large block type: "I expect to make $50,000 in Albuquerque real estate offering building lots which will increase $10,000 in value before next May 1." His claim to extraordinary profits, while doubtless exaggerated, nevertheless, encouraged the belief that Albuquerque, as a city on the move, was a good place for investors.

The platting of new suburbs kept pace with the steady increase in population. Martin P. Stamm (father of Roy and Raymond Stamm) abandoned his wholesale produce business, entered the real estate game, and launched the Park Addition between Mountain Road and New York Avenue. Bordering his property on the east was a tract developed as the Coronado Place Addition. The man behind that project was the Reverend Henry Forrester, first rector of St. John's Episcopal Church. Even men of the cloth, it seems, could not resist the temptation to cash in on the boom in land sales. Other additions progressively filled in the empty spaces that lay between the Old and New Towns and between Huning Highlands and the university on the East Mesa. As that occurred, New Albuquerque became less of the tight-knit community that it had been in the years 1880–1900, and more of a cluster of neighborhoods, each with its own character and loyalties.

In the course of municipal expansion, Railroad Avenue emerged to become, what urban historians call, the primary corridor avenue, that is, a linear thoroughfare that handles the bulk of through traffic and serves as a focus for commercial establishments and shoppers.[44] Indicative of that, Railroad Avenue was renamed Central in 1912. As intercity travel by motor car increased in the following years, Central sprouted rows of service stations and roadside hostelries, first termed auto camps, then tourist courts, and finally motels. It would remain the chief east-west artery through the city, on U.S. 66, until completion of Interstate 40 in the 1960s.

In the early part of the century, Broadway was looked upon as the principal north-south thoroughfare. At its intersection with Central was a large iron watering trough for horses, a community landmark. Chester French, a mortician with a penchant for gardening, set out thousands of flowers at his own expense, making Broadway sparkle with color. A parkway down the center of the street was planted in cottonwoods and the cool shade attracted strollers on blistering summer afternoons.

Albuquerque's favorite recreation spot, however, was Robinson Park. At the time New Albuquerque was platted, Railroad Avenue had also been laid out. To reach Old Town, it had been necessary to bend Railroad, between Eighth and Tenth Streets, with the result that it cut across the rectangular grid of the townsite and created several triangular blocks. Since the irregular shape of the land made it unsuitable for residential lots, the Townsite Company set aside part of the space as a park. For several years, it remained neglected, empty, and nameless.

In the middle of the 1880s, civic-minded matrons of some of Albuquerque's first families took a hand. They sponsored a contest to select a name and at the same time raise funds to develop the park. Young ladies were asked to stand as contestants, and the public was encouraged to select a favorite by purchasing votes. Albert Alonzo Robinson, general superintendent and chief engineer of the Santa Fe Railway, bought the largest block of votes for his daughter, Lena. Therefore, in her honor Robinson Park was named.[45]

The Albuquerque Board of Trade lent assistance with beautification by arranging a tree-planting ceremony on Arbor Day, 1885. A large crowd assembled at the Armijo House and formed a festive procession headed by Henry Jaffa and a Negro band. Some 150 citizens carried small saplings—elm, cottonwood, and Osage orange. Marching in high style to the park, they went furiously to work sowing the beginnings of a miniature forest. In the weeks that followed, school children were marshalled to carry buckets of water to the struggling trees. By century's end, their heavy boughs spread a canopy of shade over a soft and verdant lawn.[46]

The addition of three important fixtures gave special significance to Robinson Park. One was a bandstand that long drew Albuquerqueans to Sunday evening concerts in summer. Another was a memorial fountain topped by a bronze Victorian nymph erected in honor of John Braden. He was the heroic driver, it will be recalled, who in 1896 guided his flaming fireworks wagon away from parade spectators and died in the act. A third notable feature of the park were the Civil War cannons, which General Sibley had abandoned in Albuquerque upon his retreat in 1862. The unexpected recovery of the big guns, preceding their placement in Robinson Park, aroused considerable interest among local citizens and also sparked a warm controversy.

In August 1889, Major Trevanion T. Teel, a resident of El Paso, paid a visit to Albuquerque. He had been the artillery officer assigned by Sibley twenty-seven years before to bury eight cannons behind San Felipe Neri Church. "I'm certain I can find the place again," he confidently told Albuquerqueans. His announcement caused an enormous stir. Major Harry R. Whiting, long-time resident and commander of the Union veterans association, the Grand Army of the Republic (G.A.R.), took charge of the recovery operation.[47] Under his direction, a digging committee armed with shovels and pickaxes went to the site north of the plaza indicated by Teel. Sure enough, after several hours the workmen unearthed the war relics—eight guns stamped "U.S." and bearing the initials of the manufacturer, C. A. & Co., Boston. With mules and ropes, they were lifted out of the hole and moved to Trimble's corral for safekeeping. But controversy arose over the question of custody and ownership. Mayor Whiting and the G.A.R. tried to claim the cannons, but Confederate veterans about town objected strenuously. The *Albuquerque Morning Democrat* declared: "It would puzzle anyone to give a reason why the G.A.R. should have charge of the guns. Their effort to appropriate them at the expense of the city, is one which a large majority of the people of Albuquerque will most certainly condemn."[48]

The unseemly wrangle lasted for months. The Colorado Historical Society also put in a claim since it had been Colorado Volunteers who stopped the Confederate advance at Glorieta Pass and forced Sibley to withdraw from New Mexico. In the end, the Albuquerque city council shipped four of the cannon off to Denver and placed two others on display in Robinson Park. That pair remained there until 1942 when President Franklin Roosevelt asked the nation's cities to collect old cannon and bronze statues from their parks so they could be melted down as scrap for the war effort. Moved by a zealous patriotism, City Commission Chairman Clyde Tingley stated, "If donating the cannon will be of any advantage toward winning the war, we'll let the Government have them at once. The Government can have anything the city's got that'll help our cause."[49] Although the guns were removed from Robinson Park, they somehow escaped the maw of the furnaces. After the war they were discovered in storage at Albuquerque's Kirtland Air Force Base and, mounted on new carriages, were installed on the Old Town plaza.[50]

Albuquerque's municipal government at an early date recognized that parks and playgrounds should be included in long-range planning for city expansion and in 1886 it set aside a special fund for land acquisition.[51] A shortage of revenue in ensuing years, however, delayed development of any meaningful parks program. The Santa Fe Railway helped fill the vacuum by creating the narrow Depot Park along the tracks. By 1883, it boasted a stone fountain, gas lantern posts, and two bronze statues, one an idealized Indian standing seven feet tall and the other a noble stag with a wide rack of antlers. The only complaint about the park came from the *Albuquerque Morning Journal* which indelicately mentioned that, "the privy of the nearby depot gives out a very disagreeable odor and should be looked after."[52] The park later diappeared with the expansion of railroad facilities along First Street.

In spite of problems, the city's park system grew. It was pushed along by occasional land donations from private citizens. Max Nordhaus, for example, gave a small wedge of ground at Fourteenth and Central, and it was developed as the Soldiers and Sailors Park, a memorial to service men killed in World War I.[53] In 1918, the city joined with the county and began to buy up bottom land between the Barelas Bridge and New York Avenue in hopes of creating a river front park. Difficulties in acquiring title from some property holders slowed the effort so that a public recreation area facing the Rio Grande did not open until the late 1920s. The difficulties of providing parks notwithstanding, the city persevered and laid the foundation for a program that would bear fruit later in the twentieth century.

"Albuquerque is one of the cities of the West that is so openly, so rampantly healthy, so gloriously deluged with vivifying sunshine and purified with healing breezes that it invites with open arms the sick and ailing to enter its portals."[54] Such flossy statements as this flowed endlessly from the pens of journalists, writers of tourist manuals, and government propagandists. As a result, by the beginning of the twentieth century, the Territory was gaining national, indeed, international renown, as a haven for health-seekers. In fact, a French medical society issued a statement asserting that, of all habitable places in the world, New Mexico was the area most free of consumption, as tuberculosis was then called.[55]

The benefits to health derived from two favorable geographical conditions: the Territory's generally high altitude and thin atmosphere, which relieved the pressure on lungs weakened not only by consumption, but by any number of other respiratory ailments; and the relatively low humidity, which also eased the labors of persons with breathing difficulties. Colorado enjoyed the advantage of altitude, but owing to greater rainfall, not that of dry air. Southern Arizona, on the other hand, possessed a desert climate, but was comparatively low in elevation. New Mexico, then, could claim with considerable justification that it held the best qualifications to become the nation's sanatorium. The significance of that fact is apparent when it is noted that in 1909 tuberculosis was the chief cause of death in the United States.[56]

In the legions of afflicted persons, eager to escape the rigors of bad weather in the East, Albuquerque boosters perceived the basis for a profitable new industry. Advertise the city as a health haven and the wave of emigrants would provide customers for real-estate developers and merchants. The infirm would be restored to health, so the sloganeering went, and, as an inevitable corollary, the community would prosper.

By 1910, Albuquerque counted 3,000 tuberculars among a population of 13,000 (including Old Town). Six years later, statistics showed that health-seekers in the city were spending approximately 2.5 million dollars annually, precipitating a lively boom among local businesses.[57] The flood of money apparently clouded the judgment of the municipal fathers and caused them deliberately to overlook or dismiss the health problem posed by the large concentration of diseased individuals in their precincts. In the beginning, the highly communicable nature of tuberculosis was not fully understood and led to such public utterances as the following: "Unlike many localities, Albuquerque welcomes the sick, because it is realized that they are in no way a danger to the community, while it is recognized that they are a distinct economic asset."[58]

Later, when the contagious character of T.B. was well established, fervent boosters continued to minimize the perils it posed. As late as 1932, the Albuquerque Civic Council (specifically formed to publicize the city as a health center and supported by a special tax levy) was stating in one of its promotional tracts: "It is in the fact that Albuquerque has no fear of tuberculosis that its greatest attraction for a healthseeker lies. The healthseeker is welcomed here and made to feel at home."[59] While true that the community persisted in welcoming the tubercular with open arms, it is scarcely correct to say that Albuquerqueans remained unafraid of contracting the disease themselves.

The menace to public health, in actuality, was quite real. No attempt was made to confine or quarantine T.B. victims, and those who were ambulatory freely circulated among the general populace. Some people landed in Albuquerque virtually destitute expecting to find work and, as their feeble strength allowed, meet their medical expenses. The growing numbers of such individuals kept wages low, particularly for unskilled jobs, and, as they moved through the ranks of the labor force, practically all Albuquerqueans were exposed to tuberculosis. Many streetcar conductors, for example, were "lungers," as consumptives were usually called, and with the coughing and spitting that accompanied the disease, the cars had to be periodically cleaned and sterilized.[60]

By far the greater portion of sick reaching the city were persons of some means who were able to convalesce, as doctors recommended, without trying to work. A surprising number engaged servants, Indian or Hispano, to assist with domestic chores, a practice that directly contributed to the spread of the illness. Heretofore, the native people of New Mexico had been little troubled themselves by T.B., but that very

circumstance made them more susceptible when exposed, since their
bodies had no opportunity to develop a natural immunity. An examination of death certificates for the years after 1910 reveals a rising rate
of fatalities among Spanish-surnamed women from tuberculosis and other
respiratory maladies. In almost every case, the occupation of such victims
is listed as housekeeper.[61] The same situation probably prevailed among
Indian women employed as domestics, but since they would have returned
to their reservations on falling ill, their deaths and the causes leading
to them went largely unrecorded.

For several decades, every train that pulled up at the Albuquerque
station discharged another crop of disease-ridden passengers, each one
hopeful that the city's climate would work its promised magic. Some
stepped onto the platform under their own power, but many who had
made the pilgrimage as a last resort were handed down on stretchers.
The town's funeral parlors met the trains with ambulances that served
as jitneys to convey the ailing to sanatoriums, boarding houses, or private
residences. Unfailingly, the parlors would be called upon in due time to
transport some of the same persons to the cemetery.

The vast majority of new arrivals had been given up as incurables
by their physicians back in the Midwest or East. And, indeed, there
were those who proved beyond help. But for others, it was a different
story. As one writer explained it, "In the bracing atmosphere of Albuquerque they regained health and happiness, and with a merry twinkle
in their eyes, or a contented chuckle, enjoyed telling in a good-humored
manner how wrong their doctor's diagnosis had proved."[62]

Because they were so numerous and because they lived, day to day,
under the same black cloud, Albuquerque's health-seekers formed their
own tight-knit society. Much of their time was spent resting and sunning
in "chasing chairs," for in their own terminology they were "chasing the
cure." They were much given to drinking of buttermilk and sherry laced
with raw egg. And, the men at least, wore a distinctive uniform consisting
of a wide-brimmed hat, white shirt, and wild ties decorated with bright
stripes or polka dots. Such dress was intended to keep up their spirits.
"Humor," says Erna Fergusson, "was their defense and their salvation."[63]
They made jokes among themselves and poked fun at their unenviable
condition. And there was romance, too, for many sufferers were of high
school or college age. Out on the East Mesa, the University of New
Mexico had its health cottages right on campus so that students could
chase the cure and attend class simultaneously.

Soon after 1900, the swelling tide of health-seekers created an
imperative need for sanatoriums dedicated exclusively to the treatment
of tuberculosis. Doctors and pharmacists had appeared in New Albuquerque during the early years of the railroad era, but for the next two
decades medical facilities, such as hospitals and laboratories, remained
in short supply. The Atlantic and Pacific Railroad in 1881 erected a
small hospital east of its shops capable of accommodating twenty patients.
Two years later, a group of civic-minded ladies led by Ernestine Huning
established a second hospital, the Cottage Home, in a three-room adobe

house donated by Franz Huning.[64] In addition, a "pest house" to quarantine victims of smallpox was placed in the sandhills south of Fairview Cemetery. But for some twenty years, this was about all that Albuquerque could boast of in the way of health-care facilities.

The tuberculars, many of them in the last stages of terminal illness, however, required something more substantial. As a consequence, a movement was soon under way to build sanatoriums where convalescents could receive specialized treatment for lung ailments. The first of the "sans" was St. Joseph's, begun by the Catholic Sisters of Charity in 1902. The Presbyterians, Methodists, and Lutherans followed suit, and privately funded T.B. hospitals were gradually added, which eventually brought the total of such institutions to eight. Albuquerque's high concentration of patients and sanatoriums attracted pulmonary specialists from around the country, enhancing the city's reputation as a progressive medical center. Since Central, between downtown and the University, was the location of several of the sans, it was familiarly referred to as "T.B. Avenue."[65]

Not all of the lungers who came to Albuquerque seeking relief took up residence in the sanatoriums. There were dozens of convalescent homes that accepted the sick. Also available were rows of diminutive tent houses described as, "little shacks that consist chiefly of a screened porch with a bed on it."[66] The depressing nature of these structures was recalled years later by an Albuquerquean who had lived with her afflicted parents in one of them. "Our tent house was on Iron Avenue, just off High Street," she wrote. "My mother so hated the canvas walls that she painted murals on them."[67]

To meet the demand for more permanent residences, created by the influx of health-seekers, developers built scores of moderately priced cottages, all with the inevitable screened porch so necessary for effective chasing. Such buildings remain the predominant type of dwelling in many of the city's older neighborhoods. Another visible legacy of the T.B. era are aging Chinese elm trees lining the streets. The newcomers set out elms in preference to the native cottonwood because they reminded them of the eastern homes that illness had forced them to abandon.

Tuberculars left their mark on Albuquerque in other, more profound ways. Among those who survived the "white plague" and returned to a normal life could be found members of the professional class, businessmen, journalists, politicians, artists, and musicians. Upon being pronounced "cured," or at least an arrested case, many of them chose to make Albuquerque their permanent home, either because they feared a return to the rigorous climate from which they had originally fled, or simply because the unhurried pace of things on the Rio Grande had claimed their affections. They entered wholeheartedly into the life of the community and imparted to it a sophisticated and cosmopolitan air quite out of keeping with its size. As a result, Albuquerque's business, social, and civic life was immeasurably enriched.

By the late 1930s, former chasers were in evidence everywhere— in the municipal government, fraternal and religious organizations, the principal commercial establishments, and on the University faculty. Some were destined to go on and made a name beyond the limits of their adopted city: Clinton P. Anderson became a United States senator and a prime mover in the launching of America's space program; John F. Simms, governor of the state; John Gaw Meem, architect and leading spirit behind development of the Spanish-Pueblo style of building; and William Randolph Lovelace, I, founder of the Lovelace Clinic.

So important did the health industry become to Albuquerque's economy that one physician, at the height of the chasing boom, was led to remark that if a medication for the cure of tuberculosis was ever discovered, the city would tumble into financial ruin.[68] The prediction proved unwarranted, for when the introduction of new antibiotics in the 1940s brought the disease under control, banishing the chasing chair to the junk pile, Albuquerque swiftly adjusted to loss of the health-seeker's dollar. Several of the old sans, like St. Joseph's and Presbyterian, converted to regular hospitals, while others closed their doors, their specialized services no longer in demand.

Albuquerque, however, retained its greatest asset, the one that lured health-questers in the first place—a mild, invigorating, and salubrious climate. Its wholesomeness continued to be recognized in a timeless and popular refrain of the Middle Valley's Hispanic folk who, when prompted, would sagely declare: "The region is so healthy that its aged inhabitants never die, but dry up and are blown away!"[69]

Politics and Prejudice Intrude

THE UPROOTED ANGLOS who arrived in Albuquerque in an ever widening stream were decidedly conservative, both politically and morally. In temperament and outlook, most epitomized the hard-working, church-going, slightly gullible middle-class American. Whether they came for their health or strictly in search of economic opportunity, they expected the city to offer them the same sort of comfortable society to which they had grown familiar in some other corner of the country. In this they were to experience a measure of disappointment, for Albuquerque, partly because of its lingering frontier flavor and also because of its large Hispanic population, was not quite ready in the early twentieth century to bow to conformity. Nowhere was that fact more plainly manifested than in the workings of local politics.

At Albuquerque, as elsewhere in the Territory, Republicans long held the upper hand. Powerful factions within the party feuded interminably and struggled for supremacy. Anglos held tightly to the reins of authority inside the city limits, but outside, Hispanos dominated the Bernalillo County government. In both areas, however, political patronage, fraud, and vote stealing were commonplace. Beginning in the early 1880s, elections had been routinely disrupted by stuffing the ballot boxes and by "voting the sheep." The last practice, a distinctive feature of the New Mexico political scene, entailed giving names to individual sheep so that an owner could cast ballots for every member of his flock.

One man alleged to have used that voting method was Solomon Luna, vice-president of the First National Bank of Albuquerque, member of the Republican National Committee from New Mexico, and the biggest sheep raiser in the Territory. Although deeply involved in Albuquerque's business life and holding large investments in real estate, Luna was actually a resident of Los Lunas in Valencia County, just south of the city. He was the recognized *patrón,* or political boss, of that area and friend and foe alike referred to him circumspectly as "King Saul."

In one election, 4,300 votes were cast, whereas Valencia County's official population was a mere 1,800. It was apparent to all that "sheep had voted" to make up the difference.[1]

Solomon Luna died in a bizarre accident in the summer of 1912. Visiting one of his far-flung ranching operations in western New Mexico, he got up in the middle of the night to go to the privy. On the way, he evidently suffered a stroke or heart attack and fell into a huge vat of sheep dip.[2] Next morning workmen found his body floating, face down, in the slimy liquid. An Albuquerque newspaper lionized him as "a millionaire banker who was a political power in every county."[3]

For a time Bernalillo County, like Valencia County, also had its political boss, in the person of Frank A. Hubbell. His father, James, as explained earlier, had risen to prominence during the Civil War period as a prosperous south valley rancher and freighter. Through his mother, Julianita Gutiérrez, a granddaughter of former governor Francisco Javier Chávez, Frank was linked by blood to the aristocracy within the Hispano community. His standing in that quarter was enhanced by an ability to speak fluent Spanish and by a fortunate marriage to a local belle, Trinidad García. Buying up land in western New Mexico and leasing thousands of acres of graze from the railroads, Frank Hubbell built a ranching empire that, upon the death of his competitor, Solomon Luna, made him the sheep king of the Southwest.

Success in the livestock business provided Hubbell the financial resources needed to indulge his penchant for politics. In 1890, he won his first elective office, representing Bernalillo County in the territorial legislature. At that time, he was twenty-eight years old—a bright, sandy-haired, blue-eyed young man known for his polite and kindly disposition. Underneath the calm exterior, however, lurked an iron will and a tendency to be inflexible and unforgiving toward political foes.

Over the next six years, while serving in the legislature at Santa Fe, Frank Hubbell became embroiled in the bitter factionalism endemic in the Territory's Republican party. As a rule, he lined up on the side of Thomas B. Catron against a rival faction headed by Miguel A. Otero, a position that would later cost him dearly when Otero ascended to the governorship.

By 1896, Hubbell abandoned his career in the capital and turned his attention to building a solid power base in Bernalillo County. He was elected county assessor, the first of several key local offices he would hold during the next few years. His sway over the populace was strengthened by the fact that his brother, Thomas S. Hubbell, served as county sheriff between 1894 and 1905. Frank also acquired ownership of *La Bandera Americana,* a Spanish-language weekly in Albuquerque under the editorship of Nestor Montoya. That and his own family connections furnished him the means to install his machine and win control of Hispano votes in Bernalillo County.[4]

The old *patrón* system, by which a single wealthy and powerful man dominated regional politics and which had been a part of Hispanic life on the Rio Grande for generations, rendered the native folk particularly susceptible to control by a modern political machine of the kind so skillfully constructed by Frank Hubbell. Another institution, the burial society, also provided him a vehicle for winning political support. Such societies, like the Alianza Hispano-Americana, were dues-paying groups whose primary purpose was to provide funerals and wakes for members. In time, however, they had gained a tidy measure of political influence in Old Town and in the small hamlets clinging to Albuquerque's skirt. "Boss Frank," as he came to be known, often appeared at society wakes and delivered impassioned speeches that dealt more with politics than with the merits of the deceased.[5]

As the most influential Republican in Bernalillo County and a king-maker among party followers around the Territory, Hubbell counted upon the support of a large constituency. But he had formidable enemies, too, who attacked his accumulation of power and stigmatized his machine as Hubbellism.[6] Fiercest of his critics was Miguel A. Otero, appointed to the governor's office in 1897. In Hubbellism, Otero saw a challenge to his own unquestioned leadership of the Republican party. Biding his time, he finally found the chance in 1905 of dispose of his rival. Frank Hubbell was then serving as Bernalillo County treasurer and, on a rather questionable charge of mishandling of funds, Governor Otero removed him from office. Hubbell appealed his dismissal through the judicial system, and he was eventually exonerated by the territorial Supreme Court. But in the interval, the cloud hovering over his name resulted in disintegration of his machine. A final blow to his political fortunes fell in 1916 when, in a comeback attempt, he failed in his bid to win a seat in the United States Senate.[7]

Newcomers to Albuquerque in the era of Hubbellism were usually dismayed by the course of municipal politics. A boss who ran the county and owned the courts—which is how one journalist characterized Frank Hubbell—was something they were not quite prepared for.[8] In coming to New Mexico, many people anticipated escaping the evils of machine politics, then rife in eastern cities. Upon finding it entrenched on the banks of the Rio Grande, they lent their voices to a movement for reform. From such persons, the progressive Democrat Harvey Fergusson drew support to nourish both his own political aspirations and the fortunes of a growing Democratic party.

Although the attention of Albuquerqueans was riveted chiefly upon the affairs of government close at hand, increasingly they took an interest in national problems and issues. That was especially the case on those occasions when a president, touring the country by rail, would make a stopover in the city and use the opportunity to deliver a political address. One of the most popular of such illustrious guests was President Theodore Roosevelt, who paid a memorable visit to Albuquerque in 1903 and returned again in 1912, while stumping the country as a third-party candidate on the Bull Moose Ticket.

Roosevelt had a special affection for New Mexico dating back to 1898 when he had toured the Territory at the outbreak of the Spanish-American War, enlisting recruits for his famed regiment of Rough Riders.

Many Albuquerque boys had joined, and two had lost their lives in the conflict. When he came back in 1903 wearing the mantle of the presidency, Roosevelt was greeted at the depot by an exuberant throng, including many veterans of his old regiment. To the astonishment of bystanders, he called each by name, through he had not seen them since the war.

A platform had been set up near the door of the Alvarado Hotel, and the president mounted it to deliver the expected political speech. At its conclusion, civic leaders presented a dramatic tableau designed to persuade him to support statehood for New Mexico. Forty-five peach-faced girls, begowned to represent the forty-five states, posed in the background, while another fair miss, representing New Mexico, stood to the fore wringing her hands and pleading for admission. The message, so blatantly delivered, was warmly applauded by the audience.

Following the oratory and tableau, President Roosevelt was escorted to a line of waiting carriages for a triumphal parade through downtown. Led by brass bands and a troop of cavalry from Fort Wingate, the procession filed up Railroad Avenue and under a towering arch erected at the junction of Second Street. Young ladies clinging precariously to the top of the arch showered the president with flowers as he passed underneath. At the end of his ride, Roosevelt was heard to remark, "I'm surprised to see such a neat and well appearing little city."[9]

Both the civic pride and the preoccupation with statehood, in evidence on this occasion, were clearly visible six years later when President William Howard Taft paused in Albuquerque on a swing through the West. After a track-side speech late in the afternoon of October 15, 1909, he was led to a banquet at the Alvarado. In attendance were sixty-five prominent Democrats and Republicans from throughout the Territory, all men. Women's suffrage was still years away and not a single lady had been invited.

Territorial Governor George Curry served as toastmaster and introduced a series of speakers, all of whom had been instructed to politely push the statehood issue. All went well until rancher and politician Albert B. Fall took the floor, the same Fall who, as secretary of the interior in 1923, would suffer permanent disgrace in the infamous Teapot Dome Scandal. After some perfunctory remarks welcoming the president, Fall launched a stinging attack against him and the Republican party for failure to press vigorously New Mexico's campaign for statehood. As he finished, Taft leaped to his feet, seething with anger, and hotly defended his past efforts on behalf of the Territory. In spite of Mr. Fall's inflammatory words, the president assured his listeners that he was still a staunch supporter of statehood for New Mexico. The incident, according to press reports, created a sensation and much consternation.[10]

True to his word, President Taft on August 21, 1911, signed a statehood bill, using a gold-banded quill plucked from a great American eagle that had been captured near Taos. After administrative delays, New Mexico was finally admitted the following year. Albuquerqueans enthu-

siastically hailed the event as a watershed signalling the sunrise of a new
and opulent era for their city.

For some time, the men who had helped father New Albuquerque
had been passing from the scene, like dry leaves shaken from the branches
of a winter tree. Among them were William Hazeldine, claimed by death
in 1892, and Franz Huning, the salty old trader and business tycoon,
who died at seventy-eight in 1905. Of that early triumvirate of city
builders, only Elias Stover lived on into the 1920s. New men were at
the helm now, taking up where their predecessors had left off and steering
a course for the city that fitted their own notions of progress.

Out of the swirl of change that engulfed Albuquerque came a
significant development in 1917: citizens voted to adopt a new charter
establishing a commission-manager form of government. The city was
the first in New Mexico to introduce this innovative approach to municipal management. Its purpose, as attested by reformers, was to reduce
the inefficiency, incompetence, and venality that had, heretofore, characterized the conduct of city functionaries and to make local government
a responsible organ of rule. To achieve this, the plan aimed at eliminating
politics from municipal elections by rendering them nonpartisan. In so
doing, Albuquerqueans fancied that political machines would be forever
banished and that "voting the sheep" and other ballot box frauds would
remain only as an unpleasant memory.

The old system, instituted when Albuquerque incorporated as a city
in 1891, provided for the operation of government by a mayor and board
of aldermen representing the four wards. Under it, political cliques and
special-interest groups ceaselessly fought and maneuvered for advantage,
frequently bringing the administration at city hall to a standstill. As a
consequence, many Albuquerqueans became convinced that a new form
of municipal government was needed. Before that could happen, however,
the state legislature had to approve enabling legislation to allow the city
to act. To that end, Bernalillo County representatives drafted and introduced a home rule bill, which passed the state assembly March 13, 1917.
It empowered the city to appoint a commission to draft a new municipal
charter and submit it to the voters for approval.[11] One of the strongest
forces behind this movement was the newly organized Albuquerque Ro-
tary Club. Eager for a timely public project, the group campaigned
strenuously to mobilize support for the drive to modernize local government.

Architect of the proposed city charter was William P. Metcalf, a
real estate broker, graduate of Brown University, and a scholar of the
French language and literature. Surprisingly, he was also a "red-hot
Socialist," a follower of the ideas of Eugene V. Debs. The charter designed
by Metcalf provided for a commission—city manager administration and
included provision for the initiative, referendum, and recall of officials,
at the time considered by many people to be dangerous, socialist doctrine.[12]

The key feature of the new plan was the creation of the office of city manager, to be occupied by a man responsible for conducting municipal business, and to be divorced from party politics. As the chief executive, the manager was to work closely with the legislative body, composed of elected commissioners. The charter spelled out a strict separation of functions and powers, the intent being to avoid the conflicts that had plagued the previous mayor-council government. Political party affiliation, as the charter made clear, was to have no bearing on selection of commissioners. [13]

Neither Republican nor Democratic leaders at the time thought that the novel document stood a chance of being ratified by the voters. But they seriously misjudged the momentum for reform. On September 26, 1917, the charter won approval by a narrow margin. Although amended from time to time, it would remain the basic law governing Albuquerque until 1974 when the city returned to the mayor–city council form of administration.

The year 1917 was exceptional for another reason, for it was then, in April, that America entered World War I. News of the conflict filled the front page of the Albuquerque press, and patriotic fervor swept the city. When the fall session of the University opened, 70 percent of the male students, including the entire football squad, failed to appear, having enlisted. Those who did return, found a strange new campus, geared for war.

During the summer, Camp Funston had risen on vacant University land—a noisy soldiers' city of barracks and tents, Red Cross hospitals, supply houses, and horse corrals. Kwataka Hall was commandeered for officers' quarters, and military offices occupied the Administration Building. More than 1,500 members of Battery A, New Mexico National Guard, marched daily to the strains of martial music. Weekends, young soldiers, sixty at a time, crowded onto the streetcars for a ride down Central and a lark on the town. Motorettes drove the cars, the motormen having been recruited for battle. Trenches were dug on the campus to accommodate training exercises, and mesa land nearby was plowed up and irrigated for war gardens. In 1918, the National Guard departed for the fighting. Camp Funston was given over to the Student's Army Training Corps. But both training and classroom instruction ground to a halt in October when the University temporarily closed at the height of the influenza outbreak, an epidemic that girdled the globe. [14]

In the heat of war, New Mexico, like other states, succumbed to the virulent poison of prejudice, giving free rein to anti-German sentiment. The State Board of Education decreed that the German language should no longer be taught in the public schools, and journalists fanned passions by printing grim warnings to potential saboteurs. "To be quite brutally frank," said the *Santa Fe New Mexican,* "what America most needs at home right now is a considerable number of Hun tombstones. . . . The German is essentially a coward. It should be easy for the government to so put the fear of God into the hearts of all Germans in this country that . . . one would not dare attempt to poison food or drink, to use the torch or dynamite. And it would protect loyal men of German extraction from hysterical mob violence."[15]

Most German-Americans, indeed, were intensely loyal, but that did not spare some of them from the sort of violence that the *New Mexican* weakly professed to oppose. In Denver, recent immigrants from Germany were herded off to internment camps in Utah, while other persons, whose only crime was a German surname, suffered beatings in the streets and loss of their jobs.[16]

Although Albuquerque did not experience the frenzy that besmirched the name of her sister city in Colorado, there were, nevertheless, unfortunate incidents. They occurred in spite of the fact that German-Americans—not the least of whom was the late Franz Huning—had served the community nobly since the founding of New Town, and, in fact, made up the second largest ethnic minority, after Hispanics.

America's distinguished novelist Paul Horgan recalls a small and tragic drama that took place during his own boyhood in Albuquerque. The First World War was in full swing when, one hot Sunday afternoon, he leisurely pedaled his bicycle up Gold Avenue. A strange commotion in the street drew his attention and, upon approaching, he encountered a mob dragging a middle-aged man, pale with fear, by a rope around his neck. From all sides issued cries of, "German spy! Traitor! Hang him!"

The enraged crowd, with the awestruck boy trailing safely in the rear, reached the brown sandstone Commercial Club at the corner of Gold and Fourth. The leaders, clutching their helpless victim, mounted the steep flight of steps and conducted a mock ceremony. An American flag was draped over the shoulders of the "spy," rough hands forced his head down, and he was made to kiss the bunting, again and again, while the onlookers roared approval.

"I was drained of the hot day until I felt cold," reflects Horgan. "I had no idea who the victim was or what he might have done to make other people scream 'Traitor!' at him in the hysteria of their war feeling. I never knew what became of him in the end—except that there was not actually a lynching, for of that there was no subsequent news. The power of the many to abuse the one was all I saw."[17]

Mercifully, the war was brief, for the United States at least. On a cold November evening in 1918, Armistice night, jubilant Albuquerqueans brought the streetcars to a halt and built a bonfire over the tracks at First and Central. The din of their victory celebration echoed through all the streets and shops of the city.[18]

The feeling of elation did not last long. A postwar recession, brought on by a combination of drought and a fall in agricultural and livestock prices after wartime expansion, plunged New Mexico into economic despair. In the wake of the sudden turnaround, bank failures rippled across the state. Between 1920 and 1925, fifty-seven banking institutions closed. Among them was the State National Bank of Albuquerque. Local financier George A. Kaseman, however, came to its rescue by buying up the bank's assets and using them as a basis for the founding of the new

Albuquerque National Bank. His action seemed to restore a sense of confidence in the city—to remind residents that they did not have to take the hard times lying down. [19]

The same year that Kaseman formed the Albuquerque National, 1924, one hundred businessmen gathered in the large hall of Harry Strong's mortuary and organized the Civic Council. That body, as mentioned in the previous chapter, was dedicated to promoting Albuquerque as the nation's health capital. With other local industries then languishing in the doldrums, it was felt that advertising the city's peerless climate and mushrooming convalescent facilities would be just the spur needed to revitalize the economy. The Council's formation, too, helped stimulate a spirit of optimism. Partly as a result of its efforts, Albuquerque's population in the 1920s soared past 10,000, making it the first city in the state to surpass that magic number. [20]

No description of Albuquerque in the first quarter of the twentieth century would be complete without some reference to the mercurial and picturesque Elfego Baca, one of the flock of eccentric persons who lent color to the political scene. Elfego started his bumpy career as a deputy sheriff of Socorro, 80 miles south of Albuquerque. As a beardless youth of eighteen, he had won instant fame in 1884 when he single-handedly stood off in a gunfight several dozen Texas cowboys (the exact number varies according to the teller) who objected to his arresting one of their number. Later, when he had risen to the position of sheriff, Elfego's reputation for straight and quick shooting grew so large, that a short message to the worst badman, notifying him that he was under arrest, was usually sufficient to bring about a meek surrender. That, in short, is the gist of a popular legend, which seems to have had some basis in fact.

Baca was not only a man of lionlike courage, reputed to have killed seven men in stand-up fights, but he was also endowed with intellect and resourcefulness. While serving as a peace officer in Socorro, he read law and was admitted to the bar. Soon afterward, in 1910, he moved to Albuquerque to make his way as a lawyer and private detective. Dressed in a flowing cape and trailed by a bodyguard, he stalked the downtown streets handing out business cards that read on one side, "Elfego Baca, Attorney-at-Law, Fees Moderate," and on the reverse, "Private Detective; Divorce Investigations Our Specialty, Discreet Shadowing Done." [21]

Since cases came his way only irregularly, Elfego periodically ran for public office, always unsuccessfully. His first try came soon after arriving in Albuquerque, when he announced his independent candidacy for county sheriff. One afternnon during the campaign, he was talking up his qualifications with patrons at a bar near the mouth of Tijeras Canyon. Noticing some white leghorn chickens in the backyard, he asked the owner if they were for sale.

"Yes, they are. Fifty cents apiece," came the reply.

Baca pulled out his six-shooter, and without missing a shot, calmly blew off the heads of twenty chickens. Handing the owner $10.00, he threw the lifeless birds into the back of his car and sped down the mesa toward Albuquerque. The shooting exhibition was meant to demonstrate his fitness to hold the office of sheriff. He lost the election, anyway.[22]

Stories concerning Elfego's rare antics, particularly his performances while serving as an attorney in court, number in the dozens. His most memorable escapade, however, which unfolded in November 1914, occurred outside the courtroom and had international implications.

Since the overthrow of President Porfirio Díaz in 1910, the Republic of Mexico had endured unremitting political turmoil and civil war. Victoriano Huerta finally wrested control of the presidency, but he continued to be faced with challenges to the central government posed by guerrilla leaders in the northern provinces. Chief among his opponents was Pancho Villa, who controlled much of the state of Chihuahua, bordering New Mexico. Early in January 1914, General José Inés Salazar, a Huerta backer, crossed into the United States after suffering severe reverses at the hands of the Villistas. Almost at once, he was arrested and charged with violating American neutrality laws. Placed in military custody, the general was taken to Fort Wingate, near Gallup, for incarceration.

There, Salazar met Elfego Baca. The Albuquerque attorney had been engaged, at a substantial fee (put up by the Huerta government) to act as the general's legal counsel. President Huerta wanted his man out of jail and back in Mexico where he could do some good.

Elfego Baca went to Washington and tried, but failed, to persuade the State Department to release his client. Later, on November 16, General Salazar was transferred to the Bernalillo County jail at Albuquerque. Four days afterward, he made a bizarre escape.

According to the rumor, after the fact, two of Huerta's secret agents had come to the city and quietly made contact with certain local residents who were provided considerable funds to arrange the general's liberation. It was widely believed that Elfego Baca and Manuel Vigil, the Bernalillo County district attorney, were ringleaders in the plot.

If that was the case, then both men took great care to provide ironclad alibis, for on the night of the jail break, Baca was drinking with a large crowd at the Graham Bar in downtown Albuquerque, while Vigil was in Gallup, more than 160 miles away. About 9:30 in the evening, two masked men overpowered jailer Charles Armijo, bound and gagged him, and then released General Salazar. The general left the jail in an automobile and vanished. Subsequent investigation suggested that he had been taken north of the city, to Vigil's ranch house at Alameda, where he stayed hidden in a tunnel under the patio until November 28. On that date, he was given a horse, and, alone, he fled south and eventually crossed safely into Mexico.[23]

The following April 1915, a federal grand jury in Santa Fe returned indictments against Elfego Baca, Manuel Vigil, and four other Albuquerqueans, alleging that they were conspirators in the freeing of José Inés Salazar.[24] But at their trial in December, all were acquitted. After the verdict, the *Santa Fe New Mexican* asked pointedly, "Who did liberate

Salazar?" And it replied that the answer would likely remain a dark and unsolved mystery, one of the "baffling enigmas of history."[25]

It was not so baffling to the people of Albuquerque, who had been much excited by the whole affair. Almost to a man, they believed that Elfego Baca had been the mastermind behind the escape. But his association with the intrigue, far from working to his discredit, merely added glitter to an already showy personal history.

In 1944, Elfego Baca, at age seventy-nine, stood for election once more, as a candidate for district attorney. On the eve of voting, he spoke on the radio appealing for support. But, as on previous occasions, he went down to defeat. The following August 27, 1945, he died, just as Albuquerque and the rest of the world were entering the Atomic Age.

For the city, the year 1945 was a turning point, marking the beginning of a major transformation in the physical appearance and economic character of Albuquerque. But the phenomenon had long roots, extending back at least two decades to events that had commenced to unfold in the late 1920s. Largely through its own efforts, Albuquerque had managed to pull out of the recession that came on the heels of World War I. A skyscraper was completed in 1922 at Third and Central—the nine-story First National Bank Building. Other high-rise structures followed, and a distinctive skyline began to take shape. The first radio station, KGGM, went on the air in 1928, and the same year Frank Speakman and William Franklin leveled a space on the East Mesa for a small landing field, one of the first airfields in a western state. Such developments, coupled with a continuing rise in population, spoke well for Albuquerque's future. Then overnight, with the Stock Market Crash of 1929, a coal-black cloud eclipsed the beaming sun.

The crash and the ensuing national spasm of the Great Depression had their earliest and severest impact in the East. But the shock waves were soon felt in the West, and Albuquerque, like other cities, was swept up in the nationwide economic crises. The full brunt of the storm was somewhat blunted, owing to Albuquerque's geographical isolation and the relatively small number of her industrial enterprises. Nevertheless, the symptoms of illness that beset the rest of the country—business failures, bank closings, lines of unemployed, and bulging welfare rolls— were conspicuously evident.

Hard hit were the small service businesses—the motor courts, cafes, and gasoline stations strung along Central Avenue, which depended upon the tourist trade funneled in and out of the city on Highway 66. Vacationer traffic soon after 1929 dropped to half its former volume. In place of the tourists, an unending stream of broke and hungry hitchhikers, entire families as well as single men, passed through. Most were on their way to California, fleeing drought and the Dust Bowl in the Middle West. The great exodus over Route 66 was immortalized by novelist John Steinbeck in *The Grapes of Wrath*. Some out-of-work Hispanos and even a few Pueblo Indians from the Middle Valley formed another migratory current, taking the road north to the sugar beet and potato fields of Colorado, or the road south to the cotton fields of southern New Mexico.

Albuquerque retail and wholesale firms suffered their own woes. Contraction of the markets forced many to seek loans to stave off bankruptcy, but rarely was money available. Farmers and ranchers in outlying areas made stringent cutbacks in the amount of supplies purchased in the city, as their incomes plummeted alarmingly. After 1931, bankers virtually ceased making loans to cattlemen.

As conditions worsened, smaller banks in New Mexico began to close and a number of larger ones avoided collapse only by merging with other institutions. Civic leaders in Albuquerque took what meager steps they could to prop up the city banks. At one point, a run on the First National Bank appeared in the making, as fearful depositers formed long lines to withdraw their money. The president, Jack Raynolds, called on one of Albuquerque's wealthiest merchants, Louis Ilfeld, for help. Ilfeld responded. He marched into the bank lobby pushing his way through the crowd. In his hand were several thousand dollars in cash, which, with a great show of confidence, he deposited to his account. The gesture worked. When people saw Louis Ilfeld putting money in, not taking it out, they left the bank, satisfied that their funds were safe.[26]

The First National Bank had been granted a reprieve. But that is all it was, for on April 15, 1933, New Mexico's most important and influential financial institution closed its doors. Shortly afterward, an affiliate of the First National, the First Savings Bank & Trust Company of Albuquerque, followed suit. Attorney William Keleher, appointed receiver by the federal government, commented on the extent of the disaster: "The crash of the First National Bank of Albuquerque, like the falling of a huge tree in a forest, caused widespread repercussions among business and financial circles in central New Mexico and northern Arizona. The panic conditions prevailing generally throughout the United States in the spring and summer of 1933 paralyzed business in Albuquerque as elsewhere."[27]

The stagnating economy forced rigorous belt-tightening in city schools as well as at the University. A February 1933 report showed that in New Mexico generally, some 8,000 children were not receiving an education because a shortage of funds had shut down their schools.[28] But for many persons facing hunger, the state of the school system was the least of their worries.

President Herbert Hoover was opposed to direct federal relief, believing that should be left to private charities and the states. The policy changed when Franklin Roosevelt assumed the presidency in 1933 and announced his New Deal. Precious time was to elapse, however, before the ponderous bureaucratic machinery could be installed and individuals began to receive sorely needed aid from the federal government.

As late as 1935, Albuquerque experienced a near-riot when an angry crowd of destitute and unemployed workers stormed the county welfare office in Old Town. At the center of the eruption was a young newspaperman and budding politician, Clinton P. Anderson. At the height of the war, in the fall of 1917, Anderson had come to Albuquerque from his native South Dakota to chase the cure. Detraining, he checked into the Alvarado Hotel and that night suffered a lung hemorrhage that almost took his life. Next day he entered the Methodist Sanatorium where doctors, after making a physical examination, predicted he would die within five days. As happened with so many patients, New Mexico's healing climate took a hand, upset the verdict of the physicians, and by Christmas, Clinton Anderson was out of danger.

During the great influenza epidemic in 1918, H. B. Hening, editor of the *Albuquerque Herald,* knowing of Anderson's earlier journalistic experience on a small-town newspaper in South Dakota, asked him to pinch-hit for a few weeks while several regular reporters were down sick. His performance was so exemplary, Anderson was given a permanent job and assigned to cover the New Mexico legislature in Santa Fe. There he soon gained an understanding of the intricacies of state politics and made many friends among progressive Democrats, who considered theirs to be the party of reform. Working behind the scenes, Anderson within a few years was able to exert considerable influence in both the capital and Bernalillo County.

Largely on the basis of that political prestige, Governor Clyde Tingley in 1935 asked Anderson to take over the troubled county welfare office in Albuquerque. As the Depression deepened, welfare funds available for distribution by the office became scarce. The previous administrator, E. N. Boule, had been obliged to flee through a basement window one day when his door had been battered down by a hungry mob. In appointing the astute and diplomatic Anderson to the job, Governor Tingley hoped that he could find some satisfactory path out of the quagmire.

Anderson drove up to his office, located in the courthouse southeast of the Old Town plaza, to find the sidewalk jammed with people. Many knew him personally and were willing to give him a chance, but their desperate plight did not allow much delay. At once Anderson ordered his staff to begin a crash program to sort out the budget and speed at least a token payment to the needy. But wheels could not be turned fast enough and two days later, a crowd of frustrated men attacked the office and roughed up the new administrator. A deputy sheriff dispersed the invaders with a fire hose. By promising to give up his own salary, Anderson quickly got additional money from the state, enabling him to distribute relief checks. The crisis was diffused, but the emotional intensity it had generated showed the degree of hardship wrought by the Depression in Albuquerque.[29]

The unsettled conditions of the times had other effects. The Depression, for example, pushed the city's two daily newspapers, the morning *Journal* and the evening *Tribune* into a unique kind of merger. To cut down on operating expenses, they agreed to combine all business, advertising, and circulation functions under a third corporation, while each paper would retain its separate and independent editorial staff. The arrangement ensured survival of both dailies during the rough sledding of the 1930s, but it also guaranteed them an unassailable monopoly of the press, which they continue to hold to this day. The "Albuquerque Plan," as it came to be called, was later adopted by newspapers merging in other parts of the country.[30]

One category of Albuquerqueans acutely vulnerable to the economic crisis was composed of artists and writers, who found their services less and less in demand as the business climate worsened. Quaint Taos and Santa Fe had attracted the largest colonies of such persons, but Albuquerque, because of its more moderate climate, also drew members of the artistic and intellectual set. By 1930 an assortment of young artists, labelled the "Greenwich Village Group," had taken up residence in the charming, but inexpensive, area surrounding Old Town plaza. As the decade advanced and patrons fell away, their financial prospects looked exceedingly gloomy.[31]

On the other hand, public entertainment, represented by the motion picture house, theater, and symphony, found fortunes on the rise. Many citizens, it seemed, were eager to escape, however briefly, from the grim realities of the Depression by attending a stage production or concert. Albuquerque's premier theater was the Kimo, at the corner of Fifth and Central, built in 1927 by Oreste Bachechi, a founding member of Albuquerque's small but energetic Italian community. Outlandishly decorated, the Kimo was named by Pablo Abeyta, governor of Isleta Pueblo. In his language the word meant fittingly "king of its kind."[32]

The same year the Kimo was launched, 1927, a talented Broadway actress, Kathryn Kennedy, landed in Albuquerque. She had come West, as she said, because "dreams of a stage career had been stopped in mid-flight by the menace of tuberculosis."[33] Following recovery and marriage to actor James O'Connor, also a health-seeker, she and Irene Fisher, a local newspaper woman, organized the Albuquerque Little Theater. In 1930, the first production opened to a packed house on the stage of the Kimo.

Two years later, Grace Thompson founded the Albuquerque Civic Symphony. Like Kathryn Kennedy O'Connor, she, too, had come to New Mexico for her health. After becoming head of the music department at the University of New Mexico, she decided that Albuquerque, in the midst of its business slump, needed the balm of music. The first symphony was presented at the university gymnasium in 1932, with Grace Thompson directing the orchestra.[34]

While many individuals, working in a variety of ways, helped soften the traumatic consequences of the Great Depression, none exerted a stronger or more lasting influence on affairs than a gruff, thick-skinned, combative politician named Clyde Tingley. Had not merest chance brought Tingley to Albuquerque in 1911, the city over the next three decades would have had a different story to tell.

Born in a log cabin in rural Ohio, January 5, 1881, Clyde Tingley spent his early work years as a machinist and toolmaker for various automobile manufacturers. Sociable and skilled with his hands, he spoke the rough and ungrammatical language of the laboring man. An Albuquerque friend years later would say that Clyde "was not much of a reader; he probably never read a book completely on any subject."[35] But though he may have lacked polish, Tingley had a natural ability to lead.

While still in his twenties, he became superintendent of the Graham Motor Car Company in Bowling Green, Ohio. There he met and courted young Carrie Wooster, member of a wealthy and prominent family. Given the widely different social backgrounds of the two, it was a highly unlikely match. Before the relationship had ripened to marriage, however, Carrie fell ill with tuberculosis. Doctors recommended that she seek a cure in the sunshine of the Southwest and urged her to go to Phoenix. While en route to Arizona with her mother, the girl suffered a severe attack and had to be taken off the train at Albuquerque. Discovering superb health care facilities here, she decided to remain. Clyde Tingley, who to this point had scarcely heard of Albuquerque, soon joined her and they were married on April 21, 1911. They settled down, with Carrie's mother, in a small health-seeker's cottage on Iron Avenue.

Tingley's entry into Albuquerque politics came in 1916 when he entered the race for alderman on the City Commission from the Second Ward. That area included the Santa Fe Railroad shops and the Albuquerque Machine Works. Because of his own background, Clyde Tingley knew just how to appeal to members of the working class and he won his election handily. Thereafter, he was reelected to the Commission continuously until 1934, serving twelve of those years as chairman.

Tingley was a born politician. He gloried in the limelight and adroitly used the opportunity to gain public exposure that went with office-holding. He had a gift for the dramatic gesture, while his salty speech made lively newspaper copy. Reporters could always rely upon him for a good story, and they kept his name in the headlines. As City Commission chairman, Clyde adopted the ex-officio title, Mayor of Albuquerque, which had been discarded with municipal reorganization in 1917. He felt that the prestige of the city demanded that it have a mayor, even if in name only.

Autocratic in manner, Tingley often acted as if he alone knew what was good for Albuquerque. His steamroller tactics in pushing through pet civic projects aroused heated opposition. Political foes accused him of building a new machine that put the Hubbellism of yesteryear in the shade. For his conduct, the mayor offered no apology or justification. He needed none, since his tightly controlled administration had strong support from labor unions, management, and reformers, all of whom approved of his unflagging efforts to better the city. Huge political contributions passed into his hands, yet critics could never charge that he mishandled funds. Whatever other failings he may have had, Clyde Tingley was scrupulously honest. That fitted in well with his main aim in life, which was not to become rich but to get reelected.[37]

His political ambitions cultivated in him a desire to be seen and photographed with celebrities. Albuquerque, as a prime rest stop for transcontinental train passengers, provided abundant opportunity. Watching

the parade of movie stars and other notables strolling up and down the
brick walk in front of the Alvarado Hotel was a popular pastime for
townsfolk. Practically every day, Mayor Tingley was there, greeting the
likes of Rudolph Valentino, Albert Einstein, and Charles Lindbergh, and
telling them what a splendid city Albuquerque was going to be under
his leadership. Once Douglas Fairbanks and Mary Pickford, attempting
a peaceful walk, were surrounded and almost smothered by overzealous
admirers. Seeing the danger, Tingley rushed in, quickly scooped up the
lady, and, with Fairbanks running interference, carried her to safety.[38]
It was the sort of incident that characterized Tingley's flair for theatrics.

For all his showmanship, Clyde Tingley was a man who got things
done, and as a result he left a permanent imprint on the face of Albuquerque. One of his first acts, upon being elected an alderman in 1916,
was to spearhead a drive by the city to purchase the water works. That
vital utility, established in 1882 by Angus Grant, had continued under
the ownership of a private corporation, whose unwillingness to extend
new lines into subdivisions had retarded municipal growth. After months
of arm twisting and tense negotiations, the city finally acquired the water
works, a feat that delighted consumers and brought about rapid expansion
of the system. In that early fray, Tingley perceived that vigorously advancing the interest of Albuquerque pleased the voters and offered a sure
formula for promoting a successful political career.

While that knowledge, put to good use during the 1920s and 1930s,
helped Clyde Tingley become the dominant voice in community affairs,
ocasional instances of his own coarse behavior tarnished his name and
somewhat diminished his effectiveness as a politician. A case in point
occurred during the trial of fiery journalist Carl C. Magee, a close Tingley
friend.

Magee had come to Albuquerque in 1917 from Oklahoma, for what
was, by now, a familiar reason. He was seeking a more healthful climate
for his ailing wife. After arranging financing with a Kansas City bank,
he bought the *Albuquerque Morning Journal* in 1920, a Republican paper
with the largest circulation in the state. At once he began a crusade
against corruption, aiming his sharpest barbs at the Republican party.
Two of its members, Secundino Romero, political boss of San Miguel
County, and David Leahy, district judge in that county, were singled
out for editorial criticism. They and other Republican bigwigs determined to silence Magee by pressuring his financial backers to withdraw
support. As a result, he was obliged to sell the *Journal* in 1921. Nevertheless, Carl Magee was quickly back in the fight as editor of the smaller,
but still influential, *New Mexico State Tribune* (later the *Albuquerque Tribune*), which began publishing on April 5, 1923.[39]

Using the court in Las Vegas, the seat of San Miguel County, to
harass his accuser, Judge Leahy trumped up charges against Magee of
criminal libel and contempt, which resulted in a series of melodramatic
trials. Each time, Magee was convicted, and in each case the state governor pardoned him. In the course of the wrangle, the judge had declared
publicly that Carl Magee was "a greater menace to civilized society than

is the cow thief or horse thief."[40] And Magee had replied that he "had no more chance in Leahy's court than a lamb had with a butcher."[41] The personal animosity between the two eventually led to violence.

On the evening of August 9, 1925, Carl Magee was seated in a Las Vegas hotel lobby when Judge Leahy entered and began to berate him. All at once, the angry judge knocked Magee to the floor and started to beat him. The editor pulled out a concealed pistol and opened fire. Two shots hit Leahy in the arm but a third struck and killed a bystander. The following June 1926, Carl Magee was brought to trial for manslaughter.

Clyde Tingley, a warm admirer of the crusading newspaperman, decided to go to Las Vegas and lend a hand. As he drove into the city limits, a police officer arrested him for speeding and conducted him to city hall. There the pugnacious Tingley got into a fist fight with the officer. After he was clamped in a cell, a physician was summoned to dress his wound. Paying a $25 fine, Tingley emerged to find a crowd of reporters waiting. "I came up to Las Vegas," he announced, "to get Magee out of jail and here I am in jail."[42]

The undignified incident, involving Albuquerque's political prima dona, threatened to overshadow the Carl Magee trial, particularly since Magee rather promptly won acquittal. The *Albuquerque Journal,* now in the hands of Tingley's foes, used the occasion to try and bring his career to an end. In an editorial headlined "Remove the Disgrace," it urged other members of the Albuquerque City Commission "forthwith to remove this incompetent and intolerable individual from the position he now holds."[43] But the call went unheeded. Clyde Tingley survived the wrath of the press just as he would later survive, unfazed, numerous protest petitions, threats of recall, and injunctions.

Genteel members of society disliked Tingley as much for his lack of social refinement as for his unpredictability. There were even those who hinted that he was a bad influence on the manners and speech of Albuquerque school children. When the mayor heard that, he declared emphatically, "I ain't goin' to quit saying ain't."[44] And he did not. Indeed, his grammar seems to have been a decided asset in attracting the vote of the common man.

Clyde Tingley's devotion to the welfare of his adopted city was genuine. Using his authority as commission chairman to the hilt, he sponsored a series of long overdue measures to beautify Albuquerque. Trees were planted along bare avenues, unsightly weeds were cleared from vacant lots, and windblown trash was swept from gutters. In March 1927, he came out in favor of a city ordinance regulating billboards. Many property owners found it profitable to rent their vacant lots to advertisers for the placing of signs, a practice that gave the streets a cluttered look and retarded residential construction. Tingley soon had that problem under control.[45]

But it was during the dark days of the Great Depression that his ability to get things done paid the greatest dividends. In the federal relief agencies created by Franklin Roosevelt soon after his inauguration in March 1933, Clyde Tingley saw a splendid chance to alleviate some of the economic ills besetting Albuquerque. His mind became a fertile field, sprouting a bumper crop of ideas about how to get and use public project funds. When, in 1934, he was elected governor of the state on the Democratic ticket, his new rank and strong support for Roosevelt gave him direct access to the White House and to heads of administrative agencies. Tingley made at least twenty-three trips by train to Washington seeking federal aid for New Mexico, and especially for Albuquerque. He developed a close personal relationship with the president and, as the politicians would say, "had his ear." Roosevelt was deeply concerned over the plight of the city dweller and, since he was comfortable working with political bosses, his attention accorded Clyde Tingley's numerous missions to Washington is not surprising.[46] In 1936, he invited the New Mexico governor to be his special guest on a train junket circling seven western states. Tingley, with his penchant for being seen alongside celebrities, was elated.[47]

The impact on Albuquerque from funds Clyde Tingley funneled in was substantial. Numerous federal projects, like those under the Works Progress Administration (WPA) and the Civilian Conservation Corps (CCC), not only allayed unemployment, but led to the building of public facilities that the city could not have afforded on its own. These included parks, a railroad overpass at the Central Avenue crossing, the Little Theater, a zoo, an airport terminal built in Spanish-Pueblo style, the buildings for a new State Fair, which opened in 1938, and even a low, decorative stone wall (later demolished) around the perimeter of the Old Town plaza.

Clyde Tingley's hand in the furthering of additional projects is plainly evident in their names; Tingley Drive, Tingley Field, Tingley Beach (on an artificial lake adjacent to the Rio Grande), and Tingley Coliseum. Modesty was not part of his nature.

The largest single beneficiary of WPA projects was the University of New Mexico. Federal expenditures totaling more than $1,000,000 resulted in construction of the new Zimmerman Library, an administration building, a stadium, and other structures. The expansion allowed the school to accommodate a 600 percent increase in enrollment during the 1930s.[48] Despite lean times, the sunny campus was still drawing health-seekers and was also a magnet for young people looking to escape the bleakness of the Depression in the East.

Albuquerque reaped an additional windfall with the establishment of an assortment of regional federal offices in the city. A United States Veterans Hospital on the East Mesa and a new Federal Building at Fifth and Gold were constructed at a combined cost of $3,000,000. The Middle Rio Grande Conservancy District, started in 1925, accelerated its flood control efforts, which further helped to take up the slack in the work force. As Clyde Tingley had foreseen, the rapid expansion of government payrolls did much to reduce the distress suffered by "his city." But the upbeat attitude of civic leaders and plain citizens also played a part.

In 1935, businessmen conceived the idea of a three-day Golden

Jubilee celebrating Albuquerque's fifty years as an incorporated municipality. Billed as the "Biggest Birthday Party in the History of New Mexico," the event featured parades and pageants, races and regattas, fiddlers and fireworks.[49] Clyde Tingley delivered the keynote speech under the skies at Rio Grande Park. His friend, Franklin Roosevelt, sent a telegram of congratulation to the city. The purpose of the festivities was simple and direct: "to end the Depression blues and turn Albuquerqueans' thoughts to the future."[50]

The second half of the decade gave every sign that the aim had been achieved. Optimism crowded out despondency. Downtown bustled with activity. And new suburbs crept farther and farther across the East Mesa. Symbolic of Albuquerque's escape from the national economic nightmare was the ten-story Hilton Hotel completed in 1939 on the site that had once held the old Trimble Livery Stable. New Mexico–born financier Conrad Hilton believed the city was destined to go places, and that conviction was widely shared. A combination of far-reaching forces had brought Albuquerque to the edge of its greatest boom ever.

The strong trend toward economic recovery, already evident in the late 1930s, blossomed into full-scale prosperity as America entered World War II. The sudden demands of national defense found Albuquerque in a good position to become a major center for military training, wartime industries, and weapons research. One startling effect was a huge influx of government employees, servicemen, and scientists, creating a population explosion and causing a flurry of activity in the housing industry. Although there was some outward migration as well, mainly valley Hispanos seeking jobs in the larger defense plants of California, it did little to offset the city's new population gains. Beginning with approximately 35,000 people in 1940, Albuquerque started a precipitous climb, which, continuing after the war, would reach 175,000 by 1955—a growth of almost 500 percent. In the process, the casual western lifestyle, a holdover from the nineteenth century, began to be replaced by the high-pressure living typical of modern urban American.

Albuquerque's potential as a center for aviation was one of the first things that attracted the attention of the federal government. The million-dollar municipal airport on the East Mesa, opened in August 1939, had one of the longest runways in the country, and proud boosters proclaimed their city to be the "Air Capital of the Southwest."[51] Experts rated the weather in Albuquerque ideal for flying 97 percent of the year. In 1940, the United States Army Air Corps designated the city a service station for military planes. The following year, on land leased adjacent to the municipal field, it launched the Air Corps Advance Flying School to train Flying Fortress crews. Kirtland Field, as the base was named in 1942, expanded during the war to become a major defense installation.[52]

The military was also interested in New Mexico as a testing ground for all sorts of new weapons experiments that were initiated soon after Pearl Harbor. Physicists and engineers on the faculty of the University of New Mexico were enlisted, and an aerial gunnery and bombing range was established in the near-empty desert 85 miles south of Albuquerque.

The University's Dr. E. J. Workman became director of a special research project, which developed and tested the VT Fuse, an explosive projectile with both offensive and defensive capabilities. The Navy would later rate the VT second only to the atomic bomb in effectiveness as a strategic weapon.[53]

New Mexico became a focus of atomic research when in April 1943 the government established the secret Los Alamos Laboratory on the beautiful, but inaccessible, shelf of the pine-clad Pajarito Plateau 35 miles northwest of Santa Fe. The excellent air and rail facilities at Albuquerque, through which equipment and supplies could be easily shipped, figured in the final selection of the site. The Army's Albuquerque Engineering District (a branch of the Army Corps of Engineers) was assigned the task of building the laboratory and living quarters for the scientists who would be working on the hush-hush Manhattan Project.[54]

Throughout the country prominent physicsts, chemists, and mathematicians suddenly dropped from sight. Unbeknown to the public, the government had spirited them away to remote Los Alamos. People of central New Mexico were aware that mysterious doings were afoot, but so tight was security that no one had the slightest inkling that an atomic bomb was in the making. The uncertainty prompted much humorous speculation: the Army was said to be operating a nudist colony, or a home for pregnant WAC's, or an internment camp for Republicans, or a factory producing windshield wipers for submarines.[55]

Although it would not become known for some time, a serious crack had developed in the security shield. An Army corporal, David Greenglass, was a member of a soldier contingent serving at Los Alamos. He had rented a small apartment on High Street in Albuquerque and brought his wife, Ruth, out from New York. Weekends, when he could get a pass, he would drive down to the city and the couple would spend a quiet afternoon strolling along the banks of the Rio Grande. On one of those walks, Ruth suddenly dropped a bombshell. Before leaving New York, she had visited David's brother-in-law who told her that he was passing information to the Russians, and he wanted to know what was going on at Los Alamos. Would David help? The brother-in-law's name was Julius Rosenberg.

Although Greenglass hesitated at first, he was finally drawn into a web of espionage that involved a Russian agent, Harry Gold, and a Los Alamos physicist, Klaus Fuchs, who had access to the project's innermost secrets. In his High Street apartment, David Greenglass sold Gold classified documents that were quickly shipped to the Kremlin, an act that within seven years would bring about his conviction as a spy and a fifteen-year prison term.[56]

As work on the bomb progressed, a location on the gunnery range southeast of Socorro was selected as a testing ground for the first atomic explosion. The spot would become known to history as the Trinity Site. The vast quantity of materials needed to conduct and monitor the experiment were freighted to Albuquerque, addressed to Mr. J. E. Burke, University of New Mexico, Department of Physics. Everything, however, was quietly diverted to a railroad siding on the outskirts of the city where Army engineers collected the supplies and trucked them down to the Trinity Site.[57]

On July 15, 1945, the day before the scheduled detonation, a bus load of Los Alamos scientists journeyed down to Albuquerque to spend a few leisurely hours in hopes of easing the building tension. Many of them congregated in the lobby of the Hilton Hotel, engaging in strained conversation. Security agents finally ordered them to disperse since they were attracting attention. The fears of the men were real for they could not be quite sure of the after effects of the coming explosion. In Albuquerque, as in other Southwestern cities, monitors had been assigned to check the movement of the expected fallout cloud, and plans had been formulated for an emergency evacuation should that become necessary. By the evening of the 15th, all air traffic was barred between Albuquerque and El Paso.

At 5:30 the following morning, a shock-wave boom shook New Mexico and parts of Texas and Arizona. In Gallup, 235 miles from the Trinity Site, houses rattled and windows blew out. Guests in Albuquerque's Hilton Hotel tumbled from their beds in alarm and peering outside saw an awesome red glow filling the southern sky. The pyrotechnic display, visible for hundreds of miles, resembled nothing less than the fires of Hell.[58]

The world's first atomic explosion, on July 15, 1945, marked, with a mushroom-shaped exclamation point, the commencement of a new age. For New Mexico, as a center of nuclear research, the die was cast. The ancient land, which still showed on every side the influence of Indians and Spaniards, was now to become the permanent home of a growing battalion of scientists. For Albuquerque, that meant a new direction in its economy and a further swing toward the center of America's mainstream.

Reaching for the Future

ALBUQUERQUE'S BEST KNOWN CITIZEN during World War II was Pulitzer Prize–winning news correspondent Ernie Pyle. After years of roving about the country, living out of suitcases, he and his wife in 1940 finally built a white frame cottage on south Girard. For the remaining four years of his life, it was to be home base, though he seldom stayed there more than a few months at a time.

When asked why he had chosen to settle in Albuquerque, Ernie Pyle had a ready answer. "We like it," he wrote, "because we have a country mailbox instead of slot in the door; because our front yard stretches as far as you can see; and because old Mt. Taylor, 65 miles away, is like a framed picture in our front window. We like it because you aren't constantly covered with smoke and soot, . . . and because we are not stifled and smothered and hemmed in by buildings and trees and traffic and people."[1]

Ernie Pyle died on April 18, 1945, killed by a Japanese sniper's bullet on the island of Ie Shima in the Pacific. Three years later his beloved white cottage was deeded as a memorial to the city of Albuquerque, to be used for a branch library.[2] By then, the small-town atmosphere, which had proved so attractive to the harried journalist, was already giving way to the hurry and hubbub of the postwar boom. Albuquerque had been discovered—by the federal government and by a horde of Easterners who were taking flight from the smoke and soot of their own crowded, industrialized cities.

Flourishing scientific and military research installations, a bequest of World War II, were the principal contributors to rapid urban growth. During the last development stage of the atomic bomb at Los Alamos, it had become necessary to establish a cluster of support facilities on the mesa between the Albuquerque Municipal Airport and the foothills of the Manzano Mountains. Kirtland Air Force Base and adjacent Sandia Base and Sandia Laboratories soon emerged as the focus of big-budget federal projects in weaponry research. In 1949, the Atomic Energy Commission negotiated a contract with Western Electric Company, a Bell Telephone subsidiary, to operate the Sandia Laboratory as a private corporation.

As the Cold War heated up in the early 1950s, the pace of defense research accelerated. At Kirtland, engineers married nuclear weapons to aircraft and conducted atomic tests in Nevada and the Pacific. They also assembled the first air-to-air rockets with atomic warheads. Neighboring Sandia Laboratories, meanwhile, was pushing ahead in research that led to the detonation of the first experimental H-bomb in 1952. Manzano Base, a satellite of Sandia Base, was designated a storage depot for atomic bombs. A small mountain overlooking Albuquerque was hollowed out, stocked full of nuclear warheads, and surrounded by five electrified chain-link fences. Although the Defense Department understandably remained secretive about the number of bombs on hand, a probing journalist declared that, "There are more nuclear weapons in that mountain than anywhere in the country, probably more than anywhere in the world."[3]

A boost came to New Mexico's nuclear industry in 1950 with discovery of a vast uranium deposit near Grants, only 50 miles west of Albuquerque. Later strikes in the same general area, plus new advances in weaponry development at Los Alamos and Albuquerque, made the state a world leader in both uranium mining and atomic science. Private contractors, miners and other skilled laborers, engineers, technicians, and executives, were thereby lured to New Mexico, and especially to its largest city, like bees to a honeysuckle vine. The days of quiet somnolence were at an end.

The population explosion that began as a minor disturbance in the late 1940s and grew to astonishing dimensions during ensuing decades, created a new and different Albuquerque. The influx of newcomers significantly altered the city's social complexion and political structure. It included, on the one hand, a large body of well-educated persons who were cosmopolitan in their attitudes and tastes. By 1960, Albuquerque claimed more Ph.D.'s per capita than any other city in the country.[4] But this latest cycle of migration also included unskilled and displaced poor, many of them Hispano rural folk who abandoned their subsistence farms in droves to seek employment in Albuquerque's burgeoning job market. Yet, even while the number of Hispanos soared, their overall percentage within the total municipal population declined in the face of a mounting inflow of Anglos.

Another ethnic minority that also experienced change, both in size and status, was Albuquerque's Black population. A few Blacks had trickled in during the postrailroad era, working in the Santa Fe shops, establishing small businesses, or developing farms in the surrounding valley. By 1910, two churches, the African Methodist Episcopal and the Mt. Olive Baptist, had become centers of the Black community. Instances of social discrimination existed, but generally a commendable attitude of toleration prevailed. That became evident in 1928 when Ku Klux Klan organizers held a membership rally and cross-burning on the mesa.

It proved a fiasco. A crowd of curious onlookers was treated to a show as Sheriff Tony Ortiz and two deputies appeared and ordered the marchers to unmask. The Catholic Church warned the faithful to steer clear of the Klan, and the *Albuquerque Morning Journal* advised readers "not to be suckers."[5] The liberal climate, however, gradually changed as an increasing number of Southerners filtered into the city during the Depression and World War II. Albuquerque's literary light, Erna Fergusson, bitterly attributed a visible rise in prejudice to transplanted Texans who brought their outdated segregationist policies with them.[6] Nevertheless, when it became apparent that discrimination in housing and public services was gaining ground, a backlash developed. It began with students at the University of New Mexico. The school paper, the *Lobo,* commenced to list businesses that excluded Blacks, and the student senate called for a boycott of such places. The economic pressure forced some restaurants and bars to capitulate, though not all. But the matter had now become a burning public issue. A coalition of students, Hispano organizations, churches, and the local NAACP chapter carried their complaint to the Albuquerque City Commission.

After months of study to assess the depth of the problem, the City Commission acted. On Lincoln's birthday, 1952, it passed an antidiscrimination ordinance, heavily laden with penalties. Three years later when the legislature in Santa Fe introduced a statewide bill against discrimination, it received strong support from Bernalillo County representatives.[7] The success of these measures helped get Albuquerque back on the proper track, long before the Civil Rights movement precipitated social change in other parts of the country.

The postwar period also witnessed a redirection of politics. For one thing, cliques and political machines, which had exercised an easy domination over municipal affairs in the first half of the century, swiftly lost their hold as a vastly enlarged population resulted in a diversified and more sophisticated electorate. A notable casualty was Clyde Tingley. After completing his second term as governor in 1938, he had returned to Albuquerque and won back his seat on the City Commission. As chairman of the body and ex-officio mayor during the war, he ran city hall in the same personalistic and heavy-handed manner that had characterized his reign during the 1920s. But the educated voters who were swelling the suburbs on the East Mesa had little stomach for such archaic politics, and in 1947 his power was broken. Albuquerque was no longer the exclusive fiefdom of Clyde Tingley.[8]

It was about this time that political polarization on the two sides of the city first became evident. The middle-class residents swarming into the East Heights were mainly Republicans, moderately conservative in their voting habits. Indeed, by the late 1950s, they constituted one of the major vote blocks in statewide elections. In the older working-class neighborhoods of the valley, where Hispanos were numerous and the Catholic Church remained strong, Democrats predominated. The party's influence there was a legacy, in large measure, of the earlier New Deal social programs.

The division between east and west, however, ran deeper than just politics. Long a fractured city because of the continuing existence of a New Town and an Old Town, Albuquerque by mid-century began to see the original line dissolve and a new one form beyond the University. Perceptibly, though unofficially, Carlisle Boulevard emerged as the boundary separating the dynamic suburbs and shopping malls of the future from the decaying neighborhoods and waning downtown of the past. How this came about can be seen by casting a look at the patterns of residential and economic growth that developed after 1945.

Up to that time it had not become apparent that Albuquerque was destined to balloon eastward until it touched the foothills of the Sandias. Then, the most prestigious section of the city was still the Huning Castle Addition, platted in 1928 by lawyer William Keleher and contractor A. R. Hebenstreit on land acquired from Franz Huning's heirs adjacent to the Country Club and a stone's toss from the Old Town plaza. Only scarcely less desirable were a cluster of new homes built in the Pueblo and California Mission styles lying north and west of the University. But with the pull exerted by creation of the scientific-military complex on the sprawling mesa, developers began progressively to shift their housing projects east toward the mountains. Subdivisions proliferated and by 1950 the *Saturday Evening Post,* in an article on the Albuquerque phenomenon, remarked that, "New houses go up in batches of 50 to 300 at a time and transform barren mesas before you get back from lunch."[10] In the four years between 1946 and 1950, the area within the city's boundaries tripled.

Commercial business followed the lead set by the residential builders. The first shopping center, Nob Hill, at Central and Carlisle pointed the way. Other centers appeared in rapid succession,· each one more grandiose and enticing to customers than its predecessors. The culmination was reached with the introduction of massive malls encircled by wide asphalt parking lots—first the Winrock Center, opened in 1961 at a cost of $9,700,000, and two years later the neighboring Coronado Center, which in glittering opulence surpassed all that had gone before.

The trend was anything but unique to Albuquerque. From 1945 to 1960, approximately 10,000 new shopping centers were born to communities west of the Mississippi River.[11] They reflected the relentless decentralization of municipalities that occurred with the rise in popularity of suburban living. More and more, Albuquerque, like other places, became a loose agglomeration of urban neighborhoods wedded to the local shopping center and with few ties to the increasingly anachronistic downtown business district. The process, nevertheless, did not go forward without opposition.

As early as 1947, the *Albuquerque Journal* observed that unregulated growth could easily spell doom for what little physical attractiveness the city possessed and could produce blighted areas that might take years to correct.[12] But the warning went unheeded, at least for the time being. From the 1950s on, the fashionable Heights drained people, businesses, and capital away from the city's older core. Commercial and residential properties there deteriorated, and the spirit of civic pride and responsibility that had characterized Albuquerque only a generation before seemed to evaporate. The decline of downtown was hastened, moreover, by significant alterations in the city's economic base.

The once profitable health business was already a fading memory, but now it was the turn of the railway industry to wither and draw near its grave. The expansion of trucking and air freight service during wartime dealt a blow to one side of the railroad business, and a loss of passenger traffic to automobiles and planes walloped the other. Modernization of the rail system, such as the switch-over from steam to diesel locomotives, failed to stem the downhill slide. The Santa Fe line, which owned the largest fleet of diesels in the world, found that the new engines required far less maintenance, and as a result, it cut back drastically on the size of the Albuquerque shops and the payroll. The railroad's place as top employer in the city was surrendered to the military-space industry centered in the East Heights. Further, the new reliance on motor transport meant that factories and warehouses no longer had to congregate along the railway's tracks, but could disperse and seek more favorable locations near highways and away from inner-city congestion.

The wide brick platform fronting the depot and the Alvarado that had been thronged with celebrities, servicemen, tourists, health-seekers, and traveling businessmen for years, became, by the late 1960s, a neglected backroom of the city. In 1969, the Santa Fe Railroad demolished the Alvarado and replaced it with a gravel parking lot. Loss of the landmark hotel, so closely identified with Albuquerque's history, left a gaping and unsightly hole in the downtown. The continuing ebb in traffic led the railway company in 1971 to deliver its passenger operations into the hands of Amtrak. By the end of the decade, Amtrak was making strenuous efforts to eliminate the small remnant of passenger service that still remained to Albuquerque.

Coinciding with the unimpeded sink in the fortunes of the railroad was an upsurge in freeway construction. That, too, was to have a profound impact on the character and vitality of the older sections of the city. Alignment began in 1956 for the north-south Interstate 25 (the Pan American Highway) and the east-west Interstate 40, which replaced Highway 66. The interchange, where the two crossed northeast of the old commercial district, was completed in 1966. Central Avenue, whose businesses had served cross-country travelers since the advent of the automobile, fell into an economic slump.

The highway complex provided rapid access from the suburbs to the downtown area, a significant consideration, because by the late 1970s Albuquerque sprawled across 92 square miles.[13] Although many retailers had fled to the outlying shopping centers, most federal, state, county, and municipal offices remained headquartered in the center city, as did the utilities and some banking and professional firms. The federal government alone maintained more than seventy-five separate agencies and divisions, leading someone to nickname the city "Little Washington."[14] The fair abundance of jobs drew a daily stream of commuters from the far-reaching suburbs. But an unwelcome side effect of that was a rise in air pollution, especially during the cooler months when, following the morning traffic rush, the Rio Grande Valley was often left smothered under a dirty blanket of smog. Another disquieting effect was that while downtown stirred with some residual life during the day, by night it lay deserted, utterly bereft of the noisy communal activity that had enlivened its streets in times past. Perhaps no other comparable city in the West experienced such a degree of lassitude after business hours.

In tardy fashion, civic leaders finally recognized the depth of the problem. But their remedies, initially at least, did more harm than good. Hoping to lure shoppers back to the center city and encourage the return of a residential middle-class population, they used $100 million in urban renewal funds to level entire blocks and make way for futuristic style buildings, which planners had decided that the public craved. The methodical destruction of much of Albuquerque's priceless architectural heritage, in fact, left the downtown practically faceless, not to mention soulless. New towering structures with blank walls were not only unbeautiful, they intimidated pedestrians. Acres of parking lots, while useful, created huge gaps of dead space. And large-scale municipal projects like the Civic Plaza and a new City Hall, intended to symbolize Albuquerque's push-ahead commitment to modernization, came off instead as monuments to mediocrity. The public was not impressed by the novelty of it all, and downtown continued to shrivel in spirit and waste away.[15]

The problem, one common almost everywhere in America, was that Albuquerqueans were content to let technocrats and urban planners chart the destiny of their city. Such individuals think almost wholly in economic terms, equating unbridled expansion with automatic prosperity and seldom paying more than lip service to such humanistic considerations as municipal beautification and historic preservation. In 1958, Albuquerque was named an All-American City by the National Municipal League, largely on the basis of the spectacular urban growth that had occurred over the preceding decade. It was clearly a case of honoring quantity not quality.[16]

When profits become the only concern that counts, the integrity of a city suffers. Scarcely a murmur of protest could be heard in 1955 when wrecking crews assailed the venerable old Huning Castle on west Central. That stately mansion, epitomizing so eloquently the vigor and glow of the early railroad era, had become an embarrassment to those who could see no farther than the bottom line in a bank book. The prevailing attitude seemed to be that the past had no value unless it could somehow be translated into dollars and cents.

One area of historic interest that offered commercial possibilities was that adjoining Albuquerque's original plaza. Old Town had remained outside the city until 1949 when it was annexed in a bid to boost the metropolitan population for the 1950 census. Its narrow, mud-packed streets and flat-roofed adobes, left over from a more leisurely age, were suddenly recognized as a prime visitor attraction. The City Commission in 1957 created a historic zone whose expressed intent was "to preserve the unique architectural character of the district."[17] Many buildings, especially those fronting the plaza, underwent repair and renovation, but the work was designed more to preserve an illusion of authenticity that would meet the needs of the tourist industry than it was to salvage and honor a genuine remnant of Albuquerque's heritage. By the following year, the Chamber of Commerce proudly announced that Old Town had become the city's leading tourist draw.[18]

The kind of mentality that underlay the growth-at-any-price philosophy and that had countenanced the wholesale destruction by urban renewal persisted into the early 1970s. Then slowly but forcefully a new sentiment began to be felt. It found expression in the catch-phrases "downtown revitalization" and "rejuvenation of historic neighborhoods." Albuquerqueans themselves had at last taken a hand, and they pressured the business community and government managers to move in new, more thoughtful directions.

An immediate result was the adoption, in 1975, of the city's first comprehensive plan, one that gave attention to urban sprawl, pollution, and the protection of old landmarks.[19] That had been preceded the year before by a restructuring of municipal government, made possible because of the sudden interest in limited growth and public planning based on human needs. Voters replaced the commission-manager form of government with a strong full-time mayor and nine-member city council, representing a return to the type of administration that had been abandoned in 1917.[20]

Most significant in the change was the amount of power now concentrated in the office of the mayor. As chief executive over the large municipal bureaucracy, with authority to make appointments to some forty city boards and manage the more than 100-million-dollar annual budget, that official was given the means to stimulate enlightened policies and lead Albuquerque onto untried paths.[21]

The chance to do just that fell to David Rusk, son of a former secretary of state and a University of California–trained economist, who won the mayorship in the fall of 1977. Neither a promoter nor a developer in the traditional sense, he was quoted as saying, "I can't get hysterical about big factories not going up all over the countryside."[22] Downplaying the aggressive role that city government had exercised in economic development heretofore, Rusk adopted a low-key approach to industrial expansion. Instead, he brought his abundant energy and enthusiasm to bear on such pressing public issues as mass transit, conservation, upgrading city services, and, pointedly, the rescuing of downtown from further stagnation.

Mayor Rusk's stance lent hope to those Albuquerqueans who wished to see the inner city recover its urban identity. Plans were formulated to refurbish and put to new use the handful of historic buildings that had escaped demolition, including the colorful Kimo Theater, which was proposed as a performing arts facility. The city, reversing its earlier policy of condemning and removing "outdated structures," initiated a program to identify and document downtown buildings that were worthy of preservation, and in the case of the gracious old Rosenwald Building, at Fourth and Central, it offered material support to a private developer willing to underwrite restoration. At Rusk's behest, the municipality sponsored a series of social and cultural activities to encourage residents on the city's far fringes to rediscover old Albuquerque. But in spite of these successes, Mayor Rusk was defeated at the polls by Harry Kinney in 1981.

Coinciding with efforts to revitalize the business district, a grass-roots movement began, almost spontaneously, to rehabilitate the early neighborhoods that had been left to deteriorate after World War II when the middle-class decamped to the suburbs. By the early 1970s, people were seeking out long-neglected Victorian and Queen Anne homes that had fallen in disrepair and were restoring them to their former grandeur. The trend was encouraged by an active program to define residential historic districts and register them under the National Historic Preservation Act, passed in 1966. It also received impetus from the escalating prices of new homes in the suburbs and the mounting cost of gasoline, both of which made older residences within walking distance of downtown, more desirable. The urban pioneers, as those who returned to the inner city are often called, still must face high crime, pollution, and a shortage of shopping facilities. But they have brought a vitality to the heart of Albuquerque that has not been seen since the 1940s.

Through the decade of the 1970s, the municipality continued to feel the stresses that accompany the drift toward ever more intensive urbanization. As a developing area within the Sunbelt, it came to resemble a typical postindustrial city dependent upon a government- and service-oriented economy.[23] Also, there appeared a growing emphasis upon energy research and development, both by small private firms and the behemoth Sandia Laboratories, which by 1979 was spending more than 450 million dollars in that field.[24] In the same period, Albuquerque, containing one-third of New Mexico's population, further consolidated its position as the business, educational, cultural, and health-care center of the state. The University of New Mexico, with an annual enrollment of more than 20,000, attracted students from across the nation and abroad, while the smaller University of Albuquerque on the West Mesa (established originally in 1951 as the Catholic College of St. Joseph) drew heavily from the Middle Valley's Hispano population. In 1974 a new Albuquerque Public Library opened downtown, symbolizing a firm commitment to the future of that area. The University of New Mexico's College of Medicine (founded in 1956) and its Cancer Research and Treatment Center grew in stature, winning national acclaim for scientific investigation. And the Albuquerque Sunport, renamed the Albuquerque International Airport on October 1, 1971, emerged as one of the busiest air facilities in the Rocky Mountain West.

Despite these and similar achievements, which lifted community pride, there were other things that marred the history of the seventies. During early summer, 1971, young people rioted in the area of Roosevelt

Park, resulting in extensive damage to property and injury to several dozen persons. Troops of the New Mexico National Guard had to be summoned to back city police in quelling the destructive disturbance.[25] For several years following that unfortunate event, the FBI's annual *Uniform Crime Report* showed that Albuquerque had the highest crime rate in the nation. At least some of the cause could be attributed to the lively traffic in hard drugs funneled up the Rio Grande Valley from the Mexican border. And finally, Albuquerqueans, strong boosters of the University of New Mexico's sports programs, were stunned in 1979 by a major scandal that rocked the school's athletic program and led to criminal indictments against the basketball coach and members of his staff. While disheartening, these incidents failed to dissuade the majority of citizens from the belief that Albuquerque, as cities go, was an agreeable and, indeed, preferable place in which to live.

In the quarter century after explosion of the first atomic bomb, the city had experienced changes of unprecedented magnitude. In size and physical appearance, it bore scant resemblance to the lean town Ernie Pyle knew and loved in the mid-1940s. By 1980, scarcely one in five inhabitants could claim to have been born in Albuquerque. Forty percent of the people had resided there less than five years. Traffic congestion, crowding, and the blight of overcommercialization seemed to be pushing the community down the road toward unrelieved sterility, conforming with a pattern observable in so many other American cities. But Albuquerqueans of an earlier day had faced challenges no less perplexing and surmounted them. It seemed unthinkable that their successors should falter now, as they approached the opening of a new century.

Postscript

IN THE SUMMER OF 1956, Albuquerque celebrated its two hundred and fiftieth birthday. From humble beginnings in 1706 as a struggling Spanish settlement clinging to the banks of the Rio Grande, it had emerged as one of America's major cities in the Rocky Mountain West. The commemorative festivities were touted as "The Country's Greatest Celebration for 1956," and featured a resplendent parade through the spectator-lined streets of downtown and a historical pageant that handbills described as "The dramatic story of Albuquerque from wilderness to atomic center of the world." Two thousand lavishly costumed players composed the cast of the pageant, presented on nine consecutive days at the University of New Mexico's Zimmerman Stadium. By dint of much effort, a new municipal Civic Auditorium was completed in time to host other activities associated with the sumptuous event.[1]

While there was much tawdry and commercial promotion of the city connected with the affair, still, the main aim was achieved—to honor Albuquerque's past. Special dignity was lent to the occasion by the presence of the eighteenth Duke of Alburquerque, Don Beltrán Osorio y Diez de Rivera, who came from Spain as a guest of the city. In a ceremony on July 10, he presented to the people of Albuquerque a seventeenth-century embroidered tapestry, or *repostero,* bearing the coat of arms of the Duke's family.[2]

The event, involving all sectors of the community, was in the spirit and tradition of earlier celebrations beginning with that marking arrival of the railroad in 1880 and continuing through the 1935 Golden Jubilee observance commemorating fifty years as an incorporated municipality. But, from all indications, the 250 Anniversary Celebration in 1956 was to be the last of its kind.

In the years immediately following, the sense of continuity with the past and the long-held feeling that Albuquerque was a cohesive entity became casualties of the population boom. Residents miles out on the East Mesa identified strongly with their own suburbs, but scarcely at all with the older neighborhoods in the valley. When on April 25, 1980,

Mayor David Rusk manfully led a skeleton parade down Central Avenue, to salute the centennial of the founding of New Albuquerque and the advent of the railroad, the street was practically deserted. The ranks of onlookers who had packed the sidewalks and cheered the 1956 parade were nowhere in evidence. A few stray passers-by paused in bewilderment and asked what was going on. The news media barely took notice of the occasion. Their neglect was symptomatic of a New Age.

The oft-observed tendency of Americans to cut themselves off from the past, to live intensely in the present, to adopt indiscriminantly the latest fads, and to change their place of residence frequently, has the effect of weakening allegiance toward any one community. As Albuquerque increasingly conforms to the homogenized pattern that characterizes most of the nation's metropolitan areas, the difficulties of maintaining civic pride and some semblance of municipal individuality steadily mount. In an earlier time, men like Franz Huning, William McGuinness, Elias Stover, Louis Ilfeld, and Clyde Tingley made Albuquerque "their town," pegging their lives and fortunes on its future and leaving the indelible stamp of their own personalities upon its history. Today's leaders, in contrast, move hesitantly, unclear in mind about the origins of the city and its problems and unsure what direction tomorrow's events should take. Their lack of certitude is not unique; it is a condition that weighs heavily on the majority of Americans in the waning years of the twentieth century.

Albuquerque, like other cities in the Rocky Mountain West, forms a dynamic focus of human energy, expectancy, and creativity. It shares with the rest of the region a reputation of being a land of opportunity, one whose values and cultural life-styles increasingly appeal to refugees from eastern urbanism. Yet, it also suffers from woes, as we have noted, that afflict large metropolitan areas worldwide. Many of the problems, coming in the wake of technological advance, Albuquerque has inherited from older regions of urban America. But their solutions must be dealt with under new environmental conditions and within the context of the city's unique historical framework and amid distinct cultural forces.

Local pundit and social critic V. B. Price has trenchantly summarized the current dilemma. "The isolation here is as much internal as it is environmental," he affirms. "Albuquerque is a city of islands, islands of culture, geography, language, politics, occupation, and wealth. People hole up here, they don't communicate, there's no common denominator, no sense of civic identity that all can share. We're so balkanized, and so full of transients and newcomers, that decision-makers work virtually without public supervision, until they infringe upon the interests of one faction or another. . . . The only consistent and organized faction in Albuquerque is that of land speculators, developers and the construction industry."[3]

His words point to the source of the blandness, aimlessness, and even chaos that characterize so much of contemporary urban life. With all the economic, social, and educational advantages offered the city-dweller, a stiff price is exacted.

380

Modern man's malaise, which many Albuquerqueans acutely feel, has multiple causes and symptoms. But the general problem can perhaps be simply reduced to this: the inability of the individual to find meaning in himself or in his society. Albuquerque author Harvey Fergusson described it as a deep-seated longing of man to know unquestionably what he *ought* to do.[4] Past ages had their saints, heroes, shining knights, or gentle scholars to point the way. But our culture has largely given up its heroes in the mistaken belief that the ethical, courageous, noble, responsible, self-directed life is now, practically speaking, unattainable. That notion, when widespread, can dispirit and debilitate a city or an entire nation.

Acknowledged or not, the need remains to identify the boundaries of purposeful living, and as always the process is carried forward by the heroic figure who shows, by example, the fundamental potentialities to which everyone is heir. Albuquerque, by good fortune, was the home of one uncommonly gallant man who exemplified the best ideals of humanity and who, by his actions, delivered an imperishable gift into the hands of its citizens. He was Coach John Willard Baker and he died at age twenty-six on Thanksgiving Day, 1970. No more fitting close to this long narrative of Albuquerque's history could be found than one that referred to the life of the remarkable John Baker.

He grew up in the East Heights during the 1950s and early 1960s while Albuquerque was straining under the effects of its first massive expansion. There was little at first to suggest he was destined to become a star athlete, for physically he was small and slightly awkward. The first hint came at a cross-country track meet during his junior year at Manzano High School. Running a rough course in the foothills of the Sandias, he outdistanced and beat the reigning state champion through sheer nerve and pluck. When he graduated the following year, John Baker was recognized as the best miler ever to come out of New Mexico.

Showered with offers of athletic scholarships, he elected to remain in Albuquerque and attend the University of New Mexico. Over the next several years, he sparked the school team to a series of brilliant victories, trouncing some of the nation's powerhouses in track and earning the nickname "Upset John." By 1968, he was ranked eighth on the world indoor list of milers. Running twenty-five miles a day in training, Baker had his eyes set on the 1972 Olympics in Munich.

Finishing at the University, he took a position as coach at Albuquerque's Aspen Elementary School. He was eager to work with children and the job left time for his own rigorous training schedule. But bitter news was in store for John Baker. One day in May 1969, while jogging on the East Mesa, a searing pain tore through his chest and he collapsed. Later, hospital tests revealed that his body was racked with cancer. The physician gave him six months to live, at most.

Stories of young persons who struggle valiantly to cope with terminal illness are, unhappily, not rare. But John Baker's response to his plight lifted his tale far above the ordinary. With his Olympic dream in tatters and time running out, he resolved to devote all his failing energy to the school children in his charge. In a hundred ways and a hundred little incidents, he pulled his youngsters up, those with ability as well as those with emotional or physical handicaps. While a lesser man might have taken to a hospital bed and sought drugs to control the gnawing pain, John Baker kept at his task and took on a new one, coaching a youth track team, the Duke City Dashers. He became known as the "coach who cares." His own worsening condition, he kept a carefully guarded secret; only his doctor, family, and a few close friends knew.

Local author William Buchanan overheard his children, who attended Aspen, speaking of their coach as if he were half superman, half saint. Incredulous, he started making inquiries and found that the things he was hearing were true. The coach was one of those exceptional men, dedicated to some higher goal, who come along perhaps once in a lifetime. He concluded that a good story lay there and he made a mental note to follow it up. But the next thing he learned was that John Baker had died, having beaten the doctor's prediction and cheated death for an extra twelve months. A promising young athlete and dedicated coach was gone, and it seemed nothing more could be said.[5]

Albuquerque, however, refused to forget John Baker. The Jaycees held an invitational track meet and named a memorial race in his honor. A John Baker athletic scholarship was established at the University of New Mexico. He was inducted into Albuquerque's Sports Hall of Fame. And upon the insistence of the students at Aspen, the school was renamed John Baker Elementary. As the Baker legend continued to grow, Buchanan gathered his facts and in 1975 published a brief and moving biography of the man in the *Reader's Digest*. It proved to be the most popular piece in the sixty-year history of the magazine, as gauged by the number of requests for article reprints—200,000—from readers.

Buchanan followed up that success with a full-length book, *A Shining Season,* and, as it was translated into several foreign languages, the name and fame of John Baker spread around the globe.[6] Brigham Young University, Salt Lake City, produced a short inspirational film on Baker's life (though he had been a Methodist, not a Mormon), and in 1979 Columbia Pictures produced a two-hour television drama, aired on December 26, based on *A Shining Season*. Said Mayor Rusk on the occasion, "John Baker, his life and his story, are an integral part of our lives. Many of Albuquerque's citizens knew and loved him. This film is a celebration of courage and love of life."[7]

Predictions by historians about the future are always made at considerable risk. But it appears fairly safe to suggest that a thousand years hence if the name of only one Albuquerquean of the twentieth century is still remembered, that name will be John Baker.

Abbreviations

USED IN THE NOTES AND BIBLIOGRAPHY

AGN   Archivo General de la Nación, Mexico City

GAC   *Guidebook of the Albuquerque Country* (Albuquerque: New Mexico Geological Society, 1961)

NMSRCA   New Mexico State Records Center and Archives, Santa Fe

SANM   Spanish Archives of New Mexico, Santa Fe

SC,UNML   Special Collections, University of New Mexico Library, Albuquerque

Notes

CHAPTER 1:

The Geography Behind History

1. J. Paul Fitzsimmons, "Precambrian Rocks of the Albuquerque Country," in *Guidebook of the Albuquerque Country [GAC]*, ed. Stuart A. Northrop (Albuquerque: New Mexico Geological Society, 1961), pp. 90–103. *Mineral and Water Resources of New Mexico*, report prepared by the United States Geological Survey (Washington, D.C.: GPO, 1965), pp. 23–28. Vincent C. Kelley, *Albuquerque: Its Mountains, Valley, Water, and Volcanoes* (Socorro: State Bureau of Mines and Mineral Resources, 1969), pp 4–10. Vincent C. Kelley and Stuart A. Northrop, *Geology of Sandia Mountains and Vicinity, New Mexico* (Socorro: State Bureau of Mines and Mineral Resources, 1975). Perry Reiche, "Geology of the Manzanita and North Manzano Mountains, New Mexico," *Bulletin of the Geological Society of America*, 60 (1949): 1183–1212.

2. Wolfgang E. Elston, *Summary of the Mineral Resources of Bernalillo, Sandoval, and Santa Fe Counties, New Mexico* (Socorro: State Bureau of Mines and Mineral Resources, 1967), p. 15. Ron Ratkevich and Neal La Fon, *Field Guide to New Mexico Fossils* (Alamogordo: Dinograph Southwest Inc., 1978).

3. Kelley, *Albuquerque*, pp. 10–12. Paige W. Christiansen and Frank E. Kottlowski, eds., *Mosaic of New Mexico's Scenery, Rocks, and History* (Socorro: State Bureau of Mines and Mineral Resources, 1964), pp. 36–38. "Structural Problems of the Rio Grande Trough in the Albuquerque Country," in *GAC*, pp. 144–47. H. R. Joesting et al., "The Rio Grande Trough Near Albuquerque, New Mexico," in *GAC*, pp. 148–150. Frank B. Titus, Jr., "Ground-water Geology of the Rio Grande Trough in North-central New Mexico, with Sections on the Jemez Caldera and the Lucero Uplift," in *GAC*, pp. 186–192.

4. Roger Y. Anderson, "Physiography, Climate and Vegetation of the Albuquerque Region," in *GAC*, pp. 67–68.

5. Anderson, "Physiography," p. 66. Christiansen and Kottlowski, *Mosaic*, p. 37. Roy L. Griggs, *Geology and Groundwater Resources of the Los Alamos Area, New Mexico* (Washington, D.C.: GPO, 1964). Roland A. Pettitt, *Exploring the Jemez Country* (Los Alamos: Pajarito Publications, 1975), pp. 10–11.

6. Kelley, *Albuquerque*, pp. 31–33. Vincent C. Kelley et al., *Guidebook to Albuquerque Basin of the Rio Grande Rift, New Mexico* (Socorro: New Mexico Bureau of Mines and Mineral Resources, 1976). Kirk Bryan, *Geology of the Vicinity of Albuquerque* (Geological Series, Bull. no. 51; Albuquerque: University of New Mexico, 1909), pp. 12, 18–19. *The Daily New Mexican*, April 6, 1881. "Area Prone to Earthquakes," *University of New Mexico Alumnus*, 48, (1976): 4. John Fox Hammond, *A Surgeon's Report on Socorro, N.M., 1852* (Santa Fe: Stagecoach Press, 1966), p. 23. Stuart A. Northrop, "Earthquakes of Central New Mexico," in *GAC*, p. 151. In 1961 the United States Coast and Geodetic Survey built a modern seismological

laboratory on the Isleta Pueblo Reservation south of Albuquerque as part of its network of stations to monitor earthquakes.

7. Quoted in Milton Meltzer, *Bound for the Rio Grande, The Mexican Struggle, 1845–1850* (New York: Alfred A. Knopf, 1974), p. 88.

8. Marjorie Van Cleave, "Vegetative Changes in the Middle Rio Grande Conservancy District," (M.S. thesis, University of New Mexico, 1935), p. 3. Kelley, *Albuquerque*, p. 7. "Rio Grande Valley State Park," a feasibility study prepared for the New Mexico State Park and Recreation Commission, Santa Fe, 1969, p. 7. The depth of the water table fluctuates with the rise and fall of the river.

9. Karl A. Snyder, "Give Us the Good Old Days," typescript (March 13, 1933) in the Albuquerque File, Dorothy Woodward Collection, New Mexico State Records Center and Archives [NMSRCA], Santa Fe.

10. Kelley, *Albuquerque*, p. 16. "Rio Grande Valley State Park," p. 7.

11. Neil M. Clark, "Albuquerque," *Enchantorama*, official publication of Albuquerque's 250th Anniversary (1956), p. 7. (Reprinted from *Saturday Evening Post*, April 8, 1950, with corrections).

12. Kelley, *Albuquerque*, p. 27.

13. Thomas M. Pearce, ed., *New Mexico Place Names, A Geographical Dictionary* (Albuquerque: University of New Mexico Press, 1965), p. 142.

14. John Sinclair, "Mountain and River: Turtle and Snake," *El Palacio*, 82 (Summer 1976): 4–8. Edgar L. Hewett and Wayne L. Mauzy, *Landmarks of New Mexico* (Albuquerque: University of New Mexico Press, 1953), p. 76.

15. Herbert E. Ungnade, *Guide to the New Mexico Mountains* (Denver: Sage Books, 1965), pp. 111–13. The question of who Juan Tabó was has never been satisfactorily answered. One legend claims he was a priest who lived nearby, but no such name occurs in the early Church records. According to another story, Juan Tabó was an Indian sheepherder accustomed to grazing his flocks in the canyon that took his name. A prominent avenue in the East Heights is also called Juan Tabó. It is part of the irony of history that Governor Cuervo y Valdés, the man most responsible for the founding of Albuquerque, has no thoroughfare or public building honoring his name, while the mysterious Juan Tabó receives recognition on dozens of street signs.

16. Reiche, "Geology of the Manzanita and North Manzano Mountains," pp. 1183–84. Kelley, *Albuquerque*, p. 49. "Environmental Impact Statement: Tijeras Canyon Projects, Bernalillo County, New Mexico," Unpublished report prepared for the New Mexico Highway Department (1972), Santa Fe.

17. Elston, *Summary of Mineral Resources*, p. 52.

18. Ungnade, *Guide to the New Mexico Mountains*, pp. 114–18.

19. Pearce, *New Mexico Place Names*, p. 96.

20. Yi-Fu Tuan, Cyril E. Everard, and Jerold G. Widdison, *The Climate of New Mexico* (Santa Fe: State Planning Office, 1969), p. 100.

21. Ibid., pp. 17–40. Ronald U. Cooke and Richard W. Reeves, *Arroyos and Environmental Change in the American South-West* (Oxford: Clarendon Press, 1976), pp. 3–4.

22. Anderson, "Physiography, Climate, and Vegetation," p. 63. Ed Mahr, "Lofty Sandias Protect City," *Albuquerque Journal*, March 3, 1968. The rainfall average actually means little. Albuquerque receives widely variable amounts of moisture from year to year. Meteorologist Cleve Hallenbeck, writing in 1944, noted record extremes for the city ranging from as little as 3.29 inches of annual rainfall to 16.30 inches. "Choose Your Climate," *New Mexico Magazine*, 22 (June 1944): 18.

23. Martin Hardwick Hall, *Sibley's New Mexico Campaign* (Austin: University of Texas Press, 1960), p. 121. Lina Fergusson Browne, ed., *Trader on the Santa Fe Trail, The Memoirs of Franz Huning* (Albuquerque: University of Albuquerque, 1973), p. 120.

24. Mahr, "Lofty Sandias Protect City."

25. Mrs. Edward E. Ayer, trans., *The Memorial of Fray Alonso de Benavides, 1630* (Chicago: privately printed, 1916), p. 39.

26. Samuel H. Lamb, *Woody Plants of New Mexico and Their Value to Wildlife* (Bull. no. 14; Santa Fe: New Mexico Department of Game and Fish, 1971), pp. 18–19.

27. Dwight L. Clark, ed., *The Original Journals of Henry Smith Turner* (Norman: University of Oklahoma Press, 1966), p. 77.

28. Lyle H. Wright, ed., *John Udell Journal, 1859* (Los Angeles: N. A. Kovach, 1946), p. 17.

29. Lamb, *Woody Plants of New Mexico*, pp. 48–49. Robert A. Vines, *Trees, Shrubs and Woody Vines of the Southwest* (Austin: University of Texas Press, 1960), pp. 760–61.

30. Van Cleave, "Vegetative Changes in the

Middle Rio Grande Conservancy District, pp. 38–41.

31. R. DeWitt Ivey, "Ecological Notes on the Mammals of Bernalillo County, New Mexico," *Journal of Mammalogy,* 38 (1957): 490–502. Vernon Bailey, *Life Zones and Crop Zones of New Mexico* (United States Department of Agriculture, North American Fauna, no. 35; Washington, D.C.: GPO, 1913), pp. 32–33. Vernon Bailey, *Mammals of New Mexico* (U.S. Department of Agriculture, North American Fauna, no. 53; Washington, D.C.: GPO, 1931), passim.

32. George Wilkins Kendall, *Narrative of the Texan Santa Fe Expedition,* facs. ed., 2 vols. (Austin: The Steck Co., 1935), 1: 380.

33. Harvey Fergusson, *Home in the West* (New York: Duell, Sloan and Pearce, 1944), pp. 95–96.

34. Peter Matthiessen, *Wildlife in America* (New York: Viking Press, 1964), p. 167.

35. Anderson, "Physiography, Climate and Vegetation of the Albuquerque Region," p. 65. Bailey, *Life Zones and Crop Zones of New Mexico,* pp. 27–28. Robert R. Humphrey, *The Desert Grassland* (Tucson: University of Arizona Press, n.d.), p. 39.

36. George Olin, *Mammals of the Southwest Mountains and Mesas* (Globe, Ariz.: Southwestern Monuments Association, 1961), p. 21. James S. Findley et al., *Mammals of New Mexico* (Albuquerque: University of New Mexico Press, 1975), passim.

37. "Environmental Impact Statement, Tijeras Canyon Projects," pp. 3–5. Edward F. Castetter, "The Vegetation of New Mexico," *New Mexico Quarterly,* 26 (1956): 274–77. *Final Environmental Statement: Sandia Mountain Land Use Plan* (United States Department of Agriculture, 1975; copy on file, Center for Anthropological Studies, Albuquerque), pp. 27–28.

38. *Final Environmental Statement: Sandia Mountain Land Use Plan,* p. 25.

39. "A Guide to the Mammals of the Sandia Mountains," (mimeographed circular issued by Sandia Ranger District, Forest Service, United States Department of Agriculture, n.d.), pp. 1–18. Bob Lange, "Bringing Back Bighorns," *New Mexico Wildlife,* 23 (1978): 2–5, 26–28. In 1977, sixteen bighorn sheep were released in the Manzano Mountains.

40. *Final Environmental Statement: Sandia Mountain Land Use Plan,* pp. 25–26. J. Stokley Ligon, *New Mexico Birds* (Albuquerque: University of New Mexico Press, 1961), passim.

CHAPTER 2:

The Latecomers: Indians and Spaniards

1. Richard S. MacNeish, ed., *Early Man in America* (San Francisco: W. H. Freeman and Co., 1973), p. 6. See also, Jesse D. Jennings, *Ancient Native Americans* (San Francisco: W. H. Freeman & Co., 1978).

2. Ronald P. Ratkevich and William T. S. Pope, *Ice Age Animals of the Rio Grande Valley* (Albuquerque: Natural Sales Ltd., 1975), passim. Ronald P. Ratkevich, "Native Elephants in New Mexico?" *The New Mexico Independent,* April 15, 1977.

3. C. Vance Haynes, Jr., "Elephant Hunting in North America," in MacNeish, *Early Man in America,* pp. 44–52. Cynthia Irwin-Williams and C. Vance Haynes, Jr., "Climatic Change and Early Population Dynamics in the Southwestern United States," *Quaternary Research,* 1 (1970): 61–65. W. James Judge and Jerry Dawson, "PaleoIndian Settlement Technology in New Mexico," *Science,* 176 (June 1972): 1210–11.

4. W. James Judge, *PaleoIndian Occupation of the Central Rio Grande Valley in New Mexico* (Albuquerque: University of New Mexico Press, 1977), pp. 66–78. Jerry Dawson and W. James Judge, "Paleo-Indian Sites and Topography in the Middle Rio Grande Valley of New Mexico," *Plains Anthropologist,* 14 (1969): 149–63. George Agogino and Frank C. Hibben, "Central New Mexico Paleo-Indian Cultures," *American Antiquity,* 23 (1958): 422–25. Frank C. Hibben, *The Lost Americans* (New York: Thomas Y. Crowell Co., 1968), pp. 87–90.

5. The first detailed account of the Sandia Cave excavations appeared in Frank C. Hibben, *Evidences of Early Occupation in Sandia Cave, New Mexico, and Other Sites in the Sandia-Manzano Region* (Smithsonian Miscellaneous Collections 99, No. 23; Washington, D.C., 1941). An early warning concerning the difficulties of assessing the Sandia site is given by Wesley L. Bliss, "A Chronological Problem Presented by Sandia Cave, New Mexico," *American Antiquity,* 5 (1940): 200–201. A recent and full summary of the ensuing controversy is found in Dominique E. Stevens and George A.

Agogino, *Sandia Cave: A Study in Controversy* (Portales, N.M.: Eastern New Mexico University, Paleo-Indian Institute, 1975).

6. John Martin Campbell and Florence Hawley Ellis, "The Atrisco Sites: Cochise Manifestations in the Middle Rio Grande Valley," *American Antiquity*, 17 (1952): 211–21. George Agogino and Jim Hester, "The Santa Ana Pre-ceramic Sites," *El Palacio*, 60 (1953): 131–40. Agogino and Hibben, "Central New Mexico Paleo-Indian Cultures," pp. 424–25. S. McClain Staley, "The Westgate Site: Salvage Excavation in Bernalillo County, New Mexico," *Awanyu* (Archeological Society of New Mexico), 4, no.3 (1976): 6–15.

7. Irwin-Williams and Haynes, "Climatic Change and Early Population Dynamics" pp. 65–69.

8. J. W. Allen and C. H. McNutt, "A Pit House Site Near Santa Ana Pueblo, New Mexico," *American Antiquity*, 20 (1955): 241–55. Theodore R. Reinhart, "The Alameda Phase: An Early Basketmaker III Culture in the Middle Rio Grande Valley, New Mexico," *Southwestern Lore*, 33 (1967): 24–32. Theodore R. Reinhart, "The Rio Rancho Phase: A Preliminary Report on Early Basketmaker Culture in the Middle Rio Grande Valley, New Mexico," *American Antiquity*, 32 (1967): 458–70. S. Alan Skinner, "The Sedillo Site: A Pit House Village in Albuquerque," *El Palacio*, 72 (1965): 5–24. Theodore R. Frisbie, "The Excavation and Interpretation of the Artificial Leg Basketmaker III-Pueblo I Sites Near Corrales, New Mexico," (M.A. thesis, University of New Mexico, 1967). Paul Kirchhoff, "Gatherers and Farmers in the Greater Southwest: A Problem in Classification," *American Anthropologist*, 56 (1954): 529–60. Bill Hume, "Basketmaker Indian Site Discovered," *Albuquerque Journal*, October 26, 1969.

9. J. Charles Kelley and Ellen Abbott Kelley, "An Alternative Hypothesis for the Explanation of Anasazi Culture History," in *Collected Papers in Honor of Florence Hawley Ellis*, ed. Theodore R. Frisbie (Papers of the Archeological Society of New Mexico, 2; Norman, Okla.: Hooper Publishing Co., 1975), pp. 178–223.

10. Frank C. Hibben, *Kiva Art of the Anasazi at Pottery Mound* (Las Vegas, Nev.: KC Publications, 1975), pp. 2–10.

11. Bertha P. Dutton, *Sun Father's Way, The Kiva Murals of Kuaua* (Albuquerque: University of New Mexico Press, 1963), pp. 19–32. John L. Sinclair, *The Story of the Pueblo of Kuaua* (Papers of

the School of American Research, no. 45; Santa Fe, 1951).

12. H. P. Mera, *Population Changes in the Rio Grande Glaze-Paint Area* (Santa Fe: Laboratory of Anthropology, 1940), pp. 17–20. Edward P. Dozier, *The Pueblo Indians of North America* (New York: Holt, Rinehart and Winston, Inc., 1970), pp. 131–33. Albert H. Schroeder, "Rio Grande Ethnohistory," in *New Perspectives on the Pueblos*, ed. Alfonso Ortiz (Albuquerque: University of New Mexico Press, 1972), p. 43. Ezra B. W. Zubrow, *Population, Contact, and Climate in the New Mexican Pueblos* (Tucson: University of Arizona Press, 1974), p. 7.

13. George P. Hammond and Agapito Rey, eds. and trans., *Narratives of the Coronado Expedition, 1540–1542* (Albuquerque: University of New Mexico Press, 1940), p. 183.

14. Ibid., p. 183.

15. The best secondary account of Coronado's New Mexican adventure is Herbert E. Bolton, *Coronado, Knight of Pueblo and Plains* (Albuquerque: University of New Mexico Press, 1966).

16. George P. Hammond and Agapito Rey, eds. and trans., *The Rediscovery of New Mexico, 1580–1594* (Albuquerque: University of New Mexico Press, 1966), p. 221.

17. Translations of the original chronicles of the Rodríguez, Espejo, and Castaño de Sosa expeditions can be found in Hammond and Rey, *The Rediscovery of New Mexico*.

18. The location of Puaray Pueblo has been the subject of much scholarly controversy. For the most recent review of the matter, see David H. Snow, "The Identification of Puaray Pueblo," in Frisbie, *Collected Papers*, pp. 463–80.

19. The full story of the Oñate years is contained in George P. Hammond and Agapito Rey, eds. and trans., *Don Juan de Oñate, Colonizer of New Mexico, 1595–1628*, 2 vols (Albuquerque: University of New Mexico Press, 1953).

20. Ayer, *The Memorial of Fray Alonso de Benavides*, pp. 99–100.

21. France V. Scholes, "Documents for the History of the New Mexican Missions in the Seventeenth Century," *New Mexico Historical Review*, 4 (1929): 49.

22. France V. Scholes, "Civil Government and Society in New Mexico in the Seventeenth Century," *New Mexico Historical Review*, 10 (1935): 91.

23. Pearce, *New Mexico Place Names*, p. 16. On use of the name Bernalillo in the middle seven-

teenth century, see Charles Wilson Hackett, ed., *Revolt of the Pueblo Indians of New Mexico and Otermin's Attempted Reconquest, 1680–1682,* 2 vols. (Albuquerque: University of New Mexico Press, 1942), 1: 30, and Ralph Emerson Twitchell, *The Spanish Archives of New Mexico,* 2 vols. (Glendale, Calif.: Arthur H. Clark Co., 1914), 1: 338.

24. David H. Snow, "Santiago To Guache," in *Collected Papers in Honor of Marjorie Ferguson Lambert,* ed. Albert H. Schroeder (Albuquerque: Albuquerque Archaeological Society Press, 1976), p. 167. See also, *Santa Fe New Mexican,* July 12, 1880.

25. Fray Angelico Chávez, *Origins of New Mexico Families* (Santa Fe: Historical Society of New Mexico, 1954), p. 4.

26. Scholes, "Documents for the History of the New Mexican Missions," pp. 49, 55.

27. Charles Wilson Hackett, ed., *Historical Documents Relating to New Mexico, Nueva Vizcaya, and Approaches Thereto, to 1773,* 3 vols. (Washington, D.C.: Carnegie Institution, 1923–37), 3: 227. Also, Chávez, *Origins of New Mexico Families,* p. 34.

28. Hackett, *Revolt of the Pueblo Indians,* 1: 26; and Chávez, *Origins of New Mexico Families,* p. 108. Fray Angelico Chávez, in his article, "The Albuquerque Story," *New Mexico Magazine,* 34 (January 1956): 19, suggests that Doña Luisa may have been a daughter rather than the wife of Francisco.

29. J. Manuel Espinosa, ed. and trans., *First Expedition of Vargas into New Mexico, 1692* (Albuquerque: University of New Mexico Press, 1940), p. 68.

30. *Documentos para servir a la historia del Nuevo México, 1538–1778* (Madrid: Ediciones José Porrua Turanzas, 1962), p. 332.

31. Hackett, *Historical Documents,* 3: 265. Richard E. Greenleaf, "Atrisco and Las Ciruelas, 1772–1769," *New Mexico Historical Review,* 42 (1967): 5. The author postulates in this article that the signatures of citizens on the document may have been forged by the governor.

32. Jack D. Forbes, *Apache, Navajo, and Spaniard* (Norman: University of Oklahoma Press, 1960), p. 144.

33. Twitchell, *Spanish Archives of New Mexico,* 2: 57.

34. Hackett, *Revolt of the Pueblo Indians,* 1:23.

35. Ibid., 1: 26.

36. Ibid., 1: 104.

37. Ibid., 1: 27.

38. Forbes, *Apache, Navajo, and Spaniard,* p. 189.

39. Espinosa, *First Expedition of Vargas,* p. 69.

40. J. Manuel Espinosa, *Crusaders of the Rio Grande* (Chicago: Institute of Jesuit History, 1942), p. 66.

41. Ibid., p. 134.

42. Ibid., p. 221.

43. Ibid., p. 227. Snow, "Santiago to Guache," pp. 167–71. Hackett, *Historical Documents,* 3: 375. Twitchell, *Spanish Archives of New Mexico,* 1: 35, 81.

44. Twitchell, *Spanish Archives of New Mexico,* 1: 333.

45. Fray Angelico Chávez, *Archives of the Archdiocese of Santa Fe, 1678–1900* (Washington, D.C.: Academy of American Franciscan History, 1957), p. 7.

46. Hackett, *Historical Documents,* 3: 375.

CHAPTER 3:

The Bosque Becomes a Villa

1. Hackett, *Historical Documents,* 3: 379.

2. A Spanish facsimile of the original document of certification, together with an English translation, is provided by Lansing B. Bloom, ed., "Albuquerque and Galisteo, Certificate of Their Founding, 1706," *New Mexico Historical Review,* 10 (1935): 48–50.

3. *Recopilación de Leyes de los Reynos de las Indias,* facs. ed., 4 vols. (Madrid: Ediciones Cultura Hispánica, 1973), book IV, title V, law 6; and book IV, title VII, laws 1–12. The requirement of thirty families to found a villa was not a rigid one. San Antonio, Texas, was organized as a villa in 1731 with only sixteen families—Canary Islanders enlisted by the king to colonize New Spain's frontier. The enterprise was carefully superintended by the viceroy, and his instructions to the governor of Texas gave precise details as to the manner of forming a plaza, streets, residential lots, and commons. The viceroy also provided a map, *plano de la población,* to serve as a guide for forming the new villa. Lota M. Spell, ed. and trans., "The Grant and First Survey of the City of San Antonio," *Southwestern Historical Quarterly,* 66 (1962): 73–89.

4. The Spanish use of an extra "r" in Albu-

querque was dropped, through Anglo American usage, during the first half of the nineteenth century. An article in the *Rio Abajo Weekly Press,* July 7, 1863, contending that Albuquerque with a single "r" was the correct spelling in Spain, was erroneous.

5. Archivo General de la Nación, Mexico, Provincias Internas, leg. 38, exp. 8 [cited hereinafter as AGN]; and Richard E. Greenleaf, "The Founding of Albuquerque, 1706: An Historical-Legal Problem," *New Mexico Historical Review,* 39 (1964): 9–10.

6. Greenleaf, "The Founding of Albuquerque," p. 10.

7. Petition, March 8, 1892, Records of the Court of Private Land Claims, Microfilm Roll 34, NMSRCA. In this file see, also, the Plat of the City of Albuquerque Grant, showing the "imagined four square leagues." Frederic Hall in his *The Laws of Mexico* (San Francisco: A. L. Bancroft & Co., 1885), p. 51, correctly observes that the *Recopilación* specified a four square league grant only for towns founded by a private contractor. Those formed by the government, as in the case of Albuquerque, he notes, "were only limited by the discretion of the governors of the provinces, and viceroys, subject to approval or disapproval of the king. There are numerous pueblos in Mexico which have less and many that have more than four square leagues."

8. Greenleaf, "The Founding of Albuquerque," pp. 1–15; and Applicant's Brief, no. 70800, District Court Records of Bernalillo County, Albuquerque.

9. Hubert Howe Bancroft, *History of Arizona and New Mexico, 1530–1888* (San Francisco: The History Company, 1889), p. 221; and Ovidio Casado, "Don Francisco Cuerbo y Valdés, Governor of New Mexico: 1705–1707," (M.A. thesis, University of New Mexico, 1965), p. 24. The alternate spellings, "Cuervo" and "Cuerbo", are both used in the contemporary documents.

10. Before the reconquest, New Mexico governors were appointed by the viceroy. But beginning with the term of Vargas, they received their appointments directly from the king. The viceroy then could make only provisional, or interim, appointments when a governor died in office or resigned. Ted J. Warner, "Don Félix Martínez and the Santa Fe Presidio, 1693–1730," *New Mexico Historical Review,* 45 (1970): 271.

11. Archivo General de las Indias, Guadala-

jara, leg. 116, part 2 [cited hereinafter as AGI], "Méritos de Cuervo, con memorial y suplico . . ." México, October 6, 1712. See also, Casado, "Don Francisco Cuerbo y Valdés," p. 1–4.

12. Casado, "Don Francisco Cuerbo y Valdés," p. 26.

13. Spanish Archives of New Mexico, II, doc. 110, [cited hereinafter as SANM], "*Autos* and muster roll," Santa Fe, April 1705, in NMSRCA.

14. Casado, "Don Francisco Cuerbo y Valdés," p. 42.

15. John L. Kessell, *Kiva, Cross, and Crown* (Washington, D.C.: National Park Service, 1979), p. 303.

16. AGI, Guadalajara, leg. 116, part 2, "Certification of the Santa Fe Cabildo," February 23, 1706.

17. SANM, I, doc. 1136, "Inventory of the Archives of the Cabildo of Santa Fe, 1715," in NMSRCA. This grant and similar ones in the Middle Valley were probably not occupied until late 1705 or 1706.

18. Hackett, *Historical Documents,* 3: 375. Isidro Armijo, trans., "Noticias of Juan Candelaria," *New Mexico Historical Review,* 4 (1929): 276.

19. Greenleaf, "Atrisco and Las Ciruelas," p. 6.

20. See, for example, Peter Gallagher, "The Founding of Albuquerque," *Rio Grande History,* no. 7 (1977): 2–5; and Chávez, "The Albuquerque Story," pp. 18–19.

21. Ralph Emerson Twitchell, *Spanish Colonization in New Mexico in the Oñate and De Vargas Periods* (Santa Fe: Historical Society of New Mexico, 1919), p. 21.

22. That Captain Martín Hurtado, rather than Governor Cuervo carried out the actual founding of Albuquerque is confirmed by a land grant document of March 9, 1707, addressed to Hurtado as alcalde mayor of the villa. It reads: "Lorenzo de Carabajal, a resident of this town of Albuquerque and San Javier, appears before you and asking that all privileges allowed by law by given him, says that . . . on the seventeenth day of the past year of 1706, the alcalde mayor assigned to me and gave me possession of the ruins of an old house which had belonged to my father [before the revolt], and you were also pleased to set off to me a small piece of farm land on the day that you made the partition of the lands of this villa to the citizens and new settlers by virtue of the royal authority which was given you for that pur-

pose and for other purposes. . . ." Signed: Lorenzo de Carabajal. SANM, I, DOC. 156, NMSRCA.

The founding date of February 7 is given by Juan Candelaria. The reliability of this and other statements of his concerning early Albuquerque, however, has been questioned by Fray Angelico Chávez, "The Albuquerque Story," p. 51. Candelaria also claimed that the villa occupied four leagues of land. Armijo, "Noticias of Juan Candelaria," p. 275. An undated document directed to Governor Cuervo by the soldiers at Albuquerque declares that the new villa was "certified" on February 23. Cited by Gallagher, "The Founding of Albuquerque," p. 3.

Fernando Durán y Chaves and Baltazar Romero, in a petition of 1708, referred to having left their homes at Bernalillo in 1706 and gone to the new villa of Albuquerque where they were "impelled to take an oath and settle said villa." SANM, I, doc. 1205, NMSRCA.

23. Armijo, "Noticias de Juan Candelaria," p. 274. Names of the families are provided.

24. All of the preceding testimony, together with a copy of the king's original *cédula* and a viceregal order, are found in "Testimonio de unas diligencias," Santa Fe, 1712, Misc. SANM, Microfilm Roll 33, NMSRCA.

25. *Documentos para servir a la historia del Nuevo México,* p. 434.

26. Vito Alessio Robles, ed., *Diario y derrotero de Brigadier Pedro de Rivera* (México: Taller Autografico, 1946), p. 51. Hackett, *Historical Documents,* 3: 464. Eleanor B. Adams and Fray Angelico Chávez, eds. and trans., *The Missions of New Mexico, 1776* (Albuquerque: University of New Mexico Press, 1956), p. 151. Spanish law recognized the right of the citizens of a municipality to operate farms and ranches in the adjacent countryside, but it is clear that their main residence was to be in the town and not on such properties. *Recopilación,* book IV, title VIII, law 11.

27. Lino Duarte Insúa, *Historia de Alburquerque* (Badajóz, Spain: Tip. de Antonio Arqueros, 1929), pp. 25–26. Another popular, but unlikely view holds that the word Alburquerque is a corruption of the Spanish *albaricoque,* meaning "apricot." "Albuquerque," with one "r", is a common proper name in Portugal and Brazil. The Portuguese explorer Affonson de Albuquerque made the first sea expedition from Western Europe to India in 1503 and laid the foundations for Portugal's colonial empire in Asia. Clarence L. Barnhart, *The*

New Century Cyclopedia of Names, 3 vols. (New York: Appleton-Century-Crofts, Inc., 1954), 1: 84.

28. Thomas M. Pearce, *The Dukes of Alburquerque—Albuquerque, New Mexico—Old Spain and New Spain* (Albuquerque: Albuquerque Historical Society, 1977). In 1956, on the 250th anniversary of the founding of Albuquerque, the current Duke, Don Beltrán Osorio y Diez, presented the city with a wall hanging, called a *repostero,* which dates from the seventeenth century and shows the family coat of arms. It now hangs in the Albuquerque Civic Auditorium. T. M. Pearce, "The Albuquerque Repostero," *El Palacio,* 65 (1958): 169–73. Several nineteenth-century writers, among them W. W. H. Davis and L. Bradford Prince, misread the documents and erroneously referred to a Duke of Alburquerque as governor of New Mexico. Bancroft, *History of Arizona and New Mexico,* p. 228 n.

29. For a general history of the viceroy's administration in New Spain, see Manuel Rivera, *Los gobernantes de México,* 2 vols. (México: Imp. de J. M. Aguilar Ortiz, 1872), 1: 301–8; and T. M. Pearce, "The Duke," *El Palacio,* 82 (June 1976): 36–41.

30. Casado, "Don Francisco Cuerbo y Váldes," p. 85; and Pearce, "The Duke," p. 38.

31. SANM, II, doc. 265, "Claim of María Francisca García de las Rivas against the estate of Governor Cuervo y Váldes," Santa Fe, January 14, 1716, NMSRCA. In the year noted in this document, Doña Micaela de Velasco, widow of Captain Miguel García de la Riva, traveled to Santa Fe from Mexico City in an effort to discover documents in the municipal and provincial archives that would prove that her daughter, María Francisca, had an illegitimate son by former Governor Cuervo. The boy had been born while Cuervo ruled New Mexico and María Francisca resided in Santa Fe. Although no such documents could be uncovered, the alcalde Rael de Aguilar made a formal statement to the effect that it was common knowledge in the capital that Cuervo fathered a "natural" child, named Francisco Antonio Xavier y Cuervo, and that María Francisca was the mother. Micaela contended that the governor had offered to marry her daughter, provided he could get the required permission from the king, and if he failed in that, to give her 10,000 pesos. Evidently no wedding had taken place, for Micaela was attempting to win a claim on behalf of her daughter

against Cuervo's estate, for the 10,000 pesos promised. In this, she was being challenged by heirs of the governor in Mexico City.

Casado in his biography, "Don Francisco Cuerbo y Váldes," p. 1, says that the governor married María Francisca. In light of the document just cited, that would seem to be an error.

32. Adams and Chávez, *The Missions of New Mexico*, p. 146. As a footnote to this confusing story, it is worth observing that in life San Francisco Xavier, the great Jesuit missionary to the Far East, wrote a letter to San Felipe Neri, then in Rome, urging him to consider undertaking religious work in Asia. By coincidence, the two saints were both canonized in the same year, 1622. John Coulson, ed., *The Saints, A Concise Biographical Dictionary* (New York: Hawthorn Books, 1958), p. 378. See also, Fray Angelico Chávez, *From the Beginning, A Historical Survey of San Felipe Neri Church* (Albuquerque: privately printed, 1972), pp. 6–8.

33. *Recopilación,* book IV, title V, law 6.

34. Greenleaf, "The Founding of Albuquerque," pp. 10–11; and SANM, II, doc. 124, "Order of the Duke of Alburquerque," México, July 30, 1706, NMSRCA.

35. Warner, "Don Félix Martínez and the Santa Fe Presidio," p. 271.

CHAPTER 4:

Years of Struggle

1. Hackett, *Historical Documents,* 3: 507.

2. Casado, "Don Francisco Cuerbo y Váldes," p. 47.

3. Hackett, *Historical Documents,* 3: 382.

4. Greenleaf, "The Founding of Albuquerque," pp. 12–13.

5. Oakah L. Jones, Jr., *Pueblo Warriors and Spanish Conquest* (Norman: University of Oklahoma Press, 1966), p. 86.

6. Warner, "Don Félix Martínez and the Santa Fe Presidio," p. 271.

7. SANM, I, doc. 1205, "Petition of the Albuquerque settlers," 1708, NMSRCA.

8. As late as 1748, a ten-man detachment of soldiers continued to perform guard duty in Albuquerque. SANM, II, doc. 484, "Petition of Martínez Salvador," February 13, 1748, NMSRCA. In 1752, the governor detailed two additional squads of soldiers and forty Pueblo auxiliaries to patrol

the Sandia Mountains in an effort to shield Albuquerque from the Apaches. Alfred Barnaby Thomas, *The Plains Indians and New Mexico, 1751–1778* (Albuquerque: University of New Mexico Press, 1940), pp 32–33.

9. *Documentos para servir a la historía del Nuevo México,* pp. 440–41. SANM, II, doc. 154, "Decree of the governor," Santa Fe, February 21, 1709, NMSRCA.

10. SANM, II, doc. 209, "Governor's campaign report," Santa Fe, August 9, 1714, NMSRCA.

11. Quoted by F. Stanley, *The Duke City, The Story of Albuquerque, New Mexico, 1706–1956* (Pampa, Tex.: privately printed, 1963), p. 14.

12. SANM, II, doc. 534, "Governor's proclamation," Santa Fe, November 26, 1754, NMSRCA.

13. Thomas, *The Plains Indians and New Mexico,* p. 45.

14. Marc Simmons, ed. and trans., *Father Juan Agustín de Morfí's Account of Disorders in New Mexico, 1778* (Isleta, N.M.: Historical Society of New Mexico, 1977), p. 8.

15. Stanley, *The Duke City,* p. 14.

16. Thomas, *The Plains Indians and New Mexico,* pp. 44–47. Chávez, "The Albuquerque Story," p. 50.

17. Hackett, *Historical Documents,* 3: 367, 375. Armijo, "Noticias de Juan Candelaria," p. 276.

18. Twitchell, *Spanish Archives of New Mexico,* 1: 166. SANM, I, doc. 302, "Conveyance from Francisco Montes Vigil to Juan González," Santa Fe, July 18, 1712, NMSRCA. Hackett, *Historical Documents,* 3: 400. Father Domínguez inspected and described the Alameda chapel in 1776. Adams and Chávez, *The Misisons of New Mexico,* pp. 152–53, 253. For papers relating to the Alameda grant, see, Records of the Court of Private Land Claims, Microfilm Roll 34, NMSRCA. These documents show that the grant was originally entirely on the west bank of the Rio Grande. The river switched course during a flood, however, probably in the early nineteenth century, and left a narrow strip of the grant, including the village of Alameda, on the east bank. Thereafter, the eastern boundary of the grant was recognized as the "old bed of the Rio Grande," not the river itself. See Testimony of José María Lucero before the Court of Private Land Claims, March 12, 1894. Bandelier remarked in 1883 that the river at Alameda had changed course sometime within the previous seventy-five or eighty years. Charles H. Lange and Carroll L. Riley, eds., *The Southwestern Journals of*

Adolph F. Bandelier, 1880–1888, 3 vols. (Albuquerque: University of New Mexico Press, 1966–75), 2: 176.

19. Adams and Chávez, *The Missions of New Mexico*, p. 203. Candelaria states that Isleta was founded during March 1708, but clearly that is too early since Father Peña could not have reached the area until later in the year. Armijo, "Noticias de Juan Candelaria," p. 276. On Peña's service at Isleta (or Ysleta) del Sur see, Hackett, *Historical Documents*, 3: 377. Twitchell in his *Spanish Archives of New Mexico*, 2: 252, contends that Isleta was repeopled with Tiwas from Hopi. From other sources, it is evident that most, in fact, were drawn from the Rio Grande Valley.

20. Adams and Chávez, *The Missions of New Mexico*, p. 203. Ted J. Warner, "The Career of Don Félix Martínez de Torrelaguna, Soldier, Presidio Commander, and Governor of New Mexico, 1693–1726," (Ph.D. diss., University of New Mexico, 1963), p. 39. Father Peña charged Governor Peñuela with cruelty to the Indians, which upon investigation was confirmed. As a result, the governor was censured and fined 2,000 pesos. Benjamin M. Read, *Illustrated History of New Mexico* (Santa Fe: New Mexican Printing Co., 1912), p. 324.

21. Population figures quoted by Herbert O. Brayer, *Pueblo Indian Land Grants of the "Rio Abajo," New Mexico* (Albuquerque: University of New Mexico Press, 1938), p. 57. The author summarizes the history of the Isleta land grant.

22. SANM, I, doc. 1208, "Petition of genízaros," 1733, NMSRCA. Other genízaros settled near the Spanish town of Belen, founded in 1741. Nicolás de LaFora gives its population in 1766 as thirty-eight families of genízaros and Spaniards. *Relación del Viaje a los Presidios Internos* (México: Editorial Pedro Robredo, 1939), p. 96.

23. SANM, II, doc. 486, "Petition of Salvador Martínez," June 6, 1748, NMSRCA. Alfred Barnaby Thomas, ed. and trans., *Forgotten Frontiers, A Study of the Spanish Indian Policy of Don Juan Bautista de Anza, 1777–1787* (Norman: University of Oklahoma Press, 1932), p. 23.

24. SANM, I, doc. 848, "Papers relating to the founding of Sandia," 1748, NMSRCA.

25. Adams and Chávez, *The Missions of New Mexico*, p. 143. Bernalillo, whose location shifted several times during the colonial period, obtained a grant from the Mexican government in 1824 that encroached upon the lands of Sandia. The

town, as it developed in the nineteenth century, lay almost wholly within the boundaries of the pueblo. Brayer, *Pueblo Indian Land Grants*, p. 71. Bandelier reported in the 1880s that the Sandias performed kachina dances in the kiva on Thursday and Friday of Holy Week, posting guards at the perimeter of the village to exclude intruders. Lange and Riley, *The Southwestern Journals of Adolph F. Bandelier, 1880–1882*, 1: 314.

26. The actual amount later recognized and confirmed by the United States government was only 35,000 acres. Twitchell, *Spanish Archives of New Mexico*, 1: 493. Elena Gallegos's husband, Santiago Gurulé, was actually the Frenchman Jacques Grolé who had survived the tragic La Salle expedition to the Texas coast in 1684. For his unusual story, see, Marc Simmons, *Taos to Tomé, True Tales of Hispanic New Mexico* (Albuquerque: Adobe Press, 1978), pp. 41–44.

27. Wills of Elena Gallegos and Antonio Gurulé are contained in the Ranchos de Albuquerque Grant, Records of the Court of Private Land Claims, Microfilm Roll 38, NMSRCA.

28. Colonial wills and conveyances of property in this area usually speak of each narrow strip of land as extending from the river to the Sandia Mountains. In actual practice, all lands outside the irrigable valley were "held, used, and occupied in common pasturage by all the residents of the grant." The eastern limit of the grant was identified only as the Sandia Mountains, by which the colonial settlers understood, the summit of the range. Later, when the grant was confirmed by the United States government, an attempt was made to establish the foot of the mountains as the eastern boundary. Ranchos de Albuquerque Grant, Records of the Court of Private Land Claims, Microfilm Roll 38, NMSRCA.

29. For information on these and other small communities founded in the eighteenth and nineteenth centuries, see Armijo, "Noticias de Juan Candelaria," pp. 274–85; and Frank D. Reeve, *History of New Mexico*, 3 vols. (New York: Lewis Historical Publishing Co., 1961), 1: 313–18. Donaciano Gurulé, in giving testimony to the Court of Private Land Claims, November 28, 1893, asserted that the Plaza de la Magdalena, in the center of the Elena Gallegos grant, was the site of Antonio Gurulé's six-room house, that his grandfather inherited it, and that upon his death the property and town of Magdalena had been partitioned among his sons. As of 1893, the wit-

ness noted, Magdalena was largely in ruins, although a few families continued to reside there. Ranchos de Albuquerque Grant, Records of the Court of Private Land Claims, Microfilm Roll 38, NMSRCA.

30. Chávez, *Archives of the Archdiocese of Santa Fe,* p. 207. Adams and Chávez, *The Missions of New Mexico,* pp. 144, 154.

31. SANM, I, doc. 277, Petition of Bernabé Montaño et al., October 21, 1753, NMSRCA.

32. Ibid.

33. Bernabé Montaño Grant, Records of the Court of Private Land Claims, Microfilm Roll 34, NMSRCA.

34. Ibid.

35. Joseph V. Metzgar, "The Atrisco Land Grant, 1692–1977," *New Mexico Historical Review,* 52 (1977): 272–74.

36. Robert Archibald, "Cañon de Carnué: Settlement of a Grant," *New Mexico Historical Review,* 51 (1976): 316.

37. Frances Leon Swadesh, "Archeology, Ethnohistory and the First Plaza of Carnuel," *Ethnohistory,* 23 (1976): p. 36. Dolores A. Gunnerson, *The Jicarilla Apaches: A Study in Survival* (DeKalb: Northern Illinois University Press, 1974), p. 240.

38. SANM, II, doc. 636, "Criminal proceedings relating to Indians of Carnué," April 9–30, 1768, NMSRCA.

39. Quoted in Albert E. Ward, "Archeological Investigations at San Miguel de Carnué: The First Field Session," (Unpublished Report; Albuquerque: Center for Anthropological Studies, n.d.), p. 6. See also, Eleanor B. Mitchell, "A Study of an Historical Trail System Through Tijeras Canyon East of Albuquerque in Bernalillo County, New Mexico," (M.A. thesis, University of New Mexico, 1977), pp. 71–73.

40. "Cañon de Carnué Grant," Records of the Surveyor General, Microfilm Roll 27, NMSRCA.

41. Ward, "Archeological Investigations at San Miguel de Carnué," pp. 9–10. Also, Albert E. Ward, "Archeology for Albuquerque," *El Palacio,* 82 (Summer 1976): 19.

42. Swadesh, "Archeology, Ethnohistory and the First Plaza of Carnuel," p. 38.

43. SANM, I, doc. 46, "Letter of Governor Pedro Fermín de Mendinueta," March 24, 1774, NMSRCA.

44. Archibald, "Cañon de Carnué," pp. 322–24. Whether the Carnué of 1818 was founded upon the site of the original 1763 village, or in another place, remains the subject of intense controversy among scholars. Historians generally hold that the present location of Carnué, inside the canyon, was the same at the time of its founding. Archeologists, on the other hand, believe, on the basis of ceramic dating, that the site now known as Rancho de Carnué (situated outside the canyon, in the Four Hills area of Albuquerque), was the place the 1763 settlers lived, and that with the refounding of 1818, the village was moved eastward into the canyon.

45. SANM, I, doc. 156, Petition for title to lands by Lorenzo de Carvajal, Albuquerque, 1707, NMSRCA. A detailed examination of one boundary controversy is presented by Greenleaf, "Atrisco and Las Ciruelas," pp. 5–25. The alcalde mayor was the chief administrative official of the Albuquerque district. Appointed by the governor, he also possessed judicial and police powers, as well as the right to issue (though not confirm) land grants. He was assisted by lieutenant-alcaldes who served in neighboring villages.

46. Chávez, *Origins of New Mexico Families,* p. 163.

47. This statement and all material regarding the case are taken from SANM, II, doc. 299, "Criminal proceedings," Albuquerque and Santa Fe, 1719, NMSRCA. On the matter of Spanish fugitives taking refuge in churches, see Elizabeth Howard West, "The Right of Asylum in New Mexico in the Seventeenth Century," *Hispanic American Historical Review,* 8 (1928): 357–91.

48. Virginia Langham Olmstead, trans., *New Mexico Spanish and Mexican Colonial Censuses: 1790, 1823, 1845* (Albuquerque: New Mexico Genealogical Society, 1975), pp. 1–14.

49. SANM, I, doc. 94, "Inventory of Estate of Josepha Baca," 1756; doc. 341, "Inventory of Estate of Luís García," 1747; doc. 246, "Inventory of Estate of Manuel Durán de Armijo," 1764; NMSRCA. H. Bailey Carroll and J. Villasana Haggard, trans., *Three New Mexico Chronicles* (Albuquerque: Quivira Society, 1942), pp. 41–42.

50. SANM, II, doc. 421, "Petition of Albuquerque Citizens," September 3, 1737, NMSRCA.

51. SANM, II, doc. 454, "Petition of Albuquerque Citizens, May 22, 1744," NMSRCA. As late as April 1777, Governor Pedro Fermín de Mendinueta issued an order forbidding exportation of sheep and wool, because the supply was inadequate for the local population. Cited by Roland F. Dickey, *New Mexico Village Arts* (Albu-

querque: University of New Mexico Press, 1970), p. 113.

52. SANM, II, doc. 377, "Order of Governor Gervasio Cruzat y Góngora," 1732, NMSRCA.

53. Max L. Moorhead, *New Mexico's Royal Road* (Norman: University of Oklahoma Press, 1958), p. 46.

54. Hackett, *Historical Documents,* 3: 400.

55. Olmstead, *New Mexico Spanish and Mexican Colonial Censuses,* pp. 1–14. For an analysis of the 1790 census, see Antonio José Ríos-Bustamante, "New Mexico in the Eighteenth Century," *Aztlán,* 7 (1978), pp. 357–90. The appearance of intense specialization in cloth production may be misleading, since it is likely that most of those so engaged were also subsistence farmers.

56. A census table for Albuquerque during various years in the late eighteenth century is provided by Bancroft, *History of Arizona and New Mexico,* p. 279. On problems with New Mexico censuses, see a note by Alfred Barnaby Thomas, "Antonio de Bonilla and Spanish Plans for the Defense of New Mexico, 1772–1778," in *New Spain and the Anglo-American West: Contributions to Herbert Eugene Bolton,* 2 vols. (Los Angeles: privately printed, 1932), 1: 209. A church census of 1804 gives the population of the villa of Albuquerque as 3,873, but that figure beyond question includes the entire parish, which took in a considerable area north and south of the villa. See Kessell, *Kiva, Cross, and Crown,* p. 423.

57. The governor's comment and the following census are found in Ritch Papers, Microfilm Roll 2, "Padrón General," October 3, 1787, Special Collections, University of New Mexico Library, Albuquerque [cited hereinafter as SC, UNML].

58. A similar ratio, fifty-one widows to fourteen widowers, is provided by the 1790 census. Olmstead, *New Mexico Spanish and Mexican Colonial Censuses,* pp. 1–14.

59. Marc Simmons, "New Mexico's Smallpox Epidemic of 1780–1781," *New Mexico Historical Review,* 41 (1966): 321.

60. Lansing B. Bloom, *Early Vaccination in New Mexico* (Santa Fe: Historical Society of New Mexico, 1924), p. 6.

61. Ibid, p. 7.

62. SANM, II, doc. 2368, "Record of Vaccinations in Albuquerque," 1810, NMSRCA. The plazas, or hamlets, listed are Los Duranes, Los Candelarias, Los Griegos, Los Gallegos, Los Poblanos, and Los Ranchos de Gamboa. The last may

have been the same as Ranchos de Albuquerque. In this document, the plaza of Albuquerque is referred to as El Presidio, a popular designation of the period, because of the presence of the soldiers' quarters near the church.

63. Jaime Vicens Vives, *An Economic History of Spain* (Princeton: Princeton University Press, 1969), p. 617.

64. James I. Culbert, "Distribution of Spanish American Population in New Mexico," *Economic Geography,* 19 (April 1943): 175. A sharp increase in population for Albuquerque between the years 1818 and 1841 is noted by Chávez, *Archives of the Archdiocese of Santa Fe,* p. 220.

65. Adams and Chávez, *The Missions of New Mexico,* p. 146. Chávez, *From the Beginning,* p. 6.

66. Adams and Chávez, *The Missions of New Mexico,* pp. 145–47. Ritch Papers, Microfilm Roll 2, "Inventory of the Church of San Felipe de Albuquerque," October 3, 1789, SC,UNML. This document notes three small bells *(campanillas)* belonging to the church.

67. Adams and Chávez, *The Missions of New Mexico,* p. 148.

68. SANM, II, doc. 1226, "Governor's Proclamation," February 18, 1793, NMSRCA. Curiously, about 1798 the Santa Fe parish church also collapsed. Fray Angelico Chávez, "Nuestra Señora del Rosario, La Conquistadora," *New Mexico Historical Review,* 23 (1948), 177.

69. Chávez, *In the Beginning,* p. 8.

70. Lawrence and Lucia Kinnaird, "Secularization of Four New Mexican Missions," *New Mexico Historical Review,* 54 (1979): 35–41.

71. Eleanor B. Adams, ed. and trans., *Bishop Tamaron's Visitation of New Mexico, 1760* (Albuquerque: University of New Mexico Press, 1954), p. 44. At the time of his meeting with the bishop, Father Rojo, a native of Mexico City, was 42 years old. He served nineteen years in the Albuquerque parish. Adams and Chávez, *The Missions of New Mexico,* p. 80. The earlier visitation of Crespo y Monroy is referred to briefly in Guillermo Porras Muñoz, *Iglesia y Estado en Nueva Vizcaya, 1562–1821* (Pamplona, Spain: University of Navarra, 1966), p. 56.

72. The few secular priests who came from Durango never stayed long in New Mexico. A Franciscan was again ministering at Santa Fe by 1776. The Durango clergy, accustomed to some luxury and affluence, may well have found poor

and backward New Mexico not to their liking. A new move to install the seculars in New Mexico's villas is noted by Chávez, *Archives of the Archidiocese of Santa Fe*, p. 167. On the burial fees charged at Albuquerque, see, Adams and Chávez, *The Missions of New Mexico*, p. 148.

73. During his brief service at Albuquerque, Father Sida founded the Confraternity of Blessed Souls in Purgatory (Cofradía de las Benditas Animas del Purgatorio). It had been in existence in 1776 when Domínguez visited the villa, but must have lapsed, thereafter. Hence, Sida's action really represented a refounding of the confraternity. The constitution and rules of the body, which was a religious association and mutual aid society, are contained in Archives of the Archdiocese of Santa Fe [cited hereinafter as AASF], Loose Documents, 1802, no. 42, NMSRCA. Alms collected in the name of the confraternity were placed in its treasury and subsequently distributed to poor and infirm members or used to pay for special Masses.

A collection of alms made in 1802 shows that practically the entire population of the Middle Valley belonged to the confraternity. The roster lists contributions in some thirty hamlets (*plazas, puestos,* and Indian missions) surrounding Albuquerque, which together represented the ecclesiastical jurisdiction of the villa. Most of the alms were paid in kind, principally in sheep, serapes, and pairs of socks. AASF, Loose Documents, no. 30, NMSRCA.

Father Guerra continued to serve as Albuquerque's pastor until November 10, 1817 when he again handed over the parish to a secular priest, don José Francisco Leyva y Rosas. The latter remained as minister until his resignation in 1829. Chávez, *Archives of the Archdiocese of Santa Fe,* pp. 153, 220.

CHAPTER 5:

The Winds of Change

1. Simmons, *Father Juan Agustín de Morfi's Account,* p. 19.
2. In 1740 ten Frenchmen of the Mallet expedition entered New Mexico to trade. Two of the men remained in the province settling at the village of García Real near Isleta Pueblo. Thereafter, the place was often called "Canada," in honor of the original home of the French pair. Hackett, *Historical Documents,* 3: 400–401.
3. Donald Jackson, ed., *The Journals of Zebulon Montgomery Pike,* 2 vols. (Norman: University of Oklahoma Press, 1966), 1: 401.
4. Ibid., 1: 400.
5. Ibid., 1: 401.
6. Marc Simmons, *Spanish Government in New Mexico* (Albuquerque: University of New Mexico Press, 1968), pp. 206–7.
7. SANM, II, doc. 2984, "Election report," Albuquerque, June 9, 1821, NMSRCA. Although the matter is not clear, the renaming of the plaza may have actually occurred the previous year with the restoration of the Spanish constitution.
8. Mexican Archives of New Mexico, "Census," San Felipe Neri de Albuquerque, September 10, 1822, NMSRCA.
9. SANM, II, doc. 3008, "Report of Manuel Durán," San Miguel de Bado, August 21, 1821. Kessell, *Kiva, Cross, and Crown,* pp. 436–38. Daniel Tyler, "New Mexico in the 1820's: The First Administration of Manuel Armijo," (Ph.D. diss., University of New Mexico, 1970), pp. 224–26.
10. In 1833, sixty-one citizens of Albuquerque founded the village of Cubero a few miles west of Cebolleta. Myra Ellen Jenkins, "The Baltasar Baca 'Grant': History of an Encroachment," *El Palacio,* 68 (Spring 1961): 63.
11. SANM, II, doc. 2634, "Militia records," Albuquerque, December 31, 1815, NMSRCA. Baca served as governor from 1823 to 1825.
12. SANM, II, doc. 2856, "Militia records," Albuquerque, November 1, 1819, NMSRCA.
13. Participation of the Albuquerque militia in this campaign is inferred from the presence, mentioned in Vizcarra's journal, of some of the town's officers, among them Lieutenant-Colonel Manuel Armijo and Captain Julián Armijo. David M. Brugge, ed. and trans., "Vizcarra's Navajo Campaign of 1823," *Arizona and the West,* 6 (1964): 229, 233.
14. After independence, the Camino Real was formally renamed the Camino Nacional, but in New Mexico at least, the older name remained in common use among the people as late as the opening of the twentieth century.
15. Francisco Javier Chávez served briefly as interim governor in the summer of 1823.
16. Twitchell, *Leading Facts,* 2: 25 n.
17. In April 1843, Antonio José Chávez was

murdered on the Santa Fe Trail in central Kansas by outlaws.

18. Moorhead, *New Mexico's Royal Road*, p. 195. Ward Alan Minge, "Frontier Problems in New Mexico Preceding the Mexican War, 1840–1846" (Ph.D. diss., University of New Mexico, 1965), pp. 246–48.

19. Stella M. Drumm, ed., *Down the Santa Fe Trail and Into Mexico, The Diary of Susan Shelby Magoffin, 1846–1847* (New Haven: Yale University Press, 1926), p. 154.

20. Olmstead, *New Mexico Spanish and Mexican Colonial Censuses*, p. 14. Chávez, *Origins of New Mexico Families*, pp. 318–19.

21. The census of 1790 lists the couple with seven children, who, unfortunately, are not named. The youngest is mentioned as being two years old. Evidently Manuel Armijo was born after the census was taken, making a total of eight children, assuming that he was the last. His baptismal certificate has not been located so there is some question about his actual birthday. Janet LeCompte notes that in January 1851 Armijo claimed in the census records to be sixty years old. That would seem to place his date of birth in 1790, or in January of 1791. See her article, "Manuel Armijo's Family History," *New Mexico Historical Review*, 48 (1973): 252.

Further information on the matter is provided by the following document: SANM, II, doc. 2875, "Criminal case against Manuel Armijo brought by Father José Francisco Leyba," Albuquerque, January 5, 1820, NMSRCA. When questioned by the judicial investigator, the defendent gave his name as Don Manuel Antonio Armijo, age twenty-eight years, native of the villa of Albuquerque, position: militia lieutenant in the Second Company, Second Squadron. A comparison of the signature and rubric on this document with those of Manuel Armijo, the governor, confirms that we are dealing with the same man. The possibility of confusion arises from the fact that this Manuel Armijo had a cousin also named Manuel Antonio Armijo. See Chávez, *Origins of New Mexico Families*, p. 319. If Armijo was twenty-eight in 1820, that would suggest he was born in 1792. More evidence may yet be brought to light on the question.

22. Lecompte, "Manuel Armijo's Family History," p. 256. SANM, II, doc. 2856, "Militia records," Albuquerque, November 1, 1819, NMSRCA.

23. Kendall, *Narrative*, I, 360. See also, Daniel Tyler, "Gringo Views of Governor Manuel Armijo," *New Mexico Historical Review*, 45 (1970): 23–46.

24. Lansing B. Bloom, "New Mexico Under Mexican Administration, 1822–1846," *Old Santa Fe*, 1 (January 1914): 266.

25. W. H. H. Allison, "Santa Fe As It Appeared During the Winter of the Years 1837 and 1838," *Old Santa Fe*, 2 (October 1914): 172.

26. Kendall, *Narrative*, p. 350.

2. Ibid., pp. 358–59.

28. Ibid., pp. 383–85.

29. Tyler, "New Mexico in the 1820's," p. 62. Also see, Daniel Tyler, "The Mexican Teacher," *Red River Historical Review*, 1 (1974): 207–21.

30. Bloom, "New Mexico Under Mexican Administration," p. 274.

31. Tyler, "New Mexico in the 1820's," p. 60. In 1832 the salary for Albuquerque's lone teacher is listed at 300 pesos annually. Often the salary was several months in arrears. Carroll and Haggard, *Three New Mexico Chronicles*, p. 306.

32. Chávez, *Archives of the Archdiocese of Santa Fe*, pp. 155, 182. Marta Weigle, *Brothers of Light, Brothers of Blood* (Albuquerque: University of New Mexico Press, 1976), pp. 24–25. On two succeeding visitations to New Mexico, in 1845 and again in 1850 after American annexation, Bishop Zubiría was able to observe little improvement in the spiritual welfare of his flock.

33. LeRoy R. Hafen, ed., *Ruxton of the Rockies* (Norman: University of Oklahoma Press, 1950), pp. 132–33.

34. William Elsey Connelley, *Doniphan's Expedition* (Topeka: privately printed, 1907), p. 67.

35. Ross Calvin, ed., *Lieutenant Emory Reports* (Albuquerque: University of New Mexico Press, 1968), p. 68.

36. Ibid., p. 68.

37. Connelley, *Doniphan's Expedition*, pp. 68, 320.

38. Philip St. George Cooke, *The Conquest of New Mexico and California* (New York: G. P. Putnam's Sons, 1878), p. 74.

39. Ralph P. Bieber, ed. *Marching With the Army of the West, 1846–1848* (Glendale, Calif.: Arthur H. Clark Co., 1936), p. 167.

40. Alfred S. Waugh, "Desultory Wanderings in the Years 1845–46," *Bulletin of the Missouri Historical Society*, 7 (1951): 125–26.

41. Hafen, *Ruxton of the Rockies*, p. 177.

42. Bieber, *Marching With the Army of the West*, p. 168. Ruxton refers to Armijo's Albuquerque residence as a *palacio*. Hafen, *Ruxton of the Rockies*, p. 176.

43. Drumm, *Down the Santa Fe Trail and Into Mexico*, p. 152. One relative of Armijo's, an unnamed sister, did not fare so well. About September 10, Lieutenant Emory encountered her in Tomé and relates: "At the dance we found a very plain, but very intelligent woman, the sister of Armijo, who said he would return as soon as he settled his affairs in Chihuahua." Calvin, *Lieutenant Emory Reports*, p. 74. A few weeks later, volunteer Philip Ferguson mentions her again, this time at the nearby Plaza Chávez. "At night the sister of Governor Armijo came to camp on a visit to Lieutenant Mullowny. In the morning I saw this lady sitting on the ground at the corner of a house selling whiskey to the soldiers out of an old coffee pot! Who would have taken her, in this situation, for the sister of the wealthy and powerful Armijo." Beiber, *Marching With the Army of the West*, p. 328.

44. Connelley, *Doniphan's Expedition*, p. 235.

45. Ibid., p. 236.

46. Ibid., p. 236.

47. Hafen, *Ruxton of the Rockies*, p. 176.

48. Frank S. Edwards, *A Campaign in New Mexico* (Philadelphia: Casey and Hart, 1847), p. 65.

49. Sgt. Daniel Tyler, *A Concise History of the Mormon Battalion in the Mexican War, 1846–1847*, reprint ed. (Glorieta, N.M.: Rio Grande Press, 1969), p. 180.

50. Quoted in Frank McNitt, *Navajo Wars* (Albuquerque: University of New Mexico Press, 1972), p. 101.

CHAPTER 6:

New Masters, New Ways

1. Averam B. Bender, *The March of Empire* (Lawrence: University of Kansas Press, 1952), p. 154.

2. Calvin Horn, *New Mexico's Troubled Years* (Albuquerque: Horn and Wallace, 1963), p. 200.

3. Quoted in [Weightman, Richard H.], *Speech of the Hon. Richard H. Weightman of New Mexico, Delivered in the House of Representatives, March 15, 1852* (Washington, D.C.: Congressional Globe Office, 1852), p. 21.

4. Ibid.

5. Ibid.

6. Ibid., pp. 22–23. Robert W. Larson, *New Mexico's Quest for Statehood, 1846–1912* (Albuquerque: University of New Mexico Press, 1968), pp. 66–67.

7. Pearce S. Grove, Becky J. Barnett, and Sandra J. Hansen, eds., *New Mexico Newspapers: A Comprehensive Guide to Bibliographical Entries and Locations* (Albuquerque: University of New Mexico Press, 1975), p. 30. Writers sometimes mistakenly credit the *Rio Abajo Weekly Press*, founded in January 1863 by H. S. Johnson, with being Albuquerque's first paper. Porter A. Stratton, *The Territorial Press of New Mexico, 1834–1912* (Albuquerque: University of New Mexico Press, 1969), p. 5.

8. Paul Horgan, *Lamy of Santa Fe, His Life and Times* (New York: Farrar, Straus and Giroux, 1975), p. 128.

9. Ibid., p. 191.

10. W. J. Howlett, *Life of the Right Reverend Joseph P. Machebeuf* (Pueblo, Colorado: privately printed, 1908), p. 192.

11. Ibid.

12. Ibid., p. 193.

13. Ibid.

14. Ibid., p. 194.

15. On a controversy over counting the ballots in this election, see Larson, *New Mexico's Quest for Statehood*, p. 82.

16. In a race for reelection in 1853, Padre Gallegos was defeated by Miguel A. Otero, who had the backing of Lamy. Bancroft, *History of Arizona and New Mexico*, p. 650. It is of interest to the history of San Felipe Neri Church that Gallegos laid claim to personal ownership of the spacious rectory behind the church. An interior watercolor of its main *sala*, or reception hall, is shown in J. W. Abert, *Western America in 1846–1847* (San Francisco: John Howell Books, 1966), p. 40. After a protracted dispute over Gallegos's claim, Bishop Lamy paid him a sum of money as reimbursement for his investment in the property. Horgan, *Lamy of Santa Fe*, p. 197.

17. Returns from U.S. Military Posts, 1800–1916, Albuquerque Post, Microfilm Roll 13, SC, UNML. See also, S. C. Agnew, *Garrisons of the Regular U.S. Army, New Mexico, 1846–1899* (Santa Fe: Press of the Territorian, 1971), p. 21.

18. Robert W. Frazer, ed., *New Mexico in 1850: A Military View* (Norman: University of Oklahoma Press, 1968), p. 156.

19. Samuel Woodworth Cozzens, *The Marvelous Country, or Three Years in Arizona and New Mexico* (Boston: Lee and Shepard, 1876), p. 282.

20. McNitt, *Navajo Wars,* p. 134. John S. Watts, *Indian Depredations in New Mexico* (Washington, D.C.: Gideon Printers, 1858), p. 43.

21. Watts, Indian Depredations, p. 29.

22. McNitt, *Navajo Wars,* p. 169.

23. Annie Heloise Abel, comp., *The Official Correspondence of James S. Calhoun* (Washington, D.C.: GPO, 1915), p. 417.

24. Chris Emmett, *Fort Union and the Winning of the Southwest* (Norman: University of Oklahoma Press, 1965), pp. 121–22.

25. Quoted in F. Stanley, *E. V. Sumner, Major-General, United States Army* (Borger, Texas: Jim Hess Printers, 1969), pp. 152–53.

26. Bender, *March of Empire,* p. 156.

27. J. H. Beadle, *The Undeveloped West; or, Five Years in the Territories* (Philadelphia: National Publishing Co., 1873), p. 480.

28. Robert W. Frazer, ed., *Mansfield on the Condition of the Western Forts, 1853–1854* (Norman: University of Oklahoma Press, 1963), p. 45. William W. H. Davis, in 1854, noted: "The army depots are located here [Albuquerque], which causes a large amount of money to be put in circulation, and gives employment to a number of the inhabitants." *El Gringo: or New Mexico and Her People* (Santa Fe: The Rydal Press, 1938), p. 195.

29. Richard H. Dillon, ed., *A Cannoneer in Navajo Country, Journal of Private Josiah M. Rice, 1851* (Denver: Old West Publishing Co., 1970), p. 85.

30. Robert W. Frazer, "Purveyors of Flour to the Army: Department of New Mexico, 1849–1861," *New Mexico Historical Review,* 47 (1972): 216.

31. Frazer, "Purveyors of Flour," p. 226.

32. Kenyon Riddle, *Records and Maps of the Old Santa Fe Trail,* rev. ed. (Stuart, Fla.: Southeastern Printing Co., 1963), p. 14.

33. Browne, *Trader on the Santa Fe Trail,* p. 4.

34. Ibid., p. 55.

35. B. W. Kenney, "Albuquerque," WPA Manuscript, p. 1, Bernalillo County Folder, NMSRCA.

36. Browne, *Trader on the Santa Fe Trail,* p. 58.

37. Miguel Antonio Otero, *My Life on the Frontier, 1864–1882* (New York: The Press of the Pioneers, 1935), pp. 62–63.

38. General accounts of Baird's career are given in: Clarence Wharton, "Spruce McCoy Baird," *New Mexico Historical Review,* 27 (1952): 300–314; and Morris F. Taylor, "Spruce McCoy Baird: From Texas Agent to New Mexico Official, 1848–1860," *New Mexico Historical Review,* 53 (1978): 39–58.

39. Lansing B. Bloom, ed., "From Lewisburg to California in 1849," *New Mexico Historical Review,* 20 (1945): 146–47. In his journal Chamberlin actually spelled Baird's name "Beard." Several other writers of the day used the same spelling. It is possible that Judge Baird himself may have pronounced his name as if it were "Beard." See William Campbell Binkley, *The Expansionist Movement in Texas, 1836–1850* (Berkeley: University of California Press, 1925), p. 158 n.

40. Donald Dreesen, "Early Settlers of Albuquerque," Typescript in five parts, unpaginated, 1973, SC, UNML, pt. 1.

41. Ibid., pt. 5.

42. James Henry Carleton, *Diary of an Excursion to the Ruins of Abó, Quarra and Gran Quivira in New Mexico in 1853* (Santa Fe: Stagecoach Press, 1965), p. 4.

43. Davis, *El Gringo,* p. 197.

44. Court Docket Book, Socorro, May 7, 1853, NMSRCA.

45. After the first few issues, Weightman had moved the *Amigo del País* from Albuquerque to Santa Fe. When the paper foundered, he sold the press to Spruce Baird, who later sold it to the *Santa Fe Gazette.* William A. Keleher, *Turmoil in New Mexico, 1846–1868* (Santa Fe: The Rydal Press, 1952), p. 503. See, also, *Rio Abajo Weekly Press,* Albuquerque, January 20, 1863.

46. Best accounts of the fight are found in, Ralph Emerson Twitchell, *The Leading Facts of New Mexican History,* 5 vols. (Cedar Rapids, Iowa: Torch Press, 1911–17), 2: 305–8; and Donald Chaput, *Francois X. Aubry, Trader, Trailmaker and Voyageur in the Southwest, 1846–1854* (Glendale, Calif.: Arthur H. Clark Co., 1975), pp. 157–59.

47. Chaput, *Francois X. Aubry,* p. 163.

48. The identity of José Chávez has been a matter of some confusion. He is usually thought to have been the Antonio José Chávez killed on the Santa Fe Trail in 1843. But William E. Connelley, in *Doniphan's Expedition,* p. 281, writes that Henry Connelly's residence was at Peralta. "There he married Dolores Perea, widow of José Chávez, but not the man of that name who was murdered . . . at Chavez Creek [Kansas], as some suppose,

building thereon the romance of Dr. Connelly's subsequent courtship and the widow's acceptance out of gratitude for favors extended her in the troubles following the murder of her husband. . . . At the time of her marriage to Dr. Connelly, Mrs. Chávez had two children, José Francisco and Bonifacio."

Twitchell, a usually reliable authority, compounds the problem by claiming two different fathers for José Francisco, who later became one of New Mexico's foremost statesmen. In his *Leading Facts*, 2: 400 n, Twitchell declares that José Francisco Chávez was born at Los Padillas, the son of Mariano Chávez and Dolores Perea. But the same writer states in his *History of the Military Occupation of the Territory of New Mexico from 1846 to 1851* (Denver: Smith-Brooks Co., 1909), p. 366: [Connelly] "had a home at Peralta, Valencia County, where he married Dolores Perea, widow of José Chávez, the father of Colonel J. Francisco Chávez, from whom the author received most of the information contained in this sketch." Historian William Keleher writes, in *Turmoil in New Mexico*, p. 123, "In 1849 Connelly was married to the widow of Don Mariano Chávez, and maintained a pretentious ranch home at Los Pinos, near Peralta."

The certainty is that Henry Connelly married Dolores Perea. Just who her first husband, José Chávez, was remains open to question. One curious note: recently discovered records in Missouri show that she was with Antonio José Chávez at the time of his murder in 1843. See, Bill of Indictment, U.S. Circuit Court Records, September, 1843, Federal Archives and Records Center, Kansas City, Missouri.

49. Quoted in Horn, *New Mexico's Troubled Years*, p. 98.

50. Davis, *El Gringo*, p. 197.

51. McNitt, *Navajo Wars*, p. 170.

52. Connelley, *Doniphan's Expedition*, p. 282; and Twitchell, *Military Occupation of New Mexico*, p. 366.

53. Frank McNitt, *The Indian Traders* (Norman: University of Oklahoma Press, 1962), p. 143. Carol N. Callary, "A Political Biography of Frank A. Hubbell, 1862–1929," (M.A. thesis, University of New Mexico, 1967), pp. 1–3.

54. The mileage is quoted in Randolph B. Marcy, *The Prairie Traveler, A Handbook for Overland Expeditions* (New York: Harper and Brothers, 1859), p. 260. His journal is published in Grant Foreman, ed., *Marcy and the Gold Seekers* (Norman: University of Oklahoma Press, 1939).

55. Bender, *The March of Empire*, p. 70. Udell, *Journal*, pp. 14–16.

56. For Simpson's account see, Frank McNitt, ed., *Navajo Expedition* (Norman: University of Oklahoma Press, 1964).

57. Lorenzo Sitgreaves, *Report of an Expedition Down the Zuni and Colorado Rivers*, 32nd Cong., 2d sess., Senate Exec. Doc. no. 59 (Washington, D.C.: Robert Armstrong, Public Printer, 1853).

58. *Reports of Expeditions and Surveys*, 33rd Cong., 2d sess., Senate Exec. Doc. no. 78; 12 vols. (Washington, D.C.: Beverley Tucker, Printer, 1856), 3: 47.

59. Baldwin Möllhausen, *Diary of A Journey from the Mississippi to the Coasts of the Pacific*, 2 vols. (London: Longman, Brown, Green, Longman, & Roberts, 1858), 2: 10.

60. Ibid., 2: 10.

61. Ibid.

62. Ibid., 2: 6.

63. Ibid., 2: 18.

64. Ibid., 2: 20.

65. Ibid., 2: 20–21.

66. Quoted in William H. Goetzman, *Army Exploration in the American West* (New Haven: Yale University Press, 1959), p. 289.

67. Charles F. Lummis, *Flowers of Our Lost Romance* (Boston: Houghton Mifflin, 1929), p. 29. Morris F. Taylor, *First Mail West* (Albuquerque: University of New Mexico Press, 1971), pp. 55–56.

68. Lewis Burt Lesley, ed., *Uncle Sam's Camels* (Cambridge, Mass.: Harvard University Press, 1929), p. 77.

69. Lesley, *Uncle Sam's Camels*, pp. 77–78.

70. Udell, *Journal*, p. 18.

71. Adolphus Wislizenus, M.D., *Memoir of a Tour to Northern Mexico*, reprint ed. (Glorieta, N.M.: Rio Grande Press, 1969), p. 34.

72. Bloom, "From Lewisburg to California in 1849," p. 146.

73. Cozzens, *The Marvelous County*, p. 275.

74. Emmett, *Fort Union*, p. 181.

75. See Howard Bryan's column, "Off the Beaten Path," *Albuquerque Tribune*, November 27, 1962, which provides a succinct history of the building and operation of the ferry.

76. *Santa Fe Weekly Post*, November 5, 1870.

77. Sister Blandina Segale, *At the End of the*

Santa Fe Trail (Milwaukee: Bruce Publishing Co., 1948), p. 128.

78. Beadle, The Undeveloped West, p. 491. See also, E. M. Clayton, "Ferry on the Rio Grande," New Mexico Magazine, 30 (June 1952): 21, 43.

79. The flagpole was later reduced in size while undergoing repairs. It was finally removed from the plaza in 1900. Browne, Trader on the Santa Fe Trail, p. 56. John A. Hill, born 1824 in Missouri, is said to have come to Albuquerque about 1850 as a paymaster with the United States Dragoons. Prior to the Civil War, he clerked in the store of Judge Samuel Winslow of Charleston, South Carolina, who was described by Udell, Journal, p. 18, as merchant, sutler for the army, postmaster [of Albuquerque], and judge of the court. Hill represented Bernalillo and Santa Ana counties in the territorial assembly in 1862, and the following year served as deputy United States marshal. The 1880 Albuquerque census listed him as a carpenter. Franz Huning's memoirs refer to Hill as the "chief engineer" at the raising of Carleton's flagpole. Browne, Trader on the Santa Fe Trail, p. 57. For a brief biographical statement, see, Dressen, "Early Settlers of Albuquerque," pt. 2.

80. Browne, Trader on the Santa Fe Trail, p. 56.

81. Aurora Hunt, Major General James Henry Carleton, 1814–1873, Western Frontier Dragoon (Glendale, Calif.: Arthur H. Clark Co., 1958), pp. 167, 241.

82. Bloom, "From Lewisburg to California in 1849," p. 146.

83. Cozzens, The Marvelous Country, p. 271.

84. Davis, El Gringo, p. 195.

85. Susan Dewitt, Historic Albuquerque Today (Albuquerque: Historical Landmarks Survey, 1978), p. 22.

CHAPTER 7:

The Tug of War

1. Seymour V. Connor and Jimmy M. Skaggs, Broadcloth and Britches, The Santa Fe Trade (College Station: Texas A&M University Press, 1977), p. 163.

2. Quoted in Horn, New Mexico's Troubled Years, p. 100.

3. Max L. Heyman, Jr., Prudent Soldier, A Biography of Major General E. R. S. Canby, 1817–

1873 (Glendale, Calif.: Arthur H. Clark Co., 1959), p. 179.

4. Martin Hardwick Hall, "An Appraisal of the 1862 New Mexico Campaign: A Confederate Officer's Letter to Nacogdoches," New Mexico Historical Review, 51 (1976): 332.

5. Calvin Horn and William S. Wallace, eds., Confederate Victories in the Southwest, From the Official Records (Albuquerque: Horn and Wallace, 1961), pp. 104–5.

6. Keleher, Turmoil in New Mexico, p. 189.

7. Cozzens, The Marvelous Country, p. 271.

8. Browne, Trader on the Santa Fe Trail, p. 22.

9. Horn and Wallace, Confederate Victories, p. 189.

10. Emmett, Fort Union, p. 243.

11. Connor and Skaggs, Broadcloth and Britches, p. 167.

12. Connelly's grandson told Calvin Horn that the governor distributed his cattle, merchandise, and equipment to the people of Peralta to prevent seizure by the Confederates. Horn, New Mexico's Troubled Years, p. 101. On the other hand, Governor Connelly himself wrote to Secretary of State Seward that, "My own house, 90 miles from Santa Fe, was despoiled of its entire contents, including a valuable stock of goods, together with everything in the way of subsistence." Horn and Wallace, Confederate Victories, p. 196.

13. Horn and Wallace, Confederate Victories, p. 186.

14. Erna Fergusson, "When the Tejanos Came," The Albuquerque Herald, March 12, 1923.

15. Ibid.

16. Emmett, Fort Union, p. 254; and Horn and Wallace, Confederate Victories, p. 107.

17. Horn and Wallace, Confederate Victories, p. 191.

18. Ibid., p. 171.

19. Theo Noel, A Campaign from Santa Fe to the Mississippi (Houston: Stagecoach Press, 1961), p. 33.

20. Hall, Sibley's New Mexico Campaign, p. 116.

21. Santa Fe Weekly Gazette, April 26 and May 3, 1862. Horn and Wallace, Confederate Victories, p. 171. Tipton was a business partner and son-in-law of Samuel B. Watrous, a Southern sympathizer, who operated a store at La Junta on the Santa Fe Trail near Fort Union.

22. Browne, Trader on the Santa Fe Trail, p. 69.

23. Keleher, Turmoil in New Mexico, p. 189.

24. Hunt, *Major General James Henry Carleton,* p. 268.

25. *Rio Abajo Weekly Press,* March 3, 1863.

26. John O. Baxter, "Salvador Armijo: Citizen of Albuquerque, 1823–1879," *New Mexico Historical Review,* 53 (1978): 225–27.

27. Horn and Wallace, *Confederate Victories,* p. 196. Pedro José Perea's sons were José Leandro, Juan, and Faunlade. A son of Juan, Francisco Perea became an active supporter of the Union and at his own expense recruited a volunteer batallion. He was commissioned a lieutenant-colonel and was in command of volunteers at Albuquerque when the federal garrison evacuated the town upon Sibley's approach. In 1863, Francisco was elected territorial delegate to Congress. He became a friend of Lincoln's and was in Ford's Theater when the president was assassinated. Twitchell, *Leading Facts,* 2: 399 n.

28. Browne, *Trader on the Santa Fe Trail,* p. 68.

29. Harvey Fergusson, *Home in the West,* p. 9. The Huning home, La Glorieta, still stands at 1801 Central Avenue, N.W. and is currently the Manzano Day School.

30. *Santa Fe Weekly Gazette,* April 26, 1862.

31. *Rio Abajo Weekly Press,* February 10, 1863.

32. Floyd S. Fierman, *Merchant-Bankers of Early Santa Fe, 1844–1893* (El Paso: Texas Western Press, 1964), pp. 12–15.

33. Horn and Wallace, *Confederate Victories,* p. 117. Since there was no press in Albuquerque, Sibley had to wait until his forces captured Santa Fe to have his proclamation printed. On March 23, it was run off on the press of the *Santa Fe Gazette.*

34. Ebenezer Hanna, "Journal, February 10 to March 27, 1862," Manuscript, University of Texas Library, Austin.

35. *Santa Fe Gazette,* May 17, 1862; and *Las Vegas Gazette,* September 15, 1867.

36. Canby's two chief scouts who kept him informed of the Confederate movements were Colonels Miguel Pino and Manuel Cháves. While at San Antonio, he was as yet unaware of how badly his foe had been crippled by the loss of supplies at Glorieta. He feared that after regrouping in Albuquerque the rebels might return to Santa Fe. See Marc Simmons, *The Little Lion of the Southwest* (Chicago: Swallow Press, 1973), pp. 186–87.

37. Noel, *A Campaign from Santa Fe,* p. 38.

38. One account claims that part of the army crossed on the ferry and afterward sank it. William Clarke Whitford *Colorado Volunteers in the Civil War* (Denver: State Historical Society of Colorado, 1906), p. 132.

39. Keleher, *Turmoil in New Mexico,* p. 189. Another Confederate sympathizer, former territorial Surveyor General William Pelham, was arrested north of Albuquerque and jailed at Santa Fe. Emmett, *Fort Union,* p. 254.

40. Ovando J. Hollister, *Boldly They Rode, A History of the First Colorado Regiment of Volunteers* (Lakewood, Colo.: The Golden Press, 1949), p. 89. The author, who later saw Spruce Baird's house, mentions that it had an observatory on top. His is the only contemporary reference to such a feature.

41. Nolie Mumey, ed., *Bloody Trails Along the Rio Grande, The Dairy of Alonzo Ferdinand Ickis* (Denver: The Old West Publishing Company, 1958), p. 35.

42. Hollister, *Boldly They Rode,* p. 92; and Hall, *Sibley's New Mexico Campaign,* p. 180.

43. Hollister, *Boldly They Rode,* p. 95.

44. *Santa Fe Weekly Gazette,* May 3, 1862.

45. Hunt, *Major James Henry Carleton,* p. 243.

46. Ibid., p. 240.

47. Dreesen, "Early Settlers of Albuquerque," pt. 1, statement on Santiago Baca. Hunt, *Major James Henry Carleton,* p. 241.

48. Edward D. Tittmann, "The Exploitation of Treason," *New Mexico Historical Review,* 4 (1929): 133.

49. *Rio Abajo Weekly Press,* March 3, 1863.

50. Tittmann,"The Exploitation of Treason," p. 140.

51. Ibid., p. 138.

52. Browne, *Trader on the Santa Fe Trail,* p. 70.

53. Ibid.

54. Larry D. Ball, *The United States Marshals of New Mexico and Arizona Territories, 1846–1912* (Albuquerque: University of New Mexico Press, 1978), pp. 38–39.

55. Hunt, *Major James Henry Carleton,* p. 268.

56. All quotes are from the *Rio Abajo Weekly Press,* March 3, 1863. Father Chávez joined Sibley's retreating army and fled to Texas with the Armijos.

57. On the later history of Baird's Ranch, purchased initially by Samuel Archer for $1,350, see Wharton, "Spruce McCoy Baird," pp. 310–14;

and Howard Bryan's column, "Off the Beaten Path," in the *Albuquerque Tribune,* August 15, 1957, and April 12, 1977. See also, "Baird's Ranch," in Records of the Court of Private Land Claims, Microfilm Roll 36, NMSRCA. Besides his farming activities at Ranchos, Julián Tenorio was earlier involved in the Chihuahua trade. Customs records for 1844 show that in that year he shipped eighteen bales of New Mexican products to Chihuahua, Durango, and the fair at San Juan de los Lagos. Mexican Archives of New Mexico, Hacienda Records, Guías, 1844, NMSRCA.

58. Hunt, *Major James Henry Carleton,* pp. 244–45.

59. Calvin Horn and William S. Wallace, eds., *Union Army Operations in the Southwest* (Albuquerque: Horn and Wallace, Publishers, 1961), p. 98.

60. Twitchell, *Leading Facts,* 2: 414 n.

61. Gerald Thompson, *The Army and the Navajo* (Tucson: University of Arizona Press, 1976), pp. 37, 73.

62. Keleher, *Turmoil in New Mexico,* p. 502; and Edith L. Watson, *Navajo Sacred Places* (Window Rock, Ariz.: Navajo Tribal Museum, 1964), p. 7.

63. Keleher, *Turmoil in New Mexico,* p. 467; and Frank D. Reeve, "The Federal Indian Policy in New Mexico, The Bosque Redondo," *New Mexico Historical Review,* 13 (1938): 35.

64. *Albuquerque Journal,* June 30 and July 2, 1968.

65. Keleher, *Turmoil in New Mexico,* p. 383.

66. *Rio Abajo Weekly Press,* March 3, 1863. The remaining aldermen were W. H. Henrie, Tomás Gonzáles, Manuel García, and Moritz (or Morris) Miller.

67. Full text of the ordinances can be found in the *Rio Abajo Weekly Press,* May 5 and 12, 1863. They have also been published separately as, *Town Ordinances of Albuquerque, New Mexico, 1863* (Albuquerque: Vinegar Tom Press, 1970).

68. *Rio Abajo Weekly Press,* April 14, 1863.

69. Quoted in Stratton, *The Territorial Press,* p. 5.

70. Keleher, *Turmoil in New Mexico,* p. 388.

71. Frank D. Reeve, "Albert Franklin Banta: Arizona Pioneer," *New Mexico Historical Review,* 27 (1952): 97. Stratton, *The Territorial Press,* p. 17.

72. Grove et al., *New Mexico Newspapers,* p. 65. Stratton, *The Territorial Press,* p. 206.

73. Browne, *Trader on the Santa Fe Trail,* p. 72.

74. Anna Nolan Clark, "Pioneer of Progress," *New Mexico Magazine,* 15 (January 1937): 46. *Albuquerque Journal,* October 12, 1963.

75. Information available from the Albuquerque Historical Society.

76. Browne, *Trader on the Santa Fe Trail,* p. 102.

CHAPTER 8:

"Clarion Notes of Progress"

1. Beadle, *The Undeveloped West,* p. 488.

2. Ibid., pp. 489–90.

3. Alvin R. Sunseri, *Seeds of Discord, New Mexico in the Aftermath of the American Conquest, 1846–1861* (Chicago: Nelson-Hall, 1979), p. 86.

4. Horn, *New Mexico's Troubled Years,* p. 143.

5. Ibid.

6. Beadle, *The Undeveloped West,* p. 489.

7. Joseph W. Snell, ed., "By Wagon from Kansas to Arizona in 1875—The Travel Diary of Lydia E. English," *Kansas Historical Quarterly,* 36 (1970): 380.

8. Joe Wasson, "The Southwest in 1880," *New Mexico Historical Review,* 5 (1930): 273–74.

9. Howard Bryan, "Off the Beaten Path," *Albuquerque Tribune,* November 22, 1962. *Albuquerque Review,* August 29, 1879. While Brown occupied The Fort, it was his duty each Fourth of July to raise the flag and fire a cannon that served as an ornament for the plaza. Interview with Mrs. Clara Fergusson, WPA files, Bernalillo County, NMSRCA. William Brown was born in Pennsylvania in 1832. He married a native Albuquerque girl by whom he had five children. Apparently sometime in the late 1880s or early 1890s, he vacated The Fort and opened a drugstore on the south side of the plaza. Physically, he is described as being very tall and fat. See Dressen, "Early Settlers of Albuquerque," pt. 1.

10. Howard Bryan, "From Wagon Train to Railroad," *Enchantorama, 250th Anniversary of Albuquerque* (Albuquerque: 250th Anniversary Inc., 1956), p. 43. Of the arrival of the telegraph, Victor Westphall states: "On February 12, 1876, after many vexatious delays, the line was completed to the newly selected office in Major Werner's hotel. A drizzling rain, accompanied by cold winds, somewhat dampened the ardor of the people and prevented the whole town from turning out en masse; however, even with the inclement

weather, a respectable showing was made at the reception, held at five o'clock. One hour later the first message was sent to Santa Fe and finally telegraphic communication was established with the rest of the world." "History of Albuquerque, 1870–1880," (M.A. thesis, University of New Mexico, 1935), p. 58.

11. *Albuquerque Republican Review,* June 14, 1873.

12. Erna Fergusson, *Albuquerque* (Albuquerque: Merle Armitage Editions, 1947), p. 40.

13. Nicolás Armijo, a successful freighter on the Santa Fe Trail, continued to run the old Exchange as a hotel. In 1880, his establishment and Post's new Exchange offered the only lodgings in Albuquerque, Werner's Centennial having folded. Three years after Tom Post's death his building became the Sunnyside Inn, operated by Charles Böttger, whose residence at 110 San Felipe SW still stands. Later the Inn became the San Felipe Club. The historic landmark, which during Post's tenancy briefly housed such notables as General Phil Sheridan and Governor Lew Wallace, was demolished in 1960. The site of the building is now a parking lot between Central Avenue and the Old Town plaza. *Albuquerque Journal,* June 12, 1960. Westphall, "History of Albuquerque," pp. 60–61.

14. Westphall, "History of Albuquerque," p. 61. Dreesen, "Early Settlers of Albuquerque," pt. 4. In 1854, the territorial Legislature had sent a Joint Memorial to Congress seeking an appropriation of $40,000 to build two bridges across the Rio Grande, one at San Juan Pueblo and the second near the Albuquerque plaza. Its request, however, went unheeded. *Laws of the Territory of New Mexico, Passed by the Fourth Legislative Assembly* (Santa Fe: James L. Collins, Printer, 1854), p. 163.

15. Henry Allen Tice, *Early Railroad Days in New Mexico, 1880* (Santa Fe: Stagecoach Press, 1965), p. 29. The best river ford above Albuquerque was at Alameda, and below, at Isleta. The latter crossing was used by the A&P Railroad when it built a bridge in 1880 for its line leading west from Albuquerque. Toward the end of the century, Narciso Zamora maintained a ferry near Bernalillo. Post's pontoon bridge was gone at least by March 2, 1878, because on that date in the *Albuquerque Review,* he announced: "Freighters and travelers are hereby notified that I have built an excellent ferry boat at this place for the accommodation of the traveling public."

16. Terry Lehman, "Santa Fe and Albuquerque, 1870–1900: Contrast and Conflict in the Development of Two Southwestern Towns" (Ph.D. diss., Indiana University, 1974), p. 74.

17. Westphall, "History of Albuquerque," pp. 25–28. In 1876, McGuinness switched his membership from the Republican to the Democratic party. At the same time, he dropped the word Republican from the masthead of his paper so that it became simply the *Albuquerque Review.* From the house on San Felipe Street, McGuinness later moved his office to the first courthouse so that he could be in closer touch with political and judicial affairs. His residence at 201 Romero, although surviving, has been much remodeled. Tom Vinegar, *A Walk Around Old Town* (Albuquerque: Vinegar Tom Press, 1970), pp. 17, 22.

18. Lehman, "Santa Fe and Albuquerque," p. 127. C. S. Peterson, comp., *Representative New Mexicans, 1912* (Denver: C. S. Peterson, 1912), p. 286. Because of their previous positions in Arkansas and Kansas respectively, Hazeldine was commonly addressed as "Judge", and Stover as "Governor." On Stover's arrival in Albuquerque by stagecoach, see, *Albuquerque Herald,* December 26, 1922.

J. Manuel Espinosa, "Account of the First Jesuit Missionary Journey Across the Plains of Santa Fe," *Mid-America,* 20 (1938): 51–62. M. Lilliana Owens, *Jesuit Beginnings in New Mexico, 1867–1882* (El Paso: Revista Católica Press, 1950), pp. 50–52. As in Padre Gallegos's day, the rectory was privately owned by the priest. The Jesuits, upon taking over San Felipe Church, had to buy Father Truchard's house and lot for $3,600. He demanded that large figure as the sum needed to pay off his outstanding debts. Frederick G. Bohme, *A History of the Italians in New Mexico* (New York: Arno Press, 1975), p. 42.

20. Bohme, *A History of the Italians in New Mexico,* pp. 47, 56.

21. Ibid., pp. 61–63; and Albuquerque *Republican Review,* May 30, 1874.

22. James F. Meline, *Two Thousand Miles on Horseback; A Summer Tour to the Plains, the Rocky Mountains, and New Mexico* (New York: Catholic Publishing Co., 1873), p. 125.

23. Chávez, *From the Beginning,* p. 9. Dewitt, *Historic Albuquerque Today,* p. 28. Another change wrought by the Jesuits was the transfer of the San Felipe cemetery from a swampy area behind the church to the heights east of town. The first burial

in the new Santa Barbara Cemetery occurred on February 12, 1875. In later years, Anglos were "segregated" in one section called Mount Calvary, the name by which the entire cemetery is known today. Bohme, *A History of the Italians in New Mexico,* pp. 47–48.

24. Browne, *Trader on the Santa Fe Trail,* p. 102. Westphall, "History of Albuquerque," p. 75.

25. Baxter, "Salvador Armijo," p. 229. Westphall, "History of Albuquerque," p. 47. Bancroft states that Bernalillo County in 1880 had 112 farms, with 3,821 acres of improved land, producing $94,730 annually. *History of Arizona and New Mexico,* p. 787.

26. Twitchell, *Leading Facts,* 2: 396.

27. Snyder, "Give us the Good Old Times."

28. Albuquerque *Republican Review,* August 2, 1873.

29. *Albuquerque Review,* March 2, 1878.

30. Quoted in Lehman, "Santa Fe and Albuquerque," p. 96.

31. The entire episode is described in detail by Lehman, "Santa Fe and Albuquerque," pp. 91–96.

32. Typescript of an interview with José Librado Gurulé (February 16, 1940), WPA Files, Bernalillo County, NMSRCA.

33. Baxter, "Salvador Armijo," p. 229.

34. Frank H. Moore, "Sojourns in Southern Colorado and in the Territory of New Mexico," *The Trail Guide,* The Kansas City Posse of Westerners, 7 (June 1963): 12.

35. Lucile Boyle, "The Economic History of Albuquerque, 1880–1893" (M.A. thesis, University of New Mexico, 1948), p. 65.

36. Quoted in Lehman, "Santa Fe and Albuquerque," p. 83.

37. Keith L. Bryant, Jr., *History of the Atchison, Topeka, and Santa Fe Railway* (New York: Macmillan, 1974), pp. 41–45. David F. Myrick, *New Mexico's Railroads, An Historical Survey* (Golden, Colorado: Colorado Railroad Museum, 1970), p. 29.

38. Milton W. Callon, *Las Vegas, New Mexico . . . . The Town That Wouldn't Gamble* (Las Vegas, N.M.: Daily Optic, 1962), p. 184–85.

39. Quoted in Lehman, "Santa Fe and Albuquerque," p. 110.

40. Lehman, "Santa Fe and Albuquerque," p. 115.

41. Negotiations between Santa Fe and the AT&SF are discussed in Lehman, "Santa Fe and

Albuquerque," pp. 114–24; and L. L. Waters, *Steel Trails to Santa Fe* (Lawrence: University of Kansas Press, 1950), pp. 54–57.

42. *Albuquerque Review,* April 5, 1879.

43. Nathan Bibo, "The 'Making' of Albuquerque," *The Santa Fe Magazine,* 17 (January 1923): 55.

44. Bibo, "The 'Making' of Albuquerque," pp. 55–56. John Sinclair, "The Place Where DeVargas Died," *New Mexico Magazine,* 54 (August 1976): 38.

45. Beadle, *The Undeveloped West,* p. 489.

46. Erna Fergusson, *Our Southwest* (New York: Alfred A. Knopf, 1940), p. 192.

47. *Albuquerque Herald,* May 27, 1923.

48. *Albuquerque Review,* January 7, 1880.

49. *Albuquerque Review,* April 5,1879.

50. *Albuquerque Review,* June 21, 1879.

51. *Albuquerque Review,* July 8, 1879.

52. Browne, *Trader on the Santa Fe Trail,* p. 102.

53. Westphall, "History of Albuquerque," pp. 82–83.

54. Victor Westphall, "Albuquerque in the 1870's," *New Mexico Historical Review,* 23 (1948): 262–64.

55. *Albuquerque Review,* April 3, 1880. The same paper, under date of April 24, notes that Stover & Co. and Franz Huning were the largest subscribers, at $50 each, to a list of persons contributing a total of $420.20 toward expenses of the railroad celebration.

56. *Albuquerque Review,* April 3, 1880.

57. Ibid.

58. *Albuquerque Review,* April 24, 1880.

59. Ibid.

60. Westphall, "Albuquerque in the 1870's," p. 266.

61. Westphall, "History of Albuquerque," p. 102. For added details on the railroad's welcome, see Julia M. Keleher, "Old Days in Old Albuquerque," *New Mexico Magazine,* 20 (January 1942): 54; and Howard Bryan, "Off the Beaten Path," *Albuquerque Tribune,* March 24, 1966.,

CHAPTER 9:

Growing Pains

1. Tice, *Early Railroad Days in New Mexico,* p. 28; and Howard Bryan, "Off the Beaten Path," *Albuquerque Tribune,* March 24, 1966.

2. Tice, *Early Railroad Days in New Mexico,* p. 28.

3. For background on Marmon, who later became deputy surveyor of the Territory, see Austin Nelson Leiby, "The Marmon Battalion and the Apache Campaign of 1885," in *The Changing Ways of Southwestern Indians,* ed. Albert H. Schroeder (Glorieta, N.M.: Rio Grande Press, 1973), pp. 211–27.

4. Eldred Harrington, *An Engineer Writes* (Albuquerque: Calvin Horn, Publisher, 1967), p. 204.

5. Harrington, *An Engineer Writes,* p. 204; and Alan J. Oppenheimer, *The Historical Background of Albuquerque, New Mexico* (Albuquerque: City Planning Dept., 1962), p. 33.

6. Lehman, "Santa Fe and Albuquerque," p. 148.

7. Ibid., pp. 148–49; and Dewitt, *Historic Albuquerque Today,* p. 89.

8. Amy Passmore Hurt, "Oldest House Was Migratory," typescript (October 17, 1931), Museum of New Mexico Library, Santa Fe.

9. Lehman, "Santa Fe and Albuquerque," p. 151.

10. Boyle, "The Economic History of Albuquerque," p. 3.

11. Erna Fergusson, *Albuquerque,* p. 41.

12. C. M. Chase, *New Mexico and Colorado in 1881,* reprint ed. (Fort Davis, Tex.: Frontier Book Co., 1968), pp. 142–43.

13. Bernice Ann Rebord, "A Social History of Albuquerque, 1880–1885" (M.A. thesis, University of New Mexico, 1947), p. 15; and Stanley, *The Duke City,* pp. 54, 161.

14. William A. Keleher, *Memoirs: 1892–1969* (Santa Fe: The Rydal Press, 1969) pp. 19–20. *Albuquerque Morning Journal,* June 29, 1884. Howard Bryan, "Off the Beaten Path," *Albuquerque Tribune,* May 2, 1963.

15. Skip Whitson, comp., *New Mexico 100 Years Ago* (Albuquerque: Sun Publishing Company, 1977), p. 15.

16. John Joseph Ellis, "Trolly Tracts," (unpublished paper, 1978, in possession of the author), pp. 44–45. Helen Haines, *History of New Mexico* (New York: n.p., 1891), p. 384.

17. *Albuquerque Journal,* October 8, 1882.

18. Harvey Fergusson, *Home in the West,* p. 81.

19. John A. Haney and Cirino G. Scavone, "Cars Stop Here, A Brief History of Street Railways in Tucson, Arizona," *The Smoke Signal* [Tuc-son Corral of the Westerners], 23 (spring 1971): 49.

20. Erna Fergusson, *Albuquerque,* p. 42. Snyder, "Give Us the Good Old Times," p. 2.

21. *Albuquerque Herald,* July 2, 1923.

22. Snyder, "Give Us the Good Old Times," p. 2.

23. Lehman, "Santa Fe and Albuquerque," pp. 178–79.

24. William Keleher, *Memoirs,* pp. 25–26. Julia M. Keleher, "Old Days in Old Albuquerque," p. 23. The name "Armijo" was adopted February 2, 1883, and was discontinued March 1886, when the name of the plaza was changed to Old Albuquerque. See Sheldon H. Dike, *The Territorial Post Offices of New Mexico* (Albuquerque: privately printed, 1958), pp. 4, 6.

25. Lehman, "Santa Fe and Albuquerque," p. 169.

26. Ibid., pp. 180–81.

27. *Albuquerque Morning Journal,* April 7, 1886.

28. Snyder, "Give Us the Good Old Times," p. 7. Lehman, "Santa Fe and Albuquerque," p. 182. Edward Medler came to town in 1880 and three years later formed a construction firm in partnership with Alexander McKay Whitcomb, a native of Canada. Their company was responsible for the construction of the Albuquerque Indian School, the San Felipe Hotel, and the old First National Bank. Medler moved to Los Angeles in 1901. Dreesen, "Early Settlers of Albuquerque," pt. 4.

29. Donald W. Whisenhunt, *New Mexico Courthouses* (El Paso: Texas Western Press, 1979), p. 9. The courthouse of 1886 served Bernalillo County for forty years, until 1926 when county offices were moved to new quarters on Tijeras Avenue. Thereafter, the old building housed San Felipe School, until 1959 when it was condemned and demolished.

30. Santa Fe *New Mexican,* April 20, 1888.

31. Twitchell, *Leading Facts,* II, 493. Victor Westphall, *Thomas Benton Catron and His Era* (Tucson: University of Arizona Press, 1973), pp. 193–94.

32. Erna Fergusson, *Albuquerque,* p. 19. Full details of the capital removal battle are provided by Lehman, "Santa Fe and Albuquerque," pp. 245–70. In 1898, upon the urging of Territorial delegate Harvey B. Fergusson, the United States Congress passed a bill to locate the capital permanently

at Santa Fe. Larson, *New Mexico's Quest for Statehood,* p. 193.

33. Carey McWilliams, *Southern California Country, An Island on the Land* (New York: Duell, Sloan & Pearce, 1946), p. 19.

34. Boyle, "The Economic History of Albuquerque," p. 15.

35. Lehman, "Santa Fe and Albuquerque," p. 157.

36. Gladys Neel, "History of Albuquerque" (M.A. thesis, University of New Mexico, 1928), p. 11. Albuquerque's incorporation followed upon passage of two territorial laws in 1884 spelling out powers of new town governments. Charles D. Biebel, "Cultural Change on the Southwest Frontier: Albuquerque Schooling, 1870–1895," *New Mexico Historical Review,* 55 (1980): 219.

37. Morris Taylor, *Trinidad, Colorado Territory* (Trinidad: Trinidad State Junior College, 1966), pp. 106, 114. After his term as mayor, Henry Jaffa left Albuquerque for a number of years. Returning in 1899, he established the Jaffa Grocery Company, according to Dreesen ("Early Settlers of Albuquerque," pt. 3), on Railroad Avenue between First and Second, later the site of the Albuquerque National Bank. A receipt from the firm dated November 1, 1901 (ten months after Jaffa's death, January 9), however, gives the location as 115 South Second. Misc. Letterhead and Cover File, Albuquerque, NMSRCA.

38. Municipal Records, City Clerk's Office, Albuquerque, Book I, passim.

39. Judge W. C. Heacock drew up the first ordinances. For many years, town council meetings were held in the office of the municipal clerk, Jesse Wheelock, located in the Cromwell Block, on Second and Gold. *Albuquerque Herald,* August 13, 1923.

40. Neel, "History of Albuquerque," p. 12; and Haines, *History of New Mexico,* p. 294.

41. Neel, "History of Albuquerque," p. 20.

42. As noted in Chapter 2, serious doubt exists that a legal Spanish grant was ever made to the villa of Albuquerque. A summary of the secondary documentation can be seen in *Albuquerque Town Grant, Its Character and History* (Washington, D.C.: W. H. Moore, Printer, 1881).

43. Metzgar, "The Atrisco Land Grant," pp. 276–80. Neel, "History of Albuquerque," pp. 23–25.

44. Amy Passmore Hurt, "Albuquerque—Old and New," *New Mexico Magazine,* 12 (March 1935):

39. F. A. Ehmann, "The Effect of the Railroad on New Mexico," *Password,* El Paso County Historical Society, 8 (1962): 56–57.

45. Roy A. Stamm, "Boardwalk Town," *New Mexico Magazine,* 34 (March 1956): 17.

46. *Albuquerque Review,* December 31, 1879.

47. Quoted in Lehman, "Santa Fe and Albuquerque," p. 144.

48. *Albuquerque Review,* April 5, 1879.

49. Lehman, "Santa Fe and Albuquerque," p. 139.

50. *Albuquerque Journal,* April 30, 1940.

51. Janet Kromer, "History of Newspapers in Albuquerque," typescript (March 1, 1938), WPA Files, Bernalillo County, NMSRCA, p. 3.

52. Quoted in the *Albuquerque Journal,* April 30, 1930.

53. Kromer, "History of Newspapers in Albuquerque," p. 7.

54. Stratton, *The Territorial Press of New Mexico,* p. 212.

55. Kromer, "History of Newspapers in Albuquerque," p. 8.

56. Westphall, *Thomas Benton Catron,* pp. 246, 254.

57. William Keleher, *Memoirs,* p. 29.

58. Westphall, *Thomas Benton Catron,* p. 269; and Kromer, "History of Newspapers in Albuquerque," p. 8.

59. Quoted in the *Albuquerque Journal,* April 30, 1940. For contemporary accounts of the Conklin murder, see, *Santa Fe New Mexican,* December 27, 1880; and *Albuquerque Journal,* December 30, 1880. Also see Julia Keleher, "Old Days in Old Albuquerque," p. 55.

60. William J. Parish, *The Charles Ilfeld Company* (Cambridge, Mass.: Harvard University Press, 1961), p. 241. Daniel T. Kelly, *The Buffalo Head, A Century of Mercantile Pioneering in the Southwest* (Santa Fe: Vergara Publishing Co., 1972), pp. 58–59. See also Beatrice Ilfeld Meyer, *Don Luis Ilfeld* (Albuquerque: The Albuquerque Historical Society, 1973).

61. *Albuquerque Review,* January 4, 1880. Also, Lehman, "Santa Fe and Albuquerque," p. 146–47.

62. *Albuquerque Review,* January 7, 1880.

63. *Albuquerque Daily Journal,* February 8, 1881; and Boyle, "The Economic History of Albuquerque," pp. 77–78.

64. Boyle, "The Economic History of Albuquerque," pp. 46, 54.

65. *Albuquerque Morning Journal*, March 25, 1881.

66. William Keleher, *Memoirs*, pp. 24–25.

67. Cited in Frank McNitt, *The Indian Traders*, p. 315.

68. Baxter, "Salvador Armijo," p. 320.

69. *Albuquerque Morning Journal*, February 4, 1883. Parish, *The Charles Ilfeld Company*, pp. 326–29, B. W. Kenney, "Early Days in Albuquerque," typescript (June 9, 1939), Museum of New Mexico Library, Santa Fe.

70. Parish, *The Charles Ilfeld Company*, p. 330.

71. Boyle, "The Economic History of Albuquerque," pp. 50–51. It should be noted that the history of the Albuquerque stockyards was brief. In 1881, local citizens objected to their presence in the midst of New Town, so they were dismantled and removed to San Marcial below Socorro. But some loading of cattle at Albuquerque continued even after that date. See Rebord, "A Social History of Albuquerque," p. 17.

72. Bryant, *History of the Atchison, Topeka and Santa Fe Railway*, pp. 162–63.

73. Dewitt, *Historic Albuquerque Today*, p. 31. Dreesen, "Early Settlers of Albuquerque," pt. 1. Blueher built a two-story mansion, which later formed part of the Hacienda Restaurant on the Old Town plaza.

74. Boyle, "The Economic History of Albuquerque," p. 39.

75. Paul A. F. Walter, *Banking in New Mexico Before the Railroads Came* (New York: The Newcomen Society, 1955), p. 7.

76. Quoted in Browne, *Trader on the Santa Fe Trail*, p. 123. On the history of early banking in Albuquerque, see William Keleher, *Memoirs*, pp. 193–94; *Albuquerque Herald*, December 31, 1922; and Ralph L. Edgel, *A Brief History of Banking in New Mexico, 1870–1959* (Albuquerque: Bureau of Business Research, University of New Mexico, 1962), pp. 6–7.

77. LaMoine Langston, *A History of Masonry in New Mexico, 1877–1977* (Roswell, New Mexico: Hall-Poorbaugh Press, 1977), p. 182.

78. *Albuquerque Herald*, April 9, 1923.

79. *Albuquerque Morning Democrat*, January 1, 1891.

80. The Commercial Club erected a three-story red sandstone structure at Fourth and Gold, at a cost of $75,000. Historian Ralph E. Twitchell referred to the Club in its heyday as "one of the best known community organizations in the West." *Leading Facts*, 3: 9.

81. Kenneth C. Balcomb, *A Boy's Albuquerque, 1898–1912* (Albuquerque: University of New Mexico Press, 1980). p. 30. Harvey Fergusson, *Rio Grande* (New York: Tudor Publishing Co., 1945), p. 274.

82. Chase, *New Mexico and Colorado in 1881*, p. 138.

83. See *Albuquerque Morning Journal*, April 13, 1881.

84. Myrick, *New Mexico's Railroads*, p. 34.

85. Ehmann, "The Effect of the Railroad on New Mexico," p. 57.

86. Myrick, *New Mexico's Railroads*, p. 28.

87. *Albuquerque Daily Journal*, October 14, 1880.

88. Bryant, *History of the Atchison, Topeka and Santa Fe Railway*, pp. 89–90.

89. Myrick, *New Mexico's Railroads*, p. 34.

90. *Albuquerque Morning Journal*, October 21, 1883.

91. Lehman, "Santa Fe and Albuquerque," p. 177.

92. Segale, *At the End of the Santa Fe Trail*, p. 183; and Boyle, "The Economic History of Albuquerque," p. 11.

93. Stanley, *The Duke City*, p. 48. Rebord, "A Social History of Albuquerque," p. 17.

94. William Keleher, *Memoirs*, p. 22.

95. That bridge had eighteen spans and cost $60,000. It remained in use until replaced in 1928 by the present concrete structure at the Central Avenue crossing. George Fitzpatrick and Harvey Caplin, *Albuquerque—100 Years in Pictures, 1875–1975* (Albuquerque: Calvin Horn, Publisher, 1975), p. 46.

96. Bernalillo County Industrial Schedule, Census Report, June 1, 1870, NMSRCA.

97. Browne, *Trader on the Santa Fe Trail*, p. 104.

98. Harvey Fergusson, *Home in the West*, p. 41.

99. Browne, *Trader on the Santa Fe Trail*, p. 131.

100. For a general description of the Castle Huning, see, Anna Nolan Clark, "Pioneer of Progress," pp. 48, 50; Janet Kromer, "Huning Castle," typescript (July 7, 1938), Museum of New Mexico Library, Santa Fe; Browne, *Trader on the Santa Fe Trail*, pp. 127–31; and *The New Mexico Sentinel*, November 6, 1938. Franz Huning named his house Castle Huning, but in later years it was generally referred to as the Huning Castle.

101. Harvey Fergusson, *Home in the West,* p. 42. See also, Clark, "Pioneer of Progress," p. 50.

102. Harvey Fergusson, *Home in the West,* p. 44.

103. *Bernalillo County Beacon,* July 10, 1942.

104. Clark,, "Pioneer of Progress," p. 50.

105. Barbara Young Simms, "Those Fabulous Fergussons," *El Palacio,* vol. 82 (June 1976), p. 44.

106. Browne, *Trader on the Santa Fe Trail,* pp. 121–22.

107. Harvey Fergusson, *Home in the West,* p. 61.

108. Simms, "Those Fabulous Fergussons," p. 44

109. Janet Smith, "Biography of Harvey B. Fergusson, Senior," typescript (October 5, 1936), Museum of New Mexico Library, Santa Fe, p. 2.

110. Harvey Fergusson, *Home in the West,* pp. 72–73.

111. Smith, "Biography of Harvey B. Fergusson, Senior," p. 2.

112. Larson, *New Mexico's Quest for Statehood,* p. 193.

113. *Ninth U.S. Census Report,* June 1, 1870 (Washington, D.C.: GPO, 1872), p. 204.

114. Bancroft, *History of Arizona and New Mexico,* pp. 788–89.

115. Twitchell, *Leading Facts,* 2: 515.

CHAPTER 10:

Desperadoes and Disasters

1. Otero, *My Life on the Frontier,* p. 181.

2. Joseph Schmedding, *Cowboy and Indian Trader* (Albuquerque: University of New Mexico Press, 1974), pp. 60–61.

3. Erna Fergusson, "When the White Elephant Was Young and Frisky," *Albuquerque Herald,* June 11, 1923.

4. Erna Fergusson, *Albuquerque,* p. 41.

5. Chase, *New Mexico and Colorado in 1881,* p. 141.

6. William Keleher, *Memoirs,* p. 54.

7. Janet Smith, "Interview with Mrs. William C. Heacock," typescript (July 20, 1936), Museum of New Mexico Library, Santa Fe, p. 2.

8. Moore, "Sojourns in Southern Colorado and in the Territory of New Mexico," p. 22; and George F. Fitzpatrick, "Those Old-Time Tales," *Albuquerque Magazine,* 3 (September 1978): 120. A different set of dates for the abolition of gambling is given by Bohme, *A History of the Italians in New Mexico,* p. 153.

9. Bohme, *A History of the Italians in New Mexico,* p. 153.

10. Browne, *Trader on the Santa Fe Trail,* p. 155.

11. Quoted in Howard Bryan, "Off the Beaten Path," *Albuquerque Tribune,* June 20, 1974.

12. Ibid.

13. *Albuquerque Daily Review,* February 28, 1882.

14. Howard Bryan, "Off the Beaten Path," *Albuquerque Tribune,* June 20, 1974.

15. Ball, *The United States Marshals,* p. 49.

16. *Albuquerque Herald,* August 13, 1923.

17. Andy Gregg, "The Sheriff They Hanged," *Impact* [*Albuquerque Journal Magazine*], December 18, 1979, p. 9.

18. The account presented here follows Gregg, "The Sheriff They Hanged," pp. 8–11; and Howard Bryan, "Off the Beaten Path," *Albuquerque Tribune,* January 15, 1959. The two sources disagree on some details.

19. Erna Fergusson, "The First Police Force," *Albuquerque Herald,* April 23, 1923; and Howard Bryan, "Off the Beaten Path," *Albuquerque Tribune,* November 20, 1961. Fergusson claims that both Ross and Johnson were captured by a posse and hanged in Old Town, while Bryan says that they made good their escape.

20. Lansing B. Bloom, ed., "Bourke on the Southwest," *New Mexico Historical Review,* 11 (1936): 93.

21. The full story of what happened at the Martínez Bar is provided in Kyle S. Crichton, *Law and Order, Ltd.* (Santa Fe: New Mexican Publishing Corporation, 1928), pp. 16–26.

22. Henry F. Hoyt, *A Frontier Doctor* (Boston: Houghton Mifflin Co., 1929), p. 171.

23. Erna Fergusson, *Albuquerque,* p. 40. As soon as Grant, who had returned East, learned that his presidency of the company had prompted wild speculation in its stock, he resigned and the price of shares immediately plummeted. Eventually this expensive enterprise was a complete failure, mainly because after the dam was completed a lengthy drought followed and no water was to be had. Hoyt, *A Frontier Doctor,* p. 148.

24. Charles F. Lummis, *A Tramp Across the Continent* (New York: Charles Scribner's Sons, 1892), p. 125.

25. *Albuquerque Journal*, February 1, 1881.

26. Santa Fe *New Mexican*, February 4, 1881.

27. In relating the Potter episode, I have generally followed the accounts given in the *Albuquerque Journal*, April 30, 1940; and Steve Peters, *Incident on the Red River and Other True Stories of New Mexico* (Santa Fe: privately printed, 1971), pp. 29–39. Unfortunately, these and other sources vary widely in some of the details. For example, Hoyt, *A Frontier Doctor*, p. 150, claims that Pantaleón Miera, not Marino Leyba, was the gang leader.

28. Harvey Fergusson, *Home in the West*, p. 40.

29. Quoted in Howard Bryan, "Off the Beaten Path," *Albuquerque Tribune*, December 14, 1972.

30. Snyder, "Give Us the Good Old Times," p. 6.

31. Wilson, *New Mexico 100 Years Ago*, p. 31.

32. *Daily New Mexican*, April 6, 1881.

33. *Albuquerque Journal*, July 28, 1881.

34. Rebord, "A Social History of Albuquerque," p. 38.

35. Neel, "History of Albuquerque," p. 16.

36. *Albuquerque Tribune*, July 1, 1935.

37. Neel, "History of Albuquerque," p. 28.

38. Roy A. Stamm, "The Albuquerque Story—Silk Hat Days," *New Mexico Magazine*, 34 (April 1956): 19.

39. *Albuquerque Morning Journal*, March 6, 1882.

40. Meyer, *Don Luis Ilfeld*, p. 10.

41. William Keleher, *Memoirs*, p. 21.

42. Quoted in William Keleher, *Memoirs*, p. 33. In 1900, the city introduced a hose wagon pulled by horses and also created a salaried fire department, thus doing away with the old volunteer companies.

43. Lange and Riley, *The Southwestern Journals of Adolph F. Bandelier*, 2: 331.

44. Wilson, *New Mexico 100 Years Ago*, p. 26.

45. *Santa Fe New Mexican*, May 13, 1884.

46. *Albuquerque Daily Democrat*, May 28 and June 8, 1883.

47. Rufus H. Carter, Jr., "A Historical Study of Floods Prior to 1892 in the Rio Grande Watershed, New Mexico," (M.S. thesis, University of New Mexico, 1953), p. 16.

48. *Albuquerque Morning Journal*, May 27, 1884.

49. *Albuquerque Morning Journal*, May 22, 1884.

50. Carter, "A Historical Study of Floods," pp. 19–20.

51. *Albuquerque Morning Journal*, May 31, 1884.

52. Quoted in *Albuquerque Morning Journal*, June 3, 1884.

53. Lange and Riley, *The Southwestern Journals of Adolph F. Bandelier*, 2: 332; and Carter, "A Historical Study of Floods," p. 19.

54. *Albuquerque Evening Democrat*, July 20, 1885.

55. *Albuquerque Morning Journal*, July 21, 1885.

56. *Albuquerque Evening Democrat*, June 10, 1884.

57. *Daily Citizen*, April 15, 1891.

58. Fitzpatrick, "Those Old Time Tales," p. 120; and Balcomb, *A Boy's Albuquerque*, p. 54.

59. Clark, "Albuquerque," p. 7.

CHAPTER 11

The Finer Things

1. *Albuquerque Tribune*, July 1, 1935.

2. *Albuquerque Herald*, February 26, 1923.

3. Frank D. Reeve, ed., "Notes and Documents," *New Mexico Historical Review*, 24 (1949): 68. See also, Margaret Connell Szasz, "Albuquerque Congregationalists and Southwestern Social Reform: 1900–1917," *New Mexico Historical Review*, 55 (1980): 231–32.

4. Reeve, "Notes and Documents," p. 68.

5. John W. Hood, "Methodism in Albuquerque, 1879–1939," (M.A. thesis: University of New Mexico, 1947), pp. 2–5. Hood asserts that the Methodist Church was the first built in New Albuquerque. But this contradicts statements in the *Albuquerque Herald*, February 26, 1923, and in Snyder, "Give Us the Good Old Times," p. 1, which confirm that the the Congregationalists were first. Snyder's sister was one of the three original members of Ashley's congregation.

6. William Keleher, *Memoirs*, p. 30.

7. Twitchell, *Leading Facts*, 2: 351–52; and James M. Stoney, *Lighting the Candle, The Episcopal Church on the Upper Rio Grande* (Santa Fe: Rydal Press, 1961), p. 38.

8. Korber's story is told by Royce Jane Balch, "Jacob Korber, Early Businessman of Albuquerque, New Mexico, 1881–1921," (M.B.A. thesis: University of New Mexico, 1955).

9. Hood, "Methodism in Albuquerque," p. 19.

10. Stanley, *The Duke City*, p. 143; and Norton B. Stern, ed., "First Synagogue at Albuquerque, 1900," *Western States Jewish Historical Quarterly*, 11 (October 1978): 46. According to investigation by Byron Johnson, history curator, Museum of

Albuquerque, the Temple Albert's name was selected in a lottery in which members of the congregation participated. Albert Grunsfeld won the lottery and so his given name went on the temple.

11. Horgan, *Lamy of Santa Fe*, p. 343.

12. Gasparri served briefly in 1872 as Bernalillo County superintendent of schools. Bohme, *A History of the Italians in New Mexico*, p. 54. In that year the legislature at Santa Fe passed a law placing public instruction in the hands of a territorial superintendent and county school suerintendents. Not until 1884 did it enact a measure providing for the formation of local school districts. See, Benjamín M. Read, *A History of Education in New Mexico* (Santa Fe: New Mexican Printing Co., 1911), p. 18. Also, B. W. Kenney, "Early Education in New Mexico," typescript (January 19, 1938), Museum of New Mexico Library, Santa Fe. Also, consult, E. R. Vollmar, S. J., "First Jesuit School in New Mexico," *New Mexico Historical Review*, 27 (1952): 296–99.

13. Lehman, "Santa Fe and Albuquerque," p. 80; and Boyle, "The Economic History of Albuquerque," p. 19.

14. Bohme, *A History of the Italians in New Mexico*, p. 53.

15. Browne, *Trader on the Santa Fe Trail*, p. 120.

16. Segale, *At the End of the Santa Fe Trail*, p. 188.

17. Ibid.

18. Announcement in the *Albuquerque Morning Journal*, September 3, 1882.

19. Bohme, *A History of the Italians in New Mexico*, p. 118; and, Helen Stanisfer Kavanaugh, "A History of Administration in the Albuquerque Public Schools," (M.A. thesis, University of New Mexico, 1950), p. 9.

20. Segale, *At the End of the Santa Fe Trail*, p. 234.

21. Ibid., p. 239.

22. French, Sister Florita, "History of St. Vincent's Academy," (M.A. thesis, University of New Mexico, 1942), passim. And, Louis Avant, "A History of Catholic Education in New Mexico," (M.A. thesis, University of New Mexico, 1940), p. 63.

23. Quoted in Owens, *Jesuit Beginnings in New Mexico*, p. 82.

24. Howard Bryan, "Off the Beaten Path," *Albuquerque Tribune*, May 10, 1979; and Elizabeth Strong Shamberger, "A Thirty Year Educational History of Albuquerque, New Mexico"(M.A. thesis, University of New Mexico, 1928), pp. 19–20. For detailed background on the Albuquerque Academy, see, Biebel, "Cultural Change on the Southwest Frontier," pp. 213–16.

25. E. R. Harrington, "History of the Albuquerque High School, 1879–1955," typescript (1956), Woodward Collection, NMSRCA, pp. 6–7. *Albuquerque Herald*, January 8, 1923. Kavanaugh, "A History of Administration," pp. 11–14. The city of Albuquerque later acquired the Academy property, razed Perkins Hall in 1924, and erected a new public library on the site.

26. Shamberger, "A Thirty Year Educational History," p. 6.

27. Lillie G. McKinney, "History of the Albuquerque Indian School," *New Mexico Historical Review*, 20 (1945): 111–12.

28. William G. Ritch, *Illustrated New Mexico, Historical and Industrial* (Santa Fe: Bureau of Immigration, 1885), p. 93.

29. McKinney, "History of the Albuquerque Indian School," p. 118.

30. In 1934, Menaul School became a coeducational senior high school. Initially limited to Hispano pupils, it now accepts any student who applies. See, Lois Edith Huebert, "A History of Presbyterian Church Schools in New Mexico" (M.S. thesis, University of New Mexico, 1964), p. 48. For a brief history of the Menaul family (originally spelled "'McNaul") see a letter in *New Mexico Magazine*, 46 (January 1968): 36. Also consult a story on the school's 90th anniversary reported in the *Albuquerque Journal*, October 31, 1971; and Lucias E. Buck, "An Inquiry into the Presbyterian Educational Missions in New Mexico," (M.A. thesis, University of Southern California, 1949).

31. Balcomb, *A Boy's Albuquerque*, p. 59. Kavanaugh, "A History of Administration," pp. 14–16.

32. Harrington, "History of the Albuquerque High School," pp. 11–13.

33. Kavanaugh, "A History of Administration," pp. 35–36. Albuquerque's best-known superintendent was John Milne, a native of Scotland who headed the school system for almost half a century, beginning about 1910. Milne Stadium was named in his honor. In 1893, the school board lost $18,000 when the First National Bank of Albuquerque closed. For a time, it could not pay local teachers. See, Boyle, "The Economic History of Albuquerque," p. 19.

34. A so-called University of New Mexico founded at Santa Fe in 1881 by Congregational minister Horatio O. Ladd and closed in 1893, had no connection with the university which was established in Albuquerque. See, Frank D. Reeve, "The Old University of New Mexico at Santa Fe," *New Mexico Historical Review*, 8 (1933): 201–10.

35. Dorothy Hughes, *Pueblo on the Mesa, The First Fifty Years at the University of New Mexico* (Albuquerque: University of New Mexico Press, 1939), pp. 13–15; and Frank D. Reeve, "History of the University of New Mexico," (M.A. thesis, University of New Mexico, 1928), pp. 2–3. *Santa Fe New Mexican*, Aug. 7, 1885.

36. J. Francisco Chaves, comp., *Compilation of the School Laws of the Territory of New Mexico* (Santa Fe: El Boletín Popular Printing Company, 1903), p. 47.

37. Ibid.

38. Ibid.

39. B. W. Kenney, "Sidelights on Events and People of Albuquerque in the Old Days," typscript (June 27, 1938), WPA, Bernalillo County file, NMSRCA, p. 2. Also, Reeve, "History of the University of New Mexico," p. 2. Bernard Rodey later represented New Mexico in Congress, served a federal judgeship in Puerto Rico, and became United States attorney for the Territory of Alaska. His son, Pearce C. Rodey, remained in Albuquerque as a prominent lawyer, while his daughter married Raymond B. Stamm, son of a postrailroad era pioneer. See, "Familiar Names in Albuquerque Fifty Years Ago," *Albuquerque Progress*, 2 (July 1935): 8.

40. John F. Kennedy, *Profiles in Courage* (New York: Pocket Books, Inc., 1961), p. 107.

41. Howard Roberts Lamar, *The Far Southwest, 1846–1912* (New Haven: Yale University Press, 1966), pp. 176–77.

42. Edward Bumgardner, *The Life of Edmund G. Ross* (Kansas City, Mo.: Fielding-Turner Press, 1949), pp. 100–102; 109–10. Ross is buried in Fairview Cemetery on South Yale Boulevard.

43. Hughes, *Pueblo on the Mesa*, p. 17; Reeve, "History of the University of New Mexico," p.8.

44. Hughes, *Pueblo on the Mesa*, p. 17.

45. Chaves, *Compilation of the School Laws*, p. 47–48.

46. Harrington, "History of Albuquerque High School," p. 10. The census of 1890 showed that one-third of New Mexico's 154,000 population was illiterate.

47. Hughes, *Pueblo on the Mesa*, pp. 23–25.

48. George Wharton James, *New Mexico, The Land of the Delight Makers* (Boston: The Page Company, 1920), p. 422.

49. Quoted in Hughes, *Pueblo on the Mesa*, p. 29.

50. Ibid.

51. Reeve, "History of the University of New Mexico," p. 44.

52. Hughes, *Pueblo on the Mesa*, p. 29.

53. *Albuquerque Evening Herald*, May 14, 1891.

54. *Santa Fe Daily New Mexican*, August 23, 1900; and Neel, "History of Albuquerque," pp. 51; 85–86.

55. William Keleher, *Memoirs*, p. 40.

56. *Albuquerque Herald*, January 29, 1923.

57. Howard Bryan, "Off the Beaten Path," *Albuquerque Tribune*, November 30, 1972.

58. *Laws of the Territory of New Mexico Passed by the Third Legislative Assembly*, act. no. 20.

59. *Albuquerque Herald*, September 10, 1923.

60. Balcomb, *A Boy's Albuquerque*, p. 71.

61. *Albuquerque Herald*, June 18, 1923. An Albuquerque chapter of the Sons of Temperance was chartered in 1885 with an enrollment of twenty young members. There is no evidence that the organization had any significant influence on the drinking habits of local citizens. A children's temperance order, the Band of Hope, was also chartered at this time. Miss Willard was a founder and president of the national WCTU. Visiting Albuquerque, she spoke to Presbyterian women and assisted them in organizing the first temperance union. Rebord, "A Social History of Albuquerque," p. 97.

62. *Albuquerque Herald*, March 5, 1923.

63. Stamm, "Silk Hat Days," p. 18; and Balcomb, *A Boy's Albuquerque*, pp. 71–72.

64. *Albuquerque Herald*, March 5, 1923.

65. Stamm, "Silk Hat Days," p. 19.

66. *Santa Fe New Mexican Daily*, July 6 and September 20, 1882; and February 23, 1883.

67. McNitt, *The Indian Traders*, p. 340.

68. Erna Fergusson, *Albuquerque*, pp. 69–70; and Stanley, *The Duke City*, p. 180.

69. *Albuquerque Journal*, February 19, 1974; and Howard Bryan, "Off the Beaten Path," *Albuquerque Tribune*, August 26, 1978.

70. *Santa Fe New Mexican Daily*, September 23, 1882.

71. Howard Bryan, "Off the Beaten Path," *Albuquerque Tribune*, September 18, 1978.

72. Stamm, "Silk Hat Days," pp. 21, 39; and *Albuquerque Journal,* February 19, 1974.

73. *Albuquerque Journal,* January 22, 1934; and Roy A. Stamm, "Pioneers in the Air," *New Mexico Magazine,* 24 (September 1946): 18.

74. Quoted in *Line Squalls,* monthly publication of Transcontinental & Western Air, Inc., 2 (August 1934): 2.

75. *Trenton* [New Jersey] *True American,* October 4, 1912.

76. Quoted in *Albuquerque Journal,* January 22, 1934. See also, *New Mexico State Tribune,* Albuquerque, October 14, 1931.

77. Stamm, "Pioneers in the Air," p. 43.

78. *Santa Fe New Mexican Daily,* September 23, 1887.

79. Dewitt, *Historic Albuquerque Today,* p. 65

CHAPTER 12:

Trumpeting the City

1. Max Frost and Paul A. F. Walter, eds., *The Land of Sunshine* (Santa Fe: New Mexico Bureau of Immigration, 1906), p. 193.

2. Charles Riatt, "Albuquerque—Past and Present," *Santa Fe Magazine,* 3 (May 1910): 631.

3. H. B. Hening and E. Dana Johnson, *Albuquerque* (Albuquerque: Press of the Albuquerque Morning Journal, 1908), no pagination.

4. Hening and Johnson, *Albuquerque.*

5. Miguel A. Otero, *Annual Reports of the Department of the Interior: Miscellaneous Reports, Governor of New Mexico,* 58th Cong., 2d sess., House of Representatives, Exec. Doc. no. 5 (Washington, D.C.: GPO 1903), p. 321.

6. *Las Vegas Optic,* March 30, 1908; and Hening and Dana, *Albuquerque.*

7. *Albuquerque Journal Democrat,* May 11, 1902. John Conron, "The Alvarado Hotel," *New Mexico Architecture,* 11 (November–December 1969): 20; and *Albuquerque Journal,* August 25, 1968.

8. D. H. Thomas, *The Southwestern Indian Detours* (Phoenix: Hunter Publishing Co., 1978), pp. 45–50.

9. *Albuquerque Morning Journal,* September 10, 1908.

10. Ibid., September 27, 1908.

11. Ibid., September 8, 1908.

12. Ibid., September 28, 1908.

13. Ibid., September 30, 1908.

14. Ibid., September 28, 1908.

15. Hening and Johnson, *Albuquerque*; Frost and Walter, *The Land of Sunshine,* p. 197; and Balcomb, *A Boy's Albuquerque,* p. 56.

16. Neel, "History of Albuquerque," p. 37. *Albuquerque Journal,* January 23, 1966.

17. Quoted in Ellis, "Trolley Tracts," p. 8.

18. *Albuquerque Journal,* January 23, 1966.

19. Ibid., July 5, 1962.

20. Neel, "History of Albuquerque," p. 73.

21. *Albuquerque Tribune,* August 24, 1951.

22. *Albuquerque Journal,* September 4, 1966.

23. Haines, *History of New Mexico,* p. 607.

24. Erna Fergusson, *Albuquerque,* p. 43.

25. Haines, *History of New Mexico,* p. 607. See also, Balcomb, *A Boy's Albuquerque,* p. 27; and *Albuquerque Tribune,* June 12, 1969.

26. Balcomb, *A Boy's Albuquerque,* pp. 33–34; and William Keleher, *Memoirs,* p. 48.

27. Balcomb, *A Boy's Albuquerque,* p. 34.

28. *Albuquerque Herald,* February 5, 1923.

29. Meyer, *Don Luis Ilfeld,* p. 13.

30. E. Dana Johnson, "New Mexico's First State Automobile," *New Mexico Historical Review,* 11 (1936): 1–4; and Charles D. Biebel, "Paul Horgan's Early Albuquerque: Notes on a Southwest City in Transition," *New Mexico Humanities Review,* 3 (Summer 1980): 44.

31. *Albuquerque Morning Journal,* September 8, 1908.

32. *Albuquerque Journal,* December 7, 1956.

33. Neel, "History of Albuquerque," pp. 39–41.

34. *Albuquerque Morning Journal,* September 8, 1908.

35. Quoted in Ball, *The United States Marshals,* pp. 197–98.

36. Balcomb, *A Boy's Albuquerque,* p. 94.

37. Practically nothing has been written on the early history of Barelas. On San José, see, Frank C. Moore, "San José, 1946: A Study in Urbanization," (M.A. thesis, University of New Mexico, 1947). For Martineztown and Santa Barbara, consult, Susan Dewitt, "A Conversation with Felipe M. García," *La Confluencia,* 2 (March 1978): 2–7; and *Sixty Years for the Greater Glory of God,* (Albuquerque: San Ignacio Parish Historic Committee, 1976). See also, Cathy Robbins, "Martineztown—Village in the City," *New Mexico Magazine,* 58 (October 1980): 74–78, 82–84. The history of the villages north of Old Town is sum-

marized by Dewitt, *Historic Albuquerque Today,* pp. 43–59.

38. Harvey Fergusson, *Rio Grande,* p. 282.

39. Gilberto Espinosa, "New Albuquerque," *El Independiente,* October 18, 1968.

40. Advertisement in the *Albuquerque Morning Journal,* August 3, 1905, quoted in Ellis, "Trolley Tracts," p. 17. See also, Sam Bass Warner, Jr., *Streetcar Suburbs, The Process of Growth in Boston, 1870–1900* (Cambridge, Mass.: Harvard University Press, 1978), p. 14.

41. Ellis, "Trolley Tracts," pp. 8–9.

42. Ibid., pp. 15–17. The area surrounding Luna Place is now termed the Fourth Ward Historic District.

43. T. M. Pearce, *Mary Hunter Austin* (New Haven: College and University Press, 1965), pp. 56–57.

44. Lewis Mumford, *The City in History,* (New York: Harcourt, Brace & World, 1961), p. 429.

45. *Albuquerque Herald,* July 16, 1923.

46. Rebord, "A Social History of Albuquerque," pp. 50–51.

47. Major Whiting, a native of Detroit, fought at the battles of Gettysburg and the Wilderness. After being mustered out of service in 1866, he came to New Mexico as correspondent for the *New York World.* He later moved to Albuquerque as clerk of the United States District Court. One of his interests was agriculture and he became involved in several experimental farming projects. Haines, *History of New Mexico,* pp. 531–32. The burial site of the cannon was apparently near the major's home, which was on the southwest corner of Rio Grande Boulevard, one block south of Perea Road. Aurora Hunt, *The Army of the Pacific* (Glendale, Calif.: Arthur H. Clark, 1951), p. 67.

48. Quoted in William Keleher, *Turmoil in New Mexico,* p. 208.

49. *Albuquerque Journal,* August 10, 1942.

50. Ibid., November 11, 1951. Some question remains as to the actual number of cannon buried and recovered. Most sources mention eight, but others refer to only six. If in fact, eight were found, then two of them are unaccounted for. Dewitt, *Historic Albuquerque Today,* p. 23, maintains there were originally eight guns, and states, "Two can be seen in Old Town Plaza, one is in Fort Union, and others have been dispersed to other states." The gun at Ft. Union, actually, was recently brought from the East. On April 27, 1963, Major Teel's son, James T. Teel, and other descendants partic-

ipated in a dedication ceremony at the unveiling of a monument on the plaza honoring Confederate war dead. *Albuquerque Tribune,* April 27, 1963.

51. Neel, "History of Albuquerque," p. 51.

52. *Albuquerque Morning Journal,* August 21, 1883.

53. Erna Fergusson, *Albuquerque,* p. 5.

54. James, *New Mexico,* p. 453.

55. Max Frost, *New Mexico* (official publication of the Bureau of Immigration; Santa Fe: New Mexican Printing Co., 1894), p. 279.

56. W. A. Gekler, "Climate and Tuberculosis," *New Mexico Magazine,* 15 (January 1937): 22–23.

57. R. W. Wiley, "The Heart of the Well Country," *Santa Fe Magazine,* 10 (March 1916): 54.

56. Wiley, "The Heart of the Well Country," pp. 53–54.

59. *Sunshine and Health in Albuquerque* (Albuquerque: Civic Council, 1932), p. 4.

60. Interview with John Ellis, January 3, 1979.

61. Death Certificates, 1911–17, vol. II, Bernalillo County Records, Albuquerque.

62. Schmedding, *Cowboy and Indian Trader,* p. 62.

63. Erna Fergusson, *Our Southwest,* p. 233.

64. Rebord, "A Social History of Albuquerque," p. 42; and *Albuquerque Morning Journal,* April 26 and May 18, 1882.

65. Stuart W. Adler, "Health Care," in *Bicentennial '76—Albuquerque Remembers* (Albuquerque: Modern Press, 1977), p. 67.

66. Billy M. Jones, *Health-Seekers in the Southwest, 1817–1900* (Norman: University of Oklahoma Press, 1967), p. 114.

67. Rosalie Doolittle, "Plant It, Water It, It Grows," in *Enchantorama,* p. 69.

68. Quoted in Balcomb, *A Boy's Albuquerque,* p. 61.

69. Quoted in Albert D. Richardson, *Beyond the Mississippi* (Hartford, Conn.: American Publishing Co., 1867), p. 253.

CHAPTER 13:

Politics and Prejudice Intrude

1. Sister Lucretia Pittman, S.C., "Solomon Luna, Sheepmaster and Politician of New Mexico," (M.A. thesis, St. Louis University, n.d.), p. 111.

2. *Santa Fe New Mexican,* August 30, 1912.

3. Undated clipping on Solomon Luna's death, Bergere Scrapbook, Coronado Room, University of New Mexico Library, Albuquerque.

4. Callary, "A Political Biography of Frank A. Hubbell," pp. 22–24.

5. Interview with John Ellis, January 3, 1979; and Irene Fisher, *Bathtub and Silver Bullet* (Placitas, N.M.: Tumbleweed Press, 1977), p. 54.

6. Callary, "A Political Biography of Frank A. Hubbell," p. 23.

7. Curt Moyer, "The Frank A. Hubbell Company, Sheep and Cattle," *New Mexico Historical Review*, 54 (1979): 72. Otero's action in removing Hubbell from office caused such an uproar in New Mexico's Republican party that President Theodore Roosevelt asked the governor to resign, which he did. Larson, *New Mexico's Quest for Statehood*, p. 233.

8. Kromer, "History of Newspapers in Albuquerque," p. 5.

9. Howard Bryan, "Off the Beaten Path," *Albuquerque Tribune*, May 5, 1966.

10. Quoted in *Albuquerque Journal*, March 9, 1952. On this date, the president's son, Senator Robert A. Taft, was in Albuquerque, pursuing his own, unsuccessful, campaign for the presidency.

11. Dorothy I. Cline, *Albuquerque and the City Manager Plan, 1917–1948* (Albuquerque: University of New Mexico Department of Government Publication, 1951), p. 6.

12. William Keleher, *Memoirs*, p. 126.

13. Cline, *Albuquerque and the City Manager Plan*, p. 7.

14. Hughes, *Pueblo on the Mesa*, pp. 32, 137–39. *Albuquerque Journal*, July 15, 1962.

15. *Santa Fe New Mexican*, April 18, 1918.

16. Lyle W. Dorsett, *The Queen City, A History of Denver* (Boulder, Colo.: Pruett Publishing Co., 1977), pp. 180–81.

17. Paul Horgan, *Mountain Standard Time* (New York: Farrar, Straus and Cudahy, 1962), p. 201.

18. *Albuquerque Journal*, July 15, 1962.

19. William Keleher, *Memoirs*, p. 198.

20. Oppenheimer, *The Historical Background of Albuquerque*, p. 42.

21. William Keleher, *Memoirs*, p. 155.

22. Robert Hoath LaFollette, *Eight Notches and Other Stories of New Mexico* (Albuquerque: Valliant Printing Co., 1950), p. 10.

23. Ralph H. Vigil, "Revolution and Confusion: The Peculiar Case of José Inés Salazar," *New Mexico Historical Review*, 52 (1978): 163; and Crichton, *Law and Order*, pp. 140–44.

24. *Santa Fe New Mexican*, April 12, 1915.

25. Ibid., December 20, 1915.

26. Meyer, *Don Luis Ilfeld*, p. 15.

27. William Keleher, *Memoirs*, p. 193. New investors reopened the First National on October 24, 1933.

28. Gerald D. Nash, *The American West in the Twentieth Century* (Englewood Cliffs: Prentice-Hall, Inc., 1973), p. 142.

29. Clinton P. Anderson and Milton Viorst, *Outsider in the Senate, Senator Clinton Anderson's Memoirs* (New York: World Publishing Co., 1970), pp. 28–29.

30. Mark Acuff, "Newspaper Preservation Act," *The New Mexico Independent*, January 25, 1980.

31. *Art and Artists in Albuquerque* (Albuquerque: First National Bank, n.d.), p. 3.

32. Dewitt, *Historic Albuquerque Today*, p. 78.

33. Kathryn Kennedy O'Connor, *Theater in the Cow Country* (Albuquerque: Little Theater, Inc., 1966), p. 16.

34. *Albuquerque Tribune*, April 3, 1976.

35. William Keleher, *Memoirs*, pp. 120–21.

36. *Albuquerque Tribune*, December 24, 1960.

37. Erna Fergusson, "The Tingleys of New Mexico," Unpublished manuscript, Inventory no. 194, Huning-Fergusson Papers, Coronado Room, University of New Mexico Library, Albuquerque, pp. 150, 189.

38. Erna Fergusson, "The Tingleys of New Mexico," p. 158.

39. Susan Ann Roberts, "The Political Trials of Carl C. Magee," *New Mexico Historical Review*, 50 (1975): 293.

40. Ibid., p. 298.

41. Kromer, "History of Newspapers in Albuquerque," p. 11.

42. *Albuquerque Herald*, June 15, 1926.

43. Erna Fergusson, "The Tingleys of New Mexico," p. 154; and *Albuquerque Journal*, June 16, 1926.

44. *Albuquerque Journal*, June 16, 1926.

45. Erna Fergusson, "The Tingleys of New Mexico," p. 160.

46. William O. Winter, *The Urban Polity* (New York: Dodd, Mead & Co., 1970), p. 92. See also, Lyle W. Dorsett, *Franklin D. Roosevelt and the City Bosses* (Port Washington, N.Y.: Kennikat Press, 1977).

47. William Keleher, *Memoirs*, p. 140.

48. Ernest W. Hall, "State University," *New Mexico Magazine*, 15 (January 1937): 30. See also, Byron A. Johnson, "Public Works Projects in Albuquerque, 1934–1942," Unpublished paper, 1980, on file at the Museum of Albuquerque.

49. *Albuquerque Tribune*, July 1, 1935.

50. *Albuquerque Journal*, April 3, 1976.

51. Fremont Kutnewsky, "Wings Over Albuquerque," *New Mexico Magazine*, 19 (January 1941): 13.

52. Oppenheimer, *The Historical Background of Albuquerque*, p. 49.

53. Barbara Bailey, "The VT Fuse," *New Mexico Lobo*, September 28, 1945.

54. James W. Kunetka, *City of Fire, Los Alamos and the Birth of the Atomic Age, 1943–1945* (Englewood Cliffs: Prentice-Hall, 1978), p. 43.

55. Lansing Lamont, *Day of Trinity* (New York: Atheneum, 1965), p. 53.

56. Ibid., p. 10.

57. Ibid., p. 154.

58. Ibid., pp. 240–41.

CHAPTER 14:

Reaching for the Future

1. Ernie Pyle, "Why Albuquerque," *New Mexico Magazine*, 20 (January 1942): 17, 58.

2. On the city's problems in obtaining the Ernie Pyle house, see, William Keleher, *Memoirs*, pp. 229–30.

3. George Johnson, "Uneasy in the Nuclear Outback," *Harper's Weekly*, 64 (December 29, 1975): 4.

4. Nash, *The American West in the Twentieth Century*, p. 219.

5. Erna Fergusson, *New Mexico* (New York: Alfred A. Knopf, 1955), pp. 277–78. Also, John Joseph Ellis, "Albuquerque's Black Entrepreneurs, 1880–1933," Unpublished paper, 1976, in possession of the author, pp. 39–40.

6. Erna Fergusson, *New Mexico*, p. 279.

7. Albert Rosenfeld, "New Mexico's Fading Color Line: Albuquerque Shows the Way," *American Unity*, 14 (March–April 1956): 16–17.

8. Tingley died at Bataan Memorial Methodist Hospital on December 24, 1960.

9. Neal R. Peirce, *The Mountain States of America* (New York: W. W. Norton, 1972), p. 264.

10. Quoted in V. B. Price, "City Review," *New Mexico Independent*, April 28, 1978.

11. Nash, *The American West in the Twentieth Century*.

12. Howard N. Rabinowitz, "Growth Trends in the Albuquerque SMSA, 1940–1978," *Journal of the West*, 18 (July 1979): 68.

13. Ibid., p. 65.

14. Ibid., p. 63.

15. See, Susan Dewitt, "Mixing Old and New," *New Mexico Independent*, October 14, 1977.

16. *Albuquerque Journal*, February 2, 1958.

17. Ibid., September 11, 1957.

18. Ibid., November 20, 1958.

19. Rabinowitz, "Growth Trends," p. 70.

20. Paul L. Hain, F. Chris Garcia, and Judd Conway, "From Council-Manager to Mayor-Council: The Case of Albuquerque," *Nation's Cities*, 13 (October 1975): 10.

21. V. B. Price, "City Review," *New Mexico Independent*, September 30, 1977.

22. Cathy Robbins, "El Jefe," *New Mexico Business Journal*, 3 (June 1979): 47.

23. Rabinowitz, "Growth Trends," p. 63.

24. Sherry Robinson, "Albuquerque: America's Energy Savior?" *New Mexico Business Journal*, 3 (June 1979): 24.

25. *Santa Fe New Mexican*, June 14, 1971.

Postscript

1. Fitzpatrick and Caplin, *Albuquerque*, p. 108. See also, *Albuquerque's 250th Anniversary, 1706–1956* (Albuquerque: Ward Anderson Printing Co., 1956).

2. *Albuquerque Tribune*, July 2, July 10, 1956.

3. V. B. Price, "A City of Babel," *Century*, 1, no. 4 (1980): 26.

4. Harvey Fergusson, *Modern Man* (New York: Alfred A. Knopf, 1936), p. 29.

5. Therese Griffiths, "Heroes Live Next Door," *New Mexico Magazine*, 57 (April 1979): 16.

6. William Buchanan, *A Shining Season* (New York: Coward, McCann & Geoghegan, Inc., 1978).

7. Letter of Mayor David Rusk, December 16, 1979, printed in "A Shining Season: World Premier Program," (Albuquerque: n.p., 1979), p. 4.

Bibliography

ARCHIVAL COLLECTIONS

Albuquerque City Clerk's Office:
Municipal Records
Bernalillo County Court House, Albuquerque:
Death Certificates, 1911–1917
Federal Archives and Records Center, Kansas City, Missouri:
United States Circuit Court Records
Museum of New Mexico [History] Library, Santa Fe:
WPA Files
Albuquerque Vertical File
New Mexico State Records Center and Archives [NMSRCA], Santa Fe:
Mexican Archives of New Mexico
Miscellaneous Letterhead and Cover File
Records of the Court of Private Land Claims
Records of the Surveyor General
Spanish Archives of New Mexico [SANM,]
WPA File (Bernalillo County)
Woodward Collection
University of New Mexico Library, Special Collections [SC, UNML], Albuquerque:
Archivo General de Indias, Guadalajara Section, Seville, Spain [AGI], photocopies
Archivo General de la Nación, Provincias Internas Section, Mexico City [AGN], photocopies
Elfego Baca Papers
Huning-Fergusson Papers
University of Texas Archives, Austin:
Civil War Records

UNPUBLISHED PAPERS AND
DOCUMENTS

Bergere Scrapbook, in Special Collections, University of New Mexico Library [SC, UNML].
Bernalillo County Industrial Schedule, Census Report, June 1, 1870, in NMSRCA.
Court Docket Book, Socorro, in NMSRCA.
Dreesen, Donald, "Early Settlers of Albuquerque," Typescript in five parts, not paginated, 1973, in SC, UNML.
Ellis, John Joseph, "Albuquerque's Black Entrepreneurs, 1880–1933," Unpublished paper, 1976, in possession of the author.
———. "Trolly Tracts," Unpublished paper, 1978, in possession of the author.
"Environmental Impact Statement: Tijeras Canyon Projects, Bernalillo County, New Mexico," Unpublished report prepared for the New Mexico Highway Department, Santa Fe, 1972.
Fergusson, Erna. "The Tingleys of New Mexico," Unpublished manuscript, Inventory no. 194, Huning-Fergusson Papers, SC, UNML.
"Final Environmental Statement: Sandia Mountain Land Use Plan," United States Department of Agriculture, 1975; copy on file, Center for Anthropological Studies, Albuquerque.
"A Guide to the Mammals of the Sandia Mountains," Mimeographed circular issued by Sandia Ranger District, Forest Service, United States Department of Agriculture, n.d.
Hanna, Ebenezer, "Journal, February 10 to March 27, 1862," Manuscript, University of Texas Library, Austin.

Harrington, E. R. "History of the Albuquerque High School, 1879–1955," Typescript, 1956, Woodward Collection, NMSRCA.

Hurt, Amy Passmore. "Oldest House Was Migratory," Typescript, October 17, 1931, Museum of New Mexico Library, Santa Fe.

Johnson, Byron A. "Public Works Projects in Albuquerque, 1934–1942," Unpublished paper, 1980, on file at the Musuem of Albuquerque.

Kenney, B. W., "Albuquerque," WPA File, p. 1, Bernalillo County Folder, NMSRCA.

———. "Early Days in Albuquerque," Typescript, June 9, 1939, Museum of New Mexico Library, Santa Fe.

———. "Early Education in New Mexico," Typescript, January 19, 1938, Museum of New Mexico Library, Santa Fe.

———. "Sidelights on Events and People of Albuquerque in the Old Days," Typescript, June 27, 1938, WPA File, Bernalillo County Folder, NMSRCA.

Kromer, Janet, "History of Newspapers in Albuquerque," Typescript, March 1, 1938, WPA File, Bernalillo County Folder, NMSRCA.

———. "Huning Castle," Typescript, July 7, 1938, Museum of New Mexico Library, Santa Fe.

"Rio Grande Valley State Park," Feasibility study prepared for the New Mexico State Park and Recreation Commission, Santa Fe, 1969.

Smith, Janet. "Biography of Harvey B. Fergusson, Senior," Typescript, October 5, 1936, Museum of New Mexico Library, Santa Fe.

———. "Interview with Mrs. William C. Heacock," Typescript, July 20, 1936, Museum of New Mexico Library, Santa Fe.

Snyder, Karl A. "Give Us the Good Old Days," Typescript, March 13, 1933, Woodward Collection, NMSRCA.

Ward, Albert E. "Archeological Investigations at San Miguel de Carnué: The First Field Sessions," Unpublished report, Center for Anthropological Studies, n.d., Albuquerque.

THESES AND DISSERTATIONS

Avant, Louis. "A History of Catholic Education in New Mexico." (M.A. thesis, University of New Mexico, 1940).

Balch, Royce Jane. "Jacob Korber, Early Businessman of Albuquerque, New Mexico, 1881–1921." (M.B.A. thesis, University of New Mexico, 1955).

Boyle, Lucile, "The Economic History of Albuquerque, 1880–1893." (M.A. thesis, University of New Mexico, 1948).

Buck, Lucias E. "An Inquiry into the Presbyterian Educational Missions in New Mexico." (M.A. thesis, University of Southern California, 1949).

Callary, Carol N. "A Political Biography of Frank A. Hubbell, 1862–1929." (M.A. thesis, University of New Mexico, 1967).

Carter, Rufus H., Jr. "A Historical Study of Floods Prior to 1892 in the Rio Grande Watershed, New Mexico." (M.A. thesis, University of New Mexico, 1953).

Casado, Ovidio. "Don Francisco Cuerbo y Valdés, Governor of New Mexico: 1705–1707." (M.A. thesis, University of New Mexico, 1965).

French, Sister Florita. "History of St. Vincent's Academy." (M.A. thesis, University of New Mexico, 1942).

Frisbie, Theodore R. "The Excavation and Interpretation of the Artificial Leg Basketmaker III–Pueblo I Sites Near Corrales, New Mexico." (M.A. thesis, University of New Mexico, 1967).

Hood, John W. "Methodism in Albuquerque, 1879–1939," (M.A. thesis, University of New Mexico, 1947).

Huebert, Lois Edith. "A History of Presbyterian Church Schools in New Mexico." (M.A. thesis, University of New Mexico, 1964).

Kavanaugh, Helen Stanisfer. "A History of Administration in the Albuquerque Public Schools." (M.A. thesis, University of New Mexico, 1950).

Lehman, Terry. "Santa Fe and Albuquerque, 1870–1900: Contrast and Conflict in the Development of Two Southwestern Towns." (Ph.D. diss., Indiana: Indiana University, 1974).

Minge, Ward Alan. "Frontier Problems in New Mexico Preceding the Mexican War, 1840–1846," (Ph.D. diss., University of New Mexico, 1965).

Mitchell, Eleanor B. "A Study of an Historical Trail System Through Tijeras Canyon East of Albuquerque in Bernalillo County, New Mexico." (M.A. thesis, University of New Mexico, 1977).

Moore, Frank C. "San José, 1946: A Study in

Urbanization." (M.A. thesis, University of New Mexico, 1947).

Neel, Gladys. "History of Albuquerque." (M.A. thesis, University of New Mexico, 1928).

Pittman, Sister Lucretia, S.C. "Solomon Luna, Sheepmaster and Politician of New Mexico." (M.A. thesis, St. Louis University, n.d.).

Rebord, Bernice Ann. "A Social History of Albuquerque, 1880–1885." (M.A. thesis, University of New Mexico, 1947).

Reeve, Frank D. "History of the University of New Mexico." (M.A. thesis, University of New Mexico, 1928).

Shamberger, Elizabeth Strong. "A Thirty Year Educational History of Albuquerque, New Mexico." (M.A. thesis, University of New Mexico, 1928).

Tyler, Daniel. "New Mexico in the 1820's: The First Administration of Manuel Armijo." (Ph.D. diss., University of New Mexico, 1970).

VanCleave, Marjorie. "Vegetative Changes in the Middle Rio Grande Conservancy District." (M.A. thesis, University of New Mexico, 1935).

Warner, Ted J. "The Career of Don Félix Martínez de Torrelaguna, Soldier, Presidio Commander, and Governor of New Mexico, 1693–1726." (Ph.D. diss., University of New Mexico, 1963).

Westphall, Victor. "History of Albuquerque, 1870–1880." (M.A. thesis, University of New Mexico, 1935).

NEWSPAPERS

Albuquerque Daily Democrat
Albuquerque Daily Journal
Albuquerque Daily Review
Albuquerque Evening Democrat
Albuquerque Evening Herald
Albuquerque Herald
Albuquerque Journal
Albuquerque Journal Democrat
Albuquerque Morning Democrat
Albuquerque Morning Journal
Albuquerque Republican Review
Albuquerque Review
Albuquerque Tribune
Amigo del País
Bernalillo County Beacon
Daily Citizen

Daily New Mexican
El Independiente
Las Vegas Gazette
Las Vegas Optic
New Mexico Independent
New Mexico Lobo
New Mexico Sentinel
New Mexico State Tribune
Rio Abajo Weekly Press
Santa Fe Gazette
Santa Fe New Mexican
Santa Fe Weekly Gazette
Santa Fe Weekly Post
Trenton True American [New Jersey]

ARTICLES

Acuff, Mark. "Newspaper Preservation Act," The New Mexico Independent, January 25, 1980.

Adler, Stuart W. "Health Care," in Bicentennial '76—Albuquerque Remembers (Albuquerque: Modern Press, 1977), pp. 65–68.

Agogino, George, and Frank C. Hibben. "Central New Mexico Paleo-Indian Cultures," American Antiquity, 23 (1958): 422–25.

Agogino, George, and Jim Hester. "The Santa Ana Preceramic Sites," El Palacio, 60 (1953): 131–40.

Allen, J. W., and C. H. McNutt. "A Pit House Site Near Santa Ana Pueblo, New Mexico," American Antiquity, 20 (1955): 241–55.

Allison, W. H. H. "Santa Fe As It Appeared During the Winter of the Years 1837 and 1838," Old Santa Fe, 2 (October 1914): 170–83.

Anderson, Roger Y. "Physiography, Climate and Vegetation of the Albuquerque Region," in Stuart N. Northrup, ed., Guidebook of the Albuquerque Country [GAC] (Albuquerque: New Mexico Geological Society, 1961), pp. 63–71.

Archibald, Robert. "Cañon de Carnué: Settlement of a Grant," New Mexico Historical Review, 51 (1976): 313–28.

"Area Prone to Earthquakes," University of New Mexico Alumnus, 48 (1976): 4.

Armijo, Isidro, trans. "Noticias of Juan Candelaria," New Mexico Historical Review, 4 (1929): 274–97.

Bailey, Barbara. "The VT Fuse," New Mexico Lobo, September 28, 1945.

Baxter, John O. "Salvador Armijo: Citizen of Albuquerque, 1823–1879," *New Mexico Historical Review,* 53 (1978: 219–37.

Bibo, Nathan. "The 'Making' of Albuquerque," *The Santa Fe Magazine,* 17 (January 1923): 55.

Biebel, Charles D. "Cultural Change on the Southwest Frontier: Albuquerque Schooling, 1870–1895," *New Mexico Historical Review,* 55 (1980): 209–30.

———. "Paul Horgan's Early Albuquerque: Notes on a Southwest City in Transition," *New Mexico Humanities Review,* 3 (Summer 1980): 35–45.

Bliss, Wesley L. "A Chronological Problem Presented by Sandia Cave, New Mexico," *American Antiquity,* 5 (1940): 200–201.

Bloom, Lansing B., ed. "Albuquerque and Galisteo, Certificate of Their Founding, 1706," *New Mexico Historical Review,* 10 (1935): 48–50.

———, ed. "Bourke on the Southwest," *New Mexico Historical Review,* 11 (1936): 77–122.

———, ed. "From Lewisburg to California in 1849," *New Mexico Historical Review,* 20 (1945): 144–80.

———. "New Mexico Under Mexican Administration, 1822–1846," *Old Santa Fe,* 1 (January 1914): 235–87.

Brugge, David M., ed. and trans. "Vizcarra's Navajo Campaign of 1823," *Arizona and the West,* 6 (1964): 223–44.

Bryan, Howard. "From Wagon Trail to Railroad," *Enchantorama, 250th Anniversary of Albuquerque* (Albuquerque: 250th Anniversary, Inc., 1956).

———. "Off the Beaten Path," *Albuquerque Tribune,* passim.

Campbell, John Martin, and Florence Hawley Ellis. "The Atrisco Sites: Cochise Manifestations in the Middle Rio Grande Valley," *American Antiquity,* 17 (1952): 211–21.

Castetter, Edward F. "The Vegetation of New Mexico," *New Mexico Quarterly,* 26 (1956): 257–88.

Chávez, Fray Angelico. "The Albuquerque Story," *New Mexico Magazine,* 34 (January 1956): 18–19, 50–51.

Clark, Anna Nolan. "Pioneer of Progress," *New Mexico Magazine,* 15 (January 1937): 20–21, 46, 48, 50, 52.

Clark, Neil M. "Albuquerque," in *Enchantorama,* pp. 5–14.

Clayton, E. M. "Ferry on the Rio Grande," *New Mexico Magazine,* 30 (June 1952): 21, 43.

Conron, John. "The Alvarado Hotel," *New Mexico Architecture,* 11 (November–December 1969): 2–23.

Culbert, James I. "Distribution of Spanish American Population in New Mexico," *Economic Geography,* 19 (April 1943): 171–76.

Dawson, Jerry, and W. James Judge. "Paleo-Indian Sites and Topography in the Middle Rio Grande Valley of New Mexico," *Plains Anthropologist,* 14 (1969): 149–63.

Dewitt, Susan. "A Conversation with Felipe M. García," *La Confluencia,* 2 (March 1978): 2–7.

———. "Mixing Old and New," *New Mexico Independent,* October 14, 1977.

Doolittle, Rosalie. "Plant It, Water It, It Grows," in *Enchantorama,* pp. 65–70.

Ehmann, F. A. "The Effect of the Railroad on New Mexico," *Password* [El Paso County Historical Society], 8 no. 2 (1962): 56–69.

Espinosa, Gilberto, "New Albuquerque," *El Independiente,* October 18, 1968.

Espinosa, J. Manuel. "Account of the First Jesuit Missionary Journey Across the Plains to Santa Fe," *Mid-America,* 20 (1938): 51–62.

"Familiar Names in Albuquerque Fifty Years Ago," *Albuquerque Progress,* 2 (July 1935): 2–3, 8.

Fergusson, Erna. "The First Police Force," *Albuquerque Herald,* April 23, 1923.

———. "When the Tejanos Came," *The Albuquerque Herald,* March 12, 1923.

———. "When the White Elephant Was Young and Frisky," *Albuquerque Herald,* June 11, 1923.

Fitzpatrick, George. "Those Old-Time Tales," *Albuquerque Magazine,* 3 (September 1978): 120.

Fitzsimmons, J. Paul. "Precambrian Rocks of the Albuquerque Country," in *GAC,* pp. 90–103.

Frazer, Robert W., "Purveyors of Flour to the Army: Department of New Mexico, 1849–1861," *New Mexico Historical Review,* 47 (1972): 213–38.

Gallagher, Peter. "The Founding of Albuquerque," *Rio Grande History,* 7 (1977): 2–5.

Gekler, W. A. "Climate and Tuberculosis," *New Mexico Magazine,* 15 (January 1937): 22–23, 40, 42.

Greenleaf, Richard E. "Atrisco and Las Ciruelas,

1722–1769," *New Mexico Historical Review,* 42 (1967): 5–25.

———. "The Founding of Albuquerque, 1706: An Historical-Legal Problem," *New Mexico Historical Review,* 39 (1964): 9–10.

Gregg, Andy. "The Sheriff They Hanged," *Impact* [*Albuquerque Journal Magazine*], December 18, 1979, pp 8–11.

Griffiths, Therese. "Heroes Live Next Door," *New Mexico Magazine,* 57 (April 1979): 16.

Hain, Paul L., F. Chris Garcia, and Judd Conway. "From Council-Manager to Mayor-Council: The Case of Albuquerque," *Nation's Cities,* 13 (October 1975): 10–12.

Hall, Ernest W. "State University," *New Mexico Magazine,* 15 (January 1937): 30–31, 54.

Hall, Martin Hardwick. "An Appraisal of the 1862 New Mexico Campaign: A Confederate Officer's Letter to Nacogdoches," *New Mexico Historical Review,* 51 (1976): 329–35.

Hallenbeck, Cleve. "Choose Your Climate," *New Mexico Magazine,* 22 (June 1944): 18, 35, 37.

Hanley, John A., and Cirino G. Scavone. "Cars Stop Here, A Brief History of Street Railways in Tucson, Arizona," *The Smoke Signal* [Tucson Corral of the Westerners], 23 (Spring 1971): 46–64.

Haynes, C. Vance, Jr. "Elephant Hunting in North America," in MacNeish, *Early Man in America,* pp. 44–52.

Hume, Bill. "Basketmaker Indian Site Discovered," *Albuquerque Journal,* October 26, 1969.

Hurt, Amy Passmore. "Albuquerque—Old and New," *New Mexico Magazine,* 12 (March 1935): 7–9, 38–40.

Irwin-Williams, Cynthia, and C. Vance Haynes. "Climatic Change and Early Population Dynamics in the Southwestern United States," *Quaternary Research,* 1 (1970): 59–71.

Ivey, R. DeWitt. "Ecological Notes on the Mammals of Bernalillo County, New Mexico," *Journal of Mammalogy,* 38 (1957): 490–502.

Jenkins, Myra Ellen. "The Baltasar Baca 'Grant': History of an Encroachment," *El Palacio,* 68 (Spring 1961): 47–105.

Joesting, H. R., et al. "The Rio Grande Trough Near Albuquerque, New Mexico," in *GAC,* pp. 148–50.

Johnson, E. Dana. "New Mexico's First State Automobile," *New Mexico Historical Review,* 11 (1936): 1–8.

Johnson, George. "Uneasy in the Nuclear Outback," *Harper's Weekly,* 64 (December 29, 1975): 4.

Judge, W. James, and Jerry Dawson. "Paleo-Indian Settlement Technology in New Mexico," *Science,* 176 (June 1972): 1210–16.

Keleher, Julia M. "Old Days in Old Albuquerque," *New Mexico Magazine,* 20 (January 1942): 22–23, 54–55.

Kelley, J. Charles, and Ellen Abbott Kelley. "An Alternative Hypothesis for the Explanation of Anasazi Culture History," in Theodore R. Frisbie, ed., *Collected Papers in Honor of Florence Hawley Ellis* (Papers of the Archeological Society of New Mexico, 2; Norman, Oklahoma: Hooper Publishing Co., 1975), pp. 178–223.

Kinnaird, Lawrence, and Lucia Kinnaird. "Secularization of Four New Mexican Missions," *New Mexico Historical Review,* 54 (1979): 35–41.

Kirchhoff, Paul. "Gatherers and Farmers in the Greater Southwest: A Problem in Classification," *American Anthropologist,* 56 (1954): 529–60.

Kutnewsky, Fremont. "Wings Over Albuquerque," *New Mexico Magazine,* 19 (January 1941): 13–17, 37–38.

Lange, Bob. "Bringing Back Bighorns," *New Mexico Wildlife,* 23 (1978): 2–5, 26–28.

Lecompte, Janet. "Manuel Armijo's Family History," *New Mexico Historical Review,* 48 (1973): 251–58.

Leiby, Austin Nelson. "The Marmon Battalion and the Apache Campaign of 1885," in Albert H. Schroeder, ed., *The Changing Ways of Southwestern Indians* (Glorieta, N.M.: Rio Grande Press, 1973), pp. 211–27.

Letter, *New Mexico Magazine,* 46 (January 1968): 36.

McKinney, Lillie G. "History of the Albuquerque Indian School," *New Mexico Historical Review,* 20 (1945): 109–38.

Mahr, Ed. "Lofty Sandias Protect City," *Albuquerque Journal,* March 3, 1968.

Metzgar, Joseph V. "The Atrisco Land Grant, 1692–1977," *New Mexico Historical Review,* 52 (1977): 269–96.

Moore, Frank H. "Sojourns in Southern Colorado and in the Territory of New Mexico," in *The Trail Guide* [The Kansas City Posse of the Westerners], 8 (June 1963): 1–32.

Moyer, Cut. "The Frank A. Hubbell Company, Sheep and Cattle," *New Mexico Historical Review*, 54 (1979): 64–72.

Northrop, Stuart A. "Earthquakes of Central New Mexico," in *GAC*, p. 151.

Pearce, Thomas M. "The Duke," *El Palacio*, 82 (June 1976): 36–41.

Price, V. B. "City Review," *New Mexico Independent*, September 30, 1977 and April 28, 1978.

———. "A City of Babel," *Century*, 1 (1980): 25–27.

Pyle, Ernie. "Why Albuquerque," *New Mexico Magazine*, 20 (January 1942): 16–17, 56, 58.

Rabinowitz, Howard N. "Growth Trends in the Albuquerque SMSA, 1940–1978," *Journal of the West*, 18 (July 1979): 62–74.

Ratkevich, Ronald P. "Native Elephants in New Mexico?" *New Mexico Independent*, April 15, 1977.

Reeve, Frank D. "Albert Franklin Banta: Arizona Pioneer," *New Mexico Historical Review*, 27 (1952): 81–106.

———. "The Federal Indian Policy in New Mexico, The Bosque Redondo," *New Mexico Historical Review*, 13 (1938): 14–62.

———. ed. "Notes and Documents," *New Mexico Historical Review*, 24 (1949): 66–67.

———. "The Old University of New Mexico at Santa Fe," *New Mexico Historical Review*, 8 (1933): 201–10.

Reiche, Perry. "Geology of the Manzanita and North Manzano Mountains, New Mexico," *Bulletin of the Geological Society of America*, 60 (1949): 1183–1212.

Reinhart, Theodore R. "The Alameda Phase: An Early Basketmaker III Culture in the Middle Rio Grande Valley, New Mexico," *Southwestern Lore*, 33 (1967): 24–32.

———. "The Rio Rancho Phase: A Preliminary Report on Early Basketmaker Culture in the Middle Rio Grande Valley, New Mexico," *American Antiquity*, 32 (1967): 458–70.

Riatt, Charles. "Albuquerque—Past and Present," *Santa Fe Magazine*, 3 (May 1910): 627–31.

Ríos-Bustamante, Antonio José. "New Mexico in the Eighteenth Century," *Aztlán*, 7 (1978): 357–90.

Robbins, Cathy. "El Jefe," *New Mexico Business Journal*, 3 (June 1979): 47, 50–51, 53.

———. "Martineztown—Village in the City," *New Mexico Magazine*, 58 (October 1980): 74–78, 82–84.

Roberts, Susan Ann. "The Political Trials of Carl C. Magee," *New Mexico Historical Review*, 50 (1975): 291–311.

Robinson, Sherry, "Albuquerque: America's Energy Savior?" *New Mexico Business Journal*, 3 (June 1979): 21–25.

Rosenfeld, Albert. "New Mexico's Fading Color Line: Albuquerque Shows the Way," *American Unity*, 14 (March–April 1956): 16–24.

Scholes, France V. "Civil Government and Society in New Mexico in the Seventeenth Century," *New Mexico Historical Review*, 10 (1935): 71–111.

———. "Documents for the History of the New Mexican Missions in the Seventeenth Century," *New Mexico Historical Review*, 4 (1929): 45–48.

Schroeder, Albert H. "Rio Grande Ethnohistory," in Alfonso Ortiz, ed., *New Perspectives on the Pueblos* (Albuquerque: University of New Mexico Press, 1972), pp. 41–70.

Simmons, Marc. "New Mexico's Smallpox Epidemic of 1780–1781," *New Mexico Historical Review*, 61 (1966): 319–26.

Simms, Barbara Young. "Those Fabulous Fergussons," *El Palacio*, 82 (June 1976): 42–47.

Sinclair, John. "Mountain and River: Turtle and Snake," *El Palacio*, 82 (Summer 1976): 4–8.

———. "The Place Where DeVargas Died," *New Mexico Magazine*, 54 (August 1976): 33–38, 43–45.

Skinner, S. Alan. "The Sedillo Site: A Pit House Village in Albuquerque," *El Palacio*, 72 (1965): 5–24.

Snell, Joseph W., ed. "By Wagon From Kansas to Arizona in 1875—The Travel Diary of Lydia E. English," *Kansas Historical Quarterly*, 36 (1970): 369–89.

Snow, David H. "The Identification of Puaray Pueblo," in Frisbie, *Collected Papers*, pp. 463–80.

———. "Santiago to Guache," in Albert H. Schroeder, ed., *Collected Papers in Honor of Marjorie Ferguson Lambert* (Albuquerque: Albuquerque Archeological Society Press, 1976), pp. 161–81.

Spell, Lota M., ed. and trans. "The Grant and First Survey of the City of San Antonio," *Southwestern Historical Quarterly*, 66 (1962): 73–89.

Staley, S. McClain. "The Westgate Site: Salvage Excavation in Bernalillo County, New Mexico," *Awanyu* (Archeological Society of New Mexico), 4, no. 3 (1976): 6–15.

Stamm, Roy A. "The Albuquerque Story—Silk Hat Days," *New Mexico Magazine,* 34 (April 1956): 18–19, 52–54.

———. "Boardwalk Town," *New Mexico Magazine,* 34 (March 1956): 16–17, 54–55.

———. "Pioneers in the Air,"*New Mexico Magazine,* 24 (September 1946): 18–19, 43.

Stern, Norton B., ed. "First Synagogue at Albuquerque, 1900," *Western States Jewish Historical Quarterly,* 11 (October 1978): 46–48.

"Structural Problems of the Rio Grande Trough in Albuquerque," in *GAC,* pp. 144–47.

Swadesh, Frances Leon. "Archeology, Ethnohistory and the First Plaza of Carnuel," *Ethnohistory,* 23 (1976): 31–44.

Szasz, Margaret Connell. "Albuquerque Congregationalists and Southwestern Social Reform: 1900–1917," *New Mexico Historical Review,* 55 (1980): 230–52.

Taylor, Morris F. "Spruce Baird: From Texas Agent to New Mexico Official, 1848–1860," *New Mexico Historical Review,* 53 (1978): 39–58.

Thomas, Alfred Barnaby. "Antonio de Bonilla and Spanish Plans for the Defense of New Mexico, 1772–1778," in *New Spain and the Anglo-American West: Contributions to Herbert Eugene Bolton,* 2 vols (Los Angeles: privately printed, 1932), 1: 183–209.

Threlkeld, James P. "Albuquerque From the Past," *New Mexico Quarterly,* 2 (1932): 283–92.

Tittmann, Edward D. "The Exploitation of Treason," *New Mexico Historical Review,* 4 (1929): 120–45.

Titus, Frank B., Jr. "Ground-water Geology of the Rio Grande Trough in North-central New Mexico, with Sections on the Jemez Caldera and Lucero Uplift," in *GAC,* pp. 186–92.

Tyler, Daniel. "Gringo Views of Governor Manuel Armijo," *New Mexico Historical Review,* 45 (1970): 23–46.

———. "The Mexican Teacher," *Red River Historical Review,* 1 (1974): 207–21.

Vigil, Ralph H. "Revolution and Confusion: The Peculiar Case of José Inés Salazar," *New Mexico Historical Review,* 52 (1978): 145–70.

Vollmar, E. R., S.J. "First Jesuit School in New Mexico," *New Mexico Historical Review,* 27 (1952): 296–99.

Ward, Albert E. "Archeology for Albuquerque," *El Palacio,* 82 (Summer 1976): 12–21.

Warner, Ted J. "Don Félix Martínez and the Santa Fe Presidio, 1693–1730," *New Mexico Historical Review,* 45 (1970): 304.

Wasson, Joe. "The Southwest in 1880," *New Mexico Historical Review,* 5 (1930): 263–87.

Waugh, Alfred S. "Desultory Wanderings in the Years 1845–46," *Bulletin of the Missouri Historical Society,* 7 (1951): 125–26.

West, Elizabeth Howard. "The Right of Asylum in New Mexico in the Seventeenth Century," *Hispanic American Historical Review,* 8 (1928): 357–91.

Westphall, Victor. "Albuquerque in the 1870's," *New Mexico Historical Review,* 23 (1948): 253–68.

Wharton, Clarence. "Spruce McCoy Baird," *New Mexico Historical Review,* 27 (1952): 300–314.

Wiley, R. W. "The Heart of the Well Country," *Santa Fe Magazine,* 10 (March 1916): 51–55.

BOOKS AND PAMPHLETS

Abel, Annie Heloise, comp. *The Official Correspondence of James S. Calhoun* (Washington, D.C.: GPO, 1915).

Abert, J. W. *Western America in 1846–1847* (San Francisco: John Howell Books, 1966).

Adams, Eleanor B., ed. and trans. *Bishop Tamaron's Visitation of New Mexico, 1760* (Albuquerque: University of New Mexico Press, 1954).

Adams, Eleanor B., and Fray Angelico Chávez, eds. and trans., *The Missions of New Mexico, 1776* (Albuquerque: University of New Mexico Press, 1956).

Agnew, S. C. *Garrisons of the Regular U.S. Army, New Mexico, 1846–1899* (Santa Fe: Press of the Territorian, 1971).

Albuquerque Town Grant, Its Character and History (Washington, D.C.: W. H. Moore, Printer, 1881).

Albuquerque's 250th Anniversary, 1706–1956 (Albuquerque: Ward Anderson Printing Co., 1956).

Anderson, Clinton P., and Milton Viorst. *Outsider in the Senate, Clinton Anderson's Memoirs* (New York: World Publishing Co., 1970).

Art and Artists in Albuquerque (Albuquerque: First National Bank, n.d.).

Ayer, Mrs. Edward E., trans. *The Memorial of Fray*

Alonso de Benavides, 1630 (Chicago: privately printed, 1916).

Bailey, Vernon. *Life Zones and Crop Zones of New Mexico* (United States Department of Agriculture, North American Fauna, no. 35; Washington, D.C.: GPO, 1913).

———. *Mammals of New Mexico* (United States Department of Agriculture, North American Fauna, no. 53; Washington, D.C.: GPO, 1931).

Balcomb, Kenneth C. *A Boy's Albuquerque, 1898–1912* (Albuquerque: University of New Mexico Press, 1980).

Ball, Larry D. *The United States Marshals of New Mexico and Arizona Territories, 1846–1912* (Albuquerque: University of New Mexico Press, 1978).

Bancroft, Hubert Howe. *History of Arizona and New Mexico, 1530–1888* (San Francisco: The History Company, 1889).

Barnhart, Clarence L. *The New Century Cyclopedia of Names,* 3 vols. (New York: Appleton-Century-Crofts, Inc., 1954).

Beadle, J. H. *The Undeveloped West; or, Five Years in the Territories* (Philadelphia: National Publishing Company, 1873).

Bender, Averam B. *The March of Empire* (Lawrence: University of Kansas Press, 1952).

Bicentennial '76—Albuquerque Remembers (Albuquerque: Modern Press, 1977).

Bieber, Ralph P., ed. *Marching with the Army of the West, 1846–1848* (Glendale, Calif.: Arthur H. Clark Company, 1936).

Binkley, William Campbell. *The Expansionist Movement in Texas, 1836–1850* (Berkeley: University of California Press, 1925).

Bloom, Lansing B. *Early Vaccination in New Mexico* (Santa Fe: Historical Society of New Mexico, 1924).

Bohme, Frederick G. *A History of the Italians in New Mexico* (New York: Arno Press, 1975).

Bolton, Herbert E. *Coronado, Knight of Pueblo and Plains* (Albuquerque: University of New Mexico Press, 1949).

Brayer, Herbert O. *Pueblo Indian Land Grants of the "Rio Abajo," New Mexico* (Albuquerque: University of New Mexico Press, 1938).

Browne, Lina Fergusson, ed. *Trader on the Santa Fe Trail, The Memoirs of Franz Huning* (Albuquerque: University of Albuquerque, 1973).

Bryan, Kirk. *Geology of the Vicinity of Albuquerque* (Geological Series, Bulletin no. 51; Albuquerque: University of New Mexico, 1909).

Bryant, Keith L., Jr. *History of the Atchison, Topeka and Santa Fe Railway* (New York: Macmillan, 1974).

Buchanan, William. *A Shining Season* (New York: Coward, McCann & Geoghegan, Inc., 1978).

Bumgardner, Edward. *The Life of Edmund G. Ross* (Kansas City, Missouri: Fielding-Turner Press, 1949).

Callon, Milton W. *Las Vegas, New Mexico . . . The Town That Wouldn't Gamble* (Las Vegas: Daily Optic, 1962).

Calvin, Ross, ed. *Lieutenant Emory Reports* (Albuquerque: University of New Mexico Press, 1968).

Carleton, James Henry. *Diary of An Excursion to the Ruins of Abó, Quarra and Gran Quivira in New Mexico in 1853* (Santa Fe: Stagecoach Press, 1965).

Carroll, H. Bailey, and J. Villasana Haggard, trans. *Three New Mexico Chronicles* (Albuquerque: Quivira Society, 1942).

Chaput, Donald, *Francois X. Aubry, Trader, Trailmaker and Voyageur in the Southwest, 1846–1854* (Glendale Calif.: Arthur H. Clark Company, 1975).

Chase, C. M. *New Mexico and Colorado in 1881,* reprint ed. (Fort Davis, Tex.: Frontier Book Company, 1968).

Chaves, J. Francisco, comp. *Compilation of the School Laws of the Territory of New Mexico* (Santa Fe: El Boletín Popular Printing Company, 1903).

Chávez, Fray Angelico. *Archives of the Archdiocese of Santa Fe, 1678–1900* (Washington, D.C.: Academy of American Franciscan History, 1957).

———. *From the Beginning, A Historical Survey of San Felipe Neri Church* (Albuquerque: privately printed, 1972).

———. *Origins of New Mexico Families* (Santa Fe: Historical Society of New Mexico, 1954).

Christiansen, Paige W., and Frank E. Kottlowski, eds. *Mosaic of New Mexico's Scenery, Rocks, and History* (Socorro: State Bureau of Mines and Mineral Resources, 1964).

Clark, Dwight L., ed. *The Original Journals of Henry Smith Turner* (Norman: University of Oklahoma Press, 1966).

Cline, Dorothy I. *Albuquerque and the City Manager Plan, 1917–1948* (Albuquerque: University of New Mexico Department of Government Publication, 1951).

Connelley, William Elsey. *Doniphan's Expedition* (Topeka, Kansas: privately printed, 1907).

Connor, Seymour V., and Jimmy M. Skaggs. *Broadcloth and Britches, The Santa Fe Trade* (College Station: Texas A&M University Press, 1977).

Cooke, Philip St. George. *The Conquest of New Mexico and California* (New York: G. P. Putnam's Sons, 1878).

Cooke, Ronald U., and Richard W. Reeves. *Arroyos and Environmental Change in the American South-West* (Oxford: Clarendon Press, 1976).

Coulson, John, ed. *The Saints, A Concise Biographical Dictionary* (New York: Hawthorn Books, 1958).

Cozzens, Samuel Woodworth. *The Marvelous Country, or Three Years in Arizona and New Mexico* (Boston: Lee and Shepard, 1876).

Crichton, Kyle S. *Law and Order, Ltd.* (Santa Fe: New Mexican Publishing Corporation, 1928).

Davis, William W. H. *El Gringo: Or New Mexico and Her People* (Santa Fe: The Rydal Press, 1938).

Dewitt, Susan. *Historic Albuquerque Today* (Albuquerque: Historic Landmarks Survey, 1978).

Dickey, Roland F. *New Mexico Village Arts* (Albuquerque: University of New Mexico Press, 1970).

Dike, Sheldon H. *The Territorial Post Offices of New Mexico* (Albuquerque: privately printed, 1958).

Dillon, Richard H., ed. *A Cannoneer in Navajo Country, Journal of Private Josiah M. Rice, 1851* (Denver: Old West Publishing Company, 1970).

Documentos para servir a la historia del Nuevo México, 1538–1778 (Madrid: Ediciones José Porrua Turanzas, 1962).

Dorsett, Lyle W. *Franklin D. Roosevelt and the City Bosses* (Port Washington, New York: Kennikat Press, 1977).

———. *The Queen City, A History of Denver* (Boulder, Colo.: Pruett Publishing Company, 1977).

Dozier, Edward P. *The Pueblo Indians of North America* (New York: Holt, Rinehart and Winston, Inc., 1970).

Drumm, Stella M., ed. *Down the Santa Fe Trail and Into Mexico, The Diary of Susan Shelby Magoffin, 1846–1847* (New Haven: Yale University Press, 1926).

Duarte Insúa, Lino. *Historia de Alburquerque* (Badajóz, Spain: Tip. de Antonio Arqueros, 1929).

Dutton, Bertha P. *Sun Father's Way, The Kiva Murals of Kuaua* (Albuquerque: University of New Mexico Press, 1963).

Edgel, Ralph L. *A Brief History of Banking in New Mexico, 1870–1959* (Albuquerque: Bureau of Business Research, University of New Mexico, 1962).

Edwards, Frank S. *A Campaign in New Mexico* (Philadelphia: Casey and Hart, 1847).

Elston, Wolfgang E. *Summary of the Mineral Resources of Bernalillo, Sandoval, and Santa Fe Counties, New Mexico* (Socorro: State Bureau of Mines and Mineral Resources, 1967).

Emmett, Chris. *Fort Union and the Winning of the Southwest* (Norman: University of Oklahoma Press, 1965).

Enchantorama (Albuquerque: 250th Anniversary, Inc., 1956).

Espinosa, J. Manuel, *Crusaders of the Rio Grande* (Chicago: Institute of Jesuit History, 1942).

———, ed. and trans. *First Expedition of Vargas into New Mexico, 1692* (Albuquerque: University of New Mexico Press, 1940).

Fergusson, Erna. *Albuquerque* (Albuquerque: Merle Armitage Editions, 1947).

———. *New Mexico* (New York: Alfred A. Knopf, 1955). . .

———. *Our Southwest* (New York: Alfred A. Knopf, 1940).

Fergusson, Harvey. *Home in the West* (New York: Duell, Sloan and Pearce, 1944).

———. *Modern Man* (New York: Alfred A. Knopf, 1936).

———. *Rio Grande* (New York: Tudor Publishing Company, 1945).

Fierman, Floyd S. *Merchant-Bankers of Early Santa Fe, 1844–1893* (El Paso: Texas Western Press, 1964).

Findley, James S., et al. *Mammals of New Mexico* (Albuquerque: University of New Mexico Press, 1975).

Fisher, Irene. *Bathtub and Silver Bullet* (Placitas, N.M.: Tumbleweed Press, 1977).

Fitzpatrick, George, and Harvey Caplin. *Albuquerque—100 Years in Pictures, 1875–1975* (Albuquerque: Calvin Horn Publisher, 1975).

Forbes, Jack D. *Apache, Navajo, and Spaniard* (Norman: University of Oklahoma Press, 1960).

Foreman, Grant, ed. *Marcy and the Gold Seekers* (Norman: University of Oklahoma Press, 1939).

Frazer, Robert W., ed. *Mansfield on the Condition of the Western Forts, 1853–1854* (Norman: University of Oklahoma Press, 1963).

———, ed. *New Mexico in 1850: A Military View* (Norman: University of Oklahoma Press, 1968).

Frisbie, Theodore R., ed. *Collected Papers in Honor of Florence Hawley Ellis* (Papers of the Archeological Society of New Mexico, 2; Norman, Oklahoma: Hooper Publishing Company, 1975).

Frost, Max. *New Mexico* (Official Publication of the Bureau of Immigration; Santa Fe: New Mexican Printing Company, 1894).

Frost, Max, and Paul A. F. Walter, eds. *The Land of Sunshine* (Santa Fe: New Mexico Bureau of Immigration, 1906).

Goetzman, William H. *Army Exploration in the American West* (New Haven: Yale University Press, 1959).

Griggs, Roy L. *Geology and Ground-water Resources of the Los Alamos Area, New Mexico* (Washington, D.C.: GPO, 1964).

Grove, Pearce S., Becky J. Barnett, and Sandra J. Hansen, eds. *New Mexico Newspapers: A Comprehensive Guide to Bibliographical Entries and Locations* (Albuquerque: University of New Mexico Press, 1975).

Gunnerson, Dolores A. *The Jicarilla Apaches: A Study in Survival* (DeKalb: Northern Illinois University Press, 1974).

Hackett, Charles Wilson, ed. *Historical Documents Relating to New Mexico, Nueva Vizcaya, and Approaches Thereto, to 1773*, 3 vols. (Washington, D.C.: Carnegie Institution, 1923–37).

———, ed. *Revolt of the Pueblo Indians of New Mexico and Otermin's Attempted Reconquest, 1680–1682*, 2 vols. (Albuquerque: University of New Mexico Press, 1942).

Hafen, LeRoy R., ed. *Ruxton of the Rockies* (Norman: University of Oklahoma Press, 1950).

Haines, Helen. *History of New Mexico* (New York: n.p., 1891).

Hall, Martin Hardwick. *Sibley's New Mexico Campaign* (Austin: University of Texas Press, 1960).

Hammond, George P., and Agapito Rey, eds. and trans. *Don Juan de Oñate, Colonizer of New*

Mexico, 1595–1628, 2 vols. (Albuquerque: University of New Mexico Press, 1953).

———, eds. and trans. *Narratives of the Coronado Expedition, 1540–1542* (Albuquerque: University of New Mexico Press, 1940).

———, eds. and trans. *The Rediscovery of New Mexico, 1580–1594* (Albuquerque: University of New Mexico Press, 1966).

Hammond, John Fox. *A Surgeon's Report on Socorro, N.M., 1852* (Santa Fe: Stagecoach Press, 1966).

Harrington, Eldred. *An Engineer Writes* (Albuquerque: Calvin Horn, Publisher, [1967]).

Hening, H. B., and E. Dana Johnson. *Albuquerque* (Albuquerque: Press of the Albuquerque Morning Journal, 1908).

Hertzog, Peter, *Old Town Albuquerque* (Santa Fe: The Press of the Territorian, 1964).

Hewett, Edgar L., and Wayne L. Mauzy. *Landmarks of New Mexico* (Albuquerque: University of New Mexico Press, 1953).

Heyman, Max L., Jr. *Prudent Soldier, A Biography of Major General E. R. S. Canby, 1817–1873* (Glendale, Calif.: Arthur H. Clark Company, 1959).

Hibben, Frank C. *Evidences of Early Occupation in Sandia Cave, New Mexico, and Other Sites in the Sandia-Manzano Region* (Smithsonian Miscellaneous Collections 99, No. 23; Washington, D.C. 1941).

———. *Kiva Arts of the Anasazi at Pottery Mound* (Las Vegas, Nev.: KC Publications, 1975).

———. *The Lost Americans* (New York: Thomas Y. Crowell Company, 1968).

Hodge, William H. *The Albuquerque Navajos* (Tucson: University of Arizona Press, 1969).

Hollister, Ovando J. *Boldly They Rode, A History of the First Colorado Regiment of Volunteers* (Lakewood, Colo.: The Golden Press, 1949).

Horgan, Paul. *Lamy of Santa Fe, His Life and Times* (New York: Farrar, Straus and Giroux, 1975).

———. *Mountain Standard Time* (New York: Farrar, Straus and Cudahy, 1962).

Horn, Calvin. *New Mexico's Troubled Years* (Albuquerque: Horn and Wallace, Publishers, 1963).

Horn, Calvin, and William S. Wallace, eds. *Confederate Victories in the Southwest, From the Official Records* (Albuquerque: Horn and Wallace, Publishers, 1961).

———, eds. *Union Army Operations in the Southwest*

(Albuquerque: Horn and Wallace, Publishers, 1961).

Howlett, W. J. *Life of the Right Reverend Joseph P. Machebeuf* (Pueblo, Colorado: privately printed, 1908).

Hoyt, Henry F. *A Frontier Doctor* (Boston: Houghton Mifflin Company, 1929).

Hughes, Dorothy. *Pueblo on the Mesa, The First Fifty Years at the University of New Mexico* (Albuquerque: University of New Mexico Press, 1939).

Humphrey, Robert R. *The Desert Grassland* (Tucson: University of Arizona Press, n.d.).

Hunt, Aurora. *The Army of the Pacific* (Glendale, Calif.: Arthur H. Clark Company, 1951).

————. *Major General James Henry Carleton, 1814–1873, Western Frontier Dragoon* (Glendale, Calif.: Arthur H. Clark Company, 1958).

Jackson, Donald, ed. *The Journals of Zebulon Montgomery Pike,* 2 vols. (Norman: University of Oklahoma Press, 1966).

James, George Wharton. *New Mexico, The Land of the Delight Makers* (Boston: The Page Company, 1920).

Johnson, Byron A. *Old Town, Albuquerque, New Mexico, A Guide to Its History and Architecture* (Albuquerque: The Albuquerque Museum, 1980).

Jones, Billy M. *Health-Seekers in the Southwest, 1817–1900* (Norman: University of Oklahoma Press, 1967).

Jones, Oakah L., Jr. *Pueblo Warriors and Spanish Conquest* (Norman: University of Oklahoma Press, 1966).

Judge, W. James. *PaleoIndian Occupation in the Central Rio Grande Valley in New Mexico* (Albuquerque: University of New Mexico Press, 1977).

Keleher, William A. *Memoirs: 1892–1969* (Santa Fe: The Rydal Press, 1969).

————. *Turmoil in New Mexico, 1846–1868* (Santa Fe: The Rydal Press, 1952).

Kelley, Vincent C. *Albuquerque: Its Mountains, Valley, Water, and Volanoes* (Socorro: State Bureau of Mines and Mineral Resources, 1969).

Kelley, Vincent C., et al. *Guidebook to Albuquerque Basin of the Rio Grande Rift, New Mexico* (Socorro: New Mexico Bureau of Mines and Mineral Resources, 1976).

Kelley, Vincent C., and Stuart N. Northrop. *Geology of Sandia Mountains and Vicinity, New Mex-*

ico (Socorro: State Bureau of Mines and Mineral Resources, 1975).

Kelly, Daniel T. *The Buffalo Head, A Century of Mercantile Pioneering in the Southwest* (Santa Fe: Vergara Publishing Company, 1972).

Kendall, George Wilkins. *Narrative of the Texan Santa Fe Expedition,* facs. ed., 2 vols. (Austin: The Steck Company, 1935).

Kennedy, John F. *Profiles in Courage* (New York: Pocket Books, Inc., 1961).

Kessell, John L. *Kiva, Cross, and Crown, The Pecos Indians and New Mexico, 1540–1840* (Washington, D.C.: National Park Service, 1979).

Kunetka, James W. *City of Fire, Los Alamos and the Birth of the Atomic Age, 1943–1945* (Englewood Cliffs, N.J.: Prentice-Hall, 1978).

LaFollette, Robert Hoath. *Eight Notches and Other Stories of New Mexico* (Albuquerque: Valliant Printing Company, 1950).

LaFora, Nicolás de. *Relación del viaje a los presidios internos* (México: Editorial Pedro Robredo, 1939).

Lamar, Howard Roberts. *The Far Southwest, 1846–1912* (New Haven, Yale University Press, 1966).

Lamb, Samuel H. *Woody Plants of New Mexico and Their Value to Wildlife* (Bulletin no. 14; Santa Fe: New Mexico Department of Game and Fish, 1971).

Lamont, Lansing. *Day of Trinity* (New York: Atheneum, 1965).

Lange, Charles H., and Carroll L. Riley, eds. *The Southwestern Journals of Adolph Bandelier, 1880–1888,* 3 vols. (Albuquerque: University of New Mexico Press, 1966–75).

Langston, La Moine. *A History of Masonry in New Mexico, 1877–1977* (Roswell, N.M.: Hall-Poorbaugh Press, 1977).

Larson, Robert W. *New Mexico's Quest for Statehood, 1846–1912* (Albuquerque: University of New Mexico Press, 1968).

Laws of the Territory of New Mexico, Passed by the Fourth Legislative Assembly (Santa Fe: James L. Collins, Printer, 1854).

Lesley, Lewis Burt, ed. *Uncle Sam's Camels* (Cambridge, Mass.: Harvard University Press, 1929).

Ligon, J. Stokley. *New Mexico Birds* (Albuquerque: University of New Mexico Press, 1961).

Lummis, Charles F. *Flowers of Our Lost Romance* (Boston: Houghton Mifflin, 1929).

———. *A Tramp Across the Continent* (New York: Charles Scribner's Sons, 1892).

MacNeish, Richard S., ed. *Early Man in America* (San Francisco: W. H. Freeman and Company, 1973).

McNitt, Frank. *The Indian Traders* (Norman: University of Oklahoma Press, 1962).

———, ed. *Navajo Expedition* (Norman: University of Oklahoma Press, 1964).

———. *Navajo Wars* (Albuquerque: University of New Mexico Press, 1972).

McWilliams, Carey. *Southern California Country, An Island on the Land* (New York: Duell, Sloan & Pearce, 1946).

Marcy, Randolph B. *The Prairie Traveler, A Handbook for Overland Expeditions* (New York: Harper and Brothers, 1859).

Matthiessen, Peter. *Wildlife in America* (New York: Viking Press, 1964).

Meline, James F. *Two Thousand Miles on Horseback; A Summer Tour to the Plains, the Rocky Mountains, and New Mexico* (New York: Catholic Publishing Company, 1873).

Meltzer, Milton. *Bound for the Rio Grande, The Mexican Struggle, 1845–1850* (New York: Alfred A. Knopf, 1974).

Mera, H. P. *Population Changes in the Rio Grande Glaze-Paint Area* (Santa Fe: Laboratory of Anthropology, 1940).

Meyer, Beatrice Ilfeld. *Don Luis Ilfeld* (Albuquerque: Albuquerque Historical Society, 1973).

Mineral and Water Resources of New Mexico (Report prepared by the United States Geological Survey; Washington, D.C.: GPO, 1965).

Möllhausen, Baldwin, *Diary of A Journey From the Mississippi to the Coasts of the Pacific,* 2 vols. (London: Longman, Brown, Green, Longman, & Roberts, 1858).

Moorhead, Max L. *New Mexico's Royal Road* (Norman: University of Oklahoma Press, 1958).

Mumey, Nolie, ed. *Bloody Trails Along the Rio Grande, The Diary of Alonzo Ferdinand Ickis* (Denver: The Old West Publishing Company, 1958).

Mumford, Lewis. *The City in History* (New York: Harcourt, Brace & World, 1961).

Myrick, David F. *New Mexico's Railroads, An Historical Survey* (Golden, Colo.: Colorado Railroad Museum, 1970).

Nash, Gerald D. *The American West in the Twentieth Century* (Englewood Cliffs, N.J.: Prentice-Hall, Inc., 1973).

New Spain and the Anglo-American West: Contributions to Herbert Eugene Bolton, 2 vols. (Los Angeles: privately printed, 1932).

Nineth U.S. Census Report, June 1, 1870 (Washington, D.C.: GPO, 1872).

Noel, Theo. *A Campaign from Santa Fe to the Mississippi* (Houston: Stagecoach Press, 1961).

Northrop, Stuart N., ed. *Guidebook of the Albuquerque Country* [GAC] (Albuquerque: New Mexico Geological Society, 1961).

O'Connor, Kathryn Kennedy. *Theater in the Cow Country* (Albuquerque: Little Theater, Inc., 1966).

Olin, George. *Mammals of the Southwest Mountains and Mesas* (Globe, Ariz.: Southwestern Monuments Association, 1961).

Olmstead, Virginia Langham, trans. *New Mexico Spanish and Mexican Colonial Censuses: 1790, 1823, 1845* (Albuquerque: New Mexico Genealogical Society, 1975).

Oppenheimer, Alan J. *The Historical Background of Albuquerque, New Mexico* (Albuquerque: City Planning Department, 1962).

Ortiz, Alfonso, ed. *New Perspectives on the Pueblos* (Albuquerque: University of New Mexico Press, 1972).

Otero, Miguel A. *Annual Reports of the Department of the Interior: Miscellaneous Reports, Governor of New Mexico,* 58th Cong., 2nd sess., House of Rep., Doc. no. 5 (Washington, D.C.: GPO, 1903).

———. *My Life on the Frontier, 1864–1882* (New York: The Press of the Pioneers, 1935).

Owens, M. Lilliana. *Jesuit Beginnings in New Mexico, 1867–1882* (El Paso: Revista Católica Press, 1950).

Parish, William J. *The Charles Ilfeld Company* (Cambridge, Mass.: Harvard University Press, 1961).

Pearce, Thomas M. *The Dukes of Alburquerque— Albuquerque, New Mexico—Old Spain and New Spain* (Albuquerque: Albuquerque Historical Society, 1977).

———. *Mary Hunter Austin* (New Haven: College and University Press, 1965).

———, ed. *New Mexico Place Names: A Geographical Dictionary* (Albuquerque: University of New Mexico Press, 1965).

Peirce, Neal R. *The Mountain States of America* (New York: W. W. Norton, 1972).

Peters, Steve. *Incident on the Red River and Other*

True Stories of New Mexico (Santa Fe: privately printed, 1971).

Peterson, C. S., comp. *Representative New Mexicans, 1912* (Denver: C. S. Peterson, 1912).

Pettitt, Roland A. *Exploring the Jemez Country* (Los Alamos: Pajarito Publications, 1975).

Porras Muñoz, Guillermo. *Iglesia y Estado en Nueva Vizcaya, 1562–1821* (Pamplona, Spain: University of Navarre, 1966).

Ratkevich, Ron, and Neal LaFon. *Field Guide to New Mexico Fossils* (Alamogordo, N.M.: Dinograph Southwest Inc., 1978).

Ratkevich, Ronald P., and William T. S. Pope. *Ice Age Animals of the Rio Grande Valley* (Albuquerque: Natural Sales Ltd., 1975).

Read, Benjamín M. *A History of Education in New Mexico* (Santa Fe: New Mexican Printing Company, 1911).

———. *Illustrated History of New Mexico* (Santa Fe: New Mexican Printing Company, 1912).

Recopilación de Leyes de los Reynos de las Indias facs. ed., 4 vols. (Madrid: Ediciones Cultura Hispánica, 1973).

Reeve, Frank D. *History of New Mexico,* 3 vols. (New York: Lewis Historical Publishing Company, 1961).

Reports of Expeditions and Surveys, 33rd Cong., 2d sess., Senate Exec. Doc. no. 78; 12 vols. (Washington, D.C.: Beverley Tucker, Printer, 1856).

Richardson, Albert D. *Beyond the Mississippi* (Hartford, Conn.: American Publishing Company, 1867).

Riddle, Kenyon. *Records and Maps of the Old Santa Fe Trail,* rev. ed. (Stuart, Fla.: Southeastern Printing Company, 1963).

Ritch, William G. *Illustrated New Mexico, Historical and Industrial* (Santa Fe: Bureau of Immigration, 1885).

Rivera, Manuel. *Los Gobernantes de México,* 2 vols. (México: Imp. de J. M. Aguilar Ortiz, 1872).

Robles, Vito Alessio, ed. *Diario y derrotero de Brigadier Pedro de Rivera* (México: Taller Autográfico, 1946).

Schmedding, Joseph. *Cowboy and Indian Trader* (Albuquerque: University of New Mexico Press, 1974).

Schroeder, Albert H., ed. *The Changing Ways of Southwestern Indians* (Glorieta, N.M.: Rio Grande Press, 1973).

———, ed. *Collected Papers in Honor of Marjorie*

Ferguson Lambert (Albuquerque: Albuquerque Archeological Society Press, 1976).

Segale, Sister Blandina. *At the End of the Santa Fe Trail* (Milwaukee: Bruce Publishing Company, 1948).

Simmons, Marc, ed. and trans. *Father Juan Agustín de Morfi's Account of Disorders in New Mexico, 1778* (Isleta, N.M.: Historical Society of New Mexico, 1977).

———. *The Little Lion of the Southwest* (Chicago: Swallow Press, 1973).

———. *Spanish Government in New Mexico* (Albuquerque: University of New Mexico Press, 1968).

———.*Taos to Tomé, True Tales of Hispanic New Mexico* (Albuquerque: Adobe Press, 1978).

Sinclair, John L. *The Story of the Pueblo of Kuaua* (Papers of the School of American Research, no. 45; Santa Fe, 1951).

Sitgreaves, Lorenzo, *Report of an Expedition Down the Zuni and Colorado Rivers,* 32nd Cong., 2d sess., Senate Exec. Doc. no. 59 (Washington, D.C.: Robert Armstrong, Public Printer, 1853).

Sixty Years for the Greater Glory of God (Albuquerque: San Ignacio Parish Historical Committee, 1976).

Stanley, F. *The Duke City, The Story of Albuquerque, New Mexico, 1706–1956* (Pampa, Tex.: privately printed, 1963).

———. *E. V. Sumner, Major-General, United States Army* (Borger, Tex.: Jim Hess Printers, 1969).

Stevens, Dominique E., and George A. Agogino. *Sandia Cave: A Study in Controversy* (Portales, N.M.: Eastern New Mexico University, Paleo-Indian Institute, 1975).

Stoney, James M. *Lighting the Candle, The Episcopal Church on the Upper Rio Grande* (Santa Fe: Rydal Press, 1961).

Stratton, Porter A. *The Territorial Press of New Mexico, 1834–1912* (Albuquerque: University of New Mexico Press, 1969).

Sunseri, Alvin R. *Seeds of Discord, New Mexico in the Aftermath of the American Conquest, 1846–1861* (Chicago: Nelson-Hall, 1979).

Sunshine and Health in Albuquerque (Albuquerque: Civic Council, 1932).

Taylor, Morris F. *First Mail West* (Albuquerque: University of New Mexico Press, 1971).

———. *Trinidad, Colorado Territory* (Trinidad, Colo.: Trinidad State Junior College, 1966).

Thomas, Alfred Barnaby, ed. and trans. *Forgotten*

Frontiers, A Study of the Spanish Indian Policy of Don Juan Bautista de Anza, 1777–1787 (Norman: University of Oklahoma Press, 1932).

————. *The Plains Indians and New Mexico, 1751–1778* (Albuquerque: University of New Mexico Press, 1940).

Thomas, D. H. *The Southwestern Indian Detours* (Phoenix: Hunter Publishing Company, 1978).

Thompson, Gerald. *The Army and the Navajo* (Tucson: University of Arizona Press, 1976).

Tice, Henry Allen. *Early Railroad Days in New Mexico, 1880* (Santa Fe: Stagecoach Press, 1965).

Town Ordinances of Albuquerque, New Mexico, 1863 (Albuquerque: Vinegar Tom Press, 1970).

Tuan, Yi-Fu, Cyril E. Everard, and Jerold G. Widdison. *The Climate of New Mexico* (Santa Fe: State Planning Office, 1969).

Twitchell, Ralph Emerson, *The History of the Military Occupation of the Territory of New Mexico from 1846 to 1851, by the Government of the United States* (Denver: Smith-Brooks Company, 1909).

————. *The Leading Facts of New Mexican History*, 5 vols. (Cedar Rapids, Iowa: Torch Press, 1911–17).

————. *The Spanish Archives of New Mexico*, 2 vols. (Glendale, Calif.: Arthur H. Clark Company, 1914).

————. *Spanish Colonization in New Mexico in the Oñate and De Vargas Periods* (Santa Fe: Historical Society of New Mexico, 1919).

Tyler, Sergeant Daniel. *A Concise History of the Mormon Battalion in the Mexican War, 1846–1847,* reprint ed. (Glorieta, N.M.: Rio Grande Press, 1969).

Ungnade, Herbert E. *Guide to the New Mexico Mountains* (Denver: Sage Books, 1965).

Vicens, Vives Jaime. *An Economic History of Spain* (Princeton: Princeton University Press, 1969).

Vinegar, Tom. *A Walk Around Old Town* (Albuquerque: Vinegar Tom Press, 1970).

Vines, Robert A. *Trees, Shrubs and Woody Vines of the Southwest* (Austin: University of Texas Press, 1960).

Walter, Paul A. F. *Banking in New Mexico Before the Railroads Came* (New York: The Newcomen Society, 1955).

Warner, Sam Bass, Jr. *Streetcar Suburbs, The Process of Growth in Boston, 1870–1900* (Cambridge, Mass.: Harvard University Press, 1978).

Waters, L. L. *Steel Trains to Santa Fe* (Lawrence: University of Kansas Press, 1950).

Watson, Edith L. *Navajo Sacred Places* (Window Rock, Ariz.: Navajo Tribal Museum, 1964).

Watts, John S. *Indian Depredations in New Mexico* (Washington, D.C.: Gideon Printers, 1858).

[Weightman, Richard H.]. *Speech of the Hon. Richard H. Weightman of New Mexico, Delivered in the House of Representatives, March 15, 1852* (Washington, D.C.: Congressional Globe Office, 1852).

Weigle, Marta. *Brothers of Light, Brothers of Blood* (Albuquerque: University of New Mexico Press, 1976).

Westphall, Victor. *Thomas Benton Catron and His Era* (Tucson: University of Arizona Press, 1973.

Whisenhunt, Donald W. *New Mexico Courthouses* (El Paso: Texas Western Press, 1979).

Whitford, William Clarke. *Colorado Volunteers in the Civil War* (Denver: State Historical Society of Colorado, 1906).

Whitson, Skip, comp. *New Mexico 100 Years Ago* (Albuquerque: Sun Publishing Company, 1977).

Winter, William O. *The Urban Polity* (New York: Dodd, Mead & Company, 1970).

Wislizenus, Adolphus, M.D. *Memoir of a Tour to Northern Mexico,* reprint edition (Glorieta, New Mexico: Rio Grande Press, 1969).

Wright, Lyle H., ed. *John Udell Journal, 1859* (Los Angeles: N. A. Kovach, 1946).

Zubrow, Ezra B. W. *Population, Contact, and Climate in the New Mexican Pueblos* (Tucson: University of Arizona Press, 1974).

Index

Indexed by Kathleen Havill